Ɑ Y0-BCC-903

Contents

Acknowledgments   ix

Introduction   1

Part I. Beyond Eurocentrism

1. Everywhere and Nowhere   25
   Maurice Merleau-Ponty

2. Beyond Eurocentrism: The World-System and the Limits of
   Modernity   57
   Enrique Dussel

3. The Myth of the Other: China in the Eyes of the West   83
   Zhang Longxi

4. The Dream of a Butterfly   109
   Rey Chow

5. The Joy of Textualizing Japan: A Metacommentary on Roland
   Barthes's *Empire of Signs*   137
   Hwa Yol Jung

6. Under Western Eyes: Feminist Scholarship and Colonial
   Discourses   159
   Chandra Talpade Mohanty

Part II. Asian Thought in the Age of Globalization

7. Can Asians Think?   191
   Kishore Mahbubani

8. The Order of Interbeing   205
   Thich Nhat Hanh

9. The Forms of Culture of the Classical Periods of East and West
   Seen from a Metaphysical Perspective   213
   Nishida Kitarô

10. The Significance of Ethics as the Study of Man   231
    Watsuji Tetsurô

11. Beyond the Enlightenment Mentality   251
    Tu Weiming

12. Is Culture Destiny? The Myth of Asia's Anti-Democratic Values   267
    Kim Dae Jung

13. Conceptualizing Human Beings   275
    Bhikhu Parekh

Part III. Toward a Transtopia

14. The Problem of Language in Cross-Cultural Studies   305
    Lydia H. Liu

15. Universality in Culture   357
    Judith Butler

16. The Clash of Definitions   363
    Edward W. Said

17. Hermeneutical Circles, Rhetorical Triangles, and Transversal
    Diagonals   381
    Calvin O. Schrag

18. Political Prosaics, Transversal Politics, and the Anarchical
    World   397
    David Campbell

19. Polis and Cosmopolis   419
    Fred Dallmayr

Further Readings   443

Contributors   449

COMPARATIVE POLITICAL CULTURE IN THE AGE OF GLOBALIZATION

Global Encounters: Studies in Comparative Political Theory
Series Editor: Fred Dallmayr, University of Notre Dame

This series seeks to inaugurate a new field of inquiry and intellectual concern: that of comparative political theory as an inquiry proceeding not from the citadel of a global hegemony but through cross-cultural dialogue and critical interaction. By opening the discourse of political theory—today largely dominated by American and European intellectuals—to voices from across the global spectrum, we hope to contribute to a richer, multifaceted mode of theorizing as well as to a deeper, cross-cultural awareness of the requirements of global justice.

Border Crossings: Toward a Comparative Political Theory, edited by Fred Dallmayr
Race and Reconciliation in South Africa: A Multicultural Dialogue in Comparative Perspective, edited by William E. Van Vugt and G. Daan Cloete
Gandhi, Freedom, and Self-Rule, edited by Anthony J. Parel
Beyond Nationalism? Sovereignty and Citizenship, edited by Fred Dallmayr and José M. Rosales
Conversations and Transformations: Toward a New Ethics of Self and Society, by Ananta Kumar Giri
Comparative Political Culture in the Age of Globalization: An Introductory Anthology, edited by Hwa Yol Jung

COMPARATIVE POLITICAL CULTURE IN THE AGE OF GLOBALIZATION

An Introductory Anthology

Edited by
Hwa Yol Jung

LEXINGTON BOOKS
Lanham • Boulder • New York • Oxford

47863187

LEXINGTON BOOKS

Published in the United States of America
by Lexington Books
4720 Boston Way, Lanham, Maryland 20706

12 Hid's Copse Road
Cumnor Hill, Oxford OX2 9JJ, England

British Library Cataloguing in Publication Information Available

Library of Congress Cataloging-in-Publication Data

Comparative political culture in the age of globalization : an introductory anthology /
[edited by] Hwa Yol Jung.
    p.   cm.—(Global encounters)
    Includes bibliographical references and index.
    ISBN 0-7391-0317-2 (cloth : alk. paper)—ISBN 0-7391-0318-0 (pbk. : alk. paper)
    1. Political culture.   2. Globalization.   3. East and West.   I. Jung, Hwa Yol.
    II. Series.
JA75.7.C65   2002
306.2—dc21   2001038840

Printed in the United States of America

∞ ™ The paper used in this publication meets the minimum requirements of American
National Standard for Information Sciences—Permanence of Paper for Printed Library
Materials, ANSI/NISO Z39.48–1992.

To George and Alice
for their fiftieth wedding anniversary

Acknowledgments

I AM DEEPLY INDEBTED to and grateful for a number of people without whose support this project would not have seen daylight. I wish to thank my long-time friend Fred Dallmayr of the University of Notre Dame for his enthusiasm for this project as series editor of "Global Encounters: Studies in Comparative Political Theory" which was inaugurated in the wake of globalization in the multicultural world and made its auspicious beginning in 1999 with Lexington Books. I have known Fred since I published an article on Merleau-Ponty's radical humanization of politics in a European journal in 1967. My sincere gratitude goes to Serena J. Leigh (acquisitions editor), Jason Hallman (assistant editor), Martin Hayward (editorial assistant), and Michael Marino (assistant editor) of Lexington Books, for giving me their total support for this project from its very inception.

I also wish to thank my support team at Moravian College without whose diligent work this project would have been impossible. My wholehearted thanks go to Mickey Ortiz and Karen D'Angelo who have put this manuscript into its final form. I am particularly grateful to Mickey who spent an uncountable number of hours in typing and retyping it cheerfully and, I might add, other manuscripts for the past thirty years. I can say without hesitation that she has been the most indispensable person on campus for my work. I cannot thank her enough for what she has done for my scholarly pursuit. I would be remiss if I forget to express my gratitude to the following people who are the friendliest bunch I have ever known: Tom Minor, the head librarian of Reeves Library whom I have known since his undergraduate days as my student at Moravian; Debbi Gaspar and Nancy Strobel who not only take care of interlibrary loan books with lighting speed but also are willing listeners about the weekly "wisdom" of my grandson Wiley; Bonnie Falla who looked up the names and current academic affiliations of scholars on the websites; Lou Ann Vlahovic for taking care of phone calls, faxes, and office supplies; Maryann Weaver who keeps me awake with the fresh supply of caffeine; and Connie Carfagno for his duplicating services.

This project coincided with the visit of Sung Tae Lee as a Fulbright scholar in residence from Tokyo University during the academic year 2000–2001. I regret that my conversations with this young inquiring mind, like all good things in life, must come to an end after this academic year. I will miss him dearly. Thanks to Curt Keim, whose intellectual camaraderie I have cherished over the years and who is now the academic dean and a committed "transversalist," for providing an opportunity this year for faculty conversations on intercultural matters one of which was the discussion of the preliminary version of my introductory essay for the present volume.

I dedicate this volume to George and Alice Benston for their long-standing and unwavering hospitality, friendship, and generosity since my undergraduate days at Emory University where they teach.

As always, I am deeply thankful to my wife, Petee, for her inexhaustible energy for companionship for over four decades. I am delighted to say that she is the only one in this universe who reads every word I write with a critical eye.

I wish also to acknowledge my gratitude to Moravian College's Department of Political Science, Faculty Development and Research Committee, and Dean Curt Keim for providing me with funds to help defray the cost of copyright permissions.

Gratefully acknowledged are the following publishers and authors for their permission to reprint their publications: Copyright Clearance Center for Maurice Merleau-Ponty, "Everywhere and Nowhere," in *Signs*, trans. Richard C. McCleary (Evanston, IL: Northwestern University Press, 1964), pp. 121–158; Duke University Press for Enrique Dussel, "Beyond Eurocentrism: The World-System and the Limits of Modernity," in *The Cultures of Globalization*, ed. Frederic Jameson and Masao Miyoshi (1998), pp. 3–31; University of Chicago Press for Zhang Longxi, "The Myth of the Other: China in the Eyes of the West," *Critical Inquiry*, vol. 15 (1988): 108–131; Routledge, Inc., part of The Taylor & Francis Group for Rey Chow, "The Dream of a Butterfly," in *Human, All Too Human*, ed. Diana Fuss (1996), pp. 61–92; Indiana University Press for Chandra Talpade Mohanty, "Under Western Eyes: Feminist Scholarship and Colonial Discourses," in *Third World Women and the Politics of Feminism*, ed. Chandra Talpade Mohanty, Ann Russo, and Lourdes Torres (1991), pp. 51–80; Associated University Presses and Bucknell University Press for Hwa Yol Jung, "The Joy of Textualizing Japan: A Metacommentary on Roland Barthes's *Empire of Signs*," *Bucknell Review*, vol. 30, no. 2 (1987): *Self, Signs, and Symbol*, ed. Mark Neuman and Michael Payne, pp. 144–167 and Tu Weiming, "Beyond the Enlightenment Mentality," in *Worldviews and Ecology: Religion, Philosophy, and the Environment*, ed. Mary Evelyn Tucker and John A. Grim (Maryknoll, NY: Orbis Books, 1994), pp. 19–29, which is reprinted with revision in *Confucianism and Ecology*, ed. Mary Evelyn Tucker and John Berthrong (Harvard University Center for the Study of World Religions, 1998), pp. 3–21; Times Media Private Limited (Singapore) for Kishore Mahbubani, "Can Asians Think?" in *Can Asians Think?* (1998), pp. 16–33; Parallax Press for Thich Nhat Hanh, "The Order of Interbeing," in *Interbeing: Fourteen Guidelines for Engaged Buddhism*, rev. ed., ed. Fred Eppsteiner (1993), pp. 3–13; Greenwood Press for Nishida Kitaro, "The Forms of Culture of the Classical Periods of East and West Seen from a Metaphysical Perspective" and Watsuji Tetsuro, "The Significance of Ethics as the Study of Man," in *Sourcebook for Modern Japanese Philosophy*, trans. and ed. David A. Dilworth and Valdo H. Viglielmo with Agustin Jacinto Zavala (1998), pp. 21–36 and 262–278; *Foreign Affairs* for Kim Dae Jung, "Is Culture Destiny? The Myth of Asia's Anti-Democratic Values," *Foreign Affairs*, vol. 73, no. 6 (November–December, 1994), pp. 189–194; Macmillan Publishers Ltd Palgrave and Harvard University Press for Bhikhu Parekh, "Conceptualizing Human Beings," in *Rethinking Multiculturalism* (2000), pp. 114–141 and 349–350; Stanford University Press for Lydia H. Liu, "The Problem of Language in Cross-Cultural Studies," in *Translingual Practice* (1995), pp. 1–42 and 381–393; Judith Butler for "Universality in Culture," in *For Love of Country*, ed. Joshua Cohen (Beacon Press, 1996), pp. 45–52; the Wylie Agency and Harvard University Press for Edward W. Said, "The Clash of Definitions," in *Reflections on Exile* (2000), pp. 569–590; Yale University Press for Calvin O. Schrag, "Hermeneutical Circles, Rhetorical Triangles, and Transversal Diagonals," in *Rhetoric and Hermeneutics in Our Time*, ed. Walter Jost and Michael J. Hyde (1997), pp. 132–146; University of Minnesota Press for David Campbell, "Political Prosaics, Transversal Politics, and the Anarchical World," in *Challenging Boundaries*, ed. Michael J. Shapiro and Hayward R. Alker (1996), pp. 7–31; and State University of New York Press for Fred Dallmayr, "Polis and Cosmopolis," in *Margins of Political Discourse* (1989), pp. 1–21.

Introduction

Hwa Yol Jung

[T]he critique of ethnocentrism . . . should be systematically and historically contemporaneous with the destruction of the history of [Western]
metaphysics. Both belong to a single and same era.

—Jacques Derrida

The crisis of Western thought is identical to the end of imperialism. . . .
[I]t is the end of the era of Western philosophy. Thus, if philosophy of the
future exists, it must be born outside Europe or equally born in consequence of meetings and impacts between Europe and non-Europe.

—Michel Foucault

If we keep speaking the same language together, we're going to reproduce
the same history.[1]

—Luce Irigaray

COMPARATIVE POLITICAL THEORY, at last![2] The purpose of this anthology
is to bring to our attention the fact that this world is not one—not yet
anyway—but pluralistic. In the simple words of Julie Fredriekse, "There are
many maps of one place, and many histories of one time" (see McClintock,
1955: 1). Cultural pluralism or the Babel of cultures, if you will, is by necessity marked and ruled, whether we like it or not, by ambiguity, porosity, and
even promiscuity if not by con/fusion in the exact sense that Merleau-Ponty
used them throughout his philosophical career. We must always be mindful
of what might be called the *Rashomon* phenomenon after the fashion of Akira
Kurosawa's philosophical Japanese film by that name which presents four
plausibly "true" narratives of one and the same murder scene through flash-
backs: the thief's, the wife's, the dead man's, and the wood-cutter's. It is

imperative for students of the theory of comparative culture to take heed of the *Rashomon* phenomenon.[3]

Accordingly, the translation of one culture into another is a perplexing affair because of intercultural perception, misperception, and even imperception. In 1988 the noted sinologist Jonathan D. Spence wrote the fascinating book called *The Question of Hu*—a slice of Chinese history written in the entertaining style of fiction—which raises the interesting question of ethnocultural identity/difference. Hu Ruowang or John Hu was the first Chinese who traveled to the West. Hu sailed to France from Canton (Guangdon) in 1722. Because of his "strange" behavior which astonished the Parisians, he was committed to the famous lunatic asylum of Charenton (Sha-lang-dong) in 1723 and remained there until 1726 when he was ordered by the French government to return to China. Set aside the Foucauldian question of insanity as a sociocultural control mechanism; the relevance of the Hu question to this anthology is the question of whether he was committed to the asylum because he was "really mad" or because he looked mad to the "foreign" Parisians because he was "alien" to them. Perhaps the Parisians were not capable of seeing "what is ours as alien and what is alien as our own"—to repeat the language of Merleau-Ponty. Either way, the question of Hu poses the "scandalous" difficulty of translating the dynamic chiasm of intercultural understanding and misunderstanding.

This anthology introduces an important and fundamental aspect of comparative political theory with a focus on Asia. It will be of interest to advanced undergraduate and beginning graduate students in particular who are challenged today by questions and issues in intercultural and interdisciplinary (i.e., intertextual) scope in the humanities and the social sciences in the era when the world is said to be hurrying into "a global village"—to use the prophetic catchwords of the late Canadian communication theorist Marshall McLuhan. Indeed, McLuhan once had a vision of writing his *magnum opus, The Gutenberg Gallaxy* (1962), in the idiomatic medium of Chinese ideograms.[4] As a matter of fact, every text is or should be an intertext if we take seriously and sincerely the idea of multiculturalism in the age of globalization.

This anthology is divided into three parts.

The first part revolves around the demythologization or deconstruction of Eurocentrism, narcissistic or hegemonic, which refers to that habitus of mind which privileges modern Europe or the West as cultural, scientific, religious, and moral mecca and capital of the world from Montesquieu to Rousseau, Hegel, Mill, Marx, and Karl Wittfogel (who is the author of the controversial work *Oriental Despotism* [1957]). It is no more and no less than European ethnophilosophy that proclaims to be universal or global. It legislates or legitimizes itself as the privileged or anointed guardian of the historical *telos* of the entire globe. European hegemony—both epistemological and political—is implicated as soon as "universal man" (*Homo Universalis*) is *identified* (or, better, misidentified) with "European man" (*Homo Europaeus*). In fact, one may echo Derrida (1992: 36) who speaks of "a planetarization of the European model" on all fronts, on the intellect, economics, politics, and culture. *Homo Europaeus*, who lives in a "cape" of the Asian continent (Valéry's) or the "little peninsula of Asia" (Nietzsche's designation) (see Naas's "Introduction" to Derrida, 1992: lv) has a hegemonic grip over the entire globe and not just Asia. By positioning itself as the teleological temple of the world, Eurocentrism becomes a tribal idolatry. The astute observer of modernity Zygmunt Bauman (1987: 110) writes:

> From at least the seventeenth century and well into the twentieth, the writing elite of Western Europe [with] its footholds on other continents considered its own way of life as a radical break in universal history. Virtually unchallenged faith in its own mode over all alternative forms of life—contemporaneous or past—allowed it to take itself as the reference point for the interpretation of the *telos* of history. . . . Now, . . . Europe set the reference point of objective time in motion, attaching it firmly to its own thrust towards colonizing the future in the same way as it has colonized the surrounding space.

The famed American neo-pragmatist Richard Rorty's call for "continuing the conversation of the West" with itself in his influential *Philosophy and the Mirror of Nature* (1979: 394) is less than edifying.[5] Rorty not only trivializes Michael Oakeshott's original appeal for the "conversation of mankind" but also flirts with narcissistic Eurocentrism. In recent years, Eurocentrism as monocultural myopia, however, has not gone unchallenged. Kwame Anthony Appiah and Henry Louis Gates, Jr.'s, model of "global culture," for example, points to an impressive effort to respond to and challenge the Eurocentric popularity of E. D. Hirsch's *Cultural Literacy* (1987) and Allan Bloom's New York Times best-seller *The Closing of the American Mind* (1987).

The idea of deconstruction, I fear, has often been misunderstood as a purely negative or wrenching endeavor (e.g., as a boa-constrictor!). Following the phenomenological method, Heidegger (1982: 23) contends that deconstruction is "a critical process in which the traditional concepts, which at first must necessarily be employed, are de-constructed down to the sources from which they were drawn." He (1982: 23) continues: "Construction in philosophy is necessarily destruction, that is to say, a de-constructing of traditional concepts carried out in an historical recursion to the tradition. And this is not a negation of the tradition or a condemnation of it as worthless;

quite the reverse, it signifies precisely a positive appropriation of tradition." Since in Eurocentrism the power of knowledge and the power of conquest coincide, deconstructive criticism cannot afford not to be Foucauldian; for Foucault (1997: 32), philosophy as critique is "the movement by which the subject gives himself the right to question on its effects of power and question power on its discourse of truth." To paraphrase Kant, knowledge without power is empty and power without knowledge is blind.

Postmodern thinking as a mosaic polygraph of all postisms is characterized by the British cultural theorist Robert Young (1990: 19, 20) as "European culture's awareness that it is no longer the unquestioned and dominant centre of the world," and that the advent of the postmodern paradigm is tantamount to "witnessing the dissolution of 'the West' " whose pronouncement is reminiscent of Oswald Spengler's daring work called *The Decline of the West* (*Der Untergang des Abendlandes,* 1917/1922).[6]

No doubt the Enlightenment legacy is the soul of Western modernity. The unbridled optimism of the Enlightenment which promotes humanity's infinite progress based on the cultivation of pure and applied reason is the *lingua franca* of Western modernity. Kant spelled out the motto of the Enlightenment in the clearest and simplest terms: the autonomy of reason was meant to rescue and emancipate humanity—perhaps more accurately European humanity—from the dark cave of self-incurred tutelage or immaturity (*selbstverschuldeten Unmündigkeit*). In so doing, he institutionalized the major agenda of European modernity whose rationality had not been challenged until the advent of postmodernism. Foucault, for example, examined the irrationality of "enlightened reason" in discovering the "clinical body" and the "incarcerated body" in the age of Reason and revealed the very irrationality of Reason itself. While privileging and valorizing the authority and autonomy of Reason for allegedly human (material) progress and emancipation, European modernity marginalizes, disenfranchises, and denigrates the (Reason's) Other: (1) body, (2) woman, (3) nature, and (4) non-West which are four central postmodern landmarks and subversive possibilities. Needless to say, they all are interrelated issues which are blind spots of the Enlightenment itself (see Jung, forthcoming).[7]

It is most appropriate, I think, that this anthology begins with the lucid and resonating voice of Maurice Merleau-Ponty whose greatness is being tested again and again for its relevance to the contemporary world since his death in 1961. He is remarkably contemporaneous (see Madison, 1999: 185). Merleau-Ponty himself insisted that all history should be written in the present tense. One of the most enduring aspects of his philosophical legacy is an accent on philosophy's own self-reflection and vigilance not to forget its sources: the end of philosophy is the account of its beginning. It is no accident that the present volume is launched with the masterly collection of short and edifying introductory essays by Merleau-Ponty (Ch. 1) on comparative philosophy within and without the traditional of Western philosophy in *Les Philosophes célèbres* (1956) which sets the tone for the possibility of comparative political theory. His edited volume contains Western philosophers from Heraclitus to Socrates and Plato, Christian thinkers from Augustine to Aquinas, rationalism from Bacon and Descartes to Locke, from Montaigne to Kierkegaard on the discovery of history, and from Bergson to Husserl, Heidegger and Sartre on existence and the dialectic. From non-Western traditions, Merleau-Ponty included two contributions—one on Indian philosophy by Jean Fillizat and the other on Chinese philosophy by Max Kalternmark. Above all, Merleau-Ponty (1964: 120), who was sensitized, I believe, by Marcel Mauss and Claude Lévi-Strauss on the matters of anthropology and other cultures, appreciates the "diacritical value" of an "incessant testing of the self through the other person and the other person through the self" or seeing "what is ours as alien and what was alien as our own." Section 2 of Merleau-Ponty's selection, which is most pertinent to our present inquiry, encourages us to attend "the Orient's secret, mute contribution to philosophy."[8] Indeed, he is a commanding deconstructor in the honored tradition of Heidegger and the contemporary living spirit of Derrida (cf. Taylor, 1993: 334n.2). Merleau-Ponty is critical of the "cavalier fashion" of looking at Indian and Chinese thought and of drawing a Hegelian geographical distinction between philosophy (Western or Occidental) and non-philosophy (Eastern or Oriental). If philosophy is monopolized by the West, its "outside" (*dehors*) or Other is the non-philosophical East. In the end, Merleau-Ponty judiciously concludes: "Simply rallying and subordinating 'non-philosophy' to true philosophy will not create the unity of the human spirit. It already exists in each culture's lateral relationships to the others, in echoes one awakes in the other."

It is in the spirit of Merleau-Ponty that the Latin American philosopher Enrique Dussel (Ch. 2) addresses in broad strokes the conquest and the marginalization of Europe's others and non-European humanity. It is, of course, the "magisterial voice" (Spivak, 1993: 26) of Edward W. Said in his pioneering *Orientalism* (1978) which sparked a sea change in and has become the standard-bearer for contemporary postcolonial cultural studies. Inspired by Foucault's nexus of knowledge and power, he argued against Orientalism as "a fabrication of the West."[9]

Zhang (Ch. 3) registers and traces an aspect of Orientalism in China watch and evokes Gadamer's philosophical hermeneutics, particularly its formulation of the (inter-) "fusion of horizons" (*Horizontverschmelzung*), as a clue to overcoming or going beyond Orientalism. Parenthetically, Gadamer maintains that the "soul of hermeneutics" rests in the idea that the Other may be right. Chow's "The Dream of a Butterfly" (Ch. 4), which is deeply embedded in the Lacanian psychoanalytical play of fantasy/dream, involves the intriguing and intricate plot which is played out in an imagined drama of cultural identity and difference between East and West: "Madama Butterfly" by Puccini (the Italian composer)/the American film "M. Butterfly" directed by Cronenberg based on the screenplay written by the Chinese-American playwright Hwang on the one hand and Cho-cho-san (Japanese woman)/Song ("Chinese woman") and Pinkerton (American)/Gallimard (French) on the other. The title of Chow's selection alludes to the Chinese Taoist Chuang Tzu or Zhuang Zi to which the French psychoanalyst Jacques Lacan refers. According to Zhuang Zi's often-told story, one day he dreamt that he was a butterfly. When he woke up he was once again unmistakably himself, but he became befuddled because he did not know if he was Zhuang Zi who had dreamt that he was a butterfly, or a butterfly dreaming he was Zhuang Zi. In Chow, from beginning to end, the spectre of (Said's) "Orientalism" looms because she raises the question of Western representations of the non-West.

Jung (Ch. 5) cautions "prejudging" in observing matters foreign of the French structural semiologist Roland Barthes who wrote his *Empire of Signs* with bubbling enthusiasm in the backdrop of "Western narcissism" and is overjoyed ("jouissanced," as it were) with the "ideogrammic" nature of Japanese culture. Barthes should take seriously the indictment by Craig Owens (1992: 290, 296) of the visual mesmerization and reduction by Europeans of the foreign (i.e., Amerindia) others as "a distancing and a muting": to paraphrase him slightly, it is high time to stop *looking*, and *start listening* to what they may have to say.

Mohanty (Ch. 6) further counsels us not to judge the issue of "third world women" by Western standards and hopes to exorcise from it an "ethnocentric universality" or a "latent ethnocentrism." She echoes Hannah Arendt who considered the "Third World" as a "myth" rather than a "reality." As feminism, too, is heterogeneous rather than homogeneous,[10] there can be no genuine analysis of it which is transhistorical and trans-sociocultural. Indeed, there is a subtle if not radical difference between comparability and reductionism (economic or otherwise). Cross-cultural studies must take into account the sociocultural and historical specificities of women's existence. Mohanty approaches the issues of women in the Third World in the multivariant context of class, race, gender, and colonialism.

> There is not *a* philosophy which contains all philosophies; philosophy as a whole is at certain moments in each philosophy. To take up the cele-

brated phrase again, philosophy's center is everywhere and its circumference nowhere.

—Maurice Merleau-Ponty

Only connect!

—E. M. Forster

The second part of this anthology attends to the *principia* of Asian thought. In its textual organization, it is sandwiched between a critique of Orientalism and the way of multicultural hybridization in the age of globalization. The Sinitic culture of Asia is no longer "a pictograph that's lost its sound" (Liu, 1995: vii). The economic boom and success in Japan and later in four "little tigers" (South Korea, Taiwan, Hong Kong, and Singapore) drew Western attention to "Asian values."[11] Of course, culture as an interconnected corpus of meanings and values *really matters*. What the "Protestant ethic" is to the modern West, the "Confucian ethos" is to East Asia in the twentieth century. In the twenty-first century as the century of multiculturalism, thinking or rethinking multiculturalism cannot go unnoticed and cuts across disciplinary boundaries (see Parekh, 2000). It is no longer an oddity or a heresy to ask if multiculturalism is good or bad for women (see Okin, 1999) or if science itself is multicultural (see Harding, 1998).[12]

In his conversation with a visiting Japanese scholar, Heidegger (1971: 3) questions why a "true encounter" by East Asians with the European mode of existence has still not taken place despite their "assimilations and intermixtures" of the European systems of ideas, technology, and industry. In the kindred spirit of inquiry, the Singaporean intellectual/statesman Mahbubani (Ch. 7) asks the very timely but well overdue question: Can Asians think? Or can Asian societies be Asian rather than just Western replicas? He provides us with reasons for each of three possible answers—no, yes, and maybe—and challenges Asians to think about them. Mahbubani represents a significant group of Asian thinkers who question a blind faith in modernization/Westernization and its values without falling into a return to "nativism." John Gray (1995: 184), who is a British critic of Western modernity and the Enlightenment, is of the opinion that Oriental cultures have assimilated too much of the "nihilism" of Western modernity.

The prevailing opinion in the West notwithstanding, there are *philosophies* in Asia. What follows in this collection is a movement from the *disorientation* of Eurocentrism to the *reorientation* of Asian thought and Eastern/Western hybridity in terms of transversality. Nhat Hanh (Ch. 8) is a Vietnamese Zen Buddhist who established the religious "Order of Interbeing" in the mid-1960s which is simply and elegantly expressed in the two sinograms—*tiep* and *hien.* They together signify the interconnectedness and interdependence of all beings and things both human and nonhuman on earth. Indeed, Interbeing is the soul of Asian thought—Indian, Chinese, Korean, and Japanese. It, I submit, even paves the way toward the globalization of truth itself. As a matter of fact, globalism or multiculturalism is a dimension of Interbeing. Ch'an (Chinese) or Zen (Japanese) Buddhism is in its origin the hybridization of the two main currents of Asian thought—Indian and Chinese. What Interbeing (*Untersein*) is to the East from Buddha to Confucius, Lao Tzu, Dogen, Nishida, and Watsuji, Being (*Sein*) is to the West from Heraclitus to Plato, Aristotle, and Heidegger. At the same time, Eastern Interbeing is capable of "overturning" or "overcoming" Western Being.

Interbeing points to a *relational ontology,* that is, the idea that reality is nothing but a *social process,* or everything in the universe must "inter-be" with everything else. It is the synchronistic idea that everything is *interconnected* to everything else in the universe. Unlike Western ontology which focuses on the interhuman, Interbeing as relational ontology is all-encompassing in that it is both interhuman and interspeciesistic.[13] Most importantly, Interbeing is a relational ontology with an ethical face or the ethic of *compassion* for all beings and things. There is no hiatus or separation between ontology and ethics.

Among the three Japanese thinkers selected, Nishida (Ch. 9) is best known in the circle of Western students of philosophy for a good reason. He is the founder of the Kyoto School of Philosophy which accents comparative philosophy—particularly philosophy of the East and the West. Watsuji (Ch. 10) is far less known in the West. Although his treatise on the interconnection between the climatic condition and the development of human civilization is often noted and discussed, his seminal work on ethics—*Rinrigaku*—was originally published in three volumes in 1937, 1942, and 1949, but its abridged English translation was published only in 1996. It reminds me of the fact that Heidegger's *Sein und Zeit* (1927) was translated into English only in 1962.

In comparing the classical thoughts of the West and the East—Greek and Chinese—Nishida recognizes a plurality of world civilizations in location and time, that is, culture is a function of time and place.[14] Moreover, each individual culture is mediated with the other cultures of the world. The importance of Watsuji lies in the fact that ethics is the epicenter of Sinitic philosophy. Just as "existentialism" has been criticized as non-philosophical because of its focus on "irrational man," Sinitic thought has been labeled as "non-philosophical" because of its ethical predominance. Watsuji's style may be likened to Heidegger's in its attention to etymological details. What is most interesting about being human in Sinitic thought or ethics is the idea that it is characterized in terms of the interhuman much like Martin Buber's formulation of the interhuman (*das Zwischenmenschliche*) or René Girard's "interdividuality." *Ningen* or being human is symbolized in two Chinese ideograms, that is, "human" and "betweenness" (*aidagara*): etymosinologically, to be human is to be necessarily relational or interhuman (*mitmenschlich*). Tzvetan Todorov (2001) presents one of the most lucid and persuasive arguments for the *self as social*, "life in common" (*la vie commune*) or *Mitmenschlichkeit: to be alone is not to be*. What, we may ask, is language? As the primary product of culture and the primary medium of interhuman communication, it is nothing but social relationships turned directly into sound or indirectly into inscription (cf. Elias, 1978a: 117). What then is human sexuality? It is, again, nothing but social relationships turned into carnal contact. In Buber's relational ontology, there are two primary relations: "I-Thou" and "I-It." "Thou" or "It" may be human or nonhuman. The "I" of "I-Thou" and the "I" of "I-It," however, are not the same "I," but they are radically different because the "I" is defined only in relation to the other—"Thou" or "It."

Culture underwrites *ningen* or the interhuman relationships. Humans create culture, and conversely culture molds humans. The question of "what human is" and that of "what culture is" implicate each other or form a double helix, as it were. The American cultural anthropologist Clifford Geertz (1973: 49)—for whom culture is an intricate web of meaning and value and who sees that discovering heaven in a grain of sand is not a feat only poets can accomplish—puts it bluntly: "there is no such thing as a human nature independent of culture. . . . Without men, no culture, certainly; but equally, and more significantly, without culture, no men."[15]

Furthermore, it is safe to assert that ethics not only is concerned with the interhuman (and interspeciesistic) but also assumes—not unlike Confucian ethics and the ethics of the late French post-phenomenologist Emmanuel Levinas—the *primacy of the Other*. Self-absorption produces no ethics: ethics is about self-transcendence.[16] What egocentrism is to geocentrism, heterocentrism is to heliocentrism. Thus Ludwig Feuerbach's discovery of the primacy of the Other or Thou may be hailed as the Copernican revolution of social thought whose influence stretches from Marx to Buber, Levinas, and William James in the twentieth century.[17]

Tu (Ch. 11) is a prolific Confucian scholar and thinker. His selection appreciates the achievement of Western "enlightened" modernity but also shows its limits from a Sinitic or Confucian perspective. John Gray (1995: 184) comes to the conclusion that "any prospect of cultural recovery from the nihilism that the Enlightenment has spawned may lie with non-Occidental peoples" and the power of Western calculative thought or technological rationality is ruinous of the earth. Occasioned by the conference on Confucianism and ecology, Tu stresses the Confucian triad of Heaven, Earth, and human. The lack of this triadic unity is symptomatic of the ecological crisis which constitutes humanity's "ultimate concern." It is also fundamentally a political issue because in the Sinitic tradition, the political "ruler" is one who, according to its etymology, unifies Heaven, Human, and Earth.

Kim (Ch. 12) had been a long-time political dissident in South Korea and an activist in the human rights movement. He is now President of the Republic of Korea, and in 2000 he became a recipient of the Nobel Peace Prize for his relentless effort to reunify peacefully South and North Korea. In his acceptance speech in Oslo, Norway, on December 10, 2000, he reiterated the importance of human rights for advancing the cause of democracy in Korea as well as in Asia and the rest of the world. Kim's present selection is the most interesting and unorthodox view of Confucianism. It is a pithy challenge to the published conversation between Fareed Zakaria, Managing Editor of *Foreign Affairs,* and Lee Kuan Yew who is called Singapore's Confucian "patriarch." Kim rejects Lee's suggestion that "culture is destiny" (i.e., cultural determinism). Instead, Kim transcribes Confucian "rites" into the language of "human rights," as it were, which is the pillar and bastion of Western democratic values.

In Western philosophy since Plato the nature of "human nature" has been essentialized, that is, it has been held unchanging throughout time and history. Paradoxically, however, there is not one but many theories of "human nature." "Nature" and "culture," which are two of the most complex and controversial words in human language, are not independent but interdependent concepts. In the *Analects,* Confucius wisely remarks that by nature human beings are nearly alike but by practice they are widely apart. In theorizing about multiculturalism Sir Bhikhu (Ch. 13) judiciously balances "naturalism" and "culturalism." In rejecting monism, relativism, and "minimum universalism," he argues for what he calls "pluralist universalism" by whose standard he takes issue with those who champion and advance the cause of "Asian values."

> No man is an Iland, intire of it selfe; every man is a peece of the *Continent,* a part of the *maine;* . . . Any Mans *death* diminishes *me,* because I am involved in *Mankinde;* And therefore never send to know for whom the *bell* tolls; it tolls for thee.
>
> —John Donne

> He who knows himself and other,/ Will also recognise that East and/West cannot be separated.
>
> —Johann Wolfgang von Goethe

The third part of this anthology is a collection of six essays under the heading of "transtopia"—the neologism I coined after the fashion of the pivotal idea of "transversality." First, despite its spatial connotation, transtopia is meant to be chronotopical: it is a coordinate of time and place. Second, it is neither "utopian" (ou/topian), nor simply heterotopian, nor merely polytopian. Third, on account of the prefix *trans,* it means to overcome or *go beyond* the status quo. History is "an open notebook" (to use Merleau-Ponty's metaphor) in which a new future can be inscribed. Thus transversality or transtopia may be likened to the famous wooden statue of Buddha at a Zen temple in Kyoto whose face marks the dawn of awakening (*satori*) or signals the beginning of a new regime of knowledge and morals of a new world. From the crack in the middle of the old face of the Buddha's statue, there emerges an interstitial, liminal face that signifies a new transfiguration or transvaluation of cultural meanings and values. The emerging new face also symbolizes the arrival of Maitreya (i.e., the "future Enlightened One") or Middle Way—the third term which mediates intercultural border-crossings. Foucault was interested in Japan and particularly its living culture of Zen. In his brief conversation with a Japanese Buddhist priest during his second visit to Japan in 1978, Foucault (1999: 113–14) made a telling comment in response to his host's query: since Europe is "the birth place of universality," the crisis of its thought is the crisis of universality which concerns and influences the whole world. Unlike Husserl who believed that the crisis of European thought was a matter of internal concern and could be resolved from within, Foucault speculated that philosophy of the future had to be born outside Europe or born out of encounters between Europe and non-Europe.

In tune with the *Zeitgeist* of globalization whose contours are well and clearly spelled out by the British sociologist Anthony Giddens,[18] transversality (or what Merleau-Ponty calls "lateral universals") is meant to dislodge the encrustation of universality as the Eurocentric canon of truth. Universality has been a Eurocentric idea because what is particular in the West is universalized or universalizable, where what is particular elsewhere remains particularized.[19] Paul Feyerabend (1999: 252) contends that the mindset addicted to the universal/general practices the epistemological "tyranny" which intends to annihilate the local/particular. Since the enter of universality is everywhere and its circumference nowhere, truth is rather polycentric and correlative. Transversality signifies transcendence of the sovereignty of identity or self-sameness by recognizing the alterity of the Other as *Unterschied*—to use Heidegger's term—which pinpoints the sense of relatedness by way of difference (i.e., "asymmetrical reciprocity"). The popular psychologist de Bono (1968) speaks suggestively of the distinction between "vertical" and "lateral" thinking. One is analogous to digging the same hole deeper and deeper in which there is no exit, whereas the other is likened to digging a new hole in another place. Switching from vertical to lateral thinking is an act of paradigmatic change or a "New Think."[20]

By drawing insights from the broad spectrum of Heidegger, Steiner, Taylor, Benjamin, Derrida, and others, Liu (Ch. 14) puts into practice the hermeneutical principle or the principle of linguisticality (*Sprachlichkeit*) that language and cultural praxis are inseparable.[21] Hers is an "introduction" to and an exercise in cross-cultural hermeneutics. Her sophisticated and nuanced theses are the preconditions for cross-cultural studies whose discursive undertakings require the "translation" of one culture into another by way of different linguistic systems and communities. They are basic guidelines for overcoming the "language barrier" between different cultures— Eastern or East Asian and Western. Herein lies the importance of what she calls "translingual practice." Lengthy though it may be with extensive references, it is erudite and "linguistically challenged." Here Ernest Fenollosa's (1936) discovery of "etymosinology" is singularly instructive and helpful. The translation of Sinitic culture (Chinese, Korean, or Japanese) into a Western one (or vice versa) is particularly challenging because it involves the two radically different linguistic systems: one is Indo-European and the other ideographic (cf. Nakamura, 1964). Finding appropriate or matching "equivalences" (for, e.g., "Tao" and "God" with their own centuries-old conceptual careers and socio-cultural sedimentations) which fuse the two linguistic horizons, for instance, is enormously and often scandalously taxing if not insurmountable and incommensurable. The American cultural constructionist Butler (Ch. 15) is well aware of the ramifications as well as the difficulty if not the impossibility of universality as a cultural norm (see further Butler, 2000). Universality as Eurocentric idea parallels the "malestream" or "manhandled" normalization of ontology in the West: *man* is declared to be the measure of all things from the ancient Greeks to Freud thereby refusing to grant woman "an ontologically distinct category" (see Laqueur, 1990: 62, and see also Collin's [1994] argument against the "phallacy of identity"). Said is best known for his critique of the intellectual and political domination by the West of the non-Western world, particularly of the Middle East, in the name of "Orientalism." By casting a global net in light of history, here he (Ch. 16) takes to task Huntington's controversial thesis of the "clash of civilizations" which are necessarily "essentialized" (cf. Said, 1993: 305–25). According to Said, Huntington's vision perpetuates a Cold War mentality for the post–Cold War world: "Us" (the West) against "Them" (the non-West). The duality of "Us" and "Them" may be faulted in two ways. In the first place, it does not recognize a cultural and ideological diversity *within* the Western world itself as if it were monolithic and homogeneous. In the second place, by oversimplifying and rigidifying the world in terms of the "clash" between "light" and "darkness," Huntington is wrong-headed and signals trouble ahead by inciting "wasteful conflict and unedifying chauvinism" which we do not need.

The emerging concept of transversality in the American phenomenologist Carl Schrag (Ch. 17) paves the way for sustaining and promoting the cause of "transtopia" by overcoming both "Orientalism" and "Occidentalism" or what Cornel West (1990: 36) calls "ethnocentric chauvinism" and "faceless universalism" which, I submit, are often reversible phenomena. That is to say, they are two sides of the same coin, e.g., the claim of Eurocentric modernity as universal. In order to hold itself as universal, paradoxically, it must oppose the "essentialization" of individual ethnic cultures, i.e., Occidentalizing the Occidental or Orientalizing the Oriental that engenders an "ethnomania" or the Tower of ethnocultural Babel. Instead of Occidentalizing the Occidental, it universalizes the Occidental. Consequently, multiculturalism shall not be "essentialized" but rather it must always strive to transverse—diagonalize quadrilaterally or multilaterally—each of its diametrically opposite centers.[22] Some call transversality a state of "postethnicity." The transversalist is one who cuts or reaches *across* ethnocentric universalism. He or she will not easily give up the cross-cultural search for truth believing that every conclusion about truth is incomplete or inconclusive until we examine all sociocultural life-worlds. There is a lesson to be learned from a Zen *koan:* "When you get to the top of the mountain, keep climbing." It is incompleteness rather than completeness that governs the spirit of the transversalist.

Accompanied by hermeneutics and rhetoric and with its emphasis on communicability, relationality, entwinement, configuration, conjunction, col/laterality, and intersections or cross-sections, the basic grammar of transversality in Schrag provides the way of transgressing the existing topography of cultural and intellectual discourses in advancing the political and cultural agenda of globalization. For its name sake, transversal is neither totalizing uni-versal nor merely multiplying multi-versal. Rather, diagonal *crossing* opens up a new gateway that enables us to go beyond "the Scylla of a vacuous universalism" on the one hand and "the Charybdis of an anarchic historicism" on the other (see further Schrag, 1992, 1994, and 1997). Also by crossing diagonally or correlating differences, what is lacking or absent in one is complemented or compensated for by the other. To sum up: ultimately, transversality is the philosophical matrix which renders possible comparative philosophy and comparative political theory in the epoch of globalization in the multicultural world (see Jung, 1995).[23] Campbell (Ch. 18) espouses Bakhtinian dialogical prosaics and transversal politics. By transversal politics, he means to emphasize the everyday politics of nomadic and protean individuals rather than of sedentary and fixed ones.

The political philosopher Dallmayr (Ch. 19) recognizes that we are now standing at the crossroads of *polis* and *cosmopolis*. He attends, with a critical eye, Habermas's "universal pragmatics" as an exemplar of Western universalism today while criticizing fragmentary postmodern "agonistics." Rather than Habermas's universalism or postmodern agonism, Dallmayr finds a cosmopolitan outlook in Gadamer's hermeneutics and Merleau-Ponty's "lateral universals." It is befitting to have Dallmayr's selection as this anthology's concluding chapter since it echoes the voice of Merleau-Ponty's opening chapter. Their *esprit de corps* celebrates the promising arrival of a transversal world.

In conclusion, "going global" or planetary dwelling is an arduous task. Transversality is the theoretical underpinning of becoming a global citizen (*homo globatus*) or cosmopolitan who feels at home in the pluralistic world beyond the modernist division of the world as nation-states. For the transversalist, globalization means to decenter Western hegemony and disclaim Western superiority thereby empowering the non-West to participate fully in the new worldmaking as an act of hybridization or imbrication.[24] We must keep in mind Heidegger's (1958: 107) prompting us many years ago "not to give up the effort to practice planetary thinking along a stretch of the road, be it ever so short. Here too no prophetic talents and demeanor are needed to realize that there are in store for planetary building encounters to which participants are by no means equal. . . ."[25] In the age of globalization or planetary building, the transversalist is one who is willing at all cost to facilitate cross-geocultural border-crossings without passports.

Plurality or multiplicity thickens the density of the social and renders the relational always tenuous, complex, entangled and ambiguous, often paradoxical and contradictory. There is no escape from it. It embodies the human condition and its predicament for which there is no easy exit.[26] Indeed, it resembles Jackson Pollock's signature painting which charts a knotty maze of dots and intersecting lines.

By recognizing the ineluctable fact that the pluralistic world, both everyday and intellectual, is never and will never be free from conflict and contest, the transversalist welcomes and is committed to nonviolent conflict resolution as a necessary ingredient of globalization in the multicultural world.[27] Indeed, he or she is a planetary person of civility who cultivates the canny "ability to interact with strangers without holding their strangeness against them" (Bauman, 2000: 104). Transversality is predicated upon the notion that disagreement inheres in the order of the pluralistic world. On the one hand, however, disagreement is not a "clash" which connotes an irreconcilable or intolerable difference. On the other, in transversality there is no place for "Oriental inscrutability" in which the Orient (or non-West) is wrapped in an incomprehensible thus uncommunicable and intractable foreignness or mystery. In the end, the transversalist goes beyond the threshold of tolerating the other's difference, the mutual recognition of differences, or benign neglect. Rather, he or she is engaged in an active and incessant pursuit of creating and solidifying the world as the arena in which by first empowering all participants the confluence or transfusion of differences takes place. Indeed, we are living in *inter/esting* times.

Notes

1. Rich (1986: 225) writes: "The movement for change is a changing movement, changing itself, demasculinizing itself, de-Westernizing itself, becoming a critical mass that is saying in so many different voices, languages, gestures, actions: *It must change; we ourselves can change it.* We who are not the same. We who are many and do not want to be the same." Then she (1986: 231) closes her reflection with an interesting question "Who is *we?*"

2. I am echoing the voice of Culler (1995: 117–21) who prods literary comparativists "to abandon its traditional Eurocentrism and turn global." In most college textbooks the history of *Western* philosophy is simply called the history of philosophy as if there is no philosophy in the non-Western world. So-called cultural studies is Eurocentric as well as monocultural (e.g., British, American, French, German, Italian, Spanish, and Australian). Even *International Cultural Studies,* for example, is no exception and its editorial board is dominated by Western intellectuals. The talk of the Eurocentric "cultural turn" in Marxism betrays the original spirit of Marx who, in the footsteps of Diogenes, called himself "a citizen of the world." Lexington Books (Lanham, Md.) began in 1999 its series called "Global Encounters: Studies in Comparative Political Theory" under the editorship of Fred Dallmayr who also edited its first volume: *Border Crossings: Toward a Comparative Political Theory* (1999). This anthology is another volume in the series.

3. Ryunosuke Akutagawa's mystery tale of a murder (Kuriyama, 1999: 7) is no less intriguing than Kurozawa's *Rashomon.* After a bandit raped the wife, the husband was found stabbed to death. Since the bandit confessed that he killed him, the wife later confessed to the killing, and the dead husband testified through a medium that he killed himself, the mystery question is: who did *really* kill the husband? Of course, there is Jastrow's famous "rabbit/duck" perspectivism. In 1973, there was an exhibition at China's National Art Gallery in Beijing whose centerpiece was Huang Yongyu's woodcut print *Owl* with one eye open and the other closed. The *Owl* was controversial because it purported to represent the artist's subversive attitude or animosity toward China's Cultural Revolution and Socialist regime. The *Owl*'s enigmatic expression can be seen *either* as a wink *or* as a one-eye open stare. Perhaps the closed eye is simply blinded rather than an indication of any natural disposition (see Wang, 2000).

4. Rorty (1979: 371) comments in passing that "Derrida occasionally toys with the notion of the superiority of Oriental languages and of ideographic writing [to Occidental alphabetical languages]." Derrida is a stark contrast to Heidegger who once considered Greek and German the only philosophical languages.

5. Varela, Thompson, and Rosch (1991: 240–41) cite Rorty's passage while drawing our attention to Heidegger's notion of "planetary thinking" in *The Question of Being* (1958) by way of, for example, a "translingual practice" between the European and the East Asian languages since "neither one of the two is able by itself to open up this area [of planetary thinking] and to establish it." I would be remiss if I failed to mention that since his participation in the Sixth East-West Philosophers' Conference in 1989 in Honolulu, Hawaii, Rorty has been actively engaged in intercultural conversation and communication (see Balslev, 1999). Liu (1995) discusses the important issue of "translingual practice" or lack/absence of it in cross-cultural studies (see particularly, ch. 1, pp. 1–42). Gadamer's philosophical hermeneutics (1991) contends that our thinking including translating is inseparable from the question of "linguisticality" (*Sprachlichkeit*). Hermeneutics grounded in cultural phenomenology would offer great potential if not solutions for "translingual practice" in all comparative or cross-cultural studies for the "translatability of cultures" (see Budick and Iser, 1996).

6. Nussbaum (1997: 113–47) offers the rationale of studying non-Western cultures as an integral part of "cultivating humanity." Chow (1995: 112) contends that "one of the strongest justifications for studying the non-West has to do precisely with the fundamental questioning of the limits of Western discourse which is characteristic of deconstruction and poststructuralist theory." She goes on to say that "deconstruction and poststructuralist theory have very close ties with cultural studies, gender studies, gay and lesbian studies, and ethnic studies, in that the investigations of disciplines, class, race, gender, ethnicity, and so forth, however empirical, must always already contain within them the implicit *theoretical* understanding of the need to critique hegemonic signs and sign systems from without as well as from within. This kind of theoretical direction is the one in which I would like to see comparative literature continue."

7. Body, woman, nature, and non-West share something in common: all of them are regarded as feminine categories. Buruma (2000: xvi) cogently remarks that "The European idea of the Orient as female, voluptuous, decadent, amoral—in short, as dangerously seductive—long predates the European empires in India and Southeast Asia." Kant's racism in relation to the Enlightenment is well documented by Eze (1997). How and why Kant's "enlightened" logocentrism produced racism is an interesting question to be answered. Gadamer (1991: 270) points out that "there is one prejudice of the Enlightenment that defines its essence: the fundamental prejudice of the Enlightenment is the prejudice against prejudice itself, which denies tradition its power." It should also be added that the logocentric formulation in the Enlightenment of universality is not immune from prejudice. Logocentric self-complacency forgets to examine its own prejudice.

8. Eight decades ago, Fung Yu-lan (1922: 237–63), who is the most prominent historian of Chinese philosophy in the twentieth century, remarked: "To speak of things in abstract and general terms is always dangerous. But here I cannot refrain from saying that the West is *extension,* the East is *intension,* and that the West empha-

sizes what we *have*, the East emphasizes what we *are*. The question as to how to reconcile these two so that humanity may be happy both in body and in mind is at present difficult to answer. Anyway, the Chinese conception of life may be mistaken, but the Chinese experience cannot be a failure. If mankind shall afterwards become wiser and wiser, and think that they need peace and happiness in their mind, they may turn their attention to, and gain something from, the Chinese wisdom. If they shall not think so, the mind energy of the Chinese people of four thousand years will yet not have been spent in vain. The failure itself may warn our children to stop searching for something in the barren land of human mind. This is one of China's contributions to mankind."

9. See Martin and Koda (1994: 9). They refer to the influence of the East in history on Western fabric and dress.

10. Johnson (1998: 194) emphasizes placing "difference *among* women rather than exclusively between sexes. . . . [F]eminists have to take the risk of confronting and negotiating differences among women if we are ever to transform such differences into positive rather than negative forces in women's lives."

11. In rejecting the "area" study of Asia and Japan in particular, Harootunian (2000: 25–58) engages in a "disquieting," wrenching, and wide-ranging criticism of cultural studies or what he calls "dinosaurs in an intellectual Jurassic Park."

12. There is always the famous or infamous question: "Why does China have 'no science'?" Despite Joseph Needham's monumental effort to disprove the idea of "no science" in China, the phenomenological sociology of knowledge in addition to Thomas Kuhn's structuration of scientific paradigms rather than genetics might be able to produce a partial answer.

13. Stone's work (1996) is a watershed interspeciesistic argument in behalf of the Sierra Club before the Supreme Court of the United States in the landmark case of *Sierra Club v. Morton, Secretary of the Interior* (1971). It is the beginning of what may be called "Orphic jurisprudence." There are rich resources in Asian thought (Confucianism, Taoism, and Buddhism—Ch'an or Zen in particular) which are ready to be tapped for environmental philosophy.

14. Ricoeur (1965: 271–84) shares his kindred spirit with Nishida in cautioning against forging any facile "syncretism" between universalism and national cultures.

15. Speaking of biology and culture, Bruner (1990: 20–21) contends that the causes of human behavior cannot be assumed to lie in biological nature. Instead, he argues that "culture and the quest for meaning within culture are the proper causes of human action. The biological substrate, the so-called universals of human nature, is not a cause of action but, at most, a *constraint* upon it or a *condition* for it."

16. Levinas (1999: 97) writes: "When I speak of [ethics as] first philosophy, I am referring to a philosophy of dialogue that cannot not be an ethics." He made a "U-turn" in ethics, which is "de-ontologized" but not deontological, from "rights talk."

17. Here Norbert Elias's (1978b) (con)"figurational model" of *homo sociologicus* is most promising because in it humans are seen as the processual webs of interdependence in contrast to totalistic and individualistic models.

18. Geertz (2000: 218–63, "The World in Pieces: Culture and Politics at the End of the Century") gives us a short but grand tour of the condition of humanity at the end of the twentieth century.

19. In reviewing the translated work (*The August Sleepwalker*) of the Chinese poet Bei Dao, the American sinologist Stephen Owen (1990: 28) speaks of "the quintessence of cultural hegemony, when an essentially local tradition (Anglo-European) is widely taken for granted as universal." Cf. the noted Nigerian novelist Achebe (1989: 76) who writes: "In the nature of things the work of a Western writer is automatically informed by universality. It is only others who must strain to achieve it. So-and-so's work is universal; he has truly arrived! As though universality were some distant bend in the road which you may take if you travel out far enough in the direction of Europe or America, if you put adequate distance between yourself and home. I should like to see the word 'universal' banned altogether from discussions of African literature until such a time as people cease to use it as a synonym for the narrow, self-serving parochialism of Europe, until their horizon extends to include all the world."

20. Leitch (1983: 190–97) talks about "the lateral dance" in which distinction is made between two kinds of interpretation: one is vertical metaphysics and the other lateral deconstruction. The latter is an attempt to overcome the *aporia* or impasse of the former.

21. With an emphasis on Chinese ideography, Chang Tung-sun (1959) discusses such interesting issues of Chinese philosophy as the social nature of knowledge, Chinese logic as the logic of *correlation* in contrast to the Western logic of *identity*, and Chinese non-substantive or processual ontology.

22. The issue of "essentialization" is no doubt related to the essentialism/anti-essentialism debate in contemporary feminism. Schor and Weed (1994) capture the range and scope of the debate on the subject. It should also be noted that in political philosophy Leo Strauss's essentialism based on the concept of "human nature" as transhistorical, permanent, and immutable runs counter to the existentialist conception of human as *homo viator*.

23. The outstanding working of transversality or cross-fertilization in the millennia of Chinese history is evidenced in the Sinicization of (1) Indian Buddhism and (2) Western Marxism ("class essentialism"). For a detailed discussion of the second, see Jung and Jung (1975).

24. Experiencing Asian cultural hybridization or the increasingly imbricated layers of Asian interculturation may be likened to tasting transfused "Asian delicacies as the squid pizza, the curry doughnut, the bean-paste Danish, the rice burger, the kimchee burger, the tempura hot dog, the green tea milkshake, the sashimi submarine, and the ever-popular BST (that's bacon, seaweed, and tomato) sandwich" (Reid, 1999: 30).

25. Desan (1972) offers his detailed formulation of the "planetary man" as "a prelude to a united world." It is built on an epistemological and ethical edifice in the direction of *totum genus humanum* in which the nuanced term *totum* is neither totalistic nor fragmentary. Desan insists that it is "nothing but the plural" and made up of "connected parts." Virginia Woolf's *Three Guineas* (1938) is often credited by feminists with the following passage which is written in the cosmopolitan spirit of Diogenes: "As a woman I have no country. As a woman I want no country. As a woman my country is the whole world." Rich (1986, 183, 211), for example, cites it twice in one of her works without an exact reference to it. Unfortunately, however, I have not yet been able to locate it in Woolf's above-mentioned work.

26. Arendt (1998: 175–76) writes: "Human plurality, the basic condition of both action and speech, has the twofold character of equality and distinction. If men were not equal, they could neither understand each other and those who came before them nor plan for the future and foresee the needs of those who will come after them. If men were not distinct, each human being distinguished from any other who is, was, or will ever be, they would need neither speech nor action to make themselves understood. Signs and sounds to communicate immediate, identical needs and wants would be enough."

27. Collins's *The Sociology of Philosophies* (1998: 1), whose subtitle is "A Global Theory of Intellectual Change," assumes that intellectual life is continuing conflict and disagreement, and that the "heartland of disagreement is difficult to avoid; to deny it is to exemplify it." It is worth noting here that in Hans-Georg Gadamer's dialogical hermeneutics the other's disagreement is respected and welcomed with the assumption that the other may be right.

References

Achebe, Chinua (1989). *From Hopes and Impediments.* New York: Doubleday

Arendt, Hannah (1998). *The Human Condition,* 2nd ed. Chicago: University of Chicago Press

Balslev, Anindita Niyogi (1999). *Cultural Otherness: Correspondence with Richard Rorty,* 2nd ed. Atlanta: Scholars Press

Bauman, Zygmunt (1987). *Legislators and Interpreters.* Cambridge, U.K.: Polity Press
——— (2000). *Liquid Modernity.* Cambridge, U.K.: Polity Press

Budick, Sanford and Wolfgang Iser (ed.) (1996). *The Translatability of Cultures.* Stanford, Calif.: Stanford University Press

Bruner, Jerome (1990). *Acts of Meaning.* Cambridge, Mass.: Harvard University Press

Buruma, Ian (2000). *The Missionary and the Libertine.* New York: Random House

Butler, Judith (2000). "Restaging the Universal: Hegemony and the Limits of Formalism." In Judith Butler, Ernesto Laclau and Slavoj Zizek, *Contingency, Hegemony, Universality,* pp. 11–43. London: Verso

Chang, Tung-sun (1959). "A Chinese Philosopher's Theory of Knowledge." In *On Language and Our World,* ed. S. I. Hayakawa, pp. 299–324. New York: Harper and Brothers

Chow, Rey (1995). "In the Name of Comparative Literature." In *Comparative Literature in the Age of Multiculturalism,* ed. Charles Bernheimer, pp. 107–16. Baltimore: Johns Hopkins University Press

Collin, Françoise (1994). "Philosophical Differences." In *A History of Women in the West* (trans. Arthur Goldhammer), vol. 5: *Toward a Cultural Identity in the Twentieth Century,* ed. Françoise Thébaud, pp. 261–96. Cambridge, Mass.: Harvard University Press

Collins, Randall (1998). *The Sociology of Philosophies.* Cambridge, Mass.: Harvard University Press

Culler, Jonathan (1995). "Comparative Literature, At Last!" In *Comparative Litera-*

ture in the Age of Multiculturalism, pp. 117–21. Baltimore: Johns Hopkins University Press

Dallmayr, Fred (ed.) (1999). *Border Crossings: Toward a Comparative Political Theory.* Lanham, Md.: Lexington Books

De Bono, Edward (1968). *New Think.* New York: Basic Books

Derrida, Jacques (1992). *The Other Heading.* Trans. Pascale-Anne Brault and Michael B. Naas. Bloomington, Ind.: Indiana University Press

Desan, Wilfrid (1972). *The Planetary Man.* New York: Macmillan

Elias, Norbert (1978a). *The Civilizing Process*, vol. 1: *The History of Manners*, trans. Edmund Jephcott. New York: Pantheon Books

—— (1978b). *What Is Sociology?*, trans. Stephen Mennel and Grace Morrissey. New York: Columbia University Press

Eze, Emmanuel Chukwudi (ed.) (1997). *Race and the Enlightenment.* Cambridge, U.K.: Blackwell

Fenollosa, Ernest (1936). *The Chinese Written Character as a Medium for Poetry*, ed. Ezra Pound. San Francisco: City Lights Books

Feyerabend, Paul (1999). *Conquest of Abundance.* Chicago: University of Chicago Press

Foucault, Michel (1997). *The Politics of Truth.* Ed. Sylvère Lotringer and Lysa Hochroth. New York: Semiotext(e)

—— (1999). "Michel Foucault and Zen: A Stay in a Zen Temple (1978)" (trans. Richard Townsend), in *Religion and Culture*, ed. Jeremy R. Carrette, pp. 110–14. New York: Routledge

Fung, Yu-lan (1922). "Why China Has No Science—An Interpretation of the History and Consequences of Chinese Philosophy," *International Journal of Ethics*, 32: 237–63

Gadamer, Hans-Georg (1991). *Truth and Method.* 2nd rev. ed., rev. trans. Joel Weinsheimer and Donald G. Marshall. New York: Crossroad

Geertz, Clifford (1973). *The Interpretation of Cultures.* New York: Basic Books

—— (2000). *Available Light.* Princeton, N.J.: Princeton University Press

Giddens, Anthony (2000). *Runaway World.* New York: Routledge

Gray, John (1995). *Enlightenment's Wake.* New York: Routledge

Harding, Sandra G. (1998). *Is Science Multicultural?* Bloomington, Ind.: Indiana University Press

Harootunian, Harry (2000). *History's Disquiet.* New York: Columbia University Press

Heidegger, Martin (1958). *The Question of Being.* Trans. William Kluback and Jean T. Wilde. New York: Twayne

—— (1971). *On the Way to Language.* Trans. Peter D. Hertz. New York: Harper and Row

—— (1982). *The Basic Problems of Phenomenology.* Trans. Albert Hofstadter. Bloomington, Ind.: Indiana University Press

Johnson, Barbara (1998). *The Feminist Difference.* Cambridge, Mass.: Harvard University Press

Jung, Hwa Yol (1995). "The *Tao* of Transversality as a Global Approach to Truth: A Metacommentary on Calvin O. Schrag," *Man and World*, 28: 11–31

—— (forthcoming). "Enlightenment and the Question of the Other: A Postmodern Audition," *Human Studies*

Jung, Hwa Yol and Petee Jung (1975). "The Hermeneutics of Political Ideology and Cultural Change: Maoism as the Sinicization of Marxism," *Cultural Hermeneutics,* 3: 165–98

Kuriyama, Shigehisa (1999). *The Expressiveness of the Body and the Divergence of Greek and Chinese Medicine.* New York: Zone Books

Laqueur, Thomas (1990). *Making Sex.* Cambridge, Mass.: Harvard University Press

Leitch, Vincent B. (1983). *Deconstructive Criticism.* New York: Columbia University Press

Levinas, Emmanuel (1999). *Alterity and Transcendence.* Trans. Michael B. Smith. New York: Columbia University Press

Liu, Lydia H. (1995). *Translingual Practice.* Stanford, Calif.: Stanford University Press

Madison, Gary B. (1999). "The Ethics and Politics of the Flesh." In *The Ethics of Postmodernity,* ed. Gary B. Madison and Mary Fairbairn, pp. 174–90. Evanston, Ill.: Northwestern University Press

Martin, Richard and Harold Koda (1994). *Orientalism: Visions of East in Western Dress.* New York: Metropolitan Museum of Art

McClintock, Anne (1995). *Imperial Leather.* New York: Routledge

Merleau-Ponty, Maurice (1964). *Signs.* Trans. Richard C. McCleary. Evanston, Ill.: Northwestern University Press

Nakamura, Hajime (1964). *Ways of Thinking of Eastern Peoples.* Ed. Philip P. Wiener. Honolulu: East-West Center Press

Nussbaum, Martha C. (1997). *Cultivating Humanity.* Cambridge, Mass.: Harvard University Press

Okin, Susan Moller (1999). *Is Multiculturalism Bad for Women?* Ed. Joshua Cohen, Matthew Howard, and Martha C. Nussbaum. Princeton, N.J.: Princeton University Press

Owen, Stephen (1990). "What Is World Poetry?" *The New Republic,* November 19: 28–32

Owens, Craig (1992). *Beyond Recognition.* Ed. Scott Bryson, Barbara Kruger, Lynne Tillman, and Jane Weinstock. Berkeley, Calif.: University of California Press

Parekh, Bhikhu (2000). *Rethinking Multiculturalism.* Cambridge, Mass.: Harvard University Press

Reid, T. R. (1999). *Confucius Lives Next Door.* New York: Random House

Rich, Adrienne (1986). *Blood, Bread, and Poetry.* New York: W. W. Norton

Ricoeur, Paul (1965). *History and Truth.* Trans. Charles A. Kelbley. Evanston, Ill.: Northwestern University Press

Rorty, Richard (1979). *Philosophy and the Mirror of Nature.* Princeton, N.J.: Princeton University Press

Said, Edward W. (1978). *Orientalism.* New York: Pantheon Books

———— (1993). *Culture and Imperialism.* New York: Alfred A. Knopf

Schor, Naomi and Elizabeth Weed (eds.) (1994). *The Essential Difference.* Bloomington, Ind.: Indiana University Press

Spence, Jonathan D. (1988). *The Question of Hu.* New York: Alfred A. Knopf

Spivak, Gayatri Chakravorty (1993). *Outside in the Teaching Machine.* New York: Routledge

Stone, Christopher D. (1996). *Should Trees Have Standing?* Dobbs Ferry, N.Y.: Oceana Publications

Taylor, Charles (1993). "Engaged Agency and Background in Heidegger." In *The Cambridge Companion to Heidegger*, ed. Charles Guignon, pp. 317–36. New York: Cambridge University Press

Todorov, Tzvetan (2001). *Life in Common*. Trans. Katherine Golsan and Lucy Golsan. Lincoln, Nebr.: University of Nebraska Press

Varela, Francisco J., Evan Thompson, and Eleanor Rosch (1991). *The Embodied Mind*. Cambridge, Mass.: MIT Press

Wang, Eugene Y. (2000). "The Winking Owl: Visual Effect and Its Art Historical Thick Description," *Critical Inquiry*, 26: 435–73

West, Cornel (1990). "The New Cultural Politics of Difference." In *Out There*, ed. Russell Ferguson, Martha Gever, Trinh T. Minh-ha and Cornel West, pp. 19–36. Cambridge, Mass.: MIT Press

Young, Robert (1990). *White Mythologies*. New York: Routledge

Part I
Beyond Eurocentrism

1

Everywhere and Nowhere[1]

Maurice Merleau-Ponty

[I]   Philosophy and the "Outside"

PUTTING TOGETHER an anthology about famous philosophers may seem to be an inoffensive undertaking. Yet one does not attempt it without reservations. It raises the question of what idea one should have of the history of philosophy, and even of philosophy itself.

For the reader is not going to find just anecdotes in this volume, but philosophers' visible lives—the rough sketch, drawn in a few pages by different authors, of what these philosophers have tried to say throughout volumes. Even if the life, the work, or preferably the work and the life together, had been perfectly discerned in every instance, we would have only a history of philosophers or philosophies, not a history of philosophy; and so this work about philosophers would be unfaithful to what they were greatly concerned with, a truth which rises above opinions.

How could an anthology possibly have a central perspective? In order to bring out relationships, progressions, and retrogressions, we have to ask all the philosophers the same question and mark out the development of the problem in reference to it. So we cannot have the genealogy of philosophers here, nor the evolution of truth; and philosophy in our work risks being no more than a catalogue of "points of view" or "theories." A series of intellectual portraits will leave the reader with the impression of a fruitless endeavor in which each philosopher presents the whims inspired by his temper and the accidents of his life as truth, taking questions up again at their beginning and leaving them entire to his successors without there being any possibility of comparison from one mental universe to another. Since the same words— idea, freedom, knowledge—have different meanings for different philosophers, and since we lack the comprehensive witness who would reduce them to a common denominator, how could we possibly see one single philosophy developing through different philosophers?

In order to respect what they looked for and speak worthily of them, should we not on the contrary take their doctrines as aspects of one running doctrine, and preserve them in an Hegelian fashion by giving them a place in an unified system?

The system, it is true, is in its own way unconstrained: since it incorporates philosophers into an integral philosophy, it follows that it claims to lead the philosophical venture better and farther than they have led it. For a philosophy which wanted to express Being, to survive as an aspect of truth or a first draft of a final but different system is not to be preserved. When we "go beyond" a philosophy "from within," we cut the heart out of it. We insult it by retaining it without what we judge to be its "limitations"—that is, without its words and concepts—as if the meanderings of the *Parmenides* or the flow of the *Meditations* could be reduced without loss to a paragraph of the System.

In reality, the System assumes that they are known; and that is why it can go farther. Even if it brings them to a conclusion, it does not include them. We learn the full meaning of Hegelian philosophy, which wanted to "go beyond," by going to the school of other philosophers. The movement of contradictories which pass into one another, the positive which bursts into negation and the negative which establishes itself as positive, all this begins in Zeno, the *Sophist*, Descartes' doubt. The System begins in them. It is the focal point in which the rays from many mirrors are concentrated: if for one moment they stopped darting their fires toward it, it would fall into nothingness. The past transgresses upon and grows through the present; and Truth is that imaginary system, the contemporary of all philosophies, which would be able to retain their signifying power without loss. An existing philosophy is evidently no more than a crude sketch of such a system.

Hegel knows this too. "The history of philosophy," he says, "is all present history." Which means that Plato, Descartes, Kant are not true simply in what they saw, reservation made for what they did not see. The turnings which made straight the way for Hegelian philosophy are not completed; they are still permissible. More than that; they are necessary. They are the way, and Truth is only the memory of all that has been found along the way. Hegel walls history up again in the tomb of his system, but past philosophies keep on breathing and stirring within it—along with them he shut up uneasiness, movement, and the working of contingency. To say that the System is the truth of what preceded it is *also* to say that great philosophies are "indestructible."[2] Not because they saw in part what was to be fully unveiled in the System, but rather because they established landmarks—Plato's reminiscence and "ideas," Aristotle's φύσις, Descartes' *malin génie*—which posterity has not stopped recognizing.

Sartre once contrasted the Descartes who existed, lived that life, spoke those words, and wrote those works—an unshakable block and indestructible landmark—and Cartesianism, a "wandering philosophy" which necessarily escapes our grasp because it changes endlessly in the hands of its inheritors. He was right, except that no boundary marks the point where Descartes stops and his successors begin, and there would be no more sense in enumerating the thoughts which *are in Descartes* and those which *are in his successors* than there would be in making an inventory of a language. With this reservation, what counts certainly is that thinking life called Descartes, whose fortunately preserved wake is his works. The reason why Descartes is present is that—surrounded by circumstances which today are abolished, and haunted by the concerns and some of the illusions of his times—he responded to these hazards in a way which teaches us to respond to our own, even though they are different and our response is different too.

One does not enter the Pantheon of philosophers by having worked assiduously at having only eternal thoughts, and the ring of truth never resounds so long as it does when the author calls upon his life for it. Past philosophies do not survive in their spirit alone, as stages of a final system. Their access to the timeless is no museum entrance. They endure with their truths and follies as total undertakings, or they do not endure at all. Hegel himself, that mind which wanted to contain Being, lives today and gives us food for thought not only through his profundities but also through his manias and his tics. There is not *a* philosophy which contains all philosophies; philosophy as a whole is at certain moments in each philosophy. To take up the celebrated phrase again, philosophy's center is everywhere and its circumference nowhere.

Thus truth and the whole are there from the start—but as a task to be accomplished, and thus not yet there. This singular relationship between philosophy and its past generally clarifies its relationships with the outside and, for example, with personal and social history.

Like past doctrines, philosophy lives from everything which happens to the philosopher and his times. But it throws it out of focus or transports it into the order of symbols and of the truth it utters, so that there is no more sense in judging the works by the life than the life by the works.

We do not have to choose between those who think that the history of the individual or the society contains the truth of the philosopher's symbolic constructions, and those who think on the contrary that the philosophical consciousness has as a matter of principle the keys to personal and social history. The alternative is imaginary, and the proof is that those who defend one of these theses surreptitiously have recourse to the other.

One can think of replacing the internal study of philosophies with a socio-historical explanation only in reference to a history whose course and meaning one thinks he clearly knows. One assumes, for example, a certain idea of "the whole man," or a "natural" equilibrium between man and man and man and nature. Then, this historical τέλος being given, every philosophy can be presented as a diversion, an alienation, and a resistance in respect to that necessary future; or on the contrary as a step and an advance toward it. But where does the guiding principle come from, and what is it worth? The question *ought* not to be asked. To ask it is already to "resist" a dialectic which is in the course of things, to take sides against it. But how do you know it is there? By philosophy. It is just that it is a secret philosophy, disguised as Process. What is contrasted to the internal study of philosophies is never socio-historical explanation; it is always another philosophy concealed in it.

Marxists show us that Hegel conceived of alienation as he did *because* he had the alienation of capitalist society before his eyes and thought according to it. This "explanation" would account for the Hegelian idea of alienation and make it an episode of capitalism only if a society in which man objectifies himself without alienating himself could be shown. Such a society was only an idea for Marx; and even for us the least that can be said is that it is not a fact. What Marxism sets in opposition to Hegel is not a fact but an idea of the relationship between man and society as a whole. Under the name of objective explanation, it is still a way of thinking which challenges another way of thinking and denounces it as an illusion. If Marxists reply that the Marxist idea, as an historical hypothesis, clarifies the history of capitalism before and after Marx, they move to the realm of facts and historical probability. But in this realm it will be necessary to "try out" the Hegelian idea of alienation in the same way; and see, for example, whether it does not help us understand even the societies based upon the Marxist idea. It is just such an inquiry which is excluded when Marxists declare in a doctrinaire fashion that the Hegelian idea of alienation is a product of the society in which Hegel lived. Consequently, they do not stick to the realm of facts, and their historical "explanation" is a way of philosophizing without seeming to, of disguising ideas as things and thinking imprecisely. A conception of history explains philosophies only on the condition that it becomes philosophy itself, and implicit philosophy.

On their side, the philosophers who are the most smitten with interiority strangely fail to live up to their principles when they call régimes and cultures into their court and judge them from the outside, as if interiority stopped being important when it was not *their own*.

Thus the partisans of "pure" philosophy and those of socioeconomic explanation exchange roles before our very eyes, and we do not have to enter their interminable debate. We do not have to choose between a false conception of the "interior" and a false conception of the "exterior." Philosophy is everywhere, even in the "facts," and it nowhere has a private realm which shelters it from life's contagion.

We need to do many things to eliminate the twin myths of pure philosophy and pure history and get back to their effective relationships. What we would need first of all would be a theory of concepts or significations which took each philosophical idea as it is: never unburdened of historical import and never reducible to its origins. As new forms of grammar and syntax arising from the rubble of an old linguistic system or from the accidents of general history are nevertheless organized according to an expressive intention which makes a new system of them, so each philosophical idea emerging in the ebb and flow of personal and social history is not simply a result and a thing but a beginning and an instrument as well. As the discriminant in a new type of thought and a new symbolism, it sets up for itself a field of application which is incommensurable with its origins and can be understood only from within. Its origin is no more a good work than it is a sin, and it is the developed whole which must be judged, according to the view and grasp of experience it gives us. Rather than "explaining" a philosophy, the historical approach serves to show how its significance exceeds its circumstances, and how as an historical fact it transmutes its original situation into a means of understanding it and other situations. The philosophical universal lies in that instant and point where a philosopher's limitations are invested in a different history which is not parallel to the history of psychological or social facts, but which sometimes crosses and sometimes withdraws from it—or rather which does not pertain to the same dimension.

In order to understand this relationship we would also have to change our idea of psychological or historical genesis. We would have to think through psychoanalysis and Marxism again as experiences in which principles and standards are always challenged by what is judged in the light of them. This is not a matter of classifying men and societies according to their approximation to the canon of the classless society or the man without conflicts; these negative entities cannot be used to think about existing men or societies. We would especially have to understand how their contradictions function, the type of equilibrium which they have somehow managed to reach, and whether it paralyzes them or lets them live. And we would have to understand these things in all respects, taking account of job and work as well as sexual life in psychoanalysis, and as far as Marxism is concerned, of relationships in living experience as well as variables of economic analysis, of human qualities of relationships as well as production, and of clandestine social roles as well as official regulations. Although comparisons of this sort can provide a basis for preference and choice, they do not give us an ideal genetic series; and the relationship of one historical formation to another, like that of one type of man to another, will never be simply the relationship of true to false. The "healthy" man is not so much the one who has eliminated his contradictions as the one who makes use of them and drags them into his vital labors. We would also have to relativize the Marxist idea of a pre-history which is going to give way to history—of an imminence of the complete, true Society in which man is reconciled with man and nature—for although this is indeed what our social criticism demands, there is no force in history which is destined to produce it. Human history is not from this moment on so constructed as to one day point, on all its dials at once, to the high noon of identity. The progress of socio-economic history, including its revolutions, is not so much a movement toward an homogenous or a classless society as the quest, through always atypical cultural devices, for a life which is not unlivable for the greatest number. The relationships between this history which always travels from positive to positive, never overcoming itself in *pure* negation, and the philosophical concept which never breaks its ties with the world are as close as one could wish. Not that a single unequivocal meaning dwells in the rational and in the real (as both Hegel and Marx in their own way thought), but because the "real" and the "rational" are both cut from the same cloth, which is the historical existence of men, and because the real is so to speak *engaged* to reason through their common inherence in historical existence.

Even if we consider only one philosopher, he swarms with inner differences, and it is through these discordancies that we must find his "total" meaning. If I have difficulty finding the "fundamental choice" of the absolute Descartes Sartre spoke of, the man who lived and wrote once and for all three centuries ago, it is perhaps because Descartes himself did not at any moment coincide with Descartes. What he is in our eyes according to the texts, he was only bit by bit through his reaction upon himself. And the idea of grasping him in his entirety at his source is perhaps an illusory one if Descartes—instead of being some "central intuition," an eternal character, and an absolute individual—is this discourse, hesitant at first, which is affirmed through experience and use, which is apprised of itself little by little, and which never wholly stops intending the very thing it has resolutely excluded. A philosophy is not chosen like an object. Choice does not suppress what is not chosen, but sustains it marginally. The same Descartes who distinguishes so well between what arises from pure understanding and what pertains to the practice of life happens to map out at the same time the program for a philosophy which was to take as its principal theme the cohesion of the very orders he distinguishes. Philosophical choice (and doubtless all other choice) is never simple. And it is through their ambiguity that philosophy and history touch.

Although these remarks do not provide an adequate definition of philosophy, they are sufficient to absolve a work like this one, a mixture of philosophy, history, and anecdote. This disorder is a part of philosophy, which finds in it the means of creating its unity through digression and return to the center. Its unity is that of a landscape or a discourse, where everything is indirectly linked by secret references to a center of interest or central perspective which no guideline marks out in advance. Like Europe or Africa, the history of philosophy is a whole, even though it has its gulfs, its capes, its relief, its deltas and its estuaries. And even though it is lodged in a wider world, the signs of everything that is happening can be read in it. Then how could any mode of approach possibly be forbidden and unworthy of philosophers? A series of portraits is not in itself a criminal attempt on philosophy's life.

And as for the plurality of perspectives and commentators, it would disrupt the unity of philosophy only if that unity were one of juxtaposition or accumulation. But since philosophies are so many languages not immediately translatable into one another or able to be superimposed word for word upon one another, since each is necessary to the others in its own singular way, the diversity of commentators scarcely increases that of philosophies. Furthermore, if each commentator is asked, as we have asked ours, more for his reaction to a philosopher than for an "objective" account, we may find at this height of subjectivity a sort of convergence, and a kinship between the questions each of these contemporaries puts to his famous philosopher, face to face.

These problems are not settled by a preface, and need not be. If philosophy is unified by the successive reduction of differences and separations, we must necessarily encounter the difficulty of thinking about it at each stage of this book. When we come to distinguishing philosophy from Oriental thought or Christianity, we shall have to ask ourselves whether the term philosophy applies only to doctrines which are expressed conceptually, or whether it can be extended to experiences, forms of wisdom, and disciplines which do not attain to this degree or kind of consciousness, in which case we shall meet the problem of the philosophical concept and its nature again. Each time we take the risk of tracing out lines of development that philosophers themselves have clearly failed to see, and of arranging them according to themes which were not expressly their own—in a word, with each part of this work—we shall have to ask ourselves again how far our right to put past philosophies in the light of our own times extends; whether we can flatter ourselves, as Kant said, with understanding them better than they understood themselves;

and finally, up to what point philosophy is mastery of meaning. Each time we shall have to learn anew to bridge the gap between ourselves and the past, between ourselves and the Orient, and between philosophy and religion; and to find an indirect unity. And the reader will see the line of questioning we just formulated at the beginning arise again: for it is no preface to philosophy but philosophy itself.

[2]   The Orient and Philosophy

Is this huge body of thoughtful literature, which would require a volume by itself, really part of "philosophy"? Is it possible to compare it with what the West has meant by the term? *Truth* in it is not understood as the horizon of an indefinite series of investigations, nor as conquest and intellectual possession of being. It is rather a treasure scattered about in human life prior to all philosophy and not divided among doctrines. Thought does not feel called upon to extend previous efforts, or even to choose between them, and even less to really move beyond them by forming a new idea of the whole. It is presented as commentary and syncretism, echo and conciliation. The old and the new, contrasting doctrines, are all of a piece; and the uninitiated reader can see nothing acquired or completed in it all. He feels that he is in a magical world where nothing is ever finished, dead thoughts persist, and those believed to be incompatible intermingle.

Of course we must take our ignorance into consideration here: if we were to look at Western thought in such a cavalier fashion and from such a distance as we look at the thought of India and China, perhaps it too would give us the impression of a resifting, an eternal reinterpretation, an hypocritical betrayal, and an involuntary, undirected change. Yet this feeling in respect to the Orient persists in the experts. Masson-Oursel said of India: "What we are dealing with here is an immense world, without any unity at all, in which nothing appears in a wholly new way at any given time, in which nothing one might believe 'surpassed' is abolished either—a chaos of human groups, an inextricable jungle of disparate religions, a swarm of doctrines." A contemporary Chinese author writes:[3] "In certain philosophical writings, such as those of Mencius or Sun-Tse, one finds a line of reasoning and systematic arguments. But compared to Western philosophical writings, they are not yet sufficiently articulate. It is a fact that Chinese philosophers have the habit of expressing themselves in aphorisms, apothegms, or allusions and apologues. . . . The words and writings of Chinese philosophers are so inarticulate that their power of suggestion is unlimited. . . . The short sentences of Confucius' *Topics* or Lao-Tse's philosophy are not just conclusions whose premises have been lost. . . . All the ideas contained in the *Lao-Tse* can be assembled and noted down in a new book of five thousand or even five hundred thousand words. Whether it is done well or poorly, it will be a new book. It can be compared page by page with the original *Lao-Tse;* perhaps it will be a great help in understanding it, but it will never be able to replace it. Kuo Siang . . . is one of Chiang-Tse's great commentators. His commentary is in its own right a classic work of Taoist literature. He transcribed Chiang-Tse's allusions and metaphors into lines of reasoning and arguments. . . . But it can still be asked about the former's suggestive style and the articulate style of Kuo-Siang, which is better? A Ch'an or Zen Buddhist monk of a later period said one day: 'Everyone says that Kuo-Siang has written a commentary on Chiang-Tse; for my own part, I would say that it is Chiang-Tse who has written a commentary on Kuo-Siang.' "

It is true that during the last twenty centuries of Western philosophy Christian themes have persisted. And perhaps in the case of Oriental philosophy too, it is necessary, as we have been told,[4] to be *in* a civilization in order to perceive movement and history beneath the appearance of stagnation. Yet it is difficult to compare Christianity's persistence in the West to Confucianism's in China. The Christianity which persists among us is not a philosophy; it is an account of and a meditation upon an experience or a group of enigmatic events which themselves call for several philosophical elaborations and have not in fact stopped arousing philoso*phies,* even when one of these has been accorded a privileged position. Christian themes are ferments, not relics. Have we nothing comparable to the swarming of apocrypha in the Confucian tradition, to the amalgamation of themes in the neo-Taoism of the third and fourth centuries A.D., to those extravagant enterprises of over-all census-taking and conciliation to which generations of educated Chinese have devoted themselves, to that philosophical orthodoxy which was to last from Chou-Hi (1130–1200) up to the elimination of examinations in 1905? And if we go into the content of doctrines—as we would have to, since after all the external forms of Chinese philosophy are dependent upon the relationship between man and the world they express—has any Western doctrine ever taught such a strict concordance of microcosm and macrocosm? Has any ever established a name and place of *their own* for each man and thing (with not even the Stoics' mistrust as a way out), or defined "correctness" as the cardinal virtue? One has the feeling that Chinese philosophers do not understand the very idea of understanding or knowing in the same sense as Western ones do—that they do not have the intellectual genesis of the object in view or try to *grasp* the object, but simply seek to evoke it in its primordial perfection. And that is why they are suggestive; why commentary and what is commented upon, enveloping and enveloped, signifying and signified are indistinguishable in their work; why in their work concepts are as much allusions to aphorisms as aphorisms allusions to concepts.

If this is true, how are we to discover a profile, a development, a history in this inarticulate time and ontology? How are we to pin down each philosopher's contribution when they all gravitate around the same immemorial world that they do not try to think about but simply render present? The Chinese philosopher's relation to the world is a fascination which cannot be halfheartedly entered into. One is either initiated—by means of history, customs, civilization—and Chinese philosophy then becomes one of the superstructures, without inner truth, of this historical wonder; or one must give up understanding. Like everything built or instituted by man, India and China are immensely interesting. But like all institutions, they leave it to us to discern their true meaning; they do not give it to us completely. China and India are not entirely aware of what they are saying. What they need to do to have philosophies is to try to *understand* themselves and everything else.

Although these remarks are commonplace today, they do not settle the question. They come to us from Hegel. He was the one who invented the idea of "going beyond" the Orient by "understanding" it. It was he who contrasted the Western idea of truth as the total conceptual recovery of the world in all its variety to the Orient, and who defined the Orient as a failure in *the same undertaking.* It is worth recalling the terms of his condemnation before we decide whether we can accept it ourselves.

For Hegel, Oriental thought is indeed philosophy, in the sense that in it mind learns to free itself from appearances and vanity. But like many other bizarre things in the world of man, such as the Pyramids, it is only philosophy "in itself," that is, it does not contain mind in its conscious or ideal state but only gives an indication of it to the philosopher. For mind is not yet mind insofar as it is separated from and set above appearances: the counterpart of such abstract thought is the tumescence of unmastered appearances. Thus on the one hand there is an intuition "which sees nothing," a thought "which thinks nothing," the incorporeal One, the eternal substance, calm and immense, an incomparable contemplation, the mystical name of God, the indefinitely murmured syllable *om*—that is, unconsciousness and the void. And on the other hand there is a mass of absurd details, preposterous ceremonies, infinite inventories, and unbounded enumerations; a trumped-up technique of the body, respiration, and the senses from which anything in the world is expected—divination of others' thoughts, the elephant's strength, the lion's courage, and the wind's swiftness. In fakirs (as in Greek Cynics and Christianity's mendicant friars) we find a "profound abstraction from external relationships" which is itself provocative, gaudy, and picturesque. Nowhere is there mediation or passage from within toward the outside and return to self from without. India has no knowledge of "the idea's radiation in the finite," and that is why this presentiment of mind ends up in "childishness."[5]

China, for its part, has a history; it distinguishes barbarism from culture and deliberately progresses from one to the other. But it is "a culture which remains steadily within its principle" and does not develop beyond it. At another level than India, it maintains the immediate, paralyzing coexistence of the internal and the external, of the universal and a prosaic wisdom, and we see it seek the secret of the world in a tortoise shell and practice a law which is formalistic and void of any moral criticism. "A European would never think of putting the things of sense so close to abstractions."[6] Thought slides without profit from abstraction to sense, and during this time does not develop or mature.

Let us not even say, Hegel adds, that Oriental thought is religion; it is as foreign to religion in *our* sense of the term as it is to philosophy, and for the same reasons. Western religion presupposes "the principle of freedom and individuality"; it has gone through the experience of "reflecting subjectivity," of mind at work on the world. The West has learned that it is the same thing for mind to comprehend itself and to go outside itself, create itself and deny itself. Oriental thought does not have even the faintest idea of this negation which is realization; it is beyond the reach of our categories—neither theism nor atheism, neither religion nor philosophy. Brahma, Vishnu, and Siva are not individuals, nor are they the monogram and symbol of fundamental human situations, and what India tells about them does not have the inexhaustible significance of Greek myths or Christian parables. They are almost entities or philosophemes, and the Chinese flatter themselves with having the least religious and most philosophical civilization there is. In fact, it is no more philosophical than religious, since it lacks knowledge of the mind's work in contact with the immediate world. Thus Oriental thought is original; it yields its secrets to us only if we forget the terminal forms of our culture. But in our individual or collective past we have what it takes to understand it. It dwells in the unsettled region where there is *not yet* religion and *not yet* philosophy; it is the impasse of immediate mind which we have been able to avoid. It is in this way that Hegel goes beyond it by incorporating it into the true development of mind as aberrant or atypical thought.

These Hegelian views are everywhere. When the West is defined in terms of the intervention of science or capitalism, the definition is always of Hegelian inspiration. For capitalism and science can define a civilization only when they are understood as "this-worldly asceticism" or "the labor of the negative," and the reproach made to the Orient is always that it has ignored them.

So the problem is completely clear: Hegel and those who follow him grant philosophical dignity to Oriental thought only by treating it as a distant approximation of conceptual understanding. Our idea of knowledge is so demanding that it forces every other type of thought to the alternative of resigning itself to being a first sketch of the concept or disqualifying itself as irrational. Now the question is whether we can claim as Hegel did to have this absolute knowledge, this concrete universal that the Orient has shut itself off from. If we do not in fact have it, our entire evaluation of other cultures must be re-examined.

Even at the end of his career, and just when he is laying bare the *crisis of Western knowledge*, Husserl writes that "China . . . India . . . are empirical or anthropological specimens."[7] Thus he seems to be setting out again on Hegel's way. But even though he retains the privileged position of Western philosophy, he does so not by virtue of its right to it—as if its possession of the principles of all possible cultures were absolutely evident—but in the name of a fact, and in order to assign a task to it. Husserl admitted that all thought is part of an historical whole or a "life-world"; thus in principle all philosophies are "anthropological specimens," and none has any special rights. He also admits that so-called primitive cultures play an important role in the exploration of the "life-world," in that they offer us variations of this world without which we would remain enmeshed in our preconceptions and would not even see the meaning of our own lives. Yet the fact remains that the West has invented an idea of truth which requires and authorizes it to understand other cultures, and thus to recover them as aspects of a total truth. There has in fact been this miraculous turning back upon itself of an historical formation, through which Western thought has emerged from its particularity and "locality." A presumption and an intention which are still awaiting their fulfillment. If Western thought is what it claims to be, it must prove it by understanding all "life-worlds." It must bear factual witness to its unique significance beyond "anthropological specimens." So the idea of philosophy as a "rigorous science"—or as absolute knowledge—does reappear here, but from this point on with a question mark. Husserl said in his last years: "Philosophy as a rigorous science? The dream is all dreamed out."[8] The philosopher can no longer honestly avail himself of an absolutely radical way of thinking or presumptuously claim for himself intellectual possession of the world and conceptual rigor. His task is still to test himself and all things, but he is never done with it; because from now on he must pursue it through the phenomenal field, which no formal *a priori* assures him mastery of in advance.

Husserl had understood: our philosophical problem is to open up the concept without destroying it.

There is something irreplaceable in Western thought. The attempt to conceive and the rigor of the concept remain exemplary, even if they never exhaust what exists. A culture is judged by its degree of transparency, by the consciousness it has of itself and others. In this respect the West (in the broad sense of the term) is still the system of reference. It is the West which has invented the theoretical and practical means of becoming self-conscious and has opened up the way of truth.

But this possession of self and truth, which only the West has taken as its theme, nevertheless flits through the dreams of other cultures, and in the West itself it is not fulfilled. What we have learned about the historical relations of Greece and the Orient, and inversely, all the "Western" characteristics we have discovered in Oriental thought (Sophistry, Skepticism, elements of dialectics and logic), forbid us to draw a geographical frontier between philosophy and non-philosophy. Pure or absolute philosophy, in the name of which Hegel excluded the Orient, also excludes a good part of the Western past. It may be that a strict application of the criterion would spare Hegel alone.

And above all, since as Husserl said, the West has to justify its value as "historical entelechy" by new creations; since it too is an historical creation, only committed to the onerous task of understanding others; its very destiny is to re-examine everything, including its idea of truth and conceptual understanding and all institutions—sciences, capitalism, and, if you wish, the Oedipus complex—which are directly or indirectly related to its philosophy. Not necessarily in order to destroy them, but to face up to the crisis they are going through and to rediscover the source from which they derive and to which they owe their long prosperity. From this angle, civilizations lacking our philosophical or economic equipment take on an instructive value. It is not a matter of going in search of truth or salvation in what falls short of science or philosophical awareness, or of dragging chunks of mythology as such into our philosophy, but of acquiring—in the presence of these variants of humanity that we are so far from—a sense of the theoretical and practical problems our institutions are faced with, and of rediscovering the existential field that they were born in and that their long success has led us to forget. The Orient's "childishness" has something to teach us, if it were nothing more than the narrowness of our adult ideas. The relationship between Orient and Occident, like that between child and adult, is not that of ignorance to knowledge or non-philosophy to philosophy; it is much more subtle, making room on the part of the Orient for all anticipations and "prematurations." Simply rallying and subordinating "non-philosophy" to true philosophy will not create the unity of the human spirit. It already exists in each culture's lateral relationships to the others, in the echoes one awakes in the other.

We would have to apply to the problem of philosophical universality what travelers tell us of their relationships with foreign civilizations. Photographs of China give us the impression of an impenetrable universe if they stop with the picturesque—stop, that is, with precisely *our* clipping, *our* idea of China. If, on the other hand, a photograph just tries to grasp Chinese people in the act of living together, they begin paradoxically to live for us, and we understand them. If we were able to grasp in their historical and human context the very doctrines which seem to resist conceptual understanding, we would find in them a variant of man's relationships to being which would clarify our understanding of ourselves, and a sort of oblique universality. Indian and Chinese philosophies have tried not so much to dominate existence as to be the echo or the sounding board of our relationship to being. Western philosophy can learn from them to rediscover the relationship to being and initial option which gave it birth, and to estimate the possibilities we have shut ourselves off from in becoming "Westerners" and perhaps reopen them.

This is why we should let the Orient appear in the museum of famous philosophers, and why (not being able to give it as much space as a detailed study would require) we have preferred to offer in the place of generalities some rather precise samples in which the reader will perhaps discern the Orient's secret, muted contribution to philosophy.

[3]   Christianity and Philosophy

One of the tests in which philosophy best reveals its essence is its confrontation with Christianity. Not that there is Christianity unanimous on one side and philosophy unanimous on the other. On the contrary, what was striking in the famous discussion of this subject which took place twenty-five years ago[9] was that behind disagreement about the idea of Christian philosophy or about the existence of Christian philosophies, one detected a more profound debate concerning the nature of philosophy, and that on this point neither Christians nor non-Christians were agreed.

Gilson and Maritain said that philosophy is not Christian in its *essence* but only according to its status, only through the intermingling of religious thought and life in the same age and ultimately in the same man. And in this sense they were not so far from Bréhier, who distinguished philosophy as a rigorous system of ideas from Christianity as the revelation of a supernatural history of man, and concluded, for his part, that no philosophy as philosophy can be Christian. When on the other hand Brunschvicg,[10] thinking of Pascal and Malebranche, reserved the possibility of a philosophy which confirms the discordancy between existence and idea (and thus its own insufficiency), and thereby serves as an introduction to Christianity as an interpretation of existing man and the world, he was not so far from Blondel, for whom philosophy *was* thought realizing that it cannot "close the gap," locating and palpating inside and outside of us a reality whose source is not philosophical awareness. Once a certain point of maturity, experience, or criticism has been passed, what separates men or brings them together is not so much the final letter or formulation of their convictions but rather the way in which, Christians or not, they deal with their own duality and organize within themselves relationships between idea and reality.

The real question underlying debate about Christian philosophy is that of the relation between essence and existence. Shall we assume that there is an essence of philosophy or a purely philosophical knowledge which is jeopardized in human life (in this case, religious life) but nevertheless remains what it is, strictly and directly communicable, the eternal word which illuminates every man who comes into this world? Or shall we say on the contrary that philosophy is radical precisely because it digs down beneath what seems to be immediately communicable, beneath available thoughts and conceptual knowledge, and reveals a tie between men, as it does between men and the world, which precedes and founds ideality?

To prove that this alternative governs the question of Christian philosophy, we need only follow the twists and turns of the discussion which took place in 1931. Some of the discussants, having granted that in the order of principles, ideas, and possibilities, philosophy and religion are both autonomous, admit when they turn toward facts or history that religion has made a contribution to philosophy, whether it be the idea of creation, of infinite subjectivity, or of development and history. Thus in spite of essences there is an exchange between religion and reason which entirely recasts the question. For if matters of faith can in fact provide food for thought (unless faith is only the opportunity for an awareness which is equally possible without faith), we must admit that faith reveals certain aspects of being, that thought (which ignores them) does not "tie it all up," and that faith's "things not seen" and reason's evidence cannot be set apart as two *domains*. If on the contrary we follow Bréhier in going straight to history in order to show that there has been no philosophy which was Christian, we succeed only by rejecting as alien to philosophy the ideas of Christian origin which block our efforts, or be seeking their antecedents outside Christianity at no matter what cost—which proves clearly enough that we are referring to a history which has been prepared and doctored in accordance with the idea of philosophical immanence. Thus two alternatives were presented in the discussion. We may ask a factual question; but since Christian philosophy can be neither affirmed or denied on the level of "pure" history except in a wholly nominal way, the supposed factual judgment will be categorical only if it includes a conception of philosophy. Or we may openly ask the question in terms of essences, and then everything has to be begun again as soon as we pass to the order of mixtures and existing philosophies. In both cases, we miss the problem, which exists only for an historico-systematic thought capable of digging beneath essences, accomplishing the movement back and forth between them and facts, challenging essences with facts and "facts" with essences, and in particular putting its own immanence in question.

For this "open" thinking the question is in a sense settled as soon as it is asked. Since it does not take its "essences" as such for the measure of all things, since it does not believe so much in essences as in knots of significations which will be unraveled and tied up again in a different way in a new network of knowledge and experience, and which will only continue to exist as its past, we cannot see in the name of what this projecting thought would refuse the title of philosophy to indirect or imaginative modes of expression and reserve it for doctrines of the intemporal and immanent Word which are themselves placed above all history. Thus there is certainly a Christian philosophy, as there is a Romantic or a French philosophy, and a Christian philosophy which is incomparably more extensive, since in addition to the two philosophies we have mentioned it contains all that has been thought in the West for twenty centuries. How can we take ideas like those of history, subjectivity, incarnation, and positive finitude away from Christianity in order to attribute them to a "universal" reason with no birthplace?

What is not thereby settled—and what constitutes the real problem of Christian philosophy—is the relationship between this instituted Christianity, a mental horizon or matrix of culture, and the Christianity effectively lived and practiced in a positive faith. To find a meaning and an enormous historical value in Christianity and to assume it personally are two different things. To say yes to Christianity as a fact of culture or civilization is to say yes to St. Thomas, but also to St. Augustine and Occam and Nicholas of Cusa and Pascal and Malebranche, and this assent does not cost us an ounce of the pains each one of them had to take in order to be himself without default. Historical and philosophical consciousness transmutes the struggles they sustained, at times in solitude and to the death, into the benevolent universe of culture. But the philosopher or historian, precisely because he understands them all, is not one of them. Furthermore, the historian pays the same attention and infinite respect to a bit of broken pottery, formless reveries, and absurd rituals. He is only concerned with knowing what the world is made of and what man is capable of, not with getting himself burned at the stake for this proposition or having his throat cut for that truth. For the philosopher, the Christianity which fills our philosophy is the most striking sign of self-transcendence. For the Christian, Christianity is not a symbol; it is the truth. In a sense, the tension between the philosopher who understands everything as human questioning and the narrow, profound practice of the very religion he "understands" is greater than it was between a rationalism which claimed to explain the world and a faith which was only nonsense to it—because the distance between the two is shorter.

So once again philosophy and Christianity are in conflict, but the conflict is one we meet within the Christian world and within each Christian in the form of the conflict between Christianity "understood" and Christianity lived, between universality and choice. Within philosophy too, when it collides with the Manichaeism of *engagement*. The complex relationship between philosophy and Christianity would be disclosed only if a Christianity and a philosophy worked upon internally by the same contradiction were compared to one another.

The "Thomist peace" and the "Cartesian peace," the innocent coexistence of philosophy and Christianity taken as two positive orders or two truths, still conceal from us the hidden conflict of each with itself and with the other, as well as the tormented relationships which result from it.

If philosophy is a self-sufficing activity which begins and ends with conceptual understanding, and faith is assent to things not seen which are given for belief through revealed texts, the difference between them is too great even for there to be conflict. There will be conflict when rational adequation claims to be exhaustive. But if only philosophy recognizes, beyond the possibilities it is judge of, an actual world order whose detail arises from experience, and if the revealed given is taken as a supernatural experience, there is no rivalry between faith and reason. The secret of their agreement lies in infinite thought, whether it is conceiving of possibilities or creating the actual world. We do not have access to all it thinks, and its decrees are known to us only by their effects. We are thus in no position to understand the unity of reason and faith. What is certain is that it is brought about in God.

Reason and faith are thus in a state of equilibrium of indifference. Some have been astonished to see that Descartes, after having defined natural light so carefully, accepts a *different light* without difficulty, as if as soon as there are two, at least one must become relatively obscure. But the difficulty is no greater—and no differently met—than that of admitting the distinction which the understanding makes between soul and body, and, in another context, their substantial unity. There is the understanding and its sovereign distinctions, and there is the existing man (the understanding aided by imagination and joined to a body) whom we know through the practice of life because we are that man; and the two orders are a single one because the same God is both the sustainer of essences and the foundation of our existence. Our duality is reflected and surmounted in Him as the duality of his understanding and his will. We are not required to understand how. God's absolute transparency assures us of the fact, and for our part we can and must respect the difference between the two orders and live in peace on both levels.

Yet this is an unstable concordat. If man is really grafted onto the two orders, their connection is also made in him, and he should know something about it. His philosophical and his religious relationships to God should be of the same type. Philosophy and religion must symbolize. In our view, this is the significance of Malebranche's philosophy. Man cannot be part "spiritual automaton," part religious subject who receives the supernatural light. The structures and discontinuities of religious life are met with again in his understanding. In the natural order understanding is a sort of contemplation; it is vision in God. Even in the order of knowledge, we are neither our own light to ourselves nor the source of our ideas. We are our soul, but we do not have the idea of it; we only have feeling's obscure contact with it. All there can be in us of light and of intentional being comes from our participation in God. We do not have the power to conceive; our whole initiative in understanding is to address—this is what is called "attention"—a "natural prayer" to the Word which has only obligated itself to grant it always. What is ours is this invocation and the passive experience of the knowledge-events which result from it—in Malebranche's terms, "perception" and "feeling." What is also ours is this present, livelier pressure of intelligible extension on our soul, which makes us believe we see the world. In fact we do not see the world in itself. This appearance *is* our ignorance of ourselves, of our souls, and of the genesis of its modalities; and all there is of truth in our experience of the world is the fundamental certainty of an actual world existing beyond what we see and depending on which God makes us see what we do see. The slightest sense perception is thus a "natural revelation." Natural knowledge is divided between idea and perception, as religious life is divided between the light of mystical life and the chiaroscuro of revealed texts. The only thing that allows us to say that it is natural is that it obeys laws, and that God, in other words, intervenes in it only through general acts of will.

And even so the criterion is not an absolute one. If natural knowledge is woven out of religious relationships, the supernatural in return imitates nature. It is possible to sketch out a sort of dynamics of grace and glimpse laws and an order according to which the incarnate Word usually exercises its mediation. For the longitudinal cleavage between philosophy (the realm of pure understanding) and the created and existing world (the realm of natural or supernatural experience), Malebranche substitutes a transversal cleavage, and distributes the same typical structures of light and feeling, of ideal and real, between reason and religion. Natural philosophy's concepts invade theology; religious concepts invade natural knowledge. We no longer limit ourselves to evoking the infinite, which is for us incomprehensible, and in which orders that are for us distinct are believed to be unified. The articulations of nature hold only through God's action; almost all the interventions of grace are subjected to rules. God as cause is required by each idea we think of, and God as light is manifest in almost all His acts of will. No one has ever been closer to the Augustinian program: "True religion is true philosophy; and true philosophy, in turn, is true religion."

Thus Malebranche tries to think about the relationship between religion and philosophy instead of accepting it as a fact about which there is nothing to say. But can this relationship be formulated in terms of identity? Taken as contradictory, reason and faith coexist without difficulty. Similarly, and inversely, as soon as they are made identical they become rivals. The community of categories underlines the discordancy between natural revelation and natural prayer, which are open to all, and supernatural revelation and supernatural prayer, which were taught at first only to some; between the eternal and the incarnate Word; between the God we see as soon as we open our eyes and the God of the Sacraments and the Church, who must be gained and merited through supernatural life; and between the Architect divined in His works and the God of love who is reached only in the blindness of sacrifice. It is this very discordancy that one would have to take as one's theme if one wanted to construct a Christian philosophy; it is in it that one would have to look for the articulation of faith and reason. In so doing one would draw away from Malebranche, but one would also be inspired by him. For although he communicates something of reason's light to religion (and at the limit makes them identical in a single universe of thought), and although he extends the positivity of understanding to religion, he also foreshadows the invasion of our rational being by religious reversals, introducing into it the paradoxical thought of a madness which is wisdom, a scandal which is peace, a gift which is gain.

What would the relationship between philosophy and religion be in this case? Maurice Blondel[11] wrote: "Within and before itself philosophy hollows out a void which is prepared not only for the discoveries which it subsequently makes on its own grounds but also for the illuminations and contributions which it does not itself and never can really originate." Philosophy reveals a lack, a being out of focus, the expectation of forward movement. Without necessitating or presupposing positive options, it paves the way for them. It is the negative of a certain positive; not just any sort of void but precisely the lack of what faith will bring; and not hidden faith but the universally confirmable premise of a faith which remains free. We do not go from one to the other either by prolongation or simply by adjunction, but by a reversal which philosophy motivates without accomplishing.

Is the problem solved? Or does it not arise again at the suture of negative philosophy and positive faith? If, as Blondel would have it, philosophy is universal and autonomous, how could it leave responsibility for its conclusions to an absolute decision? What it roughs out with the broken lines of conceptual terms in the peace of the universal receives its full meaning only in the irreparable partiality of a life. But how could it help wanting to be a witness to this very passage from universal to particular? How could it possibly dwell in the negative and abandon the positive to a "wholly other" solicitation? It must itself recognize in a certain fullness what it sketched out beforehand in the void, and in practice at least something of what it has seen in theory. Philosophy's relationship to Christianity cannot be simply the relationship of the negative to the positive, of questioning to affirmation. Philosophical questioning involves its own vital options, and in a sense it maintains itself within a religious affirmation. The negative has its positive side, the positive its negative, and it is precisely because each has its contrary within itself that they are capable of passing into one another, and perpetually play the role of warring brothers in history.

Will this always be the case? Will there ever be a real exchange between philosopher and Christian (whether it is a matter of two men or of those two men each Christian senses within himself)? In our view this would be possible only if the Christian (with the exception of the ultimate sources of his inspiration, which he alone can judge) were to accept without qualification the task of mediation which philosophy cannot abandon without eliminating itself. It goes without saying that these lines commit their signer alone, and not the Christian collaborators who have so kindly agreed to give him their assistance. It would be a poor recognition of their aid to create the slightest ambiguity between their feelings and his. Nor does he give these lines as an introduction to their thought. They are more in the nature of reflections and questions he is writing in the margin of their texts in order to submit them to them.

These texts themselves (and on this point we are no doubt in unanimous agreement) give us a lively sense of the diversity of Christian inquiries. They remind us that Christianity has nourished more than one philosophy, no matter what privilege one of them may have been granted, that as a matter of principle it involves no single and exhaustive philosophical expression, and that in this sense—no matter what its acquisitions may be—Christian philosophy is never *something settled.*

[4] Major Rationalism

The rationalism professed or discussed in 1900, which was the scientific explanation of Being, should be called "minor rationalism." It presupposed an immense Science already inscribed in the nature of things that actually existing science would rejoin on the day it reached the end of its inquiries, and that would leave us nothing more to ask, every meaningful question having been answered. It is very difficult for us to recapture this frame of mind, even though it is very close to us. But it is a fact that men once dreamed of a time in which the mind, having enclosed "the whole of reality" in a network of relations, would thenceforth (as if in a replete state) remain at rest or have nothing more to do than draw out the consequences of a definitive body of knowledge and, by some application of the same principles, ward off the last convulsive movements of the unforeseeable.

This "rationalism" seems full of myths to us: the myth of *laws of nature* vaguely situated halfway between norms and facts, and *according to which,* it was thought, this nevertheless blind world has been constructed; the myth of *scientific explanation,* as if knowledge of relations, even extended to all observable phenomena, could one day transform the very existence of the world into an analytic and self-evident proposition. To these two myths we would have to add all those related ones which proliferated at the limits of science, for example around the ideas of life and death. It was the time when men wondered with enthusiasm or anguish whether man could create life in the laboratory; a time when rationalist orators readily spoke of "nothingness," that different and calmer milieu of life which they felt sure they would regain after this life as one regains a supersensible destiny.

But they did not think they were giving way to a mythology. They believed they were speaking in the name of reason. Reason was confused with knowledge of conditions or causes: wherever a conditioning factor was discovered, it was thought that every question had been silenced, the problem of essence resolved along with the problem of origin, and the fact brought under the jurisdiction of its cause. The issue between science and religion was only to know whether the world is a single great Process obeying a single "generative axiom," the repetition of whose mystic formula would be the only thing left to do at the end of time, or whether there are (at the point where life emerges, for example) gaps and discontinuities in which the antagonistic power of mind can be lodged. Each conquest made for determinism was a defeat for the metaphysical sense, whose victory necessarily involved the "failure of science."

The reason why this rationalism is hard for us to think of is that it was (in a disfigured, unrecognizable form) a heritage, and what we have been concerned with in our times is the tradition which had gradually produced it. It was the fossil of a major rationalism (that of the seventeenth century) rich with a living ontology, which had already died out by the eighteenth century,[12] and only a few external forms of which remained in the rationalism of 1900.

The seventeenth century is that privileged moment when natural science and metaphysics believed they had discovered a common foundation. It created the science of nature and yet did not make the object of science the rule of ontology. It assumes that a philosophy surveys science without being its rival. The object of science is an aspect or a degree of Being; it is justified in its place, perhaps it is even through it that we learn to know the power of reason. But this power is not exhausted in it. In different ways Descartes, Spinoza, Leibniz, and Malebranche recognize, beneath the chain of causal relations, another type of being which sustains the chain without breaking it. Being is not completely reduced to or flattened out upon the level of external Being. There is also the being of the subject or the soul, the being of its ideas, and the interrelations of these ideas, the inner relation of truth. And the latter universe is as extensive as the former, or rather it encompasses it. For no matter how strict the connection between external facts, it is not the external world which is the ultimate justification of the internal; they participate together in an "interior" which their connection manifests. All the problems that a scientific ontology will omit by setting itself up uncritically in external being as universal milieu, seventeenth century philosophy on the contrary never stops setting for itself. How can we understand that mind acts upon body and body upon mind, and even body upon body or mind upon another mind or upon itself, since in the last analysis, no matter how rigorous the connection between particular things within and outside us, no one of these things is ever in all respects a sufficient cause of what emerges from it? Where does the cohesion of the whole come from? Each Cartesian conceives of it in a completely different way. But all of them agree that beings and external relations present themselves for an inspection of their underlying premises. Philosophy is neither stifled by them nor compelled to contest their solidity in order to make a place for itself.

This extraordinary harmony of external and internal is possible only through the mediation of a *positive infinite* or (since every restriction to a certain type of infinity would be a seed of negation) an infinite infinite. It is in this positive infinite that the effective existence of things *partes extra partes* and extension as we think of it (which on the contrary is continuous and infinite) communicate or are joined together. If at the center and so to speak the kernel of Being there is an infinite infinite, every partial being directly or indirectly presupposes it, and is in return really or eminently contained in it. All the relationships we can have to Being must be simultaneously founded upon it. First of all our idea of truth, which is precisely what has led us to the infinite and thus cannot be called into question again by it, then all the lively and confused ideas of existing things given us by the senses. No matter how different these two kinds of understanding may be, they must have but one source; and even the sensible world (as discontinuous, partial, and mutilated as it is) must ultimately be understood, beginning with the organization of our body, as a particular case of the internal relations intelligible space is made of.

Thus the idea of the positive infinite is major rationalism's secret, and it will last only as long as that idea remains in force. Descartes had glimpsed in a flash the possibility of negative thinking. He had described mind as a being which is *neither* subtle matter, *nor* a breath of spirit, nor any existing thing, but a being which itself dwells in the absence of all positive certainty. With his gaze he had measured this power to do or not to do which, he said, admits of no degree and is thus infinite in man as it is in God—and is an infinite power of negation, since in a freedom which is freedom not to do as well as to do, affirmation can never be anything but negation denied. It is in this respect that Descartes is more modern than the Cartesians, anticipating the philosophies of subjectivity and the negative. But for him this is no more than a beginning, and he definitely moves beyond negativity when he ultimately states that the idea of the infinite precedes that of the finite in him, and that all negative thought is a shadow in this light. Whatever their differences in other respects, Cartesians will be unanimous on this point. Malebranche will say a hundred times that nothingness "has no properties" or "is not visible," and that there is thus nothing to say about this nothing. Leibniz will wonder why there is "something rather than nothing," at a certain moment positing nothingness in respect to Being; but this retreat to the near side of Being, this evocation of a possible nothingness, is for him like a proof by absurdity. It is only the basis, the minimum of shadow necessary for making Being's sovereign self-production appear. Finally, Spinoza's determination which "is negation," although subsequently understood in the sense of a determining power of the negative, can only be for him a way of underlining the immanence of determinate things in a substance which is equal to itself and positive.

Subsequent thought will never again attain this harmony between philosophy and science, this ease of going beyond science without destroying it and limiting metaphysics without excluding it. Even those of our contemporaries who call themselves and are Cartesians give a completely different philosophical function to the negative, and that is why they could not possibly recover the seventeenth century's equilibrium. Descartes said that God is conceived of but not understood by us, and this *not* expressed a privation and a defect in us. The modern Cartesian[13] translates: the infinite is as much *absence* as *presence*, which brings the negative and man into the definition of God. Léon Brunschvicg accepted all of Spinoza except the descending order of the *Ethics*. The *first book*, he used to say, is no more primary than the *fifth;* the *Ethics* ought to be read in a circle, and God presupposes man as man presupposes God. This interpretation of Cartesianism perhaps, in fact surely, extracts "its truth"; but a truth it did not itself possess. There is an innocent way of thinking *on the basis* of the infinite which made major rationalism what it was, and which nothing will ever allow us to recapture.

These words should not be taken to express nostalgia—except perhaps an indolent nostalgia for a time when the mental universe was not torn apart and man could without concessions or artificiality devote himself to philosophy, science, and (if he wished) theology. But this peace and harmony could last only as long as men remained at the entrance to the three paths. What separates us from the seventeenth century is not a decline but a growth of consciousness and experience. The intervening centuries have taught that the harmony between our evident thoughts and the existing world is not so immediate, that it is never beyond question, that our evidence can never take credit for governing the whole subsequent development of knowledge, that consequences flow back upon "principles," that we must be prepared to recast even the ideas we may believe to be "primary," that truth is not obtained by composition in going from simple to complex and from essence to properties, and that we neither can nor will be able to set ourselves up at the center of physical or even mathematical entities, but most gropingly inspect them from without, approaching them by oblique processes and questioning them like persons. A time came when the very conviction of grasping with inner certainty the principles according to which an infinite understanding conceived or conceives the world (the conviction which had sustained the Cartesians' undertakings and had long seemed justified by the progress of Cartesian science) ceased to be a stimulant of knowledge and became the threat of a new Scholasticism. Then it was indeed necessary to return to principles; reduce them to the rank of "idealizations" which are justified to the extent they give life to inquiry and disqualified when they paralyze it; learn to measure our thought by that existence which, Kant was to say, is not a predicate; go back to the origins of Cartesianism in order to go beyond it; and relearn the lesson of that creative act which, with Cartesianism, had instituted a long period of fruitful thought, but which had exhausted its force in the pseudo-Cartesianism of subsequent thinkers and from that time forward needed to be begun over again itself. It has been necessary to learn intellectual history, that queer movement by which thought abandons and preserves its old formulas by integrating them as particular and privileged cases into a more comprehensive and general thought which cannot decree itself exhaustive. This air of improvisation and the provisory, this somewhat haggard aspect of contemporary investigations (whether they be in science or philosophy, in literature or the arts), is the price we must pay in order to acquire a more mature consciousness of our relationships to Being.

The seventeenth century believed in the immediate harmony of science and metaphysics, and in another connection, of science and religion. And in this respect it is remote from our times indeed. For the past fifty years metaphysical thought has sought its way outside the physico-mathematical coordination of the world, and its role in relation to science seems to be to awaken us to the "non-relational background"[14] that science thinks about and does not think about. The fact that the most vital aspect of religious thought has taken the same course makes it consonant but also competitive with "atheistic" metaphysics. Unlike the atheism of 1900, contemporary "atheism" does not claim to explain the world "without God." It claims that the world is inexplicable, and in its view the rationalism of 1900 is a secularized theology. If the Cartesians were to come back among us, they would have the triple surprise of finding a philosophy and even a theology whose favorite theme is the radical contingency of the world, and which are rivals in just this respect. Our philosophical situation is entirely different from that of major rationalism.

And yet major rationalism is still of major importance for us, and is even close to us in that it is the indispensable way toward the philosophies which reject it, for they reject it in the name of the same exigency which gave it life. At the very moment when it was creating natural science it showed by the same movement that it was not the measure of being and carried consciousness of the ontological problem to its highest point. In this respect, it is not *past*. As it did, we seek not to restrict or discredit the initiatives of science but to situate science as an intentional system in the total field of our relationships to Being; and the only reason why passing to the infinite infinite does not seem to us to be the answer is that we are taking up again in a more radical way the task which that intrepid century had believed itself rid of forever.

[5]   The Discovery of Subjectivity

What is common to those philosophies, spread out across three centuries, which we group together beneath the banner of "subjectivity"? There is the Self which Montaigne preferred above all and Pascal hated, the Self which we take account of day by day—noticing its audacities, flights, intermittencies, and returns—and try out or put to the test like an unknown. There is the thinking Ego of Descartes and Pascal too, the Ego which rejoins itself only an instant, but in that instant exists wholly in its appearance, being everything it thinks it is and nothing else, open to everything, never fixed, and without any other mystery than this transparency itself. There is the subjective series of the English philosophers, the ideas which know themselves through a mute contact and as if by a natural property. There is the self of Rousseau, an abyss of innocence and guilt which itself organizes the "plot" in which it is aware of being implicated, and yet in the face of this destiny insists with good reason upon its incorruptible goodness. There is the transcendental subject of the Kantians, as close and closer to the world than psychological intimacy, which contemplates them both after having constructed them, and yet knows that it too is an "inhabitant" of the world. There is the subject of Biran which not only *knows* that it is in the world but is there, and could not even be subject if it did not have a body to move. There is finally subjectivity in the Kierkegaardian sense, which is no longer a region of being but the only fundamental way of relating oneself to being, which makes us *be* something instead of skimming over all things in "objective" thinking, and which in the last analysis does not really think of anything. Why make these discordant "subjectivities" stages of a single discovery?

And why "discovery"? Are we to believe then that subjectivity existed before the philosophers, exactly as they were subsequently to understand it? Once reflection had occurred, once the "I think" had been pronounced, the thought of being became so much a part of our being that if we try to express what preceded it our entire effort only succeeds in proposing a *pre-reflexive cogito*. But what is this contact of self with self before the self is revealed? Is it anything but another example of retrospective illusion? Is our investigation of it really no more than a *return* to what already *knew itself* through our life? But strictly speaking I did not know myself. Then what is this feeling of self which is not in possession of itself and does not yet coincide with itself? It has been said that to take consciousness away from subjectivity was to withdraw being from it, that an unconscious love is nothing, because to love is to see someone—actions, gestures, a face, a body—as lovable. But the *cogito* prior to reflection and the feeling of self without understanding present the same difficulty. Thus consciousness is either unaware of its origins or, if it wants to reach them, it can only project itself into them. In neither case should we speak of "discovery." Reflection has not only unveiled the unreflected, it has changed it, if only into its truth. Subjectivity was not waiting for philosophers as an unknown America waited for its explorers in the ocean's mists. They constructed, created it, and in more than one way. And what they have done must perhaps be undone. Heidegger thinks they lost being from the day they based it upon consciousness of self.

Yet we shall not give up speaking about a "discovery" of "subjectivity." These difficulties simply require us to say how we shall use the terms.

In the first place, the kinship of philosophies of subjectivity is evident as soon as they are contrasted to the others. Whatever the discordancies between them, the moderns share the idea that the being of the soul or subject-being is not a lesser being but perhaps the absolute form of being, and this is what our title is intended to indicate. Many elements of a philosophy of the subject were present in Greek philosophy. It spoke of "man the measure of all things." It recognized the soul's singular power not to know what it knows in pretending to know what it does not know, an incomprehensible capacity for error linked to its capacity for truth, a relationship to non-being just as essential to it as its relationship to being. In another connection, it conceived of a thought which is only thought of itself (Aristotle puts it at the summit of the world), and a radical freedom beyond the highest stage of our power. Thus it knew subjectivity as darkness and light. Yet the fact remains that for the Greeks the being of the subject or the soul is never the canonical form of being, that never for them is the negative at the center of philosophy, or charged with making the positive appear, assuming it, and transforming it.

From Montaigne to Kant and beyond, on the contrary, it is the same subject-being which is at issue. The discordancy of philosophies stems from the fact that subjectivity is neither thing nor substance but the extremity of both particular and universal—from the fact that it is Protean. All the philosophies of subjectivity follow its metamorphoses in one way or another, and it is this dialectic which is hidden beneath their differences. There are at bottom only two ideas of subjectivity—that of empty, unfettered, and universal subjectivity, and that of full subjectivity sucked down into the world—and it is the same idea, as can be clearly seen in Sartre's idea of nothingness which "comes to the world," drinks in the world, needs the world in order to be no matter what (even nothingness), and remains alien to the world in sacrificing itself to being.

Of course this is no discovery in the sense that America or even potassium was discovered. Yet it is still a discovery in the sense that once introduced into philosophy, "subjective" thinking no longer allows itself to be ignored.

Even if philosophy finally eliminates it, it will never again be what it was before this kind of thinking. After it, that which is true—constructed though it may be (and America is also a construction, which has just become inevitable through an infinite number of witnesses)—becomes as solid as a fact, and subjective thinking is one of these solids that philosophy will have to digest. Or let us say that once "infected" by certain ways of thinking, philosophy can no longer annul them but must cure itself of them by inventing better ones. The same philosopher who now regrets Parmenides and would like to give us back our relationships to Being such as they were prior to self-consciousness owes his idea of and taste for primordial ontology to just this self-consciousness. There are some ideas which make it impossible for us to return to a time prior to their existence, even and especially if we have moved beyond them, and subjectivity is one of them.

[6] Existence and Dialectic

We know how uncomfortable a writer is when he is asked to do a history of his thoughts. We are scarcely less uncomfortable when we have to summarize our famous contemporaries. We cannot separate them from what we have learned in reading them, or from the "climates" which have received their books and made them famous. We would have to guess what counts now that the hue and cry has died down, and what will count tomorrow for new readers (if there are any), those strangers who are going to come, lay hold of the same books, and make something else out of them. Perhaps there is a sentence—written one day in the stillness of the 16th arrondissement, in the pious stillness of Aix, in the academic stillness of Freiburg, or in the din of the rue de Rennes, or in Naples or Vésinet—which its first readers roared through like a whistle-stop and tomorrow's readers (a new Bergson, Blondel, Husserl, Alain, or Croce we cannot imagine) are going to pull up short before. To imagine them would mean distributing our evidence and questions, our hits and misses, as they will be distributed among our descendants. It would mean making ourselves different selves, and all the "objectivity" in the world cannot do that. In designating the themes of existence and dialectic the essential ones of the past half-century, we are perhaps saying what one generation saw in its philosophy, not to be sure what the following one will see in it, and far less still what the philosophers in question were conscious of saying.

Yet it is *a fact, for us,* that they all labored to go beyond critical philosophy (even those who put the most stock in it), and to unveil, on the far side of relations, what Brunschvicg used to call the "uncoordinatable" and we call existence. When Bergson made perception the fundamental mode of our relation to being; when Blondel meant to develop the implications of a thought which always in fact precedes itself, is always beyond itself; when Alain described freedom upheld by the world's flux like a swimmer on the water which holds him up and is his force; when Croce put philosophy back into contact with history; and when Husserl took the carnal presence of things as the model of obvious fact; all of them were calling the narcissism of self-consciousness into question, all of them were seeking a way between the possible and the necessary toward the real, all were pointing out our own and the world's factual existence as a new dimension of inquiry. For existential philosophy is not, as a hurried reader who limited himself to Sartre's mani-festo[15] would believe, simply the philosophy which puts freedom before essence in man. This is only a striking consequence; and behind the idea of sovereign choice there was even in Sartre's thinking (as can be seen in *Being and Nothingness*) the different and really antagonistic idea of freedom which is freedom only embodied in the world as work done upon a factual situa-tion. And from then on, even in Sartre's thinking, "to exist" is not merely an anthropological term. Facing freedom, existence unveils a wholly new face of the world—the world as a promise and threat to it; the world which sets traps for, seduces, or gives in to it; not the flat world of Kantian objects of science any more but a landscape full of routes and roadblocks; in short, the world we "exist" and not simply the theater of our understanding and free will.

Perhaps we shall have more trouble convincing the reader that in going toward existence the century was also going toward dialectic. Blondel, Alain talked about it, and Croce of course. But Bergson, Husserl? It is pretty well known that they sought intuition, and that dialectic for them was the philos-ophy of argufiers, blind and garrulous philosophy, or as J. Beaufret says, "ventriloquous" philosophy. Reading over old manuscripts, Husserl would sometimes write in the margin, *"Das habe ich angeschaut."* What do these philosophers, dedicated to what they see, positive, and systematically naive, have in common with the cunning philosopher who digs ever deeper beneath his intuition in order to find another intuition there, and who is referred back to himself by every spectacle?

To answer these questions it would be necessary to evoke the contempo-rary history of dialectic and the Hegelian revival. The dialectic our contem-poraries are rediscovering is, as von Hartmann has already pointed out, a dialectic of the real. The Hegel they have rehabilitated is not the one the nine-teenth century had turned away from, the possessor of a marvelous secret which enabled him to speak of all things without a thought by mechanically applying dialectical order and connection to them. It is the Hegel who had not wanted to choose between logic and anthropology, who made dialectic emerge from human experience but defined man as the empirical bearer of Logos, and who placed these two perspectives and the reversal which transforms them both at the center of philosophy. This dialectic and intuition are not simply compatible; there is a point at which they meet. Through Bergsonism as through Husserl's career we can follow the laborious process which gradually sets intuition in motion, changes the positive notation of "immediate data" into a dialectic of time and the intuition of essences into a "phenomenology of genesis," and links together in a living unity the contrasting dimensions of a time which is ultimately coextensive with being.

This being—which is glimpsed through time's stirrings and always intended by our temporality, perception, and our carnal being, but to which there can be no question of our being transported because to abolish its distance would be to take away its consistency of being—this being "of distances" as Heidegger will put it, which is always offered to our transcendence, is the dialectical idea of being as defined in the *Parmenides*—beyond the empirical multiplicity of existent things and as a matter of principle intended through them, because separated from them it would be only lightning flash or darkness. As for the subjective side of dialectic, modern thinkers rediscover it as soon as they want to grasp us in our *effective* relationship to the world. For then they encounter the first and most fundamental antithesis, the inaugural and never liquidated phase of dialectic, the birth of reflection which as a matter of principle separates and separates only in order to grasp the unreflected. As soon as it becomes sufficiently conscious, the search for the "immediate" or the "thing itself" is not the contrary of mediation. Mediation is only the resolute recognition of a paradox that intuition willy-nilly suffers: to possess ourselves we must begin by abandoning ourselves; to see the world itself, we must first withdraw from it.

If these remarks are just, only the logical positivism of the Anglo-Saxon and Scandinavian countries would be left outside this century's philosophy. All the philosophies we have just named speak a common language, and for logical positivism all their problems put together are meaningless. The fact can neither be hidden nor attenuated. We can only wonder if it will last. If all terms which offer no immediately assignable meaning are eliminated from philosophy, does not this purge, like all the others, reveal a crisis? Once we have set the field of apparently clear univocal meanings in order, will we not let ourselves be tempted anew by the problematic regions which lie all around it? Is it not just the contrast between a transparent mental universe and a lived universe which is less and less a contrast, is it not just this pressure of the meaningless on the meaningful, which will lead logical positivism to revise its criteria of clarity and obscurity through a development which Plato said is the development of philosophy itself? If this reversal of values were to occur, logical positivism would have to be appraised as the last and most energetic "resistance" to the concrete philosophy which, in one way or another, the beginning of this century has not stopped looking for.

A concrete philosophy is not a happy one. It must stick close to experience, and yet not limit itself to the empirical but restore to each experience the ontological cipher which marks it internally. As difficult as it is under these conditions to imagine the future of philosophy, two things seem certain: it will never regain the conviction of holding the keys to nature or history in its concepts, and it will not renounce its radicalism, that search for presuppositions and foundations which has produced the great philosophies.

It will renounce it all the less to the extent that while philosophical systems were being discredited, more advanced techniques were replacing old ones and giving new life to philosophy. At no time like the present has scientific knowledge overturned its own *a priori*. Literature has never been as "philosophical" as it has in the twentieth century; never has it reflected as much upon language, truth, and the significance of the act of writing. At no time like the present has political life shown its roots or its web and challenged its own certitudes, first those of conservatism and now those of revolution. Even if philosophers were to weaken, others would be there to call them back to philosophy. Unless this uneasiness consumes itself, and the world destroys itself in experiencing itself, much can be expected of an age which no longer believes in philosophy triumphant but is through its difficulties a permanent appeal to rigor, criticism, universality, and philosophy militant.

Perhaps it will be asked what is left of philosophy when it has lost its rights to the *a priori*, system, or construction, when it no longer dominates the whole of experience. Almost all of it is left. For system, explanation, and deduction have never been essential. These arrangements expressed—and concealed—a relation to being, other men, and the world. In spite of appearances, the system has never been more than a language (and in this respect it has been precious) for translating a Cartesian, Spinozist, or Leibnizian way of situating oneself in relation to being. And it suffices for the continuing existence of philosophy that this relationship remain problematic, that it not be take as self-evident, that there continue to exist the *tête-à-tête* between being and the one who (in every sense of the word) comes forth from it, judges it, receives it, rejects it, transforms it, and finally departs from it. It is this same relationship we are at present trying to formulate expressly, and it is for this reason that philosophy feels at home wherever it takes place—that is, everywhere—as much in the testimony of an ignorant man who has loved and lived as he could, in the "tricks" science contrives without speculative shame to get around problems, in "barbarian" civilizations, and in the regions of our life which formerly had no official existence, as in literature, in the sophisticated life, or in discussions of substance and attribute. The established human community feels problematic, and the most immediate life has become "philosophical." We cannot conceive of a new Leibniz or Spinoza entering that life today with their fundamental confidence in its rationality. Tomorrow's philosophers will have no "anaclastic line," "monad," "conatus," "substance," "attributes," or "infinite mode." But they will continue to learn in Leibniz and Spinoza how happy centuries thought to tame the Sphinx, and in their own less figurative and more abrupt fashion, they will keep on giving answers to the many riddles she puts to them.

Notes

1. Introduction to an anthology, *Les Philosophes célèbres*, published by Lucien Mazenod.
2. M. Gueroult.
3. Fung Yu-lan, *Précis d'histoire de la philosophie chinoise*, pp. 32–35.
4. C. Lévi-Strauss.
5. Hegel, *History of Philosophy*.
6. *Ibid.*
7. *Die Krisis der europäischen Wissenschaften und die transzendentale Phänomenologie;* French translation, *Les Etudes Philosophiques* (April–June, 1949), p. 140.
8. "Philosophie als strenge Wissenschaft,—der Traum ist ausgeträumt," Husserliana, VI, p. 508.
9. "La notion de philosophie chrétienne," *Bulletin de la Société française de Philosophie,* Séance du 21 mars, 1931.
10. Léon Brunschvicg, twentieth-century French philosopher and professor who influenced the young Merleau-Ponty.—Trans.
11. Maurice Blondel, twentieth-century French philosopher. For further judgments of his thought by Merleau-Ponty, see *In Praise of Philosophy.*—Trans.
12. The eighteenth century is the greatest example of a time which does not express itself well in its philosophy. Its merits lie elsewhere: in its ardor; in its passion for living, knowing, and judging; in its "spirit." As Hegel has shown so well, there is for example a second meaning of its "materialism" which makes it an epoch of the human spirit, even though, taken literally, it is a meager philosophy.
13. F. Alquié, *La découverte métaphysique de l'homme chez Descartes.*
14. Jean Wahl.
15. *Existentialism and Humanism.*

2

Beyond Eurocentrism: The World-System and the Limits of Modernity

Enrique Dussel
Translated by Eduardo Mendieta

Two opposing paradigms, the Eurocentric and the planetary, characterize the question of modernity. The first, from a Eurocentric horizon, formulates the phenomenon of modernity as *exclusvely* European, developing in the Middle Ages and later on diffusing itself throughout the entire world.[1] Weber situates the "problem of universal history" with the question: "to what combination of circumstances should the fact be attributed that in *Western civilization,* and in Western civilization only,[2] cultural phenomena have appeared which (as *we*[3] like to think) lie in a line of development having *universal* significance and value."[4] According to this paradigm, Europe had exceptional *internal* characteristics that allowed it to supersede, through its rationality, all other cultures. Philosophically, no one expresses this thesis of modernity better than Hegel: "The German Spirit is the Spirit of the new World. Its aim is the realization of absolute Truth as the unlimited self-determination (*Selbstbestimmung*) of Freedom—*that* Freedom which has its own absolute form itself as its purport."[5] For Hegel, the Spirit of Europe (the German spirit) is the absolute Truth that determines or realizes itself through itself without owing anything to anyone. This thesis, which I call the Eurocentric paradigm (in opposition to the world paradigm), has imposed itself not only in Europe and the United States, but in the entire intellectual realm of the world periphery. The chronology of this position has its geopolitics: modern subjectivity develops spatially, according to the Eurocentric paradigm, from the Italy of the Renaissance to the Germany of the Reformation and the Enlightenment, to the France of the French Revolution;[6] throughout, Europe is central. The "pseudo-scientific" division of history into Antiquity (as antecedent), the Medieval Age (preparatory epoch), and the Modern Age (Europe) is an ideological and deforming organization of history; it has already created ethical problems with respect to other cultures. Philosophy, especially ethics, needs to break with this reductive horizon in order to open itself to the "world," the "planetary" sphere.

The second paradigm, from a planetary horizon, conceptualizes modernity as the culture of the *center* of the "world-system,"[7] of the first world-system, through the incorporation of Amerindia,[8] and as a result of the *management* of this "centrality." In other words, European modernity is not an *independent*, autopoietic, self-referential system, but instead is *part* of a world-system: in fact, its *center*. Modernity, then, is planetary. It begins with the *simultaneous* constitution of Spain with reference to its "periphery" (first of all, properly speaking, Amerindia: the Caribbean, Mexico, and Peru). Simultaneously, Europe (as a diachrony that has its premodern antecedents: the Renaissance Italian cities and Portugal) will go on to *constitute* itself as center (as a superhegemonic power that from Spain passes to Holland, England, and France) over a growing periphery (Amerindia, Brazil, slave-supplying coasts of Africa, and Poland in the sixteenth century;[9] the consolidation of Latin Amerindia, North America, the Caribbean, and eastern Europe in the seventeenth century;[10] the Ottoman Empire, Russia, some Indian reigns, the Asian subcontinent, and the first penetration into continental Africa in the first half of the nineteenth century[11]). Modernity, then, in this planetary paradigm is a phenomenon proper to the system "center-periphery." Modernity is not a phenomenon of Europe as an *independent* system, but of Europe as center. This simple hypothesis absolutely changes the concept of modernity, its origin, development, and contemporary crisis, and thus, also the content of the belated modernity or postmodernity.

In addition, we submit a thesis that qualifies the previous one: the centrality of Europe in the world-system is not the sole fruit of an internal superiority accumulated during the European Middle Ages over against other cultures. Instead, it is also the fundamental effect of the simple fact of the discovery, conquest, colonization, and integration (subsumption) of Amerindia. This simple fact will give Europe the determining *comparative advantage* over the Ottoman-Muslim world, India, and China. Modernity is the fruit of these events, not their cause. Subsequently, the *management* of the centrality of the world-system will allow Europe to transform itself in something like the "reflexive consciousness" (modern philosophy) of world history; the many values, discoveries, inventions, technologies, political institutions, and so on that are attributed to it as its exclusive production are in reality effects of the *displacement* of the ancient center of the third stage of the interregional system toward Europe (following the diachronic path of the

Renaissance to Portugal as antecedent, to Spain, and later to Flanders, England, etc.). Even capitalism is the fruit and not the cause of this juncture of European planetarization and centralization within the world-system. The human experience of 4,500 years of political, economic, technological, and cultural relations of the interregional system will now be hegemonized by a Europe—which had never been the "center," and which, during its best times, became only a "periphery." The slippage takes place from central Asia to the eastern, and Italian, Mediterranean; more precisely, toward Genoa, toward the Atlantic. With Portugal as an antecedent, modernity begins properly in Spain, and in the face of the impossibility of China's even attempting to arrive through the Orient (the Pacific) to Europe, and thus to integrate Amerindia as its periphery. Let us look at the premises of the argument.

Expansion of the World-System

Let us consider the movement of world history beginning with the rupture, due to the Ottoman-Muslim presence, of the third stage of the interregional system, which in its classic epoch had Baghdad as its center (from A.D. 762 to 1258), and the transformation of the interregional system into the first *world*-system, whose center would situate itself up to today in the North Atlantic. This change in the center of the system will have its prehistory in the thirteenth through the fifteenth centuries and before the collapse of the third stage of the interregional system; the new, fourth stage of the world-system *originates* properly in 1492. Everything that had taken place in Europe was still a moment of *another* stage of the interregional system. Which state originated the deployment of the world-system? The answer is the state that will annex Amerindia, and from it, as a springboard or "comparative advantage," will go on to achieve superiority by the end of the fifteenth century. The candidates are China, Portugal, and Spain.

1

Why not China? The reason is very simple. It was impossible for China[12] to discover Amerindia (a nontechnological impossibility; that is to say, empirically, but not historically or geopolitically, possible), for it had no interest in attempting to expand into Europe. For China the center of the interregional system (in its third stage) was in the East, either in Central Asia or in India. To go toward completely "peripheral" Europe? This could not be an objective of Chinese foreign commerce.

In fact, Cheng Ho, between 1405 and 1433, was able to make seven successful voyages to the center of the system (he sailed to Sri Lanka, India, and even eastern Africa[13]). In 1479, Wang Chin attempted the same, but the archives of his predecessor were denied to him. China closed in upon itself, and did not attempt to do what, at precisely that very moment, Portugal was undertaking. Its internal politics—perhaps the rivalry of the mandarins against the new power of the merchant eunuchs[14]—prevented its exit into foreign commerce. Had China undertaken it, however, it would have had to depart *toward the west* to reach the center of the system. The Chinese went east and arrived at Alaska and, it appears, even as far as California, and still to its south, but when they did not find anything that would be of interest to its merchants, and as they went further away from the center of the interregional system, they most probably abandoned the enterprise. China was not Spain for geopolitical reasons.

However, to refute the old "evidence," which has been reinforced since Weber, we still need to ask: Was China culturally *inferior* to Europe in the fifteenth century? According to those who have studied the question,[15] China was neither technologically,[16] nor politically,[17] nor commercially, nor even because of its humanism,[18] inferior. There is a certain mirage in this question. The histories of Western science and technology do not take strictly into account that the European "jump," the technological *boom* begins to take place in the sixteenth century, but that is only in the seventeenth century that it shows its multiplying effects. The *formulation* of the modern technological paradigm (in the eighteenth century) is confused with the origin of modernity, without leaving time for the crisis of the medieval model. No notice is taken that the scientific revolution—discussed by Kuhn—departs from a modernity that has already begun, the result of a "modern paradigm."[19] It is for that reason that in the fifteenth century (if we do not consider the later European inventions) Europe does not have any superiority over China. Needham allows himself to be bewitched by this mirage, when he writes: "The fact is that the spontaneous autochthonous development of Chinese society did not produce any drastic change paralleling the *Renaissance and the scientific revolution* of the West."[20]

To treat the Renaissance and the scientific revolution[21] as being *one and the same event* (one from the fourteenth century and the other from the seventeenth century) demonstrates the distortion of which we have spoken. The Renaissance is still a European event of a peripheral culture in the third stage of the interregional system. The scientific revolution is the result of the formulation of the modern paradigm that needed more than a century of modernity to attain its maturity. Pierre Chaunu writes: "Towards the end of the XV century, to the extent to which historical literature allows us to understand it, the far East as an entity comparable to the Mediterranean . . .

does not result under any inferior aspect, at least superficially, to the far West of the Euro-Asiatic continent."[22]

Let us repeat: Why not China? Because China found itself in the easternmost zone of the interregional system, whence it looked to the center: to India in the west.

2

Why not Portugal? For the same reason: that is, because it found itself in the farthest point west of the same interregional system, and because *it also looked, and always, toward the center:* toward India in the east. Columbus's proposal (the attempt to reach the center through the West) to the king of Portugal was as insane as it was for Columbus to claim to discover a new continent (since he *only and always* attempted, and could not conceive another hypothesis, to reach the center of the third stage of the interregional system[23]).

The Italian Renaissance cities are the farthest point west (peripheral) of the interregional system, which articulated anew, after the Crusades (which failed in 1291), continental Europe with the Mediterranean. The Crusades ought to be considered a frustrated attempt to connect with the center of the system, a link that the Turks ruptured. The Italian cities, especially Genoa (which rivaled Venice's presence in the eastern Mediterranean), attempted to open the western Mediterranean to the Atlantic, in order to reach once again through the south of Africa the center of the system. The Genoese placed all their experience in navigation and the economic power of their wealth at the service of opening for themselves this path. It was the Genoese who occupied the Canaries in 1312,[24] and it was they who invested in Portugal and helped the Portuguese to develop their navigational power.

Once the Crusades had failed, and because the Europeans could not foresee the expansion of Russia through the steppes (who, advancing through the frozen woods of the North, reached the Pacific and Alaska[25] in the seventeenth century), the Atlantic was the only European door *to the center of the system.* Portugal, the first European nation already unified in the eleventh century, will transform the reconquest[26] against the Muslims into the beginning of a process of Atlantic mercantile expansion. In 1419, the Portuguese discover the Madeiras Islands, in 1431 the Azores, in 1482 Zaire, and in 1498 Vasco da Gama reaches India (the center of the interregional system). In 1415, Portugal occupies the African-Muslim Ceuta, in 1448 El-Ksar-es-Seghir, in 1471 Arzila. But all of this is the *continuation* of the interregional system whose connection is the Italian cities: "In the twelfth century when the Genoese and the Pisans first appear in Catalonia, in the thirteenth century when they first reach Portugal, this is part of the efforts of the Italians to draw the Iberian peoples into the international trade of the time. . . . As of 1317, according to Virginia Rau, 'the city and the port of Lisbon would be the great centre of Genoese trade. . . .' "[27]

A Portugal with contacts in the Islamic world, with numerous sailors (former farmers expelled from an intensive agriculture), with a money economy, in "connection" with Italy, once again opened peripheral Europe to the interregional system. But despite this it did not stop being on the periphery. Not even the Portuguese could pretend to have abandoned this situation, for although Portugal could have attempted to dominate the commercial exchange in the sea of the Arabs (the Indian sea[28]), it never could produce the commodities of the East (silk fabrics, tropical products, sub-Saharan gold, etc.). In other words, it was an intermediary and always peripheral power of India, China, and the Muslim world.

With Portugal we are in the anteroom, but still neither in modernity nor in the world-system (the fourth stage of the system, which originated, at least, between Egypt and Mesopotamia).

3

Why does Spain begin the world-system, and with it, modernity? For the same reason that it was prevented in China and Portugal. Because Spain could not reach the center of the interregional system that was in Central Asia or India, could not go east (since the Portuguese had already anticipated them, and thus had exclusivity rights) through the south Atlantic (around the coasts of Western Africa, until the cape of Buena Esperanza was discovered in 1487), Spain had only one opportunity left: to go toward the center, to India, through *the Occident*, through the West, by crossing the Atlantic Ocean.[29] Because of this Spain bumps into, finds without looking, Amerindia, and with it the entire European medieval paradigm enters into crisis (which is the paradigm of a peripheral culture, the farthest western point of the third stage of the interregional system), and thus inaugurates, slowly but irreversibly, the first *world* hegemony. This is the only world-system that has existed in planetary history, and this is the modern system, European in its center, capitalist in its economy.

This essay situates itself explicitly (is it perhaps the first practical philosophy that attempts to do so "explicitly"?) within the horizon of this modern world-system, taking into consideration not only the center (as has been done *exclusively* by modern philosophy from Descartes to Habermas, thus resulting in a *partial*, provincial, regional view of the historical ethical event), *but also* its periphery (and with this one obtains a *planetary* vision of the human experience). My position is not informative or anecdotal: it is *sensu stricto* philosophical. I have already treated the theme in another work,[30] in which I showed Columbus's existential impossibility, as a Renaissance Genoese, of convincing himself that what he had discovered was not India. He navigated, according to his own imagination, close to the coasts of the fourth Asiatic peninsula (which Heinrich Hammer had already drawn cartographically in Rome in 1489[31]), always close to the Sinus Magnus (the great gulf of the Greeks, territorial sea of the Chinese) when he transversed the Caribbean. Columbus died in 1506 without having superseded the horizon of stage 3 of the interregional system.[32] He was not able subjectively to supersede the interregional system—with a history of 4,500 years of transformations, beginning with Egypt and Mesopotamia—and to open himself to the new stage of the world-system. The first one who suspected a *new* (the *last* new) continent was Amerigo Vespucci, in 1503, and therefore, he was existentially and subjectively the first Modern, the first to unfold the horizon of the Asian-Afro-Mediterranean system as world-system, which for the first time incorporated Amerindia.[33] This revolution in the Weltanschauung of the cultural, scientific, religious, technological, political, ecological, and economic horizon is the *origin* of modernity, seen from the perspective of a world paradigm and not solely from a Eurocentric perspective. In the world-system, the accumulation in the center is for the first time accumulation on a world scale.[34] Within the new system everything changes qualitatively and radically. The very medieval European peripheral subsystem changes internally as well. The founding event was the discovery of Amerindia in 1492.[35] Spain is ready to become the first modern state;[36] through the discovery it begins to become the center of its first periphery (Amerindia), thus organizing the beginning of the slow shifting of the center of the older, third stage of the interregional system (Baghdad of the thirteenth century), which from peripheral Genoa (but the western part of the system) had begun a process of reconnection first with Portugal and now with Spain, with Seville to be precise. Genoese and other Italian wealth suddenly flows into Seville. The "experience" of the eastern Renaissance Mediterranean (and through it, of the Muslim world, of India and even China) is thus articulated with the imperial Spain of Charles V (who reaches into the central Europe of the bankers of Augsburg, to the Flanders of Amberes, and later, to Amsterdam, with Bohemia, Hungary, Austria, and Milan, and especially the kingdom of the Two Sicilies,[37] of the south of Italy, namely Sicily, Sardinia, the Baleares, and the numerous islands of the Mediterranean). But because of the economic failure of the political project of the world empire, the emperor Charles V abdicates in 1557. The path is left open for the world-system of mercantile, industrial, and, today, transnational capitalism.

To demonstrate, let us make a comparative analysis, (among the many that may be analyzed—we would not want to be criticized as being a reductive economist because of the example that we have adopted!). It is not a coincidence that twenty-five years after the discovery of the silver mines of Potosí in Peru and the mines in Zacateca in Mexico (1546)—from which a total of 18,000 tons of silver arrived in Spain between the years 1503 and 1660[38]— thanks to the first shipments of this precious metal, Spain was able to pay for, among the many campaigns of the empire, the great armada that defeated the Turks in 1571 in Lepanto. This led to the dominance of the Mediterranean as a connection with the center of the older stage of the system. However, the Mediterranean died as the road of the center toward the periphery in the west, because now the Atlantic was structuring itself as the center of the new world-system![39]

Wallerstein writes: "Bullion was desired as a preciosity, for consumption in Europe and even more for trade with Asia, but it was also a necessity for the expansion of the European economy."[40] I have read, among the many unpublished letters of the General Indian Archive of Seville, the following text of July 1, 1550, signed in Bolivia by Domingo de Santo Tomás: "It was four years ago, to conclude the perdition of this land, that a mouth of hell[41] was discovered through which every year a great many people are immolated, which the greed of the Spaniards sacrifice to their god that is gold,[42] and it is a mine of silver which is named Potosí."[43] The rest is well known. The Spanish colony in Flanders will replace Spain as a hegemonic power in the center of the recently established world-system; it liberates itself from Spain in 1610. Seville, the first modern port (along with Amberes), after more than a century of splendor, will cede its place to Amsterdam[44] (the city where Descartes in 1636 will write *Le Discours de la Méthode,* and where Spinoza will live[45]), the new port controlling naval, fishing, and crafts power; to which flow agricultural exports and great expertise in all branches of production; the city that will, in many respects, bankrupt Venice.[46] After more than a century, modernity was already visible in this city's definitive physiognomy: its port; the channels that as commercial ways reached to the houses of the bourgeoisie and the merchants (who used their fourth and fifth floors as cellars, from which boats were directly loaded with cranes); and a thousand other details of a capitalist metropolis.[47] From 1689 on, England will challenge and will end up imposing itself over Holland's hegemony—which, however, it will have to share with France, at least until 1763.[48]

Amerindia, meanwhile, constitutes the fundamental structure of the first modernity. From 1492 to 1500 approximately 50,000 square kilometers are colonized (in the Caribbean, and farm land from Venezuela to Panama).[49] In 1515 these numbers will reach 300,000 square kilometers, with about 3 million dominated Amerindians; by 1550 Spain has colonized more than 2 million square kilometers (an area greater than the whole of Europe of the center) and more than 25 million (a low figure) indigenous peoples,[50] many of whom are integrated into a system of work that produces value (in Marx's strict sense) for the Europe of the center (in the *encomienda, mita,* haciendas, etc.). We would have to add, from 1520 onward, the plantation slaves of African provenance (about 14 million until the final stage of slavery in the nineteenth century, including those in Brazil, Cuba, and the United States). This enormous space and population will give to Europe, center of the world-system, the *definitive comparative advantage* with respect to the Muslim, Indian, and Chinese worlds. It is for this reason that in the sixteenth century: "The periphery (eastern Europe and Hispanic America) used forced labor (slavery and coerced cash-crop labor [of the Amerindian]). The core, as we shall see, increasingly used free labor."[51]

For the goals of this philosophical work, it is of interest to indicate solely that with the birth of the world-system, the *"peripheral* social formations"[52] were also born: "The form of *peripheral* formation will depend, finally, at the same time on the nature of the accumulated pre-capitalist formations and the forms of external aggression."[53] These will be, at the end of the twentieth century, the Latin American peripheral formations,[54] those of the African Bantu, the Muslim world, India, Southeast Asia,[55] and China; to which one must add part of Eastern Europe before the fall of socialism (see fig. 2.1).

Modernity as "Management" of the Planetary Center and Its Contemporary Crisis

We have thus arrived at the central thesis of this essay: that modernity was the fruit of the "management" of the centrality of the first world-system. We now have to reflect on what this implies.

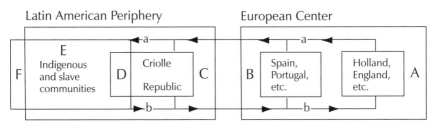

Figure 2.1. An Example of the Center-Periphery Structure in the Center and Colonial Periphery of the 18th Century

Notes: Arrow a: domination and export of manufactured goods; arrow b: transfer of value and exploitation of labor; A: power of the center; B: semiperipheral nations; C: peripheral formations; D: exploitation of Amerindian labor or slaves; E: indigenous communities; F: ethnic communities who retained a certain exteriority to the world-system

Source: Enrique Dussel, *Historia General de la Iglesia en América Latina* (Salamanca, 1983), 223.

There are, at the least, two modernities: the first is a Hispanic, humanist, Renaissance modernity, still linked to the old interregional system of Mediterranean, Muslim, and Christian.[56] In this, the "management" of the new system will be conceived from out of the older paradigm of the interregional system. That is, Spain "manages" centrality as domination through the hegemony of an integral culture, a language, a religion (and thus, the evangelization process that Amerindia will suffer); as military occupation, bureaucratic-political organization, economic expropriation, demographic presence (with hundreds of thousands of Spaniards and Portuguese who forever will inhabit Amerindia), ecological transformation (through the modification of the fauna and flora), and so on. This is the substance of the world empire project, which, as Wallerstein notes, failed with Charles V.[57] Second, there is the modernity of Anglo-Germanic Europe, which begins with the Amsterdam of Flanders and which frequently passes as the *only* modernity (this is the interpretation of Sombart, Weber, Habermas, and even the postmoderns, who will produce a "reductionist fallacy" that occludes the meaning of modernity and, thus, the sense of its contemporary crisis). This second modernity, to be able to manage the immense world-system suddenly opening itself to tiny Holland,[58] which from being a Spanish colony now places itself as the center of the world-system, must accomplish or increase its efficacy through *simplification.* It is necessary to carry out an abstraction (favoring *quantum* to the detriment of *qualitas*) that leaves out many valid variables (cultural, anthropological, ethical, political, and religious variables; aspects that are valuable even for the European of the sixteenth century) that will not allow an adequate, "factual"[59] or technologically possible management of the world-system.[60] This *simplification* of complexity[61] encompasses the totality of the life-world (*Lebenswelt*), of the relationship with nature (a new technological and ecological position that is no longer teleological), of subjectivity itself (a new self-understanding of subjectivity), and of community (a new intersubjective and political relation). A new economic attitude (practico-productive) will now establish itself: the capitalism.

The first, Hispanic, Renaissance, and humanist modernity produced a theoretical and philosophical reflection of the highest importance, which has gone unnoticed by so-called modern philosophy (which is only the philosophy of the second modernity). The theoretical-philosophical thought of the sixteenth century has contemporary relevance because it is the first, and only, that lived and expressed the originary experience during the period of the constitution of the first world-system. Thus, out of the theoretical "recourses" that were available (the scholastic-Muslim-Christian and Renaissance philosophies), the central philosophical ethical question that obtained was the following: What right has the European to occupy, dominate, and manage the recently discovered cultures, conquered by the military and in the process of being colonized? From the seventeenth century on, the conscience (*Gewissen*) of the second modernity did not have to wrestle with this question: it had already been answered in fact. From Amsterdam, London, and Paris (in the seventeenth century and from the eighteenth century onward), "Eurocentrism" (the superideology that will establish the legitimacy, without falsification, of the domination of the world-system) will *no longer* be questioned, until the end of the twentieth century—among other movements, by liberation philosophy.

In another work I have touched on this ethical question.[62] Here I will only examine the theme in general. Bartolomé de las Casas demonstrates in his numerous works, using an extraordinary bibliographic apparatus, rationally and carefully grounding his arguments, that the constitution of the world-system as European expansion in Amerindia (in anticipation of the expansion in Africa and Asia) does not have any right; it is an unjust violence, and cannot have any ethical validity:

> The common way mainly employed by the Spaniards who call themselves Christian and who have gone there to extirpate those pitiful nations and wipe them off the earth is by unjustly waging cruel and bloody wars. Then, when they have slain all those who fought for their lives or to escape the tortures they would have to endure, that is to say, when they have slain all the native rulers and young men (since the Spaniards usually spare only the women and children, who are subjected to the hardest and bitterest servitude ever suffered by man or beast), they enslave any survivors. . . . Their reason for killing and destroying such an infinite number of souls is that the Christians have an ultimate aim, which is to acquire gold, and to swell themselves with riches in a very brief time and thus rise to a high estate disproportionate to their merits. It should be kept in mind that their insatiable greed and ambition, the greatest ever seen in the world, is the cause of their villanies.[63]

Later, philosophy will no longer formulate this problematic, which showed itself unavoidable at the origin of the establishment of the world-system. For the ethics of liberation, this question remains fundamental.

In the sixteenth century, then, the world-system is established in Seville, and philosophy questions, from out of the old philosophical paradigm, the praxis of domination, but it does not reach the formulation of the *new paradigm*. However, the origin of the new paradigm ought not to be confused with the origin of modernity. Modernity begins in 1492, more than a century before the moment in which the paradigm, adequate to its own new experience, is formalized, using Kuhn's terminology; the formulation of the new modern paradigm takes place in the first half of the seventeenth century.[64]

This new paradigm corresponds to the exigencies of *efficacy,* technological "factibility" or governmentalism of the management of an enormous world-system in expansion; it is the expression of a necessary process of *simplification* through "rationalization" of the life-world, of the subsystems (economic, political, cultural, religious, etc.). Rationalization, as construed by Werner Sombart,[65] Ernst Troeltsch,[66] and Max Weber,[67] is *effect* and not cause. But the effects of that *simplifying rationalization* to *manage* the world-system are perhaps more profound and negative than Habermas or the post-moderns imagine.[68]

The corporeal Muslim-medieval subjectivity is *simplified:* subjectivity is postulated as an *ego,* an I, about which Descartes writes: "Accordingly this 'I'—that is, the soul by which I am what I am—is *entirely* distinct from the body, and indeed is easier to know than the body, and would not fail to be whatever it is, even if the body did not exit."[69] The body is a mere machine, *res extensa,* entirely foreign to the soul.[70] Kant himself writes: "The human soul should be seen as being linked in the present life to two worlds at the same time: of these worlds, inasmuch as it forms with the body a personal unity, it feels but only the material world; on the contrary, as a member of the spirit world (*als ein Glied der Geisterwelt*) [without body] it receives and propagates the pure influences of immaterial natures."[71] This dualism—which Kant will apply to his ethics, inasmuch as the maxims ought not to have any empirical or "pathological" motives—is posteriorly articulated through the negation of practical intelligence, which is replaced by instrumental reason, the one that will deal with technical, technological "management" (ethics disappears before a *more geometric* intelligence) in the *Critique of Judgment.* It is here that the conservative tradition (such as that of Heidegger) continues to perceive the *simplifying* suppression of the organic complexity of life, now replaced by a technique of the "will to power" (critiques elaborated by Nietzsche and Foucault). Galileo, with all the naïve enthusiasm of a great discovery, writes: "Philosophy is written in this grand book, the universe, which stands continually open to our gaze. But the book cannot be understood unless one first learns to comprehend the language and read the letters in which it is composed. It is written in the *language of mathematics,* and its characters are triangles, circles and other geometric figures, without which it is humanly impossible to understand a single word of it; without these, one wanders about in a dark labyrinth."[72]

Heidegger said that the "*mathematical* position"[73] one must take before entities is to have the mathematics already known, "ready-to-hand" (in the axioms of science, for example), and to approach the entities only to use them. One does not "learn" a weapon, for instance, but instead one learns to make "use" of it, because one already knows what it is: "The *mathemata* are the things insofar as we take cognizance of them as what we already know them to be in advance, the body as the bodily, the plant-like of the plant, the animal-like of the animal, the thingness of the thing, and so on."[74] The "rationalization" of political life (bureaucratization), of the capitalist enterprise (administration), of daily life (Calvinist asceticism or puritanism), the decorporalization of subjectivity (with its alienating effects on living labor, criticized by Marx, as well as on its drives, analyzed by Freud), the nonethicalness of every economic or political gestation (understood only as technical engineering, etc.), the suppression of practical-communicative reason, now replaced by instrumental reason, the solipsistic individuality that negates the community, and so on, are all examples of the diverse moments that are negated by this *simplification,* apparently necessary for the management of the centrality of a world-system that Europe found itself in need of perpetually carrying out. Capitalism, liberalism, dualism (without valorizing corporeality), and so on are *effects* of the management of this function which corresponded to Europe as center of the world-system: effects that are constituted through mediations in systems that end up totalizing themselves. Capitalism, mediation of exploitation and accumulation (effect of the world-system), is later on transformed into an *independent system* that from out of its own self-referential and autopoietic logic can destroy Europe and its periphery, even the entire planet. And this is what Weber observes, but reductively. That is to say, Weber notes part of the phenomenon but not the horizon of the world-system. In fact, the formal procedure of *simplification* that makes the world-system *manageable* produces formal rationalized subsystems that later on do not have internal standards of self-regulation within its own limits of modernity, which could be redirected at the service of humanity. It is in this moment that there emerge critiques from within the center (and from out of the periphery, such as is mine) of modernity itself. Now one (from Nietzsche to Heidegger, or with the postmoderns) attributes to *reason* all culpable causality (as object "understanding" that takes place through analysis and disintegration)—this culpability can be traced back as far as Socrates (Nietzsche) or even Parmenides himself (Heidegger). In fact, the modern *simplifications* (the dualism of an *ego*-alma without a body, teleological instrumental reason, the racism of the superiority of one's own culture, etc.) have many similarities with the *simplification* that Greek slavery produced in the second interregional system. The Greek *Weltanschauung* was advantageous to the modern man—not without complicity does he resuscitate the Greeks, as was done through the German romantics.[75] The subsumptive supercession (*Aufhebung*) of modernity will mean the critical reconsideration of *all* these simplifying reductions produced since its origin—and not only a few, as Habermas imagines. The most important of these reductions, next to that of solipsistic subjectivity, without community, is the negation of the corporeality of this subjectivity—to which are related the critiques of modernity by Marx, Nietzsche, Freud, Foucault, Levinas, and the ethics of liberation.

Because of all this, the concept that one has of modernity determines, as is evident, the claim to its realization (such as in Habermas), or the type of critique one may formulate against it (such as that of the postmoderns). In general, no debate between rationalists and postmoderns overcomes the Eurocentric horizon. The crisis of modernity (already noted by, as we have remarked frequently, Nietzsche and Heidegger) refers to internal aspects of Europe. The peripheral world would appear to be a passive spectator of a thematic that does not touch it, because it is a "barbarian," a "premodern," or, simply, still in need of being "modernized." In other words, the Eurocentric view reflects on the problem of the crisis of modernity solely with the European–North American moments (or now even Japanese), but it minimizes the periphery. To break through this "reductivist fallacy" is not easy. We will attempt to indicate the path to its surmounting.

If modernity begins at the end of the fifteenth century, with a Renaissance premodern process, and from there a transition is made to the properly modern in Spain, Amerindia forms part of "modernity" since the moment of the conquest and colonization (the mestizo world in Latin America is the only one that is as old as modernity[76]), for it contained the first "barbarian" that modernity needed in its definition. If modernity enters into crisis at the end of the twentieth century, after five centuries of development, it is not a matter only of the moments detected by Weber and Habermas, or by Lyotard or Welsch,[77] but also of those moments of a "planetary" description of the phenomenon of modernity.

To conclude, if we situate ourselves, instead, within the planetary horizon, we can distinguish at least two positions in the face of the formulated problematic. First, on the one hand, there is the "substantialist" developmentalist[78] (quasi-metaphysical) position that conceptualizes modernity as an *exclusively European* phenomenon that *expanded from the seventeenth century on* throughout all the "backward" cultures (the Eurocentric position in the center and modernizing in the periphery); thus, modernity is a phenomenon that must be concluded. Some who assume this first position (for example, Habermas and Apel), defenders of reason, do so critically, because they think that European superiority is not material, but formal, thanks to a new structure of critical questions.[79] On the other hand, there is the conservative "nihilist" position (of Nietzsche or Heidegger, for instance), which denies to modernity positive qualities and proposes practically an annihilation without exit. The postmoderns take this second position (in their frontal attack on "reason" *as such,* with differences in the case of Levinas[80]), although, paradoxically, they also defend parts of the first position, from the perspective of a developmentalist Eurocentrism.[81] The postmodern philosophers are admirers of postmodern art, of the *media,* and although they theoretically affirm *difference,* they do not reflect on the origins of these systems that are the fruit of a rationalization proper to the management of the European centrality in the world-system, before which they are profoundly uncritical, and, because of this, they do not attempt to contribute valid alternatives (cultural, economic, political, etc.) for the peripheral nations, or the peoples or great majorities who are dominated by the center and/or the periphery.

The second position, from the periphery, is the one we defend. It considers the process of modernity as the already indicated rational management of the world-system. This position intends to recoup what is redeemable in modernity, and to halt the practices of domination and exclusion in the world-system. It is a project of liberation of a periphery negated from the very beginning of modernity. The problem is not the mere superseding of instrumental reason (as it is for Habermas) or of the reason of *terror* of the postmoderns; instead, it is a project of overcoming the world-system itself, such as it has developed for the past 500 years until today. The problem is the exhaustion of a "civilizing" system that has come to its end.[82] The overcoming of *cynical managerial reason* (planetary administrative), of capitalism (as economic system), of liberalism (as political system), of Eurocentrism (as ideology), of machismo (in erotics), of the reign of the white race (in racism), of the destruction of nature (in ecology), and so on presupposes the liberation of diverse types of the oppressed and/or excluded. It is in this sense that the ethics of liberation defines itself as transmodern (because the postmoderns are still Eurocentric).

The end of the present stage of civilization is heralded by three limits of the "system of 500 years," as Noam Chomsky calls it. These limits are, first, the ecological destruction of the planet. From the very moment of its inception, modernity has constituted nature as an "exploitable" object, with the increase in the rate of profit of capital[83] as its goal: "For the first time, nature becomes purely an object for humankind, purely a matter of utility; it ceases to be recognized as a power for itself."[84] Once the earth is constituted as an "exploitable object" in favor of *quantum,* of capital, that can defeat all limits, all boundaries, the "great civilizing influence of capital" is revealed: nature now reaches its unsurmountable limit, where it is its own limit, the impassable barrier for ethical-human progress, and we have arrived at this moment: "The universality towards which it [nature] irresistibly strives encounters barriers in its own nature, which will, at a certain state of its development, allow it to be recognized as being itself the greatest barrier to this tendency, and hence will drive towards its own suspension."[85] Given that nature is for modernity only a medium of production, it runs out its fate of being consumed, destroyed, and, in addition, accumulating geometrically upon the earth its debris, until it jeopardizes the reproduction or survival of life itself. Life is the absolute condition of capital; its destruction destroys capital. We have arrived at this state of affairs. The "system of 500 years" (modernity or capitalism) confronts its first absolute limit: the death of life in its totality, through the indiscriminate use of an anti-ecological technology constituted progressively through the sole criterion of the *quantitative* management of the world-system in modernity: the increase in the rate of profit. But capital cannot limit itself. In this lies the utmost danger for humanity.

The second limit of modernity is the destruction of humanity itself. "Living labor" is the other essential mediation of capital as such; the human subject is the only one that can "create" new value (surplus value, profit). Capital that defeats all barriers requires incrementally more absolute time for work; when it cannot supersede this limit, then it augments productivity through technology; but this increase decreases the importance of human labor. It is thus that there is *superfluous* (displaced) *humanity*. The unemployed do not earn a salary, that is, money; but money is the only mediation in the market through which one can acquire commodities to satisfy needs. In any event, work that is not employable by capital increases, thus increasing unemployment and the proportion of needing subjects who are not solvent, including clients, consumers, and buyers—as much in the periphery as in the center.[86] The result is poverty, poverty as the absolute limit of capital. Today we know how misery grows throughout the entire planet. It is a "law of modernity": "Accumulation of wealth at one pole is, therefore, at the same time accumulation of misery, the torment of labour, slavery, ignorance, brutalization and moral degradation at the opposite pole. . . ."[87] The modern world-system cannot overcome this essential contradiction. The ethics of liberation reflects philosophically from this planetary horizon of the world-system, from this double limit that configures the terminal crisis of the civilizing process: the ecological destruction of the planet and the extinguishing in misery and hunger of the great majority of humanity. Before these co-implicating phenomena of planetary magnitude, the projects of many philosophical schools would seem naïve and even ridiculous, irresponsible, irrelevant, cynical, and even complicitous (certainly in the center, but even worse in the periphery, in Latin America, Africa, and Asia), for they are closeted in their "ivory towers" of sterile Eurocentric academicism. Already in 1968 Marcuse had asked, referring to the opulent countries of late capitalism:

> why do we need liberation from such a society if it is capable—perhaps in the
> distant future, but apparently capable—of conquering poverty to a greater

degree than ever before, or reducing the toil of labour and the time of labour, and of raising the standard of living? If the price for all goods delivered, the price for this comfortable servitude, for all these achievements, is exacted from people far away from the metropolis and far away from its affluence? If the affluent society itself hardly notices what it is doing, how it is spreading terror and enslavement, how it is fighting liberation in all corners of the globe?[88]

The third limit of modernity is the impossibility of the subsumption of the populations, economies, nations, and cultures that it has been attacking since its origin and has excluded from its horizon and cornered into poverty. This is the theme of the exclusion of African, Asian, and Latin American alterity and their indomitable will to survive. There is more to say on this theme, but for now I want to emphasize that the globalizing world-system reaches a limit with the exteriority of the alterity of the Other, a locus of "resistance" from whose affirmation the process of the negation of negation of liberation begins.

Notes

This essay is part of chapter 2 of *Etica de la Liberacion* (Ethics of liberation), a work in progress.

1. As a "substance" that is invented in Europe and that subsequently "expands" throughout the entire world. This is a metaphysical-substantialist and "diffusionist" thesis. It contains a "reductionist fallacy."

2. The English translation is not adequate to the expression Weber uses, "Auf dem Boden," which means *within* its regional horizon. We want to establish that "in Europe" really means the development in modernity of Europe as the "center" of a "global system," and not as an *independent* system, as if "only-from-within itself" and as the result of a solely *internal* development, as Eurocentrism pretends.

3. This "we" is precisely the Eurocentric Europeans.

4. Max Weber, *The Protestant Ethic and the Spirit of Capitalism,* trans. Talcott Parsons (New York, 1958), 13; emphasis added. Later on Weber asks: "Why did not the scientific, the artistic, the political, or the economic development there [in China and India] enter upon that path of *rationalization* which is peculiar to the Occident?" (25). To argue this, Weber juxtaposes the Babylonians, who did not mathematize astronomy, and the Greeks, who did (but Weber does not know that the Greeks learned it from the Egyptians); he also argues that science emerged in the West, but not in India or China or elsewhere, but he forgets to mention the Muslim world, from whom the Latin West learned Aristotelian "experiential," empirical exactitude (such as the Oxford Franciscans, or the Marcilios de Padua, etc.), and so on. Every Hellenistic, or Eurocentric, argument, such as Weber's, can be falsified if we take 1492 as the ultimate date of comparison between the supposed superiority of the West and other cultures.

5. Georg Wilhelm Friedrich Hegel, *The Philosophy of History*, trans. J. Sibree (New York, 1956), 341.

6. Following Hegel, in Jürgen Habermas, *Der philosophische Diskurs der Moderne* (Frankfurt, 1988), 27.

7. The world-system or planetary system of the fourth stage of the same interregional system of the Asiatic-African-Mediterranean continent, but now—correcting Frank's conceptualization—factually "planetary." See André Gunder Frank, "A Theoretical Introduction to 5000 Years of World System History," *Review* 13, no. 2 (1990): 155–248. On the world-system problematic, see Janet Abu-Lughod, *Before European Hegemony: The World System A.D. 1250–1350* (New York, 1989); Robert Brenner, "Das Weltsystem: Theoretische und Historische Perspektiven," in *Perspektiven des Weltsystems*, ed. J. Blaschke (Frankfurt, 1983), 80–111; Marshall Hodgson, *The Venture of Islam* (Chicago, 1974); Paul Kennedy, *The Rise and Fall of the Great Powers* (New York, 1987); William McNeil, *The Rise of the West* (Chicago, 1964); George Modelski, *Long Cycles in World Politics* (London, 1987); Michael Mann, *The Sources of Social Power: A History of Power from the Beginning to A.D. 1760* (Cambridge, UK, 1986); L. S. Stavarianos, *The World to 1500: A Global History* (Englewood Cliffs, NJ, 1970); William Thompson, *On Global War: Historical-Structural Approaches to World Politics* (Columbia, SC, 1989); Charles Tilly, *Big Structures, Large Processes* (New York, 1984); Immanuel Wallerstein, *The Modern World-System* (New York, 1974); Immanuel Wallerstein, *The Politics of the World-Economy* (Cambridge, UK, 1984).

8. On this point, as I already mentioned, I am not in agreement with Frank on including in the world-system the prior moments of the system, which I call interregional systems.

9. Wallerstein, *Modern World-System*, chap. 6.

10. Ibid., chaps. 4, 5.

11. Ibid., chap. 3.

12. See Owen Lattimore, *Inner Asian Frontiers of China* (Boston, 1962), and Morris Rossabi, ed., *China among Equals: The Middle Kingdom and Its Neighbors, 10th–14th Centuries* (Berkeley, 1983). For a description of the situation of the world in 1400, see Eric Wolf, *Europe and the People without History* (Berkeley, 1982).

13. In the museum of Masamba, a port city of Kenya, I have seen Chinese porcelain, as well as luxurious watches and other objects of similar origin.

14. There are other reasons for this nonexternal expansion: the existence of "space" in the neighboring territories of the empire, which needed all its power to "conquer the South" through the cultivation of rice and its defense from the "barbarian North." See Wallerstein, *Modern World-System*, 24, which has many good arguments against Weber's Eurocentrisms.

15. For example, see the following works by Joseph Needham: "The Chinese Contributions to Vessel Control," *Science* 98 (1961): 163–168; "Commentary on Lynn White's *What Accelerated Technological Change in the Western Middle Ages?*," in *Scientific Change*, ed. A. C. Crombie (New York, 1963), 117–153; and "Les contributions chinoises à l'art de gouverner les navires," *Colloque International d'Histoire Maritime* (Paris, 1966): 113–134. All of these discuss the control of shipping, which the Chinese had dominated since the first century after Christ. The Chinese use of the compass, paper, gunpowder, and other discoveries is well-known.

16. Perhaps the only disadvantages were the Portuguese caravel (invented in 1441), used to navigate the Atlantic (but which was not needed in the Indian Ocean), and the cannon, which, although spectacular, outside naval wars never had any real effect in Asia until the nineteenth century. Carlo Cipolla, in *Guns and Sails in the Early Phase of European Expansion, 1400–1700* (London, 1965), 106–107, writes: "Chinese fire-arms were at least as good as the Western, if not better."

17. The first bureaucracy (as the Weberian high stage of political rationalization) is the state mandarin structure of political exercise. The mandarin are not nobles, or warriors, or aristocratic or commercial plutocracy; they are *strictly* a bureaucratic elite whose examination system is *exclusively* based on the dominion of culture and the laws of the Chinese empire.

18. William de Bary indicates that the individualism of Wang Yang-ming, in the fifteenth century, which expressed the ideology of the bureaucratic class, was as advanced as that of the Renaissance (*Self and Society in Ming Thought* [New York, 1970]).

19. Through many examples, Thomas Kuhn in *The Structure of Scientific Revolutions* (Chicago, 1962) situates the modern scientific revolution, fruit of the expression of the new paradigm, practically with Newton (seventeenth century). He does not study with care the impact that events such as the discovery of America, the roundness of the earth (empirically proved since 1520), and others could have had on the science, the "scientific community," of the sixteenth century, since the structuration of the first world-system.

20. Needham, "Commentary on Lynn White," 139.

21. A. R. Hall places the beginning of the scientific revolution in the 1500s (*The Scientific Revolution* [London, 1954]).

22. Pierre Chaunu, *Séville et l'Atlantique (1504–1650)* (Paris, 1955), 50.

23. *Factually,* Columbus will be the first Modern, but not *existentially* (because his *interpretation of the world* remained always that of a Renaissance Genoese: a member of a peripheral Italy of the third interregional system). See Paolo Emilio Taviani, *Cristoforo Colombo: La genesi della scoperta* (Novara, 1982), and Edmundo O'Gorman, *La Invención de América* (Mexico, 1957).

24. See J. Zunzunegi, "Los orígenes de las misiones en las Islas Canarias," *Revista Española de Teología* 1 (1941): 364–370.

25. Russia was not yet integrated as periphery in the third stage of the interregional system (nor in the modern world-system, except until the eighteenth century with Peter the Great and the founding of St. Petersburg on the Baltic).

26. Already in 1095 Portugal had the rank of empire. In Algarve in 1249, the reconquest concluded with this empire. Enrique the Navigator (1394–1460) as patron introduced the sciences of cartography and astronomy and the techniques of navigation and shipbuilding, which originated in the Muslim world (he had contact with the Moroccans) and the Italian Renaissance (via Genoa).

27. Wallerstein, *Modern World-System*, 49–50. See also Charles Verlinden, "Italian Influence in Iberian Colonization," *Hispanic Historical Review* 18, no. 2 (1953): 119–209, and Virginia Rau, "A Family of Italian Merchants in Portugal," in *Studies in Honor of Armando Sapori,* ed. C. Cisalpino (Milan, 1957), 715–726.

28. See K. N. Chaudhuri, *Trade and Civilisation in the Indian Ocean: An Economic History from the Rise of Islam to 1750* (Cambridge, UK, 1985).

29. My argument would seem to be the same as in J. M. Blaut, ed., *1492: The Debate on Colonialism, Eurocentrism, and History* (Trenton, NJ, 1992), 28, but in fact it is different. It is not that Spain was "geographically" closer to Amerindia: distance was only one criterion. Spain had to go *through* Amerindia not only because it was closer, but because this was the necessary route to the center of the system, a point that Blaut does not deal with. Gunder Frank (in Blaut, *1492,* 65–80) makes the same error, because for him 1492 represents only a secondary, internal change in the same world-system. However, if it is understood that the interregional system, in its stage prior to 1492, is the "same" system but not yet a "world" system, then 1492 assumes a greater importance than Frank grants it. Even if the system *is the same,* there exists a qualitative jump, which, in other respects, is the origin of capitalism proper, to which Frank denies importance because of his prior denial of relevance to concepts such as *value* and *surplus value;* in fact, he equates *capital* with *wealth* (use-value with a virtual possibility of transforming itself into exchange-value, but not capital accumulated in stages 1 through 3 of the interregional system). This is a grave theoretical error.

30. Enrique Dussel, *The Invention of the Americas* (New York, 1995).

31. See ibid., appendix 4, where the map of the fourth Asiatic peninsula is reproduced (after the Arabian, Indian, and Malaccan), certainly a product of Genoese navigations, where South America is a peninsula attached to the south of China. This explains why the Genoese Columbus would hold the opinion that Asia would not be so far from Europe (South America = fourth peninsula of China).

32. This is what I call, philosophically, the "invention" of Amerindia seen as India, in all of its details. Columbus, existentially, neither "discovered" nor reached Amerindia. He "invented" something that was nonexistent: India in the place of Amerindia, which prevented him from "discovering" what was in front of him. See ibid., chap. 2.

33. This is the meaning of the title of chapter 2, "From the *Invention* to the *Discovery* of America," in my *Invention of the Americas.*

34. See Samir Amin, *L'accumulation à l'échelle mondiale* (Paris, 1970). This work is not yet developed on the world-system hypothesis. It would appear as though the colonial world were a *rear* or *subsequent* and *outside* space to European medieval capitalism, which is transformed "in" Europe as modern. My hypothesis is more radical: the fact of the discovery of Amerindia, of its integration as periphery, is a *simultaneous* and *coconstitutive* fact of the restructuration of Europe *from within* as center of the only new world-system that is, only now and *not before,* capitalism (first mercantile and later industrial).

35. I refer to Amerindia, and not America, because during the entire sixteenth century, the inhabitants of the continent were thought to be "Indians" (wrongly called because of the mirage that the interregional system of the third stage still produced in the still-being-born world-system. They were called Indians because of India, center of the interregional system that was beginning to fade). Anglo-Saxon North America will be born slowly in the seventeenth century, but it will be an event "internal" to a growing modernity in Amerindia. This is the *originating* periphery of modernity, constitutive of its first definition. It is the "other face" of the very same phenomenon of modernity.

36. Unified by the marriage of the Catholic king and queen in 1474, who immediately founded the Inquisition (the first ideological apparatus of the state for the creation of consensus); by a bureaucracy whose functioning is attested to in the archives of the Indies (Sevilla), where everything was declared, contracted, certified, archived; by a grammar of the Spanish language (the first national language in Europe), written by Nebrija, who in his prologue warns the Catholic kings of the importance for the empire of *only one language;* by Cisneros's edition of the Complutensian Polyglot Bible (in seven languages), which was superior to Erasmus's because of its scientific care, the number of its languages, and the quality of the imprint, begun in 1502 and published in 1522; by military power that allowed it to recoup Granada in 1492; by the economic wealth of the Jews, Andalusian Muslims, Christians of the reconquest, the Catalans with their colonies in the Mediterranean, and the Genoese; by the artisans from the antique caliphate of Cordoba, and so on. Spain in the fifteenth century is far from being the semiperipheral country that it will become in the second part of the seventeenth century—the only picture of Spain with which the Europe of the center remembers it, as Hegel or Habermas do, for example.

37. The struggle between France and the Spain of Charles V, which exhausted both monarchies and resulted in the economic collapse of 1557, was played out above all in Italy. Charles V possessed about three-fourths of the peninsula, allowing Spain to transfer through Italy to its own soil the links with the system. This was one of the reasons for all the wars with France: for the wealth and the experience of centuries were essential for whoever intended to exercise new hegemony in the system, especially if it was the first planetary hegemony.

38. This produced an unprecedented increase of prices in Europe, which was convergent with an inflation of 1000 percent during the sixteenth century. Externally this will liquidate the wealth accumulated in the Turkish-Muslim world, and will even transform India and China internally (see Earl Hamilton, *El florecimiento del capitalismo y otros ensayos de historia económica* [Madrid, 1948]; Earl Hamilton, *International Congress of Historical Sciences* [Stockholm, 1960], 144–164; and D. Ingrid Hammarström, "The *Price Revolution* of the Sixteenth Century," *Scandinavian Economic History* 1 [1957]: 118–154). Furthermore, the arrival of Amerindian gold produced a complete continental hecatomb of Bantu Africa because of the collapse of the kingdoms of the sub-Saharan savannah (Ghana, Togo, Dahomey, Nigeria, etc.) that exported gold to the Mediterranean. To survive, these kingdoms increased the selling of slaves to the new European powers of the Atlantic, with which American slavery was produced. See Pierre Bertaux, *Africa: Desde la prehistoria hasta los Estados actuales* (Madrid, 1972); V. M. Godinho, "Création et dynamisme économique du monde atlantique (1420–1670)," *Annales ESC* (1950): 10–30; Pierre Chaunu, *Séville et l'Atlantique (1504–1650)* (Paris, 1955), 57; F. Braudel, "Monnaies et civilisation: De l'or du Soudan à l'argent d'Amérique," *Annales ESC* (1946): 12–38. The whole ancient third interregional system is absorbed slowly by the modern world-system.

39. All of the subsequent hegemonic power will remain until the present on their shores: Spain, Holland, England (and France partly) until 1945, and the United States in the present. Thanks to Japan, China, and California in the United States, the Pacific appears for the first time as a counterweight. This is perhaps a novelty of the next century, the twenty-first.

40. Wallerstein, *Modern World-System*, 45.

41. This is the entrance to the mine.

42. For the past thirty years this text has kept me alert to the phenomenon of the fetishism of gold, of "money," and of "capital." See Enrique Dussel, *Las metáforas teológicas de Marx* (Estella, Spain, 1993).

43. *Archivo General de Indias* (Seville), 313. See also Enrique Dussel, *Les évêques latinoaméricains defenseurs et evangelisateurs de l'indien (1504–1620)* (Wiesbaden, 1970), 1, which was part of my doctoral thesis at the Sorbonne in 1967.

44. Wallerstein, *Modern World-System*, 165.

45. It should be remembered that Spinoza (Espinosa), who lived in Amsterdam (1632–1677), descended from an Ashkenazi family from the Muslim world of Granada, who were expelled from Spain and exiled to the Spanish colony of Flanders.

46. Wallerstein, *Modern World-System*, 214.

47. Ibid., chap. 2, "Dutch Hegemony in the World-Economy," where he writes: "It follows that there is probably only a short moment in time when a given core power can manifest *simultaneously* productive, commercial, and financial superiority *over all other core powers*. This momentary summit is what we call hegemony. In the case of Holland, or the United Provinces, that moment was probably between 1625–1675" (39). Not only Descartes, but also Spinoza, as we already indicated, constitute the philosophical presence of Amsterdam, world center of the system (and—why not?—of the self-consciousness of humanity *in its center*, which is not the same as a mere *European* self-consciousness).

48. See ibid., chap. 6. After this date, British hegemony will be uninterrupted, except in the Napoleanic period, until 1945, when it loses to the United States.

49. See Pierre Chaunu, *Conquête et exploitation des nouveaux mondes (XVIe siècle)* (Paris, 1969), 119–176.

50. Europe had approximately 56 million inhabitants in 1500, and 82 million in 1600 (see C. Cardoso, *Historia económica de América Latina* [Barcelona, 1979], 114).

51. Wallerstein, *Modern World-System*, 103.

52. See Samir Amin, *El desarrollo desigual: Ensayo sobre las formaciones sociales del capitalismo periférico* (Barcelona, 1974), 309.

53. Ibid., 312.

54. The colonial process in Latin America ends, for the most part, at the beginning of the nineteenth century.

55. The colonial process of these formations ends, for the most part, after the so-called World War II (1945), given that the North American superpower requires neither military occupation nor political-bureaucratic domination (proper only to the old European powers, such as France and England), but rather the management of the dominion of economic-financial dependence in its transnational stage.

56. *Muslim* here means the most "cultured" and civilized of the fifteenth century.

57. I think that *management* of the new world-system according to old practices had to fail because it operated with variables that made the system unmanageable. Modernity *had begun*, but it had not given itself a new way to manage the system.

58. Later on, it will also have to manage the system of the English island. Both nations had limited territories, with small populations in the beginning, without any other capacity than their creative "bourgeois attitude" to existence. Because of their

weakness, they had to greatly reform the management of the planetary metropolitan enterprise.

59. The technical "factibility" will become a criterion of truth, of possibility, of existence; Vico's "verum et *factum* conventuntur."

60. Spain, and Portugal with Brazil, undertook as states (world empire) (with military, bureaucratic, and ecclessiastical resources, etc.) the conquest, evangelization, and colonization of Amerindia. Holland, instead, founded the East India Company (1602), and later that of the "Western Indies." These companies (as well as the subsequent British, Danish, etc.) are capitalist enterprises, secularized and private, which function according to the "rationalization" of mercantilism (and later of industrial capitalism). This highlights the difference between the rational management of the Iberian companies and the management of the second modernity (a world-system not managed by a world empire).

61. In every system, complexity is accompanied by a process of "selection" of elements that allow, in the face of increase in such complexity, for the conservation of the "unity" of the system with respect to its surroundings. This necessity of selection-simplification is always a "risk" (see Niklas Luhmann, *Soziale Systeme: Grundriss einer algemeinen Theorie* [Frankfurt, 1988]).

62. See Dussel, *The Invention of the Americas,* chap. 5. During the sixteenth century there were three theoretical positions before the fact of the constitution of the world-system: (1) that of Gines de Sepulveda, the *modern* Renaissance and humanist scholar, who rereads Aristotle and demonstrates the natural slavery of the Amerindian, and thus confirms the legitimacy of the conquest; (2) that of the Franciscans, such as Mendieta, who attempt a utopian Amerindian Christianity (a "republic of Indians" under the hegemony of the Catholic religion), proper to the third Christian-Muslim interregional system; and (3) Bartolomé de las Casas's position, *the beginning of a critical "counterdiscourse" in the interior of modernity* (which, in his work of 1536, a century before *Le Discours de la Méthode,* he titles *De unico modo* [The only way], and shows that "argumentation" is the rational means through which to attract the Amerindian to the new civilization). Habermas speaks of "counterdiscourse," suggesting that it is only two centuries old (beginning with Kant). Liberation philosophy suggests, instead, that this counterdiscourse begins in the sixteenth century, perhaps in 1511 in Santo Domingo with Anton de Montesinos, decidedly with Bartolomé de las Casas in 1514 (see Dussel, *The Invention of the Americas,* 17–27).

63. Bartolomé de la Casas, *The Devastation of the Indies: A Brief Account,* trans. Herma Briffault (Baltimore, 1992), 31. I have placed this text at the beginning of volume 1 of my work *Para una ética de la liberación latinoamericana* (Buenos Aires, 1973), because it synthesizes the general hypothesis of the ethics of liberation.

64. Frequently, in the contemporary histories of philosophy, and of course of ethics, a "jump" is made from the Greeks (from Plato and Aristotle) to Descartes (1596–1650), who takes up residence in Amsterdam in 1629 and writes *Le Discours de la Méthode,* as we indicate above. That is, there is a jump from Greece to Amsterdam. In the interim, twenty-one centuries have gone by without any other content of importance. Studies are begun by Bacon (1561–1626), Kepler (1571–1630), Galileo (1571–1630), and Newton (1643–1727), and Campanella writes *Civitas Solis* in 1602. Everything would seem to be situated at the beginning of the seventeenth century, the moment I have called the second moment of modernity.

65. See Werner Sombart, *Der moderne Kapitalismus* (Leipzig, 1902), and W. Sombart, *Der Bourgeois* (Munich, 1920).

66. See Ernst Troeltsch, *Die Soziallehren der christlichen Kirchen und Gruppen* (Tübingen, 1923).

67. See Jürgen Habermas, *Theorie des kommunikativen Handelns* (Frankfurt, 1981). Habermas insists on the Weberian discovery of "rationalization," but he forgets to ask after its cause. I believe that my hypothesis goes deeper and further back: Weberian rationalization (accepted by Habermas, Apel, Lyotard, etc.) is the apparently necessary mediation of a deforming simplification (by instrumental reason) of practical reality, in order to transform it into something "manageable," governable, given the complexity of the immense world-system. It is not only the internal manageability of Europe, but also, and above all, *planetary* (center-periphery) management. Habermas's attempt to sublate instrumental reason into communicative reason is not sufficient because the moments of his diagnosis on the *origin itself of the process of rationalization* are not sufficient.

68. The postmoderns, being Eurocentric, concur, more or less, with the Weberian diagnosis of modernity. That is, they underscore certain rationalizing aspects or media (means of communication, etc.) of modernity; some they reject wrathfully as metaphysical dogmatisms, but others they accept as inevitable phenomena and frequently as positive transformations.

69. René Descartes, *Le Discours de la Méthode* (Paris, 1965).

70. See Enrique Dussel, *El dualismo en la antropología de la Cristiandad* (Buenos Aires, 1974), and Enrique Dussel, *Método para una Filosofía de la Liberación* (Salamanca, 1974). Current theories of the functions of the brain definitively put in question this dualistic mechanism.

71. Immanual Kant, *Kants Werke* (Darmstadt, 1968), 940.

72. Stillman Drake, *Discoveries and Opinions of Galileo* (New York, 1957), 237–238.

73. See Enrique Dussel, *Para una de-strucción de la historia de la ética* (Mendoza, 1973).

74. Martin Heidegger, *What Is a Thing?*, trans. W. B. Barton (Chicago, 1967), 73.

75. See Martin Bernal, *Black Athena: The Afroasiatic Roots of Classical Civilization* (New Brunswick, NJ, 1989), 224.

76. Amerindia and Europe have a premodern history, just as Africa and Asia do. Only the hybrid world, the syncretic culture, the Latin American *mestiza* race that was born in the fifteenth century has existed for 500 years; the child of Malinche and Hernán Cortés can be considered as its symbol. See Octavio Paz, *El laberinto de la soledad* (Mexico City, 1950).

77. See, among others, Jean-François Lyotard, *La condition postmoderne* (Paris, 1979); Richard Rorty, *Philosophy and the Mirror of Nature* (Princeton, NJ, 1979); Jacques Derrida, "*Violence et métaphysique*, essai sur la pensée d'Emmanuel Levinas," *Revue de Métaphysique et Morale* 69, no. 3 (1964): 322–354; Jacques Derrida, *L'Ecriture et la Différence* (Paris, 1967), and *De la Grammatologie* (Paris, 1967); Odo Marquart, *Abschied vom Prinzipiellen* (Stuttgart, 1981); Gianni Vattimo, *La fine della Modernità* (Milan, 1985).

78. This Spanish word, *desarrollismo*, which does not exist in other languages,

points to the fallacy that pretends the same development (the word *Entwicklung* has a strictly Hegelian philosophical origin) for the center as for the periphery, not taking note that the periphery is not *backward* (see Franz Hinkelammert, *Ideologías del desarrollo y dialéctica de la historia* [Santiago, 1970], and his *Dialéctica del desarrollo desigual: El caso latinoamericano* [Santiago, 1970]). In other words, it is not a temporal *prius* that awaits a development similar to that of Europe or the United States (like the child/adult), but instead it is the asymmetrical position of the dominated, the *simultaneous* position of the exploited (like the free lord/slave). The "immature" (child) could follow the path of the "mature" (adult) and get to "develop" herself, while the "exploited" (slave), no matter how much she works, will never be "free" (lord), because her own dominated subjectivity includes her "relationship" with the dominator. The "modernizers" of the periphery are developmentalists because they do not realize that the relationship of planetary domination has to be overcome as a prerequisite for "*national* development." Globalization has not extinguished, not by the least, the "national" question.

79. See Habermas, *Theorie des kommunikativen Handelns,* along with his debates with P. Winch and A. MacIntyre.

80. We will see that Levinas, the "father of French postmodernism" (from Derrida on), neither is postmodern nor negates reason. Instead, he is a critic of the *totalization* of reason (instrumental, strategic, cynical, ontological, etc.). Liberation philosophy, since the end of the decade of the 1960s, studied Levinas because of his radical critique of domination. In the preface to my work, *Philosophy of Liberation* (New York, 1985), I indicated that the philosophy of liberation is a "postmodern" philosophy, one that took its point of departure from the "second Heidegger," but also from the critique of "*totalized* reason" carried out by Marcuse and Levinas. It would seem as though we were "postmoderns" *avant la lettre.* In fact, however, we are critics of ontology and modernity from (*desde*) the periphery, which meant and *still* means something entirely different, as we intend to explain.

81. Up to now, the postmoderns remain Eurocentric. The dialogue with "different" cultures is, for now, an unfulfilled promise. They think that mass culture, the *media* (television, movies, etc.), will impact peripheral urban cultures to the extent that they will annihilate their "differences," in such a way that what Vattimo sees in Turin, or Lyotard in Paris, will be shortly the same in New Delhi and Nairobi; and they do not take the time to analyze the *hard* irreducibility of the hybrid cultural horizon (which is not *absolutely* an exteriority, but which for centuries will not be a univocal interiority to the globalized system) that receives those information impacts.

82. See Fredric Jameson, *Postmodernism, or, The Cultural Logic of Late Capitalism* (Durham, NC, 1991).

83. In Stalinist "actually existing" socialism, the criterion was the "increase in the rate of production," measured, in any event, by an approximate market value of commodities. It is a question at the same time of fetishism. See F. Hinkelammert, *Crítica a la razón utópica* (San José, Costa Rica, 1984), 123.

84. Karl Marx, *Grundrisse,* trans. Martin Nicolaus (New York, 1973), 410.

85. Ibid.

86. Pure necessity without money is no market, it is only misery, growing and unavoidable misery.

87. Karl Marx, *Capital* (New York, 1977), 799. Here we must remember that the *Human Development Report, 1992* (New York, 1992) has demonstrated in an incontrovertible manner that the richest 20 percent of the planet consumes today (as never before in global history) 82.7 percent of goods (incomes) of the planet, while the remaining 80 percent of humanity only consumes 17.3 percent of the goods. Such concentration is the product of the world-system we have been delineating.

88. Herbert Marcuse, "Liberation from the Affluent Society," in *To Free a Generation: The Dialectics of Liberation,* ed. David Cooper (New York, 1967), 181.

3

The Myth of the Other:
China in the Eyes of the West

Zhang Longxi

1

A BOOK THAT HAS BEEN hailed as one of the most important French contributions to philosophy in this century, Michel Foucault's *The Order of
Things*, first arose out of a passage in Jorge Luis Borges. As Foucault tells us
in the preface, the passage was supposedly taken from a " 'certain Chinese
encyclopaedia,' " in which we find a most curious way of classifying animals:

> "animals are divided into: (a) belonging to the Emperor, (b) embalmed, (c)
> tame, (d) sucking pigs, (e) sirens, (f) fabulous, (g) stray dogs, (h) included in
> the present classification, (i) frenzied, (j) innumerable, (k) drawn with a very
> fine camelhair brush, (l) *et cetera*, (m) having just broken the water pitcher, (n)
> that from a long way off look like flies."[1]

The strange taxonomy in this passage does not make any sense, and the
method of its classification, if there is any method at all in this madness, is
totally beyond comprehension. What else, then, can be a normal response to
this chaos but an irrepressible laughter, a laughter that points out and at the
same time ignores the illogicalness of the passage?

So Foucault laughed. In this laughter, however, he feels an uneasiness and
even distress that the outrageous absurdity has a shattering effect, that the
usual categories of thinking and naming in language are being destroyed, and
that the monstrous passage threatens to "collapse our age-old distinction
between the Same and the Other," casting a spell, an "exotic charm of
another system of thought," while showing "the limitation of our own, the
stark impossibility of thinking *that*" (*OT*, p. xv). The juxtaposition of ani-

mals in such an unthinkable order or, rather, disorder makes it impossible to find a shared space for them, not even in *utopia*. Such a strange taxonomy belongs rather to *heterotopia*, the inconceivable space that undermines the very possibility of description in language. It belongs, says Foucault, to both atopia and aphasia, the loss of correspondence between place and name. That Borges should designate China as the mythical homeland to this strange taxonomy seems most surprising, since the word *China* should immediately evoke the image of a precise region whose name alone, according to Foucault, constitutes for the West a vast reservoir of utopias:

> In our dreamworld, is not China precisely this privileged *site* of *space?* In our traditional imagery, the Chinese culture is the most meticulous, the most rigidly ordered, the one most deaf to temporal events, most attached to the pure delineation of space; we think of it as a civilization of dikes and dams beneath the eternal face of the sky; we see it, spread and frozen, over the entire surface of a continent surrounded by walls. Even its writing does not reproduce the fugitive flight of the voice in horizontal lines; it erects the motionless and still-recognizeable images of things themselves in vertical columns. So much so that the Chinese encyclopaedia quoted by Borges, and the taxonomy it proposes, lead to a kind of thought without space, to words and categories that lack all life and place, but are rooted in a ceremonial space, overburdened with complex figures, with tangled paths, strange places, secret passages, and unexpected communications. There would appear to be, then, at the other extremity of the earth we inhabit, a culture entirely devoted to the ordering of space, but one that does not distribute the multiplicity of existing things into any of the categories that make it possible for us to name, speak, and think. [*OT*, p. xix]

For the West, then, China as a land in the Far East becomes traditionally the image of the ultimate Other. What Foucault does in his writing is, of course, not so much to endorse this image as to show, in the light of the Other, how knowledge is always conditioned in a certain system, and how difficult it is to get out of the confinement of the historical a priori, the *epistemes* or the fundamental codes of Western culture. And yet he takes the Borges passage seriously and remarks on its apparent incongruity with what is usually conceived about China in the Western tradition. If we are to find any modification of the traditional image of China in Foucault's thought, it is then the association of China not with an ordered space but with a space without any conceivable arrangement or coherence, a space that makes any logical ordering utterly unthinkable. Significantly, Foucault does not give so much as a hint to suggest that the hilarious passage from that "Chinese encyclopaedia" may have been made up to represent a Western fantasy of the Other, and that the illogical way of sorting out animals in that passage can be as alien to the Chinese mind as it is to the Western mind.

In fact, the monstrous unreason and its alarming subversion of Western thinking, the unfamiliar and alien space of China as the image of the Other threatening to break up ordered surfaces and logical categories, all turn out to be, in the most literal sense, a Western fiction. Nevertheless, that fiction serves a purpose in Foucault's thought, namely, the necessity of setting up a framework for his archaeology of knowledge, enabling him to differentiate the self from what is alien and pertaining to the Other and to map out the contours of Western culture recognizable as a self-contained system. Indeed, what can be a better sign of the Other than a fictionalized space of China? What can furnish the West with a better reservoir for its dreams, fantasies, and utopias?

The passage Foucault quoted appears originally in Borges' essay on John Wilkins, a seventeenth-century English scholar and Bishop of Chester, whose mind was full of "happy curiosities" including, among other things, "the possibility and the principles of a world language."[2] As Borges shows, the idea of a precise, artificial language built on a strictly logical system of numbers or symbols ultimately originates from Descartes, that is, from within the Western philosophical tradition and its desire to classify and departmentalize all phenomena of the world. Such an attempt at universal language, however, has proved to be quite futile, and all kinds of classification of the universe are inevitably arbitrary. It is precisely the "ambiguities, redundances, and deficiencies" in Wilkins' system that have reminded Borges of similar absurdities "attributed by Dr. Franz Kuhn to a certain Chinese encyclopedia entitled *Celestial Emporium of Benevolent Knowledge*" ("AL," p. 103). In Borges' essay, however, the absurdities of the "Chinese encyclopedia" are not recalled to represent an incomprehensibly alien mode of thinking, since he mentions in the same breath "the arbitrariness of Wilkins, of the unknown (or apocryphal) Chinese encyclopedist, and of the Bibliographical Institute of Brussels," all of whom tried in vain to sort out things in the universe and exhaustively register "the words, the definitions, the etymologies, the synonymies of God's secret dictionary" ("AL," p. 104). Borges greatly admires the courageous, albeit provisional and often thwarted, human effort to penetrate the divine scheme of the universe, and the "Chinese encyclopedia" represents just part of that futile yet heroic attempt to probe God's secret. Though he mentions as his source Dr. Franz Kuhn, a German sinologist and translator of Chinese literature, and even gives the title of that "Chinese encyclopedia," the so-called *Celestial Emporium of Benevolent Knowledge* is nonexistent except in his own invention. As a matter of fact, it is not at all uncommon of Borges in his writings to mix erudition with imagination, blending real names and titles with imaginary ones.

In "The Congress," one of Borges' longest and most diffuse tales, the reader catches another glimpse of the Chinese encyclopedia. This time those fictitious volumes are put among the Britannica, the Larousse, the Brock- haus, and the other "real" encyclopedias in the Congress' reference library. "I recall," says the narrator of the story, "how I reverently fondled the silky volumes of a certain Chinese encyclopedia whose finely brushed characters seemed to me more mysterious than the spots on a leopard's skin."[3] Like the essay on Wilkins, "The Congress" depicts the ambitious intellectual effort to organize everything under the sun and to create order out of chaos. It also dramatizes the failure of this effort by portraying the burning of all the books collected by members of the Congress, including that Chinese encyclopedia. As a matter of fact, the encyclopedia is one of the recurrent images in Borges with a strong suggestion of intellectual power to create its own systematic and ideal world in language amidst the labyrinth of universe. Artificial lan- guage systems arise from the desire to impose order on the chaotic universe, and encyclopedias represent the paramount form of such orderly marshalling of things. In "Tlön, Uqbar, Orbis Tertius," one of Borges' best fantastic sto- ries, Uqbar, the strange land of ideal objects, exists nowhere except in the pages of an encyclopedia, quite specifically in Volume XLVI of *The Anglo- American Cyclopaedia*, which is, according to the narrator, "a literal but delinquent reprint of the *Encyclopaedia Britannica* of 1902." Yet the article on Uqbar is not to be found there, for it exists only in the copy Bioy Casares acquired "at some sale or other," which miraculously has four extra pages containing that article.[4] In other words, that encyclopedia exists only in Borges' fictional world to which he has, however, lent some credibility in a playful fashion by mentioning the real *Encyclopaedia Britannica* and Bioy Casares, the name of a real person. In another story, "The Garden of Forking Paths," Dr. Yu Tsun, a Chinese professor who works as a spy for the Ger- mans, finds in the library of an English sinologist "bound in yellow silk sev- eral volumes of the Lost Encyclopedia, edited by the Third Emperor of the Luminous Dynasty but never printed."[5] As in Borges' other stories, the ency- clopedia here also symbolizes a tremendous but ultimately futile effort to arrange all the irregularities of the universe; its being lost in an obscure little foreign town where a murder is about to occur intensifies the irony of its supposed function as a means to order.

Borges sees the universe as a labyrinth with its innumerable passages, cor- ridors, tortuous paths, and blind alleys, a labyrinth not without its own mys- terious order, but an order unintelligible to human beings. Thus the futile attempt at classification in the Chinese encyclopedia, like Wilkins' artificial language, symbolizes the absurd human condition in which the mind, hin- dered by the limitation of knowledge and the inadequacy of language, tries hopelessly to cope with the vast and labyrinthine creation. On the other hand, literary creation for Borges is also the making of a labyrinth. By connecting the name of a real sinologist with an invented title, Borges creates a maze that tends to puzzle and mislead his readers. Many critics have noticed Borges' "esoteric erudition," which, besides being genuine erudition, is often esoteric only because he playfully mixes his readings with inventions and blurs the boundaries between the true and the imagined as well as the generic boundaries between essay and story. Borges not only plays jokes with readers who enjoy his fantastic style but plays tricks on critics who try to track down his often obscure references. Thus, we may certainly attribute the Chinese encyclopedia to Borges the mythmaker and writer of fantastic tales, and realize that the incomprehensible passage Foucault quoted is nothing more than a good-natured joke, a fictitious representation of fictitious writing itself.

We have no reason, however, to suspect that Borges invents the Chinese encyclopedia to represent an exotic and alien culture, because in his dictionary the word *Chinese* is not synonymous with Other. Indeed, in his poem "The Keeper of the Books," as Borges recalls, he even assumes an imaginary Chinese identity: "I was trying to be as Chinese as a good student of Arthur Waley should be."[6] In his effort to transcend the limitations of space and time, and to grasp the essence of different cultures and histories, he always privileges the common nature of all human beings rather than their difference. "We love over-emphasizing our little differences, our hatreds," says Borges, "and that is wrong. If humanity is to be saved, we must focus on our affinities, the points of contact with all other human beings; by all means we must avoid accentuating our differences."[7] Borges is particularly sensitive to the problematic of the Other, and the theme of double identities runs throughout his works. In these works, the Other often turns out to be no other than the Self.[8]

2

Indeed, we do not have to go very far to seek for the Other. The need to ascertain what makes up our own being, to define our very identity and the features of the world in which we live, that is, the need to have any knowledge of ourselves and our culture, has always to be gratified by an act of differentiation. Spinoza thus formulates one of his propositions: "Every individual thing, or everything which is finite and has a conditioned existence, cannot exist or be conditioned to act, unless it be conditioned for existence and action by a cause other than itself."[9] This is, of course, one of the elementary principles of logic that postulates that the Self is invariably correlated with the Other, and that nothing can be determined by and in itself except by being differentiated from what it is not, or as Spinoza puts it, "determination is negation."[10] Since Ferdinand de Saussure, we are familiar with the structural principle of binary opposition in thinking and in language, the idea that language is a system of terms that define one another in mutual difference. When we have one thing among many and can tell the one from the others at all, what we can tell is nothing but their difference. This point is made clearly in the *Parmenides,* that otherwise enigmatic Platonic dialogue: "if we are talking about the others, things that are others must be different; 'other' and 'different' are two names for the same things."[11]

Philosophical discussions of the Other evidently bear on the problems we have to face when we try to understand different cultures, especially cultures so drastically different as the East and the West. Rudyard Kipling once said, "Oh, East is East, and West is West, and never the twain shall meet."[12] Logically, however, the fact that the poet knows East and West as two separate entities already indicates that not only have the twain met, but each has recognized the Otherness of the other. The East or the Orient, which stands for the Other over against which the West has been able to identify itself, is indeed a conceptual given in the process of self-understanding of the West, and an image built up in that formative process as much as the West itself. Thus the philosophical notion of the Other in Plato and Spinoza takes on the quality of a cultural construct in the West when it comes to represent whatever is conceived as different from traditional Western values. As a cultural entity conceived in the West, the Orient, as Edward Said argues, is almost a European invention:

> We must take seriously Vico's great observation that men make their own history, that what they can know is what they have made, and extend it to geography: as both geographical and cultural entities—to say nothing of historical entities—such locales, regions, geographical sectors as "Orient" and "Occident" are man-made. Therefore as much as the West itself, the Orient is an idea that has a history and a tradition of thought, imagery, and vocabulary that have given it reality and presence in and for the West.[13]

Though by Orient Said means the Middle East, what he says may be applied to the Far East as well, especially to China as the paradigm and locale of the Other with its own history and tradition of thought, imagery, and vocabulary. Vico's famous principle of *verum factum* is of special import for Said. It defines the criterion of truth in terms of the convertibility of the true and the made, thus elevating the humanities to a higher level than the natural sciences on the grounds that the secret of nature is known only to God the Creator. However, Vico says, "the world of civil society has certainly been made by men, and . . . its principles are therefore to be found within the modifications of our own human mind."[14] In the Greek sense of the word, men are poets, that is, makers who have not only created the world they inhabit and myths that account for their experience of the world, but they have "created themselves" (*NS*, p. 112). According to Vico, nothing can be known unless it is experienced; and nothing makes sense unless it is accommodated to the shape of the human mind, which imposes its own shape on the world and our experience of it. Studies of the modifications of the human mind from prelogical thinking in concrete images to logical conceptualization constitute the bulk of Vico's theory of knowledge, which fully recognizes the epistemological value of myth and mythic thinking in primitive societies while refusing to accept Cartesian rationalism as the sole criterion universally applicable to all times and cultures.

This seems to open a new historical vision to which Erich Auerbach enthusiastically attributes the widening of the aesthetic horizon in the West since the beginning of the nineteenth century. Owing to Vico, Auerbach declares with perfect assurance, we are now able to acknowledge the independent values of early and foreign civilizations and to cultivate the true catholicity of aesthetic taste and judgment. Under the impact of Vico's *New Science*, which for Auerbach is nothing less than a great " 'Copernican discovery' " in historical studies,

> no one would condemn a Gothic cathedral or a Chinese temple as ugly because they are not in conformity with classical models of beauty or consider the *Chanson de Roland* as a barbaric and ugly monster, unworthy of being compared to the civilized perfection accomplished in Voltaire's *Henriade*. Our historic way of feeling and judging is so deeply rooted in us that we have ceased to be aware of it. We enjoy the art, the poetry and the music of many different peoples and periods with equal preparedness for understanding.[15]

Vis-à-vis Foucault's remark on the Other, it is no wonder that Auerbach should have singled out a Chinese temple to represent an alien concept of beauty. In the eighteenth century, however, those who grew tired of the vogue of chinoiserie often mentioned the Gothic and the Chinese in tandem as equally grotesque and extravagant, as these satirical lines from Robert Lloyd's *Cit's Country Box* (1757) clearly show:

> Now bricklay'rs, carpenters and joiners,
> With Chinese artists and designers,
> Produce their schemes of alteration,
> To work this wondrous reformation.
> The trav'ler with amazement sees
> A temple, Gothic or Chinese,
> With many a bell, and tawdry rag on,
> And crested with a sprawling dragon.[16]

Since China has been for so long a myth and symbol of difference, the appreciation of the elegance of a Chinese temple would indeed be a real proof of the true spirit of cosmopolitanism, an undeniable testimony to the triumph of aesthetic historicism.

The surmounting of dogmatic precepts and provincialism, the cultivation of historical sympathy with a genuine interest in the totality of human experience of creation, and the preparedness to accept and enjoy the artistic achievements of ancient and foreign cultures may all be logical outgrowths of Vico's theory, but the recognition of the aesthetic values of Chinese architecture and Chinese art in general owes more to Auerbach's view than to Vico's. For in the *New Science,* Vico characterizes China and the Chinese in an unmistakably traditional scenario, in which China appears to be a site of space stubbornly inaccessible to the revolution of time. The Chinese, Vico observes, "are found writing in hieroglyphs just as the ancient Egyptians did"; they "boast a monstrous antiquity because in the darkness of their isolation, having no dealings with other nations, they had no true idea of time" (*NS,* pp. 32, 45). The Confucian philosophy, like "the priestly books of the Egyptians," is "rude and clumsy," almost entirely devoted to "a vulgar morality" (*NS,* p. 33). Chinese painting seems to Vico "most crude," for the Chinese "do not yet know how to make shadows in painting, against which highlights can stand out." Even Chinese porcelain fails to impress him, as he thinks the Chinese "just as unskilled as the Egyptians were in casting" (*NS,* p. 51). The comparison between the Chinese and the Egyptians Vico constantly emphasizes indicates how they both represent, as traditionally understood in the West, totally alien civilizations that are oblivious to any progress in history and lifelessly frozen in their vast, timeless immobility. The irony, however, is that this traditional image of China has itself proved to be quite frozen and timeless, as we find it almost intact in the writings of Foucault and some other contemporary thinkers who, notwithstanding the better knowledge now made available to Western scholars by the progress in sinology, still think of China in very much the same terms as Vico did some two hundred years ago: "as a civilization of dikes and dams beneath the eternal face of the sky; . . . a culture entirely devoted to the ordering of space, but one that does not distribute the multiplicity of existing things into any of the categories that make it possible for us to name, speak, and think" (*OT,* p. xix).

3

Vico's view, however, does not represent the whole picture of China in the Western mind of his time. The eighteenth century, as Adolf Reichwein argues, saw the first "metaphysical contact" between China and Europe, and the Western view was then largely favorable. Reichwein maintains that the age of the Rococo was imbued with a spirit akin to that of Chinese culture, a spirit manifested in those graceful products imported from China: "Sublimated in the delicate tints of fragile porcelain, in the vaporous hues of shimmering Chinese silks, there revealed itself to the minds of that gracious eighteenth-century society in Europe a vision of happy living such as their own optimism had already dreamed of."[17] Indeed, in Alexander Pope's *Rape of the Lock,* that famous mock-heroic drawing-room drama, one can see how important porcelain becomes as a symbol of the feminine component of the Rococo, the daintiness of eighteenth-century high society: for the cutting of the curl from fair Belinda, which forms the fatal climax and the central action of the poem, is always foreboded by the breaking of a "frail China jar" or some porcelain vessels.[18] Indeed, porcelain, silk, lacquer, wallpaper, Chinese gardening, and *ombres chinoises* all became fuels that fed the craze in Europe for things Chinese, the curious eighteenth-century vogue of chinoiserie.

Largely based on favorable reports from Jesuit missionaries and their translation of some of the Chinese classics, on the influential pioneer works by Juan González de Mendoza, Louis Daniel Le Comte, and especially Jean Baptiste Du Halde's *Description géographique, historique, chronlogique, politique, et physique de l'empire de la Chine et de la Tartarie Chinoise,* many eighteenth-century philosophers found in China and the Chinese the model of a nation well organized on the basis of lofty reason and good conduct. After Montesquieu's *Lettres persanes,* dozens of imitations commented on contemporary European life through the mouthpiece of a foreigner, including some collections of "Chinese letters." An example of this particular genre in English is Oliver Goldsmith's *Citizen of the World,* which fully exploits the opportunity for satire on the unsatisfactory conditions in contemporary England. In France, Michel de Montaigne already spoke about China in the sixteenth century as a great nation, whose history made him realize "how much wider and more various the world is than either the ancients or ourselves have discovered."[19] Donald Lach is quite right in pointing out that Montaigne "uses the East to support his beliefs about the uncertainty of knowledge, the infinite variety in the world, and the universality of moral precepts"; and that he saw in China "an example for Europe that he never discerned elsewhere in the overseas world."[20] In Montaigne as well as in Goldsmith, the use of China serves a purpose that is obviously not concerned with China per se but with learning about the self in the West.

In the eighteenth century, chinoiserie became more than just a vogue in daily social life. For Voltaire, China was *"le plus sage empire de l'univers."*[21] He admitted that the Chinese, like the French two hundred years earlier or the ancient Greeks or Romans, were not good mechanics or physicists, "but they have perfected morality, which is the first of the sciences" (*E*, 1:68). He greatly admired Confucius for counselling virtue, preaching no mysteries, and teaching in "pure maxims in which you find nothing trivial and no ridiculous allegory [*rien de bas, et rien d'une allégorie ridicule*]" (*E*, 1:70). Philosophers of the Enlightenment came to know Confucius at a time when they were extremely critical of all existing European institutions, trying to differentiate Christian morality from dogmas of the Church. They suddenly discovered, to their astonishment, that in great antiquity in China—a country whose material products had won the admiration of the average people in the market—Confucius had taught the philosophy of a state built on the basis of ethical and political *bon sens,* and that the Chinese civilization had developed for centuries on principles different from, yet in many respect superior to, those of the West. "Thus," says Reichwein, "Confucius became the patron saint of eighteenth-century Enlightenment. Only through him could it find a connecting link with China" (*CE*, p. 77).

Reichwein declares that in the year 1760, with Voltaire's *Essai sur les moeurs,* Europe's admiration of China reached its zenith. However, in a substantial study of China in English literature of the seventeenth and eighteenth centuries, Qian Zhongshu shows that Reichwein's book has unduly left out English literature and that the situation was quite different in England, where sinophilism was at its height in the seventeenth century, but suffered an eclipse in the eighteenth, particularly as seen in its literature.[22] Qian's study provides many examples of how fact and fiction about China were commingled in the minds of the English, as China was yet more legendary than real, and English men of letters could still reflect on China in a leisurely manner, with an interest more humanistic than pragmatic. For all the false information they may have had and all the strange ideas and popular misconceptions they may have helped to propagate, those writers are extremely interesting precisely because they spoke of China as the Other, as a country whose unfamiliar outline could be filled in with all sorts of fantasies, philosophical speculations, and utopian idealizations.

Of great interest is their discussion of language and writing in China. Probably based on Mendoza, Francis Bacon remarks that the Chinese "write in characters real, which express neither letters nor words in gross, but things or notions."[23] Here Bacon is talking about language as the "organ of tradition," defining, after Aristotle, words as " 'images of cogitations' " and letters as " 'images of words.' " But words, Bacon continues, are not the only medium capable of expressing cogitations, for "we see in the commerce of barbarous people, that understand not one another's language, and in the practice of divers that are dumb and deaf, that men's minds are expressed in gestures, though not exactly, yet to serve the turn."[24] It is in this context that he mentions how the Chinese use characters to communicate among themselves without understanding one another's spoken language. If that is a sign of the "barbarous," if Chinese characters express neither words nor letters—namely, images of cogitations and their transmission in alphabetic writing—the obvious inference must be that Chinese is a primitive language. And that, as we shall see, is precisely the point some writers of that age tried to prove in their vigorous quest for the "primitive language"—"primitive" in the sense of belonging to the times of the beginning or origin: the first language God created and the antediluvian people used, a language pure and simple, yet unaffected by the confusion of tongues at Babel.

Many Jesuits had propagated the view that the Chinese were descendants of Noah and had received from him the principles of natural religion, which had prepared them well for accepting the revealing light of Christianity. Under the influence of such a truly mythical view, Walter Ralegh asserts in his *History of the World* (1614) that Noah's ark finally landed in the East, somewhere between India and China; and Thomas Browne declares that "the Chineses who live at the borders of the earth . . . may probably give an account of a very ancient languadge" because by using common written characters the Chinese are yet able, in spite of their confusion in spoken language, to "make use of the workes of their magnified Confutius many hundred yeares before Christ, and in an historicall series ascend as high as Poncuus, who is conceaved to bee Noah."[25] However, it is John Webb who has presented, in a small octavo volume, the most intriguing argument on the Chinese language, and probably the first extensive treatment of this subject in the West. The thesis of his book is clearly stated in its title: *An Historical Essay Endeavoring a Probability That the Language Of the Empire of China is the Primitive Language.* In his dedicatory epistle to Charles II, dated 29 May 1668, Webb professes to "advance the DISCOVERY of that GOLDEN-MINE of Learning, which from all ANTIQUITY hath lain concealed in the PRIMITIVE TONGUE."[26] He explains that his intention is "not to dispute what in Possibility cannot, but what in Probability may be the First Speech" (*HE*, [p. iii]). Given the authority of the Bible and the "credible History" in the seventeenth century, Webb's argument must have impressed his contemporaries as logically simple and forceful. With his syllogistic argument firmly grounded on Scripture and history, Webb says:

> Scripture teacheth, that the whole Earth was of one Language until the Conspiracy at BABEL; History informs that CHINA was peopled, whilst the Earth was so of one Language, and before that Conspiracy. Scripture teacheth that the Judgment of Confusion of Tongues, fell upon those only that were at BABEL;

History informs, that the CHINOIS being fully setled before, were not there; And moreover that the same LANGUAGE and CHARACTERS which long preceding that Confusion they used, are in use with them at this very DAY; whether the Hebrew, or Greek Chronology be consulted. [*HE,* (pp. iii–iv)]

Webb did not know Chinese himself, but drawing on all the important works then available, he was able to argue with assurance that *"China* was after the Flood first planted either by *Noah* himself, or some of the sons of *Sem,* before they remove to *Shinaar,"* and that "it may with much probability be asserted, *That the Language of the Empire of CHINA, is, the PRIMITIVE Tongue, which was common to the whole World before the Flood"* (*HE,* pp. 31–32, 44). In no small feat to trace the changes of sound and spelling, he even proved to his own satisfaction that the Chinese emperor Yaus or Jaus (obviously the legendary Yao) was the same as Janus, whom many distinguished authors had identified as Noah himself! Finally he proposes "six principal guides" for discovering the primitive language: antiquity, simplicity, generality, modesty of expression, utility, and brevity, to which may be added consent of authors.[27] As he finds in Chinese plenty of these features, he has no doubt that Chinese is the primitive or first language.

Webb's enthusiasm for Chinese civilization is obvious; so are the Western values that underlie his appreciation of China. For him, as for many others in the seventeenth century who sought to see an ideal country where their dreamed values became true, China was that dreamland. He finds no difficulty in seeing China as realizing both Christian and Platonic ideals, for the Chinese are *"de civitate Dei,* of the City of God," and "their Kings may be said to be Philosophers, and their Philosophers, Kings" (*HE,* pp. 32, 93). Chinese poets win his acclaim for not stuffing their works with "Fables, Fictions, and Allegorical conceits, such as when the Authors Poetical rapture is over, himself understands not" (*HE,* p. 98). He observes that in Chinese poetry there are *"Heroick* verse[s]" for didactic purposes, poems of nature, and also poems "which treat of Love, not with so much levity nevertheless, as ours, but in such chaste Language, as not an undecent and offensive word to the most chaste ear is to be found in them." And most amusingly, he informs his readers that the Chinese "have no Letters whereby to express the *Privy parts,* nor are they to be found written in any part of all their Books." This remarkable phenomenon, he claims, is due to "the detestation of that shame, which *Noah* received by the discovery of his nakedness" (*HE,* pp. 98, 99).

For Webb as for Voltaire a century later, the perfection of morality in China, the outcome of a pure and uncorrupted state of natural religion, deserves the greatest admiration. Webb's book, as Qian comments, represents the best knowledge then available about China; it is full of inspiration and insight, putting its emphasis on "the cultural aspect of China instead of being interested in a *mélange adultère de chinoiseries.*"[28] It is therefore no exaggeration to say that in England, as the works of Webb and some other writers can testify, the enthusiasm for China and Chinese culture reached its zenith in the seventeenth century.

4

After a period of infatuation, there is bound to be disenchantment and a change of heart. And indeed we find a quite different picture of China in eighteenth-century English literature. This, of course, corresponds with the social changes in England of the time on a much larger scale. The seventeenth-century idealization of China can be partly traced to religious interests that prompted the Jesuit missionaries to go to China and study its culture. Such evangelistic zeal, however, seems less characteristic of the so-called Age of Reason: in English literature, the fictional character who goes to China is significantly not a missionary but a practical-minded fellow like Robinson Crusoe. In the second part of Daniel Defoe's novel *Robinson Crusoe,* Crusoe gives running comments as he travels through Chinese cities; his extremely negative impressions amount to a total rejection of the more favorable view we find in the literature of an earlier period. This famous earthy traveler constantly compares the "reality" he sees in China with that of Europe, predictably always to the disadvantage of the Asian country, striking a note of colonial militarism that is so typical of the time of the British Empire:

> . . . what are their buildings to the palaces and royal buildings of Europe? What is their trade to the universal commerce of England, Holland, France, and Spain? What are their cities to ours for wealth, strength, gaiety of apparel, rich furniture, and an infinite variety? What are their ports, supplied with a few junks and barks, to our navigation, our merchant fleets, our large and powerful navies? Our city of London has more trade than all their mighty empire. One English, or Dutch, or French man-of-war of eighty guns would fight and destroy all the shipping of China.[29]

If Webb saw the Chinese as being "of the City of God," Crusoe, on the contrary, finds them "a barbarous nation of pagans, little better than savages." He cannot understand why the English "say such fine things of the power, riches, glory, magnificence, and trade of the Chinese, because I saw and knew that they were a contemptible herd or crowd of ignorant, sordid slaves, subjected to a government qualified only to rule such a people."[30] If the Chinese enjoy a reputation for wisdom, says Crusoe, they are wise only "among the foolish ones"; their religion, being "all summed up in Confucius's maxims," is "really not so much as a refined paganism"; and their government is nothing but "absolute tyranny."[31]

Such a pungently critical view indeed contrasts sharply with the seventeenth-century enthusiasm for China, but Defoe's is not the only voice of depreciation. Dr. Johnson, for example, despite his "particular enthusiasm with respect to visiting the wall of China," calls the Chinese "barbarians," for he sees it as a sign of "rudeness" that "they have not an alphabet. They have not been able to form what all other nations have formed."[32] The word "rudeness" with which Johnson justifies his view reminds us of Vico, but in this case, as in many others in his conversation, the Doctor may be arguing for the sake of argument, behind which he would rather stand firm simply because Boswell is proposing a different view. Yet there is another example in his introductory note to Sir William Chambers' *Chinese Architecture,* a book with which he was much pleased. In that introduction, Johnson declares that he does not want "to be numbered among the exaggerators of Chinese excellence." He believes, in fact with very good reasons, that much of that exaggeration is due to "novelty"; and he tries to counterbalance the "boundless panegyricks which have been lavished upon the Chinese learning, policy, and arts."[33] Evidently, when French philosophers were paying very high tribute to Confucius and the Chinese civilization, their English contemporaries were having many serious doubts and reservations.

To be sure, the picture Reichwein paints of China in the perception of eighteenth-century Europe is not all that rosy. He mentions the reaction against Voltaire's excessive praise: the marked indifference of Frederick the Great; the profound skepticism, disparagement, and critique as expressed by Rousseau, Montesquieu, Frédéric-Melchior Grimm, François de Fénelon, and many others; but Reichwein dismisses all these detractors of China as "hemmed in by the limitations of an arbitrary system" (*CE,* p. 94) and presents Goethe's enthusiastic remarks on the Chinese as a kind of grand finale to his book. He regards the *Chinesisch-deutsche Jahresund Tageszeiten* as a work indicating Goethe's warm reception of the Chinese world during the last years of his life. "Everything belonging to that world," says Reichwein, "seemed to him light, delicate, almost ethereal, the relations of things cleanly and clearly defined, the inner and the outer life serene and free from convulsions, something like battledore and shuttlecock perfectly played, without a single clumsy movement" (*CE,* p. 145). But after Goethe, the concept of China underwent a radical change in nineteenth-century Europe as the influence of the Jesuits began to wane and a more practical commercial view gained the upper hand. As a result, China lost its spiritual significance for the

West, and "the idea of China as, above all, a first-rate world-market is beginning to be the sole concern of public opinion" (*CE*, p. 150).³⁴ Many misconceptions were cultivated by philosophers and historians, particularly the one
that China was in a state of eternal immobility and standstill, an idea elabo-
rately developed and explained in the works of Hegel, Leopold von Ranke,
and others—an idea that has become an integral part of the traditional image
of China in Western eyes.

In America, whose cultural roots are firmly planted across the ocean in
Europe, we find the change of attitudes and concepts often following patterns
similar to European ones. Having interviewed many people who all play an
important role in shaping the public opinion about China and India, Harold
Isaacs is convinced that there are in fact "all sorts of scratches on American
minds about Asia," that is, all sorts of images and concepts that are more or
less distorted, but all "have in common a quality of remoteness, of the exotic,
the bizarre, the strange and unfamiliar, and—until the day before yester-
day—a lack of connection with the more visibly important affairs of life."³⁵
In 1942, four months after Pearl Harbor, a national poll found that sixty
percent of Americans could not locate China or India on a world map, but by
the end of the war, because the Chinese were allies who fought the Japanese,
knowledge about China increased slightly among Americans. Evidently,
Americans have two sets of images, of which the modulation, with one
advancing and the other receding alternately, is tuned in to the social and
political atmosphere of the time. China is seen as both static and restlessly
chaotic; the Chinese are both wise and benighted, strong and weak, honest
and devious, and so on and so forth. In popular Hollywood movies, there is
on the one hand the famous villain Fu Manchu; on the other there is the
clever pseudo-Confucian sleuth Charlie Chan. Of course, the actors who
played Fu Manchu and Charlie Chan were not Chinese, and this fact speaks
for itself. As Isaacs observes, "By examining the images we hold, say, of the
Chinese and Indians, we can learn a great deal about Chinese and Indians,
but mostly we learn about ourselves."³⁶

It is indeed the image of the Self that appears through the mirror that we
call the Other, and this is no less true of the Chinese than of the Europeans
or Americans. But there is perhaps this essential difference: while the Westerners tend to see the Chinese as fundamentally Other, sometimes the Chinese would think the Westerners eager to become like the Chinese
themselves, that is, if they want to become civilized at all. In chapter 52 of
the *Dream of the Red Chamber,* also known as *The Story of the Stone,* the best-
known novel in classical Chinese literature, we find a Western girl "from the
country of Ebenash" who not only "had a perfect understanding" of Chinese
literature but "could expound the *Five Classics* and write poems in Chi-

nese."[37] In fact, the poem she composed is so good that it wins high praise from the poetically talented protagonists of that famous novel. For the Chinese of classical education, literary art was the watermark of the cultured, and here the writing of poetry would become a symbolic act of the ritual of initiation by which a foreigner was admitted into the society of culture, for which the only culture worth having was Chinese, and the Other as a cultural issue did not seem to arise.

Such an egocentric attitude may prove to be disastrous in actually dealing with the Other. When East and West first made contact, the Chinese emperor and his ministers could hardly bring themselves to understand the relation between China and other countries except in terms of an outmoded tributary framework, in which the Chinese emperor as the Son of Heaven and sovereign of the Middle Kingdom graciously accepted the respect and tribute foreign kings had to pay if they wished to contact or trade with the Celestial Dynasty. China was the sole center of civilization whereas all foreigners were regarded as barbarians. What we find in this inadequate picture of the Other is of course nothing but the incredible ignorance and arrogance of Chinese rulers. Such an attitude is shown clearly in Emperor Qianlong's letter to King George III in 1793. Here the Emperor told the King of England that "the virtue and prestige of the Celestial Dynasty having spread far and wide, the kings of the myriad nations come by land and sea with all sorts of precious things. Consequently there is nothing we lack, as your principal envoy and others have themselves observed. We have never set much store on strange or ingenious objects, nor do we need any more of your country's manufactures."[38] Not surprisingly, foreign policies based on such ignorance and arrogance later proved to be disastrous for China; in the painful experience of modern history, the Chinese—and Chinese intellectuals in particular—have recognized the significance of the presence of a powerful West. Perhaps it is no exaggeration to say that the whole history of modern China has been a long record of the clashes between cultures of the East and the West, between tradition and modernity, and that the future of China depends on a successful reconciliation of the two. To achieve that success, however, a better knowledge of the Other is absolutely vital. That explains why the desire for knowledge of the West may be said to characterize the Chinese intelligentsia during the entire modern period.

In the West, however, knowledge of China and Chinese civilization seems to be still a specialty limited to a small number of sinologists. In 1963, when Raymond Dawson edited a collection of essays on China as one of the companion volumes to the highly acclaimed *Legacy of Greece*, he felt that "a generation ago it would not have been possible to produce anything fit to occupy a place on the same shelf as the illustrious first volume of the series."[39] Even then, he still thought it necessary to entertain "a healthy scepticism" in reading anything about China. "Old misconceptions of her civilization live long and die hard," says Dawson, "for there is a certain inertia in our historical beliefs, so that they tend to be retained until they are ruthlessly questioned by original minds perhaps centuries after they have ceased to be true."[40]

Indeed, an old misconception tends to remain alive despite all improvement in knowledge and judgment, that is, the misleading idea that Chinese is a pictographic language. We have seen this idea in Bacon and Vico, and we find it again in Foucault when he talks about the difference between cultures of the East and the West in terms of different conceptions of writing. Foucault claims that in Western culture writing "refers not to a thing but to speech"; therefore, the "presence of repeated speech in writing undeniably gives to what we call a work of language an ontological status unknown in those cultures where the act of writing designates the thing itself, in its proper and visible body, stubbornly inaccessible to time."[41] The reference is obviously to nonphonetic writings in Egyptian hieroglyphs or Chinese characters, which are allegedly transparent signs of things: writings that exist not in and for themselves, not ontologically. But when Foucault describes the ontological status of writing in the sixteenth century, the "absolute privilege" and "fundamental place accorded in the West to Writing," he recalls, with Blaise de Vigenère and Claude Duret, a time when the written word was primary and the spoken word was "stripped of all its powers," when the possibility was emphasized that "before Babel, before the Flood, there had already existed a form of writing composed of the marks of nature itself" (*OT,* pp. 38, 39, 38). This naturally reminds us of Webb's view that Chinese is the primitive language before the Flood, but it reminds us even more of the sensible and accurate observation of a sixteenth-century missionary in China, Father Matthew Ricci, who noted in his diary that "from time immemorial, [the Chinese] have devoted most of their attention to the development of the written language and did not concern themselves overmuch with the spoken tongue. Even up to the present all their eloquence is to be found in their writings rather than in the spoken word."[42] If ontological status implies "privilege" and "fundamental place" as Foucault suggests, Chinese may certainly be called an ontological language in its own cultural context. As Chinese scripts are nonphonetic signs, Chinese writing is truly ontological in the sense of being detached from the spoken word. But contrary to popular misconceptions, Chinese writing is not pictographic because the characters are signs of concepts and ideas of things rather than of things themselves. When Henri Cordier, a nineteenth-century French sinologist, tried to define the Chinese writing system, he remarked with good reason that "as the graphic system is not hieroglyphic, or symbolic, or syllabic, or alphabetic, or lexigraphic, but ideophonographic, we shall, in order to avoid misconception and for the sake of brevity, call its characters *sinograms*."[43] This coinage evidently tries to differentiate Chinese written characters from both phonetic and hieroglyphic writing; the key word used here to describe Chinese scripts is "ideophonographic." More recently, George Steiner astutely uses the word "logographic" in talking about the Chinese language.[44] However, to see Chinese characters as minipictures of a myriad of things is a perennial Western misconception that simply refuses to die. Its life is made even stronger in modern times with an injection of poetic vigor by Ernest Fenollosa and Ezra Pound, who formulated one of the most powerful modern theories of poetry based on a powerful and creative misreading of the Chinese ideograms. And based on Fenollosa and Pound, Jacques Derrida sees in the nonphonetic Chinese language "the testimony of a powerful movement of civilization developing outside of all logocentrism."[45] Again the Chinese language becomes a sign of a totally different culture, which sets off, for better or for worse, whatever is conceived as Western culture. It is about time such misconceptions were questioned and the Other was recognized as truly Other, that is, the Other in its own Otherness, which is not only non-Western but may perhaps have things in common with what the West thinks of itself—the Other that does not just serve the purpose of being a foil or contrast to the Western self.[46]

5

The question is, then, can we ever know the Other as the truly Other? When we have argued with Foucault and others who entertain a variety of distorted images of China as the Other, it seems that we have argued, ironically, not against Foucault but for him completely. All we have shown is precisely the validity of his proposition that it is hardly possible to get out of the confinement of the historical a priori, the *epsitemes* or fundamental codes of cultural systems. Apparently, the misconceptions of China we find today form part of the traditional repertory of cultural concepts in the West; they are deeply rooted in its history and ideology. The image of China in the Western eye, as our discussion shows, has always been historically shaped to represent values that are considered different from Western ones. China, India, Africa, and the Islamic Orient have all served as foils to the West at one time or another, either as idealized utopias, alluring and exotic dreamlands, or lands of eternal stagnation, spiritual purblindness, and ignorance. Whatever change and progress we may make in understanding the Other, that understanding has to be mediated through language, which is itself a product of history and therefore not outside of it. As Dawson observes, the "polarity between Europe and Asia and between West and East is one of the important categories by means of which we think of the world and arrange our knowledge of it, so there can be no doubt that it colours the thoughts even of those who have a special interest in Oriental studies."[47] As there is no other language or other way of thinking available to us except our own, and no understanding of the Other except in relation to the Self, a purely "objective" or "correct" understanding unaffected by historical and ideological givens is indeed hard to find. But does that mean that our thinking and language are a kind of prisonhouse from which there is no escape? When Dawson speaks about the pervasive influence of popular misconceptions, he is speaking not only as a sinologist who understands China better than those who are yet to be initiated into the range of his knowledge, but also as a scholar and editor whose book will provide knowledge to disperse hazy fantasies and help readers understand the rich cultural legacy of China. He is, in other words, suggesting that it is not just necessary but possible to expose and rectify cultural misconceptions.

It is true to a certain extent that our thinking and knowledge are determined by the historical givens of the culture in which we are born, that we can name, speak, and think only within the boundaries of our language. Understanding begins with a set of historical givens—what Martin Heidegger describes as the fore-structure of understanding—and the process of knowing seems to move only within limits of a hermeneutic circle. Anything understood, says Heidegger, is conceptualizable through interpretation that is already "grounded in *something we have in advance*—in a *fore-having*."[48] However, the fore-structure of understanding is only a necessary but provisional beginning, not a fixation of presuppositions never to be changed and modified. "Our first, last, and constant task," says Heidegger, "is never to allow our fore-having, fore-sight, and fore-conception to be presented to us by fancies and popular conceptions, but rather to make the scientific theme secure by working out these fore-structures in terms of the things themselves."[49] In Heidegger's hermeneutic theory, therefore, while presuppositions are fully recognized, the forestructure of understanding does not preclude, but rather invites, changes and modifications based on the claims of "the things themselves." And that, as Hans-Georg Gadamer points out in a lucid gloss to this important passage, is precisely what Heidegger works out here. "The point of Heidegger's hermeneutical thinking," Gadamer observes, "is not so much to prove that there is a circle as to show that this circle possesses an ontologically positive significance."[50] To know the Other certainly begins with interpretive givens, the *epistemes* or fundamental codes of a cultural system, but as the hermeneutic process evolves, those givens will

be challenged and revised. As Gadamer remarks, in the Heideggerian hermeneutic process "interpretation begins with fore-conceptions that are replaced
by more suitable ones," and "methodologically conscious understanding will
be concerned not merely to form anticipatory ideas, but to make them conscious, so as to check them and thus acquire right understanding from the
things themselves" (*TM,* pp. 236, 239). If it is right to remember how our
language largely determines the way we can talk about the Other, it would be
wrong to forget that the Other has its own voice and can assert its own truth
against various misconceptions. What is important then is to remain open to
the claims of the Other and to listen to its voice, which will make us aware
of our own preconceptions as well as the fact that Orient and Occident as
polarized cultural entities are cultural constructs that are widely different
from the physical entities they are supposed to represent.

Images of national characters, those popular, caricaturelike generalizations, are often generated by representational systems. In 1889, Oscar Wilde
put it in clear and witty language that the discrepancy between reality and
representation can be enormous. Take Japan for example, says Wilde. "The
actual people who live in Japan are not unlike the general run of English
people; that is to say, they are extremely commonplace, and have nothing
curious or extraordinary about them. In fact the whole of Japan is a pure
invention."[51] In proclaiming that Japan as represented in art and literature is
a myth and fiction, Wilde, as Eugenio Donato argues, had dismantled the
illusion of realism and revealed "what we know only too well after Derrida,"
namely, "the play of representation."[52] As a typical aesthete Wilde certainly
prefers artistic myth to reality, but his insight into the play of representation
emphasizes precisely the false nature of cultural myths. Perhaps that is why
Wilde, though admittedly making deliberate overstatements, appears more
sober-minded than many scholars of our own time, who, for all the knowledge now made available about the language and culture of China and Japan,
seem either to take myth for reality or simply refuse to acknowledge their
difference.

An interesting modern reflection on Japan as "a fictive nation" and a consciously "invented name" is Roland Barthes' *Empire of Signs.* Like Wilde,
Barthes is fully aware that the Japan that emerges in his writing is not a real
country: "I am not lovingly gazing toward an Oriental essence—to me the
Orient is a matter of indifference, merely providing a reserve of features
whose manipulation—whose invented interplay—allows me to 'entertain'
the idea of an unheard-of symbolic system, one altogether detached from our
own."[53] He knows very well that the desire to use the language of the Other
to reveal "the impossibilities of our own," a desire Foucault shares, is merely
a "dream."[54] Having warned his reader that his writing is pure mythmaking,

Barthes is able to indulge in the dream of the totally different Other and to produce a number of charming myths about Japan when he asserts, for example, that "chopsticks are the converse of our knife (and of its predatory substitute, the fork)," setting West and East again in the frame of a fundamental polarity.[55] It would be interesting to see what symbolic meaning our modern dreamers will attribute to, say, fortune cookies, which are so popular in every Chinese restaurant in the United States but unheard of in China. And what reflections they may have on the mixture of fantasy and reality, the colorful Chinatown mythologies.

Once China or Japan is recognized as truly different, that is, not as the imaginary Other with its history of imagery in the Western tradition but as a country with its own history, and once the desire to know the Other is genuine enough, being part of the desire to expand the horizon of knowledge in the West, it becomes necessary to demythologize the myth of the Other. In the traditional imagery of the Other, however, there is always an aura of mystery, exotic beauty, or what Victor Segalen calls "the aesthetic of the Diverse." As poet and sinophile, Segalen develops a theory of the Other, celebrating the far away in space or time, which he terms *l'Exotisme*. For him China is not so much a real country as a myth that inspires his *Stèles, Equipée,* and other works; demythologization of the Other would seem to him a threat to poetic charms because exoticism, according to Segalen, is nothing but "the power to *conceive the Other*."[56] In the increasing contact of East and West, he sees a depressing loss of exoticism. "The exotic tension of the world is diminishing. Exoticism, the source of mental, asesthetic, or physical energy (though I do not like to confuse the levels), is diminishing," laments our poet. "Where is mystery? Where are the distances?"[57]

However, mystery may contribute to fear as well as to charm, and distances may blur the view of true beauty. To demythologize the Other is surely not to deny its distance, its alien nature, or the possibility of its poetic charms, but to recuperate real rather than imaginary differences. The beauty of real difference or the aesthetic of the Other cannot be truly appreciated unless various misconceptions are exposed and the false polarity between East and West is totally dismantled. To demythologize the Other is not to become self-alienated in adopting alien values, but eventually to come back to the self with rewarding experiences. Here another important concept Gadamer develops in his work may prove to be helpful, namely, the concept of Bildung.

In Hegel's concept of theoretical Bildung, there is first this move of self-alienation: "Theoretical Bildung goes beyond what man knows and experiences immediately. It consists in learning to allow what is different from oneself and to find universal viewpoints from which one can grasp the thing, 'the objective thing in its freedom', without selfish interest" (*TM*, p. 14). Yet the basic movement of the spirit is a tendency of returning to the Self from the Other; thus "it is not alienation as such, but the return to oneself, which presumes a prior alienation, that constitutes the essence of Bildung" (*TM*, p. 15). However, Bildung is not just attaining to the universal, the perfection of the absolute knowledge of philosophy, as Hegel insists. Instead Gadamer emphasizes the openness of the process: one needs "to keep oneself open to what is other, to other, more universal points of view"; for him the universal viewpoints are not absolute, "not a fixed applicable yardstick, but . . . the viewpoints of possible others" (*TM*, pp. 17–18). That is to say, to know the Other is a process of Bildung, of learning and self-cultivation, which is neither projecting the Self onto the Other nor erasing the Self with what belongs to the Other. It is rather a moment when Self and Other meet and join together, in which both are changed and enriched in what Gadamer calls "the fusion of horizons" (*TM*, p. 273). That moment of fusion would eliminate the isolated horizon of either the Self or the Other, the East or the West, and bring their positive dynamic relationship into prominence. For in the fusion of horizons we are able to transcend the boundaries of language and culture so that there is no longer the isolation of East or West, no longer the exotic, mystifying, inexplicable Other, but something to be learned and assimilated until it becomes part of our knowledge and experience of the world. Thus, in demythologizing China as the myth of the Other, the myth disappears but not the beauty, for the real differences between China and the West will be clearly recognized. China's true Otherness will be appreciated as contributing to the variety of our world and the totality of what we may proudly call the heritage of human culture.

Notes

1. Michel Foucault, *The Order of Things: An Archaeology of the Human Sciences*, trans. pub. (New York, 1973), p. xv; hereafter abbreviated *OT*.
2. Jorge Luis Borges, "The Analytical Language of John Wilkins," *Other Inquisitions, 1937–1952*, trans. Ruth L. C. Simms (Austin, Tex., 1964), p. 101; hereafter abbreviated "AL."
3. Borges, "The Congress," *The Book of Sand*, trans. Norman Thomas di Giovanni (New York, 1977), p. 37.
4. Borges, "Tlön, Uqbar, Orbis Tertius," trans. James E. Irby, *Labyrinths: Selected Stories and Other Writings*, ed. Donald A. Yates and Irby (New York, 1983), pp. 3, 4.
5. Borges, "The Garden of Forking Paths," trans. Yates, *Labyrinths*, p. 24.
6. Borges, *Borges on Writing*, ed. di Giovanni, Daniel Halpern, and Frank Mac-Shane (New York, 1973), p. 86.

7. Borges, "Facing the Year 1983," *Twenty-Four Conversations with Borges, Including a Selection of Poems*, trans. Nicomedes Suárez Araúz et al. (Housatonic, Mass., 1984), p. 12.

8. See, for example, "The Other" in *The Book of Sand*, pp. 11–20, and "Borges and I" in *Labyrinths*, pp. 246–47.

9. Benedict de Spinoza, *The Ethics, The Chief Works of Benedict de Spinoza*, trans. R. H. M. Elwes, 2 vols. (New York, 1951), 2:67.

10. Spinoza, *Correspondence, The Chief Works of Benedict de Spinoza*, 2:370.

11. Plato, *Parmenides*, trans. F. M. Cornford, *The Collected Dialogues of Plato, Including the Letters*, ed. Edith Hamilton and Huntington Cairns (Princeton, N.J., 1961), p. 954.

12. Rudyard Kipling, "The Ballad of East and West," *Collected Verse of Rudyard Kipling* (New York, 1907), p. 136.

13. Edward W. Said, *Orientalism* (New York, 1978), pp. 4–5.

14. Giambattista Vico, *The New Science*, ed. and trans. Thomas Goddard Bergin and Max Harold Fisch (Ithaca, N.Y., 1968), p. 96; hereafter abbreviated *NS*.

15. Erich Auerbach, "Vico's Contribution to Literary Criticism," in *Studia Philologica et Litteraria in Honorem L. Spitzer*, ed. A. G. Hatcher and K. L. Selig (Bern, 1958), p. 33.

16. Robert Lloyd, quoted in Qian Zhongshu [Ch'ien Chung-shu], "China in the English Literature of the Eighteenth Century (I)," *Quarterly Bulletin of Chinese Bibliography* 2 (June 1941): 31.

17. Adolf Reichwein, *China and Europe: Intellectual and Artistic Contacts in the Eighteenth Century*, trans. J. C. Powell (New York, 1925), pp. 25–26; hereafter abbreviated *CE*.

18. See Alexander Pope, *The Rape of the Lock, Selected Poetry and Prose*, 2d ed., ed. William K. Wimsatt (New York, 1972), pp. 99, 105, 110.

19. Michel de Montaigne, "On Experience," *Essays*, trans. J. M. Cohen (Harmondsworth, 1958), p. 352.

20. Donald F. Lach, *Asia in the Making of Europe*, 2 vols. (Chicago, 1965–77), 2:297.

21. François Marie Arouet de Voltaire, *Essai sur les moeurs et l'esprit des nations et sur les principaux faits de l'histoire depuis Charlemagne jusqu'à Louis XIII*, ed. René Pomeau, 2 vols. (Paris, 1963), 1:224, hereafter abbreviated *E*. All translations of Voltaire are mine.

22. See Qian Zhongshu [Ch'ien Chung-shu], "China in the English Literature of the Seventeenth Century," *Quarterly Bulletin of Chinese Bibliography* 1 (Dec. 1940): 351–84. See also Qian, "China in the English Literature of the Eighteenth Century (I)," pp. 7–48, and "China in the English Literature of the Eighteenth Century (II)," *Quarterly Bulletin of Chinese Bibliography* 2 (Dec. 1941): 113–52. I am deeply indebted to Mr. Qian for discussion of this subject.

23. Francis Bacon, *Of the Proficience and Advancement of Learning, Human and Divine, The Works of Francis Bacon*, 10 vols. (London, 1824), 1:147.

24. Ibid., 1:146.

25. Thomas Browne, "Of Languages, and Particularly of the Saxon Tongue," *The Prose of Sir Thomas Browne*, ed. Norman Endicott (Garden City, N.Y., 1967), p. 427.

26. John Webb, *An Historical Essay Endeavoring a Probability That the Language Of the Empire of China is the Primitive Language* (London, 1669), [p. ii]; hereafter abbreviated *HE*.

27. See *HE*, pp. 191–212.

28. Qian, "China in the English Literature of the Seventeenth Century," p. 371.

29. Daniel Defoe, *The Life and Strange Adventures of Robinson Crusoe, The Works of Daniel Defoe*, 8 vols., 16 pts. (Boston, 1903–4), 1:2:256–57.

30. Ibid., 1:2:257, 258.

31. Defoe, *Serious Reflections during The Life and Strange Adventures of Robinson Crusoe With his vision of The Angelic World, The Works of Daniel Defoe*, 2:3:123, 127.

32. James Boswell, *Life of Johnson*, ed. R. W. Chapman (Oxford, 1980), pp. 929, 984–85.

33. Ibid., p. 1211 n.2.

34. For a full treatment of various nineteenth-century Western concepts of China, see Mary Gertrude Mason, *Western Concepts of China and the Chinese, 1840–1876* (New York, 1939).

35. Harold R. Isaacs, *Scratches on Our Minds: American Views of China and India* (New York, 1980), p. 40.

36. Ibid., p. 381.

37. Cao Xueqin, *The Story of the Stone*, trans. David Hawkes and John Minford, 5 vols. (Harmondsworth, 1973–86), 2:539, 540.

38. Quoted in *China's Response to the West: A Documentary Survey, 1839–1923*, ed. Ssuyü Teng and John K. Fairbank (Cambridge, Mass., 1961), p. 19.

39. Raymond Dawson, "Introduction," *The Legacy of China*, ed. Dawson (Oxford, 1964), p. xiii.

40. Dawson, "Western Conceptions of Chinese Civilization," *The Legacy of China*, p. 4.

41. Foucault, "Language to Infinity," *Language, Counter-Memory, Practice: Selected Essays and Interviews*, ed. Donald F. Bouchard, trans. Bouchard and Sherry Simon (Ithaca, N.Y., 1977), p. 56.

42. Matthew Ricci, *China in the Sixteenth Century: The Journals of Matthew Ricci: 1583–1610*, trans. Louis J. Gallagher (New York, 1953), p. 28.

43. Henri Cordier, "Chinese Language and Literature," in Alexander Wylie, *Chinese Researches* (Shanghai, 1897), p. 195.

44. See George Steiner, *After Babel: Aspects of Language and Translation* (Oxford, 1975), p. 357.

45. Jacques Derrida, *Of Grammatology*, trans. Gayatri Chakravorty Spivak (Baltimore, 1976), p. 90.

46. For a discussion of Derrida's use of Chinese as a model outside logocentrism, see Zhang Longxi, "The *Tao* and the *Logos*: Notes on Derrida's Critique of Logocentrism," *Critical Inquiry* 11 (Mar. 1985): 385–98.

47. Dawson, "Western Conceptions of Chinese Civilization," p. 22.

48. Martin Heidegger, *Being and Time*, trans. John Macquarrie and Edward Robinson (New York, 1962), p. 191.

49. Ibid., p. 195.

50. Hans-Georg Gadamer, *Truth and Method*, ed. and trans. Garrett Barden and John Cumming (New York, 1975), p. 236; hereafter abbreviated *TM*.

51. Oscar Wilde, "The Decay of Lying: An Observation," *Intentions* (New York, 1905), pp. 46–47.

52. Eugenio Donato, "Historical Imagination and the Idioms of Criticism," *Boundary 2* 8 (Fall 1979): 52.

53. Roland Barthes, "Faraway," *Empire of Signs,* trans. Richard Howard (New York, 1982), p. 3.

54. Barthes, "The Unknown Language," *Empire of Signs,* p. 6.

55. Barthes, "Chopsticks," *Empire of Signs,* p. 18.

56. Victor Segalen, *Essai sur l'Exotisme: Une esthétique du divers (notes)* (Montpellier, 1978), p. 19; my translation.

57. Ibid., pp. 76, 77; my translation.

4

The Dream of a Butterfly

Rey Chow

[L]ove is of such a nature that it changes man into the things he loves.
　　　　　—Martin Heidegger (citing Meister Eckhart), "The Thing"

[I]nescapably, I passed beyond the unreality of the thing represented, I entered crazily into the spectacle, into the image, taking into my arms what is dead, what is going to die. . . .
　　　　　—Roland Barthes, *Camera Lucida*

The mystical is by no means that which is not political. . . . What was tried at the end of the last century . . . by all kinds of worthy people . . . was an attempt to reduce the mystical to questions of fucking.
　　　　　—Jacques Lacan, "God and the *Jouissance* of the Woman"

THESE DAYS WE have become complacent about our ability to criticize the racist and sexist blunders inherent in the stereotypical representations of our cultural "others." "Our" here refers to the community of intellectuals, East and West, who have absorbed the wisdom of Edward Said's *Orientalism* and who are on the alert to point out the discriminatory assumptions behind the production of cultural artifacts, in particular those that involve Western representations of the non-West. But Said's work, insofar as it successfully canonizes the demystification of Western cultural pretensions, is simply pointing to a certain direction in which much work still waits to be done—namely, the direction in which we must examine in detail the multifaceted psychical and philosophical implications of the conflict, confusion, and tragedy arising from "cross-cultural exchange" when that exchange is conditioned by the inequities and injustices of imperialist histories. This work that needs to be done cannot be done simply by repeating the debunking messages that Said has already so clearly delivered in his book. Rather, we need to explore alternative ways of thinking about cross-cultural exchange that exceed the pointed, polemical framework of "antiorientalism"—the lesson from Said's work—by continually problematizing the presumption of stable identities and also by continually asking what else there is to learn beyond destabilized identities themselves. In this chapter, I read the 1993 film *M. Butterfly* (directed by David Cronenberg, screenplay by David Henry Hwang) as an instance of such a badly needed alternative approach to the problematic of Orientalism.[1]

Let me emphasize at the outset that I am not discrediting or deemphasizing the continual need for the criticism of Orientalism. Far from it: I am saying that precisely because Orientalism has many guises—both decadent and progressivist, in the form of sexual adventures and textual devotion, *and also* in the form of political idealization, fascination with subaltern groups and disenfranchised classes, and so forth—what we need to examine ever more urgently is fantasy, a problem which is generally recognized as central to orientalist perceptions and significations.

My task is made all the more challenging because the problem of fantasy, even though it is a predominant consideration of the stage play on which the film was based, is usually dismissed moralistically, in this case also by play-wright Hwang. In responding to the real-life story of the French diplomat whose affair with a Chinese male opera singer gave him his inspiration for the play, for instance, Hwang writes confidently: "I . . . concluded that the diplomat must have fallen in love, not with a person, but with a fantasy stereotype."[2] Hwang's interest in this bizarre story is, one might say, primarily didactic, as he expresses it clearly in these remarks:

> *M. Butterfly* has sometimes been regarded as an anti-American play, a diatribe against the stereotyping of the East by the West, of women by men. Quite to the contrary, I consider it a plea to all sides to cut through our respective layers of cultural and sexual misperception, to deal with one another truthfully for our mutual good, from the common and equal ground we share as human beings.
> For the myths of the East, the myths of the West, the myths of men, and the myths of women—these have so saturated our consciousness that truthful contact between nations and lovers can only be the result of heroic effort. Those who prefer to bypass the work involved will remain in a world of surfaces, misperceptions running rampant.[3]

And yet, because the question of fantasy as stated here is already part of a conclusive understanding, of a plea for truthful human contact devoid of "misperception," there is something inherently superfluous about the representation of the story: if these layers of cross-cultural "misperception" are a fact of such crystal clarity, why not simply state it as such? Why, in other words, do we need to have a play in the first place? As a moral fable that was designed to preach a lesson well understood in advance—the lesson about the laughable "fantasy" and ludicrous "false consciousness" of the imperialist Western man—Hwang's play, it would seem, is a gratuitous act. Is the play's overwhelming success in the West due perhaps precisely to this gratuitous, stereotypical, and thus absolutely safe mockery of fantasy and false consciousness? But this success—this approval received by an Asian American playwright in the West for correctly reprimanding Western imperialist fantasies—is it not itself a sign and a warning, not of how the West has finally learned its lessons, but rather once again of the very Orientalism which Hwang intends to criticize, and to which non-Western peoples nonetheless continue to be subjected today?[4]

My interest in the film *M. Butterfly* begins where Hwang would have us stop. Rather than being my conclusion, fantasy is the beginning of my inquiry, which is framed by two major questions.

First, if fantasy is not simply a matter of distortion or willful exploitation, but is rather an inherent part of our consciousness, our wakeful state of mind,[5] what are the possibilities and implications of achieving any kind of sexual and racial identification in a "cross-cultural" exchange? Further, if the most important thing about fantasy is not the simple domination of an other but, as Laplanche and Pontalis argue, the variable positionality of the subject, whose reality consists in a constant shifting between modes of dominance and submission,[6] what could be said about the relations between East and West, woman and man, that is perhaps alternative to the ones they are assumed, in antiorientalist discourse, to have?

The second major question that concerns me, after fantasy has been sufficiently understood to be a kind of structuring and setting that is indispensable to any consideration of subjectivity, is how the film *M. Butterfly* also moves *beyond* subjectivity to philosophical issues of phenomenology and ontology. What is of particular interest is the manner in which the film relates the question of "cross-cultural" fantasy not simply to homosexuality, heterosexuality, or race, but also to the larger, open-ended question of the limits of human vision. As I will attempt to demonstrate, the film probes this other question by exploring the phenomenological effects of the image and the gaze.

"East Is East and West Is West, and Ne'er the Twain Shall Meet"

For me, what is most remarkable about the *M. Butterfly* story is, to put it in the simplest terms, the fact that it is a stereotype, in which a Western man believes he is romantically involved with an oriental woman. The story goes briefly as follows. It is 1964 in Beijing, China. René Gallimard, an accountant working at the French consulate, has just been to a performance of excerpts from Giacomo Puccini's opera *Madama Butterfly* (1904), staged at one of the foreign embassies. Gallimard finds himself drawn to the Chinese opera singer, Song Liling, who plays the role of Madame Butterfly. When he relates his fascination to his wife, who dismisses the Chinese with the familiar attitude, "East is East and West is West, and never the twain shall meet," he finds that she does not share his enthusiasm. In the rest of the film she is to become less and less significant as he embarks on a clandestine relationship with the opera singer. Song later tells Gallimard she has become pregnant; eventually she shows him a baby boy who is supposedly his son. As the Cultural Revolution progresses, the lovers are separated: Gallimard is sent back to Paris and Song put in a labor camp. Just as he is abandoning all hope, she shows up again unexpectedly in Paris outside his apartment. The lovers are happily reunited until they are arrested for passing secret information of the French government to China. But for Gallimard, the most devastating consequence of this exposure is the revelation by the French government that Song, who has all these years been his "Butterfly," is actually a male spy whose involvement with him has been for the purpose of extracting information for the Chinese government.

Precisely because of its stereotypical structure, the relationship between Gallimard and Song allows us to approach it as a kind of myth. In this myth, Gallimard occupies the role of the supposedly active and dominant white male, and Song, the role of the supposedly passive and submissive oriental female. The superimposition of the racial and sexual elements of this relationship creates the space in which the story unfolds.

In order to heighten the story's mythical quality on film, director Cronenberg dispenses with many of the complexities that characterized both the real-life story and the stage play. For instance, while in the real-life story, the "Chinese woman" that the French diplomat fell for always appeared as a man but told his beloved that he was really a woman, in the film Song always appears as a woman until the final scenes. And, while the stage play contains many farcical moments that present the Frenchman as the obvious object of ridicule, the film trims away such moments, preserving the story instead in an elegant mode, against an often hazy and darkish background, and frequently melancholic music. In thus stripping and reducing the story, Cronenberg makes its macabre structure stand out starkly. In the same vein, the usual elaborate manner in which a leading "feminine" character is fetishized is kept to a minimum. Instead of filling the movie screen with lavish physical, cosmetic, and sartorial details—such as is the case with the film with which

M. Butterfly is often compared, *Farewell My Concubine,* by Chen Kaige—the portrayal of Song is low-keyed and unglamorous. Her singing and her stage performance, in both Western and Chinese theaters, are presented only briefly and appear to have been rather unremarkable. Some critics, predisposed toward a sensational and extravagantly colorful approach whenever a non-Western culture is represented, are quick to criticize *M. Butterfly* on the basis of *verisimilitude:* they point out disparagingly, for instance, that John Lone, who plays Song, does not look like a woman and that he and Jeremy Irons are unconvincing as lovers, and so forth.[7]

In thus missing the significance of the purposefully restrained design of the film, such critics also miss its status as the uncluttered sculpting of a stereotypical story, the artful experimenting with a familiar myth. What they have utterly failed to grasp is that, as in the case of the Chinese Beijing opera, what we see is not so much realistic props as suggestive ones, which are meant to conjure and signify rather than resemble an entire ambiance.

As the effects of verisimilitude give way to those of simplified plot, sparse detail, and minimalist characterization, the object of the story—fantasy itself—becomes intensified. The film becomes literally the *setting* that typifies fantasy.[8] With little sensational visual detail to distract us, we are compelled to focus on the absurd question: what happens when a man falls in love, not with a woman or even with another man, not with a human being at all but with a thing, a reified form of his own fantasy?[9] In the context of this film, this question is mapped over the question of Orientalism, so that it becomes: what happens when a Western man falls in love with a reification of the orient, with that mysterious thing called the "oriental woman"?

In many ways, we can say that the film teaches the lesson which is summarized in that platitudinous phrase repeated by Mme. Gallimard, "East is East and West is West." The conclusion that "never the twain shall meet" could, obviously, be interpreted in accordance with the argument against Orientalism, with *M. Butterfly* serving as a piece of didacticism. Gallimard, a Frenchman working in the exotic East, harbors the typical Western male fantasy about the East and in particular about submissive oriental women. He is so enamored of this fantasy of his that he cannot tell a fake oriental woman from a real one. This fantastical relation to "the other" could then be said to be symptomatic of a deep-rooted racist, sexist, and homophobic imperialism; and Gallimard could be called a symbol of the West, with a downfall that is well deserved, and so forth.

This kind of moral is, as I already suggested, indeed what the stage play tries to point at explicitly. For Hwang, the significance of fantasy is that of a content that needs to be changed; it needs to be changed because, by using other people as objects and things, fantasy dehumanizes them. Cronenberg, on the other hand, refuses this approach to fantasy and, as in the case of most of his other films, notably *Videodrome, The Fly, Dead Ringers,* and *Naked Lunch,* explores instead the possibilities and implications of fantasy precisely as a process of dehumanization—of deconstructing the human.[10] Instead of entirely dispensing with the antiorientalist didacticism, however, Cronenberg's film makes it part of its dramatization of the Gallimard-Song relationship. In this dramatization, the film no longer simply offers a diatribe against the stereotyping of the East by the West, or of women by men, but rather raises questions about the fundamental misrecognition inherent to processes of identification, *which the encounter between an oriental woman and a Western man magnifies and thus exemplifies.* The didactic, antiorientalist criticism of the West, then, remains a significant part of the story, but it is no longer its central focus.

Consider, for instance, the scene of the lovers' first encounter, wherein Song, instead of acting flattered, reprimands Gallimard for thinking that the story of Madame Butterfly is a beautiful one. It is only because he is so grossly ignorant of the history of the atrocities committed by Japan in China, Song says, that he could think that a Chinese actress playing a Japanese woman could be convincing. Further, if the races of the roles had been reversed—if it had been a Western woman sacrificing herself for an unattractive Japanese man—the judgment would most likely be that the woman is deranged rather than beautiful:

Song: It's one of your favorite fantasies, isn't it? The submissive Oriental woman and the cruel white man.

Gallimard: Well, I didn't quite mean . . .

Song: Consider it this way: what would you say if a blonde homecoming queen fell in love with a short Japanese businessman? He treats her cruelly, then goes home for three years, during which time she prays to his picture and turns down marriage from a young Kennedy. Then, when she learns he has remarried, she kills herself. Now, I believe you would consider this girl to be a deranged idiot, correct? But because it's an Oriental who kills herself for a Westerner—ah!—you find it beautiful.

While Song's words are undoubtedly historically astute, they also serve to fuel Gallimard's imagination of the "oriental woman" rather than cure it. In other words, the fact that this piece of antiorientalist criticism is inserted in the film as part of the first dialogue between Gallimard and Song means that the film has a relationship to the didactics of antiorientalism that is not direct but mediated. Rather than simply endorsing such a didactics, the film explicitly stages Orientalism as a psychic, interpersonal structure that unfolds with a specific logic. The Western man caught in a fantasy about oriental women is here portrayed as a version of Pavlov's dog: conditioned to respond according to certain artificially induced stimuli, such creatures can, at the mere ringing of a bell or the mere appearance of an oriental woman, be expected to behave in a predictable manner—so predictable, in fact, that their behavior cannot be altered simply by an explicit exposure of the conditions that enable it. These creatures would salivate and come alive *for real* even if the stimulus had nothing "real" behind it. In Gallimard's case, the stimulus is the stereotype of the "inscrutable oriental" in the female form—and the more inscrutable she is, the more charmed he is. Simply by playing "herself," by playing her stereotypical, inscrutable role, the "oriental woman" sets the Western man's mind afire.

There is, however, another twist that makes the film decidedly different from the play. Even though she may be the relentless scheming "woman" working for the Chinese Communist Party, and even though she is fully capable of giving Gallimard lectures about the political incorrectness of his "imperialist" fantasies, Song is, as Lone plays the part, herself attracted to Gallimard. As she tells him at the end of their second encounter before saying good-bye, "sometimes, the fascination could be mutual." Is this a response spoken from her heart? Or is it also part of her role-playing? We have no way of knowing until the very end. What is crucial, nonetheless, is that this suggestion of mutual fascination takes the film beyond the one-sided antiorientalism "message" that Song verbally enunciates. And what is mutuality here if not precisely the problematic of the "meeting" between East and West, and woman and man? As I will go on to argue, mutuality in this film occurs exactly in the form of nonreciprocity, so that together, mutuality and nonreciprocity constitute a symbiotic process of fantasy which, as it draws the lovers together, also ensures that they will never meet.

"The Beauty . . . of Her Death. It's a . . . Pure Sacrifice."

Why is Gallimard so fascinated by the Madame Butterfly character? He explains: he is moved by the beauty of her death. It's a pure sacrifice, he says, for even though the man she loves is unworthy, she sacrifices herself for him. To this Song responds, as I mentioned, by pointing out the imperialist implications of his fascination. But there are other possibilities of understanding this "pure sacrifice" of the "oriental woman."

At the most immediate level, this "pure sacrifice" describes exactly the role that Song plays even as she speaks. In the course of their amorous relationship, Song does, we may say, sacrifice herself for Gallimard, a man who is not worthy of her love, by living up to his fantasy. In this instance, the "pure sacrifice" of the "oriental woman" has the status of what Lacan calls lure—that lack of a coincidence between the eye and the gaze, a lack of coincidence that, however, is often what constitutes love:

> From the outset, we see, in the dialectic of the eye and the gaze, that there is no coincidence, but, on the contrary, a lure. When, in love, I solicit a look, what is profoundly unsatisfying and always missing is that—*You never look at me from the place from which I see you.*
> Conversely, *what I look at is never what I wish to see.*[11]

In this well-known passage, Lacan shows that the essential ingredient in love is misrecognition—a circular pattern of wishing, solicitation, frustration, and desire which stems from the belief that there is something more behind what we see (in the beloved). What Lacan calls lure, Jean Baudrillard calls, in a slightly different manner, seduction. To seduce, Baudrillard writes, is to divert the other from his own truth, from the secret (of himself) that escapes him.[12] In the film, by giving Gallimard the lure, the illusion of the self-sacrificing "oriental woman," Song leads Gallimard astray from his own truth. (I will specify what I think this truth is toward the end of this chapter.) But this process of seduction is, as Song says, mutual: while she successfully lures Gallimard, Song herself is also being seduced by Gallimard in that she has been drawn into his area of *weakness*—his weakness precisely for the beauty of the self-sacrificing Madame Butterfly. As Baudrillard writes, comparing seduction and challenge:

> Challenge and seduction are quite similar. And yet there is a difference. In a challenge one draws the other into one's area of strength, which, in view of the potential for unlimited escalation, is also his or her area of strength. Whereas in a strategy (?) of seduction one draws the other into one's area of weakness, which is also his or her area of weakness. A calculated weakness; an incalculable weakness: one challenges the other to be taken in. . . .
> To seduce is to appear weak. To seduce is to render weak. We seduce with our weakness, never with strong signs or powers. In seduction we enact this weakness, and this is what gives seduction its strength.[13]

If Song seduces Gallimard with the artifice/sacrifice of the submissive "oriental woman," Gallimard seduces Song with his naïveté, his capacity for fascination, and ultimately his gullibility. In spite of her real status as a spy for the Chinese government, therefore, she too seems to have genuinely fallen in love with him.

What seduces, in other words, is not the truth of the other—what he or she really is—but the artifact, the mutual complicity in the weaving of a lure, which works as a snare over the field of encounter, ensuring that the parties meet at the same time that they miss each other, in a kind of rhythmic dance.

Furthermore, because the "pure sacrifice" of the "oriental woman" is the thing that propels and sustains the lure, the act (such as Song's in the earlier scene) of pointing out that it is a *mere* imperialist fantasy does not only not succeed in destroying this lure; it actually enhances it—makes it more alluring. Meanwhile, if the point of the film is not a straightforward antiorientalism, it is not simply homosexual love either: as in the case of the criticism of imperialist fantasy, the lure cannot be destroyed by pointing out that Gallimard is really a bisexual or closeted gay man.

A "homoerotic" reading that is intent on showing what Gallimard's sexual preference really is runs a parallel course with the "antiorientalist" reading in the sense that both readings must rely on the belief in a kind of repressed truth—repressed racism or repressed homosexuality—for their functioning. In both cases, the assumption would be that we need to look beyond the surface structure of the lure in order to locate what is "behind" or "beneath" it. In effect, critics who read this story as the story of a confused sexual identity would be lending themselves to the lure set up by the film itself, in that they would be seduced into going after the real penis, the visible body part, the "fact" of Song being a male; their re-search would be echoing the research of the antiorientalist critics, who are seduced into going after the real penis, the visible body part, the "fact" of Gallimard being a white man. Be it through the route of race or the route of sexual preference, such critics would be trapped by their own desire for a secret—the secret of cross-cultural exploitation or the secret of homosexual love, which they might think they are helping to bring to light, when in fact it is they themselves who have been seduced. In each case what seduces (them) is, shall we say, the "purity" of a secret—an indubitable Orientalism or an indubitable homoeroticism—the way the indubitable love, the pure sacrifice, of an "oriental woman" seduces Gallimard.[14]

The film *M. Butterfly,* on the other hand, is much more cunning. We can see this, for instance, in the interesting scene in Song's bedroom where she is confronted by a party cadre about her decadent behavior. Dressed in a beautiful traditional Chinese woman's jacket, reclining on her bed by herself, and reading girlie magazines featuring oriental women, Song is surprised by the visit of Comrade Chin, her connection to the party authorities. Comrade Chin contemptuously reprimands Song for indulging in "decadent trash." This scene reveals for the first time that Song is working for the Chinese Communist Party and that her relationship with Gallimard is a means to uncover American military plans in Indochina. Is Song not merely playing a role for the sole purpose of getting information from Gallimard? So why, Comrade Chin demands, is she behaving in such a degraded manner when Gallimard is not even present? Song's responses to these moralistic charges are remarkable:

> Song: Comrade, in order to better serve the Great Proletarian State, I practice my deception as often as possible! I despise this costume, yet, for the sake of the Great Helmsman, I will endure it along with all other bourgeois Western perversions!

> Comrade Chin: I am not convinced that this will be enough to redeem you in the eyes of the Party.

> Song: I am trying my best to become somebody else.

Significantly, deception, as it is described by Song, has shifted from the status of dishonesty to that of honor: the seductive "oriental woman," as we are now given to understand, is not only a romantically but also a politically self-sacrificing figure, who gives up herself—her "real" identity—for the cause of the revolution, so much so that she sacrifices even her private moments in order to immerse herself in this cause entirely, purely. The greatest deception, then, is also the greatest act of loyalty—to the people, to the country, to the "Great Helmsman." Even though, as the audience, we cannot but sense that these words of loyalty are spoken with irony—that Song's loyalty to the party is dubious precisely because she is so eloquent about it—this scene reveals that the myth of the self-sacrificing "oriental woman" far exceeds the "imperialist fantasy" that has been commonly used to decode it, and that in her artificial role, Song is faithfully serving in the intersection of two cultural symbolics—the nationalistic as well as the erotic, the intracultural as well as the intercultural.

Song does not rebel against her intended and prescribed role in either situation; rather she plays it, indeed lives it, with her truest emotions. In the relationship with Gallimard, the disguise, lure, and veil of the "oriental woman" serve the purpose of gaining access to the realm that is his trust, love, and imagination. In Gallimard's words, thus, her love is pure: she performs her artificial role to the hilt and thus sacrifices herself—gives up her "real" identity—for a man who, as he notices in the story of Madame Butterfly, is unworthy of that love. At the same time, with the revelation of Song's relationship with the party, a supplementary dimension of the myth of Madame Butterfly unfolds. In this supplementary dimension, we see for the first time that the Song-Gallimard story, which plays on the stereotype of "imperialist male fantasy," is itself the mere instrument of espionage, a means of gaining access to the forbidden realm of another country's military secrets. Gallimard's words about Madame Butterfly, then, were an unwitting description of Song's role-playing in this *other* political realm as well: for is not the "man unworthy" of her love not only Gallimard, her imperialist aggressor, her foreign enemy, but also her party leader, the Great Helmsman himself?

If, as we already said, the fascination between Gallimard and Song is mutual, we see now how this mutuality is simultaneously structured as a nonreciprocity. While the "oriental woman" remains an erotic object on the side of Gallimard, on the side of Song it is much more complex. For Song, the "oriental woman" is a means to exploit a foreigner as part of her service to the party. Gallimard, then, is not simply an erotic object or subject; rather he has been identified as a political object, a plaything that would unconsciously help Song give the party what it wants.

The Force of Butterfly; or, the "Oriental Woman" as Phallus

The foregrounding of this supplementary, political dimension of our Madame Butterfly story enables us to read the Gallimard character in a very different manner from the one originally intended by Hwang and followed by most critics. The fateful encounter between East and West takes place at a critical moment of twentieth-century world politics. For France, it is the end of the imperial empire, when Indochina was recently lost and Algeria has become independent. The emptiness of diplomatic life in Beijing is clear: officials cheat on expense accounts; women have illicit affairs; dinner parties and other gatherings are perfunctory and boring. Like a character from a Kafka novel, Gallimard has an uninspiring, low-ranking job as an accountant, but it is one that he takes seriously, so seriously that his corrupt colleagues become annoyed with him for continually exposing them. The high point of this rationalistic bookkeeping existence is tracking down the documentation from people who try to falsify their expense accounts. While we may say that Gallimard is the perfect example of the disciplined individual whose body and mind have, as Michel Foucault shows us in a work such as *Discipline and Punish,* been produced for the efficient, utilitarian functioning of its society, it is equally important to note that Gallimard is clearly a "flunky" in terms of the unspoken rules of political society. His tireless efforts to track down documentation for dubious expense accounts mean that he is out of tune with the smooth debaucheries that constitute the substance of the bureaucratic world. Precisely because he takes his job of accounting seriously, he reveals himself to be someone who does not know how to play the game. At a dinner gathering, as Gallimard sits down at the same table with his colleagues, they sneer and remind him: "You are nobody. You are worse than nobody: you are an accountant. If you are not careful we'll break all your pencils in half." To this Gallimard responds by leaving the table, clumsily dropping his silverware as he does so.

In terms of his relation to the cultural symbolic that is the world of politics, therefore, Gallimard occupies a place that is not dissimilar to that of Song in that he, too, is a bureaucratic informant, a submissive "woman" to the "man not worthy of her love"—the French government, to which he gives his loyal service. The affinity between Gallimard and Song lies in that both are manipulable and useful instruments of their respective political orders, and both respond to these orders with dedication. Gallimard's political usefulness is soon recognized by the ambassador, who sees in him the qualities of a head servant who is not smart enough to cheat and who can therefore be entrusted with the task of "coordinating a revamped intelligence division," that is, of policing the other employees. But it is obvious that in this world of complex political "intelligence," Gallimard is not at home at all as *a person in command.* As he receives, in the ambassador's office, the surprising news of his own promotion to vice-consul, we can see that he does not possess the suave body language to respond appropriately; instead his posture remains awkward and stiff, marking his destiny as someone who will remain marginal and insignificant in French diplomatic culture. When he finally sits in his office as vice consul, he lacks the presence to command the respect of those who are supposedly working for him. Instead of speaking to them with the air of mastery, he reads woodenly from a prewritten script as if he were someone being cross-examined.

It is into this impersonal but overpowering world of bureaucracy, which is echoed by a routine domestic life complete with an uncomprehending wife, classic pajamas, and bedtime tooth-brushing, that "Butterfly" intrudes with an irresistible force. Gallimard, we remember, stumbles upon "Butterfly" unexpectedly. Before the performance of the aria "Un bel dì" from Puccini's opera begins, Gallimard tells his neighbor, Frau Baden, with whom he will later have a casual affair, that he has never seen *Madama Butterfly,* even though his lack of culture is unsuspected by most people.[15] In the position of an outsider to his own European culture, then, Gallimard's eyes catch the "oriental woman" on stage, even though the situation—of a contemporary Chinese opera singer performing the role of a fetishized Japanese heroine from an Italian opera—cannot be more bizarre. If the "entrance of Butterfly" (as printed on the musicians' scores) represents a decisive marking of cultural identity and its concomitant confusion, what it marks first of all is in fact Gallimard's alienation from his own culture. Rather than simply notice the foreignness, the exoticness, of the spectacle in front of him, Gallimard finds in "Butterfly" a kind of anchorage for *himself*. (This is the reason why his behavior takes on a noticeably greater air of self-assurance from this point on.)

Because it is not fully attainable even as it is consumed through sexual contact, the fantasy of the "oriental woman" keeps the Frenchman *afloat with life* by inscribing in him an unanswerable lack. Song exists for Gallimard as the phallus in Lacan's sense of the term—that is, the Other that is always assumed to be more than it appears and that has the power to give us what we want and also to take it away. Lacan, we remember, emphasizes that the phallus functions only when it is veiled and that, once revealed, it becomes shame.[16] Song's tactic, however, includes precisely this "unveiling" of shame by deliberately calling attention to it in a letter to Gallimard: "What more do you want?" she writes. "I have already given you my shame." By feigning loss of dignity, thus, Song preserves her power as phallus, while the "shame" that has been revealed—the oriental woman's love—continues to be a sham veiling the male body that is beneath it.

The manner in which the "oriental woman" functions as a phallus is made even more clear by the fact that Gallimard seems content in love without ever experiencing Song completely naked. (Later in court, responding to the inquiry about this incredible fact, Song will describe Gallimard as a lover who has been very responsive to his " 'ancient oriental ways of love,' all of which I invented myself—just for him.") The one time Gallimard comes dangerously close to stripping her, Song tells him at the crucial moment that she is pregnant, thus shifting his sexual desire into a more paternal frame. Meanwhile, Gallimard can have what he calls an "extra extramarital affair" with Frau Baden without its intruding into his fantasy. In the scene in which he and Frau Baden are in their hotel room, Gallimard, coming out of the bathroom in his hygienic-looking undershirt, is shown to be somewhat taken aback by the sight of Frau Baden sitting casually naked on the edge of the bed. Instead of the typical sexual excitement one would expect with an illicit affair, the following matter-of-fact exchange takes place between the would-be copulants:

Gallimard: You look . . . just like I thought you would under your clothes.

Frau Baden: What did you expect? So come and get it!

While Gallimard's remark highlights the complete coincidence between the eye and the gaze, and therefore the lack precisely of a lure in his relation-

ship with this other woman, Frau Baden's notion of "getting it" comple-
ments his observation by containing sex entirely within the satiable and
short-term realm of physical need. Sex with her is but a casual meal, in which
the physical body, because it is completely available, remains a *mere* body.
The force of the phallus—and with it fantasy, the lure, and seduction—does
not come into play at all.

"Under the Robes, beneath Everything,
It Was Always Me"

One of the most moving and unforgettable scenes in this film is the one in
which, after the costume farce in the French courtroom, Song and Gallimard,
both in men's suits, sit face to face alone in the police van taking them to
prison. As the two men stare at each other, Song is the first to break the
silence: "What do you want from me?" he asks. In psychoanalytic terms, this
question is an indication of the fundamental issue in our relationship with
an other—demand. However, even though Song has brought up this fundamental issue, he has, nonetheless, posed his question imprecisely, because he
still thinks in terms of Gallimard's wanting something *from him.* Instead, as
Lacan has taught us, the significance of demand is never simply what can be
effectively enunciated by way of what the other can literally give us; rather, it
is what remains resistant to articulation, what exceeds the satisfaction provided by the other.[17] To pose the question of demand with precision, therefore, Song would have had to ask: "What do you want, by wanting me? What
is your demand, which you express through me?"

Gallimard, on the other hand, responds to (the philosophical implications
of) this question precisely: "You are my Butterfly."

With this exchange, what takes place between the former lovers is now a
new kind of nonreciprocity. If, in the past, their nonreciprocity was a matter
of their playing their respective roles in the game of erotics and politics, a
nonreciprocity that enabled them to meet through the lure, the new nonreciprocity has to do rather with Song's attempt to change the very terms of their
relationship. Instead of playing "Butterfly" the way he has for Gallimard all
these years, Song does something he has never done before: he undresses,
challenging Gallimard to see for the first time what he has always wanted but
somehow always failed to see. Kneeling completely naked in front of Gallimard, Song pleads for a rekindling of the affection that once existed between
them. As he gazes tenderly up at his former lover, Song says, in a manner
that reveals that he has indeed loved the Frenchman all along: "Under the
robes, beneath everything, it was always me."

If, until this tragic moment, the lure has been kept intact because it is upheld on both sides, Song, by the very gesture of undressing with which he tries to regain Gallimard's love, has destroyed that lure forever. While Song intends by this brave and defiant gesture a new beginning for their relationship—a beginning in which they can face each other honestly as they really are, two men physically and emotionally entangled for years—what he actually accomplishes is the death of that relationship. Song fails to see that what Gallimard "wants" is not him, Song, be he in the definitive form of a woman or a man, but, as Gallimard says, "Butterfly." Because Gallimard's desire hinges on neither a female nor a male body, but rather on the phallus, the veiled thing that is the "oriental woman," Song's candid disclosure of his physical body can only be lethal. Like Frau Baden, who, having dis-clothed herself, invites Gallimard frankly to "come and get it," Song's gesture of undressing serves not to arouse but extinguish desire.

The naked body destroys the lure once and for all by demonstrating that what lies under the veil all these years is nothing, no thing for fantasy. With the veil lifted, the phallus shows itself shamefully as merely a man, a penis, a pathetic body in all its banal vulnerability, which Gallimard rejects in abhorrence. (As many have pointed out, this moment in *M. Butterfly* is comparable to a similar one in *The Crying Game*, in which the man, in love with a transvestite whom he supposes to be a female, vomits at the sight of his beloved's actual genitalia. What has to be thrown up literally is the repugnant reality of the physical.) Song's naked body must therefore be understood ultimately as the traumatic Real that tears apart the dream of "Butterfly," forcing Gallimard to wake up in the abyss of his own self. In the two men's *parting* conversation, we see how, instead of rescuing Gallimard, Song's sincere love finally brings about the nonreciprocity that is their absolute parting of ways:

Gallimard: You, who knew me so well—how could you, of all people, have made such a mistake?

Song: What?

Gallimard: You've just shown me your true self—when all I loved was the lie. A perfect lie—it's been destroyed.

Song (genuinely hurt): You never really loved me?

Gallimard: I'm a man who loved a woman created by a man. And anything else—simply falls short.

"It's Not the Story; It's the Music"

From Gallimard's perspective, the disappearance of that "lie" he loves, that very thing in which he has found a means of anchoring his identity, means a traumatic self-awakening that is the equivalent of madness. Before examining this awakening/madness closely, I think it is necessary to discuss one more aspect of this "thing"—the music from *Madama Butterfly*—which, as much as the fetishized "oriental woman," serves as Gallimard's anchorage.

It is possible to think of the operatic music as a kind of big Other, to which the human characters submit in such a manner as to create their "fate." This fate is predicted by a remark made by Song in an early conversation with Gallimard, in regard to his fascination with the Madame Butterfly story: "The point is," she says, "it's not the story; it's the music." Indeed, one could argue that, as much as the "oriental woman," the music is the agent that engenders the plot of the story, so that it is the story which follows the lead of the music rather than the reverse. From the initial performance at the foreign embassy of "Un bel dì," which establishes contact between Gallimard and Song, we move through scenes in which the music of *Madama Butterfly* continues to haunt the characters, as if always to recall them to the primal moment of their fateful encounter. For instance, even Gallimard's wife, when she hears about his captivation by Song's performance, bursts into a spontaneous performance complete with hand gestures. In the mirror reflection that follows, we see Gallimard looking bewildered and uneasy at his wife's uncanny mimicry of the "other woman." He goes on to place a special order for the record album of the opera, noticing, upon its arrival, its cover illustration of the "oriental woman" in a submissive posture to her Western lover.

Crucially also, Gallimard's amorous relationship with "Butterfly" takes place at a time when both *Madama Butterfly* and Chinese opera singers are considered to be relics of the past.

In the China of the mid-1960s, not only were imported items such as Western operatic music considered bourgeois and imperialist; even indigenous traditional art forms such as the Beijing opera were deemed feudal and corrupt. The revolution demanded that all such ideologically suspect relics be purged and replaced by new, progressive practices. The second time Gallimard visits the Chinese theater where Song used to perform, a Maoist "model play" is being staged with a different kind of dramatic semiotics and a noticeably different didactic sentience. Such ostensible state intervention in aesthetic forms, together with the massive burning of traditional artifacts, the forced trial and punishment of intellectuals, writers, and artists, and the coerced surrender of personal ideals for the common good, made up the new reality of Chinese political life. In the film, the communist revolution establishes itself in Chinese society as a new big Other with its power to interpellate ordinary citizens with the call to repudiate the past and labor for the future. As Gallimard is finally sent back to France (since, as he is told, his foreign policy predictions about Vietnam and China were all wrong), Song is seen working with other intellectuals in a labor camp, where loudspeakers blare away with "reeducation" messages to cleanse people's souls.

If the loudspeaker of a labor camp is the apparatus for a new type of fantasy—the fantasy of revolutionized subjectivity, of proletarian agency, of nationalist progress—it is shown to compete rather weakly with that other, older and "corrupt" apparatus of interpellation, the operatic music of *Madama Butterfly*. As Song looks up strained and exhausted from her labor, she seems to hear another voice from afar, which gradually takes over the audible space hitherto occupied by the loudspeaker. As this voice becomes louder, we recognize it to be the familiar music from *Madama Butterfly*, and the grayish backdrop of the labor camp changes into Paris, 1968, when Gallimard is watching a performance of *Madama Butterfly*, with tears slowly trickling down his face, at the Paris Opera. Song and Gallimard are thus, we might say, reunited through this persistent "corrupt" big Other of "Butterfly," which was what brought them together in the first place.

This dream of a Butterfly, of an unforgettable erotic and emotional experience, inserts itself in a Paris that, as Gallimard's acquaintance in a bar tells him, is looking more like Beijing, with students shouting Maoist slogans and rioting in the streets. The juxtaposition at this point of the erotic and the political, the "personal" and the "historical," raises a question that *M. Butterfly* merely hints at but that nonetheless is crucial to any consideration of fantasy: is "revolution" itself, the film seems to say, not simply another type of "fantasy stereotype"—the fantasy stereotype that exploits in the name of the collective, the people? If we mobilize, as we must, criticism against Western "orientalist" and "imperialist" fantasies about the East, then should the cruelties committed by way of this *other* fantasy stereotype not also be under attack? The pro-Chinese communist fervor in France of the 1960s—is it an awakening from Western imperialism and Orientalism, or is it not simply the other side of that dream called Butterfly, which fetishizes the East this time not in the form of an erotic object but in the form of a political object, not in the form of the beautiful "oriental woman" but in the form of the virile oriental man, the Great Helmsman, Mao Zedong?

In his indifference to the political revolution, Gallimard will listen again to the music from *Madama Butterfly* in is own private space, away from the clamor of the streets. An evening alone in his minimalist, orientalist apartment, where a meal consists of mere bread and broth, he sits forlornly accompanied by the "Humming Chorus" played on his MCA record. As if by miracle, "Butterfly" again enters: in the midst of the melancholic music, Song has mysteriously reappeared.

Madame Butterfly, C'est Moi

After this scene of reunion, the music from *Madama Butterfly* will be heard one final time—as an accompaniment to Gallimard's performance in jail. Played on a cassette, the music has by this time become a portable object, very much like the other things that Gallimard consciously displays *on himself* in this scene. How then are we to bring together the music, the "pure sacrifice" of the "oriental woman," and Gallimard's gory suicide?

In this final one-man show, which progresses as Song is meanwhile released and sent back to China, Gallimard begins by commenting on his own "celebrity" and then proceeds to tell the story that led up to it. Gradually but steadily, as he describes his vision of the slender "oriental women" in "cheongsams and kimonos, who die for the love of unworthy foreign devils," Gallimard performs a transformation into Madame Butterfly herself. The camera shows him putting on the sash for his kimono, followed by white foundation across his face, eyelining, shiny red lip gloss, and finally a wig. As his transformation becomes complete, the transvestite pronounces: "At last, in a prison far from China, I have found her. . . . My name is René Gallimard! Also known—as Madame Butterfly!"

This scene of dramatic transformation offers, I think, one of the most compelling and complex moments in cinematic history. Because of this I must emphasize that the readings I provide below are much more experimental explorations than exact renderings of its significance.

First, what is effected in these last moments of the film seems to be a merging of two separate identities. This merging returns us, once again, to the theme of the self-sacrificing "oriental woman" discussed above, with a new twist. If Gallimard is Madame Butterfly, then this performance of his transformed identity should perhaps be described as a retroactive enactment, a slow-motion replay, of a story whose meaning has become visible only now—for the first time. In this story, Gallimard the "oriental woman" has been sacrificing himself (herself) for a man (Song) who, as Gallimard points out, is not worthy of his (her) love. This merging and swapping of identities, through which Gallimard turns into "Butterfly," is what Hwang intends as the basic "arc" of his play: "the Frenchman fantasizes that he is Pinkerton and his lover is Butterfly. By the end of the piece, he realizes that it is he who has been Butterfly, in that the Frenchman has been duped by love; the Chinese spy, who exploited that love, is therefore the real Pinkerton."[18] To return to the point of seduction I made earlier, we may add, paradoxically, that in seducing Gallimard, Song in fact led him temporarily away from his own truth—the truth of a fantasy that is not a fantasy of the other but rather *of himself as the suicidal "oriental woman."* In desiring Song, Gallimard was desiring not exactly to have her but to be her, to be the "Butterfly" that she was playing. While being the setting and structuring of fantasy, therefore, the encounter with Song served in effect to displace and postpone the fulfillment of Gallimard's wish for his own immolation. The "Butterfly" that was Song, in other words, shielded Gallimard from the "Butterfly" that is himself.

But if the relationship with Song has been a screen against the Real by giving Gallimard a conventional anchorage—a relation with a physical other and within the acceptable symbolic of heterosexual sociality—the revelation of Song's banal maleness means that this screen, which protected him but also prevented him from seeing, has evaporated. With the screen also disappear the fixed positions that are usually ascribed to man and woman, occident and orient. In a manner similar to Laplanche and Pontalis's argument about fantasy, what Gallimard's fantasy of "Butterfly" accomplishes in this final scene of monstrous transformation is ultimately a belated staging of a field of relations with multiple entry points, a field where positions of dominance and submission, of male and female, of aggressor and victim, are infinitely substitutable and interchangeable. Gallimard's transformation continues, in tandem, the series of vertiginous transvestist masquerades that began with Song.

Second, while this interpretive narrative of interchangeable racial and sexual subjectivities that I have just offered is perhaps the one most likely to be favored by critics who are invested in the utopian potential of destabilized identities, there are other elements in this transformation that far exceed such a narrative. For one thing, the conclusion that Gallimard finally discovers himself to be Madame Butterfly does not explain the power of the *visual* play of this last series of shots. How, in other words, might we understand his transformation in terms of the dynamics, the power structure of vision—of the relations between the image and the gaze? What does the interplay between Gallimard the Frenchman, Gallimard the performer, and Gallimard the Madame Butterfly signify *in terms of visuality?* For my own aid, I turn at this point to Lacan's reading of a story which has much genealogical affinity with ours.

I am referring to Lacan's consideration of the Chinese philosopher Zhuang Zi's well-known butterfly dream. Zhuang Zi wrote that one day, he dreamt that he was a butterfly happily flitting and fluttering around. He did not know he was Zhuang Zi. On waking up, he was, of course, once again solidly and unmistakably himself, but he did not know if he was Zhuang Zi who had dreamt that he was a butterfly, or a butterfly dreaming he was Zhuang Zi.[19] Lacan's analysis, which foregrounds the relations of visuality, goes as follows:

> In a dream, he is a butterfly. What does this mean? It means that he sees the butterfly in his reality as gaze. What are so many figures, so many shapes, so many colours, if not this gratuitous *showing*, in which is marked for us the primal nature of the essence of the gaze. . . . In fact, it is when he was the butterfly that he apprehended one of the roots of his identity—that he was, and is, in his essence, that butterfly who paints himself with his own colours—and it is because of this that, in the last resort, he is Choang-tsu [Zhuang Zi].[20]

What fascinates Lacan, I think, is that the dream, in which the "I"/eye of Zhuang Zi becomes this Other, the butterfly, returns Zhuang Zi for a moment to a state of nondifferentiation in which the Other exists as pure gaze.[21] In this state of nondifferentiation, one is not conscious of oneself as consciousness, as thought. This dream is so powerful that even when he wakes up, Zhuang Zi is not sure whether "he" is not simply (a lost object) dreamt by the butterfly. For Lacan, Zhuang Zi's butterfly dream is a glimpse into the truth: "it is when he was the butterfly that he apprehended one of the roots of his identity—that he was, and is, in his essence, that butterfly who paints himself with his own colours—and that it is because of this that . . . he is Choang-tsu." The conscious identity of Zhuang Zi, the "I"/eye of waking life, in other words, is the result of the butterfly's "causing" him to exist or marking him with the grid of desire.[22] Waking from this dream back into consciousness is therefore an unsettling awakening into the fact that in one life's as *cogito*, one is a captive butterfly, captivated by nothing but the inescapable law and structure of human cognition.

Lacan's reading of Zhuang Zi's dream brings us one step closer to unraveling the visual dynamics of Gallimard's transformation. Accordingly, we could see Gallimard's transformation as an equivalent to Zhuang Zi's dream, in which he, Gallimard, becomes a "Butterfly." The very image of the "oriental woman" in her strange shape and figure, in her bright colors, is then the gratuitous *showing* that Lacan mentions as the primal nature of the essence of the gaze. This gaze returns Gallimard to the roots of his identity by showing, by giving to the eye, (the knowledge) that "Butterfly" is what causes him to exist by marking him with desire. As in Zhuang Zi's story, therefore, the question implicit in Gallimard's performance is: how do "I," Gallimard, know that I, with my fantasy, my longing for the "oriental woman," am not merely an object dreamt by "Butterfly," the gaze that I (mis)took for an image? Instead of being Gallimard dreaming of a "Butterfly," might I not myself be the dream of a "Butterfly"?

Third, just as Lacan writes that Zhuang Zi is, in his essence, "the butterfly who paints himself with his own colours," so Gallimard, strictly speaking, does not simply perform but rather *paints* himself into Madame Butterfly—or more precisely, paints himself with her colors. Once this emphasis is introduced, we are able for the first time to view this scene of transformation as about a process of painting, with philosophical implications to be deduced from the relationships between the act of painting, the painted image, and the gaze.

Lacan, contrary to conventional thinking and following philosophers such as René Caillois and Maurice Merleau-Ponty, writes that painting is not really mimicry or imitation in the sense of creating a secondary, derivative form on the basis of a pre-existing one. Rather, if it is indeed mimicry or imitation in the sense of producing an image, this image is part of a process in which the painter enters a specific relation with the gaze—a relation in which the gaze (especially as embodied by the spectator) is tamed:

> To imitate is no doubt to reproduce an image. But at bottom, it is, for the subject, to be inserted in a function whose exercise grasps it. . . .
>
> The function of the picture—in relation to the person to whom the painter, literally, offers his picture to be seen—has a relation with the gaze. This relation is not, as it might at first seem, that of being a trap for the gaze. It might be thought that, like the actor, the painter wishes to be looked at. I do not think so. I think there is a relation with the gaze of the spectator, but that it is more complex. The painter gives something to the person who must stand in front of his painting which, in part, at least, of the painting, might be summed up thus—*You want to see? Well, take a look at this!* He gives something for the eye to feed on, but he invites the person to whom this picture is presented to lay down his gaze there as one lays down one's weapons. This is the pacifying, Apollonian effect of painting. Something is given not so much to the gaze as to the eye, something that involves the abandonment, the *laying down*, of the gaze.[23]

These passages indicate that painting can be described as a process of disarming the Other, of warding off the menace that comes from the Other. The means of disarming the Other is the painted image, which may thus be described as a second-order gaze, an artificial eye, a fetish in the sense of an amulet or talisman that may ward off evil. However, in using this understanding of painting as a way to read Gallimard's transformation, we are immediately confronted by the fact that Gallimard is not only the painter, nor only both painter and image, but painter, image, and spectator, all three at once. This fact considerably complicates the combative relation between the painter and the gaze that Lacan sets forth. By painting himself as Madame Butterfly, is Gallimard simply making an image to fend off the gaze (in which case he would remain in the subjectivity of the painter)? Is he not also the painted image, and is he not, as he looks at himself in the mirror, also the spectator, the one to be tamed? As "Butterfly," Gallimard appears also as a clown—but is the clown mocking us or is she the object of our mockery, and for what reason? All in all, how are we to describe this ultimate act of Gallimard's *passion*, his *passage* from painter to image to spectator?[24]

This passion/passage that is painting, we might say, is a process of making visible that which could otherwise never be directly seen. Significantly, therefore, painting here rejoins the etymological meaning of the word "fantasy," which means, precisely, "to make visible."[25] But "making visible" at the end of *M. Butterfly* is no longer simply a making visible of the multiple positions available to the subject. Rather, it is a process of throwing off the colors that make up the "self," a process of stripping and denuding that is comparable with processes of change in the natural world: "If a bird were to paint," Lacan writes suggestively, "would it not be by letting fall its feathers? a snake by casting off its scales, a tree by letting fall its leaves?"[26]

As Gallimard looks at the "Butterfly" in the mirror, he is transformed into the spectator who is invited to lay down his own gaze. This laying down of the gaze is the laying down of the weapon, the protective shield that separates us from the Other. What Gallimard finally meets, in the painted picture of himself as Madame Butterfly, is that thing which, in its muteness and absoluteness, renders him—the man Gallimard—obsolete, inoperant, excluded.[27] If the gaze is that which is always somehow eluded in our relation to the world,[28] then what Gallimard meets, in his own Butterfly image, in a manner that can no longer be eluded, is the gaze as it has all along looked at him.

If this scene of transformation could indeed be seen as a performing of enlightenment—of Gallimard's discovery that Madame Butterfly is none other than he himself—it is also enlightenment-as-self-deconstruction. From the perspective of the man with desire, this enlightenment is not progress but a regression, a passage into inertia, into the thing he loves. With this passage and passion, which we call death, the illusory independence that one achieves through the primary narcissism of the "mirror stage," which shows one as "other" but gives one the illusion of a unified "I," disappears. Significantly, therefore, the instrument of death in the film is not simply the *seppuku* dagger in the opera *Madama Butterfly* or the knife in the play *M. Butterfly*, but a mirror—a mirror, moreover, which has lost its reflective function. Being no longer the usual means with which one says, "This is me, myself," the mirror now returns to its material being as a shard of glass with which to terminate life and pass into the inorganic. Gallimard's suicide completes and fulfills the fateful plot of *Madama Butterfly*, but instead of him performing "Butterfly," it is, strictly speaking, "Butterfly" which has been performing him. As the Frenchman "sacrifices" himself and passes into his beloved spectacle, the "Butterfly" that is the character, the story, and the music—in short, the gaze—lives on.[29]

Coda: New Questions for Cultural Difference and Identity

What I have attempted to show through a more or less Lacanian reading is the ineluctability of a serious consideration of fantasy—and with it, questions of cognition—in a story of exchange that is overtly "cross-cultural." What this reading makes explicit, I hope, is that fantasy is not something that can be simply dismissed as willful deception, as "false consciousness" to be remedied by explicit didactics. Once fantasy is understood as a problem structural to human cognition, all the "cross-cultural" analyses of ideology, misogyny, and racism that are rooted in a denigration of fantasy will need to be thoroughly reexamined.

If, in this fantasy, the orient is associated with femininity itself, then the problem of coming to terms with the orient is very much similar, structurally speaking, to the problem of coming to terms with woman in psychoanalysis—in that both the orient and woman have been functioning as the support for the white man's fantasy, as the representation of the white man's *jouissance*. However, what distinguishes Cronenberg's film from many examples of such representation—one thinks, for instance, of Bernardo Bertolucci's *The Last Emperor, The Sheltering Sky,* and *The Little Buddha*—is precisely the manner in which the lavish, visible painting of fantasy finally takes place not on the female, feminized body of the other but on the white male body, so that enlightenment coincides with suicide, while the woman, the other, escapes.[30]

What remains unknown, then, is the "supplementary" *jouissance* of woman (and, by implication, of the orient) as spoken of by Lacan, who, in an aptly deconstructionist manner, puts his emphasis on the word "supplementary."[31] What does woman want, and what does the orient want? At no moment in the film *M. Butterfly* does Song's subjectivity and desire become lucid to us—we never know whether she is "genuine" or masquerading, whether her emotions are "for real" or part of her superb playacting—until in the "showdown" scene in the police van. In that scene, we see for the first time that what she "wants" is a complete overturning of the laws of desire which have structured her relationship with Gallimard. In other words, in spite of her love for the Frenchman, what the "oriental woman" wants is nothing less than the liquidation of his entire sexual ontological being—his death.

Even though Song does not get what she wants directly, her wish is vindi-
cated by the ending of the film. Gallimard's transformation into Madame
Butterfly indicates that femininity and the "oriental woman" are the very
truth of Western Man himself, and, because he is traditionally identified with
power, he is so far removed from this truth that his self-awakening must be
tragic. Gallimard's death shows that Western Man is himself no-thing more
than a French penis dreaming of (being) an oriental butterfly.

By definition, the death of the white man signals the dawn of a fundamentally different way of coming to terms with the East. The film closes with
"Butterfly" flying back to China. This "oriental woman" that existed as the
white man's symptom—what will happen to her now that the white man is
dead? That is the ultimate question with which we are left.

Notes

1. I am very grateful to David Cronenberg for providing me with a copy of the
shooting script of the film *M. Butterfly*. For related interest, see David Henry Hwang,
M. Butterfly, with an afterword by the playwright (New York: Plume, 1989). For a
discussion of the play in terms of the politics of transvestism, see Marjorie Garber,
Vested Interests: Cross-Dressing and Cultural Anxiety (New York: Routledge, 1992),
pp. 234–51. For a discussion of the play in terms of its criticism of essentialist identity
formed through Orientalism and heterosexism, see Dorinne Kondo, "*M. Butterfly*:
Orientalism, Gender, and a Critique of Essentialist Identity," *Cultural Critique*, no.
16 (Fall 1990), pp. 5–29. For a discussion of the misogynist implications of Puccini's
opera, see Catherine Clément, *Opera, or the Undoing of Women*, trans. Betsy Wing,
foreword by Susan McClary (Minneapolis: U of Minnesota P, 1988), pp. 43–47. For
a biography of Bernard Boursicot, the Frenchman whose love affair with the Chinese
opera singer Shi Peipu gave rise to the *M. Butterfly* story, see Joyce Wadler, *Liaison*
(New York: Bantam, 1993). The epigraphs at the beginning of this chapter are taken
respectively from Martin Heidegger, *Poetry, Language, Thought*, trans. Albert Hofstadter (New York: Harper Colophon, 1971), p. 176; Roland Barthes, *Camera Lucida:
Reflections on Photography*, trans. Richard Howard (New York: Hill and Wang, 1981),
p. 117; Jacques Lacan, *Feminine Sexuality: Jacques Lacan and the école freudienne*, ed.
Juliet Mitchell and Jacqueline Rose, trans. Jacqueline Rose (New York: Norton, 1985),
pp. 146–47.

2. Hwang, *M. Butterfly*, p. 94.

3. Ibid., p. 100.

4. See Kondo's essay for summaries of the vexed reactions to Hwang's play from
some members of the Asian American communities.

5. See, for instance, Freud's well-known discussion in "Creative Writers and
Day-Dreaming," *The Standard Edition of the Complete Psychological Works of Sig-
mund Freud*, vol. ix, trans. James Strachey (London: Hogarth, 1959), pp. 141–53. For
an authoritative, intensive reading of Freud's works on fantasy, see Jean Laplanche

and Jean-Bertrand Pontalis, "Fantasy and the Origins of Sexuality" (first published in the *International Journal of Psychoanalysis,* vol. 49, part 1, pp. 1–17; 1968), in *Formations of Fantasy,* edited by Victor Burgin, James Donald, and Cora Kaplan (London: Methuen, 1986), pp. 5–34. Because I am, in this chapter, primarily interested in exploring the social and cross-cultural implications of fantasy, I am not fine-tuning the various modes of conscious and unconscious fantasies as would be necessary in a more strictly clinical analysis. For the same reasons I am also using terms such as "fantasy" and "dream" interchangeably.

6. See Laplanche and Pontalis, "Fantasy and the Origins of Sexuality." Two discussions of fantasy that I have found very helpful are Cora Kaplan, *"The Thorn Birds:* Fiction, Fantasy, Femininity," *Formations of Fantasy,* pp. 142–66, and Elizabeth Cowie, "Fantasia," *The Woman in Question,* edited by Parveen Adams and Elizabeth Cowie (Cambridge, MA: MIT P, 1990), pp. 149–96.

7. Examples of these uncomprehendingly dismissive reviews: "Hwang also wrote the misguided movie version of 'M. Butterfly' for director David Cronenberg, in which Jeremy Irons and an oddly sullen John Lone act out a straightforward love story devoid of heat or plausibility. The problem is not simply that Lone's drag wouldn't fool a baby. In the magnified intimacy of the camera's eye, it's clear Hwang doesn't really know who these unlikely lovers are." David Ansen, "Much Stranger than Fiction," *Newsweek,* October 18, 1993, p. 84. "The problem with 'M. Butterfly,' both play and movie, is that the audience gets the point right away—it's too crude and too facile to miss—and has nothing to do for the rest of the evening except listen to tiresome restatements of it. . . . Cronenberg's treatment of Hwang's material has the effect of exposing it for what it really is: not a pure, incandescent work of art but an extremely ordinary piece of agitprop drama." Terrence Rafferty, "The Current Cinema: Blind Faith," *The New Yorker* 69:33 (October 11, 1993), p. 123. If one were indeed to judge the film on the basis of verisimilitude, the obvious thing to criticize, from the perspective of those who know Chinese, is the improbability of a Cantonese-speaking servant in Song's house, while every other Chinese character, including Song, speaks in Mandarin, the language most commonly used in Beijing.

8. "Fantasy involves, is characterized by, not the achievement of desired objects, but the arranging of, a setting out of, desire; a veritable *mise-en-scène* of desire. . . . The fantasy depends not on particular objects, but on their setting out; and the pleasure of fantasy lies in the setting out, not in the having of the objects. . . . It can be seen, then, that fantasy is not the object of desire, but its setting." Cowie, "Fantasia," p. 159.

9. In the early scenes of the film, Gallimard's fascination with "Butterfly" extends even to fly swatting and dragonfly gazing. In terms of the genealogy of Cronenberg's films, *M. Butterfly* is similar to its predecessors in that it stages the manner in which a man's imagination infects him like a disease, which gradually consumes and finally destroys him. For extended discussions of this—his favorite—theme, see the director's *Cronenberg on Cronenberg,* ed. Chris Rodley (London: Faber and Faber, 1992). However, two factors make *M. Butterfly* different from the earlier films. First, the restrained, minimalist design of the film is a major departure from the elaborate special effects and shocking images that are the Cronenberg trademark. Second, the biological and science-fiction modes of Cronenberg's usual film language are here

complicated by the story of a cross-cultural encounter with all its sexual, racial, and political implications. Because of these factors, I am reading *M. Butterfly* as a unique work in Cronenberg's corpus, even though the conceptual affinities with the other films are definitely present. In particular, as I will go on to argue, the significations of visuality in this film are unprecedently mind-boggling.

10. Even though Hwang too has referred to the notion of deconstruction, what he aims at deconstructing is the fantasy, the stereotype, and the cliché, rather than the human per se: "The idea of doing a deconstructivist *Madame Butterfly* immediately appealed to me. This despite the fact that I didn't even know the plot of the opera! I knew Butterfly only as a cultural stereotype; speaking of an Asian woman, we would sometimes say, 'She's pulling a Butterfly,' which meant playing the submissive Oriental number. Yet, I felt convinced that the libretto would include yet another lotus blossom pining away for a cruel Caucasian man, and dying for her love. Such a story has become too much of a cliché not to be included in the archtypal [*sic*] East-West romance that started it all. Sure enough, when I purchased the record, I discovered it contained a wealth of sexist and racist clichés, reaffirming my faith in Western culture." Hwang, *M. Butterfly*, p. 95.

11. Lacan, "The Line and Light," *The Four Fundamental Concepts of Psycho-Analysis*, edited by Jacques-Alain Miller, trans. Alan Sheridan (New York: Norton, 1981), pp. 102–103; emphases in the original.

12. See Jean Baudrillard, *Seduction*, trans. Brian Singer (New York: St. Martin's, 1990).

13. Ibid., p. 83.

14. On this point—namely, that *M. Butterfly* is not about the conflict of homosexuality and heterosexuality—Hwang is absolutely clear: "To me, this is not a 'gay' subject because the very labels heterosexual or homosexual become meaningless in the context of this story. Yes, of course this was literally a homosexual affair. Yet because Gallimard perceived it or chose to perceive it as a heterosexual liaison, in his mind it was essentially so. Since I am telling the story from the Frenchman's point of view, it is more specifically about 'a man who loved a woman created by a man.' To me, this characterization is infinitely more useful than the clumsy labels 'gay' or 'straight.'" Hwang, personal communication, 30 April 1989, quoted in Kondo, *"M. Butterfly,"* p. 21.

15. This is one of the many significant differences between the film and the play. In the play, Gallimard is familiar with the Madame Butterfly story, which he claims to like, but complains that he has only seen it "played by huge women in so much bad makeup" (Hwang, *M. Butterfly*, p. 16).

16. Lacan, "The Meaning of the Phallus," edited by Juliet Mitchell and Jacqueline Rose, trans. Jacqueline Rose (New York: Norton, 1985), p. 82.

17. See Lacan's discussion in "Feminine Sexuality in Psychoanalytic Doctrine." Responding to Freud's questions in the investigation of feminine sexuality, "What does the little girl want from her mother?" and "what does she demand of her?" Lacan writes:

"What does the little girl demand of her mother?" But it's easy! She has no shortage of words for telling us: to dress her, to make her hurt go away, to take her for a walk, to belong to her, or to her alone, in short all sorts of demands, including at times the demand to leave her alone, that is, the demand to take a rest from all demand. If, therefore, Freud's question has any meaning, it must signify something else, that is, not so much "What is she demanding *of her?*" as "What is she *demanding,* what is she really demanding, by demanding of her mother all that?"

In other words, Freud's question implies the separating out of demand onto two planes: that of the demands effectively spoken, or enounced, and that of Demand (with a capital D) which subsists within and beyond these very demands, and which, because it remains resistant to articulation, incites the little girl to make those demands at the same time as rendering them futile, both the demands and any reply they might receive. (*Feminine Sexuality,* pp. 130–31; emphases in the original)

18. Hwang, *M. Butterfly,* pp. 95–96.

19. I am following Burton Watson's English translation of Zhuang Zi's text, which appears in *Qiwulun* [a treatise on equalizing (with) all things]. See *The Basic Writings of Chuang Tzu,* trans. and ed. Burton Watson (New York: Columbia UP, 1964), p. 45.

20. Lacan, "The Eye and the Gaze," *Four Fundamental Concepts,* p. 76; emphasis in the original.

21. "When dreaming of being the butterfly, . . . he is a captive butterfly, but captured by nothing, for, in the dream, he is a butterfly for nobody." Ibid., p. 76.

22. "The butterfly may . . . inspire in him the phobic terror of recognizing that the beating of little wings is not so very far from the beating of causation, of the primal stripe marking his being for the first time with the grid of desire." Ibid., p. 76.

23. Lacan, "The Line and Light," p. 100–101; emphases in the original.

24. See Garber for an interesting discussion of "passing" in her reading of the play *M. Butterfly:* " 'What passes for a woman.' And what passes for a man. Passing is what acting is, and what treason is. Recall that the French diplomat Boursicot was accused of passing information to his Chinese contacts. In espionage, in theater, in 'modern China,' in contemporary culture, embedded in the very phrase 'gender roles,' there is, this play suggests, only passing. Trespassing. Border-crossing and border raids. Gender, here, exists only in representation—or performance." *Vested Interests,* p. 250. As my reading throughout this chapter indicates, my reading of passing—and hence of crossing, role-playing, representation, and performance—is quite different from Garber's.

25. See Cowie's discussion in "Fantasia," p. 154.

26. Lacan, "What Is a Picture?" *Four Fundamental Concepts,* p. 114.

27. The passage indicated by the previous footnote continues with these lines: "What it amounts to is the first act in the laying down of the gaze. A sovereign act, no doubt, since it passes into something that is materialized and which, from this sovereignty, will render obsolete, excluded, inoperant, whatever, coming from elsewhere, will be presented before this product." Ibid., p. 114.

28. "In our relations to things, in so far as this relation is constituted by the way of vision, and ordered in the figures of representation, something slips, passes, is transmitted, from stage to stage, and is always to some degree eluded in it—that is what we call the gaze." Lacan, "The Eye and the Gaze," p. 73.

29. This ending could also be read along the lines of Cronenberg's fascination with the resemblance of fantasy to disease. For instance, even though the vocabulary he uses is predominantly biological rather than visual, the following lines from the director could well serve as a reading of the ending of *M. Butterfly* once we substitute the word "fantasy" for the words "virus" and "disease": "To understand physical process on earth requires a revision of the theory that we're all God's creatures. . . . It should certainly be extended to encompass disease, viruses and bacteria. Why not? A virus is only doing its job. It's trying to live its life. The fact that it's destroying you by doing so is not its fault. It's about trying to understand interrelationships among organisms, even those we perceive as disease. To understand it from the disease's point of view, it's just a matter of life. It has nothing to do with disease. I think most diseases would be very shocked to be considered diseases at all. It's a very negative connotation. For them, it's very positive when they take over your body and destroy you. It's a triumph. It's all part of trying to reverse the normal understanding of what goes on physically, psychologically and biologically to [*sic*] us. . . . I identify with [the characters in *Shivers*] after they're infected. I identify with the parasites, basically. . . ." *Cronenberg on Cronenberg*, p. 82.

30. In terms of a man "painting" his fantasy, a comparison could also be made between Cronenberg's film and Hitchcock's *Vertigo*, in which the male character, Scotty, attempts to rejuvenate his fantasy world by artificially remaking—by paint-ing—Judy, his new girlfriend, into Madeleine, his supposedly dead one. Once again, in *Vertigo* it is the female body that serves as the canvas for male enlightenment and that is ultimately sacrificed; while in *M. Butterfly* it is the male body that bears the consequences of this cruel and crude act of painting.

31. Lacan, "God and the *Jouissance* of the Woman," *Feminine Sexuality*, p. 144.

5

The Joy of Textualizing Japan: A Metacommentary on Roland Barthes's *Empire of Signs*

Hwa Yol Jung

Kogo tokitsukusazare

—A Zen *jakugo*

L'écriture est . . . un *satori*.

—Roland Barthes

Nowadays the way of educating as well as the way of learning is wrong. True knowledge is not in the written word. Books are always "translations." The "original" is what *is* by its own nature.

—Okada Torajiro (Zen Master)

I

ALONG WITH Claude Lévi-Strauss, Jacques Lacan, and Michel Foucault, Roland Barthes is a major architect of French structuralism. More specifically, he is one of the most inventive masters of contemporary literary theory who fashioned its directions, modes, and trends. He is indeed, as the Japanese would say, a *meijin* of literary theory. He is called by Jonathan Culler "a cultural institution."[1] In this sense, interdisciplinarity is for Barthes not just a slogan or a theoretical speculation but is practiced in his own writings. Rather than confining himself to a particular discipline or subject matter—such as literature, anthropology, psychoanalysis, history of ideas—his intellectual taste is vast, versatile, and catholic. His versatile inventiveness as well as his *Japonisme* are evidenced in the gem of an essay, *L'Empire des signes*

(1970)[2] which is thoroughly Gallic in taking delight in the dillydally of a myriad of things in Japan. Barthes speaks fondly of Japan or "a system of signs called Japan." Versatility, however, does not mean the lack or absence of intellectual focus or unity. *Empire of Signs* is in itself the mosaic scanning by an itinerant eye of the tantalizing parade of signs each of which counts and falls in its proper place—its ordered randomness accentuates the carefree and spontaneous sense of natural balance and unity with no privileged center. It is called a "luxurious and eclectic album."[3] *Empire of Signs* is the cultural landscape or, better, the geography, of itinerant culture topics.

There is indeed some truth in saying that a great thinker thinks only one single thought. Barthes is no exception. His decentered center is semiology, whose neutral center is language and particularly "literature" as writing *(écriture)*. In his Inaugural Lecture at the Collège de France in 1977, he enunciated clearly and decisively: "I cannot function *outside* language, treating it as a target, and *within* language, treating it as a weapon."[4] And he called contemporary literature a permanent revolution of language and made it synonymous with writing or text. Writing makes knowledge festive or full of *asobi* (joyous play)—to use the expression of Japanese *geisha* culture. It is, in short, the gaiety of language in the manner of *geisha asobi*. The rhetoricity of Barthes's *Empire of Signs* is, without question, of *donjuanesque* quality: it is a seductive exercise in semiological *donjuanisme*.[5] Barthes is indeed a writer *(écrivain)* who is the homo ludens par excellence. Knowledge *(savoir)*, too, is the flavoring *(saveur)* of language or words. No wonder there is a close diatactics between the knowledge of culture and that of cooking.

Barthes's *Empire of Signs* describes Japan as the vast network of signs or a galaxy of signifiers. It is, as Susan Sontag puts it, "the ultimate accolade" of semiology.[6] As fashion is the language of fashion and the city is an ideogram, the country Japan is an "empire of signs" or an ideographic "city." Ludwig Wittgenstein wittingly likens language to a city: "Our language can be seen as an ancient city: a maze of little streets and squares, of old and new houses, and of houses with additions from various periods; and these surrounded by a multitude of new boroughs with straight and regular streets and uniform houses"[7]—and much more, more complex with, say, narrow zigzagging alleys and sometimes with unpassable subterranean tunnels which are even intriguing and befuddling to the native dwellers.

Moreover, *Empire of Signs* is inevitably an intellectual autobiography as well as *Gedankenexperiment* of his deconstructive semiology as a universal science in which Japan is one of its laboratories.[8] Barthes is indeed a *maiko*—to use the *geisha* language—in performing the semiotics of Japanese culture. Every serious endeavor is in part autobiographical—the self becoming the material subject of writing for itself as well as for others. I am here reminded of Raymond Savignac's *Astral* in which "de haut en bas" and "de bas en haut" are dialectically interchangeable. Autobiography or self-indulgence, it should be remembered, is not necessarily navel-gazing and thus acrimonious or opprobrious. For, on the contrary, radical observation is an *interrogation* for—to paraphrase Maurice Merleau-Ponty—a set of observations wherein he who observes is himself implicated by the observation. In other words, radical observation is a "metacommentary" in the sense that Fredric Jameson uses it: "every individual interpretation must include an interpretation of its own existence, must show its own credentials and justify itself: every commentary must be at the same time a metacommentary as well."[9] In this regard, *Empire of Signs* is an exotic subtext or "supplement" to Barthes's structural semiology: at least it adds colors and flavors to the texture and fabric of his written corpus as a whole. Without it the main text itself would be incomplete. The exotic in- and ex-cites his intellectual acumen. It elicits an inciting and exciting reading as well. It would be wrong to say, however, that Barthes intended to write a scholarly text on Japan and make a scholarly contribution to Oriental studies in the tradition of his countrymen Paul Masson-Oursel, Marcel Granet, Henri Maspero, and René Sieffert. Rather, he is an enthusiastic and observant amateur. Precisely because he is an amateur, he is able to pump in an air of fresh insight. Barthes's *Empire of Signs,* as Culler characterizes it judiciously, is a combination of "touristic commentary on Japan with a reflection on signs in everyday life and their ethical implications."[10] It is indeed a discerning, abecedarian account of Japanese culture as a system of signs.

In European history, Orientalism has been like a pendulum that cyclically swings back and forth from the likings and dislikings of the Orient. In French history, it fluctuates from Voltaire to Montesquieu. It is certainly a pathological swing. In an imaginary dialogue with a Japanese scholar, Martin Heidegger once expressed his puzzlement and bemusement that the Japanese forget the beginnings of their own thinking and rush to and chase after anything latest and newest in European thought. In modern history, the Oriental or Japanese love for things Occidental needs no documentation. Particularly because of the Japanese success in industrial development, now the Occidental love for the Orient—Japan in particular—abounds. In 1974 the French *Tel Quel* group including Phillippe Sollers, Julia Kristeva, and Barthes visited China. As a result, Kristeva, for example, published in 1977 *Des Chinoises* which is destined to become an important chapter in the annals of women's liberation. Before his China trip, Barthes visited and toured Japan in 1966 to lecture on structural semiology. According to the account of the French scholar who was President of the Franco-Japanese Institute in Tokyo— Maurice Pinguet to whom *Empire of Signs* was dedicated—Barthes's love for

Japan was genuine and deep. In this, I might add, he followed the footsteps of his compatriot Paul Claudel who, more than anyone else, opened up inter-cultural exchanges between France and Japan in the twentieth century. The Japanese, in turn, responded to Barthes by translating his *L'Empire des signes* four years after its original publication: *Shirushi no Teikoku* (1974).[11] And they celebrated or, better, commemorated Barthes's *oeuvre* in the June, 1980 special issue of *Gendai Shiso* which had the French subtitle—*Revue de le pen-sée d'aujourd'hui*.

The present essay is a commentary on Barthes's commentary on Japan. I think no apology, however, is necessary to the incomparable essayist Michel de Montaigne, with all due respect and seriousness, who complained about the profusion of commentaries instead of writing about the order of things *(les choses)*, that is, "interpreting *interpretations*" instead of "interpreting *things*" themselves. Montaigne's old but familiar complaint is no doubt a sober reflection on our age of "commentaries," "criticism," and "scholar-ship." On the other hand, however, we should not forget that, in the first place, as human thought is coextensive with language, the *verbum* is not the surrogate or disguise of the *res* (or *les choses*). Rather, the *verbum* is also the *res*. So "interpreting interpretations" is willy-nilly "interpreting things" themselves. In the second place, since—following the lead of Nietzsche or Harold Bloom's disputation—interpretation is, and will always be, misinter-pretation, the interpreted things or words remain to be reinterpreted. Finally, as we will see more clearly later, phenomenological reading turns and returns to the experiential to honor its validity, that is to say, it not only does not bifurcate "interpreting interpretations" and "interpreting things" but actu-ally makes the bifurcation unnecessary and superfluous because in it, as in Zen, "things" themselves are the homestead of all "interpretations."

Be that as it may, the present metacommentary will focus on Barthes's semiological observation of significant Japanese cultural signs and symbols as manifested and surfaced particularly in Zen, *haiku* and calligraphy (Sec-tion II) and then it will critically evaluate the limits of his view of the Japa-nese empire of signs from the phenomenology of lived experience (Section III). It should be noted from the outset that the question of how a given text is to be read is a controversial question in the contemporary hermeneutics of literature. No matter. I only intend to follow Barthes's own deconstructionist injunction that as there is nothing outside it, the text has an autochthonous status whose fate depends on readership rather than authorship. As, accord-ing to Barthes, there is an ineluctable dialectic or even paradox between read-ing and writing, the only explicit reading *is* writing. The only proper response to writing is another writing which is a metacommentary. By all means, Barthes intended to record in *Empire of Signs* his fascination with Japan as "the country of writing"—Japan's grammatology which is heavily picto-graphic or ideographic. As the tidal waves of deconstructive grammatology have been sweeping the contemporary literary scene, the tendency is rushing toward Chinese ideography as pure, anti-phonocentric writing.[12] Barthes is by no means the first and will not be the last Occidental who has been mes-merized by things traditionally Japanese. Nevertheless, there is a uniqueness in his *oeuvre:* unlike the other Occidental students, he *textualizes* everything in Japanese culture through deconstructive grammatology whose grand goal is to dismantle logocentrism which allegedly coincides with Western ethno-centrism. Like Igor Stravinsky who confessed that he enjoyed the activity of composing (writing) better than the music itself, deconstructive grammatol-ogists have made writing intransitive: writing is writing is writing.

II

The title of Barthes's work is, as it were, the wrapper of the content of Japa-nese culture as a system of signs. To decipher or zero in on the content, we must unwrap the wrapper. The content is packaged with a decorous plethora of cultural *bonsai* cultivated as miniaturized texts. If, however, the wrapper were the gift itself, the title would the content: there would be no inner soul separate from the textual flesh. For Barthes, Japan displays an epicurean menu of exotic icons: Zen, *satori, mu, haiku, sumotori, pachinko, ikebana, Kabuki, Bunraku, Zengakuren, hashi, miso, sashimi, sukiyaki, tempura,* etc. It would be wrong to conclude that Barthes attends only to the "wrapping" of Japanese culture while dispensing with its "contents." What is to be recog-nized here is the need to deconstruct the all-too-commonplace dichotomy between the visible and the invisible, outside and inside, appearance and real-ity, wrapping and content, surface and depth, manifest and latent, concrete and abstract, ritual and choice, text and intention, style and form, deed and word, etc. Where there is no dichotomizing doublet, there is indeed "sincer-ity."[13] Since the visible body initiates the rite of passage to the invisible soul of an alien culture by a foreign observer or tourist, let's look closer at the outer appearance. It is doubly important in understanding Japanese culture and Barthes's Japan because of the extraordinary attention paid to it by the Japanese themselves and consequently Barthes himself in *Empire of Signs.* From a semiological perspective, too, the outer is as important as, if not more than, the inner.

What is a sign? It is, according to Barthes, the union of the signifier and the signified. The term is translated in Japanese as *shirushi* (or *kigo*) which means any visible *marking*—particularly nonlinguistic marking. It is interest-

ing to see the unusual Japanese deference to the content is indicated immediately in the outer appearance of the translated copy of Barthes's *Empire of
Signs*—in addition to its addenda inside (more pictures, extra explanatory
notes and the translator's introduction). The translation is boxed and
wrapped with wax paper. The cover of the book is clothed with the printing
paper of excellent quality. Whether or not one can read Japanese, the external
appearance gives one the impression that this is an important work, indeed.

If Barthes's work is to be judged by its cover, we should attend to it. The
outer box has a separate wrapper with the photograph of a traditional, aristocratic, anonymous courtly woman which could easily depict a scene from the
Genji monogatari. The picture is explained in the French original simply as
"Fragment d'une carte postale" reminding us of Derrida's recent work on
Freud. Without doubt the woman *is* the sur/facial *centerfold* of *Empire of
Signs* which is consonant with Barthes's own semiological approach. As a picture is worth a thousand words, the woman is the *"studium"* where Barthes
displays the multicolored galaxy of signifiers in Japanese culture. First, it is a
picture. As such it *de/sign/ates* the presence of Japan in absence. In photography, according to Barthes, form and content coincide. The literal message of
the woman (denotation) is not clear, but its symbolic message (connotation)
is worth exploring. Clearly, Barthes is interested in signifying the traditional
depth of Japanese culture. Second, the courtly woman is wearing a colorful,
long garment that befits her long black hair. This garment is ingrained, as it
were, in the fabric of Barthes's text. Interestingly enough, Barthes in *The
Fashion System* discusses clothing as protecting, covering, and masking. He
quotes Hegel's aesthetics approvingly: "as pure sentience, the body cannot
signify; clothing guarantees the passage from sentience to meaning; it is, we
might say, *the signified* par excellence."[14] What then does the garment of the
courtly woman signify in relation to her pure sentience? The absolute privacy
of sex? Speaking about the absence of sex in *pachinko,* Barthes observes that
in Japan "sex is in sexuality, not elsewhere," whereas in the United States, on
the contrary, "sex is everywhere, except in sexuality."[15]

Third and the most important is the *activity* engaged in by the courtly
woman. In traditional Japan, there was a gender gap between man and
woman in the activity of writing. What Barthes describes as the country of
writing, *kanji* or ideographic calligraphy, whether or not he is aware of it, is
typically a male activity, whereas for women it was an irreverent activity.
Although there is no definite assurance that she is writing in *kanji* rather than
(hira)kana—which is highly improbably—the importance of writing is
accentuated by the woman in the act of (letter-) writing. Man in the act of
writing is normal and usual, whereas woman in the act of writing is rare. As
sexuality and textuality coincide in the portrayal of the woman in the act of

writing, the bridging of the gender gap signifies anti-phallocentrism as well as anti-logocentrism. If, however, Barthes was only interested in portraying sexuality alone, the more appropriate *centerfold* of his work would have been the "courtesan *(yugo)* with a dog" in the book, a *geisha* girl, or a *shunga* to satisfy the lascivious eye.[16]

Now, so much for the outer cover.

Zen is the inner soul of Japanese culture, and writing is for Barthes Zen's *satori*—an inner awakening or enlightenment. He is fascinated with and celebrates the graphism of all things Japanese. As a nation of ideograms or pictograms, Japan is a graphic bliss or nirvana. Barthes has a tremendous proclivity to describe nonlinguistic signs in linguistic terms: every human face—including his own shown in the *Kobe Shinbun* during his tour in Japan and that of a corpulent *sumotori*—as a written text, an inscription, or a citation; *miso* as adding "a touch of clarity"; *sukiyaki* as becoming "decentered, like an uninterrupted text"; *tempura* as a "grammar" or visibly graphic; the city as an "ideogram"; *Zengakuren* as "a syntax of actions"; the stationary store as an "ideographic marquetry," etc. In the context of his deconstructive grammatology, in short, Barthes's discovery of Japan as a nation of ideographic inscriptions may be likened to the famous wooden statue in Kyoto of the enlightened Zen monk Hoshi where the visage of divinity is emerging through a crevice of his face.

Barthes declares that writing is a *satori:* Zen and *satori* are signified by the void or empty *(le vide)*.[17] There is the *kanji* (ideogram) "void" calligraphed for Barthes by a female student. Underneath the *kanji* is the Japanese pronunciation *mu* and *le vide*. In Japan, in the country of writing whose inner soul coincides with Zen, *mu* is the abysmal "ground" or *Urgrund* of everything or everything is a metaphor of *mu*. Barthes writes:

> Writing is after all, in its way, a *satori; satori* (the Zen occurrence) is a more or less powerful (though in no way formal) seism which causes knowledge or the subject, to vacillate: it creates *an emptiness of language*. And it is also an emptiness of language which constitutes writing; it is from this emptiness that derive the features with which Zen, in the exemption from all meaning, writes gardens, gestures, houses, flower arrangements, faces, violence.[18]

The key expression to understand Barthes's Japan—and his deconstructive semiology—is "an emptiness of language." In the first place, however, there is an ambiguity in Barthes's own description of the *kanji "mu"* as *le vide*. *Mu* is *sunyata* in Sanskrit. When a Mahayana text was introduced to the Chinese in the second century, they were not able to grasp with ease the idea of *sunyata* [emptiness, *k'ung* (Chinese) and *ku* (Japanese)] as they did many other "abstract" Buddhist concepts, although they found it akin to the Taoist idea of *wu* (nothingness) as in the famous *wu-wei* (no-action) in the *Tao Te Ching*.[19] Ideogrammatically, *mu* and *ku* are two different characters. *Mu* (Japanese) or *wu* (Chinese) is *le néant*, whereas *ku* is *le vide*. The Japanese translation clearly indicates this difference.

In the second place, the expression "an emptiness of language" is "un *vide de parole*" in Barthes's original French text. Therefore, the English translation of *parole* as "language" is rather misleading inasmuch as it makes little sense to speak of writing as an emptiness of language itself. In the tradition of Saussurean linguistics, *langage* consists of *parole* and *langue*. If writing is "un vide de parole," it is contrasted with speech as event within the (Japanese) language as a system. For it, too, is an integral part of language *(langage)*. The passage cannot be understood otherwise. Writing as a *satori* is anti-phono-centric resonating with the general aim of deconstructive grammatology. The dialectical opposite of writing is not language but speech. The Japanese translation of *parole* as *kotoba* [spoken word(s)] is aware of this fundamental distinction between language as speech and language as writing. Moreover, deeply rooted in Chinese and Japanese thought is the tradition that the dialectical opposite of speech is not writing but rather silence or the "unsayable." There is, however, no glaring contradiction here because writing is always a silent transgression of verbal acts. In the Zen tradition, there is a diatactics of speech and silence: speech is the *yang* of silence and silence the *yin* of speech. Just as in John Cage's compositional techniques sound and silence are posed as complementary, Sontag considers silence not as an "incineration of consciousness" but, on the contrary, as a *pharmakon* for the pollution of language.[20] Silence may be invoked as a cupola, hyphen, punctuation, or even rupture in the dialectical flow of human communication. As such its communicative value exceeds and surpasses that of "empty talk" *(parole vide)*.[21] To Zen, as the tradition goes, silence is more suitable than eloquence.

According to D. T. Suzuki, whose name in the West is synonymous with Zen, Zen's *satori* is realized in *performance* which may be (1) verbal (speaking) or (2) actional.[22] In the first place, since Zen is an everyday occurrence in our social life, we need to communicate with one another through the medium of language. Unlike the rules of linguistics as the science of language (presumably including semiology), however, Suzuki insists that Zen verbalism is intuitive and experiential, that is, nonconceptual and lived. Cutting through the conceptual or intellectual sedimentations, Zen attempts to reach directly or im-mediately *konomama* (thisness) or *sonomama* (thatness)—i.e., "isness" the attainment of which is called *satori*. Thus the attainment of *satori* avoids conceptual detours. According to Barthes:

if this state of *a-language* is a liberation, it is because, for the Buddhist experiment, the proliferation of secondary thoughts (the thought of thought), or what might be called the infinite supplement of supernumerary signifieds—a circle of which language itself is the depository and the model—appears as a jamming: it is on the contrary the abolition of secondary thought which breaks the vicious infinity of language. In all these experiments, apparently, it is not a matter of crushing language beneath the mystic silence of the ineffable, but of *measuring* it, of halting that verbal top which sweeps into the gyration the obsessional play of symbolic substitutions. In short, it is the symbol as semantic operation which is attacked.[23]

In the second place, *satori* is a moral emancipation, that is, moral fulfillment *by doing* which is deeply Sinitic[24] (i.e., both Confucian and Taoist). Consider the famous Confucian idea of the "rectification of names" *(cheng ming)* that is addressed to the performative power of speech in human conduct *qua moral.* The only way to bridge verbalism with moral fulfillment by doing is to regard speaking itself as the act of doing (i.e., the theory of language both as speech acts and as moral acts). The Japanese as well as the Chinese consider "sincerity"—literally meaning the "completion" of "spoken words"—as the acme of moral virtue. Nishida Kitaro—the greatest Japanese philosopher of the twentieth century—regards intuition as the basis of artistic creativity as well as moral conduct. Intuition rather than the intellect is the *élan vital* of artistic and moral creativity. Mencious, too, considered "intuitive knowledge" *(liang chih* or, literally, "good knowledge") as the basis of everyday moral conduct. Culler is right, as noted earlier, that Barthes's commentary on Japan as empire of signs *is* also an ethical one.

In the Japanese as well as the Chinese tradition, painting and writing are inseparable—the fact of which has not failed Barthes's own attention. In calligraphy, writing reaches the status of an art. In it, to inscribe is to paint. As Guillaume Apollinaire "painted" his poetry as *"calligrammes,"* so does the contemporary Japanese painter Hiro Kamimura exemplify an attempt to synthesize painting with ideograms: his "Water and Ice" is a homonymous blending of painting and writing. The *Obaku* sect of Zen excels in *kanji* calligraphy which approximates painting. Painting, moreover, is invariably accompanied by ideographic inscriptions. *Sumiye* painting is an example of how painting approaches writing.[25] Japanese "photocracy"—the craze for pictograms—is too well-known to elaborate. Barthes's own 1970 painting after the Italian futurism (which is used on the front cover jacket of the recent American anthology *A Barthes Reader* edited by Susan Sontag) looks like vertiginous Chinese calligraphy. His own hand-written French transcription of a few Japanese expressions in *Empire of Signs* resembles calligraphy. Calligraphy may be characterized as a choreography of gestures. It is a ballet of ideograms in *rite* order—to paraphrase Marshall McLuhan and Harley Parker.[26] Like Picasso's *Swimmer* and *Acrobat*, calligraphy is a kinetic art: it is the human body in motion or a conversation of gestures. Although he did not have in mind Chinese ideography in particular, R. G. Collingwood is perceptive in observing that every language is a specialized form of bodily gesture and thus the dance is the mother of all languages.[27]

Haiku is a polyglot

La vieille mare:
Une grenouille saute dedans:
Oh! le bruit de l'eau.

Furu ike ya!
Kawazu tobikomu,
Mizu no oto.

The old pond:
A frog jumps in:
Oh! the sound of the water.

Barthes's unabated enthusiasm for *haiku* as the elixir of Japanese literature—indeed, all literature—cannot be doubted. *S/Z* which was published in the same year as *Empire of Signs* should perhaps be read as "Semiology/Zen" that celebrates the Japanese tradition.[28] Each of 561 lexias in *S/Z*, as noted earlier by Leitch, is a *haiku* of criticism whose packaged notation equals a cultivated *bonsai*. For Barthes, *haiku* is merely the literary branch of Zen.[29] There is indeed a three-way interfusion of writing, Zen (*satori*), and *haiku*. Barthes, too, notices the ineluctable blending of painting and *haiku* writing in the following two examples. The first is the picture of one cucumber and two eggplants on a *kakemono* by an anonymous sixteenth-century (?) author which is unfortunately omitted from the English translation. It is found in the midst of Barthes's discussion of *haiku*. The three vegetables symbolize or parallel three short lines of a *haiku*. The second is a more suggestive and seductive example than the first. It is the "mushroom picking" by the eighteenth-century Japanese artist Yokoi: three raw mushrooms are pierced through a wisp of straw above which is the following three-line *haiku* (*poème bref en trois vers*):

Il se fait cupide	He becomes greedy
aussi, le regard baissé	his eyes lowered
sur les champignons	on the mushrooms

If "rawness" *(crudité)* is the kind of "floating signifier," the painting and the *haiku* are in the state of a sexual, chiasmic invagination. The *kakemono* signifies—to use a mycophilial expression—the "bemushroomed" state of *ekstasis:* the symbolic, spiritual flight of the *haiku* and the pictured mushrooms from the body of the *kakemono.* This may explain why the composer John Cage is interested in fusing Zen and mycology, that is, in ethno-mycology. Be that as it may, Barthes goes on to ask (in handwriting) rhetorically about the "mushroom picking": "Where does the writing begin? Where does the painting begin?" Set aside the rhetoricity of the questions, one might point out that they can be raised only by those for whom Chinese ideography is an unknown art, although the pictured sketch of the three raw mushrooms pierced through a straw resembles, and may thus be mistaken easily for, a polygamous ideogram.

III

Empire of Signs is the testimonial of an itinerant pilgrim—not unlike the Zen monk Hoshi who, too, travelled to China in the beginning of the T'ang period in search of Zen *(satori)*—in search of semiological markings *(shirushi)* in all things Japanese whose epicenter is writing *(écriture).* For Barthes, we may say, Japan was a semiological *geisha* house where the freeplay *(asobi)* of signs takes place.[30] Although Barthes succeeds in "intellectual deprovincialization" and thus must be applauded for his intention and effort to overcome the conceptual "sound barriers" of Western narcissism, we cannot answer with certainty whether or not he succeeds in instituting an exagamous link between semiology and Japanese culture. To be universally valid, his semiology as the *science* of *all* signs must encompass different galaxies of markings of which Japan is only one.

To discover Japan as the country of writing is not at all contrary to the affluent exhibition of the Japanese photocracy we have all come to know so very well in recent years—the photocracy which, in an extended sense of the term, could include photography, painting, dramaturgy, fashions, packaging, gastronomy, and above all calligraphy. *Empire of Signs* is a belletrism of Japan at its best: as Barthes himself admitted, he enjoyed writing it more than any other book. No doubt the most revealing and original formulation of Barthes's work is: writing is a *satori.* As Zen is the inner soul of Japanese culture, there is all the more reason why the *écrivain* Barthes is interested in *haiku* which he views as the privileged monument of Zen. The most significant question is not how many cultural trophies Barthes gathered but whether or not *Empire of Signs*—the "ultimate accolade" of Japanese culture in the eye of a semiologist—is the insemination and dissemination of his semiology. Although every intellectual endeavor for a *savant* is, to some extent, autobiographical and Barthes's *Empire of Signs* is no exception to this rule, one hopes that it is ideally a reciprocation, as in the spirit of exchanging gifts, of the *insemination* (taking) of Zen and the *dissemination* (giving) of his semiology.

The idea of writing as *satori* already involves a semiological strategy. By strategy I mean a chosen set of calculated moves in order to "win" a conceptual game. Part of this strategy is the very selection of what signs are to be taken as significant indicators of Japanese culture. There is, however, a serious problem in relating Zen and *satori* to semiology. It is in essence the problem of reconciling the French cult of writing *(écriture)* and the Japanese cult of inner tranquility, unless, of course, writing like Zen calligraphy is the carnal "enjoyment" *(jouissance* or *asobi)* of a person as a non-utilitarian activity undertaken solely for serenity or what Martin Heidegger calls *Gelassenheit* which has been identified as the common denominator of such Zen specialists as Suzuki, Eugen Herrigel, and Karl von Dürckheim. It is also the clash between semiology as a conceptual, linguistic system and Zen as intuitive, actional experience, which is correlated with the question of the unity or duality of the inner and the outer, depth and surface, the content and the wrapping, gastronomic look and actual taste, and meaning and sign.[31] The conception of writing as *satori* raises the unresolved paradox of Zen as an *inner* awakening and writing as an *outer* ex/pression. This paradox is accentuated in Barthes's Japan because structural semiology as a method of cultural interpretation has a built-in conceptual propensity to disregard the inner in favor of the outer or, in the case of Japan, to wrap Zen with semiology. Barthes is certainly not unaware of the problem when he defines the sign as the union of the signifier and the signified, and when he acknowledges that Zen wages a war against the prevarication of meaning *(sens)* and that the meaning of a sign is polygamous, not monogamous. John Sturrock thus observes that "In Japanese culture, or at any rate Barthes's version of it, the exterior of a thing *is* the thing, there is no informing but invisible agency within. Japan is a country full of rich and intriguing signifiers whose charm is that they have no signifieds."[32]

For Barthes, there is no inner soul or privileged center in Zen's *satori* because it is *mu* or the void which is contradictory to dominant Western metaphysics. The denial of the inner or depth in favor of the outer or surface may well be a conceptual trapping of structural semiology rather than the understanding of Zen from *within*. Thus Sturrock speculates that "the opposition deep-set/flush is itself a Western not a Japanese one, and the Japanese might very well employ a different code in order to locate the Oriental soul."[33] There is always the latent danger of catching Zen with a semiological net. It is for this reason that in his important article the Chinese philosopher Chang Tung-sun identifies Western reasoning with the logic of identity, while Eastern reasoning with the logic of correlation which is neither monistic, nor dualistic, nor reductionistic.[34] As clothing is to the body, so is the sign to culture. As pure sentience without clothing, the body too cannot signify or at least cannot signify sufficiently. By the same logic, culture cannot signify without signs as external "markings" *(shirushi)*. However, a marking is only an external indication, not a meaning. There is a famous saying by the Chinese Taoist Chuang Tzu that words exist for meaning and once the meaning has been gotten, the words can be forgotten. Culture or language is not like a white onion—a subject of Basho's *haiku* of which Barthes seems fond— every layer of which is a surface without an inner core or center. Even in Zen there is mention of "the mind of no-mind" *(mushin no shin)*. It may very well be true that surface is as telling as depth, but in language the signifier without the signified is "babbling" or "doodling." Culture is like language: to understand it, we must understand the diatactics of the subjective and the objective without a facile reductionism. Cultural interpretation is the navigation of the stormy channel between the Scylla of subjectivity and the Charybdis of objectivity.

What is lacking in Barthes's structural semiology as a method of cultural interpretation, therefore, is, and is compensated for by, a phenomenology of lived experience *(l'expérience vécu)* or the life-world *(le monde vécu: Lebenswelt)*. In Barthes's case of Japan as the country of writing as well as Zen, we need to *hear* Zen's *voice* of invisibility as a prerequisite to *see* its visible surface. There is a lesson to be learned from Ralph Ellison's "invisible man" who struggles for his visibility by lighting up his basement with 1369 light bulbs. The message to be gotten here is not to disregard the outer, but rather to encourage the dialectical coupling of the inner and the outer or the invisible and the visible, that is, to abandon the facile monism, dualism, or reductionism.[35]

Without the benefit of a phenomenology of lived experience as the founding and funding matrix of *all* conceptualization, there is in cultural interpretation the ever-present danger of conceptual "entrapment" or the prevarication of meaning—especially in the interpretation of a culture, including its own linguistic system, which is unfamiliar or dissimilar to the observer's own.[36] It is not to suggest "Go native" or "Think Japanese" here, but only to intimate that a phenomenology of lived experience is the prerequisite for any cultural interpretation. Cultural interpretation is necessarily an echo of the original voice of culture as a network of intersubjective meanings—those meanings which are not just in the minds of the individual actors but rooted in their social and institutional practices including their language.

More significantly, to ignore a network of intersubjective meanings is to open—often inadvertently—the safety valve, as it were, that prevents the spillage of ethnocentrism or, as Barthes himself calls it, "Western narcissism."[37] To attend to intersubjective meanings is to respect "a local turn of mind" and not to miss the cultural contextualization of indigenous signifiers. Barthes himself observes that in the Occident the mirror is a narcissistic object for man to look at himself, whereas in the Orient it is *empty* and symbolizes the *emptiness (ku* or *le vide)* of all symbols. To be "enlightened" or to attain a *satori,* Barthes's writing on Japan must be *emptied* of the preemptive strategies of his semiology. To deconstruct (phenomenologically) Barthes's *Empire of Signs* is simply to trace the *presence* of semiological reflection in the mirror of his Japan.

There is no intimation here that Barthes is an ethnocentrist. Nor is it implied that his understanding of Japanese culture is shallow, superficial, or surfacial. What is pointed out is simply the potential danger of the categorial grid of structural semiology or, for that matter, any conceptual system that ignores consciously or unconsciously a system of intersubjective meanings. Barthes himself noted that in Japan sex is in sexuality, not anywhere else. This observation assumes, to be sure, the knowledge of the *inner* working of sexuality in Japan. Parallel to the problematic of the content of wrapping is *Kabuki's onnagata* which is in actuality the male actor playing the staged role of the female (i.e., the transvestite actor). Without knowing the *inner* working of *Kabuki,* here again, he might be easily mistaken for an actress. Let us make no mistake: a mask is *never* a real face, although the former tells on occasion a lot about the latter. Moreover, there is nothing wrong with the good looks of often decorous gastronomic Japanese dishes pleasing to our (hungry) eye, but they do not always or necessarily guarantee good taste. Taste, good or bad, is to be known only in the eating.[38] In brief, when chained to the categorial grid of structural semiology, cultural interpretation courts conceptual reification, that is to say, falsification. As, in Zen, the written is only a copy or translation of something original or real, to *textualize* the real is to *fabricate* it or, at best, to reduce it to a confessional autobiography or a cultural narcissism. In the Japanese language, not in its written but only its spoken form, there is the triple, playful distinction between *hashi-ga* (chopsticks), *haSHI-ga* (bridge), *haSHI-GA* (edge). To wit: with the slightest slip *(lapsus)* of the tongue—not a pen or brush—one can stand at the "bridge" of understanding or at the "edge" of misunderstanding, or when one means to ask for a pair of "chopsticks" at the gastronomic table, he may end up with getting a "bridge"! After having said all this, it is not altogether impossible for anyone to have missed or been "off-side" *(hors jeu)* in the *staging* of the *Bunraku* or *Kabuki* of Barthes's semiology in *Empire of Signs,* that is, the real semiological face or character behind the mask.[39] In that case, he can confess that at least he enjoyed a brief *geisha asobi* (disciplined, not promiscuous, "playfulness") of and in Barthes's house of signs without perhaps knowing its inner workings. By so doing he "supplements" the Nietzschean "freeplay" for "truth." Ultimately, perhaps we are all playing the labyrinthine game of "truth-telling" in the *Rashomon*. As the poem of the thirteenth-century Chinese Master Mumon reads:

> Gateless is the Great Tao,
> There are thousands of ways to it.
> If you pass through this barrier,
> You may walk freely in the universe.[40]

Notes

1. Jonathan Culler, *Roland Barthes* (New York: Oxford University Press, 1983), p. 9. Among the American literary notables, Susan Sontag is the most enthusiastic admirer of Barthes's literary genius. Recently she writes: "Teacher, man of letters, moralist, philosopher of culture, connoisseur of strong ideas, protean autobiographer . . . of all the intellectual notables who have emerged since World War II in France, Roland Barthes is the one whose work I am most certain will endure." ("Writing Itself: On Roland Barthes," in *A Barthes Reader,* ed. Susan Sontag [New York: Hill and Wang, 1982], p. vii.)

2. Roland Barthes, *L'Empire des signes* (Geneva: Skira, 1970); *Empire of Signs,* trans. Richard Howard (New York: Hill and Wang, 1982).

3. Guy de Mallac, "Métaphores du vide: *L'Empire des signes* de Roland Barthes," *SubStance* 1 (1971): 31.

4. *A Barthes Reader,* p. 473. For Barthes, *l'homme, c'est le langage:* "A . . . principle, particularly important in regard to literature, is that language cannot be considered as a simple instrument, whether utilitarian or decorative, of thought. Man does not exist prior to language, either as a species or as an individual. We never find a state where man is separated from language, which he then creates in order to 'express' what is taking place within him: it is language which teaches the definition of man, not the reverse." ("To Write: An Intransitive Verb?" in Richard Macksey and Eugenio Donato, eds., *The Structuralist Controversy* [Baltimore: Johns Hopkins University Press, 1972], p. 135.) Cf. the American semiotician Charles Sanders Peirce who writes that "it is sufficient to say that there is no element whatever of man's consciousness which has not something corresponding to it in the word; and the reason is obvious. It is that the word or sign which man uses *is* the man himself. For, as the fact that every thought is a sign, taken in conjunction with the fact that life is a train of thought, proves that man is a sign; so, that everything thought is an *external* sign, proves that man is an external sign. That is to say, the man and the external sign are identical, in the same sense in which the words *homo* and *man* are identical. Thus my language is the sum total of myself; for the man is the thought." (*Collected*

Papers, vol. 5, *Pragmatism and Pragmaticism,* ed. Charles Hartshorne and Paul Weiss [Cambridge, Mass.: Harvard University Press, 1960], p. 189.)

5. The terms *donjuanesque* and *donjuanisme* are borrowed from Shoshana Felman, *Le Scandale du corps parlant* (Paris: Editions du Seuil, 1980). If Felman is able to dramatize John Austin's philosophy of language as *donjuanisme* and impregnate *connaissance* with *jouissance,* we should be allowed to invent the hybrid neologism *jouinaissance* after the fashion of James Joyce. The slightest allusion of language to corporeality as hinted at by Felman—"la parole est une promesse corporelle"—elicits a filiality of the philosophy of language with (Lacanian) psychoanalysis. In *Roland Barthes: A Conservative Estimate* (Chicago: University of Chicago Press, 1983), Philip Thody observes that Barthes's *Empire of Signs* is "one of the most hedonistic of all his books, and the one in which he writes with the most enthusiasm about his subject-matter" (p. 121). Another observer comments that Barthes's thinking shifted from the themes of culture, the sign and the text to the notion of pleasure (see ibid., p. 181). Steven Ungar, too, aptly characterizes Barthes as "the professor of desire" in his recent book *Roland Barthes: The Professor of Desire* (Lincoln, Neb.: University of Nebraska Press, 1983). More specifically, John O'Neill coined the term *homotextuality* to intimate the corporeal kinship between the reader and the text in Barthes's work. See "Homotextuality: Barthes on Barthes, Fragments (RB), with a Footnote," in *Hermeneutics,* ed. Gary Shapiro and Alan Sica (Amherst, Mass.: University of Massachusetts Press, 1984), pp. 165–82.

6. "Writing Itself," p. xxiv. Speaking of *Empire of Signs,* Vincent B. Leitsch describes: "Barthes admires the Japanese custom of attending to wrapping while disregarding contents. The surface of the present, not its hidden gift, elicits appreciation. The preparations and the requisites of meaning, ritual and arbitrary, hold more interest and importance than the impatient possession of its truth. Whether the volume is ultimately empty or overfull seems less pressing than that its packaging be enjoyed. The writing of *S/Z* celebrates this non-Western tradition. Thus the lexia, a haiku of criticism, a delicacy of *S/Z,* is less violent manhandling than frail handiwork in miniature. A package of notation. Without hidden truth. A ritual of reading. Bonsai cultivated." *(Deconstructive Criticism* [New York: Columbia University Press, 1983], p. 204.)

7. *Philosophical Investigations,* trans. G. E. M. Anscombe (Oxford: Blackwell, 1953), p. 84.

8. In discussing the legacy of Saussure's linguistics, Jonathan Culler observes that "if everything which has meaning within a culture is a sign and therefore an object of semiological investigation, semiology would come to include most disciplines of the humanities and the social sciences. Any domain of human activity—be it music, architecture, cooking, etiquette, advertising, fashion, literature—could be approached in semiological terms." (*Ferdinand de Saussure* [New York: Penguin Books, 1977], p. 103. See also pp. 95 and 110–11). From a perspective of semiology, language is only one system of signs, though it is a special or privileged one. Thus, semiology broadens its jurisdiction to include all conceivable cultural objects. Barthes's *Empire of Signs* should be read in the broad sense of semiology as a cultural science.

9. Fredric Jameson, "Metacommentary," PMLA 86 (January 1971):10.

10. *Roland Barthes,* p. 11. Of course, we should not take Culler's use of the term *touristic* as nonserious or supercilious. Rather, he seems to use it after a study fashioned by Dean MacCannell, *The Tourist: A New Theory of the Leisure Class* (New York: Schocken Books, 1976).

11. Roland Barthes, *Shirushi no Teikoku,* trans. So Sacon (Tokyo: Shincho, 1974). Judging from the description of the cover of the Japanese translation, the Japanese consider the work as the "cultural criticism" of Japan. I am indebted to my friend Kazuhiko Okuda of the International University of Japan for sending me a copy of the Japanese translation of Barthes's *Empire of Signs—Shirushi no Teikoku.* At the conference on "The Languages of Criticism and the Sciences of Man" held under the auspices of the Johns Hopkins Humanities Center in 1966 (the same year in which he visited Japan), Barthes spoke of a homology between language and culture and of the intersection between literature and linguistics as "semio-criticism." (See "To Write: An Intransitive Verb?" p. 135.)

12. See the author's paper "Misreading the Ideogram: From Fenollosa to Derrida and McLuhan," *Paideuma* [13 (1984), pp. 211–27]. In this connection, we should single out the following two important recent works on Japan. One is Noël Burch, *To the Distant Observer,* rev. and ed. Annette Michelson (Berkeley: University of California Press, 1979). Burch admires Barthes's *Empire of Signs* as "a pioneer text": "it is the first attempt by any Western writer to *read* the Japanese 'text' in the light of contemporary semiotics, . . ." (p. 13). After the fashion of Barthes, Burch treats the Japanese cinema as a system of signs, that is to say, he *textualizes* it. The other is William R. LaFleur, *The Karma of Words* (Berkeley: University of California Press, 1983). LaFleur's work is concerned with the interconnection between Buddhism and the literary arts in medieval Japan. Although his methodology is self-professedly one of the Foucauldian *episteme,* the intertextuality of the religious and the literary in terms of the Japanese concept of *funi* ("nondualism") in his analysis may be likened to the interdisciplinary spirit of Barthes. I am grateful to David Pollack of the University of Rochester for suggesting these two works to me.

13. There is another Confucian ethical term that is inseparably related to sincerity: it is *fidelity* that literally means "man standing by his word." It refers to the responsibility of the speaker to his word as ethical performance. The American poet and essayist Wendell Berry dwells on the ethics of fidelity in *Standing by Words* (San Francisco: North Point Press, 1983), pp. 24–63. Ivan Morris writes about the "tragic heroes in the history of Japan" from ancient times to the time of the *kamikaze* pilots based on this single idea of "sincerity" *(makoto)* which has its origin in Confucian philosophy. (See *The Nobility of Failure* [New York: Holt, Rinehart, and Winston, 1962.]) One would immediately recognize, therefore, that I am using the notion of sincerity in an extended sense. It is preeminently that moral concept which refers to the "unity of knowledge and action" *(chih hsing ho yi)* in Confucian thought: knowledge is the beginning of action and action is the completion of knowledge.

14. *The Fashion System,* trans. Matthew Ward and Richard Howard (New York: Hill and Wang, 1973), p. 258.

15. *Empire of Signs,* p. 29.

16. From the vantage point of Barthes's own semiology, one can say that the cover "fashions" or "dresses" the text of a book. However, when he was introducing the

drawings of the fashion designer Erté in 1972, Barthes commented that fashion only seeks "clarity" (not "voluptuousness") and the cover girl is not a good erotic object because she is too preoccupied with becoming a sign. (See Thody, *Roland Barthes*, pp. 99 and 192.)

17. Cf. Isshu Miura and Ruth Fuller Sasaki, *The Zen Koan: Its History and Use in Rinzai Zen* (New York: Harcourt, Brace and World, 1965), p. 3: "The living heart of all Buddhism is enlightenment or satori, and it is upon satori that Zen Buddhism is based. But Zen is not satori, nor is a satori Zen. Satori is the goal of Zen. Moreover, the satori that is the goal of Zen is not merely the satori experience; it is the satori experience deepened through training and directed to a definite end." It would be of some interest to note that "France" and "Buddhism" begin with the same ideogram—an accidental connection between Barthes the Frenchman and his interest in (Zen) Buddhism. In the most recent collection of critical essays, *L'Obvie et l'obtus* (Paris: Editions du Seuil, 1982), Barthes declares that "Distinguons . . . le *message*, qui veut produire une information, le *signe*, qui veut produire une intellection, et le *geste*, qui produit tout le reste (le 'supplément'), sans forcément vouloir produire quelque chose" (p. 148). *Le geste* is also a *satori* presumably because it produces without being forced to produce anything at all.

18. *Empire of Signs*, p. 4. A Zen master pondered for six years on the *koan* on *mu*. Then he suddenly achieved *satori* and composed the following "Dadaist" poem:

> Mu! Mu! Mu! Mu! Mu!
> Mu! Mu! Mu! Mu! Mu!
> Mu! Mu! Mu! Mu! Mu!
> Mu! Mu! Mu! Mu! Mu!

(See Ben-Ami Scharfstein, "Introduction/Zen: The Tactics of Emptiness," in Yoel Hoffman, trans., *The Sound of the One Hand* [New York: Basic Books, 1975], p. 26.) This book is a compilation of Zen *koan*(s) with answers. To fashion a semiological *koan:* If a semiological package is made of the wrapping ("sign") and the content ("message"), what is the "content" when the "wrapping" is all peeled off? (The answer, of course, is: *mu* or the void!) In *Mind and Nature* (New York: Dutton, 1979), Gregory Bateson emphasizes zero as a message when he writes: "the deep partial truth that 'nothing will come of nothing' in the world of information and organization encounters an interesting contradiction in the circumstance that *zero*, the complete absence of any indicative event, can be a message. . . . The letter that you do not write, the apology you do not offer, the food that you do not put out for the cat—all these can be sufficient and effective messages because zero, *in context*, can be meaningful; and it is the recipient of the message who creates the context" (pp. 46–47).

19. In recounting *Empire of Signs* to Guy Scarpetta in 1971, Barthes commented that "le zen est apparemment bouddhique, mais il n'est pas du côté du bouddhisme; le clivage dont je parle n'est pas celui de l'histoire des religions; c'est précisément celui des langues, du langage." (Roland Barthes, *Le Grain de la voix: Entretiens 1962–1980* [Paris: Editions du Seuil, 1981], p. 115.)

20. See "The Aesthetics of Silence," in *Styles of Radical Will* (New York: Farrar, Straus and Giroux, 1966), pp. 3–34. For Zen all verbalism essentially represents the

pollution of reality. See Miura and Sasaki, *The Zen Koan,* p. 35: "Zen is 'without words, without explanations, without instruction, without knowledge.' Zen is self-awakening only. Yet if we want to communicate something about it to others, we are forced to fall back upon words." The positive role of silence in human communication as an ontological issue is explored extensively in Bernard P. Dauenhauer, *Silence: The Phenomenon and Its Ontological Significance* (Bloomington, Ind: Indiana University Press, 1980).

21. In speaking of psychoanalysis as the "talking cure," Jacques Lacan regards "empty speech" as an impediment to the realization of the truth of the subject: "I have tackled the function of speech in analysis from its least rewarding angle, that of 'empty' speech, where the subject seems to be talking in vain about someone who, even if he were his spitting image, can never become one with the assumption of his desire. I have pointed out the source of the growing devaluation of which speech has been the object in both theory and technique." (*Ecrits: A Selection,* trans. Alan Sheridan [New York: W. W. Norton, 1977], pp. 45–46.) In *Love's Body* (New York: Vintage Books, 1968), Norman O. Brown speaks eloquently of the metaphysics of silence in the following passages: "The ego is loquacity, the interior monologue, the soliloquy which isolates. The way of silence leads to the extinction of the ego, mortification. To become empty, to become nothing; to be free from the constrictions of the self, to have no self, to be of no mind, to be a dead man. . . . The matrix in which the word is sown is silence. Silence is the mother tongue. . . . The meaning is not in the words but between the words, in the silence. . . . The virgin womb of the imagination in which the word becomes flesh is silence; and she remains a virgin. . . . The word is made flesh. To recover the world of silence, of symbolism, is to recover the human body. . . . The true meanings of words are bodily meanings, carnal knowledge; and the bodily meanings are the unspoken meanings. What is always speaking silently is the body" (pp. 264–65).

22. Daisetz Teitaro Suzuki, *Zen and Japanese Culture* (New York: Pantheon Books, 1959).

23. *Empire of Signs,* p. 75.

24. Barthes's own term would be "Sinic." The popular French "myth" of China as a "peculiar mixture of bells, rickshaws and opium dens" is referred to by Barthes as "Sininess" or "Sinity." (*Mythologies,* trans. Annette Lavers [New York: Hill and Wang, 1972], p. 121.)

25. "Calligraphy," Bernard Karlgren writes, "is the mother of Chinese pictorial art and always its intimate ally, and an expert calligrapher has always been just as much esteemed in China as a painter of the first rank. . . . From this close connexion between script and painting it follows that the Chinese artist, who often is both calligrapher and painter, loves to insert in his picture some lines of writing, which he employs with decorative effect in a masterly way." (*Sound and Symbol in Chinese* [London: Oxford University Press, 1923], p. 67.) Another unique, interesting side of Chinese ideography is the invention of a kind of the Rorschach test based on *tsukuriji* ("made-up words") to test the attitudes of the Japanese youth. (See George Fields, *From Bonsai to Levi's* [New York: Macmillan, 1982], pp. 102–5.)

26. Marshall McLuhan and Harley Parker, *Through the Vanishing Point: Space in Poetry and Painting* (New York: Harper and Row, 1968), p. 187.

27. R. G. Collingwood, *The Principles of Art* (Oxford: Clarendon Press, 1938), pp. 243–44.

28. See Barthes, *Le Grain de la voix*, "Sur '*S/Z*' et '*l'Empire des signes*,' " pp. 69–86.

29. The reason for Barthes's liking for *haiku* lies in the fact that it enables the signified to "evaporate" or disappear, and what is left is only a thin cloud of signifier (il ne reste plus qu'un mince nuage de significant). (*Le Grain de la voix*, p. 114.) The writing of *haiku* appears to be an act of *kenosis* or even "semioclasty." It should be noted, however, that Barthes seems to have been carried away with his enthusiasm of *haiku*, that is, his assertion that *haiku* is merely the literary branch of Zen is a little hyperbolic. According to Suzuki, for example, although they are exquisitely inter-fused, "*Haiku* and Zen . . . are not to be confused. *Haiku* is *haiku* and Zen is Zen. *Haiku* has its own field, it is poetry, but it also partakes of something of Zen, at the point where a *haiku* gets related to Zen." (*Zen and Japanese Culture*, p. 229.)

30. In relation to the importance of the surfacial, the following description by Liza Crihfield Dalby on *geisha* is relevant and appropriate: "Customers are expected to give a geisha an honorarium, but the cash (preferably a stiffly virgin 5,000-yen note or two) must first be folded into a decorative envelope. A crumpled bill fished from a pocket would hardly do." ("The Art of the Geisha," *Natural History* 92 [February 1983]: 49.) For her complete treatment of Japanese *geisha* culture based on her anthropological field work and personal experience as a *geisha*, see *Geisha* (Berkeley: University of California Press, 1983). The "sociological," "cultural," and "psychoan-alytical" approaches to the role of play or playing in relation to human reality is proposed by George Herbert Mead's *Mind, Self and Society*, ed. Charles W. Morris (Chicago: University of Chicago Press, 1934), Johan Huizinga's *Homo Ludens* (Boston: Beacon Press, 1955), and Donald Woods Winnicott's *Playing and Reality* (London: Tavistock, 1971). Notwithstanding their differences, they all treat playing as a universal element of human reality. Strictly speaking, *geisha asobi* as a nightly activity which began as a male entertainment for males is close structurally to Huizinga's conception of play as an intermezzo in the flow of normal, workaday life. However, I wish to use *asobi* in Winnicott's sense of *playing as doing*. He writes that "*Psycho-therapy takes place in the overlap of two areas of playing, that of the patient and that of the therapist. Psychotherapy has to do with two people playing together. The corollary of this is that where playing is not possible then the work done by the therapist is directed towards bringing the patient from a state of not being able to play into a state of being able to play,*" and that "*it is play that is the universal,* and that belongs to health: playing facilitates growth and therefore health; playing leads into group relationships; playing can be a form of communication in psychotherapy; and, lastly, psychoanaly-sis has been developed as a highly specialized form of playing in the service of com-munication with oneself and others" (*Playing and Reality*, pp. 38 and 41). I can see no reason why what is true with playing in psychoanalysis and psychotherapy cannot be true in (Barthes's) semiology.

31. In "Maoism, Psychoanalysis, and Hermeneutics: A Methodological Critique of the Interpretation of Cultures," *Asian Thought and Society* 9 (1984), pp. 143–67, Petee Jung and I challenge shallow cultural hermeneutics and conceptual overkill that ignore a cultural phenomenology of lived experience: we point to the facile trappings of cultural interpretation in relation to Maoism as the Sinicization of Marxism.

32. John Sturrock, "Roland Barthes," in *Structuralism and Since: From Lévi-Strauss to Derrida*, ed. John Sturrock (New York: Oxford University Press, 1979), p. 77.

33. Ibid., p. 78.

34. Chang Tung-sun, "A Chinese Philosopher's Theory of Knowledge," in *Our Language and Our World*, ed. S. I. Hayakawa (New York: Harper, 1959), pp. 299–324. During the course of modernization in the Meiji Restoration whose acceleration was sloganized by a group of Japanese intellectuals as "America our mother, France our father," the Japanese unity of the inner (indigenous) and the outer (foreign) was expressed as "Eastern morality" and "Western science and technology." There may indeed be the difference here between the Eastern "logic of correlation" and the Western "logic of identity."

35. An interesting contrast can be made between the eighteenth-century anatomical sketch of the *vena cava* cited by Barthes and the nineteenth-century Japanese acupuncture figure. The contrast between the two may be depicted as that of the *universal* "semiological" man and the *particular* "Japanese" man. The *vena cava* supplements Barthes's notion of how "to write the body"—"Neither the skin, nor the muscles, nor the bones, nor the nerves, but the rest: an awkward, fibrous, shaggy, raveled thing, a clown's coat." (See Roland Barthes, *Roland Barthes*, trans. Richard Howard [New York: Hill and Wang, 1977], p. 180.) Ironically, however, Barthes's *vena cava* reveals more of the inside "depth" of the body than its counterpart, the "surfacial" body of the Japanese acupuncture figure.

36. Cf. Dean MacCannel and Juliet Flower MacCannel who write that "we have adopted the stance that comparative cultural studies cannot make sense except as a contribution to a general semiotics of culture." (*The Time of the Sign* [Bloomington, Ind.: Indiana University Press, 1982], p. 3.) This semiotic Procrusteanism might easily, I am afraid, invite conceptual hypostatization that reverses the thesis that language and culture are the masters of linguistics and anthropology. One of the anecdotes of Zen monks published around the turn of this century is an instructive parable for conceptual hypostatization or eutrophication. The edited story begins with the ideogram "emptiness" *(ku, le vide)* which is followed by the title caption "A Cup of Tea." The Zen master Nan-in served tea to a university professor who was visiting him to inquire about Zen. Nan-in poured the visitor's cup full and then kept on pouring. Watching the overflow, the professor could no longer restrain himself and said: "It is overfull. No more will go in!" Thereupon Nan-in replied: "Like this cup, you are full of your own opinions and speculations. How can I show you Zen unless you first *empty* your cup?" (Paul Reps, *Zen Flesh, Zen Bones* [Rutland, Vt.: Tuttle, 1957], p. 19, italics mine.) Zen "emptying" to which Barthes himself is so attracted should serve as a deconstructive lesson for his semiological method. If by "metacommentary" we mean the piling of conceptual construction upon conceptual construction, moreover, the word in the subtitle of this paper too should be replaced with a *"koan"* or *"teisho"*—without the pretension of being a Zen master—on Barthes's *Empire of Signs*. It also should not escape our attention that "phenomenological reduction" *(epoche)* may be called *conceptual emptying*—the technique of "suspending" all prejudgments so that the observer may construct his thought based directly on actual experience rather than piling concept upon concept (i.e., conceptual sedimentation). Zen thinking *(nen)* is compared with phenomenological reduc-

tion in Katsuki Sekida, *Zen Training*, ed. A. V. Grimstone (New York: Weatherhill, 1975), pp. 188–92. It is of course beyond the scope of this paper to compare and elaborate on Zen and phenomenology including what, as contrasted with phenomenological reduction, Alfred Schutz calls the "*epoche* of the natural attitude" which suspends "doubt" rather than "belief" in the reality of the outer world. (See *Collected Papers*, vol. 1, *The Problem of Social Reality*, ed. Maurice Natanson [The Hague: Nighoff, 1962], p. 229.) Zen can be a free variation on both types of *epoche* and more.

37. For an emphasis on the system of intersubjective meanings relevant to our discussion here, see Charles Taylor, "Interpretation and the Sciences of Man," *The Review of Metaphysics* 25 (September 1971): 3–51; Paul Ricoeur, *Hermeneutics and the Human Sciences*, trans. John B. Thompson (New York: Cambridge University Press, 1981); and Clifford Geertz, *The Interpretation of Cultures* (New York: Basic Books, 1973), especially chap. 1, "Thick Description: Toward an Interpretive Theory of Culture," pp. 3–30 and *Local Knowledge* (New York: Basic Books, 1983), especially chap. 3, " 'From the Native's Point of View': On the Nature of Anthropological Understanding," pp. 55–70. In *The Conflict of Interpretations*, ed. Don Ihde (Evanston: Northwestern University Press, 1974), Paul Ricoeur develops most fully the idea of hermeneutical phenomenology as compared with structural semiology. Cf. David Carroll, *The Subject in Question* (Chicago: University of Chicago Press, 1982), p. 15: "The structuralist critic in his effort to be *for* language, *for* the 'text,' will be for the most part militantly antisubject. In fact the problem of the subject soon passes into obscurity, into a space radically outside that is no longer analyzed, no longer pertinent. The insistence on the subject and the whole problem of consciousness associated with it is considered by structuralists to have obscured, if not negated, the problem of language (the work of the signifier); and so now, through a reversal of the problematic, language negates, displaces, and replaces the subject as origin. The subject remains only as a skeleton of its former self, as a function of language." In *The Subject of Semiotics* (New York: Oxford University Press, 1983), Kaja Silverman explores the *human subject* as the *subject* of semiotics.

38. Cf. Dalby who writes that "it is often said with justification that Japanese food is more a feast for the eyes than for the palate, so even if I didn't get to taste the banquets I witnessed, I at least got to view the beautifully orchestrated composition of dishes" (*Geisha*, p. 113).

39. The expression *hors jeu* is used by Richard Macksey during the questioning of Jacques Derrida's talk entitled "Structure, Sign, and Play in the Discourse of the Human Sciences." (See Macksey and Donato, eds., *The Structuralist Controversy*, p. 268.) The limits of the "theatrical" understanding of the world is explored by Bruce Wilshire in *Role Playing and Identity* (Bloomington, Ind.: Indiana University Press, 1982).

40. Zenkei Shibayama, *Zen Comments on the Mumonkan*, trans. Sumiko Kudo (New York: Harper and Row, 1974), p. 10.

6

Under Western Eyes: Feminist Scholarship and Colonial Discourses

Chandra Talpade Mohanty

A NY DISCUSSION of the intellectual and political construction of "third world feminisms" must address itself to two simultaneous projects: the internal critique of hegemonic "Western" feminisms, and the formulation of autonomous, geographically, historically, and culturally grounded feminist concerns and strategies. The first project is one of deconstructing and dismantling; the second, one of building and constructing. While these projects appear to be contradictory, the one working negatively and the other positively, unless these two tasks are addressed simultaneously, "third world" feminisms run the risk of marginalization or ghettoization from both mainstream (right and left) and Western feminist discourses.

It is to the first project that I address myself. What I wish to analyze is specifically the production of the "third world woman" as a singular monolithic subject in some recent (Western) feminist texts. The definition of colonization I wish to invoke here is a predominantly *discursive* one, focusing on a certain mode of appropriation and codification of "scholarship" and "knowledge" about women in the third world by particular analytic categories employed in specific writings on the subject which take as their referent feminist interests as they have been articulated in the U.S and Western Europe. If one of the tasks of formulating and understanding the locus of "third world feminisms" is delineating the way in which it resists and *works against* what I am referring to as "Western feminist discourse," an analysis of the discursive construction of "third world women" in Western feminism is an important first step.

Clearly Western feminist discourse and political practice is neither singular nor homogeneous in its goals, interests, or analyses. However, it is possible to trace a coherence of *effects* resulting from the implicit assumption of "the West" (in all its complexities and contradictions) as the primary referent in theory and praxis. My reference to "Western feminism" is by no means intended to imply that it is a monolith. Rather, I am attempting to draw attention to the similar effects of various textual strategies used by writers which codify Others as non-Western and hence themselves as (implicitly) Western. It is in this sense that I use the term *Western feminist.* Similar arguments can be made in terms of middle-class urban African or Asian scholars producing scholarship on or about their rural or working-class sisters which assumes their own middle-class cultures as the norm, and codifies working-class histories and cultures as Other. Thus, while this essay focuses specifically on what I refer to as "Western feminist" discourse on women in the third world, the critiques I offer also pertain to third world scholars writing about their own cultures, which employ identical analytic strategies.

It ought to be of some political significance, at least, that the term *colonization* has come to denote a variety of phenomena in recent feminist and left writings in general. From its analytic value as a category of exploitative economic exchange in both traditional and contemporary Marxisms (cf. particularly contemporary theorists such as Baran 1962, Amin 1977, and Gunder-Frank 1967) to its use by feminist women of color in the U.S. to describe the appropriation of their experiences and struggles by hegemonic white women's movements (cf. especially Moraga and Anzaldúa 1983, Smith 1983, Joseph and Lewis 1981, and Moraga 1984), colonization has been used to characterize everything from the most evident economic and political hierarchies to the production of a particular cultural discourse about what is called the "third world."[1] However sophisticated or problematical its use as an explanatory construct, colonization almost invariably implies a relation of structural domination, and a suppression—often violent—of the heterogeneity of the subject(s) in question.

My concern about such writings derives from my own implication and investment in contemporary debates in feminist theory, and the urgent political necessity (especially in the age of Reagan/Bush) of forming strategic coalitions across class, race, and national boundaries. The analytic principles discussed below serve to distort Western feminist political practices, and limit the possibility of coalitions among (usually white) Western feminists and working-class feminists and feminists of color around the world. These limitations are evident in the construction of the (implicitly consensual) priority of issues around which apparently *all* women are expected to organize. The necessary and integral connection between feminist scholarship and feminist political practice and organizing determines the significance and status of Western feminist writings on women in the third world, for feminist scholarship, like most other kinds of scholarship, is not the mere production of knowledge about a certain subject. It is a directly political and discursive *practice* in that it is purposeful and ideological. It is best seen as a mode of intervention into particular hegemonic discourses (for example, traditional anthropology, sociology, literary criticism, etc.); it is a political praxis which counters and resists the totalizing imperative of age-old "legitimate" and "scientific" bodies of knowledge. Thus, feminist scholarly practices (whether reading, writing, critical, or textual) are inscribed in relations of power— relations which they counter, resist, or even perhaps implicitly support. There can, of course, be no apolitical scholarship.

The relationship between "Woman"—a cultural and ideological compos- ite Other constructed through diverse representational discourses (scientific, literary, juridical, linguistic, cinematic, etc.)—and "women"—real, material subjects of their collective histories—is one of the central questions the prac- tice of feminist scholarship seeks to address. This connection between women as historical subjects and the re-presentation of Woman produced by hegemonic discourses is not a relation of direct identity, or a relation of correspondence or simple implication.[2] It is an arbitrary relation set up by particular cultures. I would like to suggest that the feminist writings I analyze here discursively colonize the material and historical heterogeneities of the lives of women in the third world, thereby producing/re-presenting a com- posite, singular "third world woman"—an image which appears arbitrarily constructed, but nevertheless carries with it the authorizing signature of Western humanist discourse.[3]

I argue that assumptions of privilege and ethnocentric universality, on the one hand, and inadequate self-consciousness about the effect of Western scholarship on the "third world" in the context of a world system dominated by the West, on the other, characterize a sizable extent of Western feminist work on women in the third world. An analysis of "sexual difference" in the form of a cross-culturally singular, monolithic notion of patriarchy or male dominance leads to the construction of a similarly reductive and homoge- neous notion of what I call the "third world difference"—that stable, ahistor- ical something that apparently oppresses most if not all the women in these countries. And it is in the production of this "third world difference" that Western feminisms appropriate and "colonize" the constitutive complexities which characterize the lives of women in these countries. It is in this process of discursive homogenization and systematization of the oppression of women in the third world that power is exercised in much of recent Western feminist discourse, and this power needs to be defined and named.

In the context of the West's hegemonic position today, of what Anouar Abdel-Malek (1981) calls a struggle for "control over the orientation, regulation and decision of the process of world development on the basis of the advanced sector's monopoly of scientific knowledge and ideal creativity," Western feminist scholarship on the third world must be seen and examined precisely in terms of its inscription in these particular relations of power and struggle. There is, it should be evident, no universal patriarchal framework which this scholarship attempts to counter and resist—unless one posits an international male conspiracy or a monolithic, ahistorical power structure. There is, however, a particular world balance of power within which any analysis of culture, ideology, and socioeconomic conditions necessarily has to be situated. Abdel-Malek is useful here, again, in reminding us about the inherence of politics in the discourses of "culture":

> Contemporary imperialism is, in a real sense, a hegemonic imperialism, exercising to a maximum degree a rationalized violence taken to a higher level than ever before—through fire and sword, but also through the attempt to control hearts and minds. For its content is defined by the combined action of the military-industrial complex and the hegemonic cultural centers of the West, all of them founded on the advanced levels of development attained by monopoly and finance capital, and supported by the benefits of both the scientific and technological revolution and the second industrial revolution itself. (145–46)

Western feminist scholarship cannot avoid the challenge of situating itself and examining its role in such a global economic and political framework. To do any less would be to ignore the complex interconnections between first and third world economies and the profound effect of this on the lives of women in all countries. I do not question the descriptive and informative value of most Western feminist writings on women in the third world. I also do not question the existence of excellent work which does not fall into the analytic traps with which I am concerned. In fact I deal with an example of such work later on. In the context of an overwhelming silence about the experiences of women in these countries, as well as the need to forge international links between women's political struggles, such work is both pathbreaking and absolutely essential. However, it is both to the *explanatory potential* of particular analytic strategies employed by such writing, and to their *political effect* in the context of the hegemony of Western scholarship that I want to draw attention here. While feminist writing in the U.S. is still marginalized (except from the point of view of women of color addressing privileged white women), Western feminist writing on women in the third world must be considered in the context of the global hegemony of Western scholarship—i.e., the production, publication, distribution, and consumption of information and ideas. Marginal or not, this writing has political effects and implications beyond the immediate feminist or disciplinary audience. One such significant effect of the dominant "representations" of Western feminism is its conflation with imperialism in the eyes of particular third world women.[4] Hence the urgent need to examine the *political* implications of our *analytic* strategies and principles.

My critique is directed at three basic analytic principles which are present in (Western) feminist discourse on women in the third world. Since I focus primarily on the Zed Press Women in the Third World series, my comments on Western feminist discourse are circumscribed by my analysis of the texts in this series.[5] This is a way of focusing my critique. However, even though I am dealing with feminists who identify themselves as culturally or geographically from the "West," as mentioned earlier, what I say about these presuppositions or implicit principles holds for anyone who uses these methods, whether third world women in the West, or third world women in the third world writing on these issues and publishing in the West. Thus, I am not making a culturalist argument about ethnocentrism; rather, I am trying to uncover how ethnocentric universalism is produced in certain analyses. As a matter of fact, my argument holds for any discourse that sets up its own authorial subjects as the implicit referent, i.e., the yardstick by which to encode and represent cultural Others. It is in this move that power is exercised in discourse.

The first analytic presupposition I focus on is involved in the strategic location of the category "women" vis-à-vis the context of analysis. The assumption of women as an already constituted, coherent group with identical interests and desires, regardless of class, ethnic or racial location, or contradictions, implies a notion of gender or sexual difference or even patriarchy which can be applied universally and cross-culturally. (The context of analysis can be anything from kinship structures and the organization of labor to media representations.) The second analytical presupposition is evident on the methodological level, in the uncritical way "proof" of universality and cross-cultural validity are provided. The third is a more specifically political presupposition underlying the methodologies and the analytic strategies, i.e., the model of power and struggle they imply and suggest. I argue that as a result of the two modes—or, rather, frames—of analysis described above, a homogeneous notion of the oppression of women as a group is assumed, which, in turn, produces the image of an "average third world woman." This average third world woman leads an essentially truncated life based on her feminine gender (read: sexually constrained) and her being "third world" (read: ignorant, poor, uneducated, tradition-bound, domestic, family-oriented, victimized, etc.). This, I suggest, is in contrast to the (implicit) self-representation of Western women as educated, as modern, as having control over their own bodies and sexualities, and the freedom to make their own decisions.

The distinction between Western feminist re-presentation of women in the third world and Western feminist self-presentation is a distinction of the same order as that made by some Marxists between the "maintenance" function of the housewife and the real "productive" role of wage labor, or the characterization by developmentalists of the third world as being engaged in the lesser production of "raw materials" in contrast to the "real" productive activity of the first world. These distinctions are made on the basis of the privileging of a particular group as the norm or referent. Men involved in wage labor, first world producers, and, I suggest, Western feminists who sometimes cast third world women in terms of "ourselves undressed" (Michelle Rosaldo's [1980] term), all construct themselves as the normative referent in such a binary analytic.

"Women" as Category of Analysis, or: We Are All Sisters in Struggle

By women as a category of analysis, I am referring to the crucial assumption that all of us of the same gender, across classes and cultures, are somehow socially constituted as a homogeneous group identified prior to the process of analysis. This is an assumption which characterizes much feminist discourse. The homogeneity of women as a group is produced not on the basis of biological essentials but rather on the basis of secondary sociological and anthropological universals. Thus, for instance, in any given piece of feminist analysis, women are characterized as a singular group on the basis of a shared oppression. What binds women together is a sociological notion of the "sameness" of their oppression. It is at this point that an elision takes place between "women" as a discursively constructed group and "women" as material subjects of their own history.[6] Thus, the discursively consensual homogeneity of "women" as a group is mistaken for the historically specific material reality of groups of women. This results in an assumption of women as an always already constituted group, one which has been labeled "powerless," "exploited," "sexually harassed," etc., by feminist scientific, economic, legal, and sociological discourses. (Notice that this is quite similar to sexist discourse labeling women weak, emotional, having math anxiety, etc.) This focus is not on uncovering the material and ideological specificities that constitute a particular group of women as "powerless" in a particular context. It is, rather, on finding a variety of cases of "powerless" groups of women to prove the general point that women as a group are powerless.

In this section I focus on five specific ways in which "women" as a category of analysis is used in Western feminist discourse on women in the third world. Each of these examples illustrates the construction of "third world women" as a homogeneous "powerless" group often located as implicit *victims* of particular socioeconomic systems. I have chosen to deal with a variety of writers—from Fran Hosken, who writes primarily about female genital mutilation, to writers from the Women in International Development school, who write about the effect of development policies on third world women for both Western and third world audiences. The similarity of assumptions about "third world women" in all these texts forms the basis of my discussion. This is not to equate all the texts that I analyze, nor is it to equalize their strengths and weaknesses. The authors I deal with write with varying degrees of care and complexity; however, the *effect* of their representation of third world women is a coherent one. In these texts women are defined as victims of male violence (Fran Hosken); victims of the colonial process (Maria Cutrufelli); victims of the Arab familial system (Juliette Minces); victims of the economic development process (Beverley Lindsay and the [liberal] WID School); and finally, victims of *the* Islamic code (Patricia Jeffery). This mode of defining women primarily in terms of their *object status* (the way in which they are affected or not affected by certain institutions and systems) is what characterizes this particular form of the use of "women" as a category of analysis. In the context of Western women writing/studying women in the third world, such objectification (however benevolently motivated) needs to be both named and challenged. As Valerie Amos and Pratibha Parmar argue quite eloquently, "Feminist theories which examine our cultural practices as 'feudal residues' or label us 'traditional,' also portray us as politically immature women who need to be versed and schooled in the ethos of Western feminism. They need to be continually challenged . . ." (1984, 7).

Women as Victims of Male Violence

Fran Hosken, in writing about the relationship between human rights and female genital mutilation in Africa and the Middle East, bases her whole discussion/condemnation of genital mutilation on one privileged premise: that the goal of this practice is "to mutilate the sexual pleasure and satisfaction of woman" (1981, 11). This, in turn, leads her to claim that woman's sexuality is controlled, as is her reproductive potential. According to Hosken, "male sexual politics" in Africa and around the world "share the same political goal: to assure female dependence and subservience by any and all means" (14). Physical violence against women (rape, sexual assault, excision, infibulation, etc.) is thus carried out "with an astonishing consensus among men in the world" (14). Here, women are defined consistently as the *victims* of male control—the "sexually oppressed."[7] Although it is true that the potential of male violence against women circumscribes and elucidates their social position to a certain extent, defining women as archetypal victims freezes them into "objects-who-defend-themselves," men into "subjects-who-perpetrate-violence," and (every) society into powerless (read: women) and powerful (read: men) groups of people. Male violence must be theorized and interpreted *within* specific societies, in order both to understand it better and to effectively organize to change it.[8] Sisterhood cannot be assumed on the basis of gender; it must be forged in concrete historical and political practice and analysis.

Women as Universal Dependents

Beverly Lindsay's conclusion to the book *Comparative Perspectives of Third World Women: The Impact of Race, Sex and Class* (1983, 298, 306) states: "dependency relationships, based upon race, sex and class, are being perpetuated through social, educational, and economic institutions. These are the linkages among Third World Women." Here, as in other places, Lindsay implies that third world women constitute an identifiable group purely on the basis of shared dependencies. If shared dependencies were all that was needed to bind us together as a group, third world women would always be seen as an apolitical group with no subject status. Instead, if anything, it is the *common context* of political struggle against class, race, gender, and imperialist hierarchies that may constitute third world women as a strategic group at this historical juncture. Lindsay also states that linguistic and cultural differences exist between Vietnamese and black American women, but "both groups are victims of race, sex, and class." Again black and Vietnamese women are characterized by their victim status.

Similarly, examine statements such as "My analysis will start by stating that all African women are politically and economically dependent" (Cutrufelli 1983, 13), "Nevertheless, either overtly or covertly, prostitution is still the main if not the only source of work for African women" (Cutrufelli 1983, 33). *All* African women are dependent. Prostitution is the only work option for African women as a *group*. Both statements are illustrative of generalizations sprinkled liberally through a recent Zed Press publication, *Women of Africa: Roots of Oppression*, by Maria Rosa Cutrufelli, who is described on the cover as an Italian writer, sociologist, Marxist, and feminist. In the 1980s, is it possible to imagine writing a book entitled *Women of Europe: Roots of*

Oppression? I am not objecting to the use of universal groupings for descriptive purposes. Women from the continent of Africa can be descriptively characterized as "women of Africa." It is when "women of Africa" becomes a homogeneous sociological grouping characterized by common dependencies or powerlessness (or even strengths) that problems arise—we say too little and too much at the same time.

This is because descriptive gender differences are transformed into the division between men and women. Women are constituted as a group via dependency relationships vis-à-vis men, who are implicitly held responsible for these relationships. When "women of Africa" as a group (versus "men of Africa" as a group?) are seen as a group precisely because they are generally dependent and oppressed, the analysis of specific historical differences becomes impossible, because reality is always apparently structured by divisions—two mutually exclusive and jointly exhaustive groups, the victims and the oppressors. Here the sociological is substituted for the biological, in order, however, to create the same—a unity of women. Thus, it is not the descriptive potential of gender difference but the privileged positioning and explanatory potential of gender difference as the *origin* of oppression that I question. In using "women of Africa" (as an already constituted group of oppressed peoples) as a category of analysis, Cutrufelli denies any historical specificity to the location of women as subordinate, powerful, marginal, central, or otherwise, vis-à-vis particular social and power networks. Women are taken as a unified "powerless" group prior to the analysis in question. Thus, it is then merely a matter of specifying the context *after the fact.* "Women" are now placed in the context of the family, or in the workplace, or within religious networks, almost as if these systems existed outside the relations of women with other women, and women with men.

The problem with this analytic strategy, let me repeat, is that it assumes men and women are already constituted as sexual-political subjects prior to their entry into the arena of social relations. Only if we subscribe to this assumption is it possible to undertake analysis which looks at the "effects" of kinship structures, colonialism, organization of labor, etc., on women, who are defined in advance as a group. The crucial point that is forgotten is that women are produced through these very relations as well as being implicated in forming these relations. As Michelle Rosaldo argues, "woman's place in human social life is not in any direct sense a product of the things she does (or even less, a function of what, biologically, she is) but the meaning her activities acquire through concrete social interactions" (1980, 400). That women mother in a variety of societies is not as significant as the value attached to mothering in these societies. The distinction between the act of mothering and the status attached to it is a very important one—one that needs to be stated and analyzed contextually.

Married Women as Victims of the Colonial Process

In Lévi-Strauss's theory of kinship structure as a system of the exchange of women, what is significant is that exchange itself is not constitutive of the subordination of women; women are not subordinate because of the *fact* of exchange, but because of the *modes* of exchange instituted, and the values attached to these modes. However, in discussing the marriage ritual of the Bemba, a Zambian matrilocal, matrilineal people, Cutrufelli in *Women of Africa* focuses on the fact of the marital exchange of women before and after Western colonization, rather than the value attached to this exchange in this particular context. This leads to her definition of Bemba women as a coherent group affected in a particular way by colonization. Here again, Bemba women are constituted rather unilaterally as victims of the effects of Western colonization.

Cutrufelli cites the marriage ritual of the Bemba as a multistage event "whereby a young man becomes incorporated into his wife's family group as he takes up residence with them and gives his services in return for food and maintenance" (43). This ritual extends over many years, and the sexual relationship varies according to the degree of the girl's physical maturity. It is only after she undergoes an initiation ceremony at puberty that intercourse is sanctioned, and the man acquires legal rights over her. This initiation ceremony is the more important act of the consecration of women's reproductive power, so that the abduction of an uninitiated girl is of no consequence, while heavy penalty is levied for the seduction of an initiated girl. Cutrufelli asserts that the effect of European colonization has changed the whole marriage system. Now the young man is entitled to take his wife away from her people in return for money. The implication is that Bemba women have now lost the protection of tribal laws. However, while it is possible to see how the structure of the traditional marriage contract (versus the postcolonial marriage contract) offered women a certain amount of control over their marital relations, only an analysis of the political significance of the actual practice which privileges an initiated girl over an uninitiated one, indicating a shift in female power relations as a result of this ceremony, can provide an accurate account of whether Bemba women were indeed protected by tribal laws *at all times*.

However, it is not possible to talk about Bemba women as a homogeneous group within the traditional marriage structure. Bemba women *before* the initiation are constituted within a different set of social relations compared to Bemba women *after* the initiation. To treat them as a unified group characterized by the fact of their "exchange" between male kin is to deny the sociohistorical and cultural specificities of their existence, and the differential *value* attached to their exchange before and after their initiation. It is to treat the initiation ceremony as a ritual with no political implications or effects. It is also to assume that in merely describing the *structure* of the marriage contract, the situation of women is exposed. Women as a group are positioned within a given structure, but there is no attempt made to trace the effect of the marriage practice in constituting women within an obviously changing network of power relations. Thus, women are assumed to be sexual-political subjects prior to entry into kinship structures.

Women and Familial Systems

Elizabeth Cowie (1978), in another context, points out the implications of this sort of analysis when she emphasizes the specifically political nature of kinship structures which must be analyzed as ideological practices which designate men and women as father, husband, wife, mother, sister, etc. Thus, Cowie suggests, women as women are not *located* within the family. Rather, it is *in* the family, as an effect of kinship structures, that women as women are *constructed*, defined within and by the group. Thus, for instance, when Juliette Minces (1980) cites *the* patriarchal family as the basis for "an almost identical vision of women" that Arab and Muslim societies have, she falls into this very trap (see especially p. 23). Not only is it problematical to speak of a vision of women shared by Arab and Muslim societies (i.e., over twenty different countries) without addressing the particular historical, material, and ideological power structures that construct such images, but to speak of the patriarchal family or the tribal kinship structure as the origin of the socioeconomic status of women is to again assume that women are sexual-political subjects prior to their entry into the family. So while on the one hand women attain value or status within the family, the assumption of a singular patriarchal kinship system (common to all Arab and Muslim societies) is what apparently structures women as an oppressed group in these societies! This singular, coherent kinship system presumably influences another separate and given entity, "women." Thus, all women, regardless of class and cultural differences, are affected by this system. Not only are *all* Arab and Muslim women seen to constitute a homogeneous oppressed group, but there is no discussion of the specific *practices* within the family which constitute women as mothers, wives, sisters, etc. Arabs and Muslims, it appears, don't change at all. Their patriarchal family is carried over from the times of the prophet Mohammed. They exist, as it were, outside history.

Women and Religious Ideologies

A further example of the use of "women" as a category of analysis is found in cross-cultural analyses which subscribe to a certain economic reductionism in describing the relationship between the economy and factors such as politics and ideology. Here, in reducing the level of comparison to the economic relations between "developed and developing" countries, any specificity to the question of women is denied. Mina Modares (1981), in a careful analysis of women and Shi'ism in Iran, focuses on this very problem when she criticizes feminist writings which treat Islam as an ideology separate from and outside social relations and practices, rather than a discourse which includes rules for economic, social, and power relations within society. Patricia Jeffery's (1979) otherwise informative work on Pirzada women in purdah considers Islamic ideology a partial explanation for the status of women in that it provides a justification for the purdah. Here, Islamic ideology is reduced to a set of ideas whose internalization by Pirzada women contributes to the stability of the system. However, the primary explanation for purdah is located in the control that Pirzada men have over economic resources, and the personal security purdah gives to Pirzada women.

By taking a specific version of Islam as *the* Islam, Jeffery attributes a singularity and coherence to it. Modares notes, " 'Islamic Theology' then becomes imposed on a separate and given entity called 'women.' A further unification is reached: Women (meaning *all women*), regardless of their differing positions within societies, come to be affected or not affected by Islam. These conceptions provide the right ingredients for an unproblematic possibility of a cross-cultural study of women" (63). Marnia Lazreg makes a similar argument when she addresses the reductionism inherent in scholarship on women in the Middle East and North Africa:

> A ritual is established whereby the writer appeals to religion as *the* cause of gender inequality just as it is made the source of underdevelopment in much of modernization theory. In an uncanny way, feminist discourse on women from the Middle East and North Africa mirrors that of theologians' own interpretation of women in Islam. . . .
>
> The overall effect of this paradigm is to deprive women of self-presence, of being. Because women are subsumed under religion presented in fundamental terms, they are inevitably seen as evolving in nonhistorical time. They virtually have no history. Any analysis of change is therefore foreclosed. (1988, 87)

While Jeffery's analysis does not quite succumb to this kind of unitary notion of religion (Islam), it does collapse all ideological specificities into economic relations, and universalizes on the basis of this comparison.

Women and the Development Process

The best examples of universalization on the basis of economic reductionism can be found in the liberal "Women in Development" literature. Proponents of this school seek to examine the effect of development on third world women, sometimes from self-designated feminist perspectives. At the very least, there is an evident interest in and commitment to improving the lives of women in "developing" countries. Scholars such as Irene Tinker and Michelle Bo Bramsen (1972), Ester Boserup (1970), and Perdita Huston (1979) have all written about the effect of development policies on women in the third world.[9] All three women assume "development" is synonymous with "economic development" or "economic progress." As in the case of Minces's patriarchal family, Hosken's male sexual control, and Cutrufelli's Western colonization, development here becomes the all-time equalizer. Women are affected positively or negatively by economic development policies, and this is the basis for cross-cultural comparison.

For instance, Perdita Huston (1979) states that the purpose of her study is to describe the effect of the development process on the "family unit and its individual members" in Egypt, Kenya, Sudan, Tunisia, Sri Lanka, and Mexico. She states that the "problems" and "needs" expressed by rural and urban women in these countries all center around education and training, work and wages, access to health and other services, political participation, and legal rights. Huston relates all these "needs" to the lack of sensitive development policies which exclude women as a group or category. For her, the solution is simple: implement improved development policies which emphasize training for women fieldworkers, use women trainees, and women rural development officers, encourage women's cooperatives, etc. Here again, women are assumed to be a coherent group or category prior to their entry into "the development process." Huston assumes that all third world women have similar problems and needs. Thus, they must have similar interests and goals. However, the interests of urban, middle-class, educated Egyptian housewives, to take only one instance, could surely not be seen as being the same as those of their uneducated, poor maids. Development policies do not affect both groups of women in the same way. Practices which characterize women's status and roles vary according to class. Women are constituted as women through the complex interaction between class, culture, religion, and other ideological institutions and frameworks. They are not "women"—a coherent group—solely on the basis of a particular economic system or policy. Such reductive cross-cultural comparisons result in the colonization of the specifics of daily existence and the complexities of political interests which women of different social classes and cultures represent and mobilize.

Thus, it is revealing that for Perdita Huston, women in the third world countries she writes about have "needs" and "problems," but few if any have "choices" or the freedom to act. This is an interesting representation of women in the third world, one which is significant in suggesting a latent self-presentation of Western women which bears looking at. She writes, "What surprised and moved me most as I listened to women in such very different cultural settings was the striking commonality—whether they were educated or illiterate, urban or rural—of their most basic values: the importance they assign to family, dignity, and service to others" (1979, 115). Would Huston consider such values unusual for women in the West?

What is problematical about this kind of use of "women" as a group, as a stable category of analysis, is that it assumes an ahistorical, universal unity between women based on a generalized notion of their subordination. Instead of analytically *demonstrating* the production of women as socioeconomic political groups within particular local contexts, this analytical move limits the definition of the female subject to gender identity, completely bypassing social class and ethnic identities. What characterizes women as a group is their gender (sociologically, not necessarily biologically, defined) over and above everything else, indicating a monolithic notion of sexual difference. Because women are thus constituted as a coherent group, sexual difference becomes coterminous with female subordination, and power is automatically defined in binary terms: people who have it (read: men), and people who do not (read: women). Men exploit, women are exploited. Such simplistic formulations are historically reductive; they are also ineffectual in designing strategies to combat oppressions. All they do is reinforce binary divisions between men and women.

What would an analysis which did not do this look like? Maria Mies's work illustrates the strength of Western feminist work on women in the third world which does not fall into the traps discussed above. Mies's study of the lace makers of Narsapur, India (1982), attempts to carefully analyze a substantial household industry in which "housewives" produce lace doilies for consumption in the world market. Through a detailed analysis of the structure of the lace industry, production and reproduction relations, the sexual division of labor, profits and exploitation, and the overall consequences of defining women as "non-working housewives" and their work as "leisure-time activity." Mies demonstrates the levels of exploitation in this industry and the impact of this production system on the work and living conditions of the women involved in it. In addition, she is able to analyze the "ideology of the housewife," the notion of a woman sitting in the house, as providing the necessary subjective and sociocultural element for the creation and maintenance of a production system that contributes to the increasing pauperization of women, and keeps them totally atomized and disorganized as workers. Mies's analysis shows the effect of a certain historically and culturally specific mode of patriarchal organization, an organization constructed on the basis of the definition of the lace makers as "non-working housewives" at familial, local, regional, statewide, and international levels. The intricacies and the effects of particular power networks not only are emphasized, but they form the basis of Mies's analysis of how this particular group of women is situated at the center of a hegemonic, exploitative world market.

This is a good example of what careful, politically focused, local analyses can accomplish. It illustrates how the category of women is constructed in a variety of political contexts that often exist simultaneously and overlaid on top of one another. There is no easy generalization in the direction of "women" in India, or "women in the third world"; nor is there a reduction of the political construction of the exploitation of the lace makers to cultural explanations about the passivity or obedience that might characterize these women and their situation. Finally, this mode of local, political analysis which generates theoretical categories from within the situation and context being analyzed, also suggests corresponding effective strategies for organizing against the exploitation faced by the lace makers. Narsapur women are not mere victims of the production process, because they resist, challenge, and subvert the process at various junctures. Here is one instance of how Mies delineates the connections between the housewife ideology, the self-consciousness of the lace makers, and their interrelationships as contributing to the latent resistances she perceives among the women:

The persistence of the housewife ideology, the self-perception of the lace makers as petty commodity producers rather than as workers, is not only upheld by the structure of the industry as such but also by the deliberate propagation and reinforcement of reactionary patriarchal norms and institutions. Thus, most of the lace makers voiced the same opinion about the rules of *purdah* and seclusion in their communities which were also propagated by the lace exporters. In particular, the *Kapu* women said that they had never gone out of their houses, that women of their community could not do any other work than housework and lace work etc. but in spite of the fact that most of them still subscribed fully to the patriarchal norms of the *gosha* women, there were also contradictory elements in their consciousness. Thus, although they looked down with contempt upon women who were able to work outside the house—like the untouchable *Mala* and *Madiga* women or women of other lower castes, they could not ignore the fact that these women were earning more money precisely because they were *not* respectable housewives but workers. At one discussion, they even admitted that it would be better if they could also go out and do coolie work. And when they were asked whether they would be ready to come out of their houses and work in one place in some sort of a factory, they said they would do that. This shows that the *purdah* and housewife ideology, although still fully internalized, already had some cracks, because it has been confronted with several contradictory realities. (157)

It is only by understanding the *contradictions* inherent in women's location within various structures that effective political action and challenges can be devised. Mies's study goes a long way toward offering such analysis. While there are now an increasing number of Western feminist writings in this tradition,[10] there is also, unfortunately, a large block of writing which succumbs to the cultural reductionism discussed earlier.

Methodological Universalisms, or: Women's Oppression Is a Global Phenomenon

Western feminist writings on women in the third world subscribe to a variety of methodologies to demonstrate the universal cross-cultural operation of male dominance and female exploitation. I summarize and critique three such methods below, moving from the simplest to the most complex.

First, proof of universalism is provided through the use of an arithmetic method. The argument goes like this: the greater the number of women who wear the veil, the more universal is the sexual segregation and control of women (Deardon 1975, 4–5). Similarly, a large number of different, fragmented examples from a variety of countries also apparently add up to a universal fact. For instance, Muslim women in Saudi Arabia, Iran, Pakistan, India, and Egypt all wear some sort of a veil. Hence, this indicates that the sexual control of women is a universal fact in those countries in which the women are veiled (Deardon 1975, 7, 10). Fran Hosken writes, "Rape, forced prostitution, polygamy, genital mutilation, pornography, the beating of girls and women, purdah (segregation of women) are all violations of basic human rights" (1971, 15). By equating purdah with rape, domestic violence, and forced prostitution, Hosken asserts its "sexual control" function as the primary explanation for purdah, whatever the context. Institutions of purdah are thus denied any cultural and historical specificity, and contradictions and potentially subversive aspects are totally ruled out.

In both these examples, the problem is not in asserting that the practice of wearing a veil is widespread. This assertion can be made on the basis of numbers. It is a descriptive generalization. However, it is the analytic leap from the practice of veiling to an assertion of its general significance in controlling women that must be questioned. While there may be a physical similarity in the veils worn by women in Saudi Arabia and Iran, the specific meaning attached to this practice varies according to the cultural and ideological context. In addition, the symbolic space occupied by the practice of purdah may be similar in certain contexts, but this does not automatically indicate that the practices themselves have identical significance in the social realm. For example, as is well known, Iranian middle-class women veiled themselves during the 1979 revolution to indicate solidarity with their veiled working-class sisters, while in contemporary Iran, mandatory Islamic laws dictate that all Iranian women wear veils. While in both these instances, similar reasons might be offered for the veil (opposition to the Shah and Western cultural colonization in the first case, and the true Islamicization of Iran in the second), the concrete *meanings* attached to Iranian women wearing the veil are clearly different in both historical contexts. In the first case, wearing the veil is both an oppositional and a revolutionary gesture on the part of Iranian middle-class women; in the second case, it is a coercive, institutional mandate (see Tabari 1980 for detailed discussion). It is on the basis of such context-specific differentiated analysis that effective political strategies can be generated. To assume that the mere practice of veiling women in a number of Muslim countries indicates the universal oppression of women through sexual segregation not only is analytically reductive, but also proves quite useless when it comes to the elaboration of oppositional political strategy.

Second, concepts such as reproduction, the sexual division of labor, the family, marriage, household, patriarchy, etc., are often used without their specification in local cultural and historical contexts. Feminists use these concepts in providing explanations for women's subordination, apparently assuming their universal applicability. For instance, how is it possible to refer to "the" sexual division of labor when the *content* of this division changes radically from one environment to the next, and from one historical juncture to another? At its most abstract level, it is the fact of the differential assignation of tasks according to sex that is significant; however, this is quite different from the *meaning* or *value* that the content of this sexual division of labor assumes in different contexts. In most cases the assigning of tasks on the basis of sex has an ideological origin. There is no question that a claim such as "women are concentrated in service-oriented occupations in a large number of countries around the world" is descriptively valid. Descriptively, then, perhaps the existence of a similar sexual division of labor (where women work in service occupations such as nursing, social work, etc., and men in other kinds of occupations) in a variety of different countries can be asserted. However, the concept of the "sexual division of labor" is more than just a descriptive category. It indicates the differential *value* placed on "men's work" versus "women's work."

Often the mere existence of a sexual division of labor is taken to be proof of the oppression of women in various societies. This results from a confusion between and collapsing together of the descriptive and explanatory potential of the concept of the sexual division of labor. Superficially similar situations may have radically different, historically specific explanations, and cannot be treated as identical. For instance, the rise of female-headed households in middle-class America might be construed as a sign of great independence and feminist progress, whereby women are considered to have *chosen* to be single parents, there are increasing numbers of lesbian mothers, etc. However, the recent increase in female-headed households in Latin America,[11] where women might be seen to have more decision-making power, is concentrated among the poorest strata, where life choices are the most constrained economically. A similar argument can be made for the rise of female-headed families among black and Chicana women in the U.S. The positive correlation between this and the level of poverty among women of color and white working-class women in the U.S. has now even acquired a name: the feminization of poverty. Thus, while it is possible to state that there is a rise in female-headed households in the U.S. and in Latin America, this rise cannot be discussed as a universal indicator of women's independence, nor can it be discussed as a universal indicator of women's impoverishment. The *meaning* of and *explanation* for the rise obviously vary according to the sociohistorical context.

Similarly, the existence of a sexual division of labor in most contexts cannot be sufficient explanation for the universal subjugation of women in the work force. That the sexual division of labor does indicate a devaluation of women's work must be shown through analysis of particular local contexts. In addition, devaluation of *women* must also be shown through careful analysis. In other words, the "sexual division of labor" and "women" are not commensurate analytical categories. Concepts such as the sexual division of labor can be useful only if they are generated through local, contextual analyses (see Eldhom, Harris, and Young 1977). If such concepts are assumed to be universally applicable, the resultant homogenization of class, race, religious, and daily material practices of women in the third world can create a false sense of the commonality of oppressions, interests, and struggles between and among women globally. Beyond sisterhood there are still racism, colonialism, and imperialism!

Finally, some writers confuse the use of gender as a superordinate category of organizing analysis with the universalistic proof and instantiation of this category. In other words, empirical studies of gender differences are confused with the analytical organization of cross-cultural work. Beverly Brown's (1983) review of the book *Nature, Culture and Gender* (Strathern and McCormack 1980) best illustrates this point. Brown suggests that nature:culture and female:male are superordinate categories which organize and locate lesser categories (such as wild/domestic and biology/technology) within their logic. These categories are universal in the sense that they organize the universe of a system of representations. This relation is totally independent of the universal substantiation of any particular category. Her critique hinges on the fact that rather than clarify the generalizability of nature:culture :: female:male as subordinate organization categories, *Nature, Culture and Gender* construes the universality of this equation to lie at the level of empirical truth, which can be investigated through fieldwork. Thus, the usefulness of the nature:culture :: female:male paradigm as a universal mode of the organization of representation within any particular sociohistorical system is lost. Here, methodological universalism is assumed on the basis of the reduction of the nature:culture :: female:male analytic categories to a demand for empirical proof of its existence in different cultures. Discourses of representation are confused with material realities, and the distinction made earlier between "Woman" and "women" is lost. Feminist work which blurs this distinction (which is, interestingly enough, often present in certain Western feminists' self-representation) eventually ends up constructing monolithic images of "third world women" by ignoring the complex and mobile relationships between their historical materiality on the level of specific oppressions and political choices, on the one hand, and their general discursive representations, on the other.

To summarize: I have discussed three methodological moves identifiable in feminist (and other academic) cross-cultural work which seeks to uncover a universality in women's subordinate position in society. The next and final section pulls together the previous sections, attempting to outline the political effects of the analytical strategies in the context of Western feminist writing on women in the third world. These arguments are not against generalization as much as they are for careful, historically specific generalizations responsive to complex realities. Nor do these arguments deny the necessity of forming strategic political identities and affinities. Thus, while Indian women of different religions, castes, and classes might forge a political unity on the basis of organizing against police brutality toward women (see Kishwar and Vanita 1984), an *analysis* of police brutality must be contextual. Strategic coalitions which construct oppositional political identities for themselves are based on generalization and provisional unities, but the analysis of these group identities cannot be based on universalistic, ahistorical categories.

The Subject(s) of Power

This last section returns to an earlier point about the inherently political nature of feminist scholarship, and attempts to clarify my point about the possibility of detecting a colonialist move in the case of a hegemonic first-third world connection in scholarship. The nine texts in the Zed Press Women in the Third World series that I have discussed[12] focused on the following common areas in examining women's "status" within various societies: religion, family/kinship structures, the legal system, the sexual division of labor, education, and finally, political resistance. A large number of Western feminist writings on women in the third world focus on these themes. Of course the Zed texts have varying emphases. For instance, two of the studies, *Women of Palestine* (Downing 1982) and *Indian Women in Struggle* (Omvedt 1980), focus explicitly on female militance and political involvement, while *Women in Arab Society* (Minces 1980) deals with Arab women's legal, religious, and familial status. In addition, each text evidences a variety of methodologies and degrees of care in making generalizations. Interestingly enough, however, almost all the texts assume "women" as a category of analysis in the manner designated above.

Clearly this is an analytical strategy which is neither limited to these Zed Press publications nor symptomatic of Zed Press publications in general. However, each of the particular texts in question assumes "women" have a coherent group identity within the different cultures discussed, prior to their entry into social relations. Thus, Omvedt can talk about "Indian women" while referring to a particular group of women in the State of Maharashtra, Cutrufelli about "women of Africa," and Minces about "Arab women" as if these groups of women have some sort of obvious cultural coherence, distinct from men in these societies. The "status" or "position" of women is assumed to be self-evident, because women as an already constituted group are *placed* within religious, economic, familial, and legal structures. However, this focus whereby women are seen as a coherent group across contexts, regardless of class or ethnicity, structures the world in ultimately binary, dichotomous terms, where women are always seen in opposition to men, patriarchy is always necessarily male dominance, and the religious, legal, economic, and familial systems are implicitly assumed to be constructed by men. Thus, both men and women are always apparently constituted whole populations, and relations of dominance and exploitation are also posited in terms of whole peoples—wholes coming into exploitative relations. It is only when men and women are seen as different categories or groups possessing different *already constituted* categories of experience, cognition, and interests as *groups* that such a simplistic dichotomy is possible.

What does this imply about the structure and functioning of power relations? The setting up of the commonality of third world women's struggles across classes and cultures against a general notion of oppression (primarily the group in power—i.e., men) necessitates the assumption of what Michel Foucault (1980, 135–45) calls the "juridico-discursive" model of power, the principal features of which are "a negative relation" (limit and lack), an "insistence on the rule" (which forms a binary system), a "cycle of prohibition," the "logic of censorship," and a "uniformity" of the apparatus functioning at different levels. Feminist discourse on the third world which assumes a homogeneous category—or group—called women necessarily operates through the setting up of originary power divisions. Power relations are structured in terms of a unilateral and undifferentiated source of power and a cumulative reaction to power. Opposition is a generalized phenomenon created as a response to power—which, in turn, is possessed by certain groups of people.

The major problem with such a definition of power is that it locks all revolutionary struggles into binary structures—possessing power versus being powerless. Women are powerless, unified groups. If the struggle for a just society is seen in terms of the move from powerless to powerful for women as a *group,* and this is the implication in feminist discourse which structures sexual difference in terms of the division between the sexes, then the new society would be structurally identical to the existing organization of power relations, constituting itself as a simple *inversion* of what exists. If relations of domination and exploitation are defined in terms of binary divisions— groups which dominate and groups which are dominated—surely the implication is that the accession to power of women as a group is sufficient to dismantle the existing organization of relations? But women as a group are not in some sense essentially superior or infallible. The crux of the problem lies in that initial assumption of women as a homogeneous group or category ("the oppressed"), a familiar assumption in Western radical and liberal feminisms.[13]

What happens when this assumption of "women as an oppressed group" is situated in the context of Western feminist writing about third world women? It is here that I locate the colonialist move. By contrasting the representation of women in the third world with what I referred to earlier as Western feminisms' self-presentation in the same context, we see how Western feminists alone become the true "subjects" of this counterhistory. Third world women, on the other hand, never rise above the debilitating generality of their "object" status.

While radical and liberal feminist assumptions of women as a sex class might elucidate (however inadequately) the autonomy of particular women's struggles in the West, the application of the notion of women as a homogeneous category to women in the third world colonizes and appropriates the pluralities of the simultaneous location of different groups of women in social class and ethnic frameworks; in doing so it ultimately robs them of their historical and political *agency*. Similarly, many Zed Press authors who ground themselves in the basic analytic strategies of traditional Marxism also implicitly create a "unity" of women by substituting "women's activity" for "labor" as the primary theoretical determinant of women's situation. Here again, women are constituted as a coherent group not on the basis of "natural" qualities or needs but on the basis of the sociological "unity" of their role in domestic production and wage labor (see Haraway 1985, esp. p. 76). In other words, Western feminist discourse, by assuming women as a coherent, already constituted group which is placed in kinship, legal, and other structures, defines third world women as subjects *outside* social relations, instead of looking at the way women are constituted *through* these very structures.

Legal, economic, religious, and familial structures are treated as phenomena to be judged by Western standards. It is here that ethnocentric universality comes into play. When these structures are defined as "underdeveloped" or "developing" and women are placed within them, an implicit image of the "average third world woman" is produced. This is the transformation of the (implicitly Western) "oppressed woman" into the "oppressed third world woman." While the category of "oppressed woman" is generated through an exclusive focus on gender difference, "the oppressed third world woman" category has an additional attribute—the "third world difference!" The "third world difference" includes a paternalistic attitude toward women in the third world.[14] Since discussions of the various themes I identified earlier (kinship, education, religion, etc.) are conducted in the context of the relative "underdevelopment" of the third world (which is nothing less than unjustifiably confusing development with the separate path taken by the West in its development, as well as ignoring the directionality of the first-third world power relationship), third world women as a group or category are automatically and necessarily defined as religious (read "not progressive"), family-oriented (read "traditional"), legal minors (read "they-are-still-not-conscious-of-their-rights"), illiterate (read "ignorant"), domestic (read "backward"), and sometimes revolutionary (read "their-country-is-in-a-state-of-war; they-must-fight!") This is how the "third world difference" is produced.

When the category of "sexually oppressed women" is located within particular systems in the third world which are defined on a scale which is normed through Eurocentric assumptions, not only are third world women defined in a particular way prior to their entry into social relations, but since no connections are made between first and third world power shifts, the assumption is reinforced that the third world just has not evolved to the extent that the West has. This mode of feminist analysis, by homogenizing and systematizing the experiences of different groups of women in these countries, erases all marginal and resistant modes and experiences.[15] It is significant that none of the texts I reviewed in the Zed Press series focuses on lesbian politics or the politics of ethnic and religious marginal organizations in third world women's groups. Resistance can thus be defined only as cumulatively reactive, not as something inherent in the operation of power. If power, as Michel Foucault has argued recently, can really be understood only in the context of resistance,[16] this misconceptualization is both analytically and strategically problematical. It limits theoretical analysis as well as reinforces Western cultural imperialism. For in the context of a first/third world balance of power, feminist analyses which perpetrate and sustain the hegemony of the idea of the superiority of the West produce a corresponding set of universal images of the "third world woman," images such as the veiled woman, the powerful mother, the chaste virgin, the obedient wife, etc. These images exist in universal, ahistorical splendor, setting in motion a colonialist discourse which exercises a very specific power in defining, coding, and maintaining existing first/third world connections.

To conclude, then, let me suggest some disconcerting similarities between the typically authorizing signature of such Western feminist writings on women in the third world, and the authorizing signature of the project of humanism in general—humanism as a Western ideological and political project which involves the necessary recuperation of the "East" and "Woman" as Others. Many contemporary thinkers, including Foucault (1978, 1980), Derrida (1974), Kristeva (1980), Deleuze and Guattari (1977), and Said (1978), have written at length about the underlying anthropomorphism and ethnocentrism which constitute a hegemonic humanistic problematic that repeatedly confirms and legitimates (Western) Man's centrality. Feminist theorists such as Luce Irigaray (1981), Sarah Kofman (see Berg 1982), and Helene Cixous (1981) have also written about the recuperation and absence of woman/women within Western humanism. The focus of the work of all these thinkers can be stated simply as an uncovering of the political *interests* that underlie the binary logic of humanistic discourse and ideology whereby, as a valuable recent essay puts it, "the first (majority) term (Identity, Universality, Culture, Disinterestedness, Truth, Sanity, Justice, etc.), which is, in fact, secondary and derivative (a construction), is privileged over and colonizes the second (minority) term (difference, temporality, anarchy, error, interestedness, insanity, deviance, etc.), which is in fact, primary and originative" (Spanos 1984), In other words, it is only insofar as "Woman/Women" and "the East" are defined as *Others*, or as peripheral, that (Western) Man/Humanism can represent him/itself as the center. It is not the center that determines the periphery, but the periphery that, in its boundedness, determines the center. Just as feminists such as Kristeva and Cixous deconstruct the latent anthropomorphism in Western discourse, I have suggested a parallel strategy in this essay in uncovering a latent ethnocentrism in particular feminist writings on women in the third world.[17]

As discussed earlier, a comparison between Western feminist self-presentation and Western feminist re-presentation of women in the third world yields significant results. Universal images of "the third world woman" (the veiled woman, chaste virgin, etc.), images constructed from adding the "third world difference" to "sexual difference," are predicated upon (and hence obviously bring into sharper focus) assumptions about Western women as secular, liberated, and having control over their own lives. This is not to suggest that Western women *are* secular, liberated, and in control of their own lives. I am referring to a *discursive* self-presentation, not necessarily to material reality. If this were a material reality, there would be no need for political movements in the West. Similarly, only from the vantage point of the West is it possible to define the "third world" as underdeveloped and economically dependent. Without the overdetermined discourse that creates the *third* world, there would be no (singular and privileged) first world. Without the "third world woman," the particular self-presentation of Western women mentioned above would be problematical. I am suggesting, then, that the one enables and sustains the other. This is not to say that the signature of Western feminist writings on the third world has the same authority as the project of Western humanism. However, in the context of the hegemony of the Western scholarly establishment in the production and dissemination of texts, and in the context of the legitimating imperative of humanistic and scientific discourse, the definition of "the third world woman" as a monolith might well tie into the larger economic and ideological praxis of "disinterested" scientific inquiry and pluralism which are the surface manifestations of a latent economic and cultural colonization of the "non-Western" world. It is time to move beyond the Marx who found it possible to say: They cannot represent themselves; they must be represented.

Notes

This is an updated and modified version of an essay published in *Boundary 2* 12, no. 3/13, no. 1 (Spring/Fall 1984), and reprinted in *Feminist Review,* no. 30 (Autumn 1988). This essay would not have been possible without S. P. Mohanty's challenging and careful reading. I would also like to thank Biddy Martin for our numerous discussions about feminist theory and politics. They both helped me think through some of the arguments herein.

1. Terms such as *third* and *first world* are very problematical both in suggesting oversimplified similarities between and among countries labeled thus, and in implicitly reinforcing existing economic, cultural, and ideological hierarchies which are conjured up in using such terminology. I use the term *"third world"* with full awareness of its problems, only because this is the terminology available to us at the moment. The use of quotation marks is meant to suggest a continuous questioning of the designation. Even when I do not use quotation marks, I mean to use the term critically.

2. I am indebted to Teresa de Lauretis for this particular formulation of the project of feminist theorizing. See especially her introduction in de Lauretis, *Alice Doesn't: Feminism, Semiotics, Cinema* (Bloomington: Indiana University Press, 1984); see also Sylvia Wynter, "The Politics of Domination," unpublished manuscript.

3. This argument is similar to Homi Bhabha's definition of colonial discourse as strategically creating a space for a subject people through the production of knowledges and the exercise of power. The full quote reads: "[colonial discourse is] an apparatus of power. . . . an apparatus that turns on the recognition and disavowal of racial/cultural/historical differences. Its predominant strategic function is the creation of a space for a subject people through the production of knowledges in terms of which surveillance is exercised and a complex form of pleasure/unpleasure is incited. It (i.e. colonial discourse) seeks authorization for its strategies by the production of knowledges by coloniser and colonised which are stereotypical but antithetically evaluated" (1983, 23).

4. A number of documents and reports on the UN International Conferences on Women, Mexico City, 1975, and Copenhagen, 1980, as well as the 1976 Wellesley Conference on Women and Development, attest to this. Nawal el Saadawi, Fatima Mernissi, and Mallica Vajarathon (1978) characterize this conference as "American-planned and organized," situating third world participants as passive audiences. They focus especially on the lack of self-consciousness of Western women's implication in the effects of imperialism and racism in their assumption of an "international sisterhood." A recent essay by Valerie Amos and Pratibha Parmar (1984) characterizes as "imperial" Euro-American feminism which seeks to establish itself as the only legitimate feminism.

5. The Zed Press Women in the Third World series is unique in its conception. I choose to focus on it because it is the only contemporary series I have found which assumes that "women in the third world" are a legitimate and separate subject of study and research. Since 1985, when this essay was first written, numerous new titles

have appeared in the Women in the Third World series. Thus, I suspect that Zed has come to occupy a rather privileged position in the dissemination and construction of discourses by and about third world women. A number of the books in this series are excellent, especially those which deal directly with women's resistance struggles. In addition, Zed Press consistently publishes progressive feminist, antiracist, and antiimperialist texts. However, a number of the texts written by feminist sociologists, anthropologists, and journalists are symptomatic of the kind of Western feminist work on women in the third world that concerns me. Thus, an analysis of a few of these particular works in this series can serve as a representative point of entry into the discourse I am attempting to locate and define. My focus on these texts is therefore an attempt at an internal critique: I simply expect and demand more from this series. Needless to say, progressive publishing houses also carry their own authorizing signatures.

6. Elsewhere I have discussed this particular point in detail in a critique of Robin Morgan's construction of "women's herstory" in her introduction to *Sisterhood Is Global: The International Women's Movement Anthology* (New York: Anchor Press/ Doubleday, 1984). See my "Feminist Encounters: Locating the Politics of Experience," *Copyright* 1, "Fin de Siecle 2000," 30–44, especially 35–37.

7. Another example of this kind of analysis is Mary Daly's (1978) *Gyn/Ecology*. Daly's assumption in this text, that women as a group are sexually victimized, leads to her very problematic comparison between the attitudes toward women witches and healers in the West, Chinese footbinding, and the genital mutilation of women in Africa. According to Daly, women in Europe, China, and Africa constitute a homogeneous group as victims of male power. Not only does this label (sexual victims) eradicate the specific historical and material realities and contradictions which lead to and perpetuate practices such as witch hunting and genital mutilation, but it also obliterates the differences, complexities, and heterogeneities of the lives of, for example, women of different classes, religions, and nations in Africa. As Audre Lorde (1983) pointed out, women in Africa share a long tradition of healers and goddesses that perhaps binds them together more appropriately than their victim status. However, both Daly and Lorde fall prey to universalistic assumptions about "African women" (both negative and positive). What matters is the complex, historical range of power differences, commonalities, and resistances that exist among women in Africa which construct African women as "subjects" of their own politics.

8. See Eldhom, Harris, and Young (1977) for a good discussion of the necessity to theorize male violence within specific societal frameworks, rather than assume it as a universal fact.

9. These views can also be found in differing degrees in collections such as Wellesley Editorial Committee, ed., *Women and National Development: The Complexities of Change* (Chicago: University of Chicago Press, 1977), and *Signs,* Special Issue, "Development and the Sexual Division of Labor," 7, no. 2 (Winter 1981). For an excellent introduction of WID issues, see ISIS, *Women in Development: A Resource Guide for Organization and Action* (Philadelphia: New Society Publishers, 1984). For a politically focused discussion of feminism and development and the stakes for poor third world women, see Gita Sen and Caren Grown, *Development Crises and Alternative Visions: Third World Women's Perspectives* (New York: Monthly Review Press, 1987).

10. See essays by Vanessa Maher, Diane Elson and Ruth Pearson, and Maila Stevens in Kate Young, Carol Walkowitz, and Roslyn McCullagh, eds., *Of Marriage and the Market: Women's Subordination in International Perspective* (London: CSE Books, 1981); and essays by Vivian Mota and Michelle Mattelart in June Nash and Helen I. Safa, eds., *Sex and Class in Latin America: Women's Perspectives on Politics, Economics and the Family in the Third World* (South Hadley, Mass.: Bergin and Garvey, 1980). For examples of excellent, self-conscious work by feminists writing about women in their own historical and geographical locations, see Marnia Lazreg (1988) on Algerian women, Gayatri Chakravorty Spivak's "A Literary Representation of the Subaltern: A Woman's Text from the Third World," in her *In Other Worlds: Essays in Cultural Politics* (New York: Methuen, 1987), 241–68, and Lata Mani's essay "Contentious Traditions: The Debate on SATI in Colonial India," *Cultural Critique* 7 (Fall 1987), 119–56.

11. Olivia Harris, "Latin American Women—An Overview," in Harris, ed., *Latin American Women* (London: Minority Rights Group Report no. 57, 1983), 4–7. Other MRG Reports include Ann Deardon (1975) and Rounaq Jahan (1980).

12. List of Zed Press publications: Patricia Jeffery, *Frogs in a Well: Indian Women in Purdah* (1979); Latin American and Caribbean Women's Collective, *Slaves of Slaves: The Challenge of Latin American Women* (1980); Gail Omvedt, *We Shall Smash This Prison: Indian Women in Struggle* (1980); Juliette Minces, *The House of Obedience: Women in Arab Society* (1980); Bobby Siu, *Women of China: Imperialism and Women's Resistance, 1900–1949* (1981); Ingela Bendt and James Downing, *We Shall Return: Women in Palestine* (1982); Maria Rosa Cutrufelli, *Women of Africa: Roots of Oppression* (1983); Maria Mies, *The Lace Makers of Narsapur: Indian Housewives Produce for the World Market* (1982); Miranda Davis, ed., *Third World/Second Sex: Women's Struggles and National Liberation* (1983).

13. For succinct discussions of Western radical and liberal feminisms, see Hester Eisenstein, *Contemporary Feminist Thought* (Boston: G. K. Hall & Co., 1983), and Zillah Eisenstein, *The Radical Future of Liberal Feminism* (New York: Longman, 1981).

14. Amos and Parmar describe the cultural stereotypes present in Euro-American feminist thought: "The image is of the passive Asian woman subject to oppressive practices within the Asian family with an emphasis on wanting to 'help' Asian women liberate themselves from their role. Or there is the strong, dominant Afro-Caribbean woman, who despite her 'strength' is exploited by the 'sexism' which is seen as being a strong feature in relationships between Afro-Caribbean men and women" (9). These images illustrate the extent to which *paternalism* is an essential element of feminist thinking which incorporates the above stereotypes, a paternalism which can lead to the definition of priorities for women of color by Euro-American feminists.

15. I discuss the question of theorizing experience in my "Feminist Encounters" (1987) and in an essay coauthored with Biddy Martin, "Feminist Politics: What's Home Got to Do with It?" in Teresa de Lauretis, ed., *Feminist Studies/Critical Studies* (Bloomington: Indiana University Press, 1986), 191–212.

16. This is one of M. Foucault's (1978, 1980) central points in his reconceptualization of the strategies and workings of power networks.

17. For an argument which demands a *new* conception of humanism in work on

third world women, see Marnia Lazreg (1988). While Lazreg's position might appear to be diametrically opposed to mine, I see it as a provocative and potentially positive extension of some of the implications that follow from my arguments. In criticizing the feminist rejection of humanism in the name of "essential Man," Lazreg points to what she calls an "essentialism of difference" within these very feminist projects. She asks: "To what extent can Western feminism dispense with an ethics of responsibility when writing about different women? The point is neither to subsume other women under one's own experience nor to uphold a separate truth for them. Rather, it is to allow them to *be* while recognizing that what they are is just as meaningful, valid, and comprehensible as what we are. . . . Indeed, when feminists essentially deny other women the humanity they claim for themselves, they dispense with any ethical constraint. They engage in the act of splitting the social universe into us and them, subject and objects" (99–100).

This essay by Lazreg and an essay by S. P. Mohanty (1989) entitled "Us and Them: On the Philosophical Bases of Political Criticism" suggest positive directions for self-conscious cross-cultural analyses, analyses which move beyond the deconstructive to a fundamentally productive mode in designating overlapping areas for cross-cultural comparison. The latter essay calls not for a "humanism" but for a reconsideration of the question of the "human" in a posthumanist context. It argues that (1) there is no necessary "incompatibility between the deconstruction of Western humanism" and such "a positive elaboration" of the human, and moreover that (2) such an elaboration is essential if contemporary political-critical discourse is to avoid the incoherences and weaknesses of a relativist position.

References List

Abdel-Malek, Anouar. 1981. *Social Dialectics: Nation and Revolution.* Albany: State University of New York Press.

Amin, Samir. 1977. *Imperialism and Unequal Development.* New York: Monthly Review Press.

Amos, Valerie, and Pratibha Parmar. 1984. "Challenging Imperial Feminism." *Feminist Review* 17:3–19.

Baran, Paul A. 1962. *The Political Economy of Growth.* New York: Monthly Review Press.

Berg, Elizabeth. 1982. "The Third Woman." *Diacritics* (Summer):11–20.

Bhabha, Homi. 1983. "The Other Question—The Stereotype and Colonial Discourse." *Screen* 24, no. 6:23.

Boserup, Ester. 1970. *Women's Role in Economic Development.* New York: St. Martin's Press; London: Allen and Unwin.

Brown, Beverly. 1983. "Displacing the Difference—Review, *Nature, Culture and Gender.*" *m/f* 8:79–89.

Cixous, Helene. 1981. "The Laugh of the Medusa." In Marks and De Courtivron (1981).

Cowie, Elizabeth. 1978. "Woman as Sign." *m/f* 1:49–63.

Cutrufelli, Maria Rosa. 1983. *Women of Africa: Roots of Oppression*. London: Zed Press.

Daly, Mary. 1978. *Gyn/Ecology: The Metaethics of Radical Feminism*. Boston: Beacon Press.

Deardon, Ann, ed. 1975. *Arab Women*. London: Minority Rights Group Report no. 27.

de Lauretis, Teresa. 1984. *Alice Doesn't: Feminism, Semiotics, Cinema*. Bloomington: Indiana University Press.

———. 1986. *Feminist Studies/Critical Studies*. Bloomington: Indiana University Press.

Deleuze, Gilles, and Felix Guattari. 1977. *Anti-Oedipus: Capitalism and Schizophrenia*. New York: Viking.

Derrida, Jacques. 1974. *Of Grammatology*. Baltimore: Johns Hopkins University Press.

Eisenstein, Hester. 1983. *Contemporary Feminist Thought*. Boston: G. K. Hall and Co.

Eisenstein, Zillah. 1981. *The Radical Future of Liberal Feminism*. New York: Longman.

Eldhom, Felicity, Olivia Harris, and Kate Young. 1977. "Conceptualising Women." *Critique of Anthropology "Women's Issue"*, no. 3.

el Saadawi, Nawal, Fatima Mernissi, and Mallica Vajarathon. 1978. "A Critical Look at the Wellesley Conference." *Quest* 4, no. 2 (Winter):101–107.

Foucault, Michel. 1978. *History of Sexuality: Volume One*. New York: Random House.

———. 1980. *Power/Knowledge*. New York: Pantheon.

Gunder-Frank, Audre. 1967. *Capitalism and Underdevelopment in Latin America*. New York: Monthly Review Press.

Haraway, Donna. 1985. "A Manifesto for Cyborgs: Science, Technology and Socialist Feminism in the 1980s." *Socialist Review* 80 (March/April):65–108.

Harris, Olivia. 1983a. "Latin American Women—An Overview." In Harris (1983b).

———. 1983b. *Latin American Women*. London: Minority Rights Group Report no. 57.

Hosken, Fran. 1981. "Female Genital Mutilation and Human Rights." *Feminist Issues* 1, no. 3.

Huston, Perdita. 1979. *Third World Women Speak Out*. New York: Praeger.

Irigaray, Luce. 1981. "This Sex Which Is Not One" and "When the Goods Get Together." In Marks and De Courtivron (1981).

Jahan, Rounaq, ed. 1980. *Women in Asia*. London: Minority Rights Groups Report no. 45.

Jeffery, Patricia. 1979. *Frogs in a Well: Indian Women in Purdah*. London: Zed Press.

Joseph, Gloria, and Jill Lewis. 1981. *Common Differences: Conflicts in Black and White Feminist Perspectives*. Boston: Beacon Press.

Kishwar, Madhu, and Ruth Vanita. 1984. *In Search of Answers: Indian Women's Voices from Manushi*. London: Zed Press.

Kristeva, Julia. 1980. *Desire in Language*. New York: Columbia University Press.

Lazreg, Marnia. 1988. "Feminism and Difference: The Perils of Writing as a Woman on Women in Algeria." *Feminist Issues* 14, no. 1 (Spring):81–107.

Lindsay, Beverley, ed. 1983. *Comparative Perspectives of Third World Women: The Impact of Race, Sex and Class*. New York: Praeger.

Lorde, Audre. 1983. "An Open Letter to Mary Daly." In Moraga and Anzaldua (1983), 94–97.

Marks, Elaine, and Isabel De Courtivron. 1981. *New French Feminisms.* New York: Schocken Books.

Mies, Maria. 1982. *The Lace Makers of Narsapur: Indian Housewives Produce for the World Market.* London: Zed Press.

Minces, Juliette. 1980. *The House of Obedience: Women in Arab Society.* London: Zed Press.

Modares, Mina. 1981. "Women and Shi'ism in Iran." *m/f* 5 and 6:61–82.

Mohanty, Chandra Talpade. 1987. "Feminist Encounters: Locating the Politics of Experience." *Copyright* 1, "Fin de Siecle 2000," 30–44.

Mohanty, Chandra Talpade, and Biddy Martin. 1986. "Feminist Politics: What's Home Got to Do with It?" In de Lauretis (1986).

Mohanty, S. P. 1989. "Us and Them: On the Philosophical Bases of Political Criticism." *Yale Journal of Criticism* 2 (March):1–31.

Moraga, Cherríe. 1984. *Loving in the War Years.* Boston: South End Press.

Moraga, Cherríe, and Gloria Anzaldúa, eds. 1983. *This Bridge Called My Back: Writings by Radical Women of Color.* New York: Kitchen Table Press.

Morgan, Robin, ed. 1984. *Sisterhood Is Global: The International Women's Movement Anthology.* New York: Anchor Press/Doubleday; Harmondsworth: Penguin.

Nash, June, and Helen I. Safa, eds. 1980. *Sex and Class in Latin America: Women's Perspectives on Politics, Economics and the Family in the Third World.* South Hadley, Mass.: Bergin and Garvey.

Rosaldo, M. A. 1980. "The Use and Abuse of Anthropology: Reflections on Feminism and Cross-Cultural Understanding." *Signs* 53:389–417.

Said, Edward. 1978. *Orientalism.* New York: Random House.

Sen, Gita, and Caren Grown. 1987. *Development Crises and Alternative Visions: Third World Women's Perspectives.* New York: Monthly Review Press.

Smith, Barbara, ed. 1983. *Home Girls: A Black Feminist Anthology.* New York: Kitchen Table Press.

Spanos, William V. 1984. "Boundary 2 and the Polity of Interest: Humanism, the 'Center Elsewhere' and Power." *Boundary 2* 12, no. 3/13, no. 1 (Spring/Fall).

Spivak, Gayatri Chakravorty. 1987. *In Other Worlds: Essays in Cultural Politics.* London and New York: Methuen.

Strathern, Marilyn, and Carol McCormack, eds. 1980. *Nature, Culture and Gender.* Cambridge: Cambridge University Press.

Tabari, Azar. 1980. "The Enigma of the Veiled Iranian Women." *Feminist Review* 5:19–32.

Tinker, Irene, and Michelle Bo Bramsen, eds. 1972. *Women and World Development.* Washington, D.C.: Overseas Development Council.

Young, Kate, Carol Walkowitz, and Roslyn McCullagh, eds. 1981. *Of Marriage and the Market: Women's Subordination in International Perspective.* London: CSE Books.

Part II
Asian Thought in the Age of Globalization

7

Can Asians Think?

Kishore Mahbubani

C AN ASIANS THINK? This is obviously a sensitive question. In this age of political correctness that we live in, just imagine the uproar that could be caused if I went to Europe or Africa and posed the question "Can Europeans think?" or "Can Africans think?" You have to be Asian to ask the question "Can Asians think?"

Given its sensitivity, let me explain both the reasons why and the context in which I am posing the question. First, if you had to ask one single, key question that could determine the future of the globe, it may well be "Can Asians think?" In 1996 Asians already made up 3.5 billion out of a global population of over 5 billion (or about 70 percent of the world population). By conservative projections, the Asian portion of the world population will increase to 5.7 billion in 2050 out of a global population of 9.87 billion, while the populations of North America and Europe will remain relatively constant at 374 million and 721 million respectively. Clearly, in the past few centuries Europe and, more recently, North America have carried the larger share of the global burden in advancing human civilisation. By 2050, when Europeans and North Americans make up one-tenth instead of one-sixth of the world's population, would it be fair for the remaining 90 percent of mankind to expect this 10 percent to continue to bear this burden? Realistically, can the rest of the world continue to rest on the shoulders of the West? If Asians double in population in the next 50 years, will they be able to carry their fair share of this burden?

Second, I am not asking this question about individual Asians in terms of limited thinking abilities. Clearly, Asians can master alphabets, add two plus two to make four, and play chess. However, throughout history, there have been examples of societies that have produced brilliant individuals yet experienced a lot of grief collectively. The classic example of this is Jewish society.

— 191 —

Per capita, Jews have contributed more brilliant minds, from Einstein to Wittgenstein, from Disraeli to Kissinger, than any other society. Yet, as a society they have suffered greatly, especially in the past century or so. Let me stress that I am not speaking about the travails of Israel in modern times. I am speaking of the period from A.D. 135, when the Jews were forced to leave Palestine, to 1948, when Israel was born. Will a similar fate befall Asian societies, or will they be able to think well and ensure a better future for themselves?

Third, the time scale in which I am posing this question is not in terms of days, weeks, months, years or even decades. I am looking at the question from the time scale of centuries, especially since we stand two years away from the new millennium. Arguably, the future course of world history in the next few centuries, as I will explain later, will depend on how Asian societies think and perform.

Back to the question "Can Asians think?" In a multiple-choice examination format, there would be three possible answers to the question: "Yes", "No" or "Maybe". Before we decide which choice to tick, let me make a case for each answer.

No, They Cannot Think

I will start with the reasons for the "No" answer, if only to refute any critics who may suggest that the question itself is manifestly absurd. If one looks at the record of the past thousand years, one can make a very persuasive case that Asians, Asian societies that is, cannot think.

Let us look at where Asian societies were 1,000 years ago, say in the year 997. Then, the Chinese and the Arabs (i.e., Confucian and Islamic civilisations) led the way in science and technology, medicine and astronomy. The Arabs adopted both the decimal system and the numbers 0 to 9 from India, and they learned how to make paper from the Chinese. The world's first university was founded just over 1,000 years ago, in the year 971, in Cairo. By contrast, Europe was then still in what has been described as the "Dark Ages", which had begun when the Roman Empire collapsed in the fifth century. As Will Durant puts it in *The Age of Faith:*

> Western Europe in the sixth century was a chaos of conquest, disintegration, and rebarbarization. Much of the classic culture survived, for the most part silent and hidden in a few monasteries and families. But the physical and psychological foundations of social order had been so disturbed that centuries would be needed to restore them. Love of letters, devotion to art, the unity and continuity of culture, the cross-fertilization of communicating minds, fell

before the convulsions of war, the perils of transport, the economies of poverty, the rise of vernaculars, the disappearance of Latin from the East and of Greek from the West.[1]

Against this backdrop, it would have been sheer folly to predict at the time that in the second millennium Chinese, Indian and Islamic civilisations would slip into the backwaters of history while Europe would rise to be the first civilisation ever to dominate the entire globe. But that, of course, is precisely what happened.

It did not come about suddenly. Until about the 16th century, the more advanced societies of Asia, while they had lost their primacy, were still on a par with those of Europe and there was no definite indication that Europe would leap far ahead. At that time, Europe's relative weaknesses were more apparent than its strengths. It was not the most fertile area of the world, nor was it particularly populous—important criteria by the measure of the day, when the soil was the source of most wealth, and human and animal muscle of most power. Europe exhibited no pronounced advantages in the fields of culture, mathematics, or engineering, navigation or other technologies. It was also a deeply fragmented continent, consisting of a hodgepodge of petty kingdoms, principalities and city-states. Further, at the end of the 15th century, Europe was in the throes of a bloody conflict with the mighty Ottoman Empire, which was pushing its way, inexorably it seemed, towards the gates of Vienna. So perduring was this threat that German princes hundreds of kilometres from the front lines had got into the custom of sending tribute— *Turkenverehrung*—to the Sublime Porte in Istanbul.

Asian cultures, on the other hand, appeared to be thriving in the 15th century. China, for example, had a highly developed and vibrant culture. Its unified, hierarchic administration was run by well-educated Confucian bureaucrats who had given a coherence and sophistication to Chinese society that was unparalleled. China's technological prowess was also formidable. Printing by movable type had already appeared in the 11th century. Paper money had expedited the flow of commerce and growth of markets. China's gargantuan iron industry, coupled with the invention of gunpowder, gave it immense military strength.

However, almost amazingly, it was Europe that leapt ahead. Something almost magical happened to European minds, and this was followed by wave after wave of progress and advance of civilisations, from the Renaissance to the Enlightenment, from the scientific revolution to the industrial revolution. While Asian societies degenerated into backwardness and ossification, European societies, propelled forward by new forms of economic organisation, military-technical dynamism, political pluralism within the continent as a whole (if not within all individual countries), and the uneven beginnings of intellectual liberty, notably in Italy, Britain and Holland, produced what would have been called at the time the "European miracle"—had there been an observing, superior civilisation to mark the event. Because that mix of critical ingredients did not exist in any of the Asian societies, they appeared to stand still while Europe advanced to the centre of the world stage. Colonisation, which began in the 16th century, and the industrial revolution in the 19th century, augmented and entrenched Europe's dominant position.

To me, coming from Singapore, with a population of 3 million, it is a source of great wonder that a small state like Portugal, also with a population of a few million, could carve out territories like Goa, Macau and Malacca from larger and more ancient civilisations. It was an amazing feat. But what is more amazing is that it was done in the 1500s. The Portuguese colonisers were followed by the Spanish, the Dutch, the French, then the British. Throughout this period, for almost three centuries or more, Asian societies lay prostrate and allowed themselves to be surpassed and colonised by far smaller societies.

The most painful thing that happened to Asia was not the physical but the mental colonisation. Many Asians (including, I fear, many of my ancestors from South Asia) began to believe that Asians were inferior beings to the Europeans. Only this could explain how a few thousand British could control a few hundred million people in South Asia. If I am allowed to make a controversial point here, I would add that this mental colonisation has not been completely eradicated in Asia, and many Asian societies are still struggling to break free.

It is truly astonishing that even today, as we stand on the eve of the 21st century, 500 years after the arrival of the first Portuguese colonisers in Asia, only one—I repeat, one—Asian society has reached, in a comprehensive sense, the level of development that prevails generally in Europe and North America today. The Japanese mind was the first to be awakened in Asia, beginning with the Meiji Restoration in the 1860s. Japan was first considered developed and more or less accepted as an equal by 1902, when it signed the Anglo-Japanese alliance.

If Asian minds can think, why is there today only one Asian society able to catch up with the West? I rest my case for the negative answer to our question. Those of you who want to tick "No" to the question "Can Asians think?" can proceed to do so.

Yes, They Can

Let me now try to draw out the arguments why we might answer "Yes" to the question "Can Asians think?"

The first, and the most obvious one, is the incredible economic performance of East Asian societies in the past few decades. Japan's success, while it has not been fully replicated in the rest of Asia, has set off ripples that now, current problems notwithstanding, have the potential to become tidal waves. Japan's economic success was first followed by the emergence of the "four tigers" (South Korea, Taiwan, Hong Kong and Singapore). But the success of these four tigers convinced other Southeast Asian countries, especially Indonesia, Malaysia and Thailand, that they could do the same. Lately they have been followed by China, which now has the potential to overtake the United States and become the world's largest economy by 2020. What is amazing is the pace of economic development. It took the British 58 years (from 1780), America 47 years (from 1839) and Japan 33 years (from the 1880s) to double their economic output. On the other hand, it took Indonesia 17 years, South Korea 11 years and China 10 years to do the same. As a whole, the East Asian miracle economies grew more rapidly and more consistently than any other group of economies in the world from 1960 to 1990. They averaged 5.5 percent annual per capita real income growth, outperforming every economy in Latin America and Sub-Saharan Africa and even the OECD economies, which averaged only 2.5 percent growth in that period.

You cannot get good grades in an examination by luck. It requires intelligence and hard work. Similarly, you cannot get good economic performance, especially of the scale seen in Asia, simply by luck. It reflects both intelligence and hard work. And it is vital to stress here that the pace and scale of the economic explosion seen in Asia is unprecedented in the history of man. The chief economist of the World Bank, Joseph Stiglitz, captured this reality well in his article in the *Asian Wall Street Journal:*

> The East Asian 'miracle' was real. Its economic transformation of East Asia has been one of the most remarkable accomplishments in history. The dramatic surge in gross domestic product which it brought about is reflected in higher standards of living for hundreds of millions of Asians, including longer life expectancy, better health and education, and millions of others have rescued themselves from poverty, and now lead more hopeful lives. These achievements are real, and will be far more permanent than the present turmoil.[2]

The confidence of East Asians has been further boosted by the numerous studies that demonstrate the impressive academic performance of East Asians, both in leading Western universities and at home. Today many of the top students produced by American universities are of Asian origin. Educational excellence is an essential prerequisite for cultural confidence. To put it baldly, many Asians are pleased to wake up to the new realisation that their minds are not inferior. Most Westerners cannot appreciate the change because they can never directly feel the sense of inferiority many Asians experienced until recently.

The second reason why we might answer "Yes" to the question "Can Asians think?" is that a vital switch is taking place in many Asian minds. For centuries, Asians believed that the only way to progress was through emulation of the West. Yukichi Fukuzawa, a leading Meiji reformer, epitomised this attitude when he said in the late 19th century that for Japan to progress, it had to learn from the West. The other leading modernisers in Asia, whether they be Sun Yat-sen or Jawaharlal Nehru, shared this fundamental attitude. The mental switch that is taking place in Asian minds today is that they no longer believe that the only way to progress is through copying; they now believe they can work out their own solutions.

This switch in Asian minds has taken place slowly and imperceptibly. Until a few decades ago, Western societies beckoned as beacons on the hill: living models of the most successful form of human societies—economically prosperous, politically stable, socially just and harmonious, ethically clean, and, all in all, providing environments that had the best possible conditions for their citizens to grow and thrive as individuals. These societies were not perfect, but they were clearly superior, in all senses of the word, to any society outside. Until recently it would have been folly, and indeed inconceivable, for any Asian intellectual to suggest, "This may not be the path we want to take". Today this is what many Asians are thinking, privately if not publicly.

However, overall, there is no question that Western societies remain more successful than their East Asian counterparts. And they retain fields of excellence in areas that no other society comes close to, in their universities, think tanks, and certainly in cultural realms. No Asian orchestra comes close in performance to the leading Western orchestras, even though the musical world in the West has been enriched by many brilliant Asian musicians. But Asians are shocked by the scale and depth of social and economic problems that have afflicted many Western societies. In North America, societies are troubled by the relative breakdown of the family as an institution, the plague of drug addiction and its attendant problems, including crime, the persistence of ghettos and the perception that there has been a decline in ethical standards. This is exemplified by statistics provided by the US government that reflect social trends for the period 1960–90. During that 30-year period, the rate of violent crime quadrupled, single parent families almost tripled, and the number of US state and federal prisoners tripled. Asians are also troubled by the addiction of Europeans to their social security nets despite the clear evidence that these nets now hold down their societies and have created a sense of gloom about long-term economic prospects. In previous decades, when East Asians visited North America and Western Europe, they envied the high standards of living and better quality of life in those societies. Today, though the high standards of living remain in the West, Asians no longer consider these societies as their role models. They are beginning to believe that they can attempt something different.

A simple metaphor may explain what Western minds would see if they could peer into Asian minds. Until recently, most of those minds shared the general assumption that the developmental path of all societies culminated in the plateau on which most Western societies now rest. Hence, all societies, with minor variations, would end up creating liberal, democratic societies, giving emphasis to individual freedoms, as they moved up the socio-economic ladder. Today Asians can still see the plateau of contentment that most Western societies rest on, but they can also see, beyond the plateau, alternative peaks to which they can take their societies. Instead of seeing the plateau as the natural end destination, they now have a desire to bypass it (for they do not wish to be afflicted by some of the social and cultural ills that afflict Western societies) and to search for alternative peaks beyond. This kind of mental horizon never existed in Asian minds until recently. It reveals the new confidence of Asians in themselves.

The third reason why we might answer "Yes" to the question "Can Asians think?" is that today is not the only period when Asian minds have begun to stir. As more and more Asians lift their lives from levels of survival, they have the economic freedom to think, reflect, and rediscover their cultural heritage. There is a growing consciousness that their societies, like those in the West, have a rich social, cultural and philosophical legacy that they can resuscitate and use to evolve their own modern and advanced societies. The richness and depth of Indian and Chinese civilisations, to name just two, have been acknowledged by Western scholars. Indeed, for the past few centuries, it was Western scholarship and endeavour that preserved the fruits of Asian civilisation, just as the Arabs preserved and passed on the Greek and Roman civilisations in the darkest days of Europe. For example, while Asian cultures deteriorated, museums and universities in the West preserved and even cherished the best that Asian art and culture had produced. As Asians delve deeper into their own cultural heritage, they find their minds nourished. For the first time in centuries, an Asian renaissance is under way. Visitors to Asian cities—from Teheran to Calcutta, from Bombay to Shanghai, from Singapore to Hong Kong—now see both a newfound confidence as well as an interest in traditional language and culture. As their economies grow and as they have more disposable income, Asians spend it increasingly on reviving traditional dance or theatre. What we are witnessing today are only the bare beginnings of a major cultural rediscovery. The pride that Asians are taking in their culture is clear and palpable.

In short, Asians who would like to rush and answer "Yes" to the question have more than ample justification for doing so. But before they do so, I would advise them to pause and reflect on the reasons for the "Maybe" answer before arriving at a final judgement.

The "Maybe" Response

Despite the travails sparked by the financial crisis in late 1997, most Asians continue to be optimistic about their future. Such optimism is healthy. Yet it may be useful for Asians to learn a small lesson in history from the experience of Europeans exactly a century ago, when Europe was full of optimism. In his book *Out of Control,* Zbigniew Brzezinski describes how the world looked then:

> The twentieth century was born in hope. It dawned in a relatively benign setting. The principal powers of the world had enjoyed, broadly speaking, a relatively prolonged spell of peace. . . . The dominant mood in the major capitals as of January 1, 1900, was generally one of optimism. The structure of global power seemed stable. Existing empires appeared to be increasingly enlightened as well as secure.[3]

Despite this great hope, the 20th century became, in Brzezinski's words:

> . . . mankind's most bloody and hateful century, a century of hallucinating politics and of monstrous killings. Cruelty was institutionalized to an unprecedented degree, lethality was organized on a mass production basis. The contrast between the scientific potential for good and the political evil that was actually unleashed is shocking. Never before in history was killing so globally pervasive, never before did it consume so many lives, never before was human annihilation pursued with such concentration of sustained effort on behalf of such arrogantly irrational goals.[4]

One of the most important questions that an Asian has to ask himself today is a simple one: Can any Asian society, with the exception of Japan (which is an accepted member of the Western club), be absolutely confident that it can succeed and do as well in a comprehensive sense as contemporary advanced societies in North America and Western Europe? If the answer is none, or even a few, then the case for the "Maybe" response becomes stronger.

There are still many great challenges that Asian societies have to overcome before they can reach the comprehensive level of achievement enjoyed by Western societies. The first challenge in the development of any society is economic. Until the middle of 1997, most East Asian societies believed that they had mastered the basic rules of modern economics. They liberalised their economies, encouraged foreign investment flows and practised thrifty fiscal policies. The high level of domestic savings gave them a comfortable economic buffer. After enjoying continuous economic growth rates of 7 percent or more per annum for decades, it was natural for societies like South Korea, Thailand, Indonesia and Malaysia to assume that they had discovered the magical elixir of economic development.

The events following the devaluation of the Thai baht on 2 July 1997 demonstrated that they had not. The remarkable thing about this financial crisis was that no economist anticipated its depth or scale. Economists and analysts are still divided on its fundamental causes. As the crisis is still unfolding as this essay is being written, it is too early to provide definitive judgements on the fundamental causes. But a few suggestions are worth making.

On the economic front, many mistakes were made. In Thailand, for example, the decision to sustain fixed exchange rates between the baht and the dollar, despite the disparity in interest rates, allowed Thai businessmen to borrow cheap in US dollars and earn high interest rates in Thai baht. This also led to overinvestments in Thailand, in the property and share markets. All this was clearly unsustainable. The IMF provided some discreet warnings. However, the relatively weak coalition governments then prevailing in Thailand were unable to administer the bitter medicine required to remedy the situation because some of it had to be administered to their financial backers. Domestically, it was a combination of economic and political factors that precipitated and prolonged the financial crisis.

There was also a huge new factor that complicated the story: the force of globalisation. The key lesson that all East Asian economic managers have learned from the 1997–98 crisis is that they are accountable not only to domestic actors but to the international financial markets and their key players. The East Asians should not have been surprised. It was a logical consequence of liberalisation and integration with the global economy. Integration has brought both benefits (in terms of significant increases in standard of living) and cost (such as loss of autonomy in economic management). But there was a clear reluctance to acknowledge and accept the loss of autonomy. This was demonstrated by the state of denial that characterised the initial East Asian response to this crisis. The denial clearly showed the psychological time lag in East Asian minds in facing up to new realities.

Significantly, the two East Asian economies that have (after the initial bouts of denial) swallowed most fully the bitter medicine administered by the IMF have been the two societies that have progressed fastest in developing middle classes that have integrated themselves into the world view of the new interconnected global universe of modern economics. South Korea and Thailand, although they continue to face serious economic challenges at the time of writing, have clearly demonstrated that their elites are now well plugged in to the new financial networks. The new finance minister of Thailand, Tarrin Nimmanhaeminda, walks and talks with ease in any key financial capital. His performance is one indicator of the new globalised Asian mind that is emerging.

The 1997–98 financial crisis also demonstrated the wisdom of the Chinese in translating the English word "crisis" as a combination of two Chinese characters, "danger" and "opportunity". Clearly, East Asian societies have experienced many dangerous moments. But if they emerge from the 1997–98 financial crisis with restructured and reinvigorated economic and administrative systems of management, they may yet be among the first societies in the world to develop strong immune systems to handle present and future challenges springing from globalisation. It is too early to tell whether this is true. And this in turn reinforces the point that on the economic front, one should perhaps give the "Maybe" answer to the question "Can Asians think?"

Second, on the political front, most Asian societies, including East Asian societies, have a long way to go before they can reach Western levels of political stability and harmony. There is little danger of a coup d'état or real civil war in most contemporary Western societies (with the possible exception, still, of Northern Ireland). Western societies have adopted political variations of the liberal democratic model, even though the presidential systems of the United States and France differ significantly from the Westminster models of the United Kingdom, Canada and Australia. These political forms are not perfect. They contain many features that inhibit social progress, from vested interest lobby groups to pork-barrel politics. Indeed, it would be fair to say that political development in most Western societies has atrophied. But it has atrophied at comfortable levels. Most of their citizens live in domestic security, fear no oppression, and are content with their political frameworks. How many Asian societies can claim to share this benign state of affairs? The answer is clearly very few. And if it is equally clear that they are *not* going to enjoy this in the very near future, then this again militates in favour of the "Maybe" answer.

Third, in the security realm, the one great advantage Western societies have over the rest of the world is that war among them has become a thing of the past. The reason for this is complex. It includes an awareness of ethnic affinity among Western tribes who feel outnumbered by the rest of the world's population and also a sense of belonging to a common civilisation. It may also reflect the exhaustion of having fought too many wars in the past.

Nevertheless, it is truly remarkable, when we count the number of wars—and truly big wars—that the English, French and Germans have fought with each other (including two in this century), that there is today almost a zero chance of war between the United Kingdom, France and Germany. This is a remarkably civilised thing to have achieved, reflecting a considerable step forward in the history of human civilisation. When will India and Pakistan, or North and South Korea, achieve this same zero prospect of war? And if the answer is not in the near future, is it reasonable to suggest that perhaps Asian minds (or the minds of Asian societies) have not reached the same level as the West?

Fourth, Asians face serious challenges in the social realm. While it is true that it took the social dislocations caused by the industrial revolution to eradicate the feudal traces of European cultures (social freedom followed economic freedom), it is still unclear whether similar economic revolutions in East Asia will have the same liberating social effects on Asian societies. Unfortunately, many feudal traces, especially those of clannishness and nepotism, continue to prevent Asian societies from becoming truly meritocratic ones, where individual citizens are able to grow and thrive on the basis of their abilities and not on the basis of their birth or connections or ethnic background.

Fifth and finally, and perhaps most fundamentally, the key question remains whether Asian minds will be able to develop the right blend of values that will both preserve some of the traditional strengths of Asian values (e.g., attachment to the family as an institution, deference to societal interests, thrift, conservatism in social mores, respect for authority) as well as absorb the strengths of Western values (the emphasis on individual achievement, political and economic freedom, respect for the rule of law as well as for key national institutions). This will be a complex challenge.

One of the early (and perhaps inevitable) reactions by some western commentators to the 1997–98 financial crisis was to suggest that it fundamentally reflected the failure of Asian values. If nothing else, this quick reaction suggested that the "Asian values debate" of the early 1990s had touched some sensitive nerves in the Western mind and soul. The desire to bury Asian values revealed the real pain that had been inflicted during that debate.

The true test of the viability and validity of values is shown not in theory but in practice. Those who try to draw a direct link of causality between adherence to Asian values and financial disaster have a tough empirical case to make because of the varied reactions of East Asian societies to the financial crisis. South Korea and Thailand, two of the three countries that were most deeply affected by the crisis (i.e., those who had to turn to the IMF for assistance), had been given the highest marks in Western minds for their moves towards democratisation. The three open economies that were least affected by the financial crisis were Taiwan, Hong Kong and Singapore, and the three had very different political systems. In short, there was no clear correlation between political systems and financial vulnerability.

The only correlation that is clear so far is that between good governance and resilience in the financial crisis. Good governance is not associated with any single political system or ideology. It is associated with the willingness and ability of the government to develop economic, social and administrative systems that are resilient enough to handle the challenges brought about in the new economic era we are moving into. China provides a good living example of this. Its leaders are not looking for the perfect political system in theory. They are searching daily for pragmatic solutions to keep their society moving forward. The population support this pragmatism, for they too feel that it is time for China to catch up. Traditionally, the Chinese have looked for good government, not minimal government. They can recognise good governance when they experience it. The fact that Japan—which is in Western eyes the most liberal and democratic East Asian society—has had great difficulties adapting to the new economic environment demonstrates that political openness is not the key variable to look at.

It is vital for Western minds to understand that the efforts by Asians to rediscover Asian values are not only, or even primarily, a search for political values. Instead, they represent a complex set of motives and aspirations in Asian minds: a desire to reconnect with their historical past after this connection had been ruptured both by colonial rule and by the subsequent domination of the globe by a Western *Weltanschauung;* an effort to find the right balance in bringing up their young so that they are open to the new technologically interconnected global universe and yet rooted in and conscious of the cultures of their ancestors; an effort to define their own personal, social and national identities in a way that enhances their sense of self-esteem in a world where their immediate ancestors had subconsciously accepted that they were lesser beings in a Western universe. In short, the reassertion of Asian values in the 1990s represents a complex process of regeneration and rediscovery that is an inevitable aspect of the rebirth of societies.

Here again, it is far too early to tell whether Asian societies can successfully both integrate themselves into the modern world and reconnect with their past. Both are mammoth challenges. Western minds have a clear advantage over Asian minds, as they are convinced that their successful leap into modernity was to a large extent a result of the compatibility of their value systems with the modern universe. Indeed, many Western minds believe (consciously or subconsciously) that without Western value systems no society can truly enter the modern universe.

Only time will tell whether Asian societies can enter the modern universe as Asian societies rather than Western replicas. Since it is far too early to pass judgement on whether they will succeed in this effort, it is perhaps fair to suggest that this too is another argument in favour of the "Maybe" answer to the question "Can Asians think?"

Conclusion

Clearly, the 21st century and the next millennium will prove to be very challenging for Asian societies. For most of the past 500 years, they have fallen behind European societies in many different ways. There is a strong desire to catch up. The real answer to the question "Can Asians think?" will be provided if they do so. Until then, Asians will do themselves a big favour by constantly reminding themselves why this question remains a valid one for them to pose to themselves. And only they can answer it. No one else can.

Notes

This is an edited and updated version of a lecture the author delivered at the 7th International Conference on thinking in Singapore on 3 June 1997. *National Interest,* Summer 1998.

1. Will Durant, *The Age of Faith,* New York, Simon & Schuster, 1950, p. 450.
2. Joseph Stiglitz, *The Asian Wall Street Journal,* 2 February 1998.
3. Zbigniew Brzezinski, *Out of Control,* New York, Charles Scribner's Sons, 1993, p. 3.
4. Ibid, pp. 4–5.

8

The Order of Interbeing

Thich Nhat Hanh

The Meaning of *Tiep Hien*

THE WORD *tiep* means "being in touch with" and "continuing." *Hien* means "realizing" and "making it here and now." For us to better understand the spirit of the Tiep Hien Order, it is helpful to begin by examining these four expressions.

What are we to be in touch with? The answer is reality, the reality of the world and the reality of the mind. To be in touch with the mind means to be aware of the processes of our inner life—feelings, perceptions, mental formations—and also to rediscover our true mind, which is the wellspring of understanding and compassion. Getting in touch with true mind is like digging deep in the soil and reaching a hidden source that fills our well with fresh water. When we discover our true mind, we are filled with understanding and compassion, which nourishes us and those around us as well. Being in touch with the true mind is being in touch with *buddhas* and *bodhisattvas,* enlightened beings who show us the way of understanding, peace, and happiness.

To be in touch with the reality of the world means to be in touch with everything that is around us in the animal, vegetal, and mineral realms. If we want to be in touch, we have to get out of our shell and look clearly and deeply at the wonders of life—the snowflakes, the moonlight, the songs of the birds, the beautiful flowers—and also the suffering—hunger, disease, torture, and oppression. Overflowing with understanding and compassion, we can appreciate the wonders of life, and, at the same time, act with the firm resolve to alleviate the suffering. Too many people distinguish between the inner world of our mind and the world outside, but these worlds are not separate. They belong to the same reality. The ideas of inside and outside are helpful in everyday life, but they can become an obstacle that prevents us from experiencing ultimate reality. If we look deeply into our mind, we see the world deeply at the same time. If we understand the world, we understand our mind. This is called "the unity of mind and world."

Modern Christianity uses the ideas of vertical and horizontal theology. Spiritual life is the vertical dimension of getting in touch with God, while social life is the horizontal dimension of getting in touch with humans. In Buddhism, there are people who also think in these terms. They speak about the higher level of practicing the Buddha's Way and the lower level of helping living beings. But this understanding does not accord with the true spirit of Buddhism, which teaches that buddhahood, the nature of enlightenment, is innate to every being and not just a transcendental identity. Thus, in Buddhism the vertical and horizontal are one. If we penetrate the horizontal, we find the vertical, and vice versa. This is the meaning of "being in touch with."

Next we come to the concept of continuation. Tiep means to tie two strings together to make a longer string. It means extending and perpetuating the career of enlightenment that was started and nourished by the buddhas and bodhisattvas who preceded us. It is helpful to remember that the word "buddha" means a person who is awake. The word "bodhisattva" also signifies an enlightened person. The way of enlightenment that was started by the buddhas and bodhisattvas should be continued, and this is the responsibility of all of us who undertake the practice of Buddhism. Sowing the seeds of enlightenment and taking good care of the tree of enlightenment are the meaning of tiep, "to continue."

The third concept is "to realize" or realization. Hien means not to dwell or be caught in the world of doctrines and ideas, but to bring and express our insights into real life. Ideas about understanding and compassion are not understanding and compassion. Understanding and compassion must be real in our lives. They must be seen and touched. The real presence of understanding and compassion will alleviate suffering and cause joy to be born. But to realize does not only mean to act. First of all, realization means transforming ourselves. This transformation creates a harmony between ourselves and nature, between our own joy and the joy of others. Once we get in touch with the source of understanding and compassion, this transformation is realized and all our actions will naturally protect and enhance life. If we wish to share joy and happiness with others, we must have joy and happiness within ourselves. If we wish to share calmness and serenity, we should first realize them within ourselves. Without a calm and peaceful mind, our actions will only create more trouble and destruction in the world.

The last expression to examine is "making it here and now." Only the present moment is real and available to us. The peace we desire is not in some distant future, but it is something we can realize in the present moment. To practice Buddhism does not mean to endure hardship now for the sake of peace and liberation in the future. The purpose of practice is not to be reborn in some paradise or buddhaland after death. The purpose is to have peace for ourselves and others right now, while we are alive and breathing. Means and ends cannot be separated. Bodhisattvas are careful about causes, while ordinary people care more about effects, because bodhisattvas see that cause and effect are one. Means are ends in themselves. An enlightened person never says, "This is only a means." Based on the insight that means *are* ends, all activities and practices should be entered into mindfully and peacefully. While sitting, walking, cleaning, working, or serving, we should feel peace within ourselves. The aim of sitting meditation is first to be peaceful and awake during sitting meditation. Working to help the hungry or the sick means to be peaceful and loving during that work. When we practice, we do not expect the practice to pay large rewards in the future, even nirvana, the pure land, enlightenment, or buddhahood. The secret of Buddhism is to be awake here and now. There is no way to peace; peace is the way. There is no way to enlightenment; enlightenment is the way. There is no way to liberation; liberation is the way.

Thus far, we have examined the meanings of the words "tiep" and "hien." In looking for an English word or phrase to express the meaning of Tiep Hien, the word "interbeing" has been proposed. It is a translation of a Chinese term found in the teaching of the *Avatamsaka Sutra*. I hope this recently invented word will be widely adopted in the near future.

Buddhist Precepts

Members of the Order of Interbeing observe fourteen precepts. The Sanskrit word *sila* means precept as an intention of mind that manifests in body and speech. Buddhist precepts are not prohibitions. They are guidelines for living mindfully. The practice of precepts does not restrict our liberty. On the contrary, the practice of precepts protects us and guarantees our liberty and prevents us from getting entangled in difficulties and confusion. The word "precept" should be understood in terms of the Threefold Training: *sila, samadhi,* and *prajña,* or precepts, concentration, and insight. Precepts lead to concentration, and concentration leads to insight. Thus, precepts are fundamentally disciplines of the mind, or mindfulness.

But, we should also understand the interbeing of the Threefold Training. Precepts lead to concentration and insight, and they themselves are concentration and insight. The same is true, at the same time, of concentration and insight. Perhaps the most appropriate definition of sila is "the practice of being awake, or mindful, during each bodily, verbal, and mental activity." It is only within this broad definition that the precepts can embrace and engender concentration and wisdom. Following the traditional commandments not to kill, not to steal, not to commit adultery, not to lie, and not to drink alcohol will bring about safety, joy, and peace, but is not enough to produce concentration and insight. In the context of practicing the Fourteen Precepts of the Order of Interbeing, the word "precept" fully embraces in itself the meaning of awakening. If we truly observe the precepts of the Order of Interbeing in our daily lives, we cultivate concentration and insight at the same time.

The Charter of the Order of Interbeing

According to the Charter of the Order of Interbeing, "the aim of the Order is to actualize Buddhism by studying, experimenting with, and applying Buddhism in modern life." Understanding can only be attained through direct experience. The results of the practice should be tangible and verifiable.

The Charter lists four principles as the foundation of the Order: nonattachment from views, direct experimentation on the nature of interdependent origination through meditation, appropriateness, and skillful means. Let us examine each of these principles.

1. Nonattachment from views: To be attached means to be caught in dogmas, prejudices, habits, and what we consider to be the Truth. The first aim of the practice is to be free of all attachments, especially attachments to views. This is the most important teaching of Buddhism.
2. Direct experimentation: Buddhism emphasizes the direct experience of reality, not speculative philosophy. Direct practice-realization, not intellectual research, brings about insight. Our own life is the instrument through which we experiment with truth.
3. Appropriateness: A teaching, in order to bring about understanding and compassion, must reflect the needs of people and the realities of society. To do this, it must meet two criteria: it must conform with the basic tenets of Buddhism, and it must be truly helpful and relevant. It is said that there are 84,000 Dharma doors through which one can enter Buddhism. For Buddhism to continue as a living source of wisdom and peace, even more doors should be opened.
4. Skillful means *(upaya)*: Skillful means consist of images and methods created by intelligent teachers to show the Buddha's way and guide peo-

ple in their efforts to practice the way in their own particular circumstances. These means are called Dharma doors.

Concerning these four principles, the Charter says, "The spirit of nonattachment from views and the spirit of direct experimentation lead to openmindedness and compassion, both in the realm of the perception of reality and in the realm of human relationships. The spirit of appropriateness and the spirit of skillful means lead to a capacity to be creative and to reconcile, both of which are necessary for the service of living beings." Guided by these principles, the Order of Interbeing has an open attitude towards all Buddhist schools. The Order of Interbeing does not consider any sutra or group of sutras as its basic text. Inspiration is drawn from the essence of the Buddhadharma as found in all sutras. The Order does not recognize any systematic arrangement of the Buddhist teachings as proposed by various schools of Buddhism. The Order seeks to realize the Dharma spirit within early Buddhism as well as the development of that spirit throughout the sangha's history and the teachings in all Buddhist traditions.

In addition, the Charter expresses a willingness to be open and to change. "The Order of Interbeing rejects dogmatism in both looking and acting. It seeks all forms of action that can revive and sustain the true spirit of insight and compassion in life. It considers this spirit to be more important than any Buddhist institution or tradition. With the aspiration of a bodhisattva, members of the Order of Interbeing seek to change themselves in order to change society in the direction of compassion and understanding by living a joyful and mindful life."

The Community

The Order of Interbeing consists of a core community and an extended community. The core community is composed of members who have taken the vows to observe the Fourteen Precepts of the Order. The extended community consists of those who attempt to live up to the spirit of the Order, but who have not formally taken the vows. Members of the extended community cooperate closely with core community members in all activities. They also participate in the recitation of the Fourteen Precepts. In order to become a member of the core community, a person undergoes a one-year apprenticeship, practicing with members of a core community. After ordination, he or she agrees to observe at least sixty days of mindfulness a year.

The Precepts of the Order of Interbeing

Buddhist precepts are not sets of rules. They are guidelines for everyday living. Most religious rules are prohibitions that begin with the control of
bodily actions—not to kill, steal, and so forth. The Fourteen Precepts of the
Order of Interbeing begin with the mind, and the first seven precepts deal
with problems associated with the mind. According to the Buddha, "The
mind is the king of all dharmas. The mind is the painter who paints everything." The Fourteen Precepts reflect very truly the Eightfold Path, the basic
teaching of both Theravada and Mahayana Buddhism. The Eightfold Path
can be described as the essential precept (Pali: *paññattisila*). The Eightfold
Path also begins with the mind—Right View and Right Thought. We can
arrange the Fourteen Precepts into three categories. The first seven deal with
the mind, the next two with speech, and the last five with the body, although
we must realize that this division is arbitrary. The mind is like a lamp of
awareness, always present. Those who regularly recite and practice the precepts will see this.

Reciting the Precepts

The Fourteen Precepts are recited at least once every two weeks. Usually, a
member of the core community is asked to lead the recitation. However, a
member of the extended community can also be invited to lead. Participants
sit in two rows facing each other. The person who sits at the beginning of the
row on the right, nearest the altar, is called the "head of the ceremony." He
or she leads the ceremony and is responsible for inviting the bell to sound.
The person who sits directly opposite him or her recites the precepts. The
recitation should be neither too slow nor too quick, as the right speed will
please the community. As the leader of the recitation, she should be visible
to everyone.

   At the beginning of the recitation, the head of the ceremony offers incense
and recites aloud the incense-offering verse. The rest of the community
stands up and, with palms joined, follows their breathing. After the incense
offering, the head of the ceremony invokes the names of Shakyamuni, Man-
jusri, Samantabhadra, Avalokitesvara, Maitreya, and all future teachers. After
each name is invoked, everyone bows together. Then the members of the
community sit down. When everyone is completely settled, the bell is invited
to sound, and the recitation begins with the sutra-opening verse. From the
very beginning of the ceremony and recitation, everyone follows his or her
breathing and practices mindfulness in each movement. When listening,

joining palms together, bowing, sitting down, or even adjusting posture, there is an appropriate verse for each movement.[1]

During the recitation, each member of the community should give full attention to the precept being read in order to receive and examine its content. Concentrating on the precepts this way will keep distracting thoughts from the mind. The person who recites the precepts should speak in a clear voice that communicates the spirit of the precepts. The community's successful concentration depends on the quality of her recitation.

She begins by asking "Brothers and Sisters, are you ready?" and each person answers silently, "Yes." After reciting each precept, she should pause for the length of three breaths, in and out, before asking, "This is the (first) precept of the Order of Interbeing. Have you studied, practiced, and observed it during the past two weeks?" This pause allows everyone to dwell on the essence and the content of the precept. The answer to the question falls somewhere between "yes" and "no." Everyone who practices mindfulness and observes the precepts is entitled to say "yes"; it would be wrong to say "no." But our "yes" is not absolutely firm, because our efforts during the past two weeks may not have been enough. So our answer is something like, "Yes, but I could have done better." We should allow time for the question to go deep into our mind and hearty and act on us during the silence of the three breaths. While allowing the question to enter us, we can follow our breathing attentively. The ceremony head should deeply observe three breaths before inviting the bell to sound, and the reciter should maintain awareness of the community's questioning. When the bell sounds, the entire community joins their palms, and the person reciting proceeds to the next precept. During this time of breathing, if anyone has a copy of the text of the ceremony, he or she should refrain from touching the page until the bell is sounded. Practicing in this way creates a serene atmosphere.

Note

1. See *Plum Village Chanting Book* (Berkeley: Parallax Press, 1991) for incense offering verse, invoking the bodhisattvas' names, and verses for various movements. See also *Present Moment Wonderful Moment: Mindfulness Verses for Daily Living* (Berkeley: Parallax Press, 1989).

9

The Forms of Culture of the Classical Periods of East and West Seen from a Metaphysical Perspective

Nishida Kitarô

1

THE FORMS OF CULTURE may be considered in various ways from various points of view. I should like to consider the essential differences between the forms of culture of East and West from the metaphysical viewpoint. By metaphysical viewpoint I mean how each culture considered the question of reality. It may be said, of course, that in China, and especially in Japan, the question of reality was not considered scientifically; the science of metaphysics may especially be said not to have been developed. But the fact that there was no distinctive science of metaphysics does not necessarily mean that there was no metaphysical orientation. As long as a specific culture has developed to any degree, it can be considered in metaphysical terms. Every culture possesses a view of life. At the basis of a view of human life there must be some kind of metaphysical thought, even though it is not consciously realized.

What, then, were the differences in the forms of culture of East and West as seen from a metaphysical perspective? I think that we can distinguish the West to have considered being as the ground of reality, the East to have taken non-being or nothingness as its ground. I shall call them reality as form and reality as the formless, respectively.

Greek culture, which became the source of Western culture, can be said to have been a culture of being, grounded on the thought of being. Needless to say, a Dionysian culture also greatly contributed to the making of Greek culture. The Greek race, like the ancient Indian race, is said to have originally also had a pessimistic view of life. Nevertheless, it was Apollonian culture which became the center of Greek culture. In Greek philosophy, that which has form and determination was regarded as the real—or, again, form itself was regarded as reality. Plato's Ideas, etymologically speaking, meant "forms." Of course, these forms did not mean physical forms in the usual sense of perceptual forms. The Platonic Ideas had a meaning contrary to this. We may call them objects of reason. In such a sense, they can rather be regarded as formless. But even as objects of reason they were not mere concepts. As we read in the *Symposium*, they were also objects of intuition. In short, the Ideas were the formative principles of this actual world.

In the rich and abundant world of Greek philosophy there were, of course, many currents of thought. The same may be said even in Plato's own thought. But Plato's philosophy of Ideas can be thought to have typified the process of the philosophical articulation of the essence of Greek culture. In Greek culture, the idea of taking absolute infinity, something which absolutely transcends actuality, as true reality, was not entertained. The One of Parmenides was not non-being but the ultimate of being. The Flux of Heraclitus was also the *Logos*. The Unbounded of Anaximander possessed the meaning of a self-contained circle. The thought of the last great Greek philosopher, Plotinus—however mystical it may be understood to have been—did nothing more than develop Plato's philosophy to its ultimate point. Even the crime of Orestes in the drama of its religiously minded author Aeschylus was redeemed through Athene. In sum, the essence of Greek culture lay in aesthetic intuition. Moreover, it was plastic and actual. Nietzsche says that the Greek man fled from the contradictions of the will through art. This is the reason that Greek culture can be considered to have been something cheerful and intellectual.

Judeo-Christian culture which, together with the Greek, became the source of Western culture, was entirely different from ancient Greek culture. Jehovah was an absolute who transcended this world—the creator of this world who dominates and commands it. God was utterly inexpressible and unnamable. There was absolutely no path from man to God, only from God to man. The original sin of Adam was saved only through the redemption of the cross of Christ.

W. R. Smith has written that the religion of the Semitic peoples developed in the distant past when social relationships between men were those of blood only. Therefore, the relation between God and man was originally that between a patriarch and his family, or, derivatively, the relation between a king and his subjects. In the case of divine worship by other ancient peoples, the relation between God and worshiper was conceived as that between a protector and those protected. This would seem to have been further developed by the people of Israel into the relationship with a God who transcended the world.

In the religion of the Israelites who worshipped Jehovah, the God of the ancient people of Mt. Sinai, the relationship between God and man was expressed as a covenant, that is, a relation between persons. Man rebels against God through his own free will, and this is sin. Sin is justified only through redemption. For people who lived on desolate and endless sands, without the color of vegetation for vast distances, the only thing which opposed the self was the infinite expanse of blue sky, and the motions of the sun, moon, and stars. This may indeed have been a reason why the Israelites, who had an indomitable spirit, created such a religion.

Christianity, into which form the Israelites' religion was deepened, contributed to Western culture the idea of personality. Of course, Roman law also contributed to the idea of the person; but the idea of a person who has free will that carries the burden of sin must be said to be based in Christianity. Augustine, at the beginning of the Middle Ages, philosophically clarified the deepest significance of personality. I do not think that Augustine's insights have been surpassed even down to the present. In medieval philosophy, reality was not a Platonic Idea but a person. God was the absolute person. The person is in essence not an object of knowledge. The personality of the absolute and infinite God must particularly transcend our knowledge. God is *Deus absconditus.* If we consider Greek philosophy as a philosophy of being, medieval Christian philosophy may be said to have already had the significance of a philosophy pointing beyond being, that is, to a philosophy of non-being. Thus, for example, the negative theology of Dionysius the Areopagite attempted to express God only in negative terms. However, the person is not nothingness, but a most determined—indeed, a most self-consciously self-determined—being. The person is endowed with free will, and, as St. Thomas says, is the highest form of existence.

2

The religion of India has run contrary to both Greek philosophy and the Judeo-Christian religion by taking the profoundest idea of nothingness as its basis. The God of the Brahmanic religion both transcends and includes all creation, and at the same time is God universally immanent. According to the account of the *Isa Upanishad*, everything in this world is enveloped by the absolute God as if wrapped in a cloak. There is only one unique reality, which is unmoving and prior to mind. God cannot be experienced by any of the senses. God moves and does not move, is both far and near. Seeing all creation in Himself and Himself in all creation, God despises nothing (according to Mounier Williams, *Hinduism*). If such a unique reality is not an absolute Idea, it is hardly personal—as with the God of the Jews—either. Both the Indian and the Greek peoples, who are of the same Aryan root, may be said to have been intellectual in contrast to the Semitic race. But they have stood diametrically opposed to one another on the question of ultimate reality. The one has seen being, the other non-being, at the root of all things. The unique reality of Parmenides is the ultimate of being. The unique reality of the Brahmanic religion is the absolute of non-being. The former is an ultimate of affirmation, the latter an absolute of negation.

The culmination of the religion of India has a focus on deep contemplation within the self and infinite compassion toward the external world. The Greeks were philosophical; the Indians are religious. When, by denying present actualities, men conceive of an absolutely infinite reality, they cannot help being religious. In this sense, the Indians may rather be said to agree with the Israelites. But the Indians also have denied personality. Thus, I believe the idea that the religion of India is pantheistic is not entirely appropriate. In the very lifeblood of the Indian religion, it is not simply that all things are merely God; there must even be a denial of all things. This has involved a dialectic of absolute negation qua affirmation. In Mahayana Buddhism, it has attained to the philosophy of the nonduality of samsara and nirvana as in the paradoxical teaching that "phenomenal being, precisely as it is, is void; voidness, precisely as it is, is phenomenal being."

3

The culture of China also has unique features. It is neither essentially "philosophical," as with Greek culture, nor "religious," as are Indian and Jewish cultures. It developed into a culture of social ritual (*Sitte*). The culture of the Chou dynasty, the source of Chinese culture for many thousands of years, was one in which human affairs—from ceremonial occasions to the ordinary affairs of daily life—were, as a whole, imbued with a religion of ritual, as expressed in the phrase "the three hundred rituals and the three thousand courtesies." As we can learn from the *Book of Rites*, ancient China was in fact a country imbued with religious ritual. The *Tso Chuan* also gives us some idea of how important ritual was in the relationships between feudal states.

When Confucius said, "I have not seen the Duke of Chou for a long time in my recurring dreams," he reflected the Chou culture and clarified its ethical significance. The *Spring and Autumn Annals*, when it praises and blames, approves and censures the affairs of the empire, was not afraid to condemn one who loses propriety, even though he have the dignity of the Son of Heaven. There is also the statement: "Yen-yüan inquired about benevolence. Confucius answered: 'To overcome selfishness and revive ritual is benevolence.' Yen-yüan further asked about the details of this, and Confucius answered: 'Do not see, do not listen, do not speak, do not act, except according to the proper ritual.' " I think that, as this statement shows, the benevolence of Confucius did not actually signify love so much as the need to follow ritual. The teachings of Confucius and Mencius were internalizations and generalizations of the religion of ritual. They cannot be understood apart from that point.

Probably the culture of every race first assumes the form of *Sitte*. They come to be deepened or developed into philosophy or religion according to their respective histories. But it can be thought that in China *Sitte* developed as *Sitte* itself. *Sitte* may be accompanied by something religious, as Fustel de Coulanges has argued concerning Greek and Roman culture. But China's case appears to be unique. Hsün-tzu said: "The sage kings considered man's nature to be evil. They regarded it to be one-sided, greedy, and perverse; to be rebellious and not peaceful. Therefore they created rituals and established systems of laws in order to reform and improve man's emotions, and thereby to rectify man."

There is also a concept of Heaven (*t'ien*) behind the teaching of the Chinese sages. In the *li yun* section of the *Book of Rites*, it is said that "ritual must be rooted in Heaven." The *Book of History* says: "Yao said: Ah, Shun! the Heaven-appointed succession now falls on your shoulders. Sincerely hold fast to the mean. If the world is in distress, the blessings of Heaven will end forever." The *Book of Songs* says: "Although Chou is an old state, its mandate is new." The Chinese emperor became such by receiving the mandate of Heaven. The Son of Heaven worshipped Heaven; and Heaven was the model for the sage king to follow. And Confucius said: "Heaven produces virtue in me; what can Huan-t'ui do to me?" Again, he said that "he fears the mandate of Heaven." In the *Mean* it says: "The Heavenly mandate is called human nature; that which rules human nature is called the Way; cultivating the Way is called the true teaching." Thus the concept of Heaven, as something moral, has been in Confucianism the foundation of the true teaching.

But in Taoism, which has been the other great source of Chinese culture alongside Confucianism, the Way is clearly said to be non-being. Lao-tzu said: "The Way that can be named is not the eternal Way. Names which can be named are not the eternal name. The nameless is the source of heaven and earth; when named, it becomes the mother of all things." And he wrote: "When the great Way is abolished, humanity and righteousness appear. When wisdom comes forth, there is great falsehood." And again: "When one looks for it, it is not visible; it is fine. When one listens for it, it is inaudible; it is infinitesimal. When one reaches out for it, one cannot grasp it; it is subtle. These three qualities cannot be investigated. Therefore, when combined they become one. There is nothing brighter above it, nothing darker below it. It can never be named. Its returning to non-being is called the form of the formless. Its form of non-being is obscure. When one meets it, one does not see its face. When one follows behind it, one does not see its back." Or again: "If one reaches to the ultimate limit of emptiness and maintains tranquillity steadfastly, then while the myriad things are flourishing, one observes their return."

However, even the Taoist teaching, reflecting special characteristics of Chinese culture, centered around human society. It was, in other words, a humanistic teaching, and not just philosophy or religion. Lao-tzu and Chuang-tzu focused on returning to Nature in itself by negating the ideas of right and wrong, good and evil of human society. Their teachings consisted of a negation of culture. Thus Taoism is also a negation of both the faith of the Jews and the wisdom of the Greeks. As Lao-tzu says, "Everything that the world considers to be beautiful is ugly, and everything that the world considers to be good is evil." Or again: "Extinguish learning and anxieties will also cease." As a result, Taoism seems to have degenerated into something sensual, at least in the case of the later Taoists.

However, Taoism does not signify a mere naturalism, but a return to the mysterious source of heaven and earth by a negation of all things. In Taoism's metaphysical sense of Nature, sensual nature has to be negated as well. "There is a being which evolves from chaos. It is born before heaven and earth. How silent and solitary! Independent and unchanging, it permeates everywhere without decrease. It can be considered the mother of heaven and earth. We do not know its name. It is called the Way. If we are forced to name it, it is called great. To say it is great means that it extends. To say that it extends means that it goes off into the distance. Going off into the distance means that it will also return. Therefore, the Way is great; earth is great; the king is also great. Within the bounds of the empire, there are four great things; the king is one of them. Man takes his model from earth, earth from heaven, heaven from the Way, the Way models itself after nature."

I note that in the ritualistic teaching of Confucianism such Taoist ideas of nature are not to be found. But even so, it was not that Confucius did not have analogous ideas at times. Thus, in the *Analects* we find: "I desire not to speak. What does Heaven say? Yet the four seasons follow one another, and the hundred things are born from it. What does Heaven say?" Again, Tzu-ssu, citing the *Book of Songs* at the end of the *Mean*, says: "Virtues are light like feathers. There are degrees even in feathers. What Heaven bears has neither sound nor smell. It is perfect." And conversely, the teachings of Lao-tzu, which negate Confucian morality, are still a moral teaching, as the title, *Lao Tzu Tao Te Ching*, indicates. And for his part Confucius, who advocated ritual, could say at times [in Taoist fashion]: "I desire not to speak." In response to Tseng-chih who said, "I bathe in the I River; the wind whirls around; I compose a verse, and return home," Confucius commented, "I give my approval to Tseng-chih." Thus, there are several metaphysical ideas—of Heaven, of the Way, and of Nature—intertwined at the root of Chinese culture.

Moreover, the Chinese concept of Nature is neither one of "evil," as in Christianity, nor "material," as conceived in modern science. It is not only the order by which the sun, moon, and stars move. Nature is the foundation of heaven, earth, and the myriad things, but also the fundamental principle of the Way of man. Thus, it is emphasized that the Way of Heaven and the Way of man are one. It is such a unifying principle of Naturalness that is considered to exist at the root of social activity as well. It functions as the natural principle of *nomos*, in which respect it may be said to have had something in common with Stoic philosophy. Yet the Romans, who were intellectual even while they were practical, gave birth to law. But the Chinese, to the very end, never went beyond a concept of ritual. Lao-tzu's statement, "man models himself after earth, earth after heaven, heaven after the Way, and the Way after Nature," probably represents such an idea of Naturalness in its consummate expression.

In this respect, the ideas of Lao-tzu and Chuang-tzu seem also to have an affinity with those of Buddhism. But the concept of nothingness in Indian religion—the creation of the intellectual Aryan people—is an intellectual one. It is a negation of knowledge by knowledge. By contrast, the naturalistic philosophy of non-being in Chinese culture may be thought to have been practical. It was a negation of practice by practice. In this regard Ch'an [Zen], while called Buddhism, can be regarded as Chinese in tone and quality. And now, another point: though Mo-tzu discussed the existence of ghosts and spirits in his chapter "Concerning Ghosts," and talked of heavenly spirits in his chapter "The Will of Heaven," these ideas too are not of the same quality as the personal God of Christianity. In general, that idea of the person is not realized in Chinese culture.

[Nishida's note:] Roman culture, in contrast to the aesthetic and intellectual culture of the Greeks, was political and legal. The Romans saw a different principle of nature at the foundation of political society. Their idea of natural law was developed from Roman law. Thus the Romans discovered the link between *logos* and *nomos* in their own forms of Stoic philosophy; and Stoicism became one of the distinctive Roman philosophies. It may be said that Chinese and Roman cultures resembled one another on the point of being cultures that centered around active society. But the Roman culture of law was rationalistic and intellectual in comparison with Chinese culture. The Chinese concept of Heaven and the Stoic concept of Nature are, in the final analysis, quite different concepts.

4

Needless to say, modern European culture was created by the confluence of two sources, the Greek and Christian cultures. We may say that all modern idealistic philosophy emerges from these two sources as well. But the special feature of modern European culture lies in its scientific—that is, its positivistic—spirit. Although it may seem to be a paradox, the scientific spirit, in one respect, signifies another negation of actuality and suggests a philosophy of nothingness. For science, as it affirms the actual world in its noematic direction (concerned as it is exclusively with cognition of the objective world), ends up negating both the "Idea" and the "person." But science also stands in diametrical opposition to Hinduism and Taoism, which negate the actual world in the direction of noetic determination (in the spirituality of knowledge itself).

However, absolute negation becomes absolute affirmation—dialectically, the absolute negation of actuality functions as its absolutely reciprocal affirmation. It has the form of actuality qua reality. Thus, while positivistic science regards the actual as thing, Buddhism (which thinks in such dialectical terms) sees it as mind. Western scholars often consider the Zen saying that "The willows are green, the flowers are red" to be directly a statement of naturalism or sensationalism. But it is actually a subtle dialectical idea from the opposite standpoint.

Now, then, things appearing in the actual present are both subjective and objective. Even in the case of perceptual objects, they both transcend us and yet are our own sensations. As natural science one-sidedly organizes them according to the forms of space, time, and causality, it universally negates the subjective. The physical world is constructed on that principle of negation. Sounds are considered to be the vibrations of air, colors to be ether waves. Taking this objectivizing direction to its logical conclusion, everything subjective must be negated—or, again, the world of lived reality, which has both subjective and objective dimensions, must be negated. This is the reason I say that the scientific spirit imports a denial of the full reality of things. (But, of course, if it entirely negates the subjectively cognitive act, there would be no things, no entities as objects of cognition.) There is a limit to taking the noematic determination of the actual—that is, of the sensory datum—as the real. This limit is reached from the standpoint of physics. But, of course, physics is not the whole of science. There are less abstract sciences. The more science becomes concrete, the more it comes to allow for the subjective.

From the above-described standpoint of natural science, the independence of personal subjectivity is not recognized. Thus it is unavoidable that, from that standpoint, the goal of human life is considered to consist of the attainment of pleasure and the avoidance of pain. The logical outcome of this is modern utilitarianism, an ethical theory predicated on a calculus of "the greatest good for the greatest number." Note that the Greeks also saw reality in the noematic direction. But the Greeks did not deny the subjective dimensions of reality. Rather, they thought of reality in terms of *logos* from the nature of *logos* in the actual present. Modern physical science, in essential contrast, considers reality from the sensory nature of the present. Thus, modern physical science may be said to be the discipline of mind that has taken the noematic side of consciousness as far as it can go. Much of modern European philosophical culture, which establishes its canon of thoroughgoing objectivity, is also rationalistic in that respect. And its rationalism that engenders such a negation of subjectivity is another form of metaphysical orientation. But then—once again—the positivistic "reason" of modern philosophy is quite different from the *nous* of Greek philosophy. It brings the negation of Greek subjectivity to its ultimate conclusion. It no longer allows for an intuitive significance, such as inspired the concept of *nous*, for example, in Plato. In this connection, Max Weber has concluded that the modern capitalistic spirit has developed from a rationalistic Protestantism, especially Calvinism, which opposed the Catholicism of the Middle Ages.

But the culture of modern Russia has its own special characteristic distinct from the culture of the other nations of the West. It may be said to have an Eastern quality—that is, to have the significance of being a culture of non-being. In its own way, it is a culture of the negation of *logos.* In its inner depths there is a dark intensity—as seen, for example, in the novels of Dostoyevsky. In such a sense, it has qualities that are even more opposed to Greek culture than all other cultures. There seems to be such a special quality even in modern Russian Marxism, despite its profession of devotion to "objective science."

5

We Japanese do not know the origins of our ancestors or how our race was formed. But, needless to say, the culture of the Japanese race, which enjoyed a unique development for thousands of years in one part of the East, was an Oriental culture. Thus, I think we can characterize Japanese culture through the idea of non-being articulated above. To be sure, our ancestors have been greatly influenced by Chinese and Indian cultures. But it can be said that the Japanese race had been essentially formed prior to those influences. The Japanese people, who already had distinctive features, formed an original and independent culture through further assimilation of Chinese and Indian cultures.

As I have stated above, a culture of non-being must, in one aspect, affirm the actual because, dialectically considered, absolute negation and absolute affirmation function in the form of reciprocal mediation. But when I speak in this way, I do not mean that there is first a culture of being out of which a culture of non-being appears through its consequent negation. Such an idea would merely be a logical abstraction. Reality has the form of being and, at the same time, of non-being; it has the reciprocally mediating form of being qua non-being and non-being qua being. Thus, it is, at the same time, subjective and objective, noetic and noematic. The poles of subjectivity and objectivity are absolutely opposite, but reality itself is the unity of subjectivity and objectivity—that is, has the form of the self-identity of their absolute opposition. Indeed, it is not that the separate poles of subjectivity and objectivity come to unite, and are then actual. Both dimensions are to be conceived as simultaneously interpenetrating—that is, as a dynamic reality that is self-determining. Self-determining reality—truly dynamic reality—must be self-contradictory in this dialectical form. One's own "self" also does not exist apart from this self-contradictory form of self-determining reality. It can only be conceived in relation to the affirmation-in-negation of reality itself. It is in this sense that I have expounded my philosophy that the world must be conceived from the standpoint of our active self. The concrete world of things must indeed be such a world. We see things through our own action.

Our world can thus be thought of as an ever self-determining reality—that is, as a world that has our active intuition as its center. Various cultural forms can be conceived from this standpoint. When a communal society (*Gemeinschaft*) is historically formed, it does so as a world of active intuition.

How, then, can we regard the cultural form of ancient Japan from this standpoint?

Let us first note that, because reality has the form of self-determination through self-contradiction, we can conceive of a transcendent world beyond actuality in both directions of its negation and affirmation. Reality can be considered as the determination of absolute infinity in both directions. Accordingly, I think we can first divide cultural forms into those that are grounded in the immanent, actual world, and those based on the transcendent, non-actual world. Thus, while Christianity and Buddhism oppose one another, both can be categorized as transcending worldviews. Christianity transcends the world in the direction of affirmation, Buddhism in the direction of negation. In contrast to them, Greek and Chinese cultures can be considered to have been aesthetic and moral cultures, respectively, but both were immanent worldviews. Both were cultures of the cities. Roman culture can also be conceived in these terms—it was a legal culture, as I noted above. Even modern scientific culture may belong to this category. But modern scientific culture has retrenched the full significance of active intuition in the development of its predominant form of rationalized, profit-motivated society (*Gesellschaft*). Objectivizing science gives the instruments of action but not its content. It ends up negating the subjective dimension, as I have said.

Considering the above distinctions, ancient Japanese culture may be taken to belong to the category of the cultural forms of the immanent worldview, similar to Greece and China. It especially resembles the cultural forms of ancient Greece. This is one reason that Japanese culture can be regarded as an aesthetic culture. However, Japanese and Greek cultures are far from having the same metaphysical basis. Greek culture was a culture of *nous* that saw the actual, even while it was actual, as an image of the eternal. Thus, while the Platonic Ideas had the significance of form, they transcended time as intelligible objects. But Japanese culture was not a culture of *nous*, or intellectual. On the contrary, its special characteristic consisted of being an emotional culture. It did not look to the eternal beyond. It moved immanently from thing to thing, without transcending time.

Japanese culture acts within time. This is also the reason that Japanese culture has been described as a "monsoon culture." Possessing such an ingenuous disposition, we Japanese do not conceive of our emotional culture as something that regulates us from without. The cultural life of the Japanese people is not a culture of Platonic *eros* that sees the eternal in a beyond to which it aspires. Nor is it a religious culture that receives and obeys the commandments of God from on high. Nor again is it a moralistic culture that receives and preserves the ritualistic teachings of sage kings. Even loyalty, the loftiest moral ideal of Japan, is the expression of pure feeling. It is expressed in the sentiment: "Though if I go by sea, and my corpse may be tossed by the waves, and though if I go over the mountains, my corpse may be covered over with grass, I shall have no regrets to die for the cause of the Emperor."

The Japanese reverence for chivalry and joy in close relationships between persons are also based on such an emotional disposition. That which regulates us is neither Idea, nor commandment, nor law, nor ritual. Emotion does not see things objectively. Therefore, where there are close bonds between persons, it becomes something family-like. The nation is the great family.

When I say feeling, because it is regarded as something internal in contradistinction to the external, it may be thought to be immediately personal. But human personality is rational; while feelings are impersonal. In fact, there is neither interior nor exterior in pure feeling. The *"aware* of things" (*mono no aware*) in the ancient Japanese aesthetic concept illustrates this modality of pure feeling.

Now, to speak once more in general terms, the self-determining real world—that is, the world of active intuition—is in one aspect temporal and in another spatial. As a spatial-and-temporal world, it determines the world of things—the world in which we directly see things. However, with respect to the self-determination of such a world, we have seen that human activity is to be conceived in the direction of its temporal determination—that is, in its subjective, noetic direction—while the effects of things are to be conceived in the direction of spatial determination—that is, in the objective, noematic direction. Subjectivity and objectivity are reciprocally mediating moments of the same concrete self-determination of the world. The world can thus be thought to determine itself in dialectical form. Or—as I have often said in my other works—the world is self-determining in both linear and circular forms. Or again, in the world of concrete actuality, things are "expressive," and we "see things" through acting—that is, in "active intuition." Or, again, the actual world determines itself expressively.

I hold that the formation of our social and historical worlds must be seen in this light. In them, the various forms of culture crystallize. The culture of the intellectual Greeks was, as it were, predominantly spatial and geometrical. The Greek sense of *eidos* can be thought to be spatial. But even the pragmatic culture of China did not have the significance of "seeing things" in the full realization of "active intuition." Its form of cultural intuition, too, was predominantly spatial, exhibiting a three-dimensional nature that is absent in the Japanese feeling for the flow of time. Roman culture was also such. Ritual and law suggest a three-dimensional organization of society. By contrast, the culture of the Japanese—which is a culture of pure feeling—can be thought to be predominantly temporal in sensibility. Emotions have a temporal flow. Thus, whereas the Greeks wrote epics and tragedies, the Japanese were already writing lyrical poetry as early as the *Man'yô* period. This is also the reason the *tanka* verse form developed in Japan. And the *haiku* poetic form captures the world from the perspective of an instant of time.

Let us say that mythology was the basis of the three-dimensional organization of society in ancient times. The various strands of Greek mythology became the cultural content of Greece as the Homeric epics, and then became the material of the Greek tragedies through which the problems of human life were considered. In Japan, mythology became the foundation for a life of feeling as the source of our national polity.

The Japanese culture of pure feeling has "the form of the formless, the sound of the soundless." It is very much a symbolic culture. It is, like time, a formless unity. Such a culture of formless emotion is, like time, creative. It is, like life itself, developmental. It receives various forms but, at the same time, gives a certain form to them. Time is not just a passing flow. If it were merely such, the unity of time would not exist. As I have often written, time has the form of the determination of what is not determinate—or, again, of "the form of the formless." In time, the formless determines form. In such a sense, time is the mirror surface of infinity. Time exists as the self-determination of absolute nothingness. In these terms, even though Japanese culture resembles Greek culture in the point of being an aesthetic culture, it is nonetheless its dialectical opposite. In aesthetic intuition, a negation of time is always implied. It may be said that Greek aesthetic intuition negated time in the spatial direction, whereas Japanese aesthetic intuition negates time in the depths of time itself. The former subsumed time within space; the latter subsumes space within time. This is the reason that I refer to the ground of Japanese culture as distinctly Eastern, a culture based on the principle of non-being.

Feelings are not ritualistic, they are spontaneous. The expression of feeling is itself an aesthetic act. In such a sense, Japanese culture differs from the Confucian culture of China and may be said to be closer to Greek culture. But Japanese aesthetics differs essentially from Greek aesthetics in that it is not an aesthetics of *eidos*. Of course, no aesthetics can exist apart from form. But Greek aesthetics saw the formless within form, while not only the distinctive quality of Japanese aesthetics but also that of all Eastern aesthetics grounded in the principle of nothingness lies in employing form to express what is formless. Eastern aesthetics does not just symbolically represent other forms but reveals the formless.

Now, I have said that the idea of being is at the root of Western culture, while the idea of non-being is at the root of Eastern culture. To conceive of the ground of the world in the direction of its spatial determination is the idea of being. To conceive of it in the direction of its temporal determination entails the idea of nothingness. The former conceives of the world in an objective direction, the latter in a subjective one. One's own "self" is something predominantly temporal. The cultures of the intellectual Greek and Indian races, as Aryan races, were philosophical. But the one sought the eternal and changeless by transcending the actual temporal-spatial world in direction of objective determination—that is, of spatial determination— while the other sought it in the direction of subjective determination, or of temporal determination. For the Indians, time is "birth and death"; their sense of temporality involves *samsara*, the rounds of birth and death. The Indians thus regarded the myriad things as having the form of impermanence. Nevertheless, Indian religion sought something beyond *samsara* in the very depths of *samsara*. Greek philosophy reached its culmination in the philosophy of Plotinus. And needless to say, while Plotinian philosophy was affine with Indian philosophy in certain respects, their fundamental orientations were quite opposite to one another.

The pragmatic culture of China resembled that of the Jewish people in several ways. Someone could say that the Confucian idea of Heaven might be developed into the Jewish idea of God. Or, the position of Christ might be given to Confucius. As a matter of fact, the ideas of the Kung-yang scholars of the Ch'ing dynasty were moving in that direction. But the Confucian idea of Heaven meant the Way of life; it cannot be thought to have been equivalent to the God of theism. In Lao-tzu and Chuang-tzu it was clearly a naturalistic Way of life based in non-being. Non-being was considered to be the beginning of heaven and earth. This Taoist idea was not conceived in the direction of an intellectual object but in the depths of spiritual practice.

Time has neither an origin from which it comes into being nor a place toward which it passes away. It arises from and returns to non-being. It must be considered to be the self-determination of absolute nothingness. Thus, in Taoism, non-being was considered as the beginning of heaven and earth. This is not to say that Lao-tzu and Chuang-tzu consciously entertained such a meaning. But, not only in Lao-tzu and Chuang-tzu but throughout Chinese philosophy, reality was considered to exist in the depths of spiritual practice. The fact that they conceived non-being in the very heart of practice must have such a significance. This would seem also to be the reason that, while the school of Legalist philosophers emerged in ancient Chinese culture, there was ultimately not a development of law as in Roman culture. Thus, despite the fact that the culture of the Chinese resembled Judaic and Roman cultures in certain respects, they were nonetheless qualitatively different.

The concept of our personhood must of course refer to something temporal. There cannot be a concept of a personal self apart from time. But it is not that the concept of person is considered in the very depths of time but in the process of time. The personal self is historical. Even though the person exists apart from space, the person must always belong to a historical world of space and time. In such a sense, it must also possess a spatial nature. Thus, the God of the Jews was thought to exist at the beginning of the historical world of space and time. In such a sense, it must also possess a spatial nature. Thus, the God of the Jews was thought to exist at the beginning of the historical world; He was the God of the creation of heaven and earth. While this

Hebrew concept of God transcended intellectual objects, it did so in the direction of intellectual objects. It was not considered to exist in the very depths of the self itself. This is another reason I refer to Judeo-Christian culture as a philosophy of being.

It is usually said that there was no concept of history in ancient India, and that it lacked an idea of time. There may therefore be some objection to my characterizing Indian culture through the category of time. However, concrete time must essentially have a spatial nature. When we take time as merely temporal, time ceases to be. And in that case, the objective world also is negated. Such a world is then conceived as the mere world of *samsara*, of impermanence.

Time, in essence, must be understood as an indeterminate determination—that is, as non-being. In time there is neither beginning nor end; it is an immediate passage from an infinite past to an infinite future. However, time does not merely fly away as a mere succession of instants. If this were so, there would be no linear unity to time. And yet, there is no link between the beginning and end of time. If the beginning and end were linked in any sense, it would not be time. Therefore, time must be considered to be the indeterminate determination of non-being. Or again, time must be what I term the self-determination of a dialectical universal.

Brahman, the absolute reality of the religion of India—who is said to embrace this world like a cloak, to be both rest and motion, to be both near and far, but invisible to the senses—presupposes the indeterminate determination of non-being in the above sense. Even Lao-tzu's concept of non-being, the mother of heaven and earth, has such an implication. But absolute negation mediates absolute affirmation. Thus, Mahayana Buddhism embodied the more adequately dialectical idea that "the willows are green, the flowers are red." In Lao-tzu and Chuang-tzu it took the form of esteem for "spontaneity" and "acting without purpose." Taoism's idea of nothingness tended both to support asceticism, on the one hand, and to encourage sensualism, on the other. Both tendencies are contained in the teaching of "following its [the Tao's] flow and riding its waves."

However, if time is considered as the determination of absolute non-being or nothingness, it must be linear; it must move from instant to instant. Here a true "momentalism" can be conceived. Time must always be considered from the present—that is, from the moving present, the self-determining present. This is precisely the reason that it can be regarded as the determination of non-being. When the present is regarded either as stationary or as determined from the past or from the future, time becomes spatialized. Only when the present is self-determining can time, as the determination of what is indeterminate, be truly understood as such. Past and future are, on the contrary, to be considered from the moving present. The self-determining present always extends. When such a present is thus considered as the form of the absolutely formless—that is, as the determination of absolute non-being—time is linear movement. I reconceive of the ancient concept of "the form of the formless, the voice of the voiceless" in this way.

This is hardly to say, however, that "the form of the formless, the voice of the voiceless" means nothing at all. It, rather, indicates that existential being in the present has the significance of not being intellectually determinable—and that it is the expression of infinite feeling. The object of feeling cannot be intellectually determined. It cannot be frozen spatially. It is infinitely dynamic. Indeed, while it has form, it is formless. It is in these terms, I think, that an emotional culture can be conceived that is adequate to grasp the essence of Japanese culture. I have shown that Japanese culture is a culture neither of *eidos* nor of ritual but one of pure feeling. The fact that the Greek aesthetic sensibility differs in essence from the Japanese aesthetic sensibility also lies herein. The mysterious quality (*yûgensei*) prized in Japanese aesthetics is a good example of this kind of culture of pure feeling.

Even if we call Taoist culture a culture of non-being, it was still imprisoned by non-being—that is, by the form of non-being. Its present was not a moving one but only an indeterminate present. The true self-determination of non-being must be infinitely active as the absolute affirmation of absolute negation. Its present is infinitely moving. It is what Moroori Norinaga refers to as "the cherry blossoms glowing in the morning sun." A merely naturalistic momentalism is still imprisoned by the determined instant. The true instant of time intersects eternity. That is the reason I like to think that the true intention of Mahayana Buddhism—which holds that "the willows are green, the blossoms are red"—is to be found exemplarily in something such as Japanese culture.

I am not saying that Japanese culture is equivalent to the Indian culture where the tendency is to affirm absolute negation with prevailing emphasis on negation. The Japanese people cannot be regarded as pessimistic. I do not know what the life of our Japanese ancestors was, but I think that, as they founded a nation on these geographically remote islands—in the fortunate condition of having no great friction among races within the country and no antagonism with other nations from without—they prospered within Japan's beautiful natural scenery so as to nourish their own ingenuous characteristic of pure feeling. That characteristic of pure feeling may be considered the source of the development of Japanese culture bearing the cultural significance expressed above. Japanese culture had already been influenced by Chinese and Indian cultures from ancient times. But when Buddhism later developed in a distinctively Japanese form it, too, became a Buddhism of feeling.

Thus, for example, although the True Pure Land Sect and the Nichiren Sect had mutually antagonistic characteristics, both were emotional forms of Buddhism. The Nichiren Sect might perhaps, rather, be called volitional in character. But it, too, was not volitional in the sense of proceeding from the basis of the rational personality. Sects [of the Nara period] such as the philosophical Kegon and Tendai and the legalistic Ritsu Sect did not in the long run become Japanese religions. As for the Shingon Sect, which was transformed into something uniquely Japanese by the Great Teacher Kôbô (Kûkai), its realistic features appealed to the Japanese nature. Later, Zen—which taught that "the willows are green and the flowers are red"—fused with Japan's warrior spirit in the Kamakura period and thus it, too, was a great influence on Japanese culture. We may even say that Zen has deeply permeated Japanese life.

The introduction of Chinese culture into Japan began, according to tradition, when Wani dedicated ten scrolls of the Confucian *Analects* and one scroll of the *Thousand Character Classic* in the ancient time of Emperor Ôjin [270–310]. (It may even have been introduced before that.) But the influence of Chinese culture on ancient Japanese culture was not especially Confucian but, rather, institutional and literary. Confucianism became a social force only later, in the Tokugawa period. Thus, I shall not belabor the point that, even though Japanese art and literature were influenced by Chinese culture, they crystallized finally into something Japanese in quality. Even the Confucianism that developed in later Japanese history was not ritualistic but rather the Neo-Confucianism of Sung China. And that Tokugawa period Sung Learning became closely linked to the Japanese Way of the Warrior. Moreover, I think that it, too, was a Confucianism of pure feeling of a depth expressed in the words:

> Heaven and earth are the great vitality. How purely it cherishes the land of the gods [Japan], whose essence is manifested in its unique mountain [Fuji], lofty and majestic through one thousand autumns. Its flowing rivers become the great ocean. How wide and deep it encircles the eight islands. It bursts forth into a myriad of cherry blossoms, beyond the compare of other flowers. It crystallizes into swords forged a hundred times, whose blades can cleave through iron pans.

6

In the above articulation, I take what are considered to be the characteristics of various cultures and discuss their metaphysical differences and relations.

Historical reality, I maintain, is spatial and temporal, objective and subjective, being and non-being. Needless to say, every culture that appears historically as a concrete reality exhibits these dialectical aspects to some extent. The more concrete it is, the more this is true.

Cultures may be said to be the realized contents of the historical world, which has the form of a contradictory identity as individual qua universal and universal qua individual. The world's cultures are, of course, essentially plural. They cannot be reduced to unity for the reason that, when they lose their specificity, they cease to be cultures. Consequently, the process of development of an authentic world culture from the standpoint of authentic culture cannot be a merely abstract advance in a single direction. That would amount to the negation of culture. A true world culture will be formed only by various cultures preserving their own respective viewpoints but simultaneously developing themselves through the mediation of the world. In that respect, first deeply considering the individual ground of each culture, we must clarify on what basis and in what relation to other cultures each individual culture stands. How do Eastern and Western cultures differ in their roots? What significance does Japanese culture have in Eastern culture? Its strong points are at once its weak points. We can learn the path along which we should truly advance only as we both deeply fathom our own depths and attain a profound understanding of other cultures.

Ed. note: Translated by David A. Dilworth, Valdo H. Viglielmo, and Agustin Jacinto Zavala.

10

The Significance of Ethics as the Study of Man

Watsuji Tetsurô

THE PRIMARY SIGNIFICANCE of my approach to ethics through the study of the Japanese term for man (*ningen*) is that it avoids the misconception of the modern world which takes ethics merely as a problem of the individual consciousness. This misconception is based upon the modern world's individualistic view of man. In itself, grasping the individual has been the achievement of the modern spirit and has an importance we must not overlook. However, individualism attempts to substitute the individual, who is merely one moment of human existence, for the totality of man. This abstraction breeds all kinds of further misconceptions. The standpoint of the isolated ego or self that is the point of departure of modern philosophy is also really nothing but one example of this. As long as this standpoint limits itself to the question of contemplation of objective nature, the misconception is not very conspicuous. For the standpoint of contemplation of nature is already one step removed from concrete human existence, and it thus is a scene which individuals as "contemplators of objects"—that is, as active subjects—can describe categorically. However, for the problem of human existence—that is, the problem of practical, behavioral relationships—the above kind of isolated subjectivity is essentially irrelevant. And yet this view of isolated subjectivity that abstracts from the behavioral relationships between men is then erroneously applied even to ethical questions. The result is that the area of ethical questions appears to parallel the relationship between human subjectivity and nature, and within that relation the sphere of the self is treated as a problem of the will in contrast to the problem of cognition. Accordingly, such considerations as the individual self's independence from nature, its autonomy, or its satisfaction of desires, are placed at the center of ethical questions. But no matter in which direction one attempts to develop a theory, the problem cannot be resolved from this standpoint alone. Ultimately, unless one introduces such concepts as a trans-individual self, or the well-being of society, or the welfare of mankind, first principles cannot be established. This serves to prove that ethical questions are not merely questions of the individual consciousness.

The place of ethical questions really lies in what is expressed in Japanese as the "between-ness between persons" (*hito to hito to no aidagara*), not in the consciousness of the isolated individual. This is why I call ethics the study of man [*ningengaku*, taking my point of departure from a study of the Japanese term *ningen*]. I hold that, except as problems of the "betweenness" between persons, the concepts of the good or evil of behavior, duty, responsibility, and virtue cannot be truly understood. Moreover, we can most readily clarify this matter by pursuing an etymological analysis of the Japanese characters for ethics (*rinri*) that we are using here.

Rinri

The concept of ethics is expressed by the term *rinri*. Now language is one of the most remarkable creations of mankind. No man can claim that he personally has created a language. And yet words, for any person, are his or her own words. This characteristic of words derives from the fact that language is the crucible which transforms the subjective relationships between persons into noematic meanings. In other words, language is the transformation into consciousness of existence that is prior to consciousness. This existence is a substantive reality that cannot be objectified but, at the same time, it involves the practical behavioral relationship among persons. Therefore, its structure is such that, as it is transformed into consciousness—despite the fact that it may be the content of this or that individual person—it does not take only individual existence as its origin. In this sense, words are indeed expressions of the subjective existence of persons and accordingly provide an access for us into their subjective existence. My following endeavor to take a philological approach in clarifying the concepts of ethics is based on such reasoning.

The word *rinri* is composed of the two characters *rin* and *ri*. *Rin* connotes "companionate association" (*nakama*). *Nakama* means a group taken as a relational structure among specific individuals but, at the same time, it refers to the individuals determined by this group. In ancient China, the relationships between father and son, lord and subject, husband and wife, older and younger brothers, and between friend and friend were called "the great relationships of man" [the Five Constant Relations]. In other words, they were the most important *nakama*. The relationship between father and son is a *rin*, a specific *nakama*. Now this does not mean that a father and son first exist as separate individuals and then create their relationship. The father acquires his title as father, and the son as son, only within this relationship. In other words, they become father and son by virtue of their being the constituent members of that *nakama*. Why, however, is it that one *nakama* determines the relationship between two men as friends, in contrast to another *nakama* determining the two men in it as father and son? It must be because a *nakama* is a specific way (*shikata*) of relationship. Consequently, *rin* means *nakama* and, at the same time, also refers to specific ways of behavioral relationship in human existence. From this, *rin* comes to mean a structure (*kimari*) or a pattern (*kata*)—or, again, an order (*chitsujo*)—within human existence. It is these *rin* that constitute the "way of man" (*ningen no michi*) in Confucianism.

The above ways of behavioral relationship do not exist in themselves apart from behavioral relationships. They always exist only as founded on behavioral relationships, as ways of transaction among individuals. However, when dynamic human existence is repeatedly realized in specific ways, persons can grasp these ways apart from their basis in dynamic existence. Such things as the Confucian *rin*—namely, "the five constant relations and the five cardinal virtues" (*gorin gojô*)—when they have been transformed into noematic meanings, are examples of this. The word *ri* that is joined to *rin* means reason (equivalent in Japanese to the words *kotowari* and *sujimichi*), and it is generally added to emphasize the way, the order, of the aforementioned behavior. Therefore, ethics refers to the order (*chitsujo*), the way (*michi*), which causes the communal existence of man to be what it is. In other words, ethics refers to the laws of social existence.

Therefore, when an ethical order already exists, does it not have meaning as a moral imperative (*tôi*)? The answer is both yes and no. As in the fifth of the Confucian five constant relations, "between friends there is trust," to the extent that a relation of friendship has become a lived reality, "trust" as the constitutive way of behavioral association already exists at the foundation of this relationship. Without this trust, there is no friendship. However, such a group (*nakama*) is not a static being but exists dynamically in the behavioral association itself. Prior behavior in a specific relationship does not render impossible later withdrawal from it. At every moment such a form of communal existence harbors the peril of its own dissolution. And yet, because human existence is human existence, it is endlessly oriented toward the realization of communal existence. And hence a way of behavioral relationship already realized provides, at the same time, the momentum by which one should continue to act. Therefore, ethics is not a mere [isolated] moral *ought* but already exists, on the one hand; yet it is not a mere law of being, but is something that can be endlessly realized, on the other.

As the above philological analysis shows, we can clarify the concept of ethics from the meaning of the term *rinri*. To be sure, the provenance of this term returns us to the intellectual history of ancient China; the more we consider the social context of ancient China in terms of the sociology of religion, the more this intellectual history comes to express a profound significance. However, I am not attempting to revive an ideology of human relationships based upon the social forms of ancient China exactly as they were. Here I am only attempting to resurrect the meaning of ethics as the way of human relationships for the sake of my position that ethics is always a question of the "betweenness between persons" (*hito to hito to no aidagara*).

At the same time that the concept of ethics thus becomes clarified, it will also become clear that the key to this clarification is nothing other than such concepts as the relations between persons, the nature of human existence, and of behavioral or practical association. *Rin*, as we saw, means *nakama*, and it also refers to the ways of behavioral association as *nakama*. However, what do *nakama* and "man" (*ningen*) signify? These are not self-evident concepts. To inquire about ethics is, in the end, nothing else than to inquire about the ways of human existence, and consequently about man. That is why I approach ethics as the study of *ningen*.

Ningen

Let me now also clarify the concept of man (*ningen*) that I have used vaguely up to this point. This is especially necessary in order to distinguish it from the philosophical anthropology that has become popular in recent times. Philosophical anthropology—as exemplified, for example, by Max Scheler in his *Die Stellung des Menschen im Kosmos*—purports to grasp a human being as the unity of spirit and the life urge. This is nothing more than a new approach within the framework of that problematic which sees the human being only from the perspective of the unity of mind and body. Scheler also reduces all the questions that he cites as archetypes of classical anthropology to the realm of this focus. (See his *Philosophische Weltanschauung*, "*Mensch und Geschichte*," 1929). These archetypes are:

1. The concept of the human being in the Christian faith: man is first created by the personal God; because of his sin he is given over to punishment and redeemed through Christ. This becomes the point of

departure of an anthropology centering on the problem of soul and body.

2. The human being is a rational being (*homo sapiens*):
   a. Man possesses spirit, that is, reason.
   b. This spirit forms the world as the world.
   c. Spirit, that is, reason, is active in itself without dependence on sensation.
   d. Spirit undergoes no historical or specific changes. (Only this last point is repudiated by Hegel. The philosophers who determined that this anthropology was the invention of the Greeks were Dilthey and Nietzsche.)

3. The human being is a working being, a technician (*homo faber*). (This anthropology conflicts with the former. There is no essential distinction between men and beasts. Man merely creates language and tools; he is differentiated from other animals only as an animal whose brain is especially developed. This is the anthropology of naturalism and positivism.)

4. The human being is sick because he possesses spirit. (This view is a new attack on *homo sapiens*.)

5. The human being has transcendent capabilities. (This is an anthropology of great personality that elevates man's self-consciousness.)

I note that Scheler's five types all abstract human being from social groups and attempt to grasp the human being as something self-existing. Consequently, the problem of man always is a question of spirit or body or the self. And therefore, even if this *Anthropologie* [the science of man] is opposed to what has been developed in anthropology or ethnology understood as physical anthropology—and even though it is advocated as philosophical anthropology in contradistinction to physical anthropology—it does not differ in its fundamental attitude of attempting to see the essence of the human being in the individual alone.

This tendency seems to be based on the fact that such words as *anthropos*, *homo*, *man*, and *Mensch* primarily mean an individual human being. In such a standpoint, such ideas as the betweenness between person and person, communal existence, and society must somehow be expressed through words which differ from the word for human being. However, if a human being is essentially a social animal, such things as betweenness between persons or society cannot be divorced from the human focus. A person must be able to exist individually and at the same time must be a social being. The word that very well expresses this double nature is the word *ningen*. Therefore, from the viewpoint of *ningen*, the fact of defining "the science of man" (*Anthropo-*

logie) and "the social sciences" as somewhat different things must be based on an attempt to abstract these moments from concrete man and isolate them. If human being (*ningen*) is to be considered in its concreteness, that consideration must be the single discipline. But at the same time, the study of human being is not some vague synthesis of the study of the individual and of social science; it must be something fundamentally different from either. For the grasping of individuals and society as constituting the twofold character of *ningen* and finding therein the deepest essence of the human being cannot even become problematic from the standpoint which takes as its premise a radical distinction in meaning between individuals and society.

How, then, can the term *ningen* signify the above kind of twofold character of human existence? In ordinary usage is not the term *ningen* synonymous with man and *Mensch*, and is not the term *ningengaku* the translation of *Anthropologie*? This is certainly the case. The term *ningen* also supports this kind of usage. However, it does not merely mean that. As shown by the very characters used for the term *ningen*, it is also a word meaning "the relation between persons"—that is, *yo no naka* or *seken*. Both terms mean "public world" or "human society," as will become clarified in the ensuing analysis. Moreover, this was the original meaning of these terms. Both in the ancient literary classics of China and the Buddhist sutras that we Japanese have taken over from China, the word "human being" (*ningen*) is always used in the sense of *yo no naka* or *seken*. And yet during their long history the Japanese people have converted these words into the meaning of individual human being, too. What mediated such a transformation were the words used in the Chinese translations of those Buddhist sutras that articulate a view of human life involving the concept of transmigration. For example, the Indian word for "the world of sentient beings" was for the sake of convenience translated as "animal life" (*chikushô*) and was always used together with the word for human being (*ningen*). From this usage, the latter word came to mean "mankind" within a perspective that distinguishes human from animal life, and also in due course it came to mean individual human beings. However, the important thing is that this was not accidental but a historical process in which, whatever the agency, the term *ningen*—originally meaning *yo no naka*—came to bear the meaning of the individual human beings as well. Poetry, aphorisms, and proverbs that speak about human being (*ningen*) became household words among the Japanese people after they were transmitted from China. In them *ningen* always means *yo no naka*. At the same time, what was said about *yo no naka* always held good for the individuals who lived within it. This accounts for the gradual transformation of the term.

Keeping this fact in mind, let us go on to consider other words that express both the whole and the parts of human life. *Nakama* means a group (*dantai*), and yet it also can refer to a single person. *Rôtô* or *rôdô* (vassals, retainers) also refer to a group, and yet an individual who belongs to it can also be spoken of as a *rôtô*. Such words as *tomodachi* (friend, or friends), *heitai* (soldier, or soldiers), *wakashû* (youth, or a youth), and *renchû* (party, or company, and the individual members of it) all have this double connotation. The usage of these words clearly indicates the fact that in human existence the whole exists in the parts and the parts exist in the whole. Therefore, it is hardly an exceptional case that the term *ningen*, which means *yo no naka* as a totality of persons, came further to signify the individual person who exists within that *yo no naka*.

The Japanese language thus possesses a very meaningful term, *ningen*. We have created the concept of human being (*ningen*) on the basis of the historical evolution of this word. *Ningen* is both the public *yo no naka* and at the same time the individuals who exist within it. Therefore, it is not merely "individuals," and at the same time it is not merely "society." Herein appears the reciprocal—dialectical—unity of the twofold character of human being (*ningen*). As long as *ningen* are individuals, they always will differ from society as a whole. Because they are not society as a whole, they are individuals. And hence one individual is not entirely the same as another individual; the self and the other are absolutely "other" to each other. And yet as long as human beings (*ningen*) are society (*yo no naka*), there is always a communal situation; there is society and not merely isolated individuals. Precisely because there are not isolated individuals there is *ningen*. Consequently, self and other, though they are absolutely "other" to one another, are nevertheless one in their mutual relatedness. Individuals, who fundamentally differ from society as a whole, are yet immersed within society. The human being (*ningen*) is this kind of relational unity of opposites. The essence of man cannot be understood without observing this dialectical structure.

Professor Yoshida Seiichi's explanation of this structure by his analogy of different centers within the same circle is extremely interesting. However, it is impossible for the same circle to have many different centers except as a unity of contradictions. Since such a thing is impossible in the case of a finite circle, he postulates that the individual centers express the individual nature of persons; he also postulates a circle of infinite radius to signify an infinity of persons. In infinity every distinction returns to identity. However, this *coincidentia* of identity and difference is a relationship between individuals and the infinite, as it were, not the relationship between individuals and a society as described above. In any shape and form a society is a finite structure of human existence—in terms of the analogy, it is a circle of finite radius. Unless the analogy of many centers of the same circle can be spoken of in terms of such a circle as well, it cannot be an analogy appropriate to our case. Hence let us postulate a case in which a circle of finite radius is the determination of a circle of infinite radius. When the infinity of the radius is negated and has become finite, a finite circle results as the realization of an infinite circle. The relationship of different centers in the infinite circle has been realized in the finite circle. Such a fact may be geometrically impossible, but human existence truly has such a structure. Thus, the finite circle that has been made the reverse side of the infinite circle comes perfectly to represent a society. While the center points are the negation of the circle and are individually distinct, as centers they are centers of the same circle. The analogy of different centers of the same circle can have significance only as the expression of such a structure.

The concept of *ningen* thus differs from *anthropos*, and has been defined in its double character of referring to both a society (*yo no naka*) and the individuals (*hito*) who compose it. However, when we did so we understood what is called society or public world (*yo no naka, seken*) by at once interchanging it with communal existence (*kyôdô sonzai*) or society (*shakai*). Was this really correct? By asking this question we have approached consideration of a central problem in modern philosophy—that is, the meaning of being-in-the-world.

Yo No Naka

When Heidegger defined man's existence as being-in-the-world, his point of departure was the idea of intentionality developed in modern phenomenology. Probing this structure a step deeper within existence, he understood it as something such as a relation with tools. Therefore, his thought is in fact exemplary as regards disclosing the subjective significance of what is expressed by human *Dasein*'s being-in-the-world. However, in Heidegger the betweenness between persons is still somewhat hidden in the shadow of man's relationship with tools. Despite the fact that he himself asserts that he is not overlooking it, it is an evident fact that the interpersonal relation is given a subordinate role. Hence his disciple Karl Löwith—in his *Das Individuum in der Rolle des Mitmenschen*, 1928—has attempted to bring this overshadowed aspect into the light and to clarify the concept of being-in-the-world principally from the perspective of the relationship between persons. Heidegger's writings are a universal phenomenological *Ontologie*, whereas Löwith departs from this ground and moves to *Anthropologie*. His *Anthropologie* does not deal with individual persons, but with the betweenness (*aidagara*) between self and other—in other words, precisely with the mutual relatedness (*kakawari*) of persons. Consequently, individuals are persons who co-exist (*tomo ni aru hito*): the world is the world of co-existence, a *mit-Welt* (*tomo ni aru sekai*)—that is, *seken*—and being-in-the-world is being-mutually-related (*tagai ni kakawariau koto*). Hence Löwith's *Anthropologie* cannot help becoming the basis of the examination of ethical questions. For what makes individuals interested in mutual dealings are matters connected with life, and thus these matters of common concern and this attitude to one another include their fundamental attitudes, their fundamental moralities—that is, their *ethos*. For this reason a study of the reciprocal structures of human existence becomes ethics. From such a perspective, Löwith's contribution consisted of analyzing the concept of being-in-the-world as the "between-ness" between men.

According to Löwith's view, in the German word *Welt* there is already a human element. (From our point of view, this element corresponds to the connotation of the Japanese *seken*.) Consider such phrases as *Ein Mann von Welt* (a man of the world), *weltkundig* (a man experienced in the ways of the world), *weltfremdig* (unversed in the ways of the world), *weltflüchtig* (misanthrope, a person who shuns society), *weltlich gesinnt* (sociable, knowledgeable), *weltverächter* (a person who looks askance at society), *alle Welt* (the world, society, life). In addition, each such term as *Männerwelt* (world of men), *Frauenwelt* (world of women), *vornehme Welt* (fashionable society), and *Halbwelt* (demimonde) serves to signify a specific social sphere. In other words, *Welt* is not the world of nature but the related-ness between men—that is, communal existence, society. In these terms the analysis of *in-der-Welt-sein* becomes an analysis of the modalities of communal life.

Now, what is said in this way about *Welt* can be said even more obviously about the Japanese *yo no naka* and *seken*. Just as the word *Welt* originally meant a generation as well as a group of individuals, *yo* also means a generation or age (*sedai*) as well as a society (*shakai*). In other words, *yo* is that which moves temporally and, at the same time, somehow has the character of a place, as in the case of a hermit "leaving the world" or someone being "a wanderer through life." However, when the terms *seken* and *yo no naka* are used, it is not merely *yo*, that is, *Welt*; it is compounded with one or other of the Japanese words that connote "within." In other words, it becomes *in-der-Welt*. And yet, unlike the German *in*, the Japanese words connoting "within" do not express merely a spatial meaning—still less, as in Heidegger, merely a relationship of involvement with tools—but in addition they clearly express human relationship. Such phrases as *danjo no aida* (relationship between man and woman), *fūfu no naka* (relationship between husband and wife), *aida o hedateru* (to break off a relationship), and *naka tagai suru* (to fall out with, be estranged from) illustrate this nuance. Indeed, such human relationships are not objective relationships which come into being in the

unity of subjects after the analogy of the relationships between two spatial
things. They are behavioral bonds of association between persons—such as in
the words *majiwari* and *kôtsû*, where one finds subjective, mutual relatedness.
Unless they behave as subjects persons cannot exist in any relational situation
at all; but at the same time they cannot behave or act except in some relational situation. Therefore "withinness" refers to a living dynamic relationship that is a subjective behavioral association. The terms *seken* and *yo no
naka* are formed from the combination of the above terms for "withinness"
and the temporal-and-spatial word *yo*. Hence the terms *seken* and *yo na naka*
are used as terms indicating something subjective, as in the phrases *seken ni
shirareru* (to be well known in society) or *yo no naka o sawagaseru* (create a
stir in society). In these examples it would seem to be clear that *seken* and *yo
no naka* signify society or communal existence as subjective entities. To be
known by only two or three friends is not to be "known in society." And one
or two people stirred up does not mean a stir created in society. *Seken* as a
subjective entity that "knows" [a public figure] or that is publicly "stirred"
must refer to a behavioral association between persons and, at the same time,
must consist of a communal subjective entity—that is, subjective communal
existence which transcends the individual subjects in this association.[1]

The superiority of the Japanese concepts of *seken* or *yo no naka* over the
German concept of *Welt* lies in the fact that they simultaneously connote
both the temporal and the spatial dimensions of subjective, communal existence. *Welt*, as we saw above, signified generation as well as group of persons
or the totality of persons understood as the communal matrices in which
individuals are set within that generation. However, with the passage of time
this kind of temporal-spatial meaning disappeared, and in the end the word
Welt inclined one-sidedly toward the meaning of the world understood as
the totality of objective natural things. However, in the case of *seken* and *yo
no naka*, even though their meanings have undergone change, the meaning
of something subjectively extended has been firmly preserved. Therefore, the
concept of *seken* continues to connote the historical, climatic, and societal
structures of human existence. *Seken* and *yo no naka* refer to human existence that is historical, climatic, and societal.

Hence, in the human being (*ningen*), comprising both society or world (*yo
no naka*) and its individuals (*hito*), I designate the previously described quality of being in the world (*yo no naka*) as the social nature or sociality of man,
whereas the quality of being an individual (*hito*) I designate as the person's
individuality. To regard *ningen* merely as *hito* is to consider the double connotation only from the aspect of individuality. This may be permissible as a
methodological abstraction but, if it is limited to that, there can be no con-

crete understanding of human being. We must always understand human being as a dialectical unity of the above two modalities.

Now, I have defined human being (*ningen*) composed in the above dual structure as always something subjective. The concept refers to subjective, communal existence in the manner of behavioral relationships and, at the same time, individuals who act in those relationships. This subjective, dynamic structure prevents our understanding the person as a reified thing or substance. A person is not a person without the behavioral relationships in which he or she is always acting. These behavioral relationships constantly both produce individuals and re-immerse them in the whole. This kind of mode of inter-relational being—rather, to speak more accurately, of dialectical mediation from being to non-being and from non-being to being and, consequently, the very mode of becoming of a human being—I should now like to articulate by the concept of existence (*sonzai*). Accordingly, my concept of existence will not exactly correspond to such Western terms as *Sein*, *einai*, or *esse*. Nor will my study of existence correspond to *Ontologie*.

Sonzai

At present the Japanese term *sonzai* is, in fact, used as equivalent to the German *Sein*. Why, then, am I attempting purposely to bring out the differences and distinguish the concept of *sonzai* from that of *Sein*? The reason is that the meaning of the word *sonzai* is extremely different from the meaning of *Sein*. The distinctive meaning that *Sein* as a central problem of philosophy has been made to bear can hardly be found in the word *sonzai*. In the point of departure of Fichte's philosophy, *Sein* was a postulate. It was the *Sein* of the proposition of identity, "*A ist A*." The *Sein* that is the point of departure of Hegel's logic, too, was the "is" (*de aru* in Japanese) of immediate indetermination; it was not what is meant by *sonzai*. In these usages the meaning of *Sein* is identical with the copula "is" as employed in formal logic, but they also intend it to function as "there is" or "there are" (*ga aru* in Japanese) in other aspects. This double intention constitutes the problem of *Sein*. Putting it the other way around, the problem of the relationship between thinking and being arose from the fact that "is"—meaning "there is" (*ga aru*) a certain thing—functions in another respect as the "is" of the logical copula. It can be said that already in Aristotle *einai* expresses this relationship of thinking to being. In Hobbes, *est* does not stop with being merely the sign of union; there is strong emphasis on its expressing the *causa* of union—in other words, *est* expresses *essentia*, not *existentia*. When it is said that the sky is blue, one and the same thing, the cause of the union of sky and blue, is expressed by *est*. In contrast to this, J. S. Mill asserts that *est* also expresses *existentia*. The copula is, indeed, as Hobbes asserts, a sign that unites the predicate to the subject. But the idea that the copula *est* on top of this expresses *existentia* is mere mysticism. Even though it can be said that a centaur is (*de aru*) a product of the poet's imagination, that the centaur exists (*ga aru*) is entirely without meaning. However, *est* does not function only as copula. In another respect *est* expresses *existentia*. In other words, *est* functions as both "is" (*de aru*) and "there is" (*ga aru*). Now, precisely this question of the relation between *essentia* and *existentia* is one of the central problems of that medieval *Ontologie* that was based on Aristotle.

However, in all these questions, what would be the result if *est* were interchanged with the word *sonzai*? Can *sonzai* function as a copula, or can it express *essentia*? By no means! Therefore, it seems one cannot help but conclude that to translate *Sein* as *sonzai* shows a blindness to the problem of *Sein*.

What, then, is the original meaning of the Japanese term *sonzai*?

The original meaning of *son* is subjective self-preservation. It is holding onto as opposed to forgetting and losing—for example, it is preserving one's life as opposed to losing it. However, the self that the subject preserves may become objectified into an ideal, or else a thing-like, intentional object. In the various expressions meaning "to be alive"—such as *sonshin* (preserve the body or person), *zonjô* (preserve life), *zommei* (preserve life), *zonroku* (preserve the record of one's life), and so forth—the self is preserved in the form of the body, one's life, or some document, respectively. Now, since the things thus preserved are by this fact able to continue to be, it also means that they themselves continue in existence. When the subjective preserves its body, it also is true that the body continues to exist. However, in this case, too, "existing" is precariously opposed to "dying." Whether one "preserves one's self" or things "exist," in either case the word for "preserve" is something that can change into "perish" at any moment—that is, it is the *son* of *sombô* (life or death, fate, destiny), where a temporal quality is made an essential part of its definition.

The original meaning of the *zai* is that a subject exists in some place. Therefore *zai* (to be in, or to remain in) is said to be the opposite of "going away." Going away is the movement from one place to another place of something that can go away of itself. Conversely, only a being that can go away of itself can remain in a certain place. Such ordinary usages as *zaishuku* (staying at an inn), *zaitaku* (being at home), *zaikyô* (being in one's native village), and *zaisei* (while alive) illustrate this point. Now, the place where a subject is will be a social place, such as an inn, his home, his native village, or the world. In other words, it is some human relationship such as a family, a village, a town, or society. Accordingly, *zai* is precisely the entering into or going out of some human relationship of an active subject while existing in such a relationship. Of course, *zai* may also be said of things, but a thing is not something that can go away of itself. That such a thing "is in some place" is essentially a personification. The determination of place is the work of a human being and, accordingly, that a thing is in some place refers merely to the fact that a human being confers upon that thing a location.

If, as in the above analysis, *son* refers to the self-maintaining of a subject and *zai* to existing in human relationships, then the compound *sonzai* is indeed the self-maintaining of the subject in the human mode of between-ness—that is, the fact of a person preserving himself or herself in relatedness. We can perhaps also say more simply that *sonzai* refers to the behavioral relationships of human beings (*ningen no kôiteki renkan*). Therefore, in the strict sense, *sonzai* is simply human existence (*ningen sonzai*). The existence of a thing is merely a personification of "the being of things" conferred by human existence.

My philological derivation of the meaning of *sonzai* demonstrates that the term does not correspond to *Sein*. It expresses the subjective, practical, dynamic structure of human existence.

In the fuller analysis, I have articulated four fundamental concepts: ethics (*rinri*), human being (*ningen*), public world or society (*yo no naka, seken*), and existence (*sonzai*). *Rinri* is the way of behavioral relations that causes human being to be human being (*ningen*). It connotes the mode of human existence. Accordingly, ethics (*rinragaku*) is the study of human being in the sense of the study of human existence. Because it investigates the practical roots of such concepts as "being" and the "consciousness of the moral ought," it also requires a fundamental place in regard to "the study of being" and "the study of the consciousness of the moral ought." Through a radical clarification of human existence we can go on to investigate such problems as how objective being comes to be established from human existence, or how the consciousness of a moral imperative comes to develop in each historical age. This kind of clarification of the hermeneutical basis—which is something prior to every being of objective nature and to every ideal ought—must always reach down to the concrete dimension of subjective, practical existence.

Ethics as the Study of Man

How this kind of clarification of subjective existence can be made is a question of methodology, which I shall take up in the next chapter. Assuming it to be possible for now, I am saying that the existential structure of man should be understood from its inherent double nature. In order to give a preliminary grasp of the problem of "ethics as the study of man," I here wish only to sketch in outline the kind of problems this double structure of human existence involves.

First of all, there is the double structure itself of human existence. No matter what part of man's daily existence we take, we can at once gain access into this double structure. When grasped in detail, this double structure is truly nothing other than a dialectical movement of negation. On the one hand, the position of the acting individual arises only as some negation of the totality of man. An individual who does not have such a meaning of negation—as an essentially independent and self-sufficient individual—is a mere hypothetical construct. On the other hand, the totality of man always arises in the negation of individuality. A totality that does not negatively include individuals is also a mere construct. These two negations reciprocally constitute the double nature of man. Moreover, they are one dialectical movement. It is precisely because individuals are the negations of the totality that they must essentially represent nothing else but the totality. Hence this negation also entails their self-consciousness of the totality. Consequently, when in negation of the whole the individual comes about, at that point the way is open to realize the whole through the reciprocal negation of the individual as well. Individual behavior is a movement of recovery of the totality. Negation develops into negation of negation—that is, into affirmation. That is the dialectical dynamic of negation.

Now, the fact that human existence is fundamentally a dynamic of dialectical negation entails that the radical source of human existence is negation itself, that is, absolute negativity. Both the individual and the totality are, in their true reality, "empty of own-being" (*kû*), and this "emptiness" or "void" is the absolute whole. From this radical source—that is, because this principle of emptiness is radical—human existence develops as a dynamic of reciprocal negations. The "negation of negation" is the self-returning, self-realizing movement of the absolute whole—and it is such that constitutes a truly human relationship. Therefore, the fundamental principle of human relations must be nothing other than realization through individuals (functioning as negations of the totality) of the totality (negation of their negations). It is ultimately the dynamic of self-realization of an original, absolute totality. In these terms, it should be clear that the fundamental principle of human relations contains two movements. The first is the moment of the individual as other over against the whole. Here lies the first step in self-consciousness. Without individuals there are no human relations. Secondly, there is the individual place within the whole; what is also called the "trans-individual will" or the "demand of a total will" in fact corresponds to this. There are also no human relations without this absorption within the whole. When the dialectics of human relationship is grasped in such terms, it also becomes evident that the basic questions of ethics—such as conscience, freedom, and good and evil—are all contained within this fundamental principle. Conscience is the voice of the original totality; freedom must be nothing other than the negative moment in the dialectical movement of negation itself; good and evil are, respectively, this movement's returning motion and its rebelling motion. However, within the scope of this principle, these questions still cannot acquire sufficiently concrete articulation. For therein only an individual person's double character in the reciprocal moments of individual and whole has come into focus. It remains to consider the structures of wholes that include many individuals.

It can be said that the whole comes about in the negation of the individual, but it does not arise in the negation of a single individual. Individuals are plural in number; a whole as a reality of communal existence comes about at the point where these plural individuals relinquish their individualities and become one. However, in any whole, individuality does not disappear entirely. The negated individual immediately in turn negates the whole and establishes its individuality, thus once more repeating the reciprocal movement of negation. The whole exists only in this dialectical interchange. Seen in this way, the dynamic structure of division into many individuals and their communal unity constitutes the concrete totality. Human existence is not only the movement of negation between individual and whole; it must also be the recovery of the concrete totality through countless individuals who stand in mutual opposition by way of a division between self and others.

A second problem for subsequent consideration focuses on the concrete structures of this communal kind of human existence. How does subjective human existence divide into self and other individuals? In the first place, what is a division of subjects? And what is the return to unity through the negation of this division? Here there arises the most fundamental problem, that of the nature of space and time. The division of subjects and their union, and the movement toward this division and union, are essentially spatial and temporal. Every kind of noematic space and time—or formal time and space as the condition for the constitution of natural objects—stems from this foundation. In a word, space and time derive from human existence and not the other way around.

It is necessary to clarify these fundamentally existential structures of spatiality and temporality that form the basis of mankind's practical behavioral relationships. In other words, human behavior can acquire its adequate modes of understanding only when this existential reference to spatiality and temporality is entertained. And from this standpoint of existential behavior the "way of man"—what since ancient times has been called the way of trust (*shinrai*) and the way of truth or sincerity (*shinjitsu*)—can be truly grasped. For the truth of human existence arises or does not arise in human behavior; the concrete modalities of human behavior are the arenas where trust and sincerity exist. Against such a background, the problems of good and evil—as well as of conscience, freedom, and justice—can also be concretely understood. The laws of human existence that arise in human space and time express their elements in the form of such questions.

Indeed, human existence involving behavioral relationships within such laws must be nothing other than various kinds of human-relational associations. It is entirely impossible to have a way of man involving action that does not involve human associations. However, human associations are by no means simple things. Hence we must turn our attention to their various forms and their special laws.

A third question will involve the structures of solidarity in such human-relational associations. We can grasp this first from our sense of the communality of existence. This togetherness can be traced in multi-layered fashion from such a simple existential communality (*Gemeinschaft*) as the union of two persons in an I-Thou relation to such a complicated form of existential communality as the unity of a nation. Each of these stages has its own distinct structure of solidarity, and each of these structures manifests a special form of the laws of human existence. Trust and sincerity, freedom and justice appear here each with special forms and names of their own. It is in these various modes of existential solidarity that each person obtains title as a determinate person and ultimately assumes concrete responsibilities and duties. Indeed, that these various forms of solidarity are built up atop one another also signifies that each kind of existential communality always possesses a private character over against a more public communality that may envelop it. A finite form of communal existence, precisely because it is finite, cannot escape this privateness. The more compact its form of togetherness in existence, the richer also is its claim to have a private character. Thus, from one aspect, the private forms of human existence mediate human relational unities, but they do not thereby cease being "private" or "ours." From another aspect, however, it may prevent the traditional ethics of human sincerity from arising. The reason is that human existence also appears in the form of deficiency of solidarity.

In the absence of an ethic of human trust and sincerity, what is called a "profit society"—or a modern society formed from selfish motives (*Gesellschaft*)—comes into being. This is a form of relationship which, while imitating the communal association's form of togetherness, falls short of making human existence truly communal. In it trust, sincerity, service, responsibility, duty, and other forms of ethical behavior degenerate into mere formalities of profit-based associations and are devoid of true moral substance and content. In other words, it is an inauthentic human-relational association. Therefore, it may be said to be a form of society in which the moral-relational (*jinrin*) plane of human existence is lost. Nevertheless, this moral deficiency in *Gesellschaft* society can still engender a strong self-consciousness of solidarity. From the perspective of togetherness in existence—and because of the spatial-temporal structure of human existence—heterogeneous kinds of togetherness cannot help but be produced. At the same time that the formality of solidarity is self-consciously realized by means of the abstraction of that true human-moral substance and content, the communality becomes some homogeneous, compact organization. The modern nation as a legal human-relational organization is an example. In the modern nation, various structures of solidarity are expressed in the form of legal institutions and responsibilities, and duties are compulsorily enjoined upon citizens. The authority of the totality in this case functions as the nation, and the destruction of human relations is prevented by authoritative power. However, the concrete nation should contain authentic forms of existential togetherness as well as profit-motivated groups as its substance and content. The true nation is more than just a legal entity. Unless the concrete nation's solidarity expressed by law possesses as background the solidarity of authentic forms of existential togetherness, it cannot be the expression of a truly ethical "way of man."

Now, human existence that possesses the above kinds of solidarity structures is essentially spatial-temporal. It forms human-relational organizations in specific places and times. Human-relational organizations floating loose without any country or age are mere abstractions. As Tönnies has said, family bonds are realized in the home, neighborly unions in the village, and friendships in the town. Home, village, and town are the concrete matrices of historical tradition, and in turn they create new historical tradition day by day. Or, better, the very unities of family, neighbors, and friends are the concrete contents of this history. Hence, when a spatial-temporal structure of human existence is realized as a human-relational organization, it must already be a climatic-cultural, historical structure of human existence.

A fourth problem is the above kind of climatic-cultural, historical structure. Here, human existence becomes concrete existence in the full sense. Such a thing as "human being in general" does not exist in reality. The concept of "universal man" spoken of by European thinkers of the past is very plainly a product of European culture. And this is by and large acceptable. But the significance of *world* history lies in the fact that the way of man is realized in various kinds of climatically and historically specific types. Just as the universal can be universal only in particulars, so too human existence can be universal only through its specific forms of existence. "Inter-national" betweenness in the true sense also becomes possible only when each historical nation strives to form the totality of humanity in its own distinct way. To try to be "inter-national" by transcending the exigency of being national is nothing but an abstract fantasy of Marxism today.

This last theme leads us to the question of Japan's national morality (*kokumin dôtoku-ron*). This problem possesses the two aspects of investigation of first principles and historical research.[2] The former involves a *theory* of a nation's morality as one part of a system of ethics; the latter refers to the ethical *history* of a given nation, and consequently, in Japan's case, is especially research into the history of ethics in Japan. The two must not be confused. However, even investigation of first principles cannot be entirely separated from questions of history. As stated above, the climatic-cultural and historical existence of man is our primary concern. A nation (*kokumin*) has meaning only when the human totality is realized in some particular type. Accordingly, the concept of nation must be elucidated from its root source as a climatic, historical entity. The very fact that the consideration of nation—that is, of national self-consciousness—is usually connected with foreign wars is itself already based on climatic and historical conditions and their limitations. A communal national structure developed through a process of division from a basis in a united Catholic world and one that has not attained a unity over and above a secular national unity—even though equally termed nations—differ in their climatic and historical structures. To investigate, in these various historically realized forms, what a nation is, and, accordingly, to elucidate the place it occupies in the movement of the human-relational whole (within which the realization of a national totality returns to its original dialectical nature through division into self and others)—these are the questions here. If we consider that in every human-relational form a national totality occupies a significant place, then the importance of this kind of inquiry should become clear of itself.

The examination of each of the above questions from the perspective of the fundamental structure of human existence is, in my opinion, the task of ethics as the study of man as an existential human being.

Notes

1. The original meaning of what is expressed by the term "behavior" (*kôi*) lies in this subjective, and hence non-objectifiable, mutual association between persons. In the past, this personal reciprocity has been neglected, and behavior has been seen

only in the relation between man and nature. Hence behavior was treated as having evident purposeful intentions or motives—passing through a process of consideration, selection, and decision-making—which were then self-consciously realized in individual actions through physical movements of individuals. However, if it were only that, behavior would merely be such individual actions, and would not necessarily become personal activity or practical human behavior. For example, to throw stones at some object in the middle of a wide riverbed or along the seashore is simply an action. But doing the same action on a school ground while aiming at a window becomes behavior. In this case, one's purposeful intentions come to include associations with other persons or groups. Such acts as deliberation, selection, and decision-making refer to one's attitudinal determinations in the above relationships. In other words, purposeful intentions, deliberations, selections, determinations, and the like function in the context of subjective, mutual relationships; it is in that context that their meanings as behavior arise. I deal with this point in detail in the second chapter of this volume.

2. The emergence of the theme of *kokumin dôtokuron* (theory of national morality), its relation to the spread of Japanism after the Sino-Japanese War by such writers as Inoue Tetsujirô, Takayama Chogyû, Kimura Takatarô, and Yumoto Takehiko—and their confusion of ideas and anachronistic use of terms for ultra-nationalistic purposes—are elaborated in Watsuji's *Nihon rinri shisôshi* (History of Japanese Ethical Thought), 1952, vol. 2, pp. 683–90.

Ed. note: Translated by David A. Dilworth, Valdo H. Viglielmo, and Agustin Jacinto Zavala.

11

Beyond the Enlightenment Mentality

Tu Weiming

THE ENLIGHTENMENT MENTALITY underlies the rise of the modern West as the most dynamic and transformative ideology in human history.[1] Virtually all major spheres of interest characteristic of the modern age are indebted to or intertwined with this mentality: science and technology, industrial capitalism, market economy, democratic polity, mass communication, research universities, civil and military bureaucracies, and professional organizations. Furthermore, the values we cherish as definitions of modern consciousness—including liberty, equality, human rights, the dignity of the individual, respect for privacy, government for, by, and of the people, and due process of law—are genetically, if not structurally, inseparable from the Enlightenment mentality. We have flourished in the spheres of interest and their attendant values occasioned by the advent of the modern West since the eighteenth century. They have made our life-world operative and meaningful. We take it for granted that, through instrumental rationality, we can solve the world's major problems and that progress, primarily in economic terms, is desirable and necessary for the human community as a whole.

We are so seasoned in the Enlightenment mentality that we assume the reasonableness of its general ideological thrust. It seems self-evident that both capitalism and socialism subscribe to the aggressive anthropocentrism underlying the modern mind-set: man is not only the measure of all things but also the only source of power for economic well-being, political stability, and social development. The Enlightenment faith in progress, reason, and individualism may have been challenged by some of the most brilliant minds in the modern Western academy, but it remains a standard of inspiration for intellectual and spiritual leaders throughout the world. It is inconceivable that any international project, including those in ecological sciences, not subscribe to the theses that the human condition is improvable, that it is desirable to find rational means to solve the world's problems, and that the dignity of the person as an individual ought to be respected. Enlightenment as human awakening, as the discovery of the human potential for global transformation, and as the realization of the human desire to become the measure and master of all things is still the most influential moral discourse in the political culture of the modern age; for decades it has been the unquestioned assumption of the ruling minorities and cultural elites of developing countries, as well as highly industrialized nations.

A fair understanding of the Enlightenment mentality requires a frank discussion of the dark side of the modern West as well. The "unbound Prometheus," symbolizing the runaway technology of development, may have been a spectacular achievement of human ingenuity in the early phases of the industrial revolution. Despite impassioned reactions from the romantic movement and insightful criticisms of the forebears of the "human sciences," the Enlightenment mentality, fueled by the Faustian drive to explore, to know, to conquer, and to subdue, persisted as the reigning ideology of the modern West. It is now fully embraced as the unquestioned rationale for development in East Asia.

However, a realistic appraisal of the Enlightenment mentality reveals many faces of the modern West incongruous with the image of "the Age of Reason." In the context of modern Western hegemonic discourse, progress may entail inequality, reason, self-interest, and individual greed. The American dream of owning a car and a house, earning a fair wage, and enjoying freedom of privacy, expression, religion, and travel, while reasonable to our (American) sense of what ordinary life demands, is lamentably unexportable as a modern necessity from a global perspective. Indeed, it has now been widely acknowledged as no more than a dream for a significant segment of the American population as well.

An urgent task for the community of like-minded persons deeply concerned about ecological issues and the disintegration of communities at all levels is to insure that both the ruling minorities and cultural elites in the modern West actively participate in a spiritual joint venture to rethink the Enlightenment heritage. The paradox is that we cannot afford to accept uncritically its inner logic in light of the unintended negative consequences it has engendered on the life-support systems; nor can we reject its relevance, with all of the fruitful ambiguities this entails, to our intellectual self-definition, present and future. There is no easy way out. We do not have an "either-or" choice. The possibility of a radically different ethic or a new value system separate from and independent of the Enlightenment mentality is neither realistic nor authentic. It may even appear to be either cynical or hypercritical. We need to explore the spiritual resources that may help us to broaden the scope of the Enlightenment project, deepen its moral sensitivity, and, if necessary, transform creatively its genetic constraints in order to realize fully its potential as a worldview for the human condition as a whole.

A key to the success of this spiritual joint venture is to recognize the conspicuous absence of the idea of community, let alone the global community, in the Enlightenment project. Fraternity, a functional equivalent of community in the three cardinal virtues of the French Revolution, has received scant attention in modern Western economic, political, and social thought. The willingness to tolerate inequality, the faith in the salvific power of self-interest, and the unbridled affirmation of aggressive egoism have greatly poisoned the good well of progress, reason, and individualism. The need to express a universal intent for the formation of a "global village" and to articulate a possible link between the fragmented world we experience in our ordinary daily existence and the imagined community for the human species as a whole is deeply felt by an increasing number of concerned intellectuals. This requires, at a minimum, the replacement of the principle of self-interest, no matter how broadly defined, with a new Golden Rule: "Do not do unto others what you would not want others to do unto you."[2] Since the new Golden Rule is stated in the negative, it will have to be augmented by a positive principle: "in order to establish myself, I have to help others to enlarge themselves."[3] An inclusive sense of community, based on the communal critical self-consciousness of reflective minds, is an ethico-religious goal as well as a philosophical ideal.

The mobilization of at least three kinds of spiritual resources is necessary to ensure that this simple vision is grounded in the historicity of the cultural complexes informing our ways of life today. The first kind involves the ethico-religious traditions of the modern West, notably Greek philosophy, Judaism, and Christianity. The very fact that they have been instrumental in giving birth to the Enlightenment mentality makes a compelling case for them to reexamine their relationships to the rise of the modern West in order to create a new public sphere for the transvaluation of typical Western values. The exclusive dichotomy of matter/spirit, body/mind, sacred/profane, human/nature, or creator/creature must be transcended to allow supreme values, such as the sanctity of the earth, the continuity of being, the beneficiary interaction between the human community and nature, and the mutuality between humankind and Heaven, to receive the saliency they deserve in philosophy, religion, and theology.

The Greek philosophical emphasis on rationality, the biblical image of man having "dominion" over the earth, and the Protestant work ethic provided necessary, if not sufficient, sources for the Enlightenment mentality. However, the unintended negative consequences of the rise of the modern

West have so undermined the sense of community implicit in the Hellenistic idea of the citizen, the Judaic idea of the covenant, and the Christian idea of fellowship that it is morally imperative for these great traditions, which have maintained highly complex and tension-ridden relationships with the Enlightenment mentality, to formulate their critique of the blatant anthropocentrism inherent in the Enlightenment project. The emergence of a communitarian ethic as a critique of the idea of the person as a rights-bearing, interest-motivated, rational economic animal clearly indicates the relevance of an Aristotelian, Pauline, Abrahamic, or Republican ethic to current moral self-reflexivity in North America. Jürgen Habermas's attempt to broaden the scope of rational discourse by emphasizing the importance of "communicative rationality" in social intercourse represents a major intellectual effort to develop new conceptual apparatuses to enrich the Enlightenment tradition.[4]

The second kind of spiritual resource is derived from non-Western, axial-age civilizations, which include Hinduism, Jainism, and Buddhism in South and Southeast Asia, Confucianism and Taoism in East Asia, and Islam. Historically, Islam should be considered an essential intellectual heritage of the modern West because of its contribution to the Renaissance. The current practice, especially by the mass media of North America and Western Europe, of consigning Islam to radical otherness is historically unsound and culturally insensitive. It has, in fact, seriously undermined the modern West's own self-interest as well as its own self-understanding. Islam and these non-Western ethico-religious traditions provide sophisticated and practicable resources in worldviews, rituals, institutions, styles of education, and patterns of human-relatedness. They can help to develop ways of life, both as continuation of and alternative to the Western European and North American exemplification of the Enlightenment mentality. Industrial East Asia, under the influence of Confucian culture, has already developed a less adversarial, less individualistic, and less self-interested modern civilization. The coexistence of market economy with government leadership, democratic polity with meritocracy, and individual initiatives with group orientation has, since the Second World War, made this region economically and politically the most dynamic area of the world. The significance of the contribution of Confucian ethics to the rise of industrial East Asia offers profound possibilities for the possible emergence of Hindu, Jain, Buddhist, and Islamic forms of modernity.

The Westernization of Confucian Asia (including Japan, the two Koreas, mainland China, Hong Kong, Taiwan, Singapore, and Vietnam) may have forever altered its spiritual landscape, but its indigenous resources (including Mahāyāna Buddhism, Taoism, Shintoism, shamanism, and other folk religions) have the resiliency to resurface and make their presence known in a new synthesis. The caveat, of course, is that, having been humiliated and frustrated by the imperialist and colonial domination of the modern West for more than a century, the rise of industrial East Asia symbolizes the instrumental rationality of the Enlightenment heritage with a vengeance. Indeed, the mentality of Japan and the Four Mini-Dragons (South Korea, Taiwan, Hong Kong, Singapore) is characterized by mercantilism, commercialism, and international competitiveness. The People's Republic of China (the motherland of the Sinic world) has blatantly opted for the same strategy of development and has thus exhibited the same mentality since the reform was set in motion in 1979. Surely the possibility for these nations to develop more humane and sustainable communities should not be exaggerated; nor should it be undermined.

The third kind of spiritual resource involves the primal traditions: Native American, Hawaiian, Maori, and numerous tribal indigenous religious traditions. They have demonstrated, with physical strength and aesthetic elegance, that human life has been sustainable since Neolithic times. The implications for practical living are far-reaching. Their style of human flourishing is not a figment of the mind but an experienced reality in our modern age.

A distinctive feature of primal traditions is a deep experience of rootedness. Each indigenous religious tradition is embedded in a concrete place symbolizing a way of perceiving, a mode of thinking, a form of living, an attitude, and a worldview. Given the unintended disastrous consequences of the Enlightenment mentality, there are obvious lessons that the modern mind-set can learn from indigenous religious traditions. A natural outcome of indigenous peoples' embeddedness in concrete locality is their intimate and detailed knowledge of their environment; indeed, the demarcations between their human habitat and nature are muted. Implicit in this model of existence is the realization that mutuality and reciprocity between the anthropological world and the cosmos at large is both necessary and desirable. What we can learn from them, then, is a new way of perceiving, a new mode of thinking, a new form of living, a new attitude, and a new worldview. A critique of the Enlightenment mentality and its derivative modern mind-set from the perspective of indigenous peoples could be thought-provoking.

An equally significant aspect of indigenous lifeways is the ritual of bonding in ordinary daily human interaction. The density of kinship relations, the rich texture of interpersonal communication, the detailed and nuanced appreciation of the surrounding natural and cultural world, and the experienced connectedness with ancestors point to communities grounded in ethnicity, gender, language, land, and faith. The primordial ties are constitutive parts of their being and activity. In Huston Smith's characterization, what they exemplify is participation rather than control in motivation, empathic

understanding rather than empiricist apprehension in epistemology, respect
for the transcendent rather than domination over nature in worldview, and
fulfillment rather than alienation in human experience. As we begin to question the soundness or even sanity of some of our most cherished ways of
thinking—such as regarding knowledge as power rather than wisdom, asserting the desirability of material progress despite its corrosive influence on the
soul, and justifying the anthropocentric manipulation of nature even at the
cost of destroying the life-support system—indigenous perspectives emerge
as a source of inspiration.

Of course, I am not proposing any romantic attachment to or nostalgic
sentiments for "primal consciousness," and I am critically aware that claims
of primordiality are often modernist cultural constructions dictated by the
politics of recognition. Rather, I suggest that, as both beneficiaries and victims of the Enlightenment mentality, we show our fidelity to our common
heritage by enriching it, transforming it, and restructuring it with all three
kinds of spiritual resources still available to us for the sake of developing a
truly ecumenical sense of global community. Indeed, of the three great
Enlightenment values embodied in the French Revolution, fraternity seems
to have attracted the least attention in the subsequent two centuries. The representation of the *Problematik* of community in recent years is symptomatic
of the confluence of two apparently contradictory forces in the late twentieth
century: the global village as both a virtual reality and an imagined community in our information age and the disintegration and restructuring of
human togetherness at all levels, from family to nation.

It may not be immodest to say that we are beginning to develop a fourth
kind of spiritual resource from the core of the Enlightenment project itself.
Our disciplined reflection, a communal act rather than an isolated struggle,
is a first step toward the "creative zone" envisioned by religious leaders and
teachers of ethics. The feminist critique of tradition, the concern for the environment, and the persuasion of religious pluralism are obvious examples of
this new corporate critical self-awareness. The need to go beyond the Enlightenment mentality, without either deconstructing or abandoning its commitment to rationality, liberty, equality, human rights, and distributive justice,
requires a thorough reexamination of modernity as a signifier and modernization as a process.

Underlying this reexamination is the intriguing issue of traditions in
modernity. The dichotomous thinking of tradition and modernity as two
incompatible forms of life will have to be replaced by a much more nuanced
investigation of the continuous interaction between modernity as the perceived outcome of "rationalization" defined in Weberian terms and traditions as "habits of the heart" (to borrow an expression from Alexis de

Tocqueville), enduring modes of thinking, or salient features of cultural self-understanding. The traditions in modernity are not merely historical sedimentation passively deposited in modern consciousness. Nor are they, in functional terms, simply inhibiting factors to be undermined by the unilinear trajectory of development. On the contrary, they are both constraining and enabling forces capable of shaping the particular contour of modernity in any given society. It is, therefore, conceptually naïve and methodologically fallacious to relegate traditions to the residual category in our discussion of the modernizing process. Indeed, an investigation of traditions in modernity is essential for our appreciation of modernization as a highly differentiated cultural phenomena rather than as a homogeneous integral process of Westernization.

Talcott Parsons may have been right in assuming that market economy, democratic polity, and individualism are three inseparable dimensions of modernity.[5] The post–Cold War era seems to have inaugurated a new world order in which marketization, democratization, and individualism are salient features of a new global village. The collapse of socialism gives the impression that market rather than planned economy, democratic rather than authoritarian polity, and individualist rather than collectivist style of life symbolize the wave of the future. Whether or not we believe in the "end of history," a stage of human development in which only advanced capitalism—characterized by multinational corporations, information superhighways, technology-driven sciences, mass communication, and conspicuous consumption—dominates, we must be critically aware of the globalizing forces which, through a variety of networks, literally transform the earth into a wired discourse community. As a result, distance, no matter how great, does not at all inhibit electronic communication and, ironically, territorial proximity does not necessarily guarantee actual contact. We can be frequent conversation partners with associates thousands of miles apart, yet we are often strangers to our neighbors, colleagues, and relatives.

The advent of the global village as virtual reality rather than authentic home is by no means congenial to human flourishing. Contrary to the classical Confucian ideal of the "great harmony" (*ta-t'ung*), what the global village exhibits is sharp difference, severe differentiation, drastic demarcation, thunderous dissonance, and outright discrimination. The world, compressed into an interconnected ecological, financial, commercial, trading, and electronic system, has never been so divided in wealth, influence, and power. The advent of the imagined, and even anticipated, global village is far from a cause for celebration.

Never in world history has the contrast between the rich and the poor, the dominant and the marginalized, the articulate and the silenced, the included and the excluded, the informed and the uninformed, and the connected and the isolated been so markedly drawn. The rich, dominant, articulate, included, informed, and connected beneficiaries of the system form numerous transnational networks making distance and, indeed, ethnic boundary, cultural diversity, religious exclusivism, or national sovereignty inconsequential in their march toward domination. On the other hand, residents of the same neighborhood may have radically different access to information, ideas, tangible resources (such as money), and immaterial goods (such as prestige). People of the same electoral district may subscribe to sharply conflicting political ideologies, social mores, and worldviews. They may also experience basic categories of human existence (such as time and space) in incommensurable ways. The severity of the contrast between the haves and the have-nots at all levels of the human experience—individual, family, society, and nation—can easily be demonstrated by hard empirical data. The sense of relative deprivation is greatly intensified by the glorification of conspicuous consumption by the mass media. Even in the most economically advanced nations, notably North America, the Scandinavian countries and other nations of Western Europe, and Japan and the Mini-Dragons, the pervasive mood is one of discontent, anxiety, and frustration.

If we focus our attention exclusively on the powerful megatrends that have exerted shaping influences on the global community since the end of the Second World War—science, technology, communication, trade, finance, entertainment, travel, tourism, migration, and disease—we may easily be misled into believing that the world has changed so much that the human condition is being structured by newly emerging global forces without any reference to our inherited historical and cultural praxis. One of the most significant *fin-de-siècle* reflections of the twentieth century is the acknowledgment that globalization does not mean homogenization and that modernization intensifies as well as lessens economic, political, social, cultural, and religious conflict in both inter- and intranational contexts. The emergence of primordial ties (ethnicity, language, gender, land, class, and faith) as powerful forces in constructing internally defensive cultural identities and externally aggressive religious exclusivities compels practical-minded global thinkers to develop new conceptual resources to understand the spirit of our time. The common practice of internationalists, including some of the most sophisticated analyzers of the world scene, of condemning the enduring strength of primordial ties as a parochial reaction to the inevitable process of globalization is simple-minded and ill-advised. What we witness in Bosnia, Africa, Sri Lanka, and India is not simply "fragmentization" as opposed to global integration. Since we are acutely aware of the explosive potential of ethnicity in the United States, language in Canada, and religious fundamentalism in all three major monotheistic religions, we must learn to appreciate that the quest for roots is a worldwide phenomenon.

Nowadays we are confronted with two conflicting and even contradictory forces in the global community: internationalization (globalization) and localization (communization). The United Nations, which came into being because of the spirit of internationalization, must now deal with issues of rootedness (all those specified above as primordial ties). While globalization in science, technology, mass communication, trade, tourism, finance, migration, and disease is progressing at an unprecedented rate and to an unprecedented degree, the pervasiveness and depth of communal (or tribal) feelings, both hidden and aroused, cannot be easily transformed by the Enlightenment values of instrumental rationality, individual liberty, calculated self-interest, material progress, and rights consciousness. The resiliency and explosive power of human-relatedness can be better appreciated by an ethic mindful of the need for reasonableness in any form of negotiation, distributive justice, sympathy, civility, duty-consciousness, dignity of person, sense of intrinsic worth, and self-cultivation.

In the Confucian perspective, human beings are not merely rational beings, political animals, tool-users, or language-manipulators. Confucians seem to have deliberately rejected simplistic reductionist models. They define human beings in terms of five integrated visions:

1. Human beings are sentient beings, capable of internal resonance not only between and among themselves but also with other animals, plants, trees, mountains, and rivers, indeed nature as a whole.
2. Human beings are social beings. As isolated individuals, human beings are weak by comparison with other members of the animal kingdom, but if they are organized to form a society, they have inner strength not only for survival but also for flourishing. Human-relatedness as exemplified in a variety of networks of interaction is necessary for human survival and human flourishing. Our sociality defines who we are.
3. Human beings are political beings in the sense that human-relatedness is, by biological nature and social necessity, differentiated in terms of hierarchy, status, and authority. While Confucians insist upon the fluidity of these artificially constructed boundaries, they recognize the significance of "difference" in an "organic" as opposed to "mechanic" solidarity—thus the centrality of the principle of fairness and the primacy of the practice of distributive justice in a humane society.
4. Human beings are also historical beings sharing collective memories, cultural memories, cultural traditions, ritual praxis, and "habits of the heart."

5. Human beings are metaphysical beings with the highest aspirations not simply defined in terms of anthropocentric ideas but characterized by the ultimate concern to be constantly inspired by and continuously responsive to the Mandate of Heaven.

The Confucian way is a way of learning, learning to be human. Learning to be human in the Confucian spirit is to engage oneself in a ceaseless, unending process of creative self-transformation, both as a communal act and as a dialogical response to Heaven. This involves four inseparable dimensions—self, community, nature, and the transcendent. The purpose of learning is always understood as being for the sake of the self, but the self is never an isolated individual (an island); rather, it is a center of relationships (a flowing stream). The self as a center of relationships is a dynamic open system rather than a closed static structure. Therefore, mutuality between self and community, harmony between human species and nature, and continuous communication with Heaven are defining characteristics and supreme values in the human project.[6]

Since Confucians take the concrete living human being here and now as their point of departure in the development of their philosophical anthropology, they recognize the embeddedness and rootedness of the human condition. Therefore, the profound significance of what we call primordial ties—ethnicity, gender, language, land, class, and basic spiritual orientation—which are intrinsic in the Confucian project, is a celebration of cultural diversity (this is not to be confused with any form of pernicious relativism). Often, Confucians understand their own path as learning of the body and mind (*shen-hsin-chih-hsüeh*) or learning of nature and destiny (*hsing-ming-chih-hsüeh*). There is a recognition that each one of us is fated to be a unique person embedded in a particular condition. By definition, we are unique particular human beings, but at the same time each and every one of us has the intrinsic possibility for self-cultivation, self-development, and self-realization. Despite fatedness and embeddedness as necessary structural limitations in our conditionality, we are endowed with infinite possibilities for self-transformation in our process of learning to be human. We are, therefore, intrinsically free. Our freedom, embodied in our responsibility for ourselves as the center of relationships, creates our worth. That alone deserves and demands respect.

In discussing the "spirit" of the Five Classics in the concluding section of *The World of Thought in Ancient China*, Benjamin Schwartz, referring to the central issue of the Neo-Confucian project, observes:

In the end the root problem was to be sought where Confucius and Mencius had sought them—in the human heart/mind. It is only the human heart/mind

. . . which possesses the capacity to "make itself sincere" and having made itself sincere to extend this transcendent capacity to realize the *tao* within the structures of human society. When viewed from this perspective, this is the essential gospel of the Four Books. At a deeper level, the Four Books also point to an ontological ground for the belief in this transcendental ethical capacity of the individual in the face of the ongoing challenge of a metaethical Taoist and Buddhist mysticism.[7]

The ontological grounding of the Neo-Confucian project on the learning of the heart-and-mind enabled Confucian intellectuals in late imperial China, premodern Vietnam, Chosŏn Korea, and Tokugawa Japan to create a cultural space above the family and below the state. This is why, though they never left home, actively participated in community affairs, or deeply engaged themselves in local, regional, or "national" politics, they did not merely adjust themselves to the world. Max Weber's overall assessment of the Confucian life-orientation misses the point. The spiritual resources that sustained their social activism came from minding their own business and included cultivating themselves, teaching others to be good, "looking for friends in history," emulating the sages, setting up cultural norms, interpreting the Mandate of Heaven, transmitting the Way, and transforming the world as a moral community.

As we are confronted with the issue of a new world order in lieu of the exclusive dichotomy (capitalism and socialism) imposed by the super powers, we are easily tempted to come up with facile generalizations: "the end of history,"[8] "the clash of civilizations,"[9] or "the Pacific century." The much more difficult and, hopefully, in the long haul, much more significant line of inquiry is to address truly fundamental issues of learning to be human: Are we isolated individuals, or do we each live as a center of relationships? Is moral self-knowledge necessary for personal growth? Can any society prosper or endure without developing a basic sense of duty and responsibility among its members? Should our pluralistic society deliberately cultivate shared values and a common ground for human understanding? As we become acutely aware of our earth's vulnerability and increasingly wary of our own fate as an "endangered species," what are the critical spiritual questions to ask?[10]

Since the Opium War (1840–1842), China has endured many holocausts. Prior to 1949, imperialism was the main culprit, but since the founding of the People's Republic of China, erratic leadership and faulty policies must also share the blame. Although millions of Chinese died, the neighboring countries were not seriously affected and the outside world was, by and large, oblivious to what actually happened. Since 1979, China has been rapidly becoming an integral part of the global economic system. More than 30 percent of the Chinese economy is tied to international trade. Natural economic territories have emerged between Hong Kong and Chuan Chou, Fujian and Taiwan, Shantung and South Korea. Japanese, European, and American, as well as Hong Kong and Taiwanese, investments are present in virtually all Chinese provinces. The return of Hong Kong to the PRC, the conflict across the Taiwan Straits, the economic and cultural interchange among overseas Chinese communities and between them and the motherland, the intraregional communication in East Asia, the political and economic integration of the Association for Southeast Asian Nations, and the rise of the Asia-Pacific region will all have substantial impact on our shrinking global community.

The revitalization of the Confucian discourse may contribute to the formation of a much needed communal critical self-consciousness among East Asian intellectuals. We may very well be in the very beginning of global history rather than witnessing the end of history. And, from a comparative cultural perspective, this new beginning must take as its point of departure dialogue rather than clash of civilizations. Our awareness of the danger of civilizational conflicts, rooted in ethnicity, language, land, and religion, makes the necessity of dialogue particularly compelling. An alternative model of sustainable development, with an emphasis on the ethical and spiritual dimensions of human flourishing, must be sought.

The time is long overdue to move beyond a mind-set shaped by instrumental rationality and private interests. As the politics of domination fades, we witness the dawning of an age of communication, networking, negotiation, interaction, interfacing, and collaboration. Whether or not East Asian intellectuals, inspired by the Confucian spirit of self-cultivation, family cohesiveness, social solidarity, benevolent governance, and universal peace, will articulate an ethic of responsibility as Chinese, Japanese, Koreans, and Vietnamese emigrate to other parts of the world is profoundly meaningful for global stewardship.

We can actually envision the Confucian perception of human flourishing, based upon the dignity of the person, in terms of a series of concentric circles: self, family, community, society, nation, world, and cosmos. We begin with a quest for true personal identity, an open and creatively transforming selfhood which, paradoxically, must be predicated on our ability to overcome selfishness and egoism. We cherish family cohesiveness. In order to do that, we have to go beyond nepotism. We embrace communal solidarity, but we have to transcend parochialism to realize its true value. We can be enriched by social integration, provided that we overcome ethnocentrism and chauvinistic culturalism. We are committed to national unity, but we ought to rise above aggressive nationalism so that we can be genuinely patriotic. We are inspired by human flourishing, but we must endeavor not to be confined by anthropocentrism, for the full meaning of humanity is anthropocosmic rather than anthropocentric. On the occasion of the international symposium on Islamic-Confucian dialogue organized by the University of Malaya (March 1995), the Deputy Prime Minister of Malaysia, Anwar Ibrahim, quoted a statement from Huston Smith's *The World's Religions*. It very much captures the Confucian spirit of self-transcendence:

> In shifting the center of one's empathic concern from oneself to one's family one transcends selfishness. The move from family to community transcends nepotism. The move from community to nation transcends parochialism and the move to all humanity counters chauvinistic nationalism.[11]

We can even add: the move towards the unity of Heaven and humanity (*t'ien-jen-ho-i*) transcends secular humanism, a blatant form of anthropocentrism characteristic of the Enlightenment mentality. Indeed, it is in the anthropocosmic spirit that we find communication between self and community, harmony between human species and nature, and mutuality between humanity and Heaven. This integrated comprehensive vision of learning to be human serves well as a point of departure for a new discourse on the global ethic.

The case against anthropocentrism through the formulation of an anthropocosmic vision embodied in the Neo-Confucian learning of the heart-and-mind is succinctly presented by Wang Yang-ming. Let me conclude with the opening statement in his *Inquiry on the Great Learning*:

> The great man regards Heaven and Earth and the myriad things as one body. He regards the world as one family and the country as one person. . . . That the great man can regard Heaven, Earth, and the myriad things as one body is not because he deliberately wants to do so, but because it is natural to the humane nature of his mind that he do so. Forming one body with Heaven, Earth, and the myriad things is not only true of the great man. Even the mind of the small man is no different. Only he himself makes it small. Therefore when he sees a child about to fall into a well, he cannot help a feeling of alarm and commiseration. This shows that his humanity (*jen*) forms one body with the child. It may be objected that the child belongs to the same species. Again, when he observes the pitiful cries and frightened appearance of birds and animals about to be slaughtered, he cannot help feeling an "inability to bear" their suffering. This shows that his humanity forms one body with birds and animals. It may be objected that birds and animals are sentient beings as he is. But when he sees plants broken and destroyed, he cannot help . . . feeling . . . pity. This shows that his humanity forms one body with plants. It may be said that plants are living things as he is. Yet even when he sees tiles and stones shattered and crushed, he cannot help . . . feeling . . . regret. This shows that his humanity forms one body with tiles and stones. This means that even the mind of the

small man necessarily has the humanity that forms one body with all. Such a mind is rooted in his Heaven-endowed nature, and is naturally intelligent, clear and not beclouded. For this reason it is called "clear character."[12]

For Confucians to fully realize themselves, it is not enough to become a responsible householder, effective social worker, or conscientious political servant. No matter how successful one is in the sociopolitical arena, the full measure of one's humanity cannot be accommodated without a reference to Heaven. The highest Confucian ideal is the "unity of man and Heaven," which defines humanity not only in anthropological terms but also in cosmological terms. In the *Doctrine of the Mean* (*Chung yung*), the most authentic manifestation of humanity is characterized as "forming a trinity with Heaven and Earth."[13]

Yet, since Heaven does not speak and the Way in itself cannot make human beings great—which suggests that although Heaven is omnipresent and may be omniscient, it is certainly not omnipotent—our understanding of the Mandate of Heaven requires that we fully appreciate the rightness and principle inherent in our heart-minds. Our ability to transcend egoism, nepotism, parochialism, ethnocentrism, and chauvinistic nationalism must be extended to anthropocentrism as well. To make ourselves deserving partners of Heaven, we must be constantly in touch with that silent illumination that makes the rightness and principle in our heart-minds shine forth brilliantly. If we cannot go beyond the constraints of our own species, the most we can hope for is an exclusive, secular humanism advocating man as the measure of all things. By contrast, Confucian humanism is inclusive; it is predicated on an "anthropocosmic" vision. Humanity in its all-embracing fullness "forms one body with Heaven, Earth, and the myriad things." Self-realization, in the last analysis, is ultimate transformation, that process which enables us to embody the family, community, nation, world, and cosmos in our sensitivity.

The ecological implications of the Confucian anthropocosmic worldview are implicit, yet need to be more carefully articulated. On the one hand, there are rich philosophical resources in the Confucian triad of Heaven, Earth, and human. On the other hand, there are numerous moral resources for developing more comprehensive environmental ethics. These include textual references, ritual practices, social norms, and political policies. From classical times Confucians were concerned with harmonizing with nature and accepting the appropriate limits and boundaries of nature. This concern manifested itself in a variety of forms cultivating virtues that were considered to be both personal and cosmic. It also included biological imagery used for describing the process of self-cultivation. To realize the profound and varied correspondences of the person with the cosmos is a primary goal of Confucianism: it is a vision with vital spiritual import and, at the same time, it has practical significance for facing the current ecological crisis. This volume itself begins to chart a course for realizing the rich resources of the Confucian tradition in resituating humans within the rhythms and limits of the natural world.

Notes

1. I wish to acknowledge, with gratitude, that Mary Evelyn Tucker and John Berthrong were instrumental in transforming my oral presentation into a written text. I would also like to note that materials from three published articles of mine have been used in this paper: "Beyond the Enlightenment Mentality," in *Worldviews and Ecology: Religion, Philosophy, and the Environment,* ed. Mary Evelyn Tucker and John A. Grim (Maryknoll, N.Y.: Orbis Books, 1994), 19–28; "Global Community as Lived Reality: Exploring Spiritual Resources for Social Development," *Social Policy and Social Progress: A Review Published by the United Nations, Special Issue on the Social Summit, Copenhagen, 6–12 March 1995* (New York: United Nations Publications, 1996), 39–51; and "Beyond the Enlightenment Mentality: A Confucian Perspective on Ethics, Migration, and Global Stewardship," *International Migration Review* 30 (spring 1996):58–75.

2. *Analects,* 12:2.

3. *Analects,* 6:28.

4. Jürgen Habermas, "What Is Universal Pragmatics?" in his *Communication and the Evolution of Society,* trans. Thomas McCarthy (Boston: Beacon Press, 1979), 1–68.

5. Talcott Parsons, "Evolutionary Universals in Sociology," in his *Sociological Theory and Modern Society* (New York: The Free Press, 1967), 490–520.

6. See Thomé H. Fang, "The Spirit of Life," in his *The Chinese View of Life: The Philosophy of Comprehensive Harmony* (Taipei: Linking Publishing, 1980), 71–93.

7. Benjamin I. Schwartz, *The World of Thought in Ancient China* (Cambridge, Mass.: Belknap Press of Harvard University Press, 1985), 406.

8. Francis Fukuyama's use of this Helena expression may have given the misleading impression that, with the end of the Cold War, the triumph of capitalism necessarily led to the homogenization of global thinking. Dr. Fukuyama's recent emphasis on the idea of "trust" by drawing intellectual resources from East Asia clearly indicates that, so far as shareable values are concerned, the West can hardly monopolize the discourse.

9. Samuel P. Huntington, "The Clash of Civilizations?" *Foreign Affairs* 72, no. 3 (summer 1993):22–49.

10. These questions are critical issues for my course, "Confucian Humanism: Self-Cultivation and the Moral Community," offered in the "moral reasoning" section of the core curriculum program at Harvard University.

11. Quoted by Anwar Ibrahim in his address at the opening of the international seminar entitled "Islam and Confucianism: A Civilizational Dialogue," sponsored by the University of Malaya, 13 March 1995. It should be noted that Huston Smith's remarks, in this particular reference to the Confucian project, are based on my dis-

cussion of the meaning of self-transcendence in Confucian humanism. If we follow my "anthropocosmic" argument through, we need to transcend "anthropocentrism" as well. See Huston Smith, *The World's Religions* (San Francisco: Harper San Francisco, 1991), 182, 193, and 195 (notes 28 and 29).

12. *A Source Book in Chinese Philosophy,* trans. Wing-tsit Chan (Princeton: Princeton University Press, 1963), 659–60.

13. *Chung yung* (Doctrine of the Mean), chap. 22. For a discussion of this idea in the perspective of Confucian "moral metaphysics," see Tu Wei-ming, *Centrality and Commonality: An Essay on Chung-yung* (Honolulu: The University Press of Hawaii, 1976), 100–141.

12

Is Culture Destiny?
The Myth of Asia's Anti-Democratic Values

Kim Dae Jung

IN HIS INTERVIEW WITH *Foreign Affairs* (March/April 1994), Singapore's former prime minister, Lee Kuan Yew, presents interesting ideas about cultural differences between Western and East Asian societies and the political implications of those differences. Although he does not explicitly say so, his statements throughout the interview and his track record make it obvious that his admonition to Americans "not to foist their system indiscriminately on societies in which it will not work" implies that Western-style democracy is not applicable to East Asia. Considering the esteem in which he is held among world leaders and the prestige of this journal, this kind of argument is likely to have considerable impact and therefore deserves a careful reply.

With the collapse of the Soviet Union in 1991, socialism has been in retreat. Some people conclude that the Soviet demise was the result of the victory of capitalism over socialism. But I believe it represented the triumph of democracy over dictatorship. Without democracy, capitalism in Prussian Germany and Meiji Japan eventually met its tragic end. The many Latin American states that in recent decades embraced capitalism while rejecting democracy failed miserably. On the other hand, countries practicing democratic capitalism or democratic socialism, despite temporary setbacks, have prospered.

In spite of these trends, lingering doubts remain about the applicability of and prospects for democracy in Asia. Such doubts have been raised mainly by Asia's authoritarian leaders, Lee being the most articulate among them. They have long maintained that cultural differences make the "Western concept" of democracy and human rights inapplicable to East Asia. Does Asia have the philosophical and historical underpinnings suitable for democracy? Is democracy achievable there?

Self-Serving Self-Reliance

Lee stresses cultural factors throughout his interview. I too believe in the importance of culture, but I do not think it alone determines a society's fate, nor is it immutable. Moreover, Lee's view of Asian cultures is not only unsupportable but self-serving. He argues that Eastern societies, unlike Western ones, "believe that the individual exists in the context of his family" and that the family is "the building brick of society." However, as an inevitable consequence of industrialization, the family-centered East Asian societies are also rapidly moving toward self-centered individualism. Nothing in human history is permanent.

Lee asserts that, in the East, "the ruler or the government does not try to provide for a person what the family best provides." He cites this ostensibly self-reliant, family-oriented culture as the main cause of East Asia's economic successes and ridicules Western governments for allegedly trying to solve all of society's problems, even as he worries about the moral breakdown of Western societies due to too much democracy and too many individual rights. Consequently, according to Lee, the Western political system, with its intrusive government, is not suited to family-oriented East Asia. He rejects Westernization while embracing modernization and its attendant changes in lifestyle—again strongly implying that democracy will not work in Asia.

Family Values (Required Here)

But the facts demonstrate just the opposite. It is not true, as Lee alleges, that Asian governments shy away from intervening in private matters and taking on all of society's problems. Asian governments intrude much more than Western governments into the daily affairs of individuals and families. In Korea, for example, each household is required to attend monthly neighborhood meetings to receive government directives and discuss local affairs. Japan's powerful government constantly intrudes into the business world to protect perceived national interests, to the point of causing disputes with the United States and other trading partners. In Lee's Singapore, the government stringently regulates individuals' actions—such as chewing bubble-gum, spitting, smoking, littering, and so on—to an Orwellian extreme of social engineering. Such facts fly in the face of his assertion that East Asia's governments are minimalist. Lee makes these false claims to justify his rejection of Western-style democracy. He even dislikes the one man, one vote principle, so fundamental to modern democracy, saying that he is not "intellectually convinced" it is best.

Opinions like Lee's hold considerable sway not only in Asia but among some Westerners because of the moral breakdown of many advanced democratic societies. Many Americans thought, for example, that the U.S. citizen Michael Fay deserved the caning he received from Singaporean authorities for his act of vandalism. However, moral breakdown is attributable not to inherent shortcomings of Western cultures but to those of industrial societies; a similar phenomenon is now spreading through Asia's newly industrializing societies. The fact that Lee's Singapore, a small city-state, needs a near-totalitarian police state to assert control over its citizens contradicts his assertion that everything would be all right if governments would refrain from interfering in the private affairs of the family. The proper way to cure the ills of industrial societies is not to impose the terror of a police state but to emphasize ethical education, give high regard to spiritual values, and promote high standards in culture and the arts.

Long Before Locke

No one can argue with Lee's objection to "foisting" an alien system "indiscriminately on societies in which it will not work." The question is whether democracy is a system so alien to Asian cultures that it will not work. Moreover, considering Lee's record of absolute intolerance of dissent and the continued crackdown on dissidents in many other Asian countries, one is also compelled to ask whether democracy has been given a chance in places like Singapore.

A thorough analysis makes it clear that Asia has a rich heritage of democracy-oriented philosophies and traditions. Asia has already made great strides toward democratization and possesses the necessary conditions to develop democracy even beyond the level of the West.

Democratic Ideals

It is widely accepted that English political philosopher John Locke laid the foundation for modern democracy. According to Locke, sovereign rights reside with the people and, based on a contract with the people, leaders are given a mandate to govern, which the people can withdraw. But almost two millennia before Locke, Chinese philosopher Meng-tzu preached similar ideas. According to his "Politics of Royal Wars," the king is the "Son of Heaven," and heaven bestowed on its son a mandate to provide good government, that is, to provide good for the people. If he did not govern righteously, the people had the right to rise up and overthrow his government in the name of heaven. Meng-tzu even justified regicide, saying that once a king loses the mandate of heaven he is no longer worthy of his subjects' loyalty. The people came first, Meng-tzu said, the country second, and the king third. The ancient Chinese philosophy of *Minben Zhengchi*, or "people-based politics," teaches that "the will of the people is the will of heaven" and that one should "respect the people as heaven" itself.

A native religion of Korea, Tonghak, went even further, advocating that "man is heaven" and that one must serve man as one does heaven. These ideas inspired and motivated nearly half a million peasants in 1894 to revolt against exploitation by feudalist government internally and imperialistic forces externally. There are no ideas more fundamental to democracy than the teachings of Confucianism, Buddhism, and Tonghak. Clearly, Asia has democratic philosophies as profound as those of the West.

Democratic Institutions

Asia also has many democratic traditions. When Western societies were still being ruled by a succession of feudal lords, China and Korea had already sustained county prefecture systems for about 2,000 years. The government of the Chin Dynasty, founded by Chin-shih huang-ti (literally, the founder of Chin), practiced the rule of law and saw to it that everyone, regardless of class, was treated fairly. For nearly 1,000 years in China and Korea, even the sons of high-ranking officials were not appointed to important official positions unless they passed civil service examinations. These stringent tests were administered to members of the aristocratic class, who constituted over ten percent of the population, thus guaranteeing equal opportunity and social mobility, which are so central to popular democracy. This practice sharply contrasted with that of European fiefdoms of that time, where pedigree more or less determined one's official position. In China and Korea powerful boards of censors acted as a check against imperial misrule and abuses by government officials. Freedom of speech was highly valued, based on the understanding that the nation's fate depended on it. Confucian scholars were taught that remonstration against an erring monarch was a paramount duty. Many civil servants and promising political elites gave their lives to protect the right to free speech.

The fundamental ideas and traditions necessary for democracy existed in both Europe and Asia. Although Asians developed these ideas long before the Europeans did, Europeans formalized comprehensive and effective electoral democracy first. The invention of the electoral system is Europe's greatest accomplishment. The fact that this system was developed elsewhere does not mean that "it will not work" in Asia. Many Asian countries, including Singapore, have become prosperous after adopting a "Western" free-market economy, which is such an integral part of a democracy. Incidentally, in countries where economic development preceded political advancement—Germany, Italy, Japan, Spain—it was only a matter of time before democracy followed.

The State of Democracy in Asia

The best proof that democracy can work in Asia is the fact that, despite the stubborn resistance of authoritarian rulers like Lee, Asia has made great strides toward democracy. In fact, Asia has achieved the most remarkable record of democratization of any region since 1974. By 1990 a majority of Asian countries were democracies, compared to a 45 percent democratization rate worldwide.[1] This achievement has been overshadowed by Asia's tremendous economic success. I believe democracy will take root throughout Asia around the start of the next century. By the end of its first quarter, Asia will witness an era not only of economic prosperity, but also of flourishing democracy.

I am optimistic for several reasons. The Asian economies are moving from a capital- and labor-intensive industrial phase into an information- and technology-intensive one. Many experts have acknowledged that this new economic world order requires guaranteed freedom of information and creativity. These things are possible only in a democratic society. Thus Asia has no practical alternative to democracy; it is a matter of survival in an age of intensifying global economic competition. The world economy's changes have already meant a greater and easier flow of information, which has helped Asia's democratization process.

Democracy has been consistently practiced in Japan and India since the end of World War II. In Korea, Burma, Taiwan, Thailand, Pakistan, the Philippines, Bangladesh, Sri Lanka, and other countries, democracy has been frustrated at times, even suspended. Nevertheless, most of these countries have democratized, and in all of them, a resilient "people power" has been demonstrated through elections and popular movements. Even in Thailand, after ten military governments, a civilian government has finally emerged. The Mongolian government, after a long period of one-party dictatorship, has also voluntarily accepted democracy. The fundamental reason for my optimism is this increasing awareness of the importance of democracy and human rights among Asians themselves and their willingness to make the necessary efforts to realize these goals. Despite many tribulations, the torch of democracy continues to burn in Asia because of the aspirations of its people.

We Are the World

As Asians increasingly embrace democratic values, they have the opportunity and obligation to learn from older democracies. The West has experienced many problems in realizing its democratic systems. It is instructive, for example, to remember that Europeans practiced democracy within the boundaries of their nation-states but not outside. Until recently, the Western democracies coddled the interests of a small propertied class. The democracies that benefited much broader majorities through socioeconomic investments were mostly established after World War II. Today, we must start with a rebirth of democracy that promotes freedom, prosperity, and justice both within each country and among nations, including the less-developed countries: a global democracy.

Instead of making Western culture the scapegoat for the disruptions of rapid economic change, it is more appropriate to look at how the traditional strengths of Asian society can provide for a better democracy. In Asia, democracy can encourage greater self-reliance while respecting cultural values. Such a democracy is the only true expression of a people, but it requires the full participation of all elements of society. Only then will it have legitimacy and reflect a country's vision.

Asian authoritarians misunderstand the relationship between the rules of effective governance and the concept of legitimacy. Policies that try to protect people from the bad elements of economic and social change will never be effective if imposed without consent; the same policies, arrived at through public debate, will have the strength of Asia's proud and self-reliant people.

A global democracy will recognize the connection between how we treat each other and how we treat nature, and it will pursue policies that benefit future generations. Today we are threatening the survival of our environment through wholesale destruction and endangerment of all species. Our democracy must become global in the sense that it extends to the skies, the earth, and all things with brotherly affection.

The Confucian maxim *Xiushen qijia zhiguo pingtianxia*, which offers counsel toward the ideal of "great peace under heaven," shows an appreciation for judicious government. The ultimate goal in Confucian political philosophy, as stated in this aphorism, is to bring peace under heaven (*pingtianxia*). To do so, one must first be able to keep one's own household in order (*qijia*), which in turn requires that one cultivate "self" (*xiushen*). This teaching is a political philosophy that emphasizes the role of government and stresses the ruling elite's moral obligation to strive to bring about peace under heaven. Public safety, national security, and water and forest management are deemed critical. This concept of peace under heaven should be interpreted to include peaceful living and existence for all things under heaven. Such an understanding can also be derived from Gautama Buddha's teaching that all creatures and things possess a Buddha-like quality.

Since the fifth century B.C., the world has witnessed a series of revolutions in thought. Chinese, Indian, Greek, and Jewish thinkers have led great revolutions in ideas, and we are still living under the influence of their insights. However, for the past several hundred years, the world has been dominated by Greek and Judeo-Christian ideas and traditions. Now it is time for the world to turn to China, India, and the rest of Asia for another revolution in ideas. We need to strive for a new democracy that guarantees the right of personal development for all human beings and the wholesome existence of all living things.

A natural first step toward realizing such a new democracy would be full adherence to the Universal Declaration of Human Rights, adopted by the United Nations in 1948. This international document reflects basic respect for the dignity of people, and Asian nations should take the lead in implementing it.

The movement for democracy in Asia has been carried forward mainly by Asia's small but effective army of dedicated people in and out of political parties, encouraged by nongovernmental and quasi-governmental organizations for democratic development from around the world. These are hopeful signs for Asia's democratic future. Such groups are gaining in their ability to force governments to listen to the concerns of their people, and they should be supported.

Asia should lose no time in firmly establishing democracy and strengthening human rights. The biggest obstacle is not its cultural heritage but the resistance of authoritarian rulers and their apologists. Asia has much to offer the rest of the world; its rich heritage of democracy-oriented philosophies and traditions can make a significant contribution to the evolution of global democracy. Culture is not necessarily our destiny. Democracy is.

Note

1. Samuel Huntington, *The Third Wave*, Norman: University of Oklahoma Press, 1991.

13

Conceptualizing Human Beings

Bhikhu Parekh

W E HAVE SEEN in the earlier chapters that neither naturalism nor culturalism is able to offer a coherent theory of moral and cultural diversity.
They are one-sided extremes and feed off each other's exaggerations. Full-
blooded naturalism insists that human beings are basically the same in all
societies and that their differences are shallow and morally inconsequential.
This provokes a legitimate reaction in the form of culturalism, whose similar
exaggerations in turn lend credibility to naturalism. Each is partial and both
undermines and reinforces the other. If we are to give a coherent account of
moral and cultural diversity, we need to critique and open up each to make
a secure space for the other, and to develop on that basis a more satisfactory
theory of human beings. Raz, Kymlicka and others have paved the way and
what follows is an attempt to build on their insights.

Human Nature

The question whether human beings have a nature cannot be answered
unless we are agreed on what we mean by human nature.[1] This is not easy.
Some writers take a substantive or thick view, and others a largely formal
view of it. Some take a teleological and others a mechanistic view. For some
it determines, and for others it only disposes human beings to act in certain
ways. Some define it to mean all that characterizes human beings including
what they share in common with animals; for others it only refers to what is
distinctive to them and marks them off as a distinct species. Given these and
other differences, the best way to discuss whether or not human beings have
a nature is to concentrate on the minimum on which different views agree
or can be expected to agree. The teleological and the mechanistic views, for

example, give very different accounts of human nature, but both are agreed that human nature is not inert or passive and that to have a nature is to be inclined to act in a certain way, which they then go on to interpret in their own different ways.

Such a minimalist view of human nature has several advantages. It encompasses a wide variety of views and does not arbitrarily exclude inconvenient ones. It is true that no view, however minimalist, can do equal justice to all of them, for it has to draw a line somewhere and cannot avoid some degree of selectivity. However, as long as the selectivity is based on good reasons and is not too narrow, it provides the only practical basis of discussion. Second, the minimalist view enables us to concentrate on the crucial questions raised by the concept of human nature without getting sidetracked into important but irrelevant questions about its content and mode of operation. Third, if we can show that the concept is problematic even in its minimalist sense, it is bound to be even more so when defined in stronger or more substantive terms.

Minimally, the term human nature refers to those permanent and universal capacities, desires and dispositions—in short, properties—that all human beings share by virtue of belonging to a common species. The properties are permanent in the sense that they continue to belong to human beings as long as they remain what they are, and that, if they were to undergo changes, human nature itself would be deemed to have changed. They are universal in the sense that they are shared by human beings in all ages and societies. This does not mean that there are no exceptions, but rather that those lacking them are to that extent defective or at least not normal. The properties are acquired by virtue of belonging to the human species and not socially or culturally derived. They belong to human beings 'by nature', as part of their inherited physical and psychological constitution, and constitute their species heritage. Although society might modify them and regulate their expression, it can never altogether eliminate them or alter their inherent tendencies. Finally, the properties are not inert and indeterminate but have a specific character or content and operate in a particular manner. To say that all human beings have a propensity or instinct to preserve themselves is to say that they tend to do all they can to avoid death and life-threatening situations. And to say that they seek to realize themselves, possess an inherent love of God, strive for happiness, have an inclination to do evil, or are naturally curious is to say that they would, as a rule, be inclined to act in a manner intimated by these impulses.

Human beings do seem to have a nature in this sense. They have a common physical and mental structure and all that follows from it. They share a common anatomy and physiological processes, stand erect, possess an identical set of sense organs which operate in an identical manner, have common bodily-derived desires, and so forth. The fact that they are embodied in a particular way is not an incidental biological fact devoid of larger significance, but structures their perceptions of themselves, the non-human species and the world at large and shapes their self-understanding. Human beings also share a common mental structure and possess capacities such as rationality, ability to form concepts, to learn language and employ complex forms of speech, self-consciousness, self-reflection, and so on. These capacities do not remain isolated but inform all aspects of human life and give rise to, and are in turn shaped by, new capacities, emotions and dispositions. If some human beings do not happen to possess the latter, they nevertheless have the potential to acquire them. These include the capacity to will, judge, fantasize, dream dreams, build theories, construct myths, feel nostalgic about the past, anticipate future events, make plans, and so on and on. At a different level human beings are also capable of a vast range of moral and non-moral emotions such as love, hate, anger, rage, sadness, sorrow, pity, compassion, meanness, generosity, self-hatred, self-esteem and vanity, and of such dispositions as curiosity, the tendency to explore new areas of experience, to seek human company, to ask questions and to seek justification of their own and others' actions. Although these capacities, emotions and dispositions are distinct and have their unique modes of operation, they are interrelated and both partially presuppose and contradict each other. Human nature is not made up of discrete, readily specifiable and mutually compatible properties as many philosophers have thought, but a complex whole composed of related but often dissonant capacities and dispositions which cannot all be reduced to a single master or foundational capacity, desire or disposition. Reason itself takes several different forms, of which theoretical and practical reasons are but two, and they are not all reducible to so many different expressions of an allegedly generic and neutral reason. And the fact that humans can reason does not by itself explain why they can also construct myths, dream dreams and imagine wholly new experiences.

Thanks to their shared physical and mental structure, human beings also share certain basic needs and common conditions of growth. They require a prolonged period of nurture and all that that implies. They also need to acquire a large body of skills, abilities and dispositions as well as a reasonably coherent conception of the world in order to hold themselves together, build up a stable self, and cope with the inevitable demands of personal and social life. In order to acquire these, they require a stable natural and social environment, close personal relationships, a measure of emotional security, moral norms, and so forth.

Human beings also go through common life-experiences. They mature slowly, reach their peak and begin to suffer losses of or diminutions in their physical and mental powers, grow old, and die. They see their loved ones die, anticipate their own death, experience joys and sorrows and moments of elation and happiness as well as disappointments and frustrations, and undergo changes of mood. They fall in and out of love, are drawn to some and not to others, cannot realize all their dreams and satisfy all their desires, make mistakes, possess limited sympathies, and fall prey to temptations. They carry a large and dimly grasped unconscious all through their lives, and sometimes not only cannot make sense of themselves but are positively puzzled by their thoughts and feelings.

Human beings, then, do seem to have a nature in the sense defined earlier—that is, capacities, emotions and dispositions which are universal, relatively permanent, acquired as part of their species-heritage or by nature, and which tend to generate certain kinds of actions. Since human beings have a certain physical and mental structure with in-built tendencies and limits, and since they go through common life experiences and life-cycles, it would be odd if they did not have a nature. If we encountered a 'human being' who was six inches or six meters tall, immoral, had unusual sense organs, never felt an emotion or fluctuations of moods, spoke a refined language at birth, never made a mistake or faced a temptation throughout his or her life, or possessed no sense of selfhood or subjectivity, we would feel profoundly disorientated in their presence and would consider that person either an aberrant member of our species or, more likely, that of another. To have a nature is to have a potency for action, a tendency to behave in a certain way, and to be subject to certain constitutional limitations. All these are true of human beings.

While acknowledging that human beings have a shared nature, we may legitimately question its conceptualization, interpretation, the explanatory and normative weight put upon it, and the ways in which it is related to culture in much of traditional philosophy. First, human nature does not exhaust all that characterizes human beings as a species. It refers to properties that inhere in or are internal to human beings and which they share in their unique isolation, excluding those that lie between or outside of them altogether. These latter include such fundamental facts as countless ties to the non-human world, being subject to ecological and other constraints, and being part of a universe structured in a certain way. They also include the fact that human beings must work to stay alive, that they are shaped by their geography, are born in a particular historical epoch and shaped by their history, live among other human beings who constrain them in various ways, and so on. These and other aspects of human existence are not internal to human beings but external or interpersonal, and form part not of human nature but of the human condition or predicament. Not surprisingly they receive little attention in many a discussion of human nature. Since they profoundly shape the context and conduct of human life and are inextricably tied up with what is internal to human beings, traditional accounts of human nature which generally ignore these cannot give an adequate account either of human beings in general or even of human nature. In other words, a conception or a theory of human beings must include, but not remain restricted to, a view of human nature.

Second, the traditional account of human nature is deeply ahistorical. It assumes that human beings begin their history endowed with a certain set of properties, and does not adequately explain how they come to acquire these in the first instance. It either leaves the question unanswered, or appeals to God with all the attendant difficulties in that, or more plausibly invokes natural evolution. This last explanation postulates a fairly neat division between evolution and history. In the former, nature holds sway, creates humans as we more or less know them today, and brings them to the threshold of history when they begin to take charge of their development.

But this is a misleading account of human nature. Evolution does not occur behind the backs of human beings, for they are active participants in it. As they acquire a posture broadly resembling their current one and some capacity to understand themselves and their world, they increasingly engage in a creative interaction with their natural environment and change it in harmony with their needs. As their environment is humanized, it provides a relatively safe island of stability which they strive to humanize yet further. In the course of this dialectic with nature, they change both themselves and their world, develop new forms of social organization, and acquire new capacities and dispositions. These historically acquired capacities and dispositions are institutionalized and reproduced during successive generations, and become part of their species heritage or nature.

Almost all distinctive human capacities and dispositions are products of such a dialectic. Our primitive ancestors possessed little of what we call reason. They had some capacity for a largely instrumental understanding of their environment, which gave them an advantage over animals, but more sophisticated forms of reason developed later as products of a semi-conscious dialectic between society and nature. This is also the case with such human capacities as willing, judging, formulating ideals, dreaming dreams of a perfect society and myth-making, as well as such motives as greed, striving for domination, and the desire for self-respect and social preeminence. What is distinctive to humans is not inherent in, nor entailed by, such primitive cognitive equipment as they acquired through their natural evolution. The equipment did start them off on their historical journey, but all that developed later was largely a human achievement. Much of human nature is thus not a product of nature but of human struggle. It is natural in the sense that it is acquired by virtue of belonging to the human species, but it is not natural in the sense that it is a result of the efforts of the species itself and forms part of its process of self-creation.

Third, contrary to what most philosophers have assumed, all attempts to discover human nature beyond what is inherent in their physicomental structure are open to two great difficulties. Since human beings have always led organized lives, their nature has been so deeply shaped by layers of social influences that we have no direct access to it in its raw or pristine form, and cannot easily detach what is natural from what is manmade or social. Some of those who appreciated the difficulty mistakenly thought they could gain access to human nature by examining the behaviour of our humanoid ancestors, primitive people, children, civilized people in times of social disintegration, or what is universally common. Since our humanoid ancestors have left no records of their thoughts and feelings, we have no knowledge of their nature, and in any case there is no good reason to assume that we must necessarily share a common nature with them. So-called primitive peoples are socially organized and shaped, and do not reveal raw human nature. Children are subject to deep social influences from the moment of their birth and even perhaps conception. When societies disintegrate, their members' behaviour does not reveal raw human nature but their socially shaped character in a climate of chaos and uncertainty. And what is common to all mankind could as well be a result of common processes of socialization rather than an expression of a common nature. In short, human nature is not a brute and empirically verifiable fact, but an inference or a theory which we have no reliable means of corroborating (Geertz, 1973, pp. 35 f, 49 §).

Another great difficulty relates to the students of human nature, who are themselves deeply shaped by their society and remain prone to the understandable tendency to mistake the normal and the familiar for the natural. This tendency is further compounded by the fact that an appeal to human nature has unique explanatory and normative advantages. To say that a particular form of behaviour is natural is to forswear the need to look for further or another explanation. And to say that certain values or ways of life are alone consistent with human nature is to give them a moral finality and to delegitimize alternative values and ways of life. Even the most rigorous and scrupulous philosophers have sometimes availed themselves of the easy advantages offered by appeals to human nature, and argued on the basis of little hard evidence that human beings have an innate tendency to pursue knowledge, love God, maximize pleasure, seek self-realization, and so on and that only such a life gives them 'true' happiness or fulfillment and is worthy of them. This does not mean that we should not appeal to human nature or seek to discover it, but rather that all references to it should be subjected to the strictest scrutiny and viewed with a healthy dose of skepticism.

Fourth and finally, human beings are culturally embedded in the sense that they are born into, raised in and deeply shaped by their cultural communities.[2] Thanks to human creativity, geographical conditions, historical experiences, and so on, different societies develop different systems of meaning, ways of looking at the world, ideals of excellence, traits of temperament and forms of moral and social life, giving different orientation and structure to universally shared human capacities and desires and cultivating wholly new ones of their own. Although skin colour, gender, height and other physical features are universally shared, they are all differently conceptualized and acquire different meaning and significance in different societies. In some societies skin colour is given a deeper metaphysical meaning and made the basis of a differential distribution of power and status, in others it is not even noticed. In some societies male–female distinctions are drawn fairly sharply; in others they are seen as overlapping categories, each sex carrying a bit of the other within itself, so that these societies draw no rigid distinction between masculine and feminine qualities or even between homosexuality and heterosexuality. In some, sexuality is viewed as a natural bodily function like 'scratching an itch', as Bentham once put it, and subjected to the fewest constraints; in others it is invested with cosmic significance, viewed as a quasi-divine activity of generating life, and surrounded with mystique and taboos. Even something as basic and inevitable as death is viewed and experienced differently in different cultures. In some it is a brute fact of life, like the falling of leaves or the diurnal setting of the sun, and arouses no strong emotions; in some others it is a release from the world of sorrow and embraced with joy; in yet others it is a symbol of human weakness, a constant reminder of inadequate human mastery over nature, and accepted with such varied emotions as regret, puzzle, incomprehension and bitterness. Different cultures, again, take different views of human life and the individual's relation to his or her body, leading to very different attitudes to suicide and manners of committing it.

Differences at the level of human capacities, emotions, motivations, values, ideals of excellence and so forth are just as great and in some respects even greater.[3] Although all human beings have the capacity to reason, different cultures cherish and cultivate different forms of it. The Greek *logos*, the Roman *ratio*, the Cartesian *cogito*, the Hobbesian reckoning with consequences, the Benthamite arithmetical reasoning, the Hegelian dialectic and the Indian *buddhi* and *prajñà* represent very different forms of human reason. Some cultures disjoin reason and feeling whereas others find their separation incomprehensible. Some distinguish between theoretical and practical reason or between thinking and willing, whereas others believe that reason has both theoretical and practical impulses built into its very structure. Different cultures also encourage different emotions and feelings. Some develop the concept of conscience and know what guilt and remorse mean; others find these emotions incomprehensible. Some have a poorly developed sense of history and cannot make sense of the desire to gain historical immortality or leave a footnote or a paragraph in history. Some others lack a sense of tradition and cannot make sense of the desire to be worthy of one's ancestors, loyal to their memories, or to cherish their heritage. Although all human beings require a prolonged period of nurture, the mode of upbringing and periodization of life vary greatly. In some cultures children graduate into adulthood without passing through adolescence, in others they never outgrow the latter. Some stress sharp individuation, self-enclosure and a tightly centered self; others encourage overlapping selves, openness to others, and a loosely held self.

Different cultures, then, define and constitute human beings and come to terms with the basic problems of human life in their own different ways. Cultures are not superstructures built upon identical and unchanging foundations, or manifestations of a common human essence, but unique human creations that reconsistute and give different meaning and orientation to those properties that all human beings share in common, add new ones of their own, and give rise to different kinds of human beings. Since human beings are culture-creating and capable of creative self-transformation, they cannot passively inherit a shared nature in the same way that animals do.

We might press the point further. As members of a cultural community, human beings *acquire* certain tendencies and dispositions, in some cases as deep and powerful as those they are deemed to possess by nature. Human beings do seek to preserve themselves, but they might develop such a strong religious commitment or patriotic spirit that they think nothing of dying for their religion or their country. They have now acquired a 'second nature' which overrides their 'natural' nature. Since the willingness to die for one's religion or country is not universally shared, it is not a part of universal human nature. However, since it is part of their culturally derived nature, it constitutes their culturally specific or shared human nature. There is no reason why we cannot say with some Chinese philosophers that some components of human nature vary from culture to culture.

The same thing also happens at the individual level. Human beings might so shape themselves that a fierce sense of independence, an uncompromising commitment to integrity, or a passionate love of God or their fellow humans might become woven into their being and become an integral part of their nature. They then not only instinctively and effortlessly act on those inclinations but might even feel helplessly driven by them. These dispositions have the same force as the tendencies deemed to be inherent in their shared human nature, and are just as inseparable and ineradicable from their being. We often call them part of their character to emphasize the fact that they represent their achievements. However, character is not external to who they are, often has the same force as human nature, and constitutes *their* nature.

This means that human beings are articulated at three different but interrelated levels: what they share as members of a common species, what they derive from and share as members of a cultural community, and what they succeed in giving themselves as reflective individuals. All three are parts of their psychological and moral constitution and relate to three different dimensions of their being. What is more, since these are distinctive to them as human beings, they are all part of their human nature. It therefore makes perfect sense to talk of their distinct *individual* natures (as the Hindus and Buddhists do), their nature as members of particular *cultural communities* (as the traditional Chinese do), and their nature as members of the *human species* (as much western thought has done over the centuries). To equate human nature with only the last is to take too narrow a view of it. Worse, it ontologically and morally privileges the species nature and marginalizes the other two.

Basis of Cultural Diversity

In the light of our discussion the concept of human nature is valid and valuable. It highlights several important facts about human beings, such as that they belong to the natural world, share several features in common, do so not accidentally but by virtue of possessing a common species-derived physical and mental structure, and are constitutionally limited in countless ways and cannot make of themselves what they will. Although for these and other reasons it has a useful explanatory and normative role, its value is limited. Human nature is only a part of, and does not exhaust, the totality of all that human beings share in common. It is largely a product of human self-creation, and although it has a certain degree of permanence, it can be altered over a long period of time. As beings who constantly push against their inherited limits and sometimes succeed in stretching them, their nature is not static and finished but subject to further development. Human nature is also culturally reconstituted and diversified, and is additionally subject to such changes as self-reflective individuals succeed in introducing. All this means that human nature alone can never explain human behaviour or justify a way of life, and that any moral and political theory that does so is inherently flawed.

Human beings share a common nature, common conditions of existence, life experiences, predicament, and so on. They also, however, conceptualize and respond to these in quite different ways and give rise to different cultures. Their identity is a product of a dialectical interplay between the universal and the particular, between what they all share and what is culturally specific. The universally shared features do not impinge on human consciousness and behaviour directly and in their raw form; they are mediated by and acquire different meaning and significance in different cultures. Cultures, however, do not exist in a vacuum nor are they created *ex nihilo*. They are embedded in, and limited by, the universally shared features of human existence including human nature. To be human is to belong both to a common species and to a distinct culture, and one only because of the other. Humans belong to a common species not directly but in a culturally mediated manner. And they belong to a cultural community by virtue of belonging to a common species. They are therefore human in very different ways, neither wholly alike nor wholly different, neither wholly transparent nor wholly opaque to one another. Their similarities and differences are both important and dialectically related. No theory of human beings can give a full account of them unless it is accompanied by a theory of culture; the reverse is just as true.

When we understand human beings in this way, we do not automatically assume that others are either basically like us as the concept of human nature encourages us to do, or totally different as the concept of cultural determinism or culturalism implies. We apprach them on the assumption that they are similar enough to be intelligible and make a dialogue possible, and different enough to be puzzling and make a dialogue necessary. We therefore neither assimilate them to our conception of human nature and deny their particularity, nor place them in a closed world of their own and deny the universality they share with us. By acknowledging their universality and particularity, we acknowledge the obligation to respect *both* their shared humanity and cultural differences. While rejecting the exaggerations and falsehoods of naturalism and culturalism, this view retains their valid insights and finds a secure space for culture within a wider theory of human beings.

As we have seen, much of the dominant tradition of moral and political philosophy gravitated towards monism because of the influence of the following five assumptions, namely:

- the uniformity of human nature;
- the ontological primacy of similarities over differences;

- the socially transcendental character of human nature;
- the total knowability of human nature; and
- human nature as the basis of the good life.

Taken together, these interrelated assumptions encourage a manner of thinking in which one cannot appreciate the depth and importance of cultural differences. Since human similarities alone are deemed to be constitutive of their humanity, their differences have no moral significance and dignity. And since the good life is taken to consist in living up to the demands of human nature, it is assumed to be the same for all and leaves no room for diversity. The fact that human beings entertain different conceptions of the good therefore appears unnatural, and is explained away in terms of such factors as human ignorance, intellectual and moral deficiencies, the hold of vested interests, and geographical and other circumstances.

In the light of our earlier discussion, each of these five assumptions is wholly or partially false. As for the first, we have already seen that the concept of human nature as it has been traditionally defined is too narrow and ahistorical to capture the full content of what constitutes human beings, or what I might call human identity. Furthermore, although human beings share in common certain capacities, desires, experiences, conditions of existence and so forth, they are also cultural beings whose cultures differently develop their universally shared capacities and cultivate additional ones that are unique to them. Their shared humanity and cultural differences interpenetrate and jointly create their human identity. This means that the second assumption is also false. Indeed, since human similarities and differences mediate each other and cannot be disengaged, the question of giving either of them ontological primacy makes no sense. The third assumption is false both because cultures transform and reconstitute human nature, and because human beings in turn constantly transform their cultures and themselves.

The fourth assumption ignores the enormously complex and elusive character of human beings. Different cultures reconstitute human beings in countless different ways, and we can hardly hope to know them all. The future, too, is not closed, and we cannot claim to know in what new directions human beings might develop. As for the last assumption, since human identity is composed of both universally common and culturally specific features, the good life cannot be defined in terms of the former alone. Furthermore, if it is to be morally relevant and practicable, a vision of the good life must take account of the capacities, desires and habits of thought and feelings of those to whom it is recommended. If it has no other basis than the abstractly shared universal properties, it can have no meaning for and carry no conviction with them.

Once we reject or reformulate these and related assumptions, we create a secure space for cultural diversity in our understanding of human beings without losing sight of their shared identity. As thinking begins who seek to make sense of themselves and the world, humans create a system of meaning and significance or culture and organize their lives in terms of it. And since they face different natural and social circumstances, are heirs to different traditions, think and dream differently, possess the capacities for creativity and imagination, and so on, the cultures they create are inescapably diverse in nature. Far from being an aberration or a source of puzzle, cultural diversity is an integral feature of human existence. This is not to say that it is underwritten by human nature as Vico, Herder and others argue and might not one day disappear, but rather that given the kinds of beings humans have made of themselves, cultural diversity has tenacious roots and that its unlikely disappearance would signify a radically new stage in their development.

Pluralist Universalism

When we understand human beings along the lines I have suggested, the question whether there are universal moral values or norms and how we can judge other cultures appears in a different light. Broadly speaking, the question has received three answers; namely relativism, monism and minimum universalism.[4] Briefly and somewhat crudely, the relativist argues that since moral values are culturally embedded and since each culture is a self-contained whole, they are relative to each society and the search for universal moral values is a logically incoherent enterprise. The monist takes the opposite view that since moral values are derived from human nature, and since the latter is universally common, we can arrive at not only them but also the best way of combining them. The minimum universalist takes the intermediate position, arguing that we can arrive at a body of universal values but that they are few and constitute a kind of floor, or a moral threshold subject to which every society enjoys what Stuart Hampshire calls a 'licence for distinctness'.

In the light of our discussion, relativism and monism are incoherent doctrines. Relativism ignores the cross-culturally shared human properties and is mistaken in its beliefs that a culture is a tightly integrated and self-contained whole, can be neatly individuated, and determines its members. Monism rests on an untenably substantive view of human nature, ignores the impossibility of deriving moral values from human nature alone, fails to appreciate its cultural mediation and reconstitution, and so on. There is much to be said for minimum universalism. It takes a minimalist view of human nature, appreciates both the cultural embeddedness of human beings and their universally shared properties, recognizes that while values can claim universal validity a way of life cannot, and so on. However, it suffers from several limitations. It naively assumes that the minimum universal values do not come into conflict, and that they are univocal and self-explanatory and mean the same thing in different cultures. Since it sees them as a set of uniform, passive and external constraints and uses them as mechanical yardsticks to judge all cultures, it also ignores the fact that different cultures are bound to balance, prioritize and relate them to their thick moral structures in their own different ways. It would seem that a dialectical and pluralist form of minimum universalism offers the most coherent response to moral and cultural diversity. As we shall see there are universal moral values and there is a creative interplay between them and the thick and complex moral structures of different societies, the latter domesticating and pluralizing the former and being in turn reinterpreted and revised in their light, thus leading to what I might call pluralist universalism.

Unlike Plato's Ideas, moral values are not self-subsistent entities occupying a transcendental realm of their own. They refer to things we consider worth cherishing and realizing in our lives. Since judgments of worth are based on reasons, values are things we have good reasons to cherish, which in our well-considered view deserve our allegiance and ought to form part of the good life. Universal moral values are those we have good reasons to believe to be worthy of the allegiance of all human beings, and are in that sense universally valid or binding. Moral values are meant for beings like us and intended to regulate our lives. Reasons relevant to a discussion of them are therefore of several kinds, such as our assessment of our moral capacities, what we take to be our basic tendencies and limits, the likely consequences of pursuing different values, their compatibility, the ease with which they can be combined into a coherent way of life, and the past and present experiences of societies that lived by them.

Although we might try to arrive at universal values by analysing human nature, universal moral consensus and so on, as philosophers have done over the centuries, the more satisfactory way to arrive at them is through a universal or cross-cultural dialogue. Since we are culturally embedded and prone to universalizing our own values, we need the dialogue to counter this tendency and help us rise to the required level of intellectual abstraction. The dialogue also brings together different historical experiences and cultural sensibilities, and ensures that we appreciate human beings in all their richness and that the values we arrive at are as genuinely universal as is humanly possible. It subjects our reasons for holding them to a cross-cultural test and requires us to ensure that they are accessible and acceptable to members of very different cultures. The dialogue has the further advantages that it shows respect for other cultures, offers those involved a motive to comply with the outcome, and gives the values an additional authority derived from democratic validation and a cross-cultural global consensus.

Moral discourse is comparative in nature and involves showing why we should subscribe to one set of values rather than their opposites. We decide in favour of the former not because we can make out a conclusive and irrefutable case for them, for such certainty is rare in human affairs, but because arguments for them are stronger and more convincing than those for their alternatives. It is therefore not enough for critics to say that our arguments are not conclusive; they need to show that a much better or an equally good case can be made out for the opposite value. If they cannot, our decision stands. For example, although we can offer powerful arguments for the equality of the sexes and races, they are unlikely to be conclusive and incontrovertible. However, if we can show, as indeed we can, that those for equality are more coherent, consistent with known facts about human beings, and so on and thus much stronger than those for inequality, we would have said enough to establish that equality is to be preferred over inequality.

Moral values have no foundations in the sense of an indisputable and objective basis, but they do have grounds in the form of intersubjectively discussable reasons and are not arbitrary. And although our defence of them is never conclusive and immune to all conceivable objections, it is conclusive for all practical purposes if it withstands criticism and is stronger than the case that can be made out for opposite values. We can, therefore, legitimately ask others to agree to these values or show us why they find our reasons unconvincing. If they do neither, we can charge them with being unreasonable. Unreasonable people participate in a dialogue and demand reasons from others, but refuse to give or be guided by them when these do not justify their preferred conclusions. Since we are prone to the human frailty of assuming our values to be self-evident and defining reasons in an ethnocentric manner, we should be extremely wary about accusing others of unreasonableness. We should make every effort to enter into their world of thought and give them every opportunity to show why they hold the views they do. If they offer no reasons or ones that are flimsy, self-serving, based on crude prejudices or ignorance of relevant facts, they are being unreasonable and have in effect opted out of the dialogue.

We can all agree that human beings have several unique and worthwhile capacities, such as the ability to think, reason, use language, form visions of the good life, enter into moral relations with one another, be self-critical and achieve increasingly higher levels of excellence. Thanks to these, they understand, control and humanize their natural environment, rise above the automatic and inexorable processes of nature, carve out spaces of freedom, create a world of aesthetic, scientific, literary, moral and other great human achievements, give depth and meaning to their lives, and introduce a novel form of existence in the world. As beings capable of creating meaning and values, they deserve to be valued themselves, and have *worth*. It is, of course, possible that their capacities and achievements are all trivial in the eyes of God or even perhaps a hitherto unknown species of unusual gifts currently inhabiting our planet or descending on it in the future, and that the high value we place on them only reveals our species-bias. However, that does not diminish their value in *our* eyes, for we have no other standards to judge them by than those derived from as detached and objective a perspective as we can bring to bear on ourselves. We cannot leap out of ourselves and pretend to be something else. Even if we believed in God and tried to look at ourselves from His point of view, we would have to rely on our own judgment as to who to accept as God and how to interpret His intentions. Since we value human beings because of their capacities, we reduce our species-bias by conferring value on apes and other higher forms of animal species that display some of these capacities.

Human beings, then, have worth because we have good reasons to value their capacities and achievements. Human worth is not a natural property like eyes and ears but something we confer upon ourselves, and hence a moral practice. Since human beings have worth, it extends to all that they deeply value and to which their sense of worth is inextricably tied. This is why we rightly confer value on objects of art, cultural and religious communities, pet animals, rare manuscripts and ancient buildings, and consider them worth preserving even, sometimes, at the cost of human life.

To say that human beings have worth or, what comes to the same thing, to adopt the moral practice of conferring worth on them, is to commit ourselves to treating them in certain ways. Negatively, we may not treat them as worthless or devoid of intrinsic value and use them as a mere means to our ends, kill them at will, torture them, use them for dangerous experiments, sacrifice them for causes they do not share, violate the integrity of their intimate relationships, and treat with contempt what they deeply value. Positively, we should cherish their sense of self-respect and self-worth, value their individual and collective achievements, encourage them to develop and express their capacities, and help create conditions in which they can lead worthy and meaningful lives.

Since human beings have unique and worthwile capacities which make them superior to animals and the rest of the natural world, they can also be said to have *dignity* or its conceptual analogues in other languages. Unlike worth, dignity is an aristocratic or hierarchical concept and describes a privileged status. It makes sense only in relation to what is judged to be inferior, and implies that our treatment of human beings should not fall below the minimum required by their status. This is why every discussion of human dignity directly or indirectly contrasts humans with animals, emphasizes their superiority, and insists that they may not be treated as if they were animals or inanimate objects. This does not mean that animals are human playthings, but rather that we can give good reasons why they should be cared for and loved but not treated as our equals and endowed with equal worth, and that there is a great moral difference between swatting a fly or trampling on an insect and killing a human being. Dignity is not inherent in human beings, but is a status they confer on themselves in acknowledgment of their uniquely shared capacities, not a natural property but a moral practice regulating their relations with each other. It is not an individual but a collective status, for the individual acquires it by virtue of belonging to the human species and possessing certain species-specific capacities.

Since human dignity is human worth seen in a comparative perspective, it is not an independent source of moral principles but it does add a new dimension to moral life. Living in a world surrounded by nonhuman beings, it is an integral part of our self-consciousness to define our ontological status in relation to them. Our identity is constituted both by what we are and are not, and whatever else we are, we are not like trees and plants and worms and insects and all the rest of the natural world. This inescapable awareness of difference, constantly reinforced by our daily experiences and activities, is an integral part of our sense of self and forms the basis of our sense of dignity. Since the concept of human dignity is based on a sharp distinction between humans and non-humans, it is central to those traditions of thought such as the Greek, the Christian and the Islamic which set much store by that distinction, and is relatively muted in those such as the Hindu and the Buddhist in which the distinction is less sharply drawn. However, even the latter stress the special and superior status of humans, and rely on a weaker notion of human dignity.

It is true that some categories of humans such as the mad or mentally handicapped may lack some of the distinctively human capacities and would therefore appear to have less or no worth. However, they are rarely devoid of these capacities altogether, and are mad and handicapped in a way that only humans can be. Besides, they are also the sons, daughters, parents, friends and so forth of normal human beings, to whom they are deeply bonded and in whose worth they therefore participate. Furthermore, madness and idiocy are not easy to define. Once we start denying worth to certain kinds of persons, we run the risk of denying it, or encouraging others to deny it, to a wider class of human beings, and hence we have good reasons not to go down that route. Conferring dignity and worth on such persons also tests, affirms and intensifies our general commitment to human worth for, if we are able to value them, we are even more likely to value our more fortunate fellow-humans. For these and other reasons, we may rightly grant them equal worth.

Human beings possess not only certain distinctive capacities but also desires and needs. They wish to continue to live, desire food and physical wholeness, loathe disease and pain, and seek sexual satisfaction. Since they live in society they also develop such socially derived desires and fears as self-respect, good opinion of others, friendship, love, and fear of rejection and humiliation. As distinct centres of self-consciousness with an inescapable inner life of their own, they require at least some measure of inviolability and privacy. They are subject to changes of mood, frustrations, anxieties and so on, and cannot come to terms with these without a relatively secure personal space and at least some measure of control over their lives. Human beings require a long period of nurture and cannot grow into sane adults without a stable, loving and stimulating environment and a sense of belonging and roots. In order to feel secure, plan their lives and form stable relationships, they need a society free from an oppressive climate of terror and total unpredictability. They also need a conducive environment in which to acquire certain existentially indispensable capacities and skills without which they cannot hold themselves together, make sense of their lives, and find their way around in the wider society.

Since human beings require certain common conditions to grow and flourish, these conditions constitute their well-being and define the content of their fundamental interests. Although different societies entertain different conceptions of the good life and differently define human well-being, the shared human capacities, needs and so forth imply that some constituents of human well-being are common to them all. These include, for example, survival, means of sustenance, physical wholeness, good health, a stable, stimulating and loving environment, access to the cultural resources of their community, freedom from the arbitrary exercise of power, a measure of privacy and control of their lives, and opportunities for self-expression. Like dignity and worth, promotion of these interests is a moral practice we adopt because we have good reasons to believe that human beings should live rather than die, grow into intelligent adults rather than zombies, enjoy health rather than suffer from diseases, and so forth.

Since human beings have equal dignity and worth and require common conditions of well-being, their claims to the latter deserve equal consideration and weight. Equality is not an empirical fact, for empirically we are either similar or different, not equal or unequal. Equality is a matter of moral judgment based on how we interpret and what weight we give to the similarities and differences. It is a moral practice we have good reasons to adopt, such as that there is a basic equality of worth, needs and so on among human beings, that the practice reinforces and nurtures our sense of dignity and worth, and that it enables each of us to lead a fulfilling personal life and contribute to the creation of a rich collective life. This does not mean that we might not admire some persons more, for that depends on their capacities and how they use them; nor that all should enjoy equal income and wealth, for human capacities vary and the incentive of inequality is often necessary to spur people to greater efforts; nor that all should enjoy equal political power, for that again is ruled out by the inequalities of talents and the needs of wider society. Equality requires, minimally, that we should acknowledge the equal dignity and worth of all human beings, accord them equal respect, and give equal consideration to their claims to the basic requirements of the good life.

It is then possible to arrive at a body of moral values which deserve the respect of all human beings. I have mentioned recognition of human worth and dignity, promotion of human well-being or of fundamental human interests, and equality, but this is only illustrative and does not exhaust the totality of possible universal moral values. The manner in which I have arrived at them is sketchy and needs to be tightened up considerably, but it should give some idea of how we might go about the task and why and how it involves appealing not just to human nature but also to the human condition, historical experiences and our judgment of the likely consequences of different forms of human relations and social life.

Although we can draw up a list of universal moral values, not all socieites have the required moral, cultural, economic and other resources to live up to their demands. Furthermore, our case for them is not equally compelling because we can offer far more powerful arguments for some of them than for others. Not all values are equally central to the good life either. We should therefore identify those that are within the reach of all, central to any form of good life, and for which we can give compelling reasons. We should consolidate global consensus around them and allow their inner momentum to generate a movement towards an increasingly higher level of consensus. As individuals and groups in different societies appeal to them in their struggles for justice and as the rest of the world responds to them, the consensus deepens, the values become a widely accepted political currency, and acquire new adherents.

In this context, the 1948 United Nations Declaration of Human Rights provides a useful starting point.[5] It was born out of the kind of cross-cultural dialogue referred to earlier and has a genuinely universal feel about it, which is why people all over the world continue to appeal to it, and all subsequent global or continental statements on the subject, while modifying it in some respects, endorse its basic values. These include respect for human life and dignity, equality of rights, respect for personal integrity and inviolability, recognition of basic human worth, and protection of fundamental human interests. These general values in turn entail and are realized by such measures as the prohibition of torture, genocide and slavery, freedom of association, liberty of conscience, equality before the law, fair trial, popular accountability of political power, protection of privacy, and respect for the integrity of familial and other intimate relationships.

Although admirable, the UN Declaration is not free of defects. It retains a distinctly liberal bias and includes rights which, though admirable, cannot claim universal validity; for example, the rights to a more or less unlimited freedom of expression, to marriage based on the 'free and full consent' of the parties involved, and to relatively unlimited property. What is even more important, it takes a statist view of human rights and emasculates their universalist and critical thrust. The rights are addressed to the state which alone is deemed to have the obligation to respect and realize them. Strictly speaking, human rights as expressions of the minimum that is both due *to* and *from* all human beings are addressed to all human beings and impose on them a duty to respect them and do all they can to facilitate their realization. Since there are good reasons to respect the autonomy of the state, human rights are its primary but not exclusive responsibility. If a state is unable to secure the conditions of their effective exercise for lack of resources, civil wars or other reasons, outsiders have a duty to render it such help as it needs and that they can afford. Universal human rights imply universal human obligations including a duty to create a global regime of justice.

The UN Declaration also makes the mistake of confusing human rights with particular institutional structures. Since the latter cannot take root and function effectively unless they suit a society's traditions and moral and political culture, they necessarily vary from society to society. We must not, therefore, hold up liberal democracy as the only acceptable political form, and condemn political systems that do not allow multiple political parties, separation of powers, and so on. We might have good reasons to believe that the desired values are more likely to be realized under one set of institutions rather than another, but we should neither be too dogmatic about our views nor so identify the institutions and the values that the latter cannot be discussed and defended independently of them.

The minimum universal values which we may legitimately insist upon are by their very nature general and need to be interpreted, prioritized, adopted to, and in case of conflict reconciled, in the light of the culture and circumstances of each society. Respect for human life is a universal value, but different societies disagree on when human life begins and ends and what respect for it entails. Again, respect for human life sometimes conflicts with that for human dignity or justice, as when a dying man has lost all control over his bodily functions, or injustices cannot be redressed without recourse to violence. Respect for human dignity requires that we should not humiliate or degrade others or treat them in a cruel and demeaning manner. What constitutes humiliation or cruelty, however, varies with cultures and cannot be universally legislated. In some societies a person would rather be slapped on her face than coldly ignored or subjected to verbal abuse. In some, human dignity is deemed to be violated when parents interfere with their offsprings' choices of spouses; in others their intervention is taken as a sign that they care enough for their offsprings' dignity and well-being to press their advice on them and save them from making a mess of their lives. Different societies might also articulate, defend and rely on different mechanisms to realize universal values. Some might prefer the language of rights and claims and rely on the state to enforce these. Others might find it too individualist, aggressive, legalistic and state-centered and prefer the language of duty, relying on social conditioning and moral pressure to ensure that their members respect each other's dignity and refrain from harming each other's fundamental interests.

Universal values might also come into conflict with the freely-accepted central values of a cultural community. Women members of some indigenous and traditional communities freely commit themselves to vows of obedience and service to men in their lives and want to have nothing to do with equality. They might be brainwashed and we need to counter that, but should not assume that those who refuse to share our values are all victims of false consciousness. Torture is bad, but members of many religious sects and even some terrorist groups welcome it as a punishment or expiation for grave moral and spiritual or political lapses. Degrading human beings is bad, yet the training for priesthood in many Christian sects involves daily public exposure and humiliation of novices suspected of harbouring 'carnal' thoughts or reading prohibited literature. Human worth is a great value, but many religious groups and even some secular communities see fit to cultivate a feeling of personal and collective worthlessness. Indeed, it is difficult to think of a single universal value which is 'absolute' or inherently inviolable and may never in practice be overriden.[6] Since we rightly consider them as constitutive of the moral minimum due to and from human beings and assign them the greatest moral weight, we must require that the overriding factors be proportionate in their importance and of at least equal moral weight.

Since different societies may legitimately define, trade-off, prioritize, and realize the universal values differently, and even occasionally override some of them, the question arises of how we can prevent them from engaging in specious and self-serving moral reasoning and reinterpreting the values out of existence or emasculating their critical thrust. There is no foolproof way of doing so. All we can do is ask their spokesmen to justify their decisions when they appear unacceptable to us. If they can provide a strong and reasonably compelling defence, we should respect their decisions. If not, we should remain sceptical and press for change.

Asian Values

A brief examination of the much-debated question of Asian values will illustrate the point.[7] Leaders of almost all East Asian countries insist that some of the rights included in the United Nations and other western-inspired declarations of human rights are incompatible with their values, traditions and self-understanding, and that western governments should be more tolerant of their attempts to define and prioritize them differently. While agreeing that these rights are universally valid, the Bangkok Declaration of 1993 insisted that they should be defined and applied in the light of local 'history, culture and religious backgrounds'. The Singapore delegation to the 1995 Vienna conference challenged the very universality of some of these rights. Urging the West not to be 'so blinded by arrogance and certainties as to lose the capacity for imagination and sympathy', the delegation asked it to take a 'more modest approach' lest it should 'fracture the international consensus on human rights'. The widespread western response is to dismiss these appeals to Asian values as self-serving attempts to justify arbitrary power, and to argue that the values are neither unique nor common to all Asian countries and cannot in any case be allowed to subvert or limit human rights.

The western response is too indiscriminate and sweeping to be convincing. The appeal to national or continental values is not unique to East Asians. Many Americans reject the European welfare state or the ban on capital punishment on the ground that they are incompatible with, and cannot be accommodated within, their way of life. And neither they nor the Europeans are prepared to follow the Singaporean or Chinese ban on hard pornography on the ground that it violates liberal values. If these societies are right to cherish their values, there is no reason why East Asians should not uphold theirs.

The other western objections to the East Asian view are no better. It would not do to say that Asian values are not unique to Asian countries, for their leaders not only make no such claim but in fact insist that the West, too, should, and indeed once did, share them and is wrong to allow them to be overridden by the liberal individualist ethos. Nor would it do to say that all East Asians do not share these values. Although East Asian countries differ in important respects, most of their citizens do cherish such 'Asian' values as social harmony, respect for authority, orderly society, a united and extended family and a sense of filial piety. The fact that some of their citizens do not share these is immaterial. After all, the racists, sexists and many conservative members of western societies do not share the value of equality, yet these societies rightly consider it central to their self-understanding and impose it on them without the slightest hesitation. In short, we should not ask the abstract and misleading question whether East Asians have a right to live by or are all agreed on their values, but what these values are and if and how they offend against universal values.

East Asian spokesmen are not a homogeneous group. They raise different kinds of objections to the universalist discourse on human rights and deserve nuanced responses. First, some find the language of rights individualist, legalistic, statist and aggressive, ideally suited in their view to the atomized western society but not to one as cohesive as theirs. They have no objection to many of the basic values underlying the discourse on human rights, but think that these are best realized within a communitarian moral framework based on mutual concern, solidarity, loyalty to the wider society, and socially responsible individualism. They prefer to rely on social and cultural institutions rather than the state, on moral and religious pressure rather than the fear of the law, and aim to foster the consciousness of individual responsibilities and duties rather than of rights. Although this is a very different way of defining and creating the good society to the liberal, it has its virtues and should be welcomed. It is vulnerable to the collectivist danger and unlikely to create a culture conducive to the development of individuality and choice. However, the liberal stress on rights, too, has its limitations, including its well-known inability to nurture the spirit of community and social responsibility vital for regulating the excesses of the culture of rights. No society so far has succeeded in striking the right balance between the individual and the community, and none can be held up as a universal model. East Asian societies should, therefore, not only be left free but encouraged to experiment with new forms of social and political organization consistent with full respect for the minimum universal values.

Second, some East Asian leaders are unhappy not so much with the language of rights as with parts of their content, which they find narrow and heavily biased towards the western liberal democratic form of government. They are better disposed to democracy than to liberalism, and take a more or less organic rather than an individualist view of the former. In their view a good polity should be just, accountable to its citizens, promote economic growth, maintain social harmony, hold society together and reflect the basic values of its people. It does not have to be liberal in the sense of a contractual association between its members pursuing no other collective goals than protecting their rights and maintaining neutrality between different conceptions of the good.

Unlike their western counterparts, East Asian societies share a broad consensus on the nature of the good life, and think that they have a right and even a duty to enforce it out of respect for both the integrity of their way of life and the wishes of the majority. Hence they wish to ban pornography, protect some of their deeply held moral and religious beliefs and practices against irresponsible attacks, and censure films and literary works that incite intercommunal hatred or mock and demean minority or majority communities. They also wish to promote the virtues of filial piety, good neighbourliness and respect for nature by such measures as giving elderly parents the right to sue their children for maintenance and imposing fines on individuals for failing to report a theft or a fire in their neighbour's house or vandalizing the environment. East Asian leaders also point to the problems involved in holding multi-ethnic societies together. Since some of their ethnic groups have no experience of living and working together, racial hostilities are easily aroused and require greater restrictions on free speech and movement than is usual in more stable societies. In many cases of racial unrest the process of trial itself inflames passions and increases tensions, making it unwise to conduct it in the normal western manner. Evidence, too, may sometimes have to be gathered by covert operations, and cannot be submitted to open courts or expected to meet the normal standards of criminal law.

This second East Asian claim respects universal values and human rights but defines, relates and prioritizes them differently. It does not justify tortures, arbitrary arrests, genocide, tyranny, racial and other forms of discrimination, and denial of free elections and basic liberties. All it maintains is that East Asian societies wish to pursue such collective goals as social harmony and cohesion, moral consensus, integrity of the family and economic development, and that these involve different kinds of rights and greater restrictions on individual freedoms than is common in liberal societies. Although some of these goals and the restrictions they entail do not find much favour among liberals, that is not an argument against them. All one can require is that the goals should promote a worthwhile, morally defensible and popularly endorsed vision of the good life, and that the measures used should be proportionate to them and represent a morally justifiable trade-off between human rights.

The third East Asian claim is quite different from the other two. Its advocates, drawn mainly from the ranks of Chinese and Vietnamese leaders, reject the very concern with human rights as bourgeois, western and incompatible with their traditional values and vision of the good life. For them, society is more important than the individual. Social solidarity, a prosperous economy and a strong and powerful state are the highest national goals. And the individual has meaning and value only to the extent that he or she serves society. Since human rights presuppose and reinforce an individualist culture and restrict the state's freedom of action, they are deemed to be inherently reactionary and part of the western design to destabilize and weaken these societies. Following the logic of this argument, the Chinese and other governments reject parts of the democratic system of free elections, multiple political parties, popular participation, peaceful protests, free speech, individual and organized dissent, and the rule of law.

Although this third claim is understandable in the context of Chinese history and is far more complex and nuanced than my brief account suggests, it violates some of the basic values mentioned earlier. It often permits terror, arbitrary arrests, gross violations of personal autonomy, destruction of the family, some of the worst forms of personal humiliation, disregard for human dignity, and the use of individuals as a mere means to collective goals. There might be some justification for some of these practices if the Chinese could show that they are the only way to promote worthwhile goals. This is not the case. Economic development does not require, and is even hampered by, repressive measures. The Great Leap forward, which killed over 20 million people and had to be reversed three years later, could have been avoided or reversed earlier if China had had a free press. The importance of economic development lies in creating the conditions of the good life, and it defeats its purpose if it violates human dignity and self-respect and renders citizens incapable of leading the good life. The same is true of national unity and social solidarity, both of which are worthwhile goals but which are bound to be subverted by the methods the Chinese propose.

The Chinese claim that human rights are incompatible with their traditional values is equally unconvincing. It is true that the traditional Chinese view of the individual requires rights to be defined in less exclusivist, proprietary and absolutist terms than is common in liberal societies. Although there is something to be said for such a view of rights, it can be easily accommodated within a suitably redefined conception of human rights. Furthermore, as their own human rights activists have pointed out, Chinese leaders misrepresent traditional values. There is no evidence that the latter justify arbitrary exercise of power or any of the other practices mentioned above. And if some of them do, they need to be changed, for no values are sacrosanct simply because they are traditional. After all, neither the communist nor even the nationalist values which the Chinese have warmly embraced are part of their tradition. Like their premodern European counterparts, the traditional Chinese society relied on intricate social and moral mechanisms to check the abuse of political power and did not stress individual rights. Their society today is quite different. The emergence of the centralized and bureaucratic state, urbanization, increased mobility of labour and capital, social differentiation, industrialization and increasing liberalization have undermined the traditional mechanisms of social self-discipline and call for effective alternatives. The only ones that have worked reasonably well so far in most societies are the institutions of human rights, constitutionally limited power, a free press, and so on. Since Chinese leaders do not propose a viable alternative, their rejection of human rights is self-serving and suspect.

Given the differences in their history, traditions and moral culture, it is both inevitable and desirable that different societies should differently interpret, prioritize and realize great moral values and integrate them with their own suitably revised thick and complex moral structures. This is the only way we can deepen our insights into the complexity and grandeur of human life and attain increasingly higher levels of moral universality. There is, however, the obvious and sadly all too familiar danger that ill-motivated governments and dominant political groups might misuse their legitimate interpretative freedom to undermine these values. This happens even in mature liberal democratic societies with regard to their constitutionally enshrined fundamental rights, a domestic political analogue of universal moral values. We rely on the courts to protect, interpret and balance these rights, and even they get things wrong from time to time and we turn to the democratic political process with all its limitations. In the international context we need, over time, to develop such judicial and political institutions, but until that happens we have nothing else to rely upon save the kind of cross-cultural interrogation referred to earlier, the moral weight of enlightened world opinion backed up by global economic and political pressure, and in rare cases humanitarian intervention.

Notes

1. The inquiry into human nature presupposes that humans can and should be clearly distinguished from non-humans, that nature and culture can and should be

separated, that we can discover human nature fairly accurately, that things of great significance depend on it, and so on. For reasons too complex to discuss here, these and related assumptions became central to western thought in a way they did not in Hindu, Buddhist, Confucian and Islamic traditions, which have therefore generally taken only limited interest in human nature. In the western tradition itself Sophists devoted little attention to it. Even Plato is primarily concerned with the structure and hierarchy of the human psyche rather than its constitutive tendencies. Aristotle seems to mark a turning point. The concept of human nature acquires enormous importance in Christianity.

2. Berger and Luckman (1966, pp. 67, 69) rightly argue that 'human-ness is socio-culturally variable' because *'Homo Sapiens* is always and in the same measure *homo socius'*. See also Geertz (1973, pp. 43f, 50–1) where he challenges the widely shared assumption that only what is uniformly shared by humans constitutes their humanity.

3. For a brief but fascinating analysis of the distinctive style of Indian thought, see Ramanujan (1990). George Fletcher (1997) offers a fascinating account of the ties between English language and the common law tradition, and the way in which the former structures legal reasoning.

4. For minimum universalism, see Hart (1961), Walzer (1994) and Tuck (1994). Walzer's 'reiterative' universalism cannot easily explain how we can tease out the commonalities between the thick and relatively self-contained moral traditions and translate the categories of one into those of another. For good critiques of Walzer, see Bellamy (1999, Chapter 3) and Carens (2000, Introduction).

5. For a good discussion of human rights across cultures, see An-Na'im (1992), especially the articles by the editor, Richard Falk, William Alford, Virginia Leary, Tom Svensson and Allan McChesney.

6. See Kekes (1993, pp. 210f). We may, of course, make some values absolute by defining them in highly formal and abstract terms, but then they have no normative and critical content. For a balanced discussion of 'Asian values', see Bell (1999), Tang (1995), *Journal of Democracy* (1997), Ames (April 1997) and Mehbubani (1999).

7. The European Court of Human Rights applies the same convention on human rights to 300 million people of very different cultural backgrounds, allowing in one case what it does not in another. Its 'variable geometry' shows one way in which general principles can be adjusted to different traditions and circumstances.

References

Ames, R. T. (1997). "Continuing the Conversation on Chinese Human Rights," *Ethics and International Affairs,* vol. 11

An-Na'im, A. (ed.) (1992). *Human Rights in Cross-Cultural Perspectives: A Quest for Consensus.* Philadelphia: University of Pennsylvania Press

Bell, D. (1999). *East Meets West: Human Rights and Democracy in Asia.* Oxford, UK: Clarendon Press

Bellamy, R. (1999). *Liberalism and Pluralism: Towards a Politics of Compromise.* London: Routledge

Berger, P. and Luckmann, T. (eds.) (1966). *The Social Construction of Reality.* Harmondsworth, UK: Penguin

Carens, J. (2000). *Culture, Citizenship and Community.* Oxford, UK: Oxford University Press

Fletcher, G. (1997). "The Case for Linguistic Self-Defence," in R. McKim and J. McMahan (eds.), *The Morality of Nationalism.* Princeton, NJ: Princeton University Press

Geertz, C. (1973). *The Interpretation of Cultures.* New York: Basic Books

Hart, H. L. A. (1961). *The Concept of Law.* Oxford, UK: Clarendon Press

Kekes, J. (1993). *The Morality of Pluralism.* Princeton, NJ: Princeton University Press

Mehbubani, L. (1999). "An Asian Perspective on Human Rights," in P. van Nees (ed.), *Debating Human Rights.* London: Routledge

Ramanujan, A. K. (1990). "Is There an Indian Way of Thinking? An Informal Essay," in M. McKim (ed.), *Indian Through Hindu Categories.* Delhi: Sage

Tang, J. T. H. (ed.) (1995). *Human Rights and International Relations in Asia Pacific.* London: Pinter

Tuck, R. (1994). "Rights and Pluralism," in J. Tully (ed.), *Philosophy in an Age of Pluralism: The Philosophy of Charles Taylor in Question.* Cambridge, UK: Cambridge University Press

Walzer, M. (1994). *Thick and Thin: Moral Arguments at Home and Abroad.* Notre Dame, IN: University of Notre Dame Press

Part III
Toward a Transtopia

14

The Problem of Language in Cross-Cultural Studies

Lydia H. Liu

S TRICTLY SPEAKING, comparative scholarship that aims to *cross* cultures can do nothing but translate. As a trope of epistemological crossing, translation always says one thing in terms of another, although it must pretend to speak the truth for the sake of fidelity (or sanity, to be more exact). But leaving aside the marital trope of fidelity and the logocentric notion of truth—concepts that readily lend themselves to deconstructionist criticism—what else do we know or can we say about translation and its implications for cross-cultural understanding? And indeed, what does it mean for a contemporary scholar to cross the "language barrier" between two or more cultures and linguistic communities?

Admittedly, much more is involved here than what is commonly known as an interlingual transaction between a source language and a target language.[1] Even before I take up the subject of this book, I find myself facing larger problems, such as certain entrenched ways of thinking about cultural difference in the Western academy. For example, disciplinary boundaries and familiar modes of intellectual inquiry often generate difficult interpretive problems regarding cultures and languages other than one's own.[2] In whose terms, for which linguistic constituency, and in the name of what kinds of knowledge or intellectual authority does one perform acts of translation between cultures? The question becomes doubly acute when one crosses from the West to the East, or vice versa. Of course, the difficulty is compounded when the object of the inquiry itself, such as modern Chinese literature, does not constitute a pristine territory of native knowledge "uncontaminated" by earlier historical forces that have coerced and conditioned similar crossings in the recent past, namely, the translation of the West

and the invention of the modern Chinese language. Although I do not presume to have an answer to these questions, I will venture these multilayered
crossings in this book, an undertaking fated to describe as well as to enact
the predicament of its subject.[3]

Perhaps, I would do better by reframing my problematic in a slightly different context. Let me evoke briefly a running debate among anthropologists
on the notion of cultural translation, a debate I believe has important ramifications for literary studies, history, and other disciplines in the humanities.
For many years, British social anthropologies have used the concept of cultural translation at its various stages of theoretical elaboration to develop a
notion of interpretation that, ideally, will account for the difference between
their own culture and the non-European societies they study. Edmund
Leach, for example, describes the typical ethnographic moment as follows:

> Let me recapitulate. We started by emphasizing how different are "the oth-
> ers"—and made them not only different but remote and inferior. Sentimen-
> tally, we then took the opposite track and argued that all human beings are
> alike; we can understand Trobrianders or the Barotse because their motivations
> are just the same as our own; but that didn't work either, "the others" remained
> obstinately other. But now we have come to see that the essential problem is
> one of translation. The linguists have shown us that all translation is difficult,
> and that perfect translation is usually impossible. And yet we know that for
> *practical purposes* a tolerably satisfactory translation is always possible even
> when the original "text" is highly abstruse. Languages are different but not so
> different as all that. Looked at in this way social anthropologists are engaged
> in establishing a methodology for the translation of cultural language. (Italics
> added)[4]

One would like to have as much faith in the power of cultural translation as
Leach, but the phrase "practical purposes" lets the cat out of the bag. To me,
the crucial thing here is not whether translation between cultures is possible
(people do it anyway), or whether the "other" is knowable, or even whether
an abstruse "text" is decipherable, but what practical purpose or needs
(which sustain one's methodological paraphernalia) bring an ethnographer
to pursue cultural translation. This is precisely the point at which the question I raised earlier should intervene: In whose terms, for which linguistic
constituency, and in the name of what kinds of knowledge or intellectual
authority does an ethnographer perform acts of translation between cultures?

In a pointed criticism of the British ethnographic tradition, Talal Asad sites
the concept of cultural translation in power relations and urges us to consider the problematic of cross-cultural interpretation with close attention to
the actual historical environment in which both the ethnographer and his
native informant live, yet do not speak the same language:

To put it crudely, because the languages of the Third World societies—including, of course, the societies that social anthropologists have traditionally studied—are "weaker" in relation to Western languages (and today, especially to English), they are more likely to submit to forcible transformation in the translation process than the other way around. The reason for this is, first, that in their political-economic relations with Third World countries, Western nations have the greater ability to manipulate the latter. And, second, Western languages produce and deploy *desired* knowledge more readily than Third World languages do.[5]

Asad's critique of the notion of cultural translation has major implications for comparative scholarship and for cross-cultural studies such as this one.[6] It warns us that the business of translating a culture into another language has little, if anything, to do with individual free choice or linguistic competence. If we have learned anything useful from Foucault, it should be clear that we must confront forms of institutional practices and the knowledge/power relationships that authorize certain ways of knowing while discouraging others. One familiar way of producing knowledge about other people and other cultures is to construct the terms of comparison on the ground of perceived linguistic equivalence. Yet that ground of equivalence itself often goes unexamined.

Tropes of Equivalence, East and West

The dictionary is based on the hypothesis—obviously an unproven one—that languages are made up of equivalent synonyms.

—Jorge Luis Borges

The idea that languages are commensurate and equivalents exist naturally between them is, of course, a common illusion that philosophers, linguists, and theorists of translation have tried in vain to dispel. Nietzsche, for example, attacked the illusion by showing that the equating of the unequal is simply a metaphorical function of language that lays claim to truth. "What therefore is truth? A mobile army of metaphors, metonymies, anthropomorphisms: in short a sum of human relations which became poetically and rhetorically intensified, metamorphosed, adorned, and after long usage seem to a nation fixed, canonic and binding; truths are illusions of which one has forgotten that they *are* illusions."[7] Gayatri Spivak explicates that Nietzsche's definition of metaphor points to the construction of an identity between dissimilar things, as the original phrase used in his essay is *Gleich machen* (make equal), "calling to mind the German word 'Gleichnis'—image, simile, similitude, comparison, allegory, parable—an unmistakable pointer to figurative practice in general."[8] Ironically, the philosopher himself has not been able to escape the fate of being translated and turned into another kind of illusion through the metaphorical equation of German and other languages. The thriving industry of bilingual dictionaries depends on the tenacity of this illusion—its will to power. It is the business of this industry to make sure that one understand "that languages are made up of equivalent synonyms."[9] The implication for cross-cultural comparison is that one relies on a conceptual model derived from the bilingual dictionary—that is, a word in language A must equal a word or a phrase in language B; otherwise one of the languages is lacking—to form opinions about other peoples or to lay philosophical grounds for discourses about other cultures and, conversely, about one's own totalized identity.

Let me illustrate the problem by reflecting on a famous passage from Heidegger's "Aus einen Gespräch von der Sprache" (Dialogue on language) between a European philosopher (Heidegger) and a Japanese interlocutor (Tezuka). The following excerpt is taken from the latter half of their dialogue (J refers to the Japanese and F [I in English] to the Fragenden or Inquirer):

J: Da Sie mir, oder besser den vermutenden Andeutungen, die ich vorbringe, zuhören, erwacht in mir ein Zutrauen, mein Zögern zu lassen, das mich bislang davor zurückhielt, Ihnen auf Ihre Frage zu antworten.

F: Sie meinen die Frage, welches Wort Ihre Sprache spricht für das, was wir Europäer "Sprache" nennen.

J: Dieses Wort scheute ich mich bis zu diesem Augenblick zu sagen, weil ich eine Übersetzung geben muß, durch die sich unser Wort für Sprache wie eine bloße Bilderschrift ausnimmt, nämlich im Vorstellungsbezirk von Begriffen; denn nur durch sie sucht die europäische Wissenschaft und ihre Philosophie das Wesen der Sprache zu fassen.

F: Wie heißt das japanische Wort für "Sprache"?

J: (nach weiterem Zögern) Es heißt *"Koto ba"*.

F: Und was sagt dies?

J: *ba* nennt die Blätter, auch und zumal die Blütenblätter. Denken Sie an die Kirschblüte und an die Pflaumenblüte.

F: Und was sagt *Koto*?

J: Diese Frage is am schwersten zu beantworten. Indessen wird ein Versuch dadurch erleichtert, daß wir das *Iki* zu erläutern wagten: das reine Entzücken der rufenden Stille. Das Wehen der Stille, die dies rufende Entzücken ereignet, ist das Waltende, das jenes Entzücken kommen läßt. *Koto* nennt aber immer zugleich das jeweils Entzückende selbst, das einzig je im unwiederholbaren Augenblick mit der Fülle seines Anmutens zum Scheinen kommt.

F: *Koto* wäre dann das Ereignis der lichtenden Botschaft der Anmut.

J: Herrlich gesagt; nur führt das Wort "Anmut" das heutige Vorstellen zu leicht in die Irre. . . .

J: The fact that you give ear to me, or better, to the probing intimations I propose, awakens in me the confidence to drop my hesitations which have so far kept me from answering your question.

I: You mean the question which word in your language speaks for what we Europeans call "language."

J: Up to this moment I have shied away from that word, because I must give a translation which makes our word for language look like a mere pictograph, to wit, something that belongs within the precincts of conceptual ideas; for European science and its philosophy try to grasp the nature of language only by way of concepts.

I: What is the Japanese word for "language"?

J: (*after further hesitation*) It is "*Koto ba.*"

I: And what does that say?

J: *ba* means leaves, including and especially the leaves of a blossom—petals. Think of cherry blossoms or plum blossoms.

I: And what does *Koto* say?

J: This is the question most difficult to answer. But it is easier now to attempt an answer because we have ventured to explain *Iki*: the pure delight of the beckoning stillness. The breath of stillness that makes this beckoning delight come into its own is the reign under which that delight is made to come. But *Koto* always also names that which in the event gives delight, itself, that which uniquely in each unrepeatable moment comes to radiance in the fullness of its grace.

I: *Koto,* then, would be the appropriating occurrence of the lightening message of grace.

J: Beautifully said! Only the word "grace" easily misleads the modern mind. . . .[10]

This exchange is illuminating in a number of ways. First, it enacts in a single dramatic performance the impossibility and yet the necessity of translation between East and West. The European Inquirer, who is undoubtedly aware of the pitfalls of translation, nonetheless insists on having a Japanese equivalent of the European concept of language. Second, before the Japanese interlocutor is compelled to answer the Inquirer's question "What is the Japanese word for 'language' "—the type of syntax that makes the nonexistence of an equivalent unthinkable without its being interpreted as a "lack"—he explains his reasons for hesitation (this hesitation, reintroduced by the parenthesized italics a few lines later, effectively disrupts the flow of the conversation). The fear that his translation would make the Japanese "equivalent" for language look like a mere pictograph is not entirely groundless because his subsequent description of *koto ba* probably succeeds in doing just that in German. Third, the Inquirer's summary of the meaning of *koto* after the lengthy description given by his interlocutor points to something other than the translation of a Japanese word. As an appropriating gesture, it leads to Heidegger's own theory of Saying or Sage, which the Inquirer describes a moment later: "Denn es müßte sich etwas ereignen, wodurch sich dem Botengang jene Weite öffnete und zuleuchtete, in der das Wesen der Sage zum Scheinen kommt" (For something would have to come about by which that vast distance in which the nature of Saying assumes its radiance, opened itself to the messenger's course and shone upon it).[11] The words "die Sage," "der Botengang," and "zuleuchten" seem to echo his free translation of the Japanese koto ba, namely, "das Ereignis der lichtenden Botschaft der Anmut" (the appropriating occurrence of the lightening message of grace; italics added), but they speak more pertinently to some of the central tropes the philosopher uses in his own meditations on Ereignis (appropriation), Eigenen (owning), Lichtung (clearing), and so on.[12] In a remarkable moment of mise en abyme, Heidegger's language acts out the appropriation that it speaks about, by illustrating the predicament of translation in the very act of translation.

"A Dialogue on Language" was a central component of Heidegger's discourse on language in his later career when the philosopher developed his important notion of language as the "house of Being." It is worth speculating, though, what the conversation would have become if the philosopher had learned Japanese and conducted and transcribed this dialogue in that language. Most likely, the questions would not have been raised or would have had to be formulated differently. This dialogue highlights a number of problematic areas in the so-called exchange between East and West in modern history, not the least of which is the language of theory that expresses or implies a universal concern but in fact bears witness to its own limitations as a European language. To me, it seems sheer folly to wield an analytical concept or category indifferently anywhere as if that which makes sense in one place must necessarily obtain elsewhere.

The implications of such language interaction between East and West are manifold. At a certain point, the crossing of language boundaries stops being a linguistic issue, for words are easily translated into analytical (often universal) categories in the hands of scholars who need conceptual models for cross-cultural studies. This happens almost daily in the scholarly realm of "pseudo-universals" criticized by Eugene Eoyang in a recent study. The subtle or not so subtle bias that informs certain comparative questions—Why is there no epic in Chinese? Is there a civil society in China? etc.—often says more about the inquirer than the object of inquiry. As Eoyang puts it well, "The obverse questions are rarely, if ever, asked. Why are there no dynastic histories in the West? Why has the West produced no counterpart to Shijing?

Are there equivalents to the *lüshi* and *zaju* forms in the West? If these challenges to lacunae in the West strike one as slightly absurd, then we must consider the possibility that the original questions might be equally pointless."[13] Eoyang attributes the problem of pseudo-universals to the fundamental confusion of premise and methodology in comparative scholarship. But are there even more firmly entrenched beliefs in what a language can or cannot do that compel such confusion? We must face the question of translation that Heidegger's dialogue raises. Are analytical categories translated less frequently into the other language than they are used in one's own? What happens in such instances of translation? What is gained or lost? Perhaps, the crux of the matter is not so much that analytical categories cannot be applied across the board because they fail to have universal relevance—the impulse to translate is in fact unstoppable—but that the crossing of analytical categories over language boundaries, like any other crossing or transgression, is bound to entail confrontations charged with contentious claims to power. To be sure, universality is neither true or false, but any intellectual claim to it should be rigorously examined in the light of its own linguistic specificity and sources of authority.

Consider some of the words frequently used and abused in this capacity across the disciplines of the humanities and social sciences: "the self," "person," and "individual." What is the Chinese, Japanese, or Arabic equivalent(s) of the word "self"? This troublesome question rests on the assumption that equivalence of meaning can readily be established between different languages. Does not the existence of bilingual dictionaries attest to this fact? I hear people ask—Isn't it true that the category of the "self" has existed all along in the Chinese philosophical tradition? What about the Confucian notion of *ji*, etc.? I find the questions themselves rather dubious because they overlook the fact that the "trope of equivalence" between the English word "self" and the Chinese *ji, wo, ziwo* and other words has been established only recently in the process of translation and fixed by means of modern bilingual dictionaries.[14] Thus any linkages that exist derive from historical coincidences whose meanings are contingent on the politics of translingual practice. Once such linkages are established, a text becomes "translatable" in the ordinary sense of the word. The point I want to stress here, and it cannot be stressed enough, is that serious methodological problems arise when a cross-cultural comparative theory is built upon the basis of an essential category, such as "self" or "individual," whose linguistic identity transcends the history of translation and imposes its own discursive priority on a different culture.[15] The assumed homogeneity between *ji, wo,* or *ziwo* and "self" inevitably blots out the history of each word and the history of translation of "self" in modern Chinese, inasmuch as difference cannot be

conceived at the ontological level without first presenting itself at the constitutive level where the question of linguistic transaction must be brought in.[16]
In a recent commentary on Leibniz's "Letter on the Natural Theology of the
Chinese," Haun Saussy points out that mutual translatability between two
languages can be assured "only after the little word 'is' has been stripped of
its meaning. Once the thing has been taken out of being, there is not much
left for ontologists to disagree about."[17]

In the past decade or so, philosophers, anthropologists, and sociologists
have discussed whether the notions of the self, person, and individual, however defined and however unstable, should continue to be used as analytical
categories in the face of poststructuralist critiques. Charles Taylor, for example, has devoted several studies to the problems of self, identity, and language
in Western philosophy, and his notions of agency, human significance, and
public space of disclosure have attracted much attention in the West lately.[18]
His *Sources of the Self*, in particular, attempts to challenge the deconstructive
critique of the Western notions of subjectivity by seeking a multilayered historical understanding of the self in the West. Taylor's approach to the genesis
of modern identity and his broad vision and integrative thinking have been
eagerly embraced by scholars across a wide array of fields and disciplines.
But, what seems to be a promising sign of intervention into deconstruction
at one level turns out to reaffirm Judaeo-Christian values at another. This
comes out strongly in Taylor's ethical thinking, when he allows the Judaeo-
Christian tradition to lay exclusive claim to the ideals of the good. Although
the author never loses sight of the historical meanings of these ideals per se,
he tends to de-emphasize certain levels of historical practice being associated
with or performed in the name of these ideals.[19] One senses a strongly evan-
gelical move as the book closes with a moralistic telos: the hope of man's
moral redemption, we are told, resides "in Judaeo-Christian theism (however
terrible the record of its adherents in history), and in its central promise of a
divine affirmation of the human, more total than humans can ever attain
unaided" (p. 521). If the violence of history can be thus contained and suppressed by parentheses, one wonders if the very ground for critical thinking
does not drop from sight altogether.[20]

Why should the self be an analytical category in the first place? "It is quite
possible to be human, to think in a human manner without any particular
'notions' of the person." British scholar Steven Collins's critique of the philosophical category of the self opens a new horizon for the possibility of
grounding the notion of the person and self in the practice of modern academic disciplines. In a re-evaluation of the Année Sociologie school, he
points out that although Durkheim and Marcel Mauss, who emphasize an
empirical or sociological approach, speak of categories developing and

changing, both rely on Kantian philosophical categories to begin with. Thus, even as empirical science compels Mauss to formulate a non-essentialist notion of the person, he nonetheless allows the *sense* of the self to stand as an overriding, philosophical category. "If the category is necessary and universal, and so in a sense a priori," Collins observes, "then in just this sense it cannot have a history."[21]

This concern is shared by a number of other British and French anthropologists who participate in rethinking the legacy of the Année Sociologie school, especially the impact of Mauss's famous 1938 essay, "A Category of the Human Mind: The Notion of the Person; the Notion of Self."[22] These scholars criticize Mauss's Eurocentrism and problematic use of philosophical categories for their universalist pretensions and try to grapple with the double bind of what Martin Hollis calls "the historical and analytic category" of the person in their own scholarship.[23] In doing so, they effectively highlight the historical conditions under which the self, person, and individual have come to be established and naturalized as analytical categories in the Western academy.

For many reasons, this kind of self-reflexive critique has done little to change the disciplinary practice of mainstream scholarship; people continue to rely on the categories of the self, person, and individual to access knowledge about the "authentic" identity of another culture as opposed to their own totalized self-perception. The knowledge obtained this way cannot be tautological: either non-Western cultures are deficient in concepts of the self, person, and individual; or their concepts essentially differ from their Western counterparts. My question is whether the precondition for this kind of knowledge exists before the categories themselves are applied. Or does it really matter? The reason I wish to draw attention to this situation is not because I think cultural relativism is more desirable than transdiscursive approaches—no one wishes to trivialize the issue on that ground—but because the situation relates to the conditioning of knowledge that predicates any attempted crossings between languages and cultures. This condition must itself be explained rather than assumed; hence the question: What induces scholars in the West to look for a singular cultural conception of the self in other cultures? Besides the inevitable exercise of power through specialized knowledge, I believe the phenomenon also has something to do with certain time-honored assumptions about translation and difference in the Western philosophical discourse on language.

Translating Difference—An Oxymoron?

We are digging the pit of Babel.

—Kafka

Tradutore, traditore. This Italian aphorism has long been a cliché in English: "The translator is a betrayer." However, as soon as one starts to take the English translation too literally, one stumbles into the epistemological trap of paying homage to the translator(s) of the aphorism who necessarily betrays the original. Apropos of this classic example of the difficulty of translation, Roman Jakobson remarked in his essay "On Linguistic Aspects of Translation" that the English translation of the Italian aphorism "would deprive the Italian rhyming epigram of all its paronomastic value. Hence a cognitive attitude would compel us to change this aphorism into a more explicit statement and to answer the questions: translator of what messages? betrayer of what values?"[24] Here Jakobson was exclusively concerned with the untranslatability of poetry where phonemic similarity and differentiation participate in semantic relationships and therefore contribute to the making of overall textual meanings. As a structural linguist who contributed much to the study of poetics, Jakobson pointed out that the aphorism *tradutore, traditore* makes sense in Italian primarily because the two words are confronted and juxtaposed in a contiguous relation within the phonemic code of that language, which cannot be reproduced in English. Consequently, the loss of the paronomastic or poetic aspect of signification in the English translation gives a prosaic turn to the aphorism, converting it into a flat indicative statement that makes a truth claim: the translator is a betrayer.

The question I want to raise in conjunction with Jakobson's example, however, is not about the metaphor of betrayal or fidelity, for this is something that Derrida and others have effectively deconstructed in their critique of the notion of originary and teleologic presence in the logocentric tradition of Western metaphysics.[25] Nor am I particularly interested in the untranslability of the phonemic code or the paronomastic aspect of a verbal code into which Jakobson and other comparative linguists have offered much insight.[26] To my mind, Jakobson's example evokes a central problematic in theories of translation that has for centuries preoccupied translators, linguists, and philosophers of language in the West. My concern with that problematic can be summarized as follows: apart from technical linguistic reasons, what theoretical assumptions about *difference* between languages prompt theorists to raise the issue of translatability and untranslatability over and over again?

The tower of Babel is often invoked by theorists of translation to symbolize the chaos of human communication. As if prefiguring the long history of Bible translation, the Babel story itself (Gen 11:6) derives in part from earlier Sumerian legend and made its way into the Hebrew Bible through adaptation and translation.[27] Babel not only figures the impossibility of translating among the irreducible multiplicity of tongues but institutes a desire for completion and for the original Logos. As George Steiner has pointed out, theologians and metaphysicians of language who strive to attenuate this second banishment from the universal grammar of Adam generally believe that "a single primal language, an *Ur-Sprache,* lies behind our present discord, behind the abrupt warring tongues which followed on the collapse of Nimrod's ziggurat."[28] However, the faith in the original Word does not help resolve the contradiction of a common language when it comes to translating the Bible into vernacular tongues. The history of Bible translation and the politics of Christianity are fraught with ambivalent practices. As Willis Barnstone puts it, "On the one hand, there is the sacred view that holds to the process of entropy, the idea that any passage between languages implies waste, corruption, and fundamental loss. On the other, there is the constant didactic and messianic need to spread the word of God to potential converts, for which Bible translation is an indispensable tool."[29]

Steiner perceives a decisive link between this earlier kabbalistic understanding of translation and modern, rational theory of language or linguistic study, in that the latter continues to debate the question whether translation is possible. In his erudite book *After Babel,* he divides the history of translation theory in the West into four periods. The first period, characterized by an immediate empirical focus, extends from Cicero's *Libellus de optimo genere oratorum* of 46 B.C. and Horace's reiteration of this formula in the *Ars poetica* some twenty years later all the way to Hölderlin's commentary on his own translations of Sophocles in 1804. The second stage is one of theory and hermeneutic inquiry initiated by Friedrich Schleiermacher's decisive essay *Über die verschiedenen Methoden des Übersetzens* (1813) and taken up by A. W. Schlegel, Humboldt, Goethe, Schopenhauer, Ezra Pound, Walter Benjamin, and others. After this age of philosophic-poetic theory, Russian and Czech scholars, heirs to the Formalist movement, introduced the third period of translation theory by applying structural linguistics and information theory to the discussion of interlingual exchange. Andrei Fedorov's *Introduction to the Theory of Translation* (*Vvedenie v teoriiu perevoda*; Moscow, 1953) is representative of this collaborative scientific effort. Somewhat overlapping with the scientific stage—a necessary contradiction in Steiner's attempt to periodize—the fourth period begins in the early 1960's when the rediscovery of Walter Benjamin's paper "Die Aufgabe des Übersetzers" (The task of the translator), originally published in 1923, together with the influence of Heidegger and Hans-Georg Gadamer, caused a reversion to hermeneutic inquiries into translation and interpretation.[30] Although Steiner's periodization may well be disputed, his critical survey provides remarkable insights into some of the major concerns with the theories of translation examined by his book.[31] For instance, he argues that all theories of translation—formal, pragmatic, chronological—are only variants of a single, inescapable question. In what ways can or ought fidelity to be achieved? What is the optimal correlation between the A text in the source-language and the B text in the receptor-language? The issue has been debated for over two thousand years. But is there anything of substance to add to Saint Jerome's statement of the alternatives: *verbum e verbo*, word by word in the case of the mysteries, but meaning by meaning, *sed sensum exprimere de sensus*, everywhere else? (pp. 261–62)

Steiner's observation runs the risk of oversimplifying the situation of translation theory, but it is a risk worth taking because it raises issues that more than compensate for its reductive approach. Focusing on the ways in which the perennial question of translatability has been asked in translation theories, Steiner offers a historical critique of the metaphysical foundation of Western philosophical tradition and, in particular, its universalist notion of language. His criticism brings a widely held assumption into question, namely, that

the underlying structure of language is universal and common to all men. Dis-similarities between human tongues are essentially of the surface. Translation is realizable precisely because those deep-seated universals, genetic, historical, social, from which all grammars derive can be located and recognized as opera-tive in every human idiom, however singular or bizarre its superficial forms. To translate is to descend beneath the exterior disparities of two languages in order to bring into vital play their analogous and, at the final depths, common princi-ples of being. (p. 73)

Is Steiner overstating his case? Readers might object that Sapir and Whorf's cultural relativism can hardly fit into this totalizing picture; in fact, Sapir and Whorf were bent on undermining a universalist understanding of language and reality. According to their familiar theses, no two languages are sufficiently similar to be considered as representing the same social reality, and different societies live in distinct, linguistically determined worlds, not the same world that happens to have different labels attached to it. This met-alinguistics of "thought worlds" or cultural relativism, which aspires to a universal condition in its own way, has come under attack on various intel-lectual fronts, empirical and philosophical, from ethnographers and linguists. What interests me here is not the validity of the Sapir-Whorf hypothesis about the linguistic worldview of a given community, but an undisputed area of intellectual thinking inhabited by both universalists and cultural relativists, one that predicates a mode of knowledge on translation while ostensibly con-testing the possibility of translation. This contradiction simply brings in the old question of translatability and untranslatability through the back door, as the following passage from Whorf illustrates very well:

> In translating into English, the Hopi will say that these entities in process of causation "will come" or that they—the Hopi —"will come to" them, but in their own language, there are no verbs corresponding to our "come" and "go" that mean simple and abstract motion, our purely kinematic concept. The words in this case translated "come" refer to the process of eventuating without calling it motion—they are "eventuates to here" (*pew'i*) or "eventuates from it" (*angqö*) or "arrived" (*pitu*, pl. *öki*) which refers only to the terminal manifestation, the actual arrival at a given point, not to any motion preceding it.[32]

By performing a literal translation between English and Hopi on the spot, the author inadvertently undermines his own theory of well-defined boundaries of ethno-linguistic communities. One might want to ask, following Steiner, "if languages were monads with essentially discordant mappings of reality, how then could we communicate interlingually? How could we acquire a second tongue or transverse into another language-world by means of translation?"[33] To push these questions further in the direction of a politics of interlingual transaction, it seems that the very theoretical language that helped Whorf arrive at his conclusion that Hopi could not be understood except on its own terms somehow also entitled him to a free translation of this "exotic" language to an English-speaking audience.

Perhaps, it would be useful to turn to Walter Benjamin's essay "The Task of the Translator" at this point, for not only is Benjamin self-reflexive about his role as a practicing translator but his formulation of cross-linguistic communication follows a new mode of inquiry that promises to take us outside the familiar terrain of universalism and cultural relativism. The essay in question, which prefaces Benjamin's translation of Baudelaire's *Tableaux parisiens,* is an attempt to rethink the question of translatability beyond the problematic of the original and translated text. "The question of whether a work is translatable has a dual meaning," said Benjamin, "Either: Will an adequate translation ever be found among the totality of its readers? Or, more pertinently: Does its nature lend itself to translation and, therefore, in view of the significance of the mode, call for it?"[34] He dismissed the factor of readers' reception or the "ideal" receiver as a useful approach to the theoretical issues under question. In his view, the original in the source language and its translation in the receptor language must yield to a third concept, *die reine Sprache,* or pure language, which "no longer means or expresses anything but is, as expressionless and creative Word, that which is meant in all languages."[35] This conceptualization may be said to anticipate French deconstructive theory in its displacement of the notions of fidelity, originality, presence, and authenticity, which explains Benjamin's popularity among poststructuralists in our own time.[36] But there are tensions in his thought that seem to point away from deconstructionist concerns toward something else. For instance, Benjamin stated that the telos of translation is the possibility of God's messianic return.[37] The messianic troping Benjamin used throughout his essay must be taken seriously because it suggests important linkages between his thinking and the earlier theoretical/theological concerns that Steiner describes. What is pure language? It binds both the original and translation to Holy Writ and belongs to the realm of God's remembrance where the original and translation co-exist in a complementary relationship (Derrida later picks up the idea of complementarity). It is in this sense that "the translatability of linguistic creations ought to be considered even if men should prove unable to translate them."[38] Not surprisingly, Bible translation serves as "the prototype or the ideal of all translation."[39] In his desire to rid translation of its indebtedness to the original text, Benjamin reveals, wittingly or not, his own profound indebtedness to the story of Babel.

But can the Babel story not be questioned on its own ground? Has the story itself not been translated into and read in numerous tongues and, therefore, always already contradicted the myth of the origin? Derrida raises this question in his essay "Des Tours de Babel." Through a "complementary" re-reading of Maurice de Gandillac's French translation of Benjamin, he offers a deconstructionist approach to the problematic of translation theory. He reminds us that the irony surrounding the story of Babel is that "one pays little attention to this fact: it is in translation that we most often read this narrative" and yet one continues to reiterate the impossibility of translation.[40] Here we have come full circle from the double bind of Jakobson's example of *tradutore, traditore,* with the vital exception that the structural linguist's concern with the original and its untranslatability is now replaced by a fundamental questioning of the metaphysical status of the original and originary text.

Benjamin's notion of complementarity thus acquires a fresh importance in Derrida's reconsideration of the concepts of origin, intention, and the relations between the languages involved in translation processes. That is to say, translation is no longer a matter of transferring meaning between languages "within the horizon of an absolutely pure, transparent, and unequivocal translatability."[41] The original and translation complement each other to produce meanings larger than mere copies or reproduction: "These languages relate to one another in translation according to an unheard-of-mode. They complete each other, says Benjamin; but no other completeness in the world can represent this one, or that symbolic complementarity."[42] In this sense, the question of translatability/untranslatability that earlier theorists and structural linguists have raised becomes a moot point. The irreducible multiplicity of languages cannot be reduced to anything other than itself, and yet, like proper names, these languages are bound to call for interpretation, translation, and complementarity. Babel and God are examples of such names that simultaneously command and forbid one to translate.

Derrida's reading of Benjamin leads to a radical rethinking of the problematic of translation theory in the manner of what Steiner would call the mode of philosophic-poetic inquiry in the contemporary West. Here translation becomes an oxymoron: inasmuch as nothing can be reduced to anything else and translation cannot but say one thing in terms of another, the epistemic violence is committed out of necessity—a condition that circumscribes cognitive understanding itself and must, therefore, be grasped in its proper context. Through Benjamin, Derrida is able to contribute new insights to an old problematic in his powerful critique of Western metaphysics. But precisely because his attention is fixed on Western metaphysics, his critique cannot break away from the hold of the object of his critique to allow him to ask such mundane questions as How does hypothetical equivalence get established and maintained between concrete languages? What needs are served by such acts of equation historically? These are not just technical or linguistic issues that one may hope to resolve in a case-by-case study; rather, they point to forms of practice and power that deserve our foremost attention in cross-cultural and translingual inquiries.

Perhaps the thing to do is go beyond the deconstructionist stage of trying to prove that equivalents do not exist and look, instead, into their *manner of becoming*. For it is the making of hypothetical equivalences that enables the modus operandi of translation and its politics. For instance, historically when and how do equivalents or tropes of equivalence get established between languages? Is it possible that at certain levels of practice some equivalents might cease to be mere illusions? What enables such changes? Under what conditions does difference, which is the perceived ground for the inscription of equivalence, become translatable in "other words"? When we are confronted with languages that are radically different from the Indo-European languages, such as classical and modern vernacular Chinese, in what terms should that difference be conceptualized for the purpose of understanding translation and translingual practice?

Steiner, for example, gives an interesting description of the Chinese language (a language he did not know) in order to illustrate what he takes to be the radical difference of a non-European language. "Chinese is composed mainly of monosyllabic units with a wide range of diverse meanings. The grammar lacks clear tense distinctions. The characters are logographic but many contain pictorial rudiments or suggestions. The relations between propositions are paratactic rather than syntactic and punctuation marks represent breathing pauses far more than they do logical or grammatical segmentations."[43] Somewhat curious about the sources of information Steiner uses here, I checked the article he cites, which was written by Achilles Fang, a renowned sinologist in the 1950's and 1960's. A quick comparison of the two texts reveals that Fang's discussion, which addresses the difficulty of translating classical Chinese *shi* and *wen*, is taken out of its immediate context and used by Steiner to generalize about the Chinese language. To be sure, Fang would probably have never used the verb "lack" to characterize classical Chinese vis-à-vis European languages or describe Chinese as composed of monosyllabic units any more than he would say Indo-European languages were full of redundant grammatical units. In the context of his outdated essay, entitled "Some Reflections on the Difficulty of Translation," Fang stressed the need for a translator of classical Chinese texts to attend to the elements of rhetoric, quotation and allusion, sentiment, punctuation, parataxis, particles, context, and so on. He brought up the question of grammar in criticizing sinologists "who still think Chinese (classical Chinese) is a 'language' in the conventional sense."[44] Interestingly, Steiner overlooks the implied critique of the Western notion of "language," which might have proved useful in strengthening his own critique of the Western philosophy of language. Of course, in order to create a genuine confrontation between these languages, one not only needs a firsthand knowledge of the languages involved, but must guard vigilantly against easily assuming an equivalence between any pair of words, idioms, or languages.

But a question lingers: Can we talk about an "uncontaminated" Chinese notion of language *in English*? And can we do so even in Chinese in the wake of all that has happened in the past one and a half centuries? Languages change, and Chinese is no exception. Since the latter half of the nineteenth century, massive (unidirectional) interactions between Chinese, Japanese, and modern European languages have taken place. If Chinese remains one of the most difficult languages to translate, the chances are that the difficulty lies in the growing number of hypothetical equivalents between Chinese and other languages, rather than the lack thereof. Modern Chinese words and concepts as well as those from the classical language, which are increasingly mediated through modern Chinese, often present hidden snares, even though on the surface they seem relatively transparent. Edward Gunn's recent *Rewriting Chinese* offers some brilliant insights in this respect by documenting the major innovations in modern Chinese prose style since the turn of the twentieth century. His detailed stylistic analysis reveals, for example, that as many as 21 out of the 44 major types of innovations that he categorizes according to the criteria of grammatical construction, rhetorical invention, and sentence cohesion result from exposure to European languages and Japanese through translation.[45]

In the area of loanword studies, mainland Chinese linguists Gao Mingkai and Liu Zhengtan have identified 1,266 onetime neologisms that are now part of the mainstream vocabulary of modern Chinese; of these 459 compounds were borrowed from Japanese *kanji* (Chinese character) translations of European words, mainly English.[46] This pioneering work was published in 1958; in the same year, a linguist named Wang Lida came up with a list of 588 loanwords from *kanji* translation independently.[47] Based on the findings of these linguists, Japanese sinologist Sanetō Keishū pinpointed 830 loanwords from Japanese *kanji* translations, of which 98 percent are nouns (note, however, that a Chinese word may often belong to two or more parts of speech; many of the words Sanetō classifies as nouns can also function as verbs).[48] Yue-him Tam's research in late Qing and early Republican publications has added 233 more to Sanetō's list, which brings the neologisms from Japanese *kanji* translation to the grand total of 1,063.[49] Even then, as Tam reminds us, the list is far from exhaustive, but it serves to illustrate the extent to which the infusion of loanword neologisms has changed the Chinese language since the nineteenth century. Moreover, many of these terms also entered the Korean and Vietnamese languages—which heretofore had been dominated by the Chinese writing system—at the turn of the century. A more recent study done by Italian linguist Federico Masini further complicates this picture by showing that up to a quarter of the total number of what were previously considered Japanese loans in modern Chinese had actually been invented in Chinese first by nineteenth-century Protestant missionaries and their native collaborators in the process of translating secular texts (mainly English) and that it was not until the second half of the nineteenth century that the Japanese began to adopt those neologisms in their own second-hand translations of the same texts and to create their own calques (loan-translations) and semantic loans.[50]

Needless to say, lexical borrowing or loan translation is unique neither to China nor to modern times. The Japanese had long borrowed from classical Chinese before the two-way and reverse process began in the late nineteenth century.[51] Calques, semantic, and other loans from Central Asian, Arabic, and Northern Asian sources found their way into Chinese as early as the Han dynasty, and translations of Buddhist texts in the Six Dynasties period introduced a fairly large number of Sanskrit terms.[52] But the massive influx of neologisms in the late nineteenth century and the first quarter of the twentieth century was unprecedented in terms of scale and influence. It fundamentally transformed the Chinese language at almost every level of linguistic experience, rendering classical Chinese nearly obsolete. The situation reminds one of Bakhtin's description of vernacular translations in sixteenth-century Europe: "An intense interorientation, interaction, and mutual clarification of languages took place during that period. The two languages frankly and intensely peered into each other's faces, and each became more aware of itself, its potentialities and limitations, in the light of the other. This line drawn between the languages was seen in relation to each object, each concept, and each point of view."[53] Perhaps the analogy with sixteenth-century Europe is not so appropriate after all, because the interactions among Chinese, modern Japanese, and European languages have predominantly been unidirectional rather than mutual.[54] The need to account for the cause and manner of this imbalance cries out for a radically different approach, one that Bakhtin's otherwise excellent study of hybrid linguistic interactions in the European context cannot provide.

Earlier in this chapter, I criticized transhistorical uses of concepts of the individual and self in certain areas of contemporary scholarship. What I would like to do now is explore alternative avenues for cross-cultural and cross-linguistic inquiry, since the rejection of universal categories on linguistic grounds does not preclude the possibility of talking about cross-cultural issues on those same grounds. Once again, to evoke the archetypal question, what is the Chinese equivalent(s) of the English word X or Y? If questions like this seem inevitable, as indeed they are in comparative studies, can we pose them in a way that will help open up, rather than assume, the hypothetical equivalence of meanings between the languages—an assumption so jealously guarded by bilingual dictionaries? As I argue above, analytical categories cannot operate fruitfully in a transhistorical and transdiscursive mode. But neither do I think that cultural relativism provides a viable solution in this fast shrinking world of ours, in which geopolitical boundaries are constantly being redrawn and crossed, and in which the need for translation and interaction is literally thrust on people who had little contact before. It seems to me that, to eschew the transhistorical/transdiscursive approach on the one hand and cultural relativism on the other, one must turn to the occurrences of historical contact, interaction, translation, and the travel of words and ideas between languages.

Take, for example, the term *geren zhuyi* in modern Chinese, which is a neologistic equivalent, via the Japanese *kanji* translation *kojin shugi,* of English "individualism." The trajectory of the discourse of *geren zhuyi* in China, which I discuss at length in Chapter 3, offers a good example of the complex ways in which ideas operate through translation and translingual practice. In this case, one can talk about linkages between "individualism" and *geren zhuyi* meaningfully in a historical/translingual context without using the one or the other as an absolute category of analysis. My point can be stated simply: a cross-cultural study must examine its own condition of possibility. Constituted as a translingual act itself, it enters, rather than sits above, the dynamic history of the relationship between words, concepts, categories, and discourse. One way of unraveling that relationship is to engage rigorously with those words, concepts, categories, and discourses beyond the real of common sense, dictionary definition, and even historical linguistics.

Traveling Theory and the Postcolonial Critique

What happens when a word, category, or discourse "travels" from one language to another? In nineteenth-century colonial and imperialist discourse, the travel of ideas and theories from Europe to the rest of the world usually evoked notions of expansion, enlightenment, progress, and teleological history. In recent years, the move to historicize and decolonize knowledge in various academic disciplines has led to a growing number of studies that scrutinize these notions. The word "travel" is no longer seen as innocent and is often put in quotation marks. Edward Said's notion of "traveling theory" has gained wide circulation in the past decade and is worth critical reflection here. This notion registers a tendency to push contemporary Marxian theory beyond some of its dominant models, such as the mode of production, consumption, and the like, to arrive at a more fluid sense of literary practice. With the help of what he terms "critical consciousness"—a notion ill-defined but daring enough to evoke a space beyond (not outside) theory—Said introduces a concept of literary practice that emphasizes creative borrowing, appropriation, and the movement of ideas and theories from place to place in an international environment.[55] Apropos of the manner in which theories and ideas travel, Said sees four main stages:

> First, there is the point of origin, or what seems like one, a set of initial circumstances in which the idea came to birth or entered discourse. Second, there is a distance traversed, a passage through the pressure of various contexts as the idea moves from an earlier point to another time and place where it will come into a new prominence. Third, there is a set of conditions—call them conditions of acceptance or, as an inevitable part of acceptance, resistances—which then confronts the transplanted theory or idea, making possible its introduction or toleration, however alien it might appear to be. Fourth, the now full (or partly) accommodated (or incorporated) idea is to some extent transformed by its new uses, its new position in a new time and place.[56]

Having introduced his general framework, Said then examines the intellectual development of three major Marxian literary critics, Georg Lukács,

Lucien Goldmann, and Raymond Williams, with Foucault thrown in toward the end, and measures the career of each critic against his historical environment. For some inexplicable reason, however, his discussion does not go beyond the usual argument that theory is always a response to changing social and historical circumstances, and the traveling aspect of his theory is abandoned along the way. As I tried to figure out an explanation for this, it occurred to me that perhaps the notion itself lacked the kind of intellectual rigor needed for its own fulfillment. Indeed, who does the traveling? Does theory travel? If so, how? Granting theory such subjectivity leads to a further question: What is the means of transportation? Is it the aircraft, automobile, rickshaw, train, man-of-war, or space shuttle? Commenting on Said's oversight, James Clifford suggests that "Lukácsian Marxism in his essay seems to travel by immigrant boat; theory nowadays takes the plane, sometimes with round-trip tickets."[57] I would take this point a step further: not only does the concept of traveling theory tend to affirm the primacy of theory (or Western theory in the context of Said's book) by endowing the latter with full-fledged, mobile subjectivity, but it fails to account for the vehicle of translation. With the suppression of that vehicle, travel becomes such an abstract idea that it makes no difference in which direction theory travels (from West to East or vice versa) and for what purpose (cultural exchange, imperialism, or colonization?), or in which language and for what audience.

It is not as if Said has paid little attention to the question of translation elsewhere. In fact, his widely influential *Orientalism* and later writings all tackle the representation and translation of cultural difference in the Orientalist textual tradition of the West, and Said himself has become a leading contemporary critic of the history of colonialism, imperialism, and ethnocentrism in the West.[58] It is ironic, therefore, that his notion of traveling theory is generally interpreted as if theory (read Western theory) were a hero from a European picaresque narrative who initiates the trip, encounters obstacles en route, and always ends up being accommodated one way or another by the host country.[59] Inasmuch as language transaction is always a contested territory in national and international struggles, one must rethink one's priorities in theorizing the migration of ideas and theory and ask what role translation and related practices play in the construction of relations of power between the so-called First and Third Worlds. Indeed, what happens when languages meet during the East-West encounter? Are the relations of power between the two always reducible to patterns of domination and resistance? Is the cultural critic not risking too much for granting too little to the agency of non-Western languages in these transactions?

Recent work in poststructuralist and postcolonial studies has initiated an important rethinking of the problem of language and translation in historical terms. The idea of historicity used in this body of scholarship is pitted against teleological History written with a capital H. It emphasizes, instead, "effective history," an idea borrowed from Nietzsche (*wirkliche Historie*) and Gadamer (*Wirkungsgeschichte*) that refers to the part of the past that is still operative and meaningful in the present.[60] This understanding of historicity enables postcolonial critics to raise questions about the "effective history" of the text: "Who uses/interprets the text? How is it used, and for what?"[61] In putting their questions this way, these critics are not trying to reduce history to texts, but are emphasizing texts as social facts like any other facts, capable of being deployed for political or ideological purposes. As Mary Louise Pratt puts it in a recent study of travel writing and European colonialism:

> How has travel and exploration writing *produced* "the rest of the world" for European readerships at particular points in Europe's expansionist trajectory? How has it produced Europe's differentiated conceptions of itself in relation to something it became possible to call "the rest of the world"? How do such signifying practices encode and legitimate the aspirations of economic expansion and empire? How do they betray them?[62]

The study of language has acquired a fresh urgency in these various historical projects. Words, texts, discourse, and vocabulary enter one's scholarship as veritable historical accounts per se, not just as sources of historical information about something more important than themselves. Obviously, Foucault's work has greatly influenced this line of thinking among those who study former European colonies in Asia, America, and Africa. For example, in research on the relationship between colonial control and the use of Swahili as a lingua franca in the former Belgian Congo, anthropologist Johannes Fabian expounds the relevance of the Foucaultian notion of discourse to his own work:

> Here the notion of discourse is of methodological value. The assumption is that ideas and ideologies expressing as well as informing colonial praxis are formulated and perpetuated (and occasionally changed) in ways of talking and writing about the *oeuvre civilisatrice*. In interpreting this sort of talk as discourse one is less interested in the truth value of specific statements, in the question, for instance, whether a certain author really expressed his convictions, gave an accurate report of facts, and so on. Instead one seeks to appreciate the documentary value of a "style" by discerning key notions, rules of combining these and theoretical devices used to build arguments. In short, one concentrates on elements which determined the shape and content of colonial thought irrespective of individual intentions.[63]

Fabian's analysis of Swahili language manuals and other colonial documents relating to Katanga demonstrates that promotion of this language was

a vital part of the promotion of the symbolic power of the colonial administration.[64] One might object that there is nothing new about languages being
used to serve political and ideological goals.[65] But Fabian raises an important
question by placing language practice at the heart of colonial history while
linking that "effective history" with a series of genealogies of imperialist
expansion and of the development of modern linguistics and anthropology
as scientific disciplines.[66] For instance, he reminds us that one of the earliest
linguistic undertakings to include African and Asian languages for comparative research in Europe was an ambitious collection of vocabularies called
Linguarum totius orbis vocabularia comparativa . . . , a project conceived and
initiated by Catherine the Great, Empress of Russia, and completed by Peter
Simon Pallas (Moscow, 1787 and 1789). Vocabulary lists were sent to the
governors of the Russian empire to be forwarded to official interpreters and
translators and, through Russian ambassadors in Madrid, London, and the
Hague, they reached Spanish, English, and Dutch colonies, and even China.
George Washington took a personal interest and asked the governors of the
United States to participate in the collection of material.[67] Thus "translations
were regarded as official business and the wordlists became documents of
state, witnessed to with stamps and signatures."[68]

In a recent study of colonial India and postcoloniality, Tejaswini Niranjana
raises a similar point about translation and sees it as "part of the colonial
discourse of Orientalism" and "British efforts to obtain information about
the people ruled by the merchants of the East India Company." She defines
colonial discourse as "the body of knowledge, modes of representation, strategies of power, law, discipline, and so on, that are employed in the construction and domination of 'colonial subjects.' " Based on an interesting re-
reading of Benjamin, de Man, and Derrida, she proposes a postcolonial concept of translation and history and stresses the linkage between the two in
the desire to "re-translate" and to "re-write history." "To read existing translations against the grain," she says, "is also to read colonial historiography
from a post-colonial perspective, and a critic alert to the ruses of colonial
discourse can help uncover what Walter Benjamin calls 'the second tradition,' the history of resistance."[69] Niranjana's re-reading of colonial discourse
is enabled by what she calls "a post-colonial perspective." But in the course
of doing so, she unwittingly privileges European languages as a host language
(or target language) where meanings are decided. If the postcolonial critic
continues to emphasize European languages in these accounts of East-West
linguistic transactions and to leave the unspoken part of that history/story
unaddressed, how far can she go toward fulfilling her own promise of rewriting history? The irony is that one often remembers only to forget. By refresh-
ing our memories of the past crimes committed by imperialism, the

postcolonial critic inadvertently erases traces of the previous histories of anti-imperialist struggle to which he or she rightly belongs.[70] Why are Mao and Gandhi often forgotten as Derrida or Benjamin is evoked as the oppositional voice to the hegemony of the West? If poststructuralism is the driving force that gives a new impetus and new meaning to the contemporary criticism of colonialism and imperialism, then one must take account of the fact that the critique of "cultural imperialism" has its own genealogies and has long been part of the anti-imperialist legacies of non-Western peoples.

What happens when a European text gets translated into a non-European language? Can the power relationship between East and West be reinvented (if not reversed) in that case? If so, how? These are the questions that Vicente Rafael has tried to address in his study of Spanish evangelization and the emergence of Tagalog colonial society in the Philippines. He compares the different modes of translation in Tagalog and Castilian and shows that this difference greatly complicated the process of native conversion and often confounded the missionaries' expectations. Something interesting happens when two languages are brought into confrontation in these moments:

> For in setting languages in motion, translation tended to cast intentions adrift, now laying, now subverting the ideological grounds of colonial hegemony. The necessity of employing the native vernaculars in spreading the Word of God constrained the universalizing assumptions and totalizing impulses of a colonial-Christian order. It is this contradiction precipitated by translation that we see played out in the history of Tagalog conversion.[71]

Rafael's insight is important. His acute understanding of the complexities of linguistic transaction between East and West is not without some relevance to the concept of translingual practice I discuss here.[72] However, the idea of resistance and subversion that runs throughout his book and prevails in current postcolonial theory in general needs a critical re-examination. To the extent that the postcolonial critic wishes to decolonize certain kinds of knowledge that have dominated the world for the past few hundred years, resistance describes his or her own condition of being just as much as it does that of the colonial world s/he describes. But the same idea also runs the risk of reducing the power relationship between East and West to that of native resistance and Western domination, as I point out above.[73] There is a certain amount of danger in reifying the patterns of resistance and domination, however complicated they are, along the East/West divide, since the boundaries between the two are frequently permeable and subject to changing conditions. As Lisa Lowe puts it well in her critique of the notions of Occident and Orient, "When we maintain a static dualism of identity and difference, and uphold the logic of the dualism as the means of explaining how a discourse expresses domination and subordination, we fail to account for the differences inherent in each term."[74] In my own study of translingual practice, I argue that a non-European language does not automatically constitute a site of resistance to European languages. Rather, I see it as a much neglected area where complex processes of domination, resistance, and appropriation can be observed and interpreted from within the discursive context of that language as well as in connection with other linguistic environments.

Host Language and Guest Language

In the following pages I propose the notion of translingual practice to ground my study of an earlier moment of historical transaction between China and the West in language practices. Since the modern intellectual tradition in China began with translation, adaptation, appropriation, and other interlingual practices related to the West, it is inevitable that this inquiry should take translation as its point of departure. Yan Fu's interpretive translation of Thomas Huxley's *Evolution and Ethics* (1898) and other Western texts had an enormous impact on China and helped fashion an entire generation of Chinese intelligentsia.[75] In literature, Lin Shu's immensely popular renderings of over a hundred foreign works into literary Chinese predated publication of Lu Xun's first modern short story (1918) by many years.[76] Literary historian A Ying (Qian Xingcum) estimates that of the at least 1,500 published works of fiction in the last decade of the Qing, two-thirds are translations of foreign literature and many are English and French works.[77] (The word "translation" should be understood here as a shorthand for adaptation, appropriation, and other related translingual practices.) As several studies have pointed out, the rise of modern journalism and major publishing businesses such as the Commercial Press in China's metropolitan centers had a direct bearing on the growing popularity of translated literature.[78] The majority of modern Chinese writers first tried their hand at translation and then moved on to other literary activities.[79] Lu Xun translated numerous Russian and Japanese works into Chinese, and his very first book, a collaboration with his brother Zhou Zuoren during their student days in Japan, was a collection of translations called *Yuwai xiaoshuo ji* (Anthology of foreign fiction; 1909).[80] Throughout his life, he translated and encouraged translation of foreign works and continued to do so after he stopped writing fiction. Among other well-known figures in May Fourth literature, Yu Dafu translated Rousseau, and Guo Moruo's rendering of Goethe's *Die Leiden des jungen Werthers* into the modern vernacular became a bestseller among urban youths.

However, I must hasten to add that the point of translingual practice is not to study the history of translation, much less the technical aspects of translation, although one could benefit from excursions into the one or the other.[81] I am interested in theoretical problems that lead up to an investigation of the *condition of translation* and of discursive practices that ensue from initial interlingual contacts between languages. Broadly defined, the study of translingual practice examines the process by which new words, meanings, discourses, and modes of representation arise, circulate, and acquire legitimacy within the host language due to, or in spite of, the latter's contact/ collision with the guest language. Meanings, therefore, are not so much "transformed" when concepts pass from the guest language to the host language as invented within the local environment of the latter. In that sense, translation is no longer a neutral event untouched by the contending interests of political and ideological struggles. Instead, it becomes the very site of such struggles where the guest language is forced to encounter the host language, where the irreducible differences between them are fought out, authorities invoked or challenged, ambiguities dissolved or created, and so forth, until new words and meanings emerge in the host language itself. I hope the notion of translingual practice will eventually lead to a theoretical vocabulary that helps account for the process of adaptation, translation, introduction, and domestication of words, categories, discourses, and modes of representation from one language to another, and, furthermore, helps explain the modes of transmission, manipulation, deployment, and domination within the power structure of the host language. My goal is to reconceptualize the problematic of "language" in a new set of relationships that is not predicated on some of the familiar premises of contemporary theories of language, which tend to take metropolitan European tongues as a point of departure.

A word of explanation about some of the terms I use here. If it is true that the translator or some other agent in the host language always initiates the linguistic transaction by inviting, selecting, combining, and reinventing words and texts from the guest language and, moreover, if the needs of the translator and his/her audience together determine and negotiate the meaning (i.e., usefulness) of the text taken from the guest language, then the terms traditional theorists of translation use to designate the languages involved in translation, such as "source" and "target/receptor," are not only inappropriate but misleading. The idea of source language often relies on concepts of authenticity, origin, influence, and so on, and has the disadvantage of reintroducing the age-old problematic of translatability/untranslatability into the discussion. On the other hand, the notion of target language implies a teleological goal, a distance to be crossed in order to reach the plenitude of meaning; it thus misrepresents the ways in which the trope of equivalence is conceived in the host language, relegating its agency to secondary importance. Instead of continuing to subscribe to such metaphysical concerns perpetuated by the naming of a source and a target, I adopt the notions "host language" and "guest language" in this book (the Chinese equivalents, *zhufang yuyan* and *kefang yuyan,* would even more radically alter the relationship between the original and translation), which should allow me to place more emphasis on the host language than it has heretofore received. In this light, the knowledge/power dyad that Talal Asad so lucidly describes in the passage quoted at the beginning of this chapter should be re-examined, for his description overlooks the possibility that a non-European host language may violate, displace, and usurp the authority of the guest language in the process of translation as well as be transformed by it or be in complicity with it. These complex forms of mediations during the historical contact between China and the West are the main concerns of the individual chapters in this book.

Theory of Change, Neologisms, and Discursive Histories

It is my contention that the study of modern Chinese history must take the history of translingual practice into account. The prominence of the problem of language in the Chinese imagination of modernity can hardly be disputed. "What is so 'modern' about modern Chinese history and literature?" asks Leo Ou-fan Lee in a recent article. "In what ways did the May Fourth generation, and their predecessors, attempt to define their difference from the past and articulate a new range of sensibilities which they would consider 'modern'?"[82] Indeed, the quoted status of the word "modern" highlighted here by Lee alerts one to the question of "translated" modernity in the history of translingual practice between China and the West. Rather than continuing to argue about tradition and modernity as essential categories, one is compelled to ask How do twentieth-century Chinese *name* the condition of their existence? What kind of language do they use in talking about their differences from whatever contingent identities they perceive as existing before their own time or being imposed from the outside? What rhetorical strategies, discursive formations, naming practices, legitimizing processes, tropes, and narrative modes impinge upon the historical conditions of the Chinese experience of the modern?

The problem of methodology in Chinese historical studies has not gone unexamined in the past decades. For example, in a critique of American historical writings about China since John Fairbank and Joseph Levenson, Paul Cohen urges historians to rethink their priorities in explaining the recent changes in Chinese history. He focuses on three dominant conceptual paradigms in his book *Discovering History in China* and suggests an alternative he terms the "China-centered approach." To summarize his poignant criticism in a somewhat reductive fashion, the impact-response theory, the first of the three paradigms he discusses, emphasizes China's response to the Western challenge and often "prompts historians to define aspects of recent Chinese history that had no obvious connections with the Western presence as unimportant—or, alternatively, as important *only* insofar as they shed light on China's response to the West." The second of these approaches—the tradition-modernity model—has deep roots in nineteenth-century ethnocentrism and imposes on Chinese history an external—"parochially Western—definition of what change is and what kinds of change are important." The third, or the imperialism, approach falls into "the ahistorical trap of *assuming* for Chinese history a 'natural' or 'normal' course of development with which Western (and later Japanese) imperialism interfered."[83] As a corrective to the above, Cohen draws attention to the work of a younger generation of China historians who have turned to a *China-centered* approach. In his view, this approach has the advantage of avoiding imported criteria by beginning with Chinese problems set in a Chinese context, whether these problems are generated by the West or have no Western connection at all.

This new approach, which effectively challenges the established way of writing Chinese history, has important implications for literary studies as well. Instead of continuing to do so-called influence studies in the time-honored sense of comparative literature, one could stress the agency of the host language (modern Chinese in this case) in the meaning-making process of translation so that the guest language need not carry a signature of authenticity around in order to make sense in the new context. On the other hand, at least in sinological studies, one can afford to be China-centered without ceasing to adopt the Western-centered perception of what is important or unimportant for scholarship. I am reminded of a criticism Rey Chow made some time ago: "In sinology and Chinese studies, where the emphases on 'heritage' are clearly immovable, the homage to the West has long been paid in the form of what seems to be its opposite—in the idealist insistence on a separate, self-sufficient 'Chinese tradition' that should be lined up against the Western one because it is as great if not greater. The 'rejection' of the West in this instance is solemnly respectful; by upholding 'China,' it repeats the hegemonic overtones of that which is rejected."[84]

Indeed, to draw a clear line between the indigenous Chinese and the exogenous Western in the late twentieth century is almost an epistemological impossibility. The fact that one writes about China for an English-speaking academic audience further complicates the situation. Interestingly, the theoretical impulse for the China-centered approach does not originate in China but draws its inspiration from the works of objectivist sociologists and anthropologists in the contemporary West who emphasize the "regional approach" as a more valid one than those they have discredited. As Pierre Bourdieu aptly puts it, "What is at stake here is the power of imposing a vision of the social world through principles of di-vision which, when they are imposed on a whole group, establish meaning and a consensus about meaning, and in particular about the identity and unity of the group, which creates the reality of the unity and the identity of the group."[85] In other words, regionalist discourse is a performative discourse that seeks to legitimate a new definition of the frontiers whereby the *region,* a reality thus named, becomes the site of the struggle to *define* reality, rather than simply the "reality" itself. It is not difficult to see that the theoretical frontiers in this case are, once again, set and framed by contemporary Western academic discourses.[86]

Consider, on the other hand, the situation in which one does historiography strictly for a Chinese academic audience in the Chinese language. Would one not be using a language already thoroughly "contaminated" by the influx of neologisms and theories from China's earlier and current contact with the West? Paradoxically, contemporary Chinese scholars in China can assume "China-centeredness" in their own work even as they speak and write an *ouhua* or Europeanized Chinese language.[87] There, as much as here, the "indigenous Chinese" can no longer be so easily separated out from the "exogenous Western." Given these difficulties and constraints, my question is whether one can still talk about change and transaction between East and West in twentieth-century China without privileging the West, modernity, progress, or other post-Enlightenment notions on the one hand and without holding on to a reified idea of indigenous China on the other.

Since the death of Levenson in 1969, as Theodore Huters has recently pointed out, there has been "a curious and very marked silence concerning the traumatic choices that the coming of the West presented to China. This silence is striking in that modern Chinese literature has traditionally dated itself as beginning in a movement to discard the native literary language in favor of a literary language explicitly based on Western models."[88] Indeed, Levenson's totalizing statements about Confucian China and its modern fate may no longer obtain, but the question of how to explain the "traumatic choices" made by the Chinese since their violent encounters with Western imperialism does not easily go away. This is a historical question as well as a theoretical challenge to contemporary scholarship. Recently, Gayatri Spivak has brought attention to a theory of change developed by contemporary South Asian historians that I find interesting and not without relevance to what I am trying to talk about here.

> The work of the Subaltern Studies group offers a theory of change. The insertion of India into colonialism is generally defined as a change from semi-feudalism into capitalist subjection. Such a definition theorizes the change within the great narrative of the modes of production and, by uneasy implication, within the narrative of the transition from feudalism to capitalism. Concurrently, this change is seen as the inauguration of politicization for the colonized. The colonial subject is seen as emerging from those parts of the indigenous élite which come to be loosely described as "bourgeois nationalist." The Subaltern Studies group seems to be revising this general definition and its theorization by proposing at least two things: first, that the moment(s) of change be pluralized and plotted as *confrontations* rather than *transition* (they would thus be seen in relation to histories of domination and exploitation rather than within a great modes-of-production narrative) and, secondly, that such changes are signalled or marked by a functional change in sign-systems.[89]

The theoretical model advanced by the South Asian historians is thought-provoking in that they eschew the idea of "transition," at least in Spivak's interpretation of it—whether from East to West, from tradition to modernity, or from feudalism to capitalism—and turn, instead, to the notion of "confrontation," which provides a new perspective for understanding the kinds of changes that have occurred since the encounter of East and West. Their approach renders the old problematic of tradition and modernity uninteresting and opens modern history to alternative avenues of interpretation.[90]

One could object that this theory does not apply to the Chinese situation on the grounds that India was a British colony and China was not. I wonder, however, if the real issue here is one of compatibility at the level of "experience." Behind the obvious truthfulness of this objection, is there an anxiety or intellectual bias that gravitates toward European theory as a universal bearer of meaning and value? Objections to the use of European theory in the China field are, however, seldom raised on the same ground—namely, that Western theory fails to apply to China because the former has linkages with a colonial/imperialist past whereas the latter has had an opposite "experience." On the contrary, the terms of difference are almost always constructed along the line of Western theory versus Chinese reality.[91] In that sense, the work of the Subaltern historians is inspiring, for they do not assume a hegemonic divide between Western theory and someone else's reality. To them, the realities of the West, India, and other places are to be equally

subjected to theoretical critique and interrogated in light of the history of
their mutual involvement and contention. Needless to say, the terms of such
critique need to be constantly negotiated between these different localities.

I emphasize historical *linkages*—rather than commonalities—between
these localities, the kind of linkages that Lu Xun, for example, discerned in
writing "Moluo shili shuo" (On the power of Mara poetry) in 1907. Commenting on how his compatriots treated their less fortunate neighbors or
nations that had been colonized by the imperialist forces, he said:

> One need only step out into the streets of any major Chinese city, to meet with
> soldiers sauntering about the marketplace, serenading us with martial airs that
> rebuke the servility of India and Poland; these have become so widespread as to
> practically constitute a national anthem for us. This is due to the fact that
> China, in spite of her present situation, is always anxious to jump at any chance
> to cite at length her past glories, yet now she feels deprived of the capacity to
> do so, and can only resort to comparisons of herself with captive neighbors that
> have either fallen under the yoke of servitude or ceased to exist, hoping thereby
> to show off her own superiority.[92]

Lu Xun is alluding to two popular songs allegedly composed by the reformer
Zhang Zhidong entitled *Xuetang ge* (Song for the new-style school) and *Jun
ge* (Army song). The first contains the lines: "Poland lies shattered, India is
done, / The last of the Jews to the four winds is flung!" and the second:
"Prithee look toward India vast, / As slaves enchained, they'll never last!"[93]
Lu Xun's critique of the self-perception of the Chinese in the larger context
of colonialism and imperialism is a useful reminder of the dangers of exag-
gerating China's uniqueness at the expense of erasing the traces of its involvement (and collusion) with other localities and histories. At issue, therefore,
is not who was colonized and who was not, but how to interpret the interconnected moments of confrontation between those who sought to conquer
the world and those who struggled to survive under such enormous pres-
sures.

This new emphasis inevitably turns our concern with abstract questions of
continuity or transition in modern history to contingencies, struggles, and
surprising twists and turns of events at each moment of confrontation
between nations or different groups of people. In my study of translingual
practice, I am interested in conditions under which "confrontations" occur
between China, Japan, and the West at the site of translation or wherever the
languages happen to meet, for this is where the irreducible differences
between the host language and the guest language are fought out, authorities
invoked or challenged, and ambiguities dissolved or created. In short, the con-

frontations register a meaning-making history that cuts across different national languages and histories.

The trope for change in the context of translingual practice is neologism or neologistic construction. This metaphorical projection of linguistic mediations will be better understood after we take a close look at the actual routes by which modern neologisms, especially Sino-Japanese-European ones, traveled and took residence in modern Chinese.[94] According to Gao Mingkai and Liu Zhengtan, the influx of calques, semantic, and other loans into late nineteenth-century and early twentieth-century literary and vernacular Chinese followed a typical pattern; that is, the Japanese used *kanji* (Chinese characters) to translate European terms, and the neologisms were then imported back into the Chinese language. The majority of these borrowings fall under three headings: (1) two-character compounds made up of Chinese characters that are found only in pre-modern Japanese and do not appear in classical Chinese. Examples are *renli che* (rickshaw; *jinrikisha*), *changhe* (occasion; *baii*), and *zongjiao* (religion; *shūkyō*);[95] (2) classical Chinese expressions used by the Japanese to translate Western terms that were then imported back into Chinese with a radical change in meaning, such as *geming* (revolution; *kakumei*), *wenhua* (culture; *bunka*), *jingji* (economy; *keizai*); and *kexue* (science; *kagaku*).[96] (3) modern Japanese compounds that have no equivalent in classical Chinese, such as *zhongzu* (race; *shūzoku*), *meishu* (art; *bijutsu*), *meixue* (aesthetics; *bigaku*), and *guoji* (international; *kokusai*).[97] Chapter 2 of this book is devoted to the trajectory of one such loanword translation: the Japanese *kanji* rendering of "national character," *kokuminsei*, which became the Chinese *guomin xing* through loanword translation. This translation is one of several discursive occurrences that have profoundly transformed the sensibilities of generations of the Chinese in the twentieth century. I evoke the word "occurrences" here in the sense that Paul de Man uses it in discussing Benjamin's essay on translation: "When Luther translated, translated the Bible, something occurred—at that moment, something happened—not in the immediate sense that from then on there were wars and then the course of history was changed—that is a by-product. What really occurred was that . . . translation. Then there are, in the history of texts, texts which are occurrences."[98] As Chapter 2 demonstrates, the loanword translation of "national character" into Chinese is an example of just such an event that catalyzes another important event, which, in Lu Xun's view, is no less than the invention of modern Chinese literature itself.

Of the three types of loanwords identified by Gao and Liu, the second is the most deceptively transparent, because these "return graphic loans" are easily mistaken as direct derivatives from classical Chinese.[99] Gao and Liu warn that one should be careful about equating these loanwords with their classical counterparts. For example, the modern meaning of *wenhua* (culture) derives from the Japanese *kanji* compound *bunka*, and it is through borrowing that an equivalence was established between the Chinese *wenhua* and the English "culture" (French *culture*; German *die Kultur*). In classical Chinese, *wenhua* denoted the state of refinement or artistic cultivation as opposed to *wu* or military prowess, carrying none of the ethnographic connotations of "culture" commonly associated with the two-character compound in today's usage.[100] Chapter 9 of this book pursues the ways in which this translingual notion of *wenhua* or culture—an omnipotent cliché that has generated some of the most vibrant and contentious debates in the modern world—evolved into a central bearer of meaning and difference between countries and peoples in the intellectual discourse of late Qing and Republic China.

The massive influx of semantic translations and "return graphic loans" *interrupt* the classical etymons in ways that profoundly change their meanings and status. Because of this historical interruption, one can no longer bypass the Japanese *bunka* to explicate the meaning of *wenhua* as if the existence of a classical Chinese term written with the same characters would automatically account for the meaning of its modern counterpart. Of course, the etymological routes taken by these Sino-Japanese-English semantic and loan translations were by no means limited to the three as proposed above by Gao and Liu. A newly published study by Federico Masini shows that the Japanese had borrowed nineteenth-century neologisms, calques, and semantic translations from Chinese before the reverse process began in China some years later. These new terms were invented by Protestant missionaries and their Chinese assistants in the collaborative rendering of secular texts from the West around the early and mid-nineteenth century. The Japanese adopted some of these terms in their *kanji* translations and began to coin their own neologisms in Chinese characters in a similar fashion. To complicate the picture further, many of these early Chinese translations of European terms had had relatively limited impact within China, and the Japanese borrowing was often instrumental to their widespread influence at home. In fact, the Japanese role was so crucial in the "round-trip" dissemination of these autochthonous neologisms that some of them came to be regarded as Japanese loanwords by the Chinese themselves.[101]

This round-trip dissemination of autochthonous neologisms, which is often hard to distinguish from the etymological route taken by return graphic loans from Japan, accounts for linguists' difficulty in trying to determine the origins of some of the modern Chinese lexicon. For example, scholars since Gao and Liu have long considered the compound *wenxue* in its present usage a return graphic loan from the Japanese *bungaku*, that is, a *kanji* translation of the English term "literature."[102] According to Masini, however, *wenxue* with this new meaning dates at least as early as American missionary Elijah C. Bridgman's *Meiligeguo zhilüe* (Short history of America; 1831), a Chinese-language history of America that included neologisms such as *wenxue* (literature), *maoyi* (trade), *falü* (law), *huolunchuan* (paddleboat powered by steam), *huolunche* (steam-powered train), *huoche* (train), *gongsi* (United East India Company).[103] These and a host of other Chinese neologisms traveled to Japan in the 1860's and 1870's when the Japanese started translating Wei Yuan's *Haiguo tuzhi* (Maps and documents on maritime countries; 1844), a multivolume anthology that contained excerpts from Bridgman's book and other missionary works. "These works and the neologisms would have probably remained confined to a very narrow circle had the texts not been included in the *Haiguo tuzhi*. Their fate is therefore linked to the diffusion of Wei Yuan's work first in China and then in Japan."[104] Indeed, the etymology of these neologisms is so inextricably bound up with their patterns of diffusion in China, Japan, and back again in China that, in reflecting on their history, one cannot afford to dwell on a single point of origin as the exclusive locus of meaning but must, instead, allow for a fluid sense of etymology. In other words, the patterns of diffusion sometimes prove to be just as decisive as the moment of invention. It is possible that if Yan Fu had coined his neologisms before the 1860's and had been translated into Japanese, some of his creations might have survived and, through the Japanese mediation, found their way back into the modern Chinese lexicon.

Wenxue, a direct neologistic translation of the English term "literature" by an American missionary, may not qualify as a return loan from Japanese but, through a process of round-trip diffusion via Japan, this term became widespread and evolved into a standard translation of "literature" in China.[105] For want of a better word, one might want to call it a round-trip neologism to underscore this interesting connection with the Japanese *bungaku*. Chapter 8 is devoted to discussing this translingual concept of literature in the making of a modern canon known as *The Compendium of Modern Chinese Literature*. Published in 1935–36, the famous anthology took fiction, poetry, drama, and familiar prose to be "proper" *wenxue* forms while relegating all other forms of writing to the status of non-*wenxue*. This is certainly a far cry from the classical concept of *wenxue*, although nowadays not even classical works can escape contamination by this translingual notion of literature. Witness the numerous histories and anthologies of classical Chinese *wenxue* published in the twentieth century where poetry, fiction, drama, and, to a lesser degree, familiar prose are similarly designated as *wenxue*, whereas the rest of the classical genres are redistributed along the lines of *lishi* (history), *zongjiao* (religion), *zhexue* (philosophy), and other spheres of knowledge that are themselves created on the basis of neologistic translations of Western concepts. In short, classical Chinese "literature" is subjected to radical reinvention in terms of modern literature even as the latter invents itself at the same time.

European-Japanese loanwords that take up residence in modern Chinese sometimes start out by competing with transliterations. As Appendixes F and G illustrate, some neologisms began as a Chinese transliteration of a foreign word or, at least, ran parallel to the European-Japanese semantic and loan translation of the same word. Before long the translation took over and rendered the transliteration obsolete. This is attributable to the ideographic character of Chinese writing, which favors semantic or loan translation over phonemic transliteration.[106] The translation of the word "democracy" is a case in point. For a period of time, the transliteration *demokelaxi* and its loan translation *minzhu* (*minshu*) coexisted, but the loan translation soon replaced the awkward sounding transliteration to become the only acceptable equivalent of "democracy" in use today. To complicate the situation further, the loan translation *minzhu* happens to coincide with one of the oldest expressions in classical Chinese (see Appendix A). But it would be a serious mistake to equate the classical *minzhu* with the loan translation on the basis of their identical written forms. Classical *minzhu* has a genitive structure (roughly, "ruler of the people"), which cannot be further removed from the subject-predicate semantic structure of the modern compound ("people rule").[107]

Needless to say, not all neologisms were semantic or loan translations. In fact, one of the most fascinating neologisms invented in this period was the gendering of the third-person pronoun in written Chinese, which occurred directly between European languages and Chinese.[108] The original form of the Chinese character for the pronoun *ta* contains an ungendered *ren* radical (denoting the human species), and the gendering of this pronoun arose from circumstances of translation. For thousands of years, the Chinese had lived comfortably with the ungendered form of *ta* and other ungendered deictic forms. Suddenly they discovered that Chinese had no equivalent for the third-person feminine pronoun in English, French, and other European languages.[109] Some Chinese perceived the absence of an equivalent as an essential lack in the Chinese language itself, and efforts were made to design neologisms to fill this lack. (It seems to me that this anxiety reflects a historical situation of perceived inequality between languages rather than a failing in the language itself. For instance, one does not experience much inconvenience when translating the French feminine plural *elles* into the ungendered English "they.") After a few years of experiments with regional forms, such as *yi* from the Wu dialect, writers and linguists finally settled on writing the feminine *ta* with a *nü* (woman) radical.[110] For instance, Lu Xun's use of the third-person pronoun in his fiction reflects this interesting period of experimentation. As one study has pointed out, he started out by using *ta* written with its usual ungendered radical *ren* interchangeably with the Wu dialect word *yi* when he referred to his female characters in some of the early stories, such as "Tomorrow" (1920).[111] The feminine pronoun written with a *nü* radical did not appear in his works until "New Year's Sacrifice," which was written in 1924. A year later, Lu Xun began to adopt another neologism, *ta* with a *niu* (cattle), radical, to refer to animals, as in "Regret for the Past" (1925).

The appearance of the feminine and animal/neuter pronouns succeeded in converting the ungendered *ta* into a masculine pronoun, even though the ungendered written form underwent not the slightest morphological change. In other words, the invention of the gendered neologisms forced the original *ta* to assume a masculine character, which is, nonetheless, contradicted by its ungendered radical *ren*. This is a perfect illustration of the Saussurian principle of differentiation whereby meanings become possible only when elements of a language enter a relation of similarity and differentiation. In the case of *ta* and related neologisms, the morphology of written Chinese characters rather than pronunciation serves to differentiate the different meanings. As far as pronunciation is concerned, the feminine *ta* and the animal/neuter *ta* are indistinguishable from the masculine *ta*.

Liu Fu (Liu Bannong), who is credited with the invention of the feminine *ta*, once attempted to introduce an element of differentiation at the phonemic level as well.[112] In a 1920 essay "Ta zi wenti" (The problem of feminine *ta*), he argued:

> The most difficult task facing us is how to pronounce this sign. Mr. Zhou Zuoren prefers *yi* to the feminine *ta* mainly because the latter is indistinguishable from the masculine *ta* to the ear, as Mr. Han Bing has rightly pointed out, even though the difference seems clear enough visually. Admittedly, *yi* is pronounced differently from the masculine *ta,* but it has the following disadvantages that seem to make the feminine *ta* a better choice in the final analysis. First, when it comes to colloquial speech, *yi* cannot have popular appeal because its usage as a third-person pronoun is restricted to a small local area. Second, the word is not marked by a female radical as in the case of the feminine *ta.* Third, *yi* smacks of the classical language and sounds awkward when used in the vernacular. I suggest that we adopt the feminine *ta* and make some slight changes to the way it is pronounced. Originally the masculine *ta* had two pronunciations in Mandarin: /t'a/ in colloquial speech and /t'uo/ in literary reading. What we can do is to keep the first pronunciation for the masculine *ta* and use the second one for the feminine pronoun.[113]

For the reasons Liu Fu mentioned, *yi* as a feminine third-person pronoun soon dropped out of written vernacular Chinese to be replaced by *ta* as the acceptable feminine pronoun, although the alternative pronunciation /t'uo/ proposed by Liu has never materialized. Here, one can probably glimpse how *guoyu* (national language), or *putongyu* (Standard Mandarin) as Liu terms it, achieved its hegemonic status over regional dialects.[114] On the other hand, one must also keep the ideographic nature of written Chinese characters in mind; that is, written modern Chinese overlaps, but cannot be simply equated, with spoken Mandarin syllables, unlike romanized characters that are supposed to represent sound. For instance, the character *ta* written with a feminine radical is now widely recognized as a third-person feminine pronoun in written Chinese by Mandarin speakers as well as by other dialect groups, although no one, as far as I know, can produce a pronunciation that separates it from its masculine and animal/neuter counterparts either in Mandarin or in regional dialects.

The gendering of the third-person pronoun in the written language has important implications for the study of translingual representations of gender in modern Chinese literature. The splitting of a formerly ungendered Chinese *ta* into feminine and masculine forms introduced a level of symbolic reality that had never existed in written Chinese. It is not as if women and men have not been perceived or spoken of as sexual beings or *yin/yang* categories prior to the twentieth century, but the deictic relationship—in the manner of man speaking to and about woman, or woman speaking to and about man, and the like—that is enabled by such a split at the symbolic level of the pronoun allows gender to shape social relations of power in a new language. For instance, the Shen Congwen story I analyze in Chapter 6 contains a narrative of class that is consistently played out in terms of deictic construction of gender and desire. In it, an anonymous gentrywoman designated by the feminine pronoun *ta* is admired by three aspiring lower-class men who are addressed by the narrator in the first-person plural, *women* (we/us), constructed specifically as masculine and lower class in the story. These men cannot hope to enter "her" world because the deictic impasse between "her" class and "our" class is insurmountable.[115] Or consider Lu Xun's "New Year's Sacrifice" where a deictic narrative about class and gender captures a reverse situation—the upper-class narrator "I" speaks to and about a lower-class woman *ta*. In a broader sense, deictic constructions of gender reflect and participate in a larger gendering process under way since the turn of the twentieth century, as Chinese men, women, and the state discover separately for themselves and in terms of one another that they all have a stake in deciding how gender difference should be constructed and what kind of political investment that difference should or could represent in China's pursuit of modernity.[116] The tensions generated between some of these constructed positions in literary criticism are discussed at length in Chapters 5, 6, and 7.

Neologisms in modern Chinese do more than bear physical witness to historical change. I am reminded of a statement Adorno once made in a different context: "Every foreign word contains the explosive material of enlightenment, contains in its controlled use the knowledge that what is immediate cannot be said in unmediated form but only expressed in and through reflection and mediation."[117] Catapulted into existence through translingual interaction with foreign words, neologisms and neologistic constructions occupy an intermediary position of past and present that demands a different reading of historical change. For one thing, change can hardly be a transition from an intact past to the present, for there exist multiple mediations from an intact past to the present, for there exist multiple mediations that do not substantiate the claims of a reified past.[118] For another thing, the transformation of a native language cannot be explained simply in terms of impact from the outside as, for example, Levenson would have argued, because foreign terms are subjected to the same logic of translingual reading as is the native classical language through the mediation of translation. In *Confucian China and Its Modern Fate*, Levenson asserts that "what the West has probably done to China is to change the latter's language—what China has probably done to the West is to enlarge the latter's vocabulary."[119] Although this observation accurately captures the power relationship between China and the West, Levenson's underlying assumptions about what change is and how it occurs prevent him from taking the processes of linguistic mediation seriously or literally (for he is using "language" and "vocabulary" as metaphors) and from re-examining the meaning of Chinese agency. The round-trip words and other neologisms in modern Chinese embody an idea of change that renders the question of historical continuity and discontinuity less than meaningful. Rather than continuing to debate how modernized (read Westernized) China is or how traditional it still remains—these being two contradictory positions frequently articulated among scholars of differing intellectual persuasion[120]—one might do well to focus on the ways in which intellectual resources from the West and from China's past are cited, translated, appropriated, or claimed in moments of perceived historical contingency so that something called *change* may be produced. In my view, this change is always already different from China's own past and from the West, but have profound linkages with both.

Arif Dirlik provides a useful insight into this problematic of change in his recent study of Chinese anarchism.[121] He shows, for example, that nationalism in modern Chinese intellectual discourse pointed to "a new kind of universalism that pushed against the boundaries imposed by a national reorganization of society." At issue is not the collapse of a Confucian order in the Levensonian sense, but the emergence of a new dialectical view of the nation and global society that enabled the "redefinition of China as a nation in a world of nations" while eliciting "as its dialectical counterpoint a new vision of a world in which nations would once again disappear and human-kind would discover a world of unity." The utopian goal of such universalism is always already embedded in something more than the ancient Chinese ideal of *datong* (great unity), a term often appropriated by Chinese intellectu-als in writing about China's future. Rather, as Dirlik describes so well in his discussion of Kang Youwei's *Datong shu* (The book of great unity):

> Kang's society of Great Unity represented the final stage of human progress, following stages of familism and nationalism, in that order. The utopia drew its name and virtues from a native Chinese utopian tradition, but already its inspiration came from the future—a future, moreover, that transcended Chi-na's own world and took as its scope the global society of which China had just become an integral part.[122]

Indeed, Confucianism was reinterpreted and appropriated by Kang to solve the crisis of China's positioning in the modern world. His disciple Tan Sitong did something similar by establishing a hypothetical equivalence between "the ideal of 'great unity' (*datong*) in the *Book of Rites* and what would appear to be a reference to Edward Bellamy's *Looking Backward*" (pp. 56–57). These acts of *equating* ideas from the Chinese classics and concepts imported from the West are significant in that they introduced a level of mediated reality or change that came into existence only after the act of equating had been initiated.

Neologism or neologistic construction is an excellent trope for change, because it has been invented simultaneously to represent and to replace for-eign words, and in so doing, it identifies itself as Chinese and foreign locked in linguistic tension. One does not translate between equivalents; rather, one creates tropes of equivalence in the middle zone of interlinear translation between the host and the guest languages. This middle zone of hypothetical equivalence, which is occupied by neologistic imagination, becomes the very ground for change, a change that cannot be reduced to an essentialist under-standing of modernity, for that which is untraditional is not necessarily West-ern and that which is called modern is not necessarily un-Chinese. A question may be asked: What do we make of those words and symbolic con-structions that are exclusively of indigenous origin and have not been touched by neologistic loanwords? To answer this question, I would like to recall an example I gave earlier of the engendering of the masculine pronoun *ta*. Morphologically speaking, this character has not changed a bit, yet because of the differential intervention of the feminine *ta* and the animal/neuter *ta* in the overall system of modern Chinese, the word no longer means what it used to mean and has been made to stand for the masculine third-person singular. This *relational* transformation behind the appearance of an unchanging construction applies, I think, to other aspects of modern vernacular written Chinese as well. The presence of neologisms points to a much more widely based and deep-seated revolutionary process that has fundamentally changed the linguistic landscape of China.

It is commonplace in speech-act theory that words exist not simply to reflect external reality but to make things happen. My emphasis on translingual practice by no means reduces historical events to linguistic practices; rather, it aims to expand the notion of history by treating language, discourse, text (including historical writing itself), as genuine historical events, not the least of which is the power of discursive acts to produce the terms of legitimation in shaping the historical real.[123] To conclude this discussion, I anticipate Chapter 3 by offering a few remarks on the power of words to shape what is often termed reality. That chapter discusses the changing meaning of the translingual notion of *geren zhuyi* (individualism) in the Chinese theory of modern nation-state in the early Republican period. The point I would make here in light of that analysis is that, after 1949, the discursive struggle surrounding the meaning of individualism begins to play a remarkable role in China's reinvention of the relationship both between East and West and between the state and its intelligentsia. The state has a political stake in presenting the idea of individualism to its people as *un-Chinese*, with the consequence that the idea becomes a synecdoche for a negative West. Paradoxically, the anti-Western rhetoric of the state is most effective when it causes its opponents to rally around individualism in the predictable gesture of pro-Western defiance. What tends to be neglected, forgotten, or suppressed in these endless contentions for or against the West is precisely the potent history surrounding the discourse of individualism within China, a century-long history of translingual practice fraught with political exigencies. As late as the mid-1980's, there was a major controversy over critic Liu Zaifu's theory of literary subjectivity in mainland China.[124] In many ways, that controversy carried over some familiar overtones from earlier debates on individualism, but it also took on a character of violence reminiscent of the Cultural Revolution.[125] Yet, there is another kind of violence not so acutely felt but all the more damaging, which is amnesia, a forgetting of the discursive history of the past. I myself feel deeply connected with that history, not only because I grew up during the Cultural Revolution but, more important, because I have a utopian desire to resist that amnesia. So let this book be an embodiment of that desire.

Notes

[*Ed. note:* For complete references, see "Selected Bibliography," in *Translingual Practice,* pp. 433–58.]

1. These traditional concepts of translation theory will be replaced by "guest language" and "host language" in my formulation of translingual practice.

2. Anthropologists, sociologists, and poststructuralist critics have discussed the politics of culture along this line and raised numerous questions about knowledge, power, scholarship, and academic disciplines. See, e.g., Bourdieu, *Distinction*; and idem, *Homo Academicus.*

3. A word about my own positioning in this book. Since I work simultaneously with two languages, Chinese and English, I find myself occupying a shifting position: moving back and forth between these languages and learning to negotiate the irreducible differences. The concept of translingual practice, therefore, applies to my personal situation as an analyst just as much as to the earlier historical encounter between China and the West that I explore here. Of course, this book would have a different look if I were to write it in Chinese. But writing for a Chinese-speaking audience, as I do from time to time, does not automatically solve the problem of intellectual authority and one's positioning in a given situation. It simply raises different questions in a different context and must be dealt with in terms of that context.

4. Edmund R. Leach, "Ourselves and Others"; as quoted in Talal Asad, "The Concept of Cultural Translation in British Social Anthropology," in Clifford and Marcus, p. 142.

5. Asad, in Clifford and Marcus, pp. 157–58.

6. The main target of Asad's critique is Ernest Gellner, but the essay also mentions other anthropologists in the field including Godfrey Lienhardt, John Beattie, Edmund Leach, Max Gluckman, and Rodney Needham.

7. Nietzsche, "On Truth and Falsity in Their Ultramoral Sense" (1873), in *The Complete Works of Nietzsche,* 2: 180.

8. Spivak, "Translator's Preface," in Derrida, *Of Grammatology,* p. xxii.

9. Borges, p. 51.

10. Heidegger, *Unterwegs zur Sprache,* pp. 141–43; idem, *On the Way to Language,* p. 45.

11. Ibid., p. 153; trans., p. 53.

12. For a discussion of Heidegger's interest in the philosophies of Asia, see Park[es].

13. Eoyang, p. 238.

14. For the concept of the "trope of equivalence," see Robinson, who uses this notion to criticize the idea of substantial equivalence that prevails in the traditional theories of translation and language.

15. To give a few examples, in *Expressions of Self in Chinese Literature,* co-edited by Robert E. Hegel and Richard C. Hessney, the concept of the self appears as a gen-

eral rubric under which essays that focus on a number of different issues are supposed to fall: author's psyche, identity, individual, female image, literary characterization, and so forth. It is interesting that no two essays in this collection seem to share a homogeneous view of the self, and some of the views differ vastly from one another. This suggests that not only is the concept of self extremely elusive—a situation that can hardly be remediated by a better definition, since meaning defies fixing—but one may be treading precarious ground when using the notion as a transhistorical category. *Culture and Self,* edited by Anthony J. Marsella et al., seeks to critique logical positivism by introducing the concept of the self into social science theory and using it as a comparative basis for cultural studies. While all the essays in this volume exhibit a genuine desire to understand cultural differences (Western, Chinese, Japanese, Hindu, etc.), the deployment of the self as a universal category is taken for granted, as the editors put it: "All of the chapters proceed from the premise that the self is a necessary construct for explaining those emergent qualities of human behaviour that proceed from person-context relationships" (p. ix). However, the category of the self we often find used in comparative studies has evolved only recently in the scholarly practices of the West.

16. Tu Wei-ming, the foremost Confucian theorist in the U.S. to expound on the differences between Neo-Confucian *ji* and the Western notion of the self, assumes the mutual translatability of the two words. In fact, his humanist notion of *ji* is predicated on the idea that the former can be readily translated into the English word "self" without the mediation of the modern history of translation. In a number of his works, such as *Humanity and Self-Cultivation: Essays in Confucian Thought* and *Confucian Thought: Selfhood as Creative Transformation,* his argument appears tautological: the Neo-Confucian *ji* differs from (by which he means is superior to) the Western notion of the self, but it remains a notion of the "self." For a discussion of the relegitimation of Neo-Confucianism in the international context, see the section on the *Critical Review* in Chapter 9 of this book.

17. Saussy, p. 185.

18. In an earlier essay entitled "The Person," Taylor defines the agent as a human being who encompasses purposes and to whom things matter (i.e., human significance), whereas the notion of the public space of disclosure is associated with his view of language as social intercourse.

19. Taylor, *Sources of the Self,* esp. "The Self in Moral Space," chap. 2, pt. I, pp. 2–5, and "A Digression on Historical Explanation," chap. 12, pt. II, pp. 199–207. In the latter, Taylor anticipates criticism of his philosophical/religious approach, explaining that the advantage of such an approach lies in its emphasis on the question of *idées-forces,* of which reductive Marxism has not given an adequate account. But it is by no means clear why he refuses to engage post-Althusserian Marxism, which has already moved beyond the base-structure/superstructure paradigm. Although Taylor seems to have a well-developed notion of "practice" (pp. 204–5), there is little evidence that this notion is integrated with his study of philosophical ideas.

20. Taylor's totalistic impulse sometimes leads to a slippage between the notion of the person and that of the human species, which stands out strikingly in his tendency to stress the distinction between the person and non-human (rather than non-person) categories such as animal and machine, as if the stakes remain the same as

those of Enlightenment philosophy, which was obsessed with the human-beast distinction and their hierarchical order. This is also true of his earlier essay, "The Person," where he re-introduces a universal, albeit modern, concept of the person
capable of explaining all human conditions.

21. Collins, "Categories, Concepts or Predicaments? Remarks on Mauss's Use of
Philosophical Terminology," in Carrithers et al., pp. 68–69.

22. See Marcel Mauss, "A Category of the Human Mind: The Notion of Person;
the Notion of Self" (pp. 1–25); J. S. La Fontaine, "Person and Individual: Some
Anthropological Reflections" (pp. 123–40); Mark Elvin, "Between the Earth and the
Heaven: Conceptions of the Self in China" (pp. 156–89); Martin Hollis, "Of Masks
and Men" (pp. 217–33); and Michael Carrithers, "An Alternative Social History of
the Self" (pp. 234–56); all in Carrithers et al.

23. See Martin Hollis, "Of Masks and Men," in Carrithers et al., p. 217.

24. Roman Jakobson, "On Linguistic Aspects of Translation," in idem, p. 435.
Jakobson (p. 423) defines "paranomasia" as "a semantic confrontation of phonemi-
cally similar words irrespective of any etymological connection."

25. Derrida, Of Grammatology; see also Barbara Johnson, pp. 142–48; and Niranjana, pp. 57–58. In a study of the modern theory of translation and German romanticism, Antoine Berman (p. 35) points out that Treue (fidelity) was given distinct
marital overtones by Breitinger, Voss, and Herder in the second half of the eighteenth
century, whereas, at about the same time, French translators continued their tradition of embellishing and poeticizing in a more or less free vein. Also, the idea of
double fidelity can be traced back to Rosenzweig, who held the view that to translate
is "to serve two masters": the foreign work and the foreign language on the one hand,
and one's own public and one's own language on the other. It stands to reason that
a double fidelity is incessantly threatened by the specter of a double treason.

26. Following Jakobson, comparative linguists have done much work on the kind
of formal analysis of the translation process we observe in his essay, including the
technical problem of translatability. See Catford; Popoviōc; and Mounin.

27. For the prehistory of the Babel story and its implication for the theory of
translation, see Barnstone, pp. 135–52.

28. Steiner, p. 58.

29. Barnstone, p. 43. And, indeed, there is a great deal more at stake politically
surrounding the translation of the Scriptures. As we know, Martin Luther's revolutionary Verdeutschung of the Bible into common German became the cornerstone of
the Protestant Reformation in Germany. He was also celebrated as a great writer,
creator of literary German by Herder and Klopstock.

30. See Steiner, pp. 236–38.

31. For a critique of Steiner's periodization, see Berman, p. 2.

32. Whorf, p. 60; as quoted in Steiner, pp. 90–91.

33. Steiner, p. 94.

34. Benjamin, p. 70.

35. Ibid., p. 80.

36. See Derrida, "Des Tours de Babel," discussed below. See also de Man, Resistance to Theory, pp. 73–105.

37. Martin Jay (esp. chap. 12, "Politics of Translation: Siegfried Kracauer and

Walter Benjamin on the Buber-Rosenzweig Bible," pp. 198–216) situates Benjamin's language in the context of the so-called Jewish Renaissance in Germany, particularly the important twentieth-century translation of the Old Testament (1926–61) by Martin Buber and Franz Rosenzweig.

38. See Benjamin, pp. 70, 82.

39. Ibid. He has Luther and others in mind who "have extended the boundaries of the German language" through translation (p. 80).

40. Derrida, "Des Tours de Babel," p. 171.

41. Derrida, *Positions*, p. 20.

42. Derrida, "Des Tours de Babel," p. 201.

43. Steiner, p. 357.

44. Fang, p. 130.

45. I am referring to the numbers 3.1 through 4.12 in Gunn's appendix, pp. 217–70.

46. See Gao Mingkai and Liu Zhengtan. Portions of their work are mentioned and cited in Liu Yu-ning and Zdneka Novotná. The percentage of direct borrowings from the Indo-European languages in the period Gao and Liu have documented (ca. 1900's–1950's) is much lower than borrowing of loanwords of Japanese *kanji* origin. See the Appendixes.

47. See Wang Lida, pp. 90–94.

48. See Sanetō, *Kindai Nitchū kōshō shiwa*, pp. 311–27.

49. See Tam, *Jindai Zhong-Ri wenhua guanxi yanjiu*, pp. 317–49; and idem, "Meiji Japan and the Educational and Language Reforms in Late Ch'ing China," p. 71. If we include loanwords from sources other than Japanese *kanji*, the total figure reached by these scholars should be around 1,600. The Appendixes to this book contain slightly over 1,800 loanwords and neologisms, mainly because I have included a sampling of neologistic affixes.

50. See Masini, pp. 157–223.

51. For studies and dictionaries of loanwords in Japanese, see Arakawa's *Japanized English* and his dictionaries of loanwords. See also Shi Qun; and Chen Shanlong. In an earlier comparison of Japanese and Chinese, Miller (pp. 235–68) makes a curious suggestion that "Chinese, in all of its historical forms and modern Chinese as well, has generally reacted to outside linguistic stimulus in this extremely conservative fashion, preferring to translate new lexical items made necessary by its contacts with the outside world, rather than to take them over as loanwords" (p. 236). As far as modern Chinese is concerned, Miller's conclusion is easily contradicted by the research of linguists and other scholars, such as Gao Mingkai, Liu Zhengtan, Sanetō Keishū, Edward Gunn, Tam Yue-him, and Federico Masini.

52. See Gao Mingkai and Liu Zhengtan, esp. chap. 2 on a description and list of earlier Chinese loanwords from Persian, Sogdian, Sanskrit, Mongolian, Manchu, and other Asian languages. For further discussions, see Luo; Chmielewski; and Mair, "Buddhism."

53. Bakhtin, *Rabelais and His World*, p. 465.

54. Although Ezra Pound's translation and introduction of Chinese poetry marks a major turning point in modernist literature, it has not shaken the fundamentals of the English language as the latter has done to Chinese.

55. For a critique of the notion of "critical consciousness," see Dhareshwar.
56. Said, *The World, the Text, and the Critic,* pp. 226–27.
57. Clifford, p. 185.
58. See Said's recent *Culture and Imperialism.*
59. The journal *Inscriptions* published a special issue entitled "Traveling Theories and Traveling Theorists" in 1989. This, I believe, is a major collective effort to apply and revise Said's theory. Nearly all the eight fine essays and three commentaries contained in this volume center on the question of location. Lata Mani's essay, "Multiple Mediations: Feminist Scholarship in the Age of Multinational Reception," illustrates the politics of location by comparing the differing receptions of her own history of *sati* in the United States, Great Britain, and India. Following Chandra Mohanty's definition of the politics of location as "the historical, geographic, cultural, psychic and imaginative boundaries which provide the ground for political definition and self definition," Mani emphasizes that "location" is not a fixed point but a "temporality of struggle" and that its politics is characterized by processes of movement "between cultures, languages, and complex configurations of meaning and power" (p. 5). By focusing on the complexity of the self-positioning of the theorist in the postcolonial context, this move helps revise Said's original conception of traveling theory. At the same time, however, traveling theory is replaced by the postcolonial traveling theorist as the privileged subject in the multiple mediations of different locations. To the extent that the fuzzy notion of location helps cut a discursive space for postcolonial theory and the Third World "diaspora" in the First World, it might work very well, but it is not clear to me exactly how the postcolonial theorist relates to the "Third World" except that s/he travels in and out of it and points out its difference from that of the "First World."

David Scott's analysis of the postcolonial situation in "Locating the Anthropological Subject: Postcolonial Anthropologists in Other Places" in the same issue suggests that the direction in which the postcolonial travels matters just as much as the difference of locations as s/he leaves one place for another:

> The postcolonial is now, in Derek Walcott's felicitously ironic phrase, a "fortunate traveller." However, even as we recognize this irreversible redistribution of the postcolonial map (one which Louise Bennett has so inimitably satirized in such poems as "Colonization in Reverse"), we should not lose sight of the fact that these movements are rather *one* way than the other. Colonial and postcolonial peoples were/are going *west.* (p. 75)

Ironically, as immigrants arrive in large numbers in the *West,* theory is simultaneously penetrating the *East.* In her essay "Postcolonial Feminists in the Western Intellectual Field: Anthropologists *and* Native Informants?" Mary E. John points out that "the choice of the term itself is telling—not emigrant, but immigrant" (p. 57).

The linkages between the two phenomena can hardly escape one's notice. In this respect it is doubtful that the postcolonial condition differs that much from that of the colonial era. But I will defer the subject of immigrant culture to the scholars of diaspora, whose excellent work has attracted increased attention in the United States, and concentrate instead on the subject of traveling theory between East and West. My question is this: What happens when theory produced in one language gets translated into another?

60. See Niranjana, p. 37. For the concepts of *wirkliche Historie* and *Wirkungsge-schichte*, see Nietzsche's *The Use and Abuse of History*; and Hans-Georg Gadamer, *Truth and Method*.

61. Niranjana, p. 35.

62. Pratt, p. 5.

63. Fabian, *Language and Colonial Power*, p. 79.

64. Ibid., p. 137. For more on colonialism in Africa, see Chinweizu et al., vol. 1; and JanMohamed.

65. For the development of languages in relation to the formation of modern nation-states and the history of colonialism and imperialism, see Certeau et al.; Maz-rui; B. Anderson; Cooper; Burke and Porter; Bourdieu, *Language and Symbolic Power*; and Pratt.

66. Fabian, *Language and Colonial Power*, p. 73. See also Fabian's other influential book, *Time and Other: How Anthropology Makes Its Object*.

67. See Fabian, *Language and Colonial Power*, pp. 1–2.

68. Fodor; as cited in Fabian, *Language and Colonial Power*, p. 1.

69. Niranjana, pp. 11, 7, 172. The convergence of poststructuralism and postcolo-nial theory in the study of colonial India has produced some exciting research in the past decade. For an informed study of the ideological uses of English literature in the colonial period, see Viswanathan.

70. Eric Cheyfitz's *Poetics of Imperialism*, which offers a strong critique of the colo-nialist and imperialist impulses of modern European literature, also exemplifies some of the problems I mention here.

71. Rafael, p. 21.

72. See also Homi Bhabha's essay on this issue as it pertains to British India, "Signs Taken for Wonders: Questions of Ambivalence and Authority Under a Tree Outside Delhi, May 1817," in Gates, *"Race," Writing, and Difference*, pp. 163–84.

73. Among scholars of postcolonial history, Partha Chatterjee is aware of this problem and tries to negotiate it in his *Nationalist Thought and the Colonial World: A Derivative Discourse*.

74. Lowe, p. 7.

75. See Schwartz, *In Search of Wealth and Power*.

76. See Lee, *Romantic Generation*, p. 44.

77. Qian Xingcun (A Ying), *Wanqing xiaoshuo shi*, p. 1. Perry Link (p. 135*n*27) has compared two editions of A Ying's study—the Taiwanese Renren wenku edition (1968) and the Hong Kong edition (1973)—and discovered a discrepancy in the esti-mated figure. The former gives about 1,500 titles, whereas the latter mentions 1,000. He argues convincingly that the Taiwan edition makes better sense: "Ch'ien [Qian] states that 'almost 400' titles of translated novels and 'about 120' original novels appear in *Han-fen-lou hsin-shu fen-lei mu-lu*. He then states that his own estimate is 'about three times' what appears in this index." In a recent study, Chen Pingyuan (p. 20) has come up with a figure of 1,145 fiction titles published between 1898 and 1911. Of these, 647 were translated novels, and 498 indigenous creations. The ratio of translated fiction to original compositions in this case is roughly three to two.

78. On the rise of modern publishing institutions in the late Qing and Republican periods, see Link, esp. chap. 3; Lee and Nathan; Barnett, "Silent Evangelism"; Qian

Xingcum (A Ying), *Wanqing wenyi baokan shulüe;* Zhang Jinglu, *Zhongguo jindai chuban shiliao;* idem, *Zhongguo xiandai chuban shiliao,* vols. 1–4; idem, *Zhongguo chuban shiliao bubian;* and Lin Yutang.

79. Literary historians tend to emphasize the importance of the journal *Xiaoshuo yuebao* (The short story magazine, 1910–32) in terms of its contribution to the rise of modern fiction—which is part of an official narrative about the beginnings of modern literature—and often mention in passing the journal's commitment to the translation of foreign literatures. In fact, the evidence calls for a different interpretation. Between its conversion from a Butterfly magazine to a "serious" modern literary journal by the Literary Association in 1921 (vol. 12, no. 1) and its demise in January 1932, this monthly set up sections and numerous programs aimed at introducing foreign literature, theory, and criticism. By comparison, the original works of fiction and poetry we now call "modern" literature occupy only a fraction of the total space. Among the regular sections featured by the journal were a "translation series," a "literature abroad" feature, and a "criticism" section. Well over half of the essays in the last section were devoted to the discussion of foreign literature. In addition, there were serialized studies on foreign literature, including Russian literature (supplementary issue, 1921) and French literature (supplementary issue, 1924); and a special number "Literature of the Abused Nations" (1921), which contained translations of the literature of marginal European nations such as Poland, Finland, Greece, and others, to mention a few. For a full-length study of Russian influence on early modern Chinese writers, see Ng.

80. Although it is common knowledge, I emphasize that modern Japan played a central role during this period as Chinese students who had studied there brought back numerous translations and a massive infusion of loanwords and neologisms into the Chinese language. See Sanetō, *Zhongguoren liuxue Riben shi.*

81. For a study of Chinese translations of foreign literature and related publications in this period, see Ma Zuyi, *Zhongguo fanyi jianshi.*

82. Lee, "In Search of Modernity," p. 110.

83. Cohen, *Discovering History in China,* pp. 3, 4.

84. Rey Chow, p. xv.

85. Bourdieu, *Language and Symbolic Power,* p. 221.

86. For a salient critique of Cold War social science and regional studies in the China field, see Barlow, "Postwar China Studies."

87. It is important to keep in mind that what has happened to modern Chinese is not restricted to the elite Chinese alone. Although they were the ones who introduced or invented the neologisms and for whom the problematic of East and West has been a preoccupation (the very reason we must take this problematic seriously in any critique of the East-West binary opposition), words do not stay with those who invent them but travel and circulate in other areas of social discourses as well. Like other verbal signs, neologisms in modern Chinese have long penetrated the popular and lower levels of Chinese society.

88. Huters, "Ideologies of Realism in Modern China," p. 149.

89. Spivak, *In Other Worlds,* p. 197. See also Guha and Spivak. Guha's preface to this volume summarizes the genesis of this historiography.

90. This is not to downplay some of the problematic areas in the historical writ-

ings of this group, such as their treatment of various class formations criticized in O'Hanlon; Hershatter; and Chen Xiaomei.

91. A recent example is the debate on the notions of the public sphere and civil society in *Modern China* 19 (1993).

92. *LXQJ*, 1: 196. Jon Kowallis's translation. I am grateful to Kowallis for allowing me to use his unpublished translations of Lu Xun's early essays (p. 7).

93. *LXQJ*, 1: 516*n*18. The original lyrics are "Bolan mie, Yindu wang, / Youtai yimin san si fang"; "Qing kan Yindu guotu bing fei xiao, / wei nu wei ma bude tuo long lao." The English translation is by William A. Lyell, as quoted in Kowallis (p. 4).

94. In a recent article, Wang Liwei argues that the Japanese had borrowed modern Chinese character translations of English terms from nineteenth-century missionary dictionaries, in particular, Robert Morrison's *Dictionary of the Chinese Language* (1815), long before the reverse process began. He (p. 281) suggests 1875(?) as the date when this one-way traffic in lexical borrowing gave way to the predominantly Chinese importation of Japanese *kanji* compounds; Japanese translators had ordered bilingual dictionaries compiled by Protestant missionaries (Morrison, Williams, and Medhurst) from China and relied heavily on them in their translations until the first English-Japanese dictionary appeared in 1862. Wang's study complicates our view of the flow of neologisms between Chinese and Japanese, but it tends to exaggerate the situation by attributing a greater role to these early missionary dictionaries in the rise of modern Japanese *kanji* compounds than can be fully substantiated by textual evidence. I have not been able to verify more than a limited number of such earlier compounds in Morrison's dictionary that coincide exactly with the Sino-Japanese-European loanwords that Gao, Liu, and others have pointed out. For these particular compounds, see the footnotes to the Appendixes. A more reliable source of Japanese borrowing from missionary works would be in their translations of Wei Yuan's *Hai-guo tuzhi*. See the discussion below.

95. Gao and Liu (pp. 82–83) list of total of 91 items in this category. A native speaker of Chinese cannot usually tell that some of these words did not exist in Chinese before the twentieth century. Further examples are *bu jingji* (recession; *fukeiki*), *changsuo* (site; *basho*), *paichusuo* (police station; *hashutsujo*), *fuwu* (service; *fukumu*), *gebie* (individual; *kobetsu*), *juli* (distance; *kyori*), *neirong* (contents; *naiyō*), *zhibu* (party branch; *shibu*). In Appendix C, I modify and correct this list with my findings and those of other scholars.

96. The pre-loanword meaning of *geming* (now revolution) was "to follow the Mandate of Heaven"; *wenxue* (now literature) meant "the state of being learned or erudite"; *jingji* (now economy) used to mean "governing and assisting" (the people). *Kexue* (now science), which is not considered a return-graphic loan by Gao, Liu, and Masini but which I reassigned to the present category (see Appendix D), originally meant "study programs for the civil service examination." For a fascinating account of the Chinese translation of the word "science" in the Ming dynasty as *gezhi* and its later replacement by the Japanese *kanji* term *kagaku* or *kexue* in modern Chinese, see Wang Hui. Gao and Liu (pp. 83–88) list 67 lexical items in this category. Further examples are *wenxue* (literature; *bungaku*), *wenming* (civilization; *bunmei*), *fenxi* (analysis; *bunseki*), *fengjian* (feudal; *hōken*), *falü* (law; *hōritsu*), *ziyou* (freedom; *jiyū*), *jieji* (class; *kaikyū*), *laodong* (labor; *rōdō*), *zhengzhi* (politics; *seiji*), *sixiang* (thought;

shisō), *yundong* (movement; *undō*), *weiyi* (only/sole; *yuiitsu*). Masini has contested some of these terms, such as *wenxue*. See the discussion below as well as the Appendixes, especially A and D.

97. This is by far the largest of the three groups of loanwords. Gao and Liu (pp. 88–98) list 100 compounds in this category; with few exceptions, all are *kanji* translations of English terms. Other examples are *yihui* (parliament; *gikai*), wuzhi (matter/ substance; *busshitsu*), *fandui* (oppose/opposition; *hantai*), *xianshi* (reality; *genjitsu*), *zhexue* (philosophy; *tetsugaku*). See Appendix B.

98. De Man, *Resistance to Theory,* p. 104.

99. The term is Masini's. An alternative label, "round-trip words," was coined by Victor Mair ("Anthologizing and Anthropologizing," p. 3). Either term should be helpful in specifying the second of the three categories of Sino-Japanese-European neologisms that Gao Mingkai and Liu Zhengtan classify.

100. I am not implying that the meaning of classical Chinese *wenhua* or the English "culture" did not go through mutations in its separate existence. It certainly did (see Williams, *Keywords,* pp. 76–82). What I am trying to do here is to call attention to a unique historical situation within a limited period of time between the nineteenth and early twentieth centuries. During this time—neither before nor after—a large number of Chinese compounds were reinvented, radically, via the mediation of Japanese *kanji* translations of European terms.

101. It is well known that Yan Fu had to defend the Chinese lexicon against the influx of Japanese loanwords when he started translating John Mill, Thomas Huxley, Herbert Spencer, Adam Smith, and other Westerners at the turn of the century. He preferred to use ancient terms or coin his own, refusing to adopt those existing in contemporary works. For example, he uses *mucai* to translate "capital" instead of the return-graphic loanword *ziben* (*shihon*) and renders "bank" as *chaodian, chaoshang,* or *banke* (a transliteration) in place of the already known Japanese loan *yinhang* (*ginkō*). Interestingly, despite the great impact of Yan Fu's translations on his generation, his neologisms were quickly rendered obsolete by the growing popularity of Japanese loanword translations (Schwartz, *In Search of Wealth and Power,* pp. 95– 96). Joshua Fogel ("Recent Translation Theory") has tried to reopen the question of exactly how Yan Fu's idiosyncratic neologism should be viewed in relation to Japanese loanwords in this time. Speculating on why *tianyanlun,* Yan Fu's famous coinage for the "theory of evolution," was soon replaced in the new Chinese lexicon by the Japanese term *shinkaron* (Chinese *jinhualun*), Fogel (p. 28) says

> Why such terms did not "take" in China cannot simply be sluffed off on the fact that they were too literary or assumed too profound a knowledge of classical Chinese lore. When Yan Fu was writing, there was no widespread vernacular Chinese language in use, and most of those who were able to read his translations undoubtedly understood his allusions (even if the Western ideas behind them remained partially obscured). Was Yan Fu aware of the Japanese translations by Nakamura Keiu of the same texts he labored over? Has anyone ever compared the vocabularies devised by Nakamura and Yan to render Western philosophical, political, and economic concepts?

Masini's recent study of late Qing neologisms and loanwords in the Chinese lexicon sheds oblique light on these questions—oblique in the sense that he does not tackle directly the comparative question along the lines suggested by Fogel. He (p. 115) shows that even Yan Fu himself had trouble keeping all Japanese-associated neologisms out of his own translations. The examples he gives are *yiyuan* (parliament; *giin*), *ziyou* (freedom; *jiyū*), *wenxue* (literature; *bungaku*), etc. (Note that the modern term *wenxue*, unlike *ziyou*, is not exactly a return-graphic loan; however, its round-trip dissemination through the mediation of Japanese *bungaku* has much to do with the establishment of the new translingual meaning of *wenxue* in the modern Chinese lexicon. See the discussion below.) Also worth mentioning is the important point Masini makes about Yan Fu's translation of the English terms "economy" and "sociology," which would substantiate Fogel's point. Yan Fu's renderings *jixue* and *qunxue* were soon replaced by the Japanese *jingji* and *shehuixue*, which later became standard. Did Yan Fu oppose the Japanese loans or was he unaware of their existence? As far as Yan Fu is concerned, it would probably have come to the same result; a more interesting question has to do with the complex circumstances under which Yan Fu made the choices he did. Masini's study claims that no evidence of the Japanese loan-words *jingji* and *shehuixue* could be found in the earlier Chinese translations of Western texts he examined—that is, before Yan Fu's invention of *jixue* and *qunxue* in 1898. if true, this would establish Yan Fu as "first and foremost an innovator and not only an opponent of Japanese loans" (Masini, p. 115).

102. See also Mair, "Anthologizing and Anthropologizing," p. 3.

103. Masini, pp. 24–25. For a fascinating account of the changing meaning of *gonsi*, see ibid., p. 174.

104. Ibid., 25.

105. The original meaning of *wenxue* goes back to the Confucian *Analects* (II.2), where it denotes "the state of being learned or erudite." Masini (p. 204) proposes that the term with this modern meaning of "literature" should be dated further back to Jesuit missionary Giulio Aleni's work *Zhifang waiji* (Record of the places outside the jurisdiction of the Office of Geography; 1623). He cites as evidence the phrase *ouluoba zhuguo shang wenxue*, which he renders as "all Western countries highly esteem literature." This translation strikes me as anachronistic, since "literature" or whatever its Italian counterpart happened to be covered a different and much broader semantic field in the seventeenth century than what we mean by "literature" in the post-Enlightenment era.

106. There remain, however, a number of transliterations that have not been replaced by loanword translations. See Appendixes F and G.

107. Before *minzhu* became a standard translation for "democracy," it had been used in this modern sense of "people rule" by missionary W.A.P. Martin to render the word "republic" (now *gonghe*) in his 1864 *Wanguo gongfa*, a translation of Henry Wheaton's *Elements of International Law*. This earlier transvaluation of *minzhu* via the translation of "republic" contributed indirectly to the reversal of its classical meaning. Masini (pp. 189–90) speculates that the Japanese probably picked up this two-character compound through their secondhand translation of *Wanguo gongfa* in 1865 and later used it to translate "democracy" (*minshu*).

108. This is probably because deictic words are more closely tied to the logic of indigenous word formation than other parts of speech, such as nouns and verbs.

109. For the fascinating debate on the invention of the feminine third-person sin-

gular in 1920, see the following articles published in *Xue deng* (Scholarly lamp), a supplement to the Shanghai newspaper *Shishi xinbao* (Current affairs), plus one published in the journal *Xin ren* (New humans): Sun Zuji, " '*Ta*' zi de yanjiu"; Han Bing, "Bo '*ta* zi de yanjiu' "; Sun Zuji, "Fei 'Bo *ta* zi de yanjiu' "; Meng Shen; Han Bing, "Zhe shi Liu Bannong de cuo"; and Liu Fu (Liu Bannong), "Ta zi wenti." For a comparative study of the personal pronoun in modern and classical Chinese, see Wang Li, 2: 1–60; Gao Mingkai; Lu Shuxiang and Huang Shengzhang.

110. The invention of the feminine *pronoun* should not be confused here with the existence of the same character written with the *nü* radical, which used to be a noun and bore no etymological relationship with the original Chinese pronoun *ta* written with a *ren* radical. According to Morohashi (*Dai Kanwa jiten*, 3: 626), the premodern character *ta* is pronounced /ch'i/ or /jie/ (the same as in *jie*, sister), signifying "mother" in the Sichuan dialect.

111. See Shan Shi. At the same time the feminine pronoun was invented, the neuter form of *ta* was also considered; see Liu Fu, "Ta zi wenti."

112. Edward Gunn mentions Zhou Zuoren as one of the sources of information on the circumstances surrounding Liu Fu's invention of the feminine pronoun *ta* (p. 305*n*24). In addition, Lu Xun also refers to this fact in his "Yi Liu Bannong" (Remembering Liu Bannong), in *LXQJ*, 6: 55. Chinese linguist Wang Li (2: 351*n*22) cites two more sources: Hu Shi's memorial speech at the funeral service for Liu Fu (Liu Bannong) in which he describes Liu as the engineer of the neologism and Lin Yutang's book *Kaiming Yingwen wenfa* (An illuminating English grammar) in which the author pinpoints the year 1917 as the exact date of the birth of the character.

113. See Liu Fu, "Ta zi wenti."

114. Interestingly, during Liu's term as the president of Women's College in Beijing, he issued an order forbidding female students to use the fashionable transliteration *misi* of the English word "miss" as a form of address and insisting on the adoption of indigenous Chinese terms, such as *guniang* (girl or unmarried woman), *xiaojie* (young lady), and *nüshi* (lady). See his interview with a journalist from *Shijie ribao*, Apr. 1, 1931.

115. The pluralizing suffix *men*, which is tagged on to nouns and pronouns, was another hot subject of debate during the language reform; see Gunn, pp. 266–68.

116. For a discussion of the modern statist construction of gender from a poststructuralist and feminist point of view, see Barlow, "Theorizing Women."

117. Adorno, 2: 190.

118. For a discussion of the invention of tradition in modern national histories, see Hobsbawm and Ranger.

119. Levenson, p. 157.

120. Thomas Metzger's continuity model, which is meant to criticize Levenson's impact theory, operates, nevertheless, on the same reified binaries (tradition/modernity; China/West) as Levenson used. Metzger argues (p. 17) that "to a large extent, it was the indigenous, intense, centuries-old desire to escape from a metaphysical, psychological, political, and economic predicament which led many Chinese enthusiastically to devote their lives to the overthrow of traditionally revered institutions and the adoption of strange and foreign ways." This attempt to minimize the presence of a mediated West in favor of a self-explanatory indigenous past cannot, however,

explain the process by which the "modern" and the "West" get legitimized in twentieth-century Chinese intellectual discourse.

121. There are two translations for anarchism: the Chinese transliteration as *anaqi zhuyi* and the Japanese *kanji* translation as *museifu shugi*. The *kanji* translation, pronounced *wuzhengfu zhuyi* in Mandarin, eventually replaced the transliteration. See Appendix F.

122. Dirlik, *Anarchism,* pp. 50, 55.

123. I am concerned with an order of reality that might sometimes coincide with, but should by no means be leveled down to, the state's brute regulation and manipulation of the written and spoken word. For a discussion of the latter in China, see Schoenhals.

124. For a discussion of this debate, see Liu Kang, "Subjectivity, Marxism, and Cultural Theory in China," in Liu Kang and Xiaobing Tang, pp. 23–55.

125. See Liu Zaifu. Initially published in *Wenxue pinglun* (Literary criticism) (1985, no. 6, and 1986, no. 1), Liu's essay was attacked by an official critic named Chen Yong.

15

Universality in Culture

Judith Butler

CONSIDER THAT IT MAY be a mistake to declare one's affiliation by stating an order of priorities: I am X first and then Y. It may be that the ordering of such identifications is precisely the problem produced by a discourse on multiculturalism which does not yet know how to relate the terms that it enumerates. It would be a great consolation, I suppose, to return to a ready-made universal perspective, and to compel everyone to identify with a universal moral attitude before they take on their various specific and parochial concerns. The problem emerges, however, when the meaning of "the universal" proves to be culturally variable, and the specific cultural articulations of the universal work against its claim to a transcultural status.

This is not to say that there ought to be no reference to the universal or that it has become, for us, an impossibility. On the contrary. All it means is that there are cultural conditions for its articulation that are not always the same, and that the term gains its meaning for us precisely through these decidedly less than universal conditions. This is a paradox that any injunction to adopt a universal attitude will encounter. For it may be that in one culture a set of rights are considered to be universally endowed, and that in another those very rights mark the limit to universalizability, i.e., "If we grant those people those rights we will be undercutting the foundations of the universal as we know it." This has become especially clear to me in the field of lesbian and gay human rights, where *the universal* is a contested term, and where various cultures and various mainstream human rights groups voice doubt over whether lesbian and gay people ought properly to be included in "the human" and whether their putative rights fit within the existing conventions governing the scope of rights considered universal.

Consider that to claim that there are existing conventions governing the scope of rights described as universal is not to claim that that scope has been decided once and for all. In fact, it may be that the universal is only partially articulated, and that we do not yet know what forms it may take. The contingent and cultural character of the existing conventions governing the scope of universality does not deny the usefulness or importance of the term *universal*. It simply means that the claim of universality has not been fully or finally made and that it remains to be seen whether and how it will be further articulated. Indeed, it may well be politically important to claim that a given set of rights are universal even when existing conventions governing the scope of universality preclude precisely such a claim. Such a claim runs the good risk of provoking a radical rearticulation of universality itself. Whether the claim is preposterous, provocative, or efficacious depends on the collective strength with which it is asserted, the institutional conditions of its assertion and reception, and the unpredictable political forces at work. But the uncertainty of success is not enough of a reason to refrain from making the claim.

Mari Matsuda has recently argued that hate speech—in particular, racially degrading speech—ought not to qualify as protected speech precisely because it sends a message of racial inferiority, and that message has been refuted by universally accepted codes of law.[1] Setting aside for the moment whether or not hate speech ought to be unprotected for that reason, the argument raises other kinds of questions. Is Matsuda's view one which only isolates kinds of speech that ought not to be part of public discourse, or is it also a normative position concerning what ought to be the positive boundaries of legitimate speech—namely, speech that is constrained by *existing* notions of universality?[2] How would we reconcile such a view with that of Étienne Balibar, for instance, who argues that racism informs our current notions of universality?[3] How might we continue to insist upon more expansive reformulations of universality, if we commit ourselves to honoring only the provisional and parochial versions of universality currently encoded in international law? Clearly, such precedents are enormously useful for political arguments in international contexts, but it would be a mistake to think that such conventional formulations exhaust the possibilities of what might be meant by "the universal." Are we to expect that we will know in advance the meaning to be assigned to the utterance of universality, or is this utterance the occasion for a meaning that is not to be fully or concretely anticipated?

If standards of universality are historically articulated, then it would seem that exposing the parochial and exclusionary character of a given historical articulation of universality is part of the project of extending and rendering substantive the notion of universality itself. "Speech that contests current standards governing the universal reach of political enfranchisement" characterizes racist speech, to be sure. But there are other sorts of speech that constitute valuable contestations crucial to the continuing elaboration of the universal itself, and which it would be a mistake to foreclose. An example of the latter would be a situation in which subjects who have been excluded from enfranchisement by existing conventions (including racist conventions) governing the exclusionary definition of the universal seize the language of enfranchisement and set into motion a "performative contradiction": claiming to be covered by that universal, they thereby expose the contradictory character of previous conventional formulations of the universal.

This kind of speech appears at first to be impossible or contradictory, but it constitutes one way to expose the limits of current notions of universality, and to constitute a challenge to those existing standards to revise themselves in more expansive and inclusive ways. In this sense, being able to utter the performative contradiction is hardly a self-defeating enterprise; on the contrary, it is crucial to the continuing revision and elaboration of historical standards of universality proper to the futural movement of democracy itself. To claim that the universal has not yet been articulated is to insist that the "not yet" is proper to an understanding of the universal itself: that which remains "unrealized" by the universal constitutes it essentially. The universal begins to become articulated precisely through challenges to its existing formulation, and this challenge emerges from those who are not covered by it, who have no entitlement to occupy the place of the "who," but who nevertheless demand that the universal as such ought to be inclusive of them. The excluded, in this sense, constitutes the contingent limit of universalization. And the universal, far from being commensurate with its conventional formulation, emerges as a postulated and open-ended *ideal* that has not been adequately encoded by any given set of legal conventions.[4] If existing and accepted conventions of universality *constrain* the domain of the speakable, this constraint produces the speakable, marking a border of demarcation between the speakable and the unspeakable.

The border that produces the speakable through the exclusion of certain forms of speech becomes an operation of censorship exercised through the very postulation of the universal. Does every postulation of the universal as an existent, as a given, not codify the exclusions by which that postulation of universality proceeds? In this instance and through this strategy of relying on *established conventions of universality,* do we unwittingly stall the process of universalization within the bounds of established convention, naturalizing its exclusions, and preempting the possibility of its radicalization? The universal can be articulated only in response to a challenge from (its own) outside. What constitutes the community that might qualify as a legitimate community that might debate and agree upon this universality? If that very community is constituted through racist exclusions, how shall we trust it to deliberate on the question of racist speech?

The above definition of universality is distinct from an idealizing presupposition of consensus, one that is in some ways already there. A universality that is yet to be articulated might well defy or confound the existing conventions that govern our anticipatory imaginings. This last is something other than a pre- or postconventional idealization (Habermas) conceived as always already there, or as one already encoded in given international law (Matsuda), a position that equates present and ultimate accomplishments. It is the futural anticipation of a universality that has not yet arrived, one for which we have no ready concept, one whose articulations will only follow, if they do, from a contestation of universality at its already imagined borders.

The notion of "consensus" presupposed by either of the first two views proves to be a prelapsarian contention, one which short-circuits the necessarily difficult task of forging a universal consensus from various locations of culture, to borrow Homi Bhabbha's title and phrase, and the difficult practice of translation among the various languages in which universality makes it varied and contending appearances.⁵ The task of cultural translation is one that is necessitated precisely by the performative contradiction that takes place when one with no authorization to speak within and as the universal nevertheless lays claims to the terms. Or, perhaps more appropriately phrased, the extension of universality through the act of translation takes place when one who is excluded from the universal, and yet belongs to it nevertheless, speaks from a split situation of being at once authorized and deauthorized (so much for delineating a neatly spatialized "site of enunciation"). That translation is not the simple entry of the deauthorized into the authorized, whereby the former term simply alters its status and the latter domain simply makes room for what it has unwittingly failed to accommodate. If the norm is itself predicated on the exclusion of the one who speaks, one whose speech calls into question the foundation of the universal itself, then translation on such occasions is to be something more and different than an assimilation to an existing norm. The kind of translation that exposes the alterity within the norm (an alterity without which the norm would not assume its borders and "know" its limits) exposes the failure of the norm to effect the universal reach for which it stands, exposes what we might underscore as the promising ambivalence of the norm.

The failure of the norm is exposed by the performative contradiction enacted by one who speaks in its name even as the name is not yet said to designate the one who nevertheless insinuates his or her way into the name enough to speak "in" it all the same. Such double-speaking is precisely the temporalized map of universality's future, the task of a postlapsarian translation the future of which remains unpredictable. The contemporary scene of cultural translation emerges with the presupposition that the utterance does not have the same meaning everywhere, indeed that the utterance has become a scene of conflict (to such a degree, in fact, that we seek to prosecute the utterance in order, finally, to "fix" its meaning and quell the conflicts to which it gives rise). The translation that takes place at this scene of conflict is one in which the meaning intended is no more determinative of a "final" reading than the one that is received, and no final adjudication of conflicting positions can emerge. Without this final judgment, an interpretive dilemma remains, and it is that interpretive dilemma that is the dynamic mark of an emerging democratic practice.

Thus it makes little sense to imagine the scene of culture as one that one might enter to find bits and pieces of evidence that show an abiding faith in an already established notion of universality. If one were to enter various domains of culture in order to find examples of world citizens, one would invariably cull from those various examples the selfsame lesson, the selfsame universal bearing. But is the relation between culture and the universal appropriately construed as that between an example and the moral dictum it is said to support? In such cases, the examples are subordinate to the universal, and they all indicate the universal in the same way. The futural articulation of the universal, however, can happen only if we find ways to effect cultural translations between those various culture examples in order to see which versions of the universal are proposed, on what exclusions they are based, and how the entry of the excluded into the domain of the universal requires a radical transformation in our thinking of universality. When competing claims to the universal are made, it seems imperative not to presume that the cultural moments at issue exemplify a ready-made universal. The claim is part of the ongoing cultural articulation of universality, and the complex process of learning how to read that claim is not something any of us can do outside of the difficult process of cultural translation. This translation will not be an easy one in which we reduce every cultural instance to a presupposed universality, nor will it be the enumeration of radical particularisms between which no communication is possible.

The risks will be that translation will become an imposition of a universal claim on a culture that resists it, or that those who defend the universal will domesticate the challenge posed by alterity by invoking that very cultural claim as an example of its own nascent universality, one which confirms that such a universality is already achieved. What kind of cultural imposition is it to claim that a Kantian may be found in every culture? For whereas there may be something like a world reference in moral thinking or even a recourse to a version of universality, it would sidestep the specific cultural work to be done to claim that we have in Kant everything we might want to know about how moral reasoning works in various cultural contexts.

Importantly, then, the task that cultural difference sets for us is the articulation of universality through a difficult labor of translation. That labor seeks to transform the very terms that are made to stand for one another, and the movement of that unanticipated transformation establishes the universal as that which is yet to be achieved and which, in order to resist domestication, may never be fully or finally achievable.

Notes

1. Mari J. Matsuda, "Public Response to Racist Speech: Considering the Victim's Story," in *Words that Wound,* eds. Mari J. Matsuda, Charles R. Lawrence III, Richard Delgado, Kimberlè Williams Crenshaw (Boulder, Colo.: Westview Press, 1993), pp. 26–31.

2. The following discussion on universality is taken in revised form from a forthcoming essay, "Sovereign Performatives in the Contemporary Scene of Utterance," *Critical Inquiry.*

3. Étienne Balibar, "Racism as Universalism," in *Masses, Classes, and Ideas,* trans. James Swenson (New York: Routledge, 1994).

4. See the comparable views of ideals and idealization in Drucilla Cornell and Owen Fiss.

5. Much of this discussion is indebted to Homi Bhabha's use of Walter Benjamin's notion of "translation" for thinking about the problem of exclusion in cultural politics. See Bhabha, *The Location of Culture* (New York: Routledge, 1993).

16

The Clash of Definitions

Edward W. Said

S AMUEL P. HUNTINGTON's essay "The Clash of Civilizations?" appeared in *Foreign Affairs* in the summer of 1993, announcing in its first sentence that "world politics is entering a new phase." By this he meant that whereas in the recent past world conflicts were between ideological factions grouping the first, second, and third worlds into warring camps, the new style of politics would entail conflicts between different, and presumably clashing, civilizations: "The great divisions among humankind and the dominating source of conflict will be cultural . . . The clash of civilizations will dominate global politics." Later Huntington explains that the principal clash will be between Western and non-Western civilizations, and indeed he spends most of his time in the article discussing the fundamental disagreements, potential or actual, between what he calls the West on the one hand and the Islamic and Confucian civilizations on the other. In terms of detail, a great deal more attention is paid to Islam than to any other civilization, including the West.

Much of the subsequent interest taken in Huntington's essay, as well as the ponderously ineffective book that followed it in 1995, I think, derives from its timing, rather than exclusively from what it actually says. As Huntington himself notes, there have been several intellectual and political attempts since the end of the Cold War to map the emerging world situation; this included Francis Fukuyama's contention about the end of history and the thesis put about during the latter days of the Bush administration, the theory of the so-called New World Order. More recently Paul Kennedy, Conor Cruise O'Brien, and Eric Hobsbawm—all of whom have looked at the new millennium—have done so with considerable attention to the causes of future conflict, which has given them all reason for alarm. The core of Huntington's vision (not really original with him) is the idea of an unceasing clash, a concept of conflict which slides somewhat effortlessly into the politi-

cal space vacated by the unremitting bipolar war of ideas and values embodied in the unregretted Cold War. I do not, therefore, think it is inaccurate to
suggest that what Huntington is providing in this essay of his—especially
since it is primarily addressed to Washington-based opinion and policy-
makers who subscribe to *Foreign Affairs*, the leading U.S. journal of foreign
policy discussion—is a recycled version of the Cold War thesis, that conflicts
in today's and tomorrow's world will remain not economic or social in
essence but ideological; and if that is so then one ideology, the West's, is the
still point or locus around which for Huntington all others turn. In effect,
then, the Cold War continues, but this time on many fronts, with many more
serious and basic systems of values and ideas (like Islam and Confucianism)
struggling for ascendancy and even dominance over the West. Not surprisingly, therefore, Huntington concludes his essay with a brief survey of what
the West might do to remain strong and keep its putative opponents weak
and divided (it must "exploit differences and conflicts among Confucian and
Islamic states; . . . support in other civilizations groups sympathetic to Western values and interests; . . . strengthen international institutions that reflect
and legitimate Western interests and values and . . . promote the involvement
of non-Western states in those institutions," p. 49).

So strong and insistent is Huntington's notion that other civilizations necessarily clash with the West, and so relentlessly aggressive and chauvinistic is
his prescription for what the West must do to continue winning, that we are
forced to conclude that he is really most interested in continuing and
expanding the Cold War by means other than advancing ideas about understanding the current world scene or trying to reconcile different cultures. Little in what he says expresses the slightest doubt or skepticism. Not only will
conflict continue, he says on the first page, but "conflict between civilizations
will be the latest phase in the evolution of conflict in the modern world." It
is as a very brief and rather crudely articulated manual in the art of maintaining a wartime status in the minds of Americans and others that Huntington's
essay has to be understood. I would go so far as to say that it argues from the
standpoint of Pentagon planners and defense industry executives who may
have temporarily lost their occupations after the end of the Cold War, but
have now discovered a new vocation for themselves. Huntington at least has
the merit of underlining the cultural component in relationships among different countries, traditions, and peoples.

The sad part is that "the clash of civilizations" is useful as a way of exagger-
ating and making intractable various political or economic problems. It is
quite easy to see how, for instance, the practice of Japan-bashing in the West
can be fueled by appeals to the menacing and sinister aspects of Japanese
culture as employed by government spokespersons, or how the age-old

appeal to the "yellow peril" might be mobilized for use in discussions of ongoing problems with Korea or China. The opposite is true in the practice throughout Asia and Africa of Occidentalism, turning "the West" into a monolithic category that is supposed to express hostility to non-White, non-European, and non-Christian civilizations.

Perhaps because he is more interested in policy prescription than in either history or the careful analysis of cultural formations, Huntington in my opinion is quite misleading in what he says and how he puts things. A great deal of his argument depends on second- and third-hand opinion that scants the enormous advances in our concrete and theoretical understanding of how cultures work, how they change, and how they can best be grasped or apprehended. A brief look at the people and opinions he quotes suggests that journalism and popular demagoguery rather than scholarship or theory are his main sources. For when you draw on tendentious publicists, scholars, and journalists like Charles Krauthammer, Sergie Stankevich, and Bernard Lewis you already prejudice the argument in favor of conflict and polemic rather than true understanding and the kind of cooperation between peoples that our planet needs. Huntington's authorities are not the cultures themselves but a small handful of authorities picked by him because they emphasize the latent bellicosity in one or another statement by one or another so-called spokesman for or about that culture. The giveaway for me is the title of his essay—"The Clash of Civilizations"—which is not his phrase but Bernard Lewis's. On the last page of Lewis's essay "The Roots of Muslim Rage," which appeared in the September 1990 issue of *The Atlantic Monthly,* a journal that has on occasion run articles purporting to describe the dangerous sickness, madness, and derangement of Arabs and Muslims, Lewis speaks about the current problem with the Islamic world: "It should by now be clear that we are facing a mood and a movement far transcending the level of issues and policies and the governments that pursue them. This is no less than a clash of civilizations—the perhaps irrational but surely historic reactions of an ancient rival against our Judeo-Christian heritage, our secular present, and the worldwide expansion of both. It is crucially important that we on our side should not be provoked into an equally historic but also equally irrational reaction against that rival."

I do not want to spend much time discussing the lamentable features of Lewis's screed; elsewhere I have described his methods—the lazy generalizations, the reckless distortions of history, the wholesale demotion of civilizations into categories like irrational and enraged, and so on. Few people today with any sense would want to volunteer such sweeping characterizations as the ones advanced by Lewis about more than a billion Muslims, scattered throughout at least five continents, speaking dozens of differing languages, and possessing various traditions and histories. All he says about them is that they are all enraged at Western modernity, as if a billion people were but one and Western civilization were no more complicated a matter than a simple declarative sentence. But what I do want to stress is first of all how Huntington has picked up from Lewis the notion that civilizations are monolithic and homogenous, and second, how—again from Lewis—he assumes the unchanging character of the duality between "us" and "them."

In other words, I think it is absolutely imperative to stress that like Bernard Lewis, Samuel Huntington does not write a neutral, descriptive, and objective prose, but is himself a polemicist whose rhetoric not only depends heavily on prior arguments about a war of all against all, but in effect perpetuates them. Far from being an arbiter between civilizations, therefore, Huntington is a partisan, an advocate of one so-called civilization over all others. Like Lewis, Huntington defines Islamic civilization reductively, as if what matters most about it is its supposed anti-Westernism. For his part Lewis tries to give a set of reasons for his definition—that Islam has never modernized, that it never separated between Church and State, that it has been incapable of understanding other civilizations—but Huntington does not bother with them. For him Islam, Confucianism, and the other five or six civilizations (Hindu, Japanese, Slavic-Orthodox, Latin American, and African) that still exist are separate from one another, and consequently potentially in a conflict which he wants to manage, not resolve. He writes as a crisis manager, not as a student of civilization, nor as a reconciler between them.

At the core of his essay, and this is what has made it strike so responsive a chord among post–Cold War policy-makers, is this sense of cutting through a lot of unnecessary detail, of masses of scholarship and huge amounts of experience, and boiling all of them down to a couple of catchy, easy-to-quote-and-remember ideas, which are then passed off as pragmatic, practical, sensible, and clear. But is this the best way to understand the world we live in? Is it wise as an intellectual and a scholarly expert to produce a simplified map of the world and then hand it to generals and civilian law-makers as a prescription for first comprehending and then acting in the world? Doesn't this method in effect prolong, exacerbate, and deepen conflict? What does it do to minimize civilizational conflict? Do we *want* the clash of civilizations? Doesn't it mobilize nationalist passions and therefore nationalist murderousness? Shouldn't we ask the question, Why is one doing this sort of thing: to understand or to act? to mitigate or to aggravate the likelihood of conflict?

I would begin to survey the world situation by commenting on how prevalent it has become for people to speak now in the name of large, and in my opinion undesirably vague and manipulable, abstractions like the West or Japanese or Slavic culture, Islam or Confucianism, labels that collapse religions, races, and ethnicities into ideologies that are considerably more unpleasant and provocative than those of Gobineau and Renan 150 years ago. Strange as it may seem, these examples of group psychology run rampant are not new, and they are certainly not edifying at all. They occur in times of deep insecurity, that is, when peoples seem particularly close to and thrust upon one another, as either the result of expansion, war, imperialism, and migration, or the effect of sudden, unprecedented change.

Let me give a couple of examples to illustrate. The language of group identity makes a particularly strident appearance from the middle to the end of the nineteenth century as the culmination of decades of international competition between the great European and American powers for territories in Africa and Asia. In the battle for the empty spaces of Africa—the dark continent—France and Britain as well as Germany and Belgium resort not only to force but to a whole slew of theories and rhetorics for justifying their plunder. Perhaps the most famous of such devices is the French concept of civilizing mission, *la mission civilisatrice,* an underlying notion of which is the idea that some races and cultures have a higher aim in life than others; this gives the more powerful, more developed, more civilized the right therefore to colonize others, not in the name of brute force or raw plunder, both of which are standard components of the exercise, but in the name of a noble ideal. Joseph Conrad's most famous story, *Heart of Darkness,* is an ironic, even terrifying enactment of this thesis, that—as his narrator Marlow puts it—"the conquest of the earth, which mostly means the taking it away from those who have a different complexion or slightly flatter noses than ourselves, is not a pretty thing when you look into it too much. What redeems it is the idea only. An idea at the back of it, not a sentimental pretence but an idea; and an unselfish belief in the idea—something you can set up, and bow down before, and offer a sacrifice to."

In response to this sort of logic, two things occur. One is that competing powers invent their own theory of cultural or civilizational destiny in order to justify their actions abroad. Britain had such a theory, Germany had one, Belgium had one, and of course in the concept of manifest destiny, the United States had one, too. These redeeming ideas dignify the practice of competition and clash, whose real purpose, as Conrad quite accurately saw, was self-aggrandizement, power, conquest, treasure, and unrestrained self-pride. I would go so far as to say that what we today call the rhetoric of identity, by which a member of one ethnic or religious or national or cultural group puts that group at the center of the world, derives from that period of imperial competition at the end of the nineteenth century. And this in turn provokes the concept of "worlds at war" that quite obviously is at the heart of Huntington's article. It received its most frightening futuristic application

in H. G. Wells's fable *The War of the Worlds,* which, recall, expands the concept to include a battle between this world and a distant, interplanetary one.
In the related fields of political economy, geography, anthropology, and historiography, the theory that each "world" is self-enclosed, has its own
boundaries and special territory, is applied to the world map, to the structure
of civilizations, to the notion that each race has a special destiny, psychology,
ethos, and so on. All these ideas, almost without exception, are based not on
the harmony but on the conflict, or clash, between worlds. It is evident in
the works of Gustav LeBon (cf. *The World in Revolt*) and in such relatively
forgotten works as F. S. Marvin's *Western Races and the World* (1922) and
George Henry Lane-Fox Pitt Rivers's *The Clash of Culture and the Contact of
Races* (1927).

The second thing that happens is that, as Huntington himself concedes,
the lesser peoples, the objects of the imperial gaze, so to speak, respond by
resisting their forcible manipulation and settlement. We now know that
active primary resistance to the white man began the moment he set foot in
places like Algeria, East Africa, India, and elsewhere. Later, primary resistance
was succeeded by secondary resistance, the organization of political and cultural movements determined to achieve independence and liberation from
imperial control. At precisely the moment in the nineteenth century that a
rhetoric of civilizational self-justification begins to be widespread among the
European and American powers, a responding rhetoric among the colonized
peoples develops, one that speaks in terms of African or Asian or Arab unity,
independence, self-determination. In India, for example, the Congress party
was organized in 1880 and by the turn of the century had convinced the
Indian elite that only by supporting *Indian* languages, industry, and commerce could political freedom come; these are ours and ours alone, runs the
argument, and only by supporting our world against *theirs*—note the us-versus-them construction here—can we finally stand on our own. One finds a
similar logic at work during the Meiji period in modern Japan. Something
like this rhetoric of belonging is also lodged at the heart of each independence movement's nationalism, and shortly after World War Two it achieved
the result not only of dismantling the classical empires, but of winning independence for dozens and dozens of countries thereafter. India, Indonesia,
most of the Arab countries, Indochina, Algeria, Kenya, and so on: all these
emerged onto the world scene sometimes peacefully, sometimes as the effect
of internal developments (as in the Japanese instance), ugly colonial wars, or
wars of national liberation.

In both the colonial and the post-colonial context, therefore, rhetorics of
general cultural or civilizational specificity went in two potential directions,
one a utopian line that insisted on an overall pattern of integration and har-

mony among all peoples, the other a line which suggested that all civilizations were so specific and jealous, monotheistic, in effect, as to reject and war against all others. Among instances of the first are the language and institutions of the United Nations, founded in the aftermath of World War Two, and the subsequent development out of the U.N. of various attempts at world government predicated on coexistence, voluntary limitations of sovereignty, and the harmonious integration of peoples and cultures. Among the second are the theory and practice of the Cold War and, more recently, the idea that the clash of civilizations is, if not a necessity for a world of so many different parts, then a certainty. According to this view, cultures and civilizations are basically *separated* from each other. I do not want to be invidious here. In the Islamic world there has been a resurgence of rhetorics and movements stressing the inimicability of Islam with the West, just as in Africa, Europe, Asia, and elsewhere, movements have appeared that stress the need for excluding designated others as undesirable. White apartheid in South Africa was such a movement, as is the current interest in Afrocentrism and a totally independent Western civilization to be found in Africa and the United States respectively.

The point of this short cultural history of the idea of the clash of civilizations is that people like Huntington are products of that history, and are shaped in their writing by it. Moreover, the language describing the clash is laced with considerations of power: the powerful use it to protect what they have and what they do, the powerless or less powerful use it to achieve parity, independence, or a comparative advantage with regard to the dominant power. Thus to build a conceptual framework around the notion of us-versus-them is in effect to pretend that the principal consideration is epistemological and natural—our civilization is known and accepted, theirs is different and strange—whereas in fact the framework separating us from them is belligerent, constructed, and situational. Within each civilizational camp, we will notice, there are official representatives of that culture or civilization who make themselves into its mouthpiece, who assign themselves the role of articulating "our" (or for that matter "their") essence. This always necessitates a fair amount of compression, reduction, and exaggeration. So on the first and most immediate level, then, statements about what "our" culture or civilization is, or ought to be, necessarily involve a contest over the definition. This is certainly true of Huntington, who writes his essay at a time in U.S. history when a great deal of turmoil has surrounded the very definition of Western civilization. Recall that in the United States many college campuses have been shaken during the past couple of decades over what the canon of Western civilization is, which books should be taught, which ones read or not read, included, or otherwise given attention. Places like Stanford and

Columbia debated the issue not simply because it was a matter of habitual academic concern but because the definition of the West and consequently of America was at stake.

Anyone who has the slightest understanding of how cultures work knows that defining a culture, saying what it is for members of the culture, is always a major and, even in undemocratic societies, a democratic contest. There are canonical authorities to be selected and regularly revised, debated, re-selected, or dismissed. There are ideas of good and evil, belonging or not belonging (the same and the different), hierarchies of value to be specified, discussed, re-discussed, and settled or not, as the case may be. Moreover, each culture defines its enemies, what stands beyond it and threatens it. For the Greeks beginning with Herodotus, anyone who did not speak Greek was automatically a barbarian, an Other to be despised and fought against. An excellent recent book by the French classicist François Hartog, *The Mirror of Herodotus*, shows how deliberately and painstakingly Herodotus sets about constructing an image of a barbarian Other in the case of the Scythians, more even than in the case of the Persians.

The official culture is that of priests, academies, and the state. It provides definitions of patriotism, loyalty, boundaries, and what I have called belonging. It is this official culture that speaks in the name of the whole, that tries to express the general will, the general ethos and idea which inclusively holds in the official past, the founding fathers and texts, the pantheon of heroes and villains, and so on, and excludes what is foreign or different or undesirable in the past. From it come the definitions of what may or may not be said, those prohibitions and proscriptions that are necessary to any culture if it is to have authority.

It is also true that in addition to the mainstream, official, or canonical culture there are dissenting or alternative unorthodox, heterodox cultures that contain many anti-authoritarian strains that compete with the official culture. These can be called the counter-culture, an ensemble of practices associated with various kinds of outsiders—the poor, the immigrants, artistic bohemians, workers, rebels, artists. From the counter-culture comes the critique of authority and attacks on what is official and orthodox. The great contemporary Arab poet Adonis has written a massive account of the relationship between orthodoxy and heterodoxy in Arabic culture and has shown the constant dialectic and tension between them. No culture is understandable without some sense of this ever-present source of creative provocation from the unofficial to the official; to disregard this sense of restlessness within each culture, and to assume that there is complete homogeneity between culture and identity, is to miss what is vital and fecund.

In the United States the debate about what is American has gone through a large number of transformations and sometimes dramatic shifts. When I was growing up, the Western film depicted Native Americans as evil devils to be destroyed or tamed; they were called Red Indians, and insofar as they had any function in the culture at large—this was as true of films as it was of the writing of academic history—it was to be a foil to the advancing course of white civilization. Today that has changed completely. Native Americans are seen as victims, not villains, of the country's Western progress. There has even been a change in the status of Columbus. There are even more dramatic reversals in the depictions of African Americans and women. Toni Morrison has noted that in classic American literature there is an obsession with whiteness, as Melville's Moby Dick and Poe's Arthur Gordon Pym so eloquently testify. Yet she says the major male and white writers of the nineteenth and twentieth centuries, men who shaped the canon of what we have known as American literature, created their works by using whiteness as a way of avoiding, curtaining off, and rendering invisible the African presence in the midst of our society. The very fact that Toni Morrison writes her novels and criticism with such success and brilliance now underscores the extent of the change from the world of Melville and Hemingway to that of Du Bois, Baldwin, Langston Hughes, and Toni Morrison. Which vision is the real America, and who can lay claim to represent and define it? The question is a complex and deeply interesting one, but it cannot be settled by reducing the whole matter to a few clichés.

A recent view of the difficulties involved in cultural contests whose object is the definition of a civilization can be found in Arthur Schlesinger's little book *The Disuniting of America.* As a mainstream historian Schlesinger is understandably troubled by the fact that emergent and immigrant groups in the United States have disputed the official, unitary fable of America as it used to be represented by the great classical historians of this country, men like Bancroft, Henry Adams, and more recently Richard Hofstadter. They want the writing of history to reflect, not only an America that was conceived of and ruled by patricians and landowners, but an America in which slaves, servants, laborers, and poor immigrants played an important but as yet unacknowledged role. The narratives of such people, silenced by the great discourses whose source was Washington, the investment banks of New York, the universities of New England, and the great industrial fortunes of the Middle West, have come to disrupt the slow progress and unruffled serenity of the official story. They ask questions, interject the experiences of social unfortunates, and make the claims of frankly lesser peoples—of women, Asian and African Americans, and various other minorities, sexual as well as ethnic. Whether or not one agrees with Schlesinger's *cri de coeur,* there is no disagreeing with his underlying thesis that the writing of history is the royal road to the definition of a country, that the identity of a society is in large part a function of historical interpretation, which is fraught with contested claims and counter-claims. The United States is in just such a fraught situation today.

There is a similar debate inside the Islamic world today which, in the often hysterical outcry about the threat of Islam, Islamic fundamentalism, and terrorism that one encounters so often in the Western media, is often lost sight of completely. Like any other major world culture, Islam contains within itself an astonishing variety of currents and counter-currents, most of them undiscerned by tendentious Orientalist scholars for whom Islam is an object of fear and hostility, or by journalists who do not know any of the languages or relevant histories and are content to rely on persistent stereotypes that have lingered in the West since the tenth century. Iran today—which has become the target of a politically opportunistic attack by the United States—is in the throes of a stunningly energetic debate about law, freedom, personal responsibility, and tradition that is simply not covered by Western reporters. Charismatic lecturers and intellectuals—clerical and non-clerical alike—carry on the tradition of Shariati, challenging centers of power and orthodoxy with impunity and, it would seem, great popular success. In Egypt two major civil cases involving intrusive religious interventions in the lives of an intellectual and a celebrated filmmaker respectively have resulted in the victory of both over orthodoxy (I refer here to the cases of Nasir Abu Zeid and Yousef Chahine). And I myself have argued in a recent book (*The Politics of Dispossession*, 1994) that far from there being a surge of Islamic fundamentalism as it is reductively described in the Western media, there is a great deal of secular opposition to it, in the form of various contests over the interpretation of *sunnah* in matters of law, personal conduct, political decision-making, and so on. Moreover, what is often forgotten is that movements like Hamas and Islamic Jihad are essentially protest movements that go against the capitulationist policies of the PLO and mobilize the will to resist Israeli occupation practices, expropriation of land, and the like.

I find it surprising and indeed disquieting that Huntington gives no indication anywhere in his essay that he is aware of these complex disputes, or that he realized that the nature and identity of a civilization are never taken as unquestioned axioms by every single member of that civilization. Far from the Cold War being the defining horizon of the past few decades, I would say that it is this extremely widespread attitude of questioning and skepticism toward age-old authority that characterizes the post-war world in both East and West. Nationalism and decolonization forced the issue by bringing whole populations to consider the question of nationality in the era after the white colonist had left. In Algeria, for example, today the site of a bloody contest between Islamists and an aging and discredited government, the debate has taken violent forms. But it is a real debate and a fierce contest nonetheless. Having defeated the French in 1962, the National Front for the Liberation of Algeria (FLN) declared itself to be the bearer of a newly liberated Algerian, Arab, and Muslim identity. For the first time in the modern history of the place, Arabic became the language of instruction, state socialism its political creed, non-alignment its foreign affairs posture. In the process of conducting itself as a one-party embodiment of all these things, the FLN grew into a massive, atrophied bureaucracy, its economy depleted, its leaders stagnating in the position of an unyielding oligarchy. Opposition arose not only from Muslim clerics and leaders but from the Berber minority, submerged in the all-purpose discourse of a supposedly single Algerian identity. The political crisis of the past few years, then, represents a several-sided contest for power, and for the right to decide the nature of Algerian identity: what is Islamic about it, and what kind of Islam, what is national, what Arab and Berber, and so on.

To Huntington, what he calls "civilization identity" is a stable and undisturbed thing, like a roomful of furniture in the back of your house. This is extremely far from the truth, not just in the Islamic world but throughout the entire surface of the globe. To emphasize the differences among cultures and civilizations—incidentally, I find his use of the words "culture" and "civilization" extremely sloppy, precisely because for him the two words represent fixed and reified objects, rather than the dynamic, ceaselessly turbulent things that they in fact are—is completely to ignore the literally unending debate or contest (to use the more active and energetic of the two words) about defining the culture or civilization within those civilizations, including various "Western" ones. These debates completely undermine any idea of a fixed identity, and hence of relationships between identities, what Huntington considers to be a sort of ontological fact of political existence, to wit the clash of civilizations. You don't have to be an expert on China, Japan, Korea, and India to know that. There is the American instance I mentioned earlier. Or there is the German case, in which a major debate has been taking place ever since the end of World War Two about the nature of German culture, as to whether Nazism derived logically from its core, or whether it was an aberration.

But there is more to the question of identity even than that. In the field of cultural and rhetorical studies, a series of recent discoveries/advances has given us a much clearer insight not only into the contested, dynamic nature of cultural identity, but into the extent to which the very idea of identity itself involves fantasy, manipulation, invention, construction. During the 1970s Hayden White published an extremely influential work called *Metahistory*.

It is a study of several nineteenth-century historians—Marx, Michelet, and Nietzsche among them—and how their reliance upon one or a series of tropes (figures of speech) determines the nature of their vision of history. Thus Marx, for instance, is committed to a particular poetics in his writing which allows him to understand the nature of progress and alienation in history according to a particular narrative model, stressing the difference in society between form and substance. The point of White's extremely rigorous and quite brilliant analysis of Marx and the other historians is that he shows us how their histories are best understood, not according to criteria of "realness" but rather according to how their internal rhetorical and discursive strategies work: it is these, rather than facts, that make the visions of Tocqueville or Croce or Marx actually work as a system, not any external source in the so-called real world.

The effect of White's book, as much as the effect of Michel Foucault's studies, is to draw attention away from the existence of veridic confirmations for ideas that might be provided by the natural world, and focus it instead on the kind of language used, which is seen as shaping the components of a writer's vision. Rather than the idea of clash, for instance, deriving from a real clash in the world, we would come to see it as deriving instead from the strategies of Huntington's prose, which in turn relies on what I would call a managerial poetics, a strategy for assuming the existence of stable and metaphorically defined studies called civilizations which the writer proceeds quite emotively to manipulate, as in the phrase "the crescent-shaped Islamic bloc, from the bulge of Africa to central Asia, has bloody borders." I am not saying that Huntington's language is emotive and shouldn't be, but rather that quite revealingly it is, the way all language functions in the poetic way analyzed by Hayden White. What is evident from Huntington's language is the way he uses figurative language to accentuate the distance between "our" world— normal, acceptable, familiar, logical—and, as an especially striking example, the world of Islam, with its bloody borders, bulging contours, and so on. This suggests not so much analysis on Huntington's part but a series of determinations which, as I said earlier, creates the very clash he seems in his essay to be discovering and pointing to.

Too much attention paid to managing and clarifying the clash of cultures obliterates the fact of a great, often silent exchange and dialogue between them. What culture today—whether Japanese, Arab, European, Korean, Chinese, or Indian—has not had long, intimate, and extraordinarily rich contacts with other cultures? There is no exception to this exchange at all. One wishes that conflict managers would have paid attention to and understood the meaning of the mingling of different musics, for example, in the work of Olivier Messiaen or Toru Takemitsu. For all the power and influence of the various national schools, what is most arresting in contemporary music is that no one can draw a boundary around any of it; cultures are often most naturally themselves when they enter into partnerships with one another, as in music with its extraordinary receptivity to developments in the musics of other societies and continents. Much the same is true of literature, where readers of, for example, García Márquez, Mahfuz, and Oe exist far beyond the boundaries imposed by language and nation. In my own field of comparative literature there is an epistemological commitment to the relationships between literatures, to their reconciliation and harmony, despite the existence of powerful ideological and national barriers between them. And this sort of cooperative, collective enterprise is what one misses in the proclaimers of an undying clash between cultures: the lifelong dedication that has existed in all modern societies among scholars, artists, musicians, visionaries, and prophets to try to come to terms with the Other, with that other society or culture that seems so foreign and so distant. One thinks of Joseph Needham and his lifelong study of China, or in France, of Louis Massignon, his pilgrimage within Islam. It seems to me that unless we emphasize and maximize the spirit of cooperation and humanistic exchange—and here I speak not simply of uninformed delight or of amateurish enthusiasm for the exotic, but rather of profound existential commitment and labor on behalf of the other—we are going to end up superficially and stridently banging the drum for "our" culture in opposition to all others.

Two other recent seminal works of cultural analysis are relevant here. In the compilation of essays entitled *The Invention of Tradition* and edited by Terence Ranger and Eric Hobsbawm, two of the most distinguished historians alive today, the authors argue that tradition, far from being the unshakable order of inherited wisdom and practice, is frequently a set of invented practices and beliefs used in mass societies to create a sense of identity at a time when organic solidarities—such as those of family, village, and clan—have broken down. Thus the emphasis on tradition in the nineteenth and twentieth centuries is a way that rulers can claim to have legitimacy, even though that legitimacy is more or less manufactured. In India, as a case in point, the British invented an impressive array of rituals to celebrate Queen Victoria's receipt of the title of Empress of India in 1872. By doing so, and by claiming that the durbars, or grand processions, commemorating the event had a long history in India, the British were able to give her rule a pedigree that it did not have in fact, but came to have in the form of invented traditions. In another context, sports rituals like the football game, a relatively recent practice, are regarded as the culmination of an age-old celebration of sporting activity, whereas in fact they are a recent way of diverting large numbers of people. The point of all this is that a great deal of what used to be thought of as settled fact, or tradition, is revealed to be a fabrication for mass consumption in the here and now.

To people who speak solely of the clash of civilizations, there exists no inkling of this possibility. For them cultures and civilizations may change, develop, regress, and disappear, but they remain mysteriously fixed in their identity, their essence graven in stone, so to speak, as if there were a universal consensus somewhere agreeing to the six civilizations Huntington posits at the beginning of his essay. My contention is that no such consensus exists, or if it does, it can hardly withstand the analytic scrutiny brought to bear by analyses of the kind provided by Hobsbawm and Ranger. So in reading about the clash of civilizations we are less likely to assent to analysis of the clash than we are to ask the question, Why do you pinion civilizations into so unyielding an embrace, and why then do you go on to describe their relationship as one of basic conflict, as if the borrowing and overlappings between them were not a much more interesting and significant feature?

Finally, my third example of cultural analysis tells us a great deal about the possibilities of actually creating a civilization retrospectively and making that creation into a frozen definition, in spite of the evidence of great hybridity and mixture. The book is *Black Athena,* the author, the Cornell political scientist Martin Bernal. The conception most of us have today about classical Greece, Bernal says, does not at all correspond with what Greek authors of that period say about it. Ever since the early nineteenth century, Europeans and Americans have grown up with an idealized picture of Attic harmony and grace, imagining Athens as a place where enlightened Western philosophers like Plato and Aristotle taught their wisdom, where democracy was born, and where, in every possible significant way, a Western mode of life completely different from that of Asia or Africa held sway. Yet to read a large number of ancient authors accurately is to note that many of them comment on the existence of Semitic and African elements in Attic life. Bernal takes the further step of demonstrating by the skillful use of a great many sources that Greece was originally a colony of Africa, more particularly of Egypt, and that Phoenician and Jewish traders, sailors, and teachers contributed most of what we know today as classical Greek culture, which he sees as an amalgam therefore of African, Semitic, and later northern influences.

In the most compelling part of *Black Athena,* Bernal goes on to show how with the growth of European, and in particular German, nationalism the original mixed portrait of Attic Greece that obtained into the eighteenth century was gradually expunged of all its non-Aryan elements, just as many years later the Nazis decided to burn all books and ban all authors considered non-German, non-Aryan. So from being the product of an invasion from the South—that is, Africa—as in reality it really was, classical Greece was progressively transformed into the product of an invasion from the Aryan north. Purged of its troublesome non-European elements, Greece thereafter has stood in the Western self-definition—an expedient one to be sure—as its fons et origo, its source of sweetness and light. The principle underlined by Bernal is the extent to which pedigrees, dynasties, lineages, and predecessors are changed to suit the political needs of a later time. Of the unfortunate results this produced in the case of a self-created white Aryan European civilization none of us need to be convinced.

What is even more troubling to me about proclaimers of the clash of civilizations is how oblivious they seem of all we now know as historians and as cultural analysts about the way definitions of these cultures themselves are so contentious. Rather than accepting the incredibly naive and deliberately reductive notion that civilizations are identical with themselves, and that is all, we must always ask which civilizations are intended, created, and defined by whom, and for what reason. Recent history is too full of instances in which the defense of Judeo-Christian values has been urged as a way of quelling dissent or unpopular opinions for us passively to assume that "everyone" knows what those values are, how they are meant to be interpreted, and how they may or may not be implemented in society.

Many Arabs would say that their civilization is really Islam, just as some Westerners—Australians and Canadians and some Americans—might not want to be included in so large and vaguely defined a category as Western. And when a man like Huntington speaks of the "common objective elements" that supposedly exist in every culture, he leaves the analytic and historical world altogether, preferring instead to find refuge inside large and ultimately meaningless categories.

As I have argued in several of my own books, in today's Europe and the United States what is described as "Islam" belongs to the discourse of Orientalism, a construction fabricated to whip up feelings of hostility and antipathy against a part of the world that happens to be of strategic importance for its oil, its threatening adjacence to the Christian world, and its formidable history of competitiveness with the West. Yet this is a very different thing from what, to Muslims who live within its domain, Islam really is. There is a world of difference between Islam in Indonesia and Islam in Egypt. By the same token, the volatility of today's struggle over the meaning of Islam is evident in Egypt, where the secular powers of society are in conflict with various Islamic protest movements and reformers over the nature of Islam. In such circumstances the easiest, and the least accurate, thing is to say: *that* is the world of Islam, and see how it is all terrorists and fundamentalists, and see also how different *they* are from us.

But the truly weakest part of the clash of civilizations thesis is the rigid separation assumed among civilizations, despite the overwhelming evidence that today's world is in fact a world of mixtures, of migrations, of crossings over. One of the major crises affecting countries like France, Britain, and the United States has been brought about by the realization now dawning everywhere that no culture or society is purely one thing. Sizeable minorities—North Africans in France, the African and Caribbean and Indian populations in Britain, Asian and African elements in the United States—dispute the idea that civilizations that prided themselves on being homogenous can continue to do so. There are no insulated cultures or civilizations. Any attempt made to separate them into the water-tight compartments alleged by Huntington does damage to their variety, their diversity, their sheer complexity of elements, their radical hybridity. The more insistent we are on the separation of cultures and civilizations, the more inaccurate we are about ourselves and others. The notion of an exclusionary civilization is, to my way of thinking, an impossible one. The real question, then, is whether in the end we want to work for civilizations that are separate or whether we should be taking the more integrative, but perhaps more difficult, path, which is to try to see them as making one vast whole whose exact contours are impossible for one person to grasp, but whose certain existence we can intuit and feel. In any case, a number of political scientists, economists, and cultural analysts have for some years been speaking of an integrative world system, largely economic, it is true, but nonetheless knitted together, overriding many of the clashes spoken of so hastily and imprudently by Huntington.

What Huntington quite astonishingly overlooks is the phenomenon referred to frequently in the literature as the globalization of capital. In 1980 Willy Brandt and some associates published *North-South: A Program for Survival.* In it the authors noted that the world was now divided into two vastly uneven regions: a small industrial North, comprising the major European, American, and Asian economic powers, and an enormous South, comprising the former Third World plus a large number of new, extremely impoverished nations. The political problem of the future would be how to imagine their relationships as the North would get richer, the South poorer, and the world more interdependent. Let me quote now from an essay by the Duke political scientist Arif Dirlik that goes over much of the ground covered by Huntington in a way that is more accurate and persuasive:

> The situation created by global capitalism helps explain certain phenomena that have become apparent over the last two or three decades, but especially since the eighties: global motions of peoples (and, therefore, cultures), the weakening of boundaries (among societies, as well as among social categories), the replications in societies internally of inequalities and discrepancies once associated

with colonial differences, simultaneous homogenization and fragmentation within and across societies, the interpenetration of the global and the local, and the disorganization of a world conceived in terms of three worlds or nation-states. Some of these phenomena have also contributed to an appearance of equalization of differences within and across societies, as well as of democratization within and among societies. What is ironic is that the managers of this world situation themselves concede that they (or their organizations) now have the power to appropriate the local for the global, to admit different cultures into the realm of capital (only to break them down and remake them in accordance with the requirements of production and consumption), and even to reconstitute subjectivities across national boundaries to create producers and consumers more responsive to the operations of capital. Those who do not respond, or the "basket cases" that are not essential to those operations—four-fifths of the global population by the managers' count—need not be colonized; they are simply marginalized. What the new flexible production has made possible is that it is no longer necessary to utilize explicit coercion against labor at home or in colonies abroad. Those peoples or places that are not responsive to the needs (or demands) of capital, or are too far gone to respond "efficiently," simply find themselves out of its pathways. And it is easier even than in the heyday of colonialism or modernization theory to say convincingly: It is their fault. (*Critical Inquiry,* Winter 1994, 351)

In view of these depressing and even alarming actualities, it does seem to me ostrich-like to suggest that we in Europe and the United States should maintain our civilization by holding all the others at bay, increasing the rifts between peoples in order to prolong our dominance. That is, in effect, what Huntington is arguing, and one can quite easily understand why it is that his essay was published in *Foreign Affairs,* and why so many policy-makers have drifted toward it as allowing the United States to extend the mind-set of the Cold War into a different time and for a new audience. Much more productive and useful is a new global mentality that sees the dangers we face from the standpoint of the whole human race. These dangers include the pauperization of most of the globe's population; the emergence of virulent local, national, ethnic, and religious sentiment, as in Bosnia, Rwanda, Lebanon, Chechnya, and elsewhere; the decline of literacy and the onset of a new illiteracy based on electronic modes of communication, television, and the new global information superhighway; the fragmentation and threatened disappearance of the grand narratives of emancipation and enlightenment. Our most precious asset in the face of such a dire transformation of tradition and of history is the emergence of a sense of community, understanding, sympathy, and hope which is the direct opposite of what in his essay Huntington has provoked. If I may quote some lines by the great Martiniqean poet Aimé Césaire that I used in my recent book *Culture and Imperialism:*

Edward W. Said

> but the work of man is only just beginning
> and it remains to man to conquer all
> the violence entrenched in the recesses of his passion
>
> And no race possesses the monopoly of beauty,
> of intelligence, of force, and there
> is a place for all at the rendez-vous of victory.

In what they imply, these sentiments prepare the way for a dissolution of cultural barriers as well as of the civilizational pride that prevents the kind of benign globalism already to be found, for instance, in the environmental movement, in scientific cooperation, in the universal concern for human rights, in concepts of global thought that stress community and sharing over racial, gender, or class dominance. It would seem to me, therefore, that efforts to return the community of civilizations to a primitive stage of narcissistic struggle must be understood not as descriptions about how in fact they behave but rather as incitements to wasteful conflict and unedifying chauvinism. And that seems to be exactly what we do not need.

17

Hermeneutical Circles, Rhetorical Triangles, and Transversal Diagonals

Calvin O. Schrag

THE AIM OF THIS ESSAY is to provide a thought experiment on how to maneuver an alliance of hermeneutics with rhetoric. I argue that hermeneutics is delimited by the practice of rhetoric, and in turn both hermeneutics and rhetoric need to be refigured within the space of transversal communication.

Hermeneutics and the Search for Meaning

Hermeneutics as theory and practice of interpretation stimulates an economy of meanings, latent as well as manifest, that is at play in texts and actions, in text analogues and action analogues, while it addresses both actual and potential misunderstandings. Hermeneutics constitutes its operating matrix as a part-whole relationship and finds its root metaphor in the circle. The aim of hermeneutical understanding is to comprehend the part through the whole and the whole through the part. Whether dealing with a text complex or a configuration of action, the hermeneut attends to the parts of the text and particular acts in relation to other parts and other acts, all of which have meaning only recursively as they are placed back into the context of a configurative whole. Meaning is garnered to the degree that an intercalation of part and whole is achieved, evincing the circularity of movement from part to whole and whole to part. Charles Taylor articulates this point with some felicity when, addressing the matter of the circularity of text interpretation, he states the case as follows: "The circle can also be put in terms of part-whole relations: we are trying to establish a reading for the whole text, and for this we appeal to readings of its partial expressions; and yet because we are dealing with meaning, with making sense, where expressions only make sense or not in relation to others, the readings of partial expressions depend on those of others, and ultimately of the whole."[1]

There is, however, another display of circularity in the hermeneutical undertaking. Not only is there a circular to and fro between part and whole, there is also a circularity of interpretive understanding in the variation and expansion of perspectives on the part-whole configuration itself. Within this circularity of perspectives there is only a movement between and among perspectives; there is no movement beyond perspectivity to a vantage point outside the circle of understanding. To be sure, advances and refinements in the quest for meaning are possible through a revision of perspectives that results from an encounter with other perspectives, but there appears to be no exit from the circularity of perspectivity as such. This marks another dimension of the circularity of hermeneutical thought and discourse.

It is of vital importance, however, that we not mistake the circularity of hermeneutical thought and discourse for the obtrusive *circulus vitiosus* that invalidates linear and quantitative calculating and reckoning. The hermeneutical circle is not a "vicious circle," an aberration of proper entailment that would be avoidable by carefully attending to the rules of inference. Hermeneutics is not governed by the rules of linear/representational thinking. True, such rules may have utility in an analytical explanation of the constitutive parts of a portion of text or a pattern of action and in this manner contribute to the understanding of a part-whole complex. Such would be the case, for example, in attending to the rules of grammar in analyzing an obscure and problematic sentence structure within a wider portion of text. The comprehension of a perspective on a part-whole intercalation, however, proceeds not from rules of method somehow determined in advance but rather from a *taking as* posture. Hence, the propriety of the vocabulary of the "hermeneutical as." A text under consideration is *taken as* a certain genre of discourse— for example, a scientific document, a political satire, a homily, a historical account, a piece of fiction, a treatise on morality. A display of behavior is *taken as* an expression of meaningful action—a friendly gesture, a physical threat, an obscene sign, a cry for help.

Whether interpreting a text or an action, there is always a foregrounding of both the texture and range of meanings that come to bear. The task of hermeneutics is to sort out, consolidate, describe, and redescribe these meanings by attending to the partial expressions as they relate to other partial expressions in pursuit of an understanding and articulation of the whole. Indeed, different perspectives on the integration of part and whole may arise, requiring a "correction" of any particular perspective through a contrastive

comparison with another actual or possible perspective. This strategy of correction is not a matter of landing on the correct perspective and finally getting it right but rather a dynamics of opening up new possibilities through
which delivered perspectives might be enriched. But there is no escape from
the circling from part to whole nor from the circularity of revisable perspectives. Given this state of affairs, Heidegger's advice may be peculiarly judicious: "What is decisive is not to get out of the circle but to come into it in
the right way."[2]

The consequences of the hermeneutical requirement to come into the circle in the right way, one soon finds out, are both broad and deep. The scope
of hermeneutics does appear to enjoy a kind of ubiquity, prompting some
hermeneuts to speak of a "universal hermeneutics."[3] One can readily observe
that hermeneutics has spread its mantle over a variety of discourses and disciplines. In the pantheon of Hermes one finds hermeneutics of the social sciences and hermeneutics of the natural sciences; hermeneutics of texts and
hermeneutics of action; hermeneutics of jurisprudence and hermeneutics of
medical practices; hermeneutics of culture forms and heremeneutics of *Exis-
tenz*. The range of hermeneutics is broad. It is also deep. In each of the discourses and disciplines that exhibit its traces it goes all the way down. There
is no terminus ad quem in the hermeneutical project, no end point, no coming to rest in a brute, isolated, hard-knob, indubitable *fact*. Indeed, there are
no facts without interpretation. Facts become facts only when they are *taken
as* such within a constituted disciplinary matrix. The interior dynamics of
hermeneutics is that of a progression from one interpretation-fact complex
to another. This is the sense in which interpretation goes all the way down.
Clearly, it does not go all the way down in the sense of reaching a stable
foundation of incorrigible facts and unimpeachable assertoric claims. In this
respect, hermeneutics is antifoundationalist both in attitude and strategy.
The break with epistemological foundationalism is decisive.[4]

The entwinement of fact and interpretation and the ensuing rapture with
epistemological foundationalism have certain consequences for the classical
problem of meaning and reference as defined in the annals of modernity.
Hermeneutics remains a quest for meaning, but the understanding and use
of *meaning* is significantly refigured. Meaning is no longer understood simply
as a concept or a set of concepts issuing from an insular and sovereign cogito
seeking commerce with an epistemic "object" (physical body, sense datum,
intuited essence, proposition, etc.). Hermeneutics effects a *Verstellung,* a
dissimulation, of both the knowing subject and the object as known. The
subject-object dichotomy as enframed by modern epistemology is dismantled from both sides, as it were. The abstract Cartesian thinking subject is
refashioned into an embodied, self-interpreting, discursive, and agentive sub-

ject; the object of reference is reinscribed as a figure-against-a-background. In the move from objectifying ostensive reference to hermeneutical reference, the referent is no longer determined as an isolatable and self-identical datum but is refigured as that which shows itself against the contours of an intentionality-laden background. Discourse remains discourse about something, but the "aboutness" in question does not turn on the isolation of discrete properties and relations. The aboutness, the terminus of reference, if you will, is more global, having to do with the *world-as-experienced* in perception, discourse, and action.

Let us suppose that a portion of discourse turns on the life and times of former president John F. Kennedy. John F. Kennedy as the proper referent at issue in the discussion has its aboutness, its power of indication, fulfilled only through the insinuation of a background of political institutions and social practices that situate Kennedy as "the former president of the United States." One could say, in the vocabulary of phenomenology, that what is referred to is John F. Kennedy's "being-in-the-world." Meanings put into play by self-interpreting speakers and actors find their fulfillment in a reference to a *lifeworld*. Such is the route of hermeneutical reference, which, as I have argued elsewhere, is complemented by a hermeneutical self-implicature, through which the subject, deconstructed as an epistemological sovereign ego-cogito, is reclaimed as an implicate in the life of discourse and action.[5]

Although the response of hermeneutics to the classical problem of meaning and reference, by way of a refiguration of the problem itself, comprises a notable advance, there are certain emergent issues in this response that require further critical attention. To be sure, within a hermeneutical posture there is a move beyond epistemological protocols of verification and truth conditions legislated in advance of inquiry; however, there remains a gesture in the direction of coherence as a quasitheory of truth, given the strong commitment to holism. In its antifoundationalist stance, hermeneutics severs relations with the classical representational theory of knowledge and the correspondence theory of truth. However, it continues to make purchases on the coherence theory of truth in defining the project of interpretive understanding as one of integrating part with whole and whole with part.

This appetition for a holism, in both practical and theoretical understanding, confers a certain privilege upon unity and totality. The dynamics of hermeneutical understanding is that of a shuttling to and from parts and wholes, oriented toward an agreement on the meaning of a particular part-whole configuration. But this accentuation of a quest for unity and solidarity of agreement among the community of interpreters invites a troublesome *aporia* in the face of insurmountable conflicts of interpretation. It is precisely at this juncture, where the orientation toward common understanding and shared perspectives encounters a conflict of interpretation—or, indeed, as in some cases, a radical dissensus—that delimitation of the hermeneutical project is required. We need to effect a shift of inquiry standpoint, involving a suspension of the heavy demands for unity, coherence, and consensus in our sundry projects of understanding and explanation. The hermeneutical circle lacks the requisite resources for productively addressing conflicts of interpretation. Its presuppositions do not allow a move to the outside of the circle, to a supplementary standpoint from which resolutions to conflict situations and ruptures of consensus would be productively addressed. Might such a delimitation of and supplement to the hermeneutical circle be found in the rhetorical triangle?

The Consequences of Rhetoric

Although the hermeneutical demand is both broad and deep in its orientation toward a solidarity of consensus against the backcloth of a valorization of unity and totality, it encounters difficulties in dealing with the intrusion of difference in situations of conflicts of interpretation. Let us now explore possible resources in rhetoric for addressing the difficulties occasioned by the event of difference within the hermeneutical economy.

It is important to keep in mind that hermeneutics and rhetoric have traveled together over a considerable length of time. Heidegger has called our attention to Aristotle's *Rhetoric* as comprising "the first systematic hermeneutics of the everydayness of Being with one another."[6] Gadamer, and on this point quite in accord with Heidegger, concludes that "the rhetorical and hermeneutical aspects of human linguisticality completely interpenetrate each other."[7] If such is indeed the case, then it would clearly follow that Gadamer's call for a "universal hermeneutics" needs to be supplemented with a call for a "universal rhetoric." Rhetoric, like hermeneutics, goes all the way down and all the way back. They enjoy a co-primordial ubiquity.

Surely there is a close connection between hermeneutics and rhetoric. Yet the one cannot be simply analyzed into the other. They overlap, they interconnect, they supplement each other; but one cannot be reduced to the other. As Paul Ricoeur has well stated, rhetoric and hermeneutics each speaks for itself. "Rhetoric remains the art of arguing with a view to persuading an audience that one opinion is preferable to its rival. . . . Hermeneutics remains the art of interpreting texts within a context which is distinct from that of the author and from that of the texts' original audience with a view to discovering new dimensions of reality."[8] Closely related yet distinct, the required task thus becomes the articulation of the lines of force and vectors of interplay that stimulate the amalgamated hermeneutical-rhetorical economy.

The thesis I wish to propose concerning the hermeneutic-rhetoric connection is that rhetoric at once delimits and enriches hermeneutical understanding in accentuating the role of the other and the play of difference. In performing this service rhetoric reins in the hermeneut's strong proclivities to unity, solidarity, and consensus. The recognition of alterity and difference, in turn, has certain consequences for addressing the *aporia* of the conflict of interpretations, which hermeneutics by itself is unable to resolve.

The role of the other and the play of alterity in the rhetorical situation come to prominence through the triangulation of rhetor and interlocutor intersecting the *topoi* that occasion the discourse. Whereas the root metaphor of hermeneutics is the circle, the root metaphor of rhetoric is the triangle.[9] Rhetoric, properly understood as collaborative discourse and action designed for the purpose of persuasion, is a project of communication to, for, and with *the other*. The aim of rhetoric is communication. The modes of this communication vary from confronting the face of the other in a dialogic transaction, to addressing a wider audience on issues of public concern, to the uses of texts and the technology of telecommunication, to forms of personal behavior and institutional action. In attending to the modes of persuasive communication in the rhetorical situation it is important to recognize the integrity of a rhetoric of action that is not simply reducible to a rhetoric of the spoken or the written word. One persuades by actions as well as by words. Kenneth Burke's notion of "administrative rhetoric" is particularly illustrative of this point.[10]

The alterity at issue in the dynamics of persuasive communication is inscribed on two nodal points in the triangulation of the rhetorical economy. Not only is there the otherness of the interlocutor/addressee/reader, there is also the otherness of the *topoi*, the topics, which have to do with the plethora of beliefs, practices, and institutions that congeal into a variety of forms of life. Language is already on the scene and social practices and institutions are already in play when a rhetor engages an interlocutor. Various meanings and lifestyles are already extant, insinuated within the delivered discourses and practices. When a rhetor seeks to persuade an interlocutor to vote for a particular candidate for a state or national office, the meanings of democracy and representational government are already inscribed in a lifeworld that antedates their conversations. When an adherent to a religion of the East engages an adherent to a religion of the West in dialogue, the background of religious thought and practices that divide East and West impinge, sometimes obtrusively, upon the participants in the dialogue. It is thus that the rhetorical situation exhibits an alterity that antedates the otherness in the rhetor-interlocutor dyad, an alterity of lifeworld horizons to which each in different ways responds.

The lifeworld, with its multiple patterns of meaning, is indeed the proper referent in the rhetorical situation, enabling one to speak of a dynamics of "rhetorical reference" that at once delimits, supplements, and enriches the dynamics of the circularity of "hermeneutical reference." Rhetorical reference is centrifugal rather than centripetal, adventitious, coming from the outside as it were, impinging upon rhetor and interlocutor alike, effecting an incursive disclosure, setting the requirement for each speaker to respond to the discourses and actions of a lifeworld that is not of his or her doing. Rhetoric thus finds its occasion not in a condemnation to subjective freedom (à la Jean-Paul Sartre) nor even in a condemnation to meaning (à la Maurice Merleau-Ponty) but more specifically in a condemnation to responsibility (à la Emmanuel Levinas) in which mortals—indeed, by virtue of their mortality—are called upon to respond to discourses and actions that are always already extant.

The requirement to respond to an incursive alterity of multiple and often heterogeneous beliefs and practices confers upon rhetoric its peculiar dynamics of communication—a communication that remains an existential struggle because of the diversity of perspectives that define our sociohistorical inherence. Given the multiplicity and heterogeneity of voices that invade the rhetorical situation, our projected goals of solidarity and consensus will need to be somewhat attenuated. It may be that the principle of unity that informs the ontology of the part-whole framework of hermeneutical inquiry will require modifications, as will the hermeneutical definition of understanding as a quest bent upon the attainment of solid agreement. The realities of the rhetorical situation appear to be such that any privileging of unity and totality and any prescription of a consensual solidarity will inevitably lead to a profound metaphysical disappointment.

The topography of rhetoric is more amenable than that of hermeneutics to the settlements of otherness on its terrain, and it is thus more ready to accept diversity and difference. In its dealings with diversity and difference, rhetoric is required to experiment with new strategies of argumentation and persuasion, probing possibilities for new forms of behavior and social organization. It is thus that rhetoric is able to place a premium on novelty, invention, and creativity. It supplements the weight placed on tradition in hermeneutical understanding by experimenting with the new and the untried. It conserves the past without succumbing to conservatism. It speaks from the past as it heeds the call of the future. In this manner rhetoric is forced to reckon with time, effecting a preserving function in its liaison with the discursive and institutional practices of the tradition as it engenders a creating function in its projection of new forms of discourse and action.[11]

In its distanciation from the discursive and institutional sediments within the tradition, intervening while it invents, rhetoric is able to supply a needed critical function, a standpoint for critique of tradition, convention, and ideology. The rationality of rhetoric finds a decisive expression in this critical function. One of the principal tasks of rhetoric is to bring traditional beliefs and practices to the bar of critical discernment and evaluation. We are thus able to find in this posture of critique what Hans Blumenberg seeks when he sets out to find in rhetoric "a form of rationality itself—a rational way of coming to terms with the provisionality of reason."[12] Inventing the new does not necessitate a toppling of the old, but it does call for a critical assessment and a mustering of arguments for an acceptance of some practices and cultural forms and a jettisoning of others. The rhetorician J. Robert Cox sees the critical principle of rhetoric emerging from a "dialectic of repetition and disavowal," which provides a space for a *critical* appropriation of traditional forms of life. Thanks to the dynamics of disavowal, the contents of a tradition are always placed under scrutiny, questioned, reevaluated, refigured, or indeed overturned.[13]

Cognizant of the incursion of alterity and the need for a critical assessment of the delivered contents of the tradition, rhetoric effects a delimitation of hermeneutics without simply jettisoning it. Rhetoric is more like a supplement to and complement of hermeneutics than a displacement of it, addressing the *aporia* of the conflict of interpretations bequeathed by hermeneutics in such a manner as to problematize the ideals of solidarity and consensus in recognition of the need to live with multiplicity and difference. Yet there is a troublesome tendency that travels with this delimitation of the quest for common understanding and solidifying agreement while accentuating the multiple, the different, and the other. The tendency is to valorize and celebrate difference over sameness to the point that the hermeneutic problematic of the conflict of interpretations is stood on its head. The consequences of such an embrace of difference is that conflict, the disruption of consensus, no longer poses a problem; the problem is placing a value on agreement and collaborative activity in the first place. Indeed, the proper disposition of discourse is then seen as being dissensus rather than consensus, disagreement rather than agreement.

This tendency has found its most illustrious avatar in the "rhetorical agonistics" proposed by the arch postmodernist Jean-François Lyotard. Rhetorical agonistics portrays rhetoric as a veritable agon, a war of minds and wills bent toward conflict rather than dialogue. Lyotard separates the "partisans of agonistics" from the "partisans of dialogue," extolling the economy of difference over the economy of sameness.[14] What underwrites the economy of rhetorical agonistics, if indeed one can speak of underwriting on such matters as these, is what Lyotard has named the *différend,* which as distinct from a litigation is an irremediable conflict between two parties that resists resolution for want of a common rule of judgment.[15]

It should be noted that a consequence of some effect ensues from Lyotard's hermeneutical agonistics, namely, that the proper end of discourse is dissensus rather than consensus, paralogy rather than commensurability. "As I have shown in the analysis of the pragmatics of science, consensus is only a particular state of discussion, not its end. Its end, on the contrary, is paralogy."[16] This rhetorical turn to an economy of agonistics, privileging dissensus over consensus, issues a bankruptcy notice to any hermeneutic of meaning oriented toward mutual understanding and solidarity in thought and discourse. The apparently ineradicable multiplicity and heterogeneity of beliefs and practices, courting at every juncture an irremediable conflict of interpretations and institutional programs, forestalls anything that would approximate a consensus or a meeting of minds. The hermeneutical circle is ruptured by a dissolution of its economy of coherence and unity—its appetition for part-whole totalization; it is replaced by a triangulation of rhetor, interlocutor, and heterogeneous practices, producing a situation in which the rhetor remains at war with the interlocutor in the face of insurmountable *différends.* The partisans of agonistics thus provide a somewhat curious resolution to the hermeneutical *aporia* of conflicting interpretations. Conflict, which for the hermeneut, as a partisan of dialogue, is a negativity to be avoided, becomes for the partisan of agonistics a state of affairs to be cultivated.

Transversal Communication

In this section I propose to delimit and resituate the hermeneutical and rhetorical tasks discussed in the previous sections in an effort to think beyond the resultant *aporias* in each. This will involve a reconsideration of the aims of discourse and the dynamics of communication by way of experimentation with a new grammar and a new root metaphor. The grammar is that of transversality, and the root metaphor is the diagonal instead of the circle or the triangle. Admittedly, the concept of transversality is not of recent invention. For some time it has been an underlaborer in the disciplines of mathematics, physics, physiology, anatomy, psychology, and philosophy. One of the more prominent philosophical uses of transversality occurs in Sartre's existentialist description of consciousness as "play of transversal intentionalities."[17] Sar-

tre's project is to displace a self-identical consciousness, grounded in a transcendental ego, with a consciousness that overruns any stable presence of
consciousness by way of concrete transversal intentionalities that bind it to
past consciousness through a recursive functioning.

The sense of transversality as it plays in the multiple disciplines is diagonal
transgression, lying across, extending over surfaces and lines, longitudinal
mass, bands of fibers, vertebrae, or moments of consciousness. In their lying
across and extending over, transversal vectors and lines of force exhibit a
convergence without coincidence, a conjuncture without identity. The root
metaphor of the diagonal is thus peculiarly apt, conveying the sense of cutting across and intersecting without coming to rest at any particular point,
surface, or moment.

Although Sartre's appropriation of the figure of transversality in his
description of the dynamics of consciousness is insightful and has its own
rewards, the figure has a wider applicability in the arenas of discourse and
action that mark out our variegated communicative engagements. Transversality as a feature of our social practices of discourse, action, and institutional
involvements defines the dynamics of moving across multiple contexts and
forms of human association, oriented toward an understanding of these multiple contexts without violating their otherness. Transversal thought and
communication recognizes the integrity of the beliefs and practices of the
other and critically engages the other so as to enhance an understanding of
that which is one's own. It enriches both self-understanding and the understanding of the other. The principle task is not to change the beliefs and practices of the other (although this may result from an ongoing communication)
but rather to understand the other. In its orientation toward an enriched
understanding of self and other, transversal communication continues the
hermeneutical project of seeking the better understanding (Besserverstehen)
that was proposed by Wilhelm Dilthey. However, it does so without the
heavy ontological investments in a unity-based holism that defined the classical hermeneutical program.

The dynamics of transversality is such that due regard is given to the particularity and historical specificity of social practices and culture forms. It
proceeds in recognition of the contextuality and conditionality of the multiple knowledge claims and valuations that define our historical situatedness.
Claims for contextless and unconditioned sources of universal truths are rendered problematic. Thought is informed by the trans-versal rather than the
universal. However, the recognition of the contextuality and historical specificity of our beliefs and practices need not catapult us into a historical relativism that views all thought and action as simply determined by the
particularities of our personal and social existence. Such would be the case

only if we failed to distinguish the *context conditioned* from the *context determined*. To say that the amalgam of our thought, discourse, and action is context conditioned is to recognize that a variety of cultural and historical influences inform what is believed, asserted, and practiced. But this surely is not to say that the totality of human thought and action is determined by particular contexts, which themselves would house, in a mysterious fashion, causal or quasi-causal forces that produce thought in the way electricity produces light. The transversal feature of thought and action enables a movement both *within* and *across* traditional beliefs and practices. Thought and action remain contextualized, but they are not determined by the particularities of any specific context within any specific tradition. It is thus that transversal lines of force are able to create a passage between the Scylla of a vacuous universalism and the Charybdis of an anarchic historicism. Transversal thought is *trans*-historical, neither ahistorical nor historicist, neither suspended above the historical nor suffocated within it.

Against the backdrop of the space and dynamics of transversality, effecting convergences without coincidence, situated betwixt and between the claims for universality and identity on the one hand and the valorization of particularity and difference on the other, I intend to address the resultant *aporias* in the hermeneutical and rhetorical endeavors. Because of its ontological commitments to unity and totality, marginalizing heterogeneity and alterity, hermeneutical understanding overdetermines the requirement for agreement and solidarity, thus lacking the resources to deal with conflicts of interpretation. Rhetoric, cognizant of the irruption of otherness and the play of multiplicity, supplements interpretation with argumentation and defines the field of our communicative practices as a battlefield, an agon of disputation, in which the most forceful argument has the best chance to persuade, if only for the moment.

To put the matter simply, we need to find a way of maneuvering between the imperatives of consensus and the celebration of dissensus, between solid agreement and intractable discord, between the commensurable and the incommensurable. Transversal communication is peculiarly fitted for the task, splitting the difference, as it were, between the partisans of dialogue and the partisans of agonistics, moderating the hermeneutical appetitions for unity and common understanding while mitigating the combative posture of rhetoric.

There are a number of points that require special emphasis in this particular task, which is one of splitting the difference between consensus and dissensus. A point to be underscored is the need for a refiguration of the phenomenon of intersubjectivity, accenting the "inter" rather than the "subjective" side of the phenomenon. Intersubjectivity must no longer be understood as the end result of a phenomenological constitution on the part of a monadic, constituting subject, whereby the other is called to presence via the projection of an alter ego and an accompanying analogical transfer of sense. Rhetoric has done well to recognize the exteriority of the other, encountered in advance of constitution, and announced by way of an intrusion of social practices and cultural forms of life that are alien to the projects of subjectivity. Yet the differences that are inscribed through the incursion of alterity need not congeal into the impermeability of a Lyotardian *différend*. Indeed a *différend* in the guise of an *absolute* exteriority, impermeable and nonrelational, remains at most a limit to thought and to the experience of a lifeworld. The array of differences encountered in the lifeworld—the other self, the other text, the other set of mores, the other institution, the other culture—turn on a *topos*, a topography, a space of engagement, a being-with-that-which-is-other, that binds, however loosely, rhetor and interlocutor, citizen and alien, friend and foe.

It is thus that Lyotard's sharp demarcation of "partisans of dialogue" from "partisans of agonistics," against the backdrop of an intractable *différend*, appears to be somewhat overdrawn. Apparently the partisans of agonistics wage war not only on the partisans of dialogue but also on each other. But then in what sense do they continue to function as partisans? Whence issues the collaborative zeal to march shoulder to shoulder as party affiliates? If the agon is so firmly entrenched in the economy of discourse, how is it that one partisan of agonistics is able to communicate with another? Have we not learned from Plato that there needs to be honor even among thieves? Might it not be that one can learn from Lyotard (in a somewhat serendipitous manner to be sure) that even a rhetorical agonistics requires a measure of collaboration and solidarity among its partisans?

The point to be underscored at this juncture is that a new sketch of the terrain of intersubjectivity is needed to account for being with others in the midst of conflict and strife. As antagonist I wage a war with a protagonist, registering total disagreement, to the point of rupturing the dialogue and eventually removing myself from the conversation. But what I cannot do is remove him or her from the intersubjective space we share. The facticity of the situation is such that "the other," whether protagonist or antagonist, remains inscribed as "the one with whom one differs." Even in the throes of disagreement, partisans of dialogue and partisans of agonistics continue to face each other as they announce to the world, "*We* cannot agree!"

It is on this new topography of intersubjectivity as a we-experience amid occurrent differences that something like an ethic of transversal communication is able to take root—an ethic that is able to tolerate differences in its response to the diversity of beliefs and practices. The dynamics of such an ethic resides in the cognition of the alterity of the other as an *acknowledgement* of the other as other. The grammar of acknowledgement is already a mixed grammar, both descriptive and normative. Acknowledging the other is at once a demonstration, by discourse or action, word or deed, that one has *knowledge of* and *respect for* the rights, claims, and authority issuing from the other; *regard* for incurred debts, promises, and duties; and an *avowal* of the integrity of the other as other. All these senses, in mixing the descriptive and the prescriptive, travel with the event of acknowledgment. Acknowledging the other as other is a mode of being-with-others, an event of intersubjectivity within a concrete lifeworld, that is already infused with moral predicates. Contextualized within an ethos that defines the character of rhetor and interlocutor alike, acknowledgment conveys respect for the integrity of the other, soliciting the ethical as the requirement for a fitting response to the discourses and the actions of the other that are always already in force.

The economy of transversal communication, stimulated by the ethic of the fitting response, refigures both the hermeneutic orientation toward understanding and the rhetorical stance on alterity, effecting a passage between the unacceptable alternatives of pure consensus and unqualified dissensus as the proper ends of discourse. The search for understanding, the appetition for agreement and shared meaning, the drive toward solidarity—these all remain. However, the hermeneutical project is recast in such a manner as to become a struggle with irremovable risks, given the play of difference in the diverse agenda of beliefs and social practices. This recasting enables an acceptance of the conflict of interpretations and the clash of convictions as indigenous features of existence in a cosmopolitan lifeworld.

These conflicts of interpretations and clashes of convictions in public life arise from intricate interlacings of political, economic, moral, and religious perspectives. Such is the case in the longstanding divergent points of view separating the British Crown and the Irish Republican Army, the Palestinian Arab and the Zionist Jew, the Eastern Orthodox Serb and the Catholic Croat, the Eastern mystic and the Western rationalist. To demand consensus amid such profound differences is to court resignation and cynicism. Each perspective is shaped within a hermeneutical circle of agreed-upon beliefs and practices, and each perspective is bounded by another hermeneutical circle exterior to it. There are no trade routes from the circulating beliefs and practices in the one economy to another. Any opening of routes from one circle to another will require a diagonal extending across the multiple circles of interpretation, a transversal communicative performance that seeks an understanding of that which is other without aspiring to a coincidence of perspectives. The other understood transversely is the other understood *in spite of* differing commitments and points of view. Transversal communication is bent neither toward a solid agreement with the other nor toward a displacement of the other.

The rhetoric of transversal communication labors within the space between the rhetor and the interlocutor, but it does not seek to fill this space by establishing a point of identity through conversion or coercion, nor does it strive to annihilate the space of the other. The proper end of the rhetoric of transversal communication is convergence without coincidence, conjuncture without identity; it exhibits a self-understanding that works with an understanding of the other, geared to possible agenda for collaboration in spite of difference. Amid the heterogeneity of discursive and institutional practices, it acknowledges the other as a coinhabitant of a common earth. It is thus that transversal communication can split the difference between consensus and dissensus. The diagonal of transversality ruptures the closure of the hermeneutical circle as it keeps the triangulation of rhetoric from subjugation to an absolute exteriority.

Notes

1. Charles Taylor, *Philosophy and the Human Sciences: Philosophical Papers* (Cambridge: Cambridge University Press, 1985), 18.

2. Martin Heidegger, *Being and Time,* trans. John Macquarrie and Edward Robinson (New York: Harper and Row, 1962), 195.

3. See particularly Hans-Georg Gadamer, "The Universality of the Hermeneutical Problem," in Gadamer, *Philosophical Hermeneutics,* trans. David E. Linge (Berkeley: University of California Press, 1976), 3–17.

4. For an extensive critical discussion of the *aporias* of epistemological foundationalism, see Richard Rorty, *Philosophy and the Mirror of Nature* (Princeton: Princeton University Press, 1979), esp. chap. 7, "From Epistemology to Hermeneutics," 315–56.

5. See Calvin O. Schrag, *Communicative Praxis and the Space of Subjectivity* Bloomington: Indiana University Press, 1986), esp. parts I and II.

6. Heidegger, *Being and Time,* 178.

7. Gadamer, "Rhetoric, Hermeneutics, and Ideology-Critique," in *Philosophical Hermeneutics,* 25. See Chapter 15, this volume.

8. Paul Ricoeur, "Rhetoric—Poetics—Hermeneutics," in *From Metaphysics to Rhetoric,* ed. Michel Meyer (Dordrecht: Kluwer, 1989), 149. See Chapter 2, this volume.

9. For an extended discussion of the figuration of the triangle in rhetoric and communication, see James L. Kinneavy, *A Theory of Discourse* (New York: Norton, 1971).

10. Burke uses the designator *administrative rhetoric* to describe a rhetoric that illustrates a dynamics of persuasion not confined to discursive forms. His example is Theodore Roosevelt sending the United States fleet to Germany on a "goodwill

mission"—ostensibly a friendly visit but more specifically an unequivocal message warning the German emperor of Roosevelt's military buildup. See Kenneth Burke, *Language as Symbolic Action* (Berkeley: University of California Press, 1968), 301.

11. For a discussion of the role of invention in rhetoric, see Michael J. Hyde and Craig R. Smith, "Aristotle and Heidegger on Emotion and Rhetoric: Questions of Time and Space," in *The Critical Turn: Rhetoric and Philosophy in Postmodern Discourse*, ed. Ian Angus and Lenore Langsdorf (Carbondale: Southern Illinois University Press, 1993), 68–99.

12. Hans Blumenberg, "An Anthropological Approach to the Contemporary Significance of Rhetoric," trans. Robert M. Wallace, in *After Philosophy: End or Transformation?* ed. Kenneth Baynes, James Bohman, and Thomas McCarthy (Cambridge: MIT Press, 1987), 452.

13. J. Robert Cox, "Cultural Memory and the Public Moral Argument," The Van Zelst Lecture in Communication (Evanston, Ill.: Northwestern University School of Speech, 1987), 10. Cox's vocabulary of "dialectic of repetition and disavowal" is informed by Heidegger's use of *Wiederholung* and *Widerruf* in working out the dynamics of historical understanding. Cox has shown that these two moments are operative in the dynamics of the rhetorical art.

14. Jean-François Lyotard, *The Differend: Phrases in Dispute*, trans. George Van Den Abbeele (Minneapolis: University of Minnesota Press, 1988), 26.

15. "As distinguished from a litigation, a differend [*différend*] would be a case of conflict between (at least) two parties, that cannot be equitably resolved for lack of a rule of judgment applicable to both arguments" (Lyotard, *Differend*, xi).

16. Jean-François Lyotard, *The Postmodern Condition: A Report on Knowledge*, trans. Geoff Bennington and Brian Massumi (Minneapolis: University of Minnesota Press, 1984), 66.

17. Jean-Paul Sartre, *The Transcendence of the Ego: An Existentialist Theory of Consciousness*, trans. Forrest Williams and Robert Kirkpatrick (New York: Noonday Press, 1957), 39. The grammar of transversality has also received intermittent usage in the French scene of postmodern thought, in particular, by Gilles Deleuze and Félix Guattari. For a sustained discussion of the uses of transversality in postmodern philosophy as well as of the applicability of the concept for understanding the dynamics of reason in communicative praxis as an interplay of discourse and action, see Calvin O. Schrag, *The Resources of Rationality: A Response to the Postmodern Challenge* (Bloomington: Indiana University Press, 1992), esp. chap. 6, "Transversal Rationality," 148–79.

18

Political Prosaics, Transversal Politics, and the Anarchical World

David Campbell

IN THE DOCUMENTARY PHOTOGRAPHY of Sebastiao Salgado can be found one powerful representation of the multiple realities of world politics. Salgado's depiction of workers at Brazil's Serra Pelda gold mine, in the blazing oil fields of Kuwait, and in the cattle slaughterhouses of South Dakota; his evocative pictures of the "uncertain grace" possessed by the inhabitants of the African Sahel in their struggle with drought and famine; and his empathetic portrayal of the daily lives of people in central and southern America open a window onto what Nietzsche called the rich ambiguity of existence.[1]

Yet Sebastiao Salgado's photographs are not merely representations of individuals; they are testament to the way lives in the modern world are bound and shaped, constrained and constituted, by a complex manifold of social forces often unseen and often from elsewhere. For in the faces of those photographed, and through the environments in which they are situated, flow the many and varied effects of an increasingly globalized political economy in tension with a range of identities and practices.[2] As a *New York Times* critic remarked, the photographs "carry a sense of smoldering energy, of passion too big to be held in check by any body, any job, any relationship or any political system."[3]

Salgado's photographs can thus be read as manifesting what Fredric Jameson has called "the geopolitical aesthetic."[4] For Jameson, our location in what he calls "the new world system of late capitalism"[5] poses innumerable representational problems for politics, principal among them being our "structural incapacity . . . to construct a narrative that can map totality."[6] To come to terms with this challenge, and as a means of fashioning "a conceptual instrument for grasping our new being-in-the-world,"[7] Jameson reads a

range of films (such as Pakula's *All the President's Men*) as attempts to figure
the intersection of two incommensurable levels of being, the individual subject and the concealed network of the social order in which they can be
located.[8] What is being allegorized in Jameson's reading of these films is the
way in which "the local items of the present and the here-and-now can be
made to express and to designate the absent, unrepresentable totality; how
the individuals can add up to more than their sum; what a global or world
system might look like after the end of cosmology."[9]

For Jameson, reading films in this light highlights a larger issue, that "all
thinking today is *also*, whatever else it is, an attempt to think the world system as such."[10] In this context, Jameson's argument concerning the geopolitical aesthetic is a development of his earlier concern to move toward what he
has called "an aesthetic of cognitive mapping—a pedagogical political culture
which seeks to endow the individual subject with some new heightened sense
of its place in the global system." As Jameson maintains, such a project is
anything but a nostalgic call for returning to a "transparent national space."
Instead, "the new political art (if it is possible at all) will have to hold to the
truth of postmodernism, that is to say, to its fundamental object—the world
space of multinational capital—at the same time at which it achieves a break-
through to some as yet unimaginable new mode of representing."[11]

Jameson's framing of the issue has a number of limitations, perhaps the
greatest of which is the reinscription of a new and determinate ground in
terms of a conventionally rendered multinational space as the basis for politics.[12] Specifically, Jameson argues that the study of capital "is now our true
ontology. It is indeed the new world system, the third stage of capitalism,
which is for us the absent totality, Spinoza's God or Nature, the ultimate
(indeed, perhaps the only) referent, the true ground of Being of our own
time."[13] Such certainty in the face of ambiguity and contingency may be mis-
placed. As such, reframing Jameson's argument in chronopolitical rather
than geopolitical terms (or at least some combination of the two) might be
more suggestive.[14] Nonetheless, recognizing both the need for, yet current
inability to achieve, the representation of the local and the global, spaces and
flows, Jameson has identified a major problematic.

Moreover, Jameson's argument has (indirectly at least) issued a substantial
challenge to the discipline of international relations. As that subfield of the
social sciences to which the task of thinking about world politics has either
fallen or been arrogated, international relations has a responsibility to consider the best way in which to participate in the project of cognitive mapping
in a manner that directly addresses the multiple realities of Salgado's photographs. International relations must address the basic question of whether it
is adequate as a mode of understanding global life given the increasing irrup-

tions of accelerated and nonterritorial contingencies upon our political horizons, irruptions in which a disparate but powerful assemblage of flows—flows of people, goods, money, ecological factors, disease, ideas, etc.—contest borders, put states into question (without rendering them irrelevant), rearticulate spaces, and re-form identities.[15]

This essay argues that because of the continued hegemony of spatial modes of representation, specifically the geopolitics of the levels of analysis, international relations is unrealistic. In an effort to point the way to modes of representation that could possibly be considered more adequate, the argument here suggests that a form of inquiry, which might be termed "political prosaics," concerned with the *transversal* (instead of trans*national*) character of politics in an an-archical world (as distinct from anarchy) is worth pursuing.

Representing Transformations

The discipline of international relations has not been blind to the increasingly transnational transformations and the theoretical and practical challenges to which they give rise. Indeed, for more than the last two decades, the literature of international relations has made a concerted attempt to come to grips with what it perceives as major changes in world order. Although some have pointed out that this awakening was induced more by the declining fortunes of American power subsequent to the Vietnam War than a disinterested appreciation for the globalization of politics,[16] there can be no doubt that those who have written about transnationalism, interdependence, international regimes, hegemonic stability, and, particularly, international political economy have sought to make more complicated the state-centric view of the world, in which the "billiard ball" model was the metaphor of choice and the levels of analysis were the preferred mode of understanding.

Nonetheless, even a cursory examination of some of these literatures shows—for all the fanfare of theoretical innovation and the claims of cumulative knowledge in the social sciences—some remarkably persistent assumptions about what is significant in international relations/world politics. In particular, even when transformations like those discussed earlier are cited as important, what demands our attention is the way in which the issue has been posed, the question raised, or the problem stated. What we find when these representational concerns are our focus is, first, that these transformations are understood in terms of the rise of "nonstate" actors and, second, that the "nonstate" problematization of the issues does not seek to displace the state from the core of a regulative ideal of interpretation.[17]

A number of textual references from the international political economy literature could be offered in support of this proposition, but an influential argument by Robert Gilpin provides an exemplary illustration. Writing in 1971, Gilpin posed the specific issue of transnational economic actors in terms that are still very familiar:

> In specific terms the issue is whether the multinational corporation has become or will become an important actor in international affairs, supplanting, at least in part, the nation-state. If the multinational corporation is indeed an increasingly important and independent international actor, what are the factors that have enabled it to break the political monopoly of the nation-state? What is the relationship of these two sets of political actors, and what are the implications of the multinational corporation for international relations?[18]

Nearly twenty years later, theorists critical of realism, who drew upon a disparate range of sources divergent from those which underpinned Gilpin's thoughts, put forward similar formulations.[19] Nor is the framing of the debate in terms of state/nonstate the only formulation of interest and concern in these literatures. A number of other related assumptions—especially those concerning autonomy and power—figure often and prominently. For example, in the same year as Gilpin wrote, Joseph Nye and Robert Keohane set forth a world politics paradigm—parts of which they later retracted because it moved too far from the state—in which, because they defined politics "in terms of the conscious employment of resources," they argued that "the central phenomenon [of world politics] is bargaining between a variety of autonomous or semiautonomous actors."[20]

Although far from a comprehensive survey, I will venture to suggest that the literatures of which these formulations might be representative exhibit a number of common assumptions:

> They recur to the presence of certain agents (such as states, corporations, intergovernmental organizations, etc.), thereby exhibiting a preference for a sovereign presence as the organizing principle around which understanding can be constructed.

> Autonomy and semiautonomy are said to be important conditions, such that actors are taken to be separate from and prior to the relationships in which they are implicated.

> The capacity to wield power as a (usually material, though sometimes symbolic) resource over other agents is an important proviso of agency.

> Any complexity surrounding the issue of actors and agency is represented by additional levels of analysis—such as the supplementing of national and inter-

national with local and global—rather than by any sustained questioning of the assumptions of agency that might be challenged. This is most obvious in the way that complexity is always anchored in a "something-national" formulation, whether it be "international," "multinational," or "transnational."[21]

Such concerns are, of course, perfectly legitimate, such questions are certainly worth asking, and such formulations make sense given those concerns and questions. The worry is, why have these formulations triumphed over nearly all others as a means of understanding the wide-ranging and truly radical transformations of the global political economy and world order in the postwar period?

Much of the new literature in international relations, especially that concerned with transnational epistemic communities, multilateralism, and the importance of knowledge as a source of power, contains impressive evidence and valuable insights on some of the changes in global life.[22] At least as far as it goes. Which may not be very far—that is, not as far as it either should or could go—given the broader purview of world politics rather than international relations.[23] To illustrate this limitation, I want to consider two valuable and recent contributions to the international relations literature that are both cognizant of these empirical developments and (apparently) open to developments in social and political theory from which others have sought inspiration to raise anew fundamental issues of representation in world politics.

Alexander Wendt, who has argued strongly for the appreciation of the mutually constituted and codetermined nature of agents and structures in international relations,[24] recently concluded that the appropriate research agenda for international relations was a state-centric one. "The significance of states relative to multinational corporations, new social movements, transnationals, and intergovernmental organizations is clearly declining, and 'postmodern' forms of world politics merit more research attention than they have received," he wrote. "But I also believe, with realists, that in the medium run sovereign states will remain the dominant political actors in the international system."[25] Although Wendt did not seek to delegitimize other research concerns, he recognized that the priority he accorded state-centrism would be "depressingly familiar" to many. But what is of particular interest is how Wendt's self-professed modernist constructivism re-endorses state-centric realism, and how this explanation might shed light on the broader issues of this essay.

One possible answer may lie in the often explicit social-scientific preferences exhibited in the argument, most evident in the concern that international relations theorists structure their work in terms of a "research agenda" that can offer "causal" and "empirical" answers.[26] Another important, though related, argument is that for all the effort to go beyond the bounds of the "rationalist problematique" that binds neorealists and neoliberals together,[27] Wendt exhibits an overwhelming but underrecognized commitment to many of the general tenets of that disposition. Wendt wanted to maintain that "philosophies of science are not theories of international relations" (hence we should avoid spending too much time on "questions of ontology"),[28] but there seems little escape from the fact that consciously or not international relations theorists are philosophers of knowledge. After all, as Wendt acknowledges, "All theories of international relations are based on social theories of the relationship between agency, process, and social structure."[29] The real question is whether we want to take the constitution and nature of agency seriously—which would by definition require considerable attention to the question of ontology—or whether we are happy in the final instance to merely posit the importance of certain agents. To do the latter involves gliding over a point well made by Judith Butler:

> Agency belongs to a way of thinking about persons as instrumental actors who confront an external political field. But if we agree that politics and power exist already at the level at which the subject and its agency are articulated and made possible, then agency can be *presumed* only at the cost of refusing to inquire into its construction . . . In a sense, the epistemological model that offers us a pregiven subject or agent is one that refuses to acknowledge that *agency is always and only a political prerogative.*[30]

Although Wendt might initially agree that "politics and power exist already at the level at which the subject and its agency are articulated and made possible" (hence his focus on identity- and interest-formation amongst states), a powerful rationalist pull in his argument curtails the logical consequence of pushing the constitutive nature of political agency to its limits. This commitment can be observed at two key points: when the anthropomorphism of the individual-state analogy is defended by Wendt,[31] and when it is argued that the body is the "material substrate of agency" that remains for the individual once the constitutive properties of the self are stripped away.[32] The latter point is particularly telling, on two counts. First, one of the major contributions of recent political theorizing, particularly feminist scholarship, has been to put in question the assumption of pregiven, material bodies as the unproblematic ground for identity and politics.[33] To overlook such arguments in favor of a (seemingly commonsense) resolution of this complex issue forecloses Wendt's potential to come to terms with "postmodern" politics. The second count of interest is that Wendt retreats in the end to the (supposedly) secure foundations of the body politic because of his moral commitment to an "epistemic realism" whereby the world comprises objects independent of ideas or beliefs about them.[34]

Another instance in which a rationalist faith overcomes postmodern potential is John Gerard Ruggie's attempts to problematize modernity in international relations through an analysis of the status of territoriality.[35] Ruggie contends that in the face of developments similar to those outlined earlier, visualizing "long-term challenges to the system of states only in terms of entities that are institutionally substitutable for the state" is evidence of "an extraordinarily impoverished mind-set at work." The inability, Ruggie argues, to even conceive of these developments in terms of "the possibility of fundamental institutional discontinuity in the system of states" is "because, among other reasons, prevailing modes of analytical discourse simply lack the requisite vocabulary."[36]

Few should disagree with such a contention. But from a broader perspective, a tension is evident between this proposition and the manifest limits of Ruggie's own analytical discourse. Like Wendt, Ruggie frames the quest for knowledge in overtly social-scientific terms, with his article marking "a relatively modest and pretheoretical task: to search for a vocabulary and for the dimensions of a research agenda by means of which we can start to ask systematic questions about the possibility of fundamental international transformation today."[37] Pretheoretical. Research agenda. Systematic questions. The rationalist commitment is evident.

Most interestingly, Ruggie reveals that this commitment—which John Lewis Gaddis has argued was utterly incapable of coming to terms with the end of the Cold War (and thus the emergence of the issues driving Ruggie's argument)[38]—is made possible by an irrational fear of the irrational. For what is striking about Ruggie's argument is his disavowal of the possibility that postmodern analytics may have something to say about the cultural category of postmodernity. Arguing via secondhand sources that within international relations postmodern theorizing has been at best "symptomatic" and "preoccupied with style and method" and offers "limited substantive insight," Ruggie attempts to drive the nail into the postmodern coffin by declaring that "the Paul de Man saga, especially the shameful defense of de Man by several leading deconstructivists, shows poignantly how deleterious the political consequences can be that follow from the moral vacuum—if not moral vacuity—the French fries would have us inhabit."[39]

One hardly need to be a defender of de Man's offensively fascist and sometimes openly anti-Semitic writings for the (then German-controlled) Belgian newspaper *Le Soir* between December 1940 and November 1942—writings which Derrida painfully noted manifested "an alliance with what has always been for me the very worst"[40]—to recognize the anti-intellectual and highly polemical nature of Ruggie's caricature. It seems to be based upon the dubious proposition that periods in the life of an individual taint irrevocably an intellectual tradition for all subsequent interpreters, an argument which to be sustained would require supreme confidence that one's own theoretical debts were to discourses made possible only by saints. Of course, as Christopher Norris contends, such a defense is no substitute for "serious, responsible debate" *except* in cases of "crude *ad hominem* abuse."[41] But many moments in the controversy surrounding Paul de Man—including David Lehman's book, upon which Ruggie relies for his attack[42]—have been marked by ad hominem arguments. A great deal could and should be said about this debate, for it has many implications for our understandings of ethics, politics, and theory, but given the space here I will restrict my remarks to a couple of observations, worthy of further development, that are relevant to the immediate argument.

The first is that de Man and his wartime writings are taken by the critics (including, it seems, Ruggie) to be indissolubly linked with a body of theory, such that "the primary goal of the rage in question is a settling of accounts with 'deconstruction.' "[43] It is for this reason that the entire first half of Lehman's book is concerned with deconstruction rather than de Man. But logic of this type, even assuming that de Man as a thinker can be said to stand in for a varied tradition assembled under the heading "deconstruction," is far from being shared by all those justifiably critical of the wartime politics of de Man (and Heidegger). With respect to the latter, Jürgen Habermas, certainly no apologist for Heidegger's politics, has argued that "Illumination of the political conduct of Martin Heidegger cannot and should not serve the purpose of a global depreciation of his thought."[44]

At the same time—and somewhat paradoxically—it can be said that deconstruction is not really on trial, for "it has already proved its usefulness, even in the work of many who now attack it."[45] This is, one suspects with unintended irony, abundantly evident in Lehman's book, where for all the lamentations about the perfidious influence of textuality as one of deconstruction's central ideas,[46] the focus of his argument and the target of his wrath are texts and their politics: de Man's wartime writings and the responses of those, like Derrida, who have so outraged the critics.[47] In this vein, it is remarkable that the same angry critics who are so keen to maintain a sharp distinction between the world and the text have no hesitation in referring to de Man as an "academic Waldheim," an act of moral leveling that equates the actions of an officer in a German army unit known for its record of atrocities with the words of a newspaper columnist and reviewer.[48]

More importantly, especially for those prepared to think beyond the fear that the only certain alternative to specific commands of the Enlightenment tradition is a dark period of evil doings, Ruggie's off-the-cuff gestures ignore a growing literature on the ethical character of postmodern theorizing and its political entailments.[49]

Indeed, at one time, it seemed as though Ruggie himself wished to cultivate the interpretive possibilities of postmodern analytics with respect to postmodern politics. Writing during the great European political upheavals symbolized most obviously by the collapse of the Berlin Wall, Ruggie noted that what was most intriguing about the modernity/postmodernity debates in European social theory was how postmodern insights—concerning "detotalized, decentered, and fragmented discourses and practices; multiple and field-dependent referents in place of single-point fixed referents; flow-defined spaces and sequential temporal experiences; the erosion of sovereign or macro powers over society coupled with the diffusion of disciplinary or micro powers within society"—sounded familiar to the student of international political economy sensitive to "certain recently emerged global systems of economic transaction."[50] One should perhaps not overstate Ruggie's seeming interest in the nexus of postmodern inquiry and postmodern practices, for his subsequent questions concerning the issue of authority relations in a global context were still framed in terms of "how states see themselves in relation to one another; how they stand in relation to private actors."[51] Nonetheless the absence of ill-informed characterizations in 1989 is to be contrasted to the calculated closing down and willful writing off of postmodern possibilities a mere four years later. Any number of things could account for Ruggie's change in tone, but perhaps it was an instance of the belief that the accelerating globalization and simultaneous fragmentation of the post–Cold War world order was beyond understanding.

The Problematic of Sovereignty

Of course, theorists of Wendt's and Ruggie's caliber do not want to reduce everything to states, territory, or the international system. Yet in framing their concerns in a manner that gives those or other grounds some priority, they seem to be exhibiting a fear, a (Cartesian) anxiety, that if one pushes to the logical conclusions of their arguments, and avoids the defensive maneuvers whose sole purpose is to ward off "foreign" theoretical traditions, no longer will it be possible to speak again of the state, or any other foundation of politics upon which one can ethically secure the good life. I want to argue that what is behind this anxiety and fear is an often unstated yet unequivocal commitment enabled by a narrow rationalism to "the sovereignty problematic" that restricts the interpretive possibilities of world politics understood as international relations.

Sovereignty, as Derrida noted, "is presence, and the delight in presence."[52] The sovereignty problematic is thus an articulation of two of Derrida's central concepts, the metaphysics of presence and logocentrism, whereby order can be said to result from a conformity to first principles, such that we make sense of the world by differentiating and normalizing contingency in terms of a hierarchical understanding of sovereignty/anarchy (or agent/structure, endogenous/exogenous, inside/outside, domestic/foreign, etc.). *Sovereignty* (or the equivalent first term) comes to be thought of as a center of decision presiding over a unitary self, whereas *anarchy* (or the equivalent second term) is that which cannot or will not be assimilated to this prior subjectivity.[53]

The idea of sovereignty, of presence, of the ground of first principles, is closely connected to the metanarrative of subjectivity from which we derive the interpretive resources for making sense of politics and transformations. Identified by Stephen White as the strong tradition of Western thought that is "oriented to the consciousness of a subject (singular or collective) who is faced with the task of surveying, subduing, and negotiating *his* way through a world of objects, other subjects, and his own body,"[54] the metanarrative of subjectivity underpins the way in which, through a proper name ("the keystone of logocentrism"),[55] we turn "dynamic, interconnected phenomena into static, disconnected things."[56]

The desire for presence and the fear of absence favor geopolitical grounds, the levels of rigid political segmentarity that devolve from those grounds, and the presumption of agency. It is because of these interpretive debts that the dynamics of global transformations have been represented through statements—of the sort that pronounce that "Non-state actors such as multinational corporations and banks may increase in importance, but there are few signs that they are edging states from center stage"[57]—that both depend upon and reproduce logocentric vocabularies. These analytic discourses, part of the "extraordinarily impoverished mind-set" that Ruggie decried but did not escape, continually reinscribe three assumptions through their operation: (1) that there is a "center stage" or pinnacle of power from which most if not all relationships can be governed, (2) that the site of power can only ever be occupied by one source of authority, and (3) that the presiding source of authority has to be an easily identifiable, unitary agent, endowed with relative autonomy and capable of purposively wielding material resources. It is in these terms that those international relations literatures that have sought to represent the complexity of world politics have been hampered in their task by a commitment to the problematic of sovereignty.

To this point I have focused on the sovereignty problematic and its assumptions about the centrality of geopolitical space and agency as presence. But inescapably intertwined with this are assumptions about power, because hand in hand with the sovereignty problematic goes an economistic conception of power,[58] whereby power is regarded as a commodity to be wielded by agents. Such a perspective is, however, wholly inadequate as a basis for understanding our postmodern time. Only if we understand power—in a manner that recalls recent observations about corporate structures in the global economy—"as something which circulates, or rather as something which only functions in the form of a chain . . . [as] employed and exercised through a net-like organisation,"[59] can we begin to grasp the economic and political globalization of the last thirty years. As Wendy Brown has observed:

> Postmodern capitalist power, like postmodern state power, is monopolized without being concentrated or centered: it is tentacular, roving, and penetrating, paradoxically advancing itself by diffusing and decentralizing itself . . . Postmodernity decenters, diffuses, and splays power and politics. Postmodern power incessantly violates, transgresses, and resituates social boundaries; it flows on surfaces and irrigates through networks rather than consolidating in bosses and kings; it is ubiquitous, liminal, highly toxic in small and fluid doses.[60]

Moreover, this theorization of power, in combination with the many globalizing tendencies discussed earlier, identifies a powerful reason for the unwillingness-cum-inability of theorists like Wendt and Ruggie, let alone the mainstream of international relations, to go beyond the sovereignty problematic. It is that in a time marked by this "centrifugation of power," a sense of dislocation and homelessness can prevail: indeed, as Brown notes, "we are today very susceptible to getting lost."[61] Or, as Daniel Warner has poignantly suggested, "we are all refugees."[62]

In response to this sense of dislocation and homelessness, identity politics (i.e., understanding and practicing politics in terms of ethnicity, race, gender, sexuality, region, continent, nation, state, etc.) emerges to provide a sense of situation, a feeling of location, and an air of certainty about our place in the world. In Brown's formulation, "Identity politics emerges as a reaction, in other words, to an ensemble of distinctly postmodern assaults upon the integrity of communities producing identity."[63] In this context, international relations as a discipline, because of its propensity to discursively recur to the state as the organizing identity in the face of both empirical and theoretical assaults, might be better understood as a particular though powerful *discourse of identity politics,* writers indebted to the sovereignty problematic might be understood as particular though powerful *theorists of identity politics,* and the state might be understood as a particular though powerful *for-*

mation of identity politics. All of which gives, by definition, only limited purchase on the complexities of world politics.

The issue, then, is, can we represent world politics in a manner less indebted to the sovereignty problematic? What would be highlighted in place of the sovereign presence of agents and the relationships between them? Can we think international relations and world politics beyond the sovereignty problematic?

Toward a Political Prosaics

The challenge for a mode of representation adequate to our postmodern time is therefore to articulate an understanding of world politics attuned to the need to move beyond the sovereignty problematic, with its focus on geopolitical segmentarity, settled subjects, and economistic power, that appreciates the significance of flows, networks, webs, and the identity formations located therein but does not resort simply to the addition of another level of analysis or of more agents to the picture.

Some attempts in this direction are being made outside of international relations in a burgeoning literature on globalization.[64] What I want to suggest is that thinking in terms of a *political prosaics* that understands the *transversal* nature of politics and the *an-archical* condition of postmodern life is one way of approaching the issue. Such an effort, however, should *not* be thought of in terms of constructing a theory, much less a new theory of international relations. Rather, it is part of an aspiration to encourage genealogically inclined critique of the sort Foucault indicated in his thoughts on Kant and the Enlightenment:

> The critical ontology of ourselves has to be considered not, certainly, as a theory, a doctrine, nor even as a permanent body of knowledge that is accumulating; it has to be conceived as an attitude, an ethos, a philosophical life in which the critique of what we are is at one and the same time the historical analysis of the limits that are imposed on us and an experiment with the possibility of going beyond them.[65]

This ethos begins with the notion of "prosaics," derived from the Russian literary theorist Mikhail Bakhtin, which signifies two associated yet discrete concepts.[66] The first is the antonym of "poetics" and comes from one of the central themes of Bakhtin's work: that the prose of the novel rather than poetics constituted the highest art form, because of the novel's ability to convey what Bakhtin called the heteroglossia of life.[67] This focus upon the contribution of prose to human understanding finds a (perhaps unlikely) resonance in John Lewis Gaddis's argument concerning international relations theory at the end of the Cold War. Faulting the pretensions of social-scientific theory in the discipline—and particularly its failure to offer any insights on the end of the Cold War—Gaddis argues that like historians and novelists, "we 'model' human actions by falling back upon the only known simulative technique that successfully integrates the general and the specific, the regular and the irregular, the predictable and the unpredictable: we construct narratives."[68]

Heteroglossia—the panoply of discordant voices, abundance of disorder, and the clash between centrifugal (unofficial) forces and centripetal (official) forces that, without apparent reason, seek to construct order out of the disorder that is the norm—is the basis for the second of the two notions of prosaics, that which understands these features as part and parcel of an antisystematic philosophy of the everyday and ordinary.[69]

This attitude (in a manner that resonates with Derrida's notion of undecidability) is understood by the "all-purpose carrier" concept of "unfinalizability," which signifies the conviction that the world is a messy, open, and plural place.[70] Concomitant with this is the importance of dialogue as something like a model of the world.[71] But Bakhtin's notion of dialogue (and of dialogism as a nonteleological dialectics)[72] exceeds the idea of argument or debate. Instead, the notion of dialogue brings into question certain assumptions linked to the conventional view of discussion, specifically those of interacting and autonomous monads. For Bakhtin, communication is so central to existence that to separate out particular identities from their conditions of possibility is an instance of "theoretism" (the mistaken belief that events should be understood in terms of rules or structures to which they purportedly conform).[73]

For the conventional modes of understanding world politics these concepts have some significant ramifications. In the first instance, an interpretive disposition indebted to prosaics reverses the burden of proof to focus analysis on the intellectual and political constitution of order rather than disorder, and the constructed rather than discovered character of selfhood and ethics.[74] The presumption of agency and the naturalness of autonomy are thus called into question. But even more importantly, Bakhtin's thoughts—akin again to a Derridean notion, this time of the trace—highlight the way in which individual and collective subjects are "extraterritorial, partially 'located outside' themselves," such that Bakhtin can speak of the " 'nonself-sufficiency' of the self."[75] With respect to individuals, Bakhtin maintains:

I achieve self-consciousness, I become myself only by revealing myself to another, through another, with another's help. The most important acts, consti-

tutive of self-consciousness, are determined by their relation to another consciousness (a 'thou'). Cutting oneself off, isolating oneself, closing oneself off,
those are the basic reasons for loss of self . . . It turns out that every internal
experience occurs on the border, it comes across another, and this essence
resides in this intense encounter . . . The very being of man (both internal and
external) is a *profound communication*. *To be* means to *communicate* . . . To be
means to be for the other, and through him, for oneself. Man has no internal
sovereign territory; he is all and always on the boundary; looking within himself, he looks *in the eyes of the other* or *through the eyes of the other* . . . I cannot
do without the other; I cannot become myself without the other; I must find
myself in the other, finding the other in me (in mutual reflection and perception).[76]

These thoughts also have important implications for collective subjects
(such as states, etc.), because they point to the limitations of "territory" and
"boundary" as metaphors, stressing that "cultural entities are, in effect, *all*
boundary."[77] As Bakhtin notes, "One must not, however, imagine the realm
of culture as some sort of spatial whole, having boundaries but also having
internal territory. The realm of culture has no internal territory: it is entirely
distributed along the boundaries, boundaries pass everywhere, through its
every aspect."[78] And without boundaries, rigid segmentarity (the levels of
analysis problem) is no more.

Were one constructing a theory, the next question would inevitably be,
How are such concerns to be made more concrete?, or (even more scientifically) How are these ideas to be operationalized? But as I am interested in no
more than—because it is quite sufficient—a critical attitude or ethos toward
our limits and that which lies beyond them, the animus behind those queries
can be answered by saying "This philosophical attitude has to be translated
into the labor of diverse inquires."[79] And the labor of those diverse inquiries
might be organized around a number of related attitudes that intersect with
the ethos of prosaics.

The first would be "philosophical anthropology," a term that Bakhtin used
to encompass his reflections on alterity, being, boundaries, the self, and the
other (some of which are presented earlier). Philosophical anthropology,
drawn out by Tzvetan Todorov as that which holds the key to most of Bakhtin's work, is that ethos which refers to Bakhtin's "general conception of
human existence, where the *other* plays a decisive role. This is then the fundamental principle: it is impossible to conceive of any being outside of the relations that link it to the other."[80]

Although Todorov draws attention to a fundamental principle, a second
element of this ethos is that life is not organized in terms of first principles.
An interpretation that moves toward a political prosaics and philosophical

anthropology of the postmodern world thus does more than reverse the priority of sovereignty over anarchy in conditioning political possibilities. Instead, a political prosaics subverts those terms by thinking of action and agency in terms of anarchy, not anarchy in the sense of being without a central authority or existing in a state of nature (its common rendering within international relations) but in terms of its Greek etymology, *an-arche*, that is, being without first principles, foundations, or grounds.[81]

Given life is understood in terms of being without first principles, the ethos articulated here pays particular attention to thinking that presumes the importance of the quotidian facts of daily life. This disposition is found in (among others) the histories of Fernand Braudel, the philosophy of Henri Lefebvre, and the genealogies of Michel Foucault.[82] But this is not to suggest that there exists some sort of positivist level of analysis called "everyday life" to which we can turn for the truth. One the contrary, our "life-world" is one in which competing discourses and interpretations about reality are already folded into the reality we are seeking to grasp.[83] Nor is it to suggest a return to presumptive social atomism and individuation as the basis for everyday life. Instead, and in keeping with Bakhtin's philosophical anthropology, a focus on everyday life depends upon the recognition that "a relation (always social) determines its terms, and not the reverse, and that each individual is a locus in which an incoherent (and often contradictory) plurality of such relational determinations interact."[84]

Likewise, neither is "everyday life" a synonym for the local level, for in it global interconnections, local resistances, transterritorial flows, state politics, regional dilemmas, identity formations, and so on are always already present. Everyday life is thus a *transversal* site of contestations rather than a fixed level of analysis. It is transversal because it "cannot be reconciled to a Cartesian interpretation of space."[85] And it is transversal because the conflicts manifested there not only transverse all boundaries; *they are about those boundaries*, their erasure or inscription, and the identity formations to which they give rise.[86]

In the "labor of diverse inquiries" that might employ such notions, the situation in the former Yugoslavia serves as a powerful example of the limitations and problems associated with international relations' standard modes of representation. Indeed, few instances in recent world politics better illustrate the way in which alterity, boundaries, and questions of self/other erupt in transversal conflicts incapable of being understood in geopolitical terms. Nonetheless, to try and read the Balkan conflict in a conventional manner, many analyses have struggled between understanding the conflict in terms of, on the one hand, "civil war" and, on the other, a "war of aggression," a vacillation made possible by doubts as to whether the war is "internal" or "external" to the space of the former Yugoslavia. In recent times, another sovereign interpretation, the idea that the bloodshed is the natural playing out of ancient animosities formerly suppressed, has stepped to the fore to shore up doubts about what is going on.[87]

The trouble with this perspective, particularly its fatalistic determinism, is that it is ethnographically dubious. Its inattentiveness to history overlooks the important fact that in the federal state of Yugoslavia the communist leadership did not suppress nationalist identifications but rather constitutionally enshrined and utilized them to further its authority. And its inattentiveness to the prosaics of everyday life overlooks the fact that at the same time as news accounts have spread the line on permanent enmity, they have also contained statements from Bosnian residents that speak to the lie of centuries-old hatreds.[88] In one such report, an eighty-two-year-old (Serbian) Bosnian—whose own son, a doctor, was killed by Serb nationalist forces because he refused to join "ethnic cleansing operations"—was mystified at the Vance-Owen plan: "We have lived together for a thousand years . . . Where did they come up with this crazy plan to divide us up? Why don't they come and talk to us?"[89]

A good question, indeed, and one that points to the necessity of understanding the violence as constitutive of, rather than a response to, settled borders and absolute alterity. It is because of instances like this that I contend that for international relations to be about world politics in our postmodern time it should incorporate a prosaics of everyday life and order to replace the Olympian detachment and reifications of the sovereignty problematic, and it should recognize that the an-archical condition of postmodern, globalized life is better represented as a series of transversal struggles rather than as a complex of inter-national, multi-national, or trans-national relations, because of their being modes of representation that have powerful investments in the very borders being questioned. In these terms, international relations—or at least that part of it that wants to understand world politics—might be better understood as a *philosophical anthropology of everyday life on a global scale*, an understanding that is, most surely, incapable of representation in exclusively geopolitical, segmented terms.

Notes

1. Sebastiao Salgado, *An Uncertain Grace,* essays by Eduardo Galeano and Fred Ritchin (New York and San Francisco: Aperture/San Francisco Museum of Modern Art, 1990), and Salgado, *Workers: An Archeology of the Industrial Age* (New York: Aperture, in association with the Philadelphia Museum of Art, 1993).

2. This location is made explicit in the text accompanying the photographs in Salgado, *Workers.*

3. Matthew L. Wald, "The Eye of the Photojournalist," *New York Times Magazine*, June 9, 1991, p. 58, quoting Michael Brenson.

4. Fredric Jameson, *The Geopolitical Aesthetic: Cinema and Space in the World System* (Bloomington and Indianapolis: Indiana University Press, 1992).

5. Ibid., p. 49.

6. Ibid., p. 41.

7. Ibid., p. 3.

8. Ibid., p. 33.

9. Ibid., p. 10.

10. Ibid., p. 4.

11. Fredric Jameson, *Postmodernism, or The Cultural Logic of Late Capitalism* (Durham: Duke University Press, 1991), p. 54.

12. Jameson, *The Geopolitical Aesthetic*, p. 1.

13. Ibid., p. 82.

14. For a discussion of chronopolitics and international relations, see James Der Derian, *Antidiplomacy: Spies, Terror, Speed, and War* (Cambridge: Blackwell, 1992), especially ch. 6.

15. The literature on these developments is obviously large, but the texts I have found particularly useful include Mike Davis, *City of Quartz: Excavating the Future in Los Angeles* (New York: Verso, 1990); David Harvey, *The Condition of Postmodernity* (Oxford: Basil Blackwell, 1989); Saskia Sassen, *Global City: New York, London, Tokyo* (Princeton: Princeton University Press, 1991); and Timothy W. Luke, "Discourses of Disintegration, Texts of Transformation: Re-Reading Realism in the New World Order," *Alternatives* 18 (1993), pp. 229–58.

16. Robert Cox, "Social Forces, States, and World Orders: Beyond International Relations Theory," in *Neorealism and Its Critics*, ed. Robert O. Keohane (New York: Columbia University Press, 1986).

17. Richard K. Ashley, "Untying the Sovereign State: A Double Reading of the Anarchy Problematique," *Millennium* 17 (1988), especially pp. 244–51.

18. Robert Gilpin, "The Politics of Transnational Economic Relations," in *The Theoretical Evolution of International Political Economy: A Reader*, ed. George T. Crane and Abla Amawi (New York: Oxford University Press, 1991), p. 170.

19. Stephen Gill and David Law, *The Global Political Economy* (Baltimore: Johns Hopkins University Press, 1988), p. 204: "Ultimately, different interpretations of the role and impact of transnationals have to focus on the relationship between these firms and the states they deal with. How far are the policies, strategies and goals of the state influenced by transnationals? How far can states influence the behavior of transnational corporations so as to meet 'national goals.' "

20. Joseph Nye and Robert Keohane, "Transnational Relations and World Politics: A Conclusion," *International Organization* 25 (1971), p. 730. The retraction comes in Keohane and Nye, *Power and Interdependence*, 2d ed. (Glenview, Ill.: Scott Foresman, 1989). As they note in the preface to the first edition (p. vi), "In this book we try to understand world politics by developing explanations at the level of the international system."

21. See, for example, Robert C. North, *War, Peace and Survival: Global Politics and Conceptual Synthesis* (Boulder: Westview, 1990), one of a number of works that has added a fourth (global) tier to the levels of analysis to accommodate recent transformations. This tendency is also succinctly manifested by Rosenau when he writes that the relocation of authority involves movement "both outward toward supranational entities and inward toward subnational groups." James N. Rosenau, "Governance, Order, and Change in World Politics," in *Governance without Government: Order and Change in World Politics*, ed. James N. Rosenau and Ernst-Otto Czempiel (Cambridge: Cambridge University Press, 1992), pp. 2–3. As Walker observes, notwithstanding "the importance of global processes, the spatial imagery of levels necessarily provides an inappropriate guide to what these processes involve." R. B. J. Walker, *Inside/Outside: International Relations as Political Theory* (Cambridge: Cambridge University Press, 1993), p. 206n.

22. See, for example, Peter Haas, ed., "Knowledge, Power, and International Policy Coordination," *International Organization* 46 (1992), pp. 1–390; and "Symposium: Multilateralism," *International Organization* 46 (1992), pp. 561–708.

23. A good illustration of this unrealized potential is James N. Rosenau, *Turbulence in World Politics: A Theory of Change and Continuity* (Princeton: Princeton University Press, 1990). Although the argument, premised on the idea of a new era of "postinternational politics" and sensitive to the limitations of the "non-state actor" mode of representation (see p. 36), seems to want to go beyond the levels of analysis problem, some of its later formulations seem to lapse back into a form of segmented representation. Specifically, the central idea of the "two worlds of global politics" (ch. 10)—i.e., the state-centric world vs. the multi-centric world—depends upon qualitative distinctions between the domains, and thus reinforces the notion of distinct levels, neither of which seems to call into question the other.

24. See Alexander Wendt, "The Agent-Structure Problem in International Relations Theory," *International Organization* 41 (1987), pp 335–70. For commentaries and criticisms, see David Dessler, "What's at Stake in the Agent-Structure Debate," *International Organization* 43 (1989), pp. 441–73; Richard K. Ashley, "Living on Borderlines: Man, Poststructuralism, and War," in *International/Intertextual Relations: Postmodern Readings of World Politics*, ed. James Der Derian and Michael J. Shapiro (Lexington: Lexington Books, 1989), pp. 276–77; and Barry Buzan, Charles Jones, and Richard Little, *The Logic of Anarchy: Neorealism to Structural Realism* (New York: Columbia University Press, 1993), ch. 6.

25. Alexander Wendt, "Anarchy Is What States Make of It: The Social Construction of Power Politics," *International Organization* 46 (1992), p. 424.

26. Ibid., pp. 425–26. For one discussion of why this stricture is problematic, see the discussion of a similar argument made by Robert Keohane, in Walker, *Inside/Outside*, pp. 99–100.

27. Wendt, "Anarchy Is What States Make of It," pp. 391–92.

28. Ibid., p. 425.

29. Ibid., p. 422.

30. Judith Butler, "Contingent Foundations: Feminism and the Question of Postmodernism," in *Feminists Theorize the Political*, ed. Judith Butler and Joan W. Scott (New York: Routledge, 1992), p. 13.

31. Wendt, "Anarchy Is What States Make of It," p. 397, note 21.

32. Ibid., p. 402.

33. See, in particular, Judith Butler, *Bodies That Matter: On the Discursive Limits of "Sex"* (New York: Routledge, 1993). Of importance here is the writing of Michel Foucault with respect to the concept of "biopower." See Foucault, *The History of Human Sexuality*, vol. 1, *An Introduction*, trans. Robert Hurley (New York: Vintage Books, 1980), part 5. I have attempted to connect some of these insights to the state and foreign policy in David Campbell, *Writing Security: United States Foreign Policy and the Politics of Identity* (Minneapolis: University of Minnesota Press, 1992), especially pp. 8–10, 87–92.

34. Campbell, *Writing Security*, p. 4; and William E. Connolly, "Democracy and Territoriality," *Millennium* 20 (1991), p. 483n.

35. John Gerard Ruggie, "Territoriality and Beyond: Problematizing Modernity in International Relations," *International Organization* 47 (1993), pp. 139–74.

36. Ibid., p. 143.

37. Ibid., p. 144.

38. John Lewis Gaddis, "International Relations Theory and the End of the Cold War," *International Security* 17 (Winter 1992–93), pp. 5–58.

39. Ibid., pp. 145–46. See also the critical remarks concerning so-called "postmodernist epistemologues" at p. 170, where Ruggie protests the "fetishistic parent (he[re]tical) obscurantism" of degenerate postmodernist method (his terms) by offering as evidence—in an argument that praises "straightforward scientific methods"—nothing more than a secondhand bibliography.

40. Jacques Derrida, "Like the Sound of the Sea Deep within a Shell: Paul de Man's War," trans. Peggy Kamuf, in *Responses: On Paul de Man's Wartime Journalism*, ed. Werner Hamacher, Neil Hertz, and Thomas Keenan (Lincoln: University of Nebraska Press, 1989), p. 132.

41. Christopher Norris, *What's Wrong with Postmodernism: Critical Theory and the Ends of Philosophy* (Baltimore: Johns Hopkins University Press, 1990), p. 223.

42. David Lehman, *Signs of the Times: Deconstruction and the Fall of Paul de Man* (New York: Poseidon Press, 1991).

43. Rodolphe Gasché, "Edges of Understanding," in *Responses*, ed. Hamacher et al., p. 208.

44. Jürgen Habermas, "Work and Weltanschauung: The Heidegger Controversy from a German perspective," *Critical Inquiry*, 15 (1989), p. 433.

45. Gerald Graff, "Looking Past the de Man Case," in *Responses*, ed. Hamacher et al., p. 248.

46. Lehman, *Signs of the Times*, pp. 67, 84–85, 106–7.

47. Derrida's response to the rage is his "Like the Sound of the Sea Deep within a Shell." One can safely say that this is not the critique Ruggie would have written, but one can say with equal assurance that neither is it made possible by a "moral vacuum" let alone "moral vacuity."

48. The comparison was made by Jon Wiener in *The Nation*, and later reprinted in his *Professors, Politics and Pop* (New York: Verso, 1991), p. 3. Critical responses can be found in Gasché, "Edges of Understanding," p. 209; and J. Hillis Miller, "An Open Letter to Professor Jon Wiener," in *Responses*, ed. Hamacher et al., p. 335.

49. See, for example, William Connolly, *The Augustinian Imperative: A Reflection on the Politics of Morality* (Newbury Park, Calif.: Sage, 1993); Drucilla Cornell, *The Philosophy of the Limit* (New York: Routledge, 1992); *Deconstruction and the Possibility of Justice,* ed. Drucilla Cornell, Michael Rosenfeld, and David Gray Carlson (New York: Routledge, 1992); and Simon Critchely, *The Ethics of Deconstruction: Derrida and Levinas* (Oxford: Blackwell, 1992). My attempts to begin thinking about this issue can be found in David Campbell and Michael Dillon, "The Political and the Ethical," in *The Political Subject of Violence,* ed. David Campbell and Michael Dillon (Manchester: Manchester University Press, 1993); and David Campbell, *Politics without Principle: Sovereignty, Ethics, and the Narratives of the Gulf War* (Boulder, Colo.: Lynne Rienner, 1993), especially ch. 6. For a recognition of the importance to international relations of postmodern theorizing on these issues—even as he takes issue with some of its formulations—see Steve Smith, "The Forty Years Detour: The Resurgence of Normative Theory in International Relations," *Millennium* 21 (1992), pp. 489–506.

50. John Gerard Ruggie, "International Structure and International Transformation: Space, Time, and Method," in Ernst-Otto Czempiel and James N. Rosenau, *Global Changes and Theoretical Challenges: Approaches to World Politics for the 1990s* (Lexington: Lexington Books, 1989), p. 30.

51. Ibid., p. 31.

52. Jacques Derrida, *Of Grammatology,* trans. Gayatri Spivak (Baltimore: Johns Hopkins University Press, 1976), p. 296.

53. See Ashley, "Untying the Sovereign State," p. 230; and Ashley, "Living on Borderlines," pp. 261–62.

54. Stephen K. White, *Political Theory and Postmodernism* (Cambridge: Cambridge University Press, 1991), p. 6.

55. Geoffrey Bennington and Jacques Derrida, *Jacques Derrida,* trans. Geoffrey Bennington (Chicago: University of Chicago Press, 1993), p. 105.

56. Wolf, *Europe and the People without History,* p. 2.

57. Mark W. Zacher, "The Decaying Pillars of the Westphalian Temple: Implications for International Order and Governance," in *Governance without Government,* ed. Rosenau and Czempiel, p. 64.

58. See Michel Foucault, "Two Lectures," in *Power/Knowledge: Selected Interviews and Other Writings* 1972–1977, ed. Colin Gordon (New York: Pantheon, 1980).

59. Ibid., p. 98.

60. Wendy Brown, "Feminist Hesitations, Postmodern Exposures," *differences: A Journal of Feminist Cultural Studies* 3 (1) 1991, p. 64.

61. Ibid., p. 66.

62. Daniel Warner, "We Are All Refugees," *International Journal of Refugee Law* 4 (1992), pp. 365–72.

63. Brown, "Feminist Hesitations, Postmodern Exposures," pp. 66–67.

64. See, for example, *Global Culture: Nationalism, Globalization and Modernity,* ed. Mike Featherstone (London: Sage, 1990); Arjun Appadurai, "Disjuncture and Difference in the Global Cultural Economy," *Public Culture* 2 (spring 1990), pp. 1–24; *Culture, Globalization and the World-System: Contemporary Conditions for the Representation of Identity,* ed. Anthony D. King (Department of Art and Art History,

State University of New York at Binghamton, 1991); Ulf Hannerz, *Cultural Complexity: Studies in the Social Organization of Meaning* (New York: Columbia University Press, 1992). There is not space here to pose the question of whether this literature does in the end exceed the sovereignty problematic, but it is worth asking.

65. Michel Foucault, "What Is Enlightenment?" in *The Foucault Reader*, ed. Paul Rabinow (New York: Pantheon, 1984), p. 50.

66. Although Bakhtin used the notion of prosaic, "prosaics" is a neologism constructed by Morson and Emerson. Gary Saul Morson and Caryl Emerson, *Mikhail Bakhtin: Creation of a Prosaics* (Stanford: Stanford University Press, 1990), p. 15.

67. Ibid., pp. 30, 139–42.

68. Gaddis, "International Relations Theory," p. 56.

69. Ibid., pp. 23–25, 27–30, 32–36.

70. Ibid., pp. 36–40.

71. Ibid., p. 49.

72. Robert Young, "Back to Bakhtin," *Cultural Critique* 2 (1985), p. 76.

73. Morson and Emerson, *Mikhail Bakhtin*, pp. 49–50.

74. See Gary Saul Morson, "Prosaics: An Approach to the Humanities," *American Scholar* 57 (1988), pp. 515–28.

75. Morson and Emerson, *Mikhail Bakhtin*, p. 50. Derrida's notion of the trace accents the way identity is constituted in relation to difference. As Bennington and Derrida argue, "if every element of the system only get its identity in its difference from the other elements, every element is in this way marked by all those it is not; it thus bears the trace of those other elements." Accordingly, "no element is anywhere present (nor simply absent), there are only traces." What this means is that "in referring to a stimulus or a self-presence of the subject, we are not finally referring to a fundamental presence with respect to which we might then comfortably envisage all the ambiguity one might wish, but still to a network of traces." Bennington and Derrida, *Jacques Derrida*, pp. 74–75, III.

76. Mikhail Bakhtin, "Toward a Reworking of the Dostoyevsky Book," Appendix 2 in his *Problems of Dostoyevsky's Poetics*, ed. and trans. Caryl Emerson (Minneapolis: University of Minnesota Press, 1984), quoted in Tzvetan Todorov, *Mikhail Bakhtin: The Dialogical Principle*, trans. By Wlad Godzich (Minneapolis: University of Minnesota Press, 1984), p. 96. Emphasis in the original.

77. Morson and Emerson, *Mikhail Bakhtin*, p. 51.

78. Quoted in ibid.

79. Foucault, "What Is Enlightenment?" p. 50. As an example of one path such labors might take, consider George E. Marcus, ed., *Perilous States: Conversations on Culture, Politics, and Nation* (Chicago: University of Chicago Press, 1993). In addition, I will furnish my own example later to satisfy this concern.

80. Todorov, *Mikhail Bakhtin: The Dialogical Principle*, p. 94. Todorov's own work has been inspired by this ethos. See especially his *Conquest of America: The Question of the Other*, trans. Richard Howard (New York: Harper and Row, 1984).

81. This theme is central to Reiner Schurmann's, *Heidegger on Being and Acting: From Principles to Anarchy*, trans. Christine Marie Gros in collaboration with Reiner Schurmann (Bloomington: Indiana University Press, 1987). As Schurmann declares, "the turn beyond metaphysics . . . reveals the essence of praxis: exchange deprived of

principle" (p. 18). I take the political implications that devolve from this to be radically democratic. See Campbell and Dillon, "The Political and the Ethical," where various readings of Schurmann's argument are discussed.

82. See Fernand Braudel, *Afterthoughts of Material Civilization and Capitalism*, trans. Patricia Ranum (Baltimore: Johns Hopkins University Press, 1977); Henri Lefebvre, *Everyday Life in the Modern World*, trans. Sacha Rabinovitch (New Brunswick, N.J.: Transaction Publishers, 1984); and Lefebvre, *Critique of Everyday Life*, trans. John Moore (New York: Verso, 1991).

83. Edith Wyschogrod, *Spirit in Ashes: Hegel, Heidegger, and Man-Made Mass Death* (New Haven: Yale University Press, 1985), especially pp. 9–24.

84. Michel de Certeau, *The Practice of Everyday Life*, trans. Steven Rendall (Berkeley: University of California Press, 1984), p. xi.

85. Ashley, "Living on Borderlines," p. 296.

86. Ibid., pp. 270, 296–97.

87. Among many examples, see Richard Cohen, "Serbs Savour Ancient Hatreds," *Manchester Guardian Weekly*, December 27, 1992, p. 15; "Hostages to a Brutal Past," *U.S. News and World Report*, February 15, 1993; and "Meddling in the Balkans: A Peril of the Ages," *New York Times*, April 11, 1993, p. E5.

88. For example, "Besieged Muslims Place Their Dignity over Life," *New York Times*, March 7, 1993, p. E3.

89. Maggie O'Kane, "A Public Trial in Bosnia's Sniper Season," *Manchester Guardian Weekly*, March 21, 1993, p. 10.

19

Polis and Cosmopolis

Fred Dallmayr

THE PROSPECTS AND PERILS of our age have reached global proportions. This is due to a host of technological, economic, and cultural-political factors. In the latter sense, ours is the first age ever to give rise to something like a genuinely global history: nations and continents previously hovering in the shadow or on the sidelines of history have stirred from this condition and have become co-shapers and co-definers of the future of mankind. Economically, the spreading of capital markets has for some time eroded traditional national boundaries and fostered the emergence of ever-larger trading zones, partially monitored by multinational organizations. Technologically, the contemporary informational revolution—with its corollaries of tele-communications and jet travel—has tended to reduce the world increasingly to a global village where news from every corner is almost instantly available, at the same rate as the diffusion of technical gadgets is promoting a uniform world culture. While promising and exhilarating in many respects, global tendencies of this kind, however, are fraught with matching dangers—foremost among them the danger of a nuclear holocaust or of the collective self-destruction of the Spaceship Earth. Blending together the promising features of our age, Karl Jaspers at one point anticipated the possibility of a new axial age giving birth to a truly universal civilization in which different cultures would cooperate in shouldering jointly the stewardship of the human race. A generation earlier, however, Friedrich Nietzsche had projected the twentieth century as the arena of an unparalleled battle: namely, the battle for the domination of the globe in which the vastness of the stakes is equaled by the enormity of devastation.[1]

From the vantage of lived experience, the latter prophecy seems to be close to the mark. Without prejudging the dispute between Jaspers and Nietzsche, their disagreement—in my view—points up an important theoretical issue, one which cannot readily be settled by empirical tendencies or statistical fore-casts: namely, the question how something like a global city or a cosmopolis can at all be conceived and plausibly articulated. On this point, the history of (Western) philosophy and political thought is not entirely silent, but also not very conclusive. There is a strong universalist streak in Western thought, a streak ranging from the Stoics over the medieval theory of universals to Enlightenment rationalism and beyond. Relying on universal principles and essential definitions, the guiding assumption of those perspectives is that mankind at bottom is (and has always been) one, with cultural diversities constituting at best surface variations on a common theme. Despite its specu-lative vigor, the defects of this assumption are not hard to detect and have frequently been stated: from nominalism to Romanticism and beyond, critics of universalism have pointed to its high-flown, often tautological abstract-ness and its aloofness from concrete cultural content. This complaint has been reinforced in our century by language philosophy with its accent on language games and diverse cultural narratives; the latter accent, in turn, has been exacerbated by post-Nietzscheans insisting on the primacy of cultural and political discord or struggle. In the following pages I hope to make some headway in this complex thicket of arguments, focusing chiefly on recent debates. In the first section I intend to discuss versions of universalist approaches from the Stoics to Habermas. The second section explores the particularist (or anti-totalist) challenge to these approaches, emphasizing motifs stretching from Herder to Lyotard. Taking its bearings from (late) hermeneutics and post-structuralism, the concluding part sketches a tenta-tive cross-cultural avenue, in the hope of shedding some theoretical light on the prospect of a global city.

I

In Western thought, universalism or the notion of the oneness of mankind arose first in a philosophically ambitious and politically relevant manner with the Stoics. To be sure, classical Greek philosophy had not been devoid of universal categories (as is evident in Plato's "forms" and Aristotle's teleol-ogy); however, in the context of the Greek city-states, these categories retained at best an embryonic and practically circumscribed character—a sit-uation which changed during Hellenism and later with the expansion of the Roman Empire. The founders of Stoicism were Greeks of the post-classical age, but subsequently the center of the school gravitated toward Rome until finally it became a cornerstone of Roman imperial culture. As propounded by a succession of thinkers, a key tenet of Stoicism was the notion of a divine spark or *logos* operative in the universe as a creative potency, a potency in which all human beings were meant to share regardless of race, creed or nationality. Translated as "reason" (or as *ratio et oratio*) this *logos* also functioned as the hidden law governing nature and society alike, and in this capacity it furnished the yardsticks for human behavior and legislation, that is, for rules of practical conduct. In ethical and political terms, the task of a Stoic was to practice citizenship in a given *polis* so that it would be compatible with, and a gateway to, citizenship in a universal "cosmopolis of reason" embracing all mankind. What saved this vision from speculative abstractness was ultimately its linkage with concrete legal institutions and practices. From Cicero to the imperial jurists, persistent efforts were afoot to assimilate the law of reason with the emerging *ius gentium* (law of nations) of the far-flung Empire, in contradistinction to the more restricted civil law of Rome.[2]

To a large extent, the Middle ages remained heir to the Roman legacy of universalism (or the merger of universalism with concrete institutions). Starting roughly with Charlemagne, the Holy Roman Empire kept its spiritual center in Rome or the Roman church while seeking to combine this center politically with loose transnational structures. On a philosophical plane, the medieval theory of universals was a blending of Platonic and Aristotelian essences with the Stoic belief in a rational *logos* governing the cosmos and human thought, a blending which came to serve as backbone to scholastic logic and epistemology. At the same time, in line with the Stoic example, the equation of *logos* and reason was the source of a complex system of rules or norms, and especially of the Thomistic distinction between the "law of nature" (applicable to all mankind) and the "human law" (applicable to a given *polis*). To be sure, rational argument in the Middle Ages tended to be a handmaiden of theology, a circumstance which surfaced in the superimposition of divine and eternal norms on principles of natural reason. To this extent, medieval thought sponsored the idea of a "cosmopolis of faith" as contrasted with Roman or pre-Christian modes of rationalism. As in the case of the Roman precedent, the medieval vision was concretized and rendered partly workable by practical institutional arrangements. Thus, the reception of the Roman law throughout the Continent provided European kingdoms with a semblance of cultural unity, just as feudalism furnished a transnational framework of economic interdependence.[3]

Renaissance and Reformation shattered and relegated to the past Europe's political and spiritual unity—but by no means all universalist aspirations. As has frequently been noted, Renaissance humanism was in many ways affected by Stoic beliefs, especially by the notion of a common or universal human nature. This conception was intensified during the Baroque and Enlightenment periods, chiefly through the assumption—favored by contractarian

theorists—of a pristine "state of nature" (outside and prior to social conventions) in which humans are rigorously free and equal and only subject to a
universal law of nature (or reason). The latter point, in turn, was corrobo-
rated by Enlightenment rationalism from Descartes to Leibniz with its insistence on a universal structure of the human mind giving rise to an absolute,
quasi-mathematical form of knowledge (a *mathesis universalis*) valid everywhere irrespective of cultural variations. The metaphysical underpinnings of
this kind of rationalism were severely attacked by Kant (and also by Hume).
In his three *Critiques* Kant divided reason or rationality into three domains—
science, ethics, and art—but without in any way challenging the a priori
structure of human consciousness or the possibility of achieving a universally
valid, objective type of knowledge. During the nineteenth century, the universalist direction of Enlightenment thought was further pursued by liberal
utilitarians and by Marx; however, their hope was grounded less in a common structure of reason than in the globalizing effects of the capitalist market
and the advances of modern technology. In contrast to liberal utilitarians,
Marxism envisaged a dénouement of social conflicts in the emergence of the
proletariat as the 'universal class' embodying the promise of human freedom
and equality.[4]

Apart from the continuing effects of these perspectives, twentieth-century
thought has engendered its own initiatives in this domain, ranging from the
unified science movement (wedded to a universal model of knowledge) to
linguistic universalism (stressing syntactical depth structures). Instead of
exploring this array of approaches, I want to concentrate here on one prominent example: the modified universalism endorsed in Habermas's "critical
theory." This theme has emerged in varying guises and formulations in
Habermas's steadily evolving opus—but without damage to a persistent
common direction. His epistemological treatise, *Knowledge and Human
Interests* (1968), was a concerted assault on logical positivism and its equation
of genuine knowledge with that produced by empirical science. However, as
one should note, the attack did not call into question the value and objectivity of empirical science but only the restrictedness of the positivist focus: its
neglect of historical-hermeneutical knowledge and of critical self-reflection
(or ideology critique). Thus, in lieu of the unified science program, *Knowledge and Human Interests* proposed a three-tiered or tripartite model
embracing science, hermeneutics and reflection—a model distantly patterned on Kant's three *Critiques;* only a correlation of these three types of
cognition, the study claimed, could furnish a truly comprehensive and universal theory of knowledge. In line with the study's title, modes of cognition
were linked with underlying interests or motivations, namely, the technical
interest in control, the practical interest in understanding, and the emancipa-

tory interest in self-knowledge and free self-realization. These interests, in turn, were presented as universal species dispositions (said to be endowed with a quasi-transcendental status as well as being involved in an historical learning process). As the Appendix of the study asserted, accentuating the universal character of interests and their moorings in both nature and culture: "The achievements of the transcendental subject have their basis in the natural history of the human species. . . . My second thesis is that knowledge equally serves as an instrument and transcends mere (natural) self-preservation." Alerting to the social context of technical, practical, and reflective orientations, the Appendix also affirmed that interests "take form in the medium of labor, language, and power."[5]

The years following publication of *Knowledge and Human Interests* brought several changes in the study's framework. For present purposes, two such modifications were particularly significant: the loosening of the linkage between knowledge and underlying cognitive motivations; and the reassessment of self-reflection particularly when seen as methodological cornerstone of critical social science. In the first rubric—without canceling the linkage entirely—Habermas introduced a crucial distinction or separation between experience and knowledge, between "experiential a priori" and "argumentative a priori" or, more generally, between praxis and discourse. While in ordinary life-praxis, experiences are gathered and integrated into a set of taken-for-granted beliefs, discourses in this scheme bracket or suspend immediate action constraints or ordinary experiences with the sole purpose of permitting the rigorous testing of knowledge claims. Extricated from the opacity of the life-world, discourses function as warrants of the validity and objectivity of cognitive propositions, especially of assertions or empirical 'truth' and normative 'rightness.' Even more dramatic—and pregnant with long-term implications—was the second revision. Distancing himself from the emancipatory model invoked in *Knowledge and Human Interests*, Habermas noted that the model was too closely tailored to therapeutic endeavors to serve properly as paradigm for critical knowledge. Dropping this restriction he prepared a new bifurcation, this time within the emancipatory cognitive domain: namely, the bifurcation between self-reflection and rational reconstruction or, more simply, between critique and reconstructive inquiry. While self-reflection centers on particular life stories or on processes of individual and collective identity formation, rational reconstruction uncovers anonymous rule systems as well as general depth-structures of knowledge and behavior. As leading exemplars of reconstructive inquiry Habermas invoked Wittgenstein's analysis of rule-following, Chomsky's explorations of generative grammar and of universal modes of linguistic competence, and—on a more behavioral level—the findings of developmental psychology (as practiced by Piaget). As he pointed out, it is reconstructive inquiries of this kind which "today step into the place of a (transformed) transcendental philosophy. To the extent that it derives universal rules of a communicative ethics from the basic norms of rational speech, even moral philosophy will establish itself as a reconstructive science."[6]

Both revisions gave direction to Habermas's subsequent investigations. In a prominent manner, the combination of discursive knowledge and reconstructive methodology surfaced in his formulation of universal pragmatics as a general theory of communication. As he stated in his study on the topic (1976), the task of universal pragmatics is "to identify and reconstruct universal conditions of possible understanding and consensus (*Verständigung*)." Drawing on his conception of discursive validation, Habermas portrayed these conditions as the "validity basis of speech," arguing that (rational) communication necessarily involves basic validity claims—specifically the four claims of factual truth, normative rightness, personal truthfulness, and linguistic comprehensibility. While ordinary exchanges rely on taken-for-granted beliefs, the disruption of direct understanding brings these validity claims to the fore—whose operation can be uncovered through reconstructive analysis. According to Habermas, the latter analysis was not restricted to linguistic depth structures (in Chomsky's sense) nor to the level of general concepts, but could be extended to the pragmatics of speech and communication; universal pragmatic (or formal-pragmatic) inquiry thus supplemented formal semantics and generative grammar. "I would defend the thesis," he wrote, "that not only language (*langue*) but speech too—that is the employment of sentences in utterances—is accessible to formal analysis," in the sense that utterances can be studied "in the methodological attitude of a reconstructive science." Reconstruction in this case aimed at uncovering the depth capacity or "intuitive rule consciousness" of speakers—what Habermas called their "communicative competence." In contrast to the interpretation of meaning contents, and also to individual self-reflection, reconstructive inquiry was said to relate to "pretheoretical knowledge of a general sort" or to "universal capabilities" of speech; to this extent, "what begins as an explication of meaning aims at the reconstruction of species competences." In comparison with a general linguistic or grammatical know-how, universal-pragmatic theory (we read) "postulates a corresponding communicative rule competence, namely, the competence to employ sentences in speech acts. It is further assumed that communicative competence has just as universal a core as linguistic competence."[7]

Seen as a general theory of communication, universal pragmatics was a broad-gauged program buttressing reconstructive endeavors in a variety of fields, including the domains of empirical truth and normative rightness. In

line with his earlier anticipation, Habermas soon embarked on the reconstruction of moral philosophy by focusing on the rightness claims implicit in
speech acts and their discursive validation. Deviating from non-cognitive and
emotivist stances, Habermasian communicative ethics (or discourse ethics)
provides a linguistic grounding for categorical standards—standards which
are now seen as embedded in communication and amenable to testing in
practical discourses. Simultaneously with the analysis of depth assumptions
or capabilities, Habermas turned to the reconstruction of developmental (or
diachronic) processes—in line with his view that universal competences are
both natural (or species endowments) and historically generated. Thus, his
study on universal pragmatics was accompanied and succeeded by a number
of essays dealing in detail with human cognitive development, with stages of
moral consciousness, with the formation of ego identity, and with the progressive maturation of behavioral and linguistic faculties. In large measure,
these essays were indebted to psychologists like Piaget and Lawrence Kohl-
berg; however, the latter's framework was significantly expanded, especially
by means of analogies with "phylo-genetic" evolution, that is, with the
sequential transformation of group life in the course of social development
and modernization.[8] Analytical-synchronic and developmental considerations were linked in Habermas's major work of sociological theory: *The
Theory of Communicative Action*. The central concept of the study—communicative rationality and action—was basically a restatement of the validity
basis of speech, embracing (in contrast to instrumental behavior) the full
range of validity claims embedded in communicative exchanges. At the same
time, relying in part on Weberian teachings, the study portrayed modernization as a process of societal rationalization along sequential stages of cognitive and normative development. Rationality in both dimensions was said to
be not simply a Western-cultural bias but (at least potentially) a universal
category. In Habermas's words: "Theory formation is in danger of being limited from the start to a particular, culturally or historically bound perspective—unless fundamental concepts are constructed in such a way that the
concept of rationality implicit in them is encompassing and general, that is,
satisfies universalistic claims."[9]

II

While captivating in its theoretical élan, Western universalism has always
been suspect: both because of its abstractness and its proclivity to ethnocentrism (if not cultural paternalism). Throughout the history of Western
thought, assertions of oneness and universal principles have consistently

been opposed by perspectives stressing contingency and cultural diversity. Thus, the Stoic doctrine of the *logos* unifying mankind was challenged by a long string of skeptical thinkers—from Carneades to Sextus Empiricus—counseling a more patient and sober concern with concrete detail and particular circumstances. Similarly, the medieval theory of universals did not hold undisputed sway, but was contested with growing intensity by nominalists insisting on the verbal and ultimately vacuous character of universal categories (in comparison with the concrete reality of particulars). During the eighteenth century, Enlightenment rationalism was critiqued by both skeptics and *Sturm-und-Drang* thinkers—the latter precursors of the Romantic movement—questioning the belief in the linear evolution of mankind along the path of growing rationalization. To some extent, Johann Gottlieb Herder— the contemporary of Voltaire—was illustrative of this counterpoint. In his philosophical reflections on the "formation of mankind," Herder emphasized the language- and context-bound quality of human thought and action. In contrast to a uniform evolutionary pattern or telos, history in his view was dispersed or disseminated among diverse peoples, cultures and periods; moreoever, these cultures and periods needed to be judged on their own terms rather than being subjected to a general measuring-rod, invariably taken from a later and presumably more advanced vantage. As he wrote: "The enlightened man of the later age—not only does he wish to listen to everything, but he also pretends to be the final synthesis of all voices, mirror of the entire past, and representative of the goal of the entire historical production. The precocious child blasphemes."[10]

From Herder an intellectual line might be drawn—with some caution—over the Romantics and Nietzsche to contemporary expressions of postmodern or anti-foundational thought. With regard to Habermas Richard Rorty has extended his indictment of foundationalism also to the rational (and quasi-Kantian) universalism of critical theory. As he observes in *Philosophy and the Mirror of Nature,* Habermas as well as Karl-Otto Apel have labored to create a new transcendental vista "enabling us to do something like what Kant tried to do," namely, by formulating a "universal pragmatics" or a "transcendental hermeneutics"—efforts which he finds "very suspicious" and misguided. As he adds, the notion that we can overcome positivistic reductions "only by adopting something like Kant's transcendental standpoint seems to me the basic mistake in programs like that of Habermas." Rorty's assessment could be fleshed out by reference to recent developments in scientific theory calling into question the univocal objectivity of scientific inquiry (including reconstructive science). According to a leading spokesman of post-empiricism, Mary Hesse, it has been "sufficiently demonstrated that the language of theoretical science is irreducibly metaphorical and unformalizable and that the logic of science is circular interpretation, reinterpretation and self-correction of data in terms of theory, theory in terms of data."[11] Habermasian universalism, in my view, is particularly flawed from a practical and political perspective. For, if the oneness of mankind is already assured by a priori categories and built-in universal capabilities, what need is there to engage in interaction and transcultural dialogue with a view toward achieving (a measure of) political concord? Theory at this point seems to preempt practice—unless the latter is seen simply as (technical-deductive) implementation of preordained formulas.[12]

Critiquing human oneness, to be sure, can entail different conclusions. In the case of many postmodern or post-foundational thinkers, anti-universalism tends to give rise to a frank endorsement of cultural segregation or separatism. Thus, in several of his writings, Rorty gleefully celebrates his native habitat—North American culture—with its attachment to technology, social engineering, and human mastery of the environment; in contrast to global philosophical schemes, his preference is for local, even parochial narratives and their deliberate continuation. "Whereas Habermas compliments 'bourgeois ideals' by reference to the 'elements of reason' contained in them," he states at one point, "it would be better just to compliment those untheoretical sorts of narrative discourse which make up the political speech of the Western democracies. It would be better to be frankly ethnocentric."[13] In Rorty's case—due to his liberal-pluralistic leanings—ethnocentrism retains a somewhat benign or noncombative flavor—which differentiates his outlook sharply from other, more radical formulations of postmodernism. Partly under the influence of Nietzschean motifs, these formulations construe the exit from universalism as warrant for cultural incompatibility and relentless reciprocal contestation. Once general foundations are removed, all cultural contexts or discourses are said to be radically politicized—in the sense that given contexts reflect political choices or preferences which necessarily are in conflict with competing political frameworks or interpretations. A major representative of conflictual or agonal analysis is Jean-François Lyotard—some of whose works I select to illustrate this version of anti-universalism.

In the English-speaking world, Lyotard first emerged as a spokesman or standard-bearer of postmodernism through a book whose main epistemological content only obliquely matched its startling title: *The Postmodern Condition: A Report on Knowledge* (of 1979/1984). In condensed form, the Introduction summarized the thrust of the book's argument. As used in the study, the term *modern* was said to designate any science or knowledge form that legitimates itself through reference to a universal "metadiscourse" or by appealing to "some grand narrative such as the dialectics of spirit, the hermeneutics of meaning, the emancipation of the rational or working subject, or the creation of wealth." By contrast, the term *postmodern* denoted a basic "incredulity toward metanarratives," an incredulity or skepsis fostered by the contemporary crisis of metaphysics as well as the malaise of the "university institution" erected on metaphysical grounds. What happened as a result of this skepsis, according to Lyotard, was the dismantling of metanarratives and their dispersal into heterogeneous discourses or "clouds of narrative language elements." In lieu of grand unifying schemes, postmodernism tolerates only a "pragmatics of language particles" arranged in many diverse "language games"—a pragmatics giving rise to institutionalization only "in patches— local determinism." Such localism stands in opposition to the dictates of total systems—governed by efficiency criteria—but also to neo-universalist schemes stressing rational consensus. Turning to the Habermasian model of communicative agreement, Lyotard insisted: "Such consensus does violence to the heterogeneity of language games. And invention is always born of dissension." Postmodern knowledge, he added, can no longer be accommodated in universalizing frameworks; rather, it "refines our sensitivity to differences and reinforces our ability to tolerate the incommensurable. Its principle is not the expert's homology, but the inventor's paralogy"—where "paralogy" means a disruption of paradigms.[14]

Congruent with its subtitle, a large portion of *The Postmodern Condition* dealt with changing modes of knowledge or science, and particularly with the computerization of knowledge associated with the contemporary informational revolution. No longer a part of character formation or individual training, Lyotard observed, scientific knowledge in our time has become a marketable commodity and, in fact, the chief force of production in developed countries; to this extent, such knowledge "is already, and will continue to be, a major—perhaps *the* major—stake in the worldwide competition for power." Together with computerization, our age has accentuated another feature of knowledge or cognition: its basically linguistic character, that is, the status of cognitive frameworks as discursive formations or language games. In a manner reminiscent of Habermas—but without universalist ambitions—*The Postmodern Condition* endorsed the primacy of the pragmatics of language: the notion that—far from simply copying an external reality—cognitive statements or assertions should be seen as utterances or speech acts executed in the context of rule-governed linguistic conventions. Deviating from Habermas, the study placed the emphasis of pragmatics less on the 'illocutionary' than the 'perlocutionary' quality of speech: the ability of speakers to parry objections or counter-proposals and ultimately to defeat opponents as part of a competitive struggle or contest. Normally, opponents are other speakers or interlocutors; but even in their absence, there remains

"at least one adversary, and a formidable one: the accepted language or connotation." In Lyotard's presentation, every utterance must be seen as a
"move" within a game—where "move" signifies a combative strategy or
challenge. This, he writes, "brings us to the first principle underlying our
method as a whole: to speak is to fight, in the sense of playing, and speech
acts fall within the domain of a general agonistics."[15]

The arguments concerning linguistic moves carry over into social and
political interactions and ultimately shape the nature of the social bond in
our time. According to Lyotard two traditional models or construals of the
social bond can be distinguished: the models of integral holism and of binary
opposition or conflict. The first model had been inaugurated by the French
founders of sociology and was developed by functionalist theorists from
Malinowski to Talcott Parsons. In our own time, the same model has been
further refined by systems theory and cybernetics—approaches exclusively
wedded to operational efficiency. What remained constant throughout these
historical variations is the view of society as "a unified totality, a 'unicity'."
In opposition to this view, Marxism adopted a dualistic model stressing the
class struggle between workers and management. As Lyotard points out,
however, the Marxist alternative has largely lost its salt: either by being
coopted in Western welfare societies, or else by being transformed into a
functional holism in communist countries. Returning to the notion of linguistic pragmatics, the study reaffirms the centrality of language games—
actually a multiplicity of games—which function as the only remaining social
bond in a postmodern context. Contrary to the pretense of integral holism
or of the grand narratives of the past, our age is said to witness the " 'atom-
ization' of the social into flexible networks of language games"—with each
speaker or participant being located at particular "nodal points" of competing communication circuits. Instead of being submerged in social harmony,
the "atoms" of society are perceived as operating at the "crossroads of pragmatic relationships" and involved in perpetual moves and countermoves—an interplay which exceeds predictable stimulus-response processes.
While reactive responses are no more than programmed effects, genuine
countermoves are seen as enhancing displacement in the games and even a
disorientation encouraging unexpected moves. "What is needed," Lyotard
comments, "if we are to understand social relations in this manner, on whatever scale we choose, is not only a theory of communication but a theory of
games which accepts agonistics as a founding principle." Such games approximate a general state of war—but the war is "not without rules."[16]

As the study recognizes, forms of knowledge are not self-sufficient but
dependent on some kind of legitimation; typically such legitimation in the
past has assumed a narrative cast. Thus, Plato's theory of forms was embed-

ded in a dialogical context, while Cartesian and post-Cartesian thought relied on a mental narrative—the story of the development and clarification of mind. In the wake of the Enlightenment, two major legitimation stories or grand narratives are distinguished in the study: the conception of a dialectic of spirit (or of spirit coming to itself) promulgated by German idealism, and the notion of popular emancipation initiated by the French Revolution and later translated into proletarian emancipation. Both types of stories, in Lyotard's view, have collapsed or lost their plausibility: speculative idealism has been undermined by the proliferation of language games following different rules—an experience first formulated by Nietzsche; regarding popular emancipation, the presumed theory-praxis nexus has been dissolved due to the segregation of denotative and prescriptive language games. In our own time, a new metanarrative has been propounded by cybernetics and systems theory with the accent on technical efficiency or performativity; but the latter principle offers at best a de facto legitimation and can by no means account for itself. As a result, we are faced today with a lack or erosion of general narratives or universal metalanguages and accordingly confined to a multitude of competing narrative accounts. Realization of this situation first dawned in *fin-de-siècle* Vienna, among philosophers and scientists as well as artists: "They carried awareness of and theoretical and artistic responsibility for delegitimation as far as it could be taken." Wittgenstein's accomplishment, in particular, is said to reside in his delineation of the theory of language games without recourse to either grand narratives or sheer performativity: "That is what the postmodern world is all about."[17]

In its conclusion, the study points to various developments in contemporary science, all illustrative of the postmodern situation of polymorphous non-universalism. Contrary to the focus on ultra-stability endemic to systems theory, postmodern scence is said to be embarked on a search for instabilities and even the exploration of logical paradoxes. Quantum mechanics and microphysics have shifted the accent from steady, predictable processes to the study of discontinuity and indeterminacy; the same is true of recent mathematical theory with its focus on Brownian movements and the description of reversals or catastrophes in phenomena. Following René Thom, Lyotard sees the catastrophe model as reducing all casual processes to a single one: namely, "conflict, the father of all things according to Heraclitus." What remains at this point are at best "islands of determinism," while catastrophic antagonism is "literally the rule." The lesson to be drawn from these scientific developments is that the "continuous differential equation" has lost its preeminence for contemporary science; instead, by concerning itself with "undecidables, the limits of precise control, . . . 'fracta', catastrophes, and pragmatic paradoxes" postmodern science is grasping its own evolution as "discontinuous, catastrophic, nonrectifiable, and paradoxical." After the demise of the grand narratives, the only remaining legitimation of knowledge is one based on paralogy or the transgression of paradigms. In contrast to the consensual model favored by rationalism, Lyotard insists, "it is now dissension that must be emphasized." While paradigmatic research tends to stabilize and domesticate, he states, one must posit "the existence of a power that destabilizes the capacity for explanation, manifested in the promulgation of new norms for understanding" and knowledge.[18]

Lyotard's "dissensual" or combative-agonal approach is fleshed out and amplified in a number of other writings, particularly in *Le Différend* (of 1983)—a complex study to which I can only briefly allude. Elaborating on the study's title, the opening section distinguishes sharply between contest *(différend)* and juridical litigation *(litige)*. "In contrast to a litigation," we read, "an agonal contest is a conflict between (at least) two parties which cannot properly be decided due to the absence of a decision rule applicable to both sides of the argument. The legitimacy of one side does not entail the illegitimacy of the other." If the same decision rule is applied to both sides, the contest is transformed into a litigation—with damaging results for at least one party, and possibly both. As Lyotard adds, the title of the book suggests that "generally there is no universal rule applicable to diverse modes of discourse." As in his previous work, this circumstance is traced to the pragmatics of language games, particularly to the rule-governed character of sentences and discourses. A sentence, he writes, is formed "in accordance with a set or system of rules," and there are several systems of sentence formation. Sentences, in turn, are part of discourses or discursive structures which are equally rule-governed. Here is the linguistic source of agonal contestation. For, sentences belonging to diverse or heterogeneous rule systems "cannot be translated into each other"; they can only be connected in compliance with a given discursive goal. Similarly, the diversity of discursive structures engenders on inter-discursive conflict or contest—one unable to be settled by a higher authority (due to the absence of a universal discourse). According to Lyotard, philosophical reflection emerges precisely at the boundaries of discourses and language games. The aim of his study, he notes, is to convince the reader "that thinking, knowledge, ethics, politics, and being are at stake at the margins between sentences," and to counter the prejudice that there is something like "man" as such or "language" as such. In this sense, the study seeks to make a contribution to "philosophical politics," by bearing witness to contestation.[19]

Philosophical politics of this kind stands in contrast to traditional, nonpolitical metaphysics. The change in outlook is attributed chiefly to the "linguistic turn" in Western thought, a turn accompanied by the "decline of universalistic discourses." In a more personal vein, Lyotard lists as his main sources of inspiration two works (whose combination is certainly uncommon): namely, Kant's *Critique of Judgment* (together with his historical-political writings) and Wittgenstein's *Philosophical Investigations.* Kant's teachings are invoked because of his denial of intellectual intuition, and Wittgenstein because of his pragmatic definition of meaning. Both thinkers, Lyotard states, attest the demise of "universalistic doctrines": their works are "epilogues of modernity and prologues of a significant postmodernity"; thus they prepare the "thought of dispersal" (or the thinking in diaspora) befitting our postmodern context. In line with Kantian initiatives, contestation is opposed to all forms of holism, including intuited universals or substantive-general ideas. As a rule, the study observes, the categories of the whole (or the absolute) cannot characterize objects of cognition; the thesis affirming the opposite "might be called 'totalitarism'." Totalist tendencies are encouraged by several contemporary frameworks, including cybernetic communication models and also theories of complete rational consensus. In contrast to such synthetizing approaches, agonal contest is said to demarcate a situation of instability where different discursive options are still open and the outcome hangs in the balance. Properly conceived, politics means the possibility or threat of contestation. In Lyotard's words: Politics "is not a mode of discourse but rather denotes their multiplication, the diversity of goals and especially the question of their connection. . . . Politics arises from the fact that language is not one language but sentences, and being not one being but different instances of '*Es gibt*'. It is mere being which is (also) not—one of its names."[20]

III

I do not mean here to question the importance and even profundity of many of Lyotard's insights—a depth which is unfairly curtailed by my condensed and selective reading of his texts. My concern is mainly with certain accents and perhaps overstatements marking these texts, particularly with the heavy accentuation of dissensus and conflict. One source of my concern is the similarity of Lyotard's arguments with perspectives arising on very different soil: particularly contemporary neo-utilitarianism and (naturalistic) behavioralism. According to the former, politics is basically a struggle for advantage among individuals (or groups), with each participant seeking to maximize interests or benefits over losses; according to the latter, politics is an arena of power where the strong invariably dominate the weak. No doubt, Lyotard—like other post-Nietzscheans—would want to distance himself from these approaches whose premises, he might argue, are still moored in traditional subject-centered (or "logocentric") versions of metaphysics and thus oblivious of the linguistic turn. On a different level, this is also his central objection to Habermasian universalism and his model of rational consensus. Yet, rationalist metaphysics may be more difficult to vanquish than is often assumed. Generally speaking—and this is my basic concern or apprehension— metaphysics can scarcely be overcome by inverting its premises or priorities. Such an inversion (I am afraid) is manifest at many junctures of Lyotard's work: particularly in the reversal from consensus to dissensus, from paradigm to paralogy, from holism to dispersion, and from totality to agonal contests. What these reversals neglect is the complex interlacing of the paired opposites and the ambivalent status of their meaning. Most importantly, placed in radical opposition, the terms tend to replicate or mirror each other's defects. This applies prominently to the (so-called) social bond. In the absence of mutual—and more than contingent-accidental—relations, the contending parties are liable to lapse into self-centeredness. Differently put: unless contest involves more than combat and mutual repulsion, competing discourses or language games are bound to suffer the very enclosure rightly bemoaned in the case of integral holism.[21]

What these considerations suggest is that universalism and agonistics (or holism and contest) are not mutually exclusive but rather correlated and interlocking vistas—though correlated neither on the level of a priori categories nor that of accidental contacts. Something like this correlation seems to have been involved in the universality claim of hermeneutics as originally formulated by Hans-Georg Gadamer (in 1966). Universality in this case did not denote a complete transparency of understanding predicated on abstract categories of reason; nor, conversely, was it compatible with radical fragmentation. As Gadamer stated in his essay on the topic: "The claim to universality proper to the hermeneutic dimension means this: understanding is tied to language" or a linguistic context, and language is not an abstract "system of signals" nor an anonymous rule structure which could be generalized and computerized. Viewed ontologically, understanding is always context-bound and embedded in a given mode of being fraught with various judgments and prejudgments. According to Gadamer, however, this feature did not vindicate a "linguistic relativism"—because (he wrote) there "cannot be an enclosure in language, not even in one's mother tongue. This we all experience when we learn a foreign language and especially in traveling insofar as we somehow master a foreign idiom." To this extent, every living language had to be viewed as unlimited or "infinite," and it was "entirely erroneous" to derive from the diversity of languages something like a dispersal or fragmentation of understanding. "The opposite is true," Gadamer stated (somewhat exuberantly): "Precisely the experience of the finitude and particularity of our being—a finitude manifest in the diversity of languages—opens the road to the infinite dialogue in the direction of ontological truth" (or the truth "that we are").[22]

The same point was reinforced in Gadamer's rejoinder to Habermas's critique of universal hermeneutics (in 1971). As Gadamer observed at the time in his defense, hermeneutical experience is not the experience of universal meaning or the discernment of a general "plan of reason"—an ambition plausible only *sub specie aeternitatis;* by contrast, hermeneutical inquiry is an "ever renewed attempt to decode the meaning fragments of history, fragments limited by the opaque contingency of reality and especially by the twilight zone in which the future hovers from the vantage of the present." The notion of universal hermeneutics had to be seen in the same subdued light: understanding was universal only in the sense of being an inescapable feature of the human mode of life, a mode articulating itself (in the first instance) in ordinary language and common-sense beliefs—into which even alien or abstracted idioms have ultimately to be translated. Recapitulating arguments advanced in *Truth and Method,* Gadamer presented understanding not so much as a method or a methodologically trained exegesis but rather as the "medium of human social life which, in the last analysis, has the character of a linguistic or dialogical community" (though not one geared to uniform consensus). In this sense, hermeneutics reflected not a universal reason but the plurality of modes of rational argumentation as well as "the pluralism which combines and connects mutually opposed or conflicting elements in society."[23]

In many ways, the path beyond universalism and agonistics had been prepared by Gadamer's teacher, Martin Heidegger. In several of his writings of the interbellum period, Heidegger had articulated a mode of relationship between diverse elements which eluded the alternatives of both coincidence (or synthesis) and radical separation. Thus, the lectures on "The Origin of the Work of Art" (of 1936) differentiated between two dimensions or modalities—namely, 'world' and 'earth'—whose precarious interplay was said to constitute the central trademark of artworks. In this juxtaposition, the term *world* designated the aspect of meaning-disclosure or the "self-disclosing openness" of cultural understanding and of narrative-historical meaning-contexts; the term *earth* by contrast pointed to the aspect of "permanent self-seclusion or sheltering," that is, to the dimension of concealment (of meaning), of non-understanding and non-reason. In Heidegger's presentation, the two modalities were not simply factual domains standing in a relation of causal or functional dependence (which would reduce one to a variable of the other). Most importantly, their interplay in art-works did not yield a facile blend but rather amounted to a strenuous contest or agonal "strife." "In resting upon the earth," he noted, "world strives to surmount the latter; as disclosing openness it cannot endure anything secluded. On the other hand, earth in its mode of sheltering tends to embrace and harbor the world in its own ambience." Yet, strife in this case was not synonymous with hostile collision or mutual repulsion; rather, art-works had the distinctive ability to sustain the strife while raising or lifting the contesting parties into a tensional unity or non-synthetic harmony (that is, a harmony preserving heterogeneity). As the lectures stated: "The work-being of the work consists in the enactment of the strife between world and earth. It is because the strife achieves its culmination in the simplicity of mutual intimacy that this enactment yields the unity of the works. . . . The serene repose of a work at peace with itself reflects the intimacy of the strife."[24]

Heidegger's comments on agonal concord were fleshed out and amplified in his postwar discussion of 'identity and difference' and also in his conception of a complex fourfold constellation *(das Geviert)* combining contest and sympathy. Roughly at the same time, strides in a similar direction were undertaken by another student or successor of Husserlian philosophy: Maurice Merleau-Ponty, especially through his notions of 'intertwining' and 'chiasm'—terms meant to designate the tensional intersection of meaning and non-meaning, of culture and nature, immanence and transcendence, and of self and other. Defining chiasm also as a mode of reversibility—"the finger of the glove that is turned inside out"—Merleau-Ponty saw such an intersection at work particularly in the arena of intersubjective or self-other relations: "In reality there is neither me nor the other as tangible, positive subjectivities. There are two caverns, two opennesses, two stages where something will take place—and which both belong to the same world, to the stage of being." In another context, he extended the perspective of intertwining explicitly to the domain of inter- or cross-cultural relations, coining at that point the suggestive concept of a 'lateral universalism.' Objecting to an abstract type of structuralism concerned with invariant categories, Merleau-Ponty observed: "Even if these invariants exist, even if social science were to find beneath structures a metastructure to which they conformed (as phonology does beneath phonemes), the universal we would thus arrive at could no more be substituted for the particular than general geometry annuls the local truth of Euclidean spatial relations." The antidote or necessary complement to a structuralist focus had to be found in anthropological field work, in lived experience which exposes the analyst to concrete modes of cultural diversity. In this manner a new path opened up to cross-cultural understanding or to "the universal: no longer the overarching universal of a strictly objective method, but a sort of lateral universal which we acquire through ethnological experience and its incessant testing of the self through the other person and the other person through the self."[25]

Merleau-Ponty's intimations of lateral connectedness and agonal reversibility have been further pursued by one of his leading German followers: the philosopher Bernhard Waldenfels. Translating or recasting agonal concord as the problem of the contingent ordering of social life, his *Order at Twilight* portrays social and cross-cultural relations as patterned on the model of agonal dialogue, a model highlighting the inevitable asymmetry between question and answer, challenge and response. Since in dialogues—Waldenfels observes—questions are typically unprovoked and unpredictable and there usually is room for multiple answers, communicative exchanges cannot be subsumed under (either deductively or inductively constructed) holistic systems and retain instead an open-ended, multivocal character. The communicative model can be extended to concrete social practices and interactions, where it surfaces as the interplay between "stimulus" (seen as enticement or provocation) and "reaction" (seen as responding action or countermove). "If it is true," he notes, "that every question opens up a field of possibilities and thus permits several responses and not only one, then there emerges a rift between question and reply," between stimulus and response. The rift here has the nature of an agonal contest—but one which does not cancel the connectedness of the contending parties. Dialogical exchange thus implies a "peculiar" kind of correlation: one which "simultaneously links and separates"; for a given response "may meet the point of a question—but without thereby exhausting the possibilities and need of responding." Reflecting this asymmetrical structure, acts of social ordering are never fully transparent but fraught with ambivalence and contingency; far from achieving rational wholeness or consensus, such ordering requires continuous negotiation and renegotiation of the terms of interaction. According to *Order at Twilight*, this fact ultimately derives from the tensional intertwining of meaning and non-meaning, culture and nature. Since ordering always presupposes non-order or the backdrop of the unordered—a domain it can never completely eradicate—social order is bound to inhabit a twilight zone *"entre chien et loup"*— just as human thought and existence can never shed traces (in Merleau-Ponty's terms) of *"a pensée sauvage* and an *etre sauvage."*[26]

Among political theorists or philosophers, a similar outlook has been formulated by Ernesto Laclau and Chantal Mouffe—though with greater emphasis on hegemonic arrangements or the asymmetrical distribution of political power. In their presentation, hegemony signifies a contingent or selective mode of ordering, in sharp contrast to foundational or essentialist political conceptions—conceptions stressing either an integral holism or the complete segregation (and self-enclosure) of opposing camps. Generally speaking, politics in their view is an articulated practice or a creatively constructive enterprise, a practice which can never achieve total rational transparency or logical unity but only a precarious blend of meaning and non-meaning, of concord and dissent. Seen as constructive enterprises, political formations only selectively structure a given social domain without being able to exhaust available possibilities; differently phrased: discursive orders or practices always are silhouetted against the horizon of the unordered and unarticulated or against the broader field of discursivity with its inherent surplus of meaning. This aspect is the deeper source of social conflict or antagonism. Due to their finite and selective character, political formations inevitably are in tension with alternative types of ordering. Antagonism, however, results not only from the confrontation of empirical structures but from the intrinsic contingency of political order as such, that is, from the built-in limit and negative potency challenging its positive arrangements. Hegemonic order, in this sense, is located at the margins not only of meaning and non-meaning, but also of presence and absence, positivity and negativity. Yet, just as positive structures can never be fully integrated or stabilized, negativity cannot be synonymous with total opposition (without canceling the ambivalence of political articulation). This is particularly true in the case of democracy. According to Laclau and Mouffe, democracy cannot be equated with a holistic system nor with a polar conflict between opposed camps—despite the persistence of agonal tensions. "Between the logic of complete identity and that of pure difference," they write, "the experience of democracy should consist of the recognition of the multiplicity of social logics along with the necessity of their (hegemonic) articulation"—an articulation which needs to be "constantly re-created and renegotiated."[27]

The preceding formulations apply primarily to domestic (or intra-societal) relations—but they can readily be extended to the field of cross-cultural and international politics. In the latter arena, the vista of an agonal universalism or a tensional cosmopolis has been articulated by a number of political thinkers, including Eric Voegelin—though chiefly with reference to the Hellenistic age. Pondering the difference between regional or "ecumenic" orders and the idea of a "universal mankind," Voegelin presents the former as historical instantiations or anticipations of the universal idea—which in itself remains a symbol or index of a hidden meaning. "Universal mankind," he writes (in *The Ecumenic Age*), "is not a society existing in the world, but a symbol" expressing obliquely the sense of human destiny—in the form of an "eschatological index." On a broader philosophical level, the notion of mankind as a "calling"—or rather as a reciprocal calling and invocation—has been expressed by Merleau-Ponty, with specific reference to contemporary global contacts between East and West. "The relationship between Orient and

Occident," he observed, is "not that of ignorance to knowledge or of non-philosophy to (rational) philosophy; it is much more subtle, making room on the part of the Orient for all kinds of anticipations and 'prematurations'." Against this background, it is not merely the Orient's task to learn from the West, but also the Occident's task to reassess itself by remembering aban-doned possibilities. Indian and Chinese thought, we read, have tried "not so much to dominate existence as to be the sounding board of our relationship to being"; Western philosophy can learn from this example by seeking to rediscover this relationship and to "estimate the options we have shut ourselves off from in becoming 'Westerners' and perhaps reopen them." As Merelau-Ponty concluded, the unity of mankind is not a bland synthesis but rather "exists in each culture's lateral relations to the others, in the echoes one awakens in the other."[28]

Notes

1. See Karl Jaspers, *The Origin and Goal of History*, trans. M. Bullock (New Haven: Yale University Press, 1953), also *The Future of Mankind*, trans. E. B. Ashton (Chicago: University of Chicago Press, 1961); Friedrich Nietzsche, *Ecce Homo: How One Becomes What One Is*, trans. R. J. Hollingdale (New York: Penguin Books), p. 127 ("Why I Am A Destiny," section 1).

2. See E. Vernon Arnold, *Roman Stoicism* (Cambridge: University Press, 1911), and Max Pohlenz, *Die Stoa* (Göttingen: Vandenhoek and Ruprecht, 1940).

3. See e.g. M. H. Carré, *Realists and Nominalists* (London: Oxford University Press, 1946); R. I. Aaron, *The Theory of Universals* (London: Oxford University Press, 1952); and I. M. Bochénski et al., *The Problem of Universals* (Notre Dame: University of Notre Dame Press, 1956). The unifying factors mentioned above must be supple-mented by the institutions of the Catholic Church and by the use of Latin as common language among scholars and intellectuals. In emphasizing the doctrine of universals, and later nominalism, I shortchange the medieval theory of *analogia entis* (with its linkage of universals and particulars).

4. The following statements from the *Communist Manifesto* are still instructive: "The bourgeoisie, by the rapid improvement of all instruments of production, by the immensely facilitated means of communication, draws all nations, even the most barbarian, into civilization. The cheap prices of its commodities are the heavy artil-lery with which it batters down all Chinese walls, with which it forces the barbarians' intensely obstinate hatred of foreigners to capitulate. It compels all nations, on pain of extinction, to adopt the bourgeois mode of production. . . . The bourgeoisie has subjected the country to the rule of towns. It has created enormous cities, has greatly increased the urban population as compared with the rural, and has rescued a con-siderable part of the population from the idiocy of rural life. Just as it has made the country dependent on the towns, so it has made barbarian and semi-barbarian coun-tries dependent on the civilized ones, nations of peasants on nations of bourgeois,

the East on the West." See Karl Marx and Frederick Engels, *The Communist Manifesto* (New York: International Publishers, 1948), p. 13.

5. Jürgen Habermas, *Knowledge and Human Interests*, trans. Jeremy J. Shapiro (Boston: Beacon Press, 1971), pp. 312–313. The Appendix actually was Habermas's inaugural address at the University of Frankfurt in 1965.

6. Habermas, "A Postscript to *Knowledge and Human Interests*," *Philosophy of the Social Sciences*, vol. 3 (1975), pp. 157–189. Compare also "Some Difficulties in the Attempt to Link Theory and Practice" in Habermas, *Theory and Practice*, trans. John Viertel (Boston: Beacon Press, 1973), pp. 13–24; and my "Critical Epistemology Criticized" in *Beyond Dogma and Despair* (Notre Dame: University of Notre Dame Press, 1981), pp. 246–269.

7. See "What is Universal Pragmatics?" in Habermas, *Communication and the Evolution of Society*, trans. Thomas McCarthy (Boston: Beacon Press, 1979), pp. 1–3, 6, 9, 12–14, 26. Referring to structural linguistics Habermas observes (pp. 14, 20) that "it is the great merit of Chomsky to have developed this idea (i.e., of universal capabilities) in the case of grammatical theory"; at the same time, toning down the "essentialist" claims of linguistics, he states that Chomsky's "maturationist" assumption (regarding the correlation of depth grammar and mental development) "seems to me too strong"—a point which leads him in the direction of Piaget's developmental psychology. Although acknowledging an affinity with "transcendental hermeneutics" as proposed by Karl-Otto Apel, Habermas differentiates his approach by pointing to the distinction between a (Kantian) constitution of experiences and the generation of utterances and also to the at least quasi-empirical status of reconstructive analysis (pp. 23–25).

8. See the essays on "Moral Development and Ego Identity" and "Historical Materialism and the Development of Normative Structures" in *Communication and the Evolution of Society*, pp. 69–94, 95–129; also *Legitimation Crisis*, trans. Thomas McCarthy (Boston: Beacon Press, 1975), esp. Part 3, pp. 95–117, and *Moralbewusstsein und kommunikatives Handeln* (Frankfurt-Main: Suhrkamp, 1983), esp. pp. 53–125.

9. Habermas, *The Theory of Communicative Action*, vol. 1: *Reason and the Rationalization of Society*, trans. Thomas McCarthy (Boston: Beacon Press, 1984), p. 137. The latter claims were hedged in by various caveats but not abandoned in the study. As Habermas added, with reference to the rational structure of communicative action: "If the requirement of objectivity is to be satisfied, this structure would have to be shown to be *universally valid* in a specific sense. This is a very strong requirement for someone who is operating without metaphysical support and is also no longer confident that a rigorous transcendental-pragmatic program, claiming to provide ultimate grounds, can be carried out." The universalistic aspirations are still maintained in the more recent study on the "discourse of modernity." Through modern forms of communication, Habermas states, "processes of opinion and consensus formation get institutionalized which depend upon diffusion and mutual interpenetration no matter how specialized they are. The boundaries are porous; each public sphere is open to other public spheres. To their discursive structures they owe a (barely concealed) universalist tendency. . . . The European Enlightenment elaborated this experience and adopted it into its programmatic formulas." See Habermas,

The Philosophical Discourse of Modernity: Twelve Lectures, trans. Frederick Lawrence (Cambridge, MA: MIT Press, 1987), p. 360.

10. Johann Gottlieb Herder, Auch eine Philosophie der Geschichte zur Bildung der Menschheit (1774; Frankfurt-Main: Suhrkamp, 1967), p. 106. To be sure, Herder was not simply a defender of particularism against universalism, or of immanence against transcendence—as Gadamer persuasively shows in his "Postscript" (pp. 146–177). Compare also my "Abeunt studi in mores: Berlin on Vico and Herder" in Twilight of Subjectivity (Amherst, MA: University of Massachusetts Press, 1981), pp. 257–263.

11. Richard Rorty, Philosophy and the Mirror of Nature (Princeton: Princeton University Press, 1979), pp. 379–382; Mary Hesse, Revolutions and Reconstructions in the Philosophy of Science (Bloomington: Indiana University Press, 1980), p. 173.

12. This point has been forcefully made by Agnes Heller, "Habermas and Marxism," in John B. Thompson and David Held, eds. Habermas: Critical Debates (Cambridge, MA: MIT Press, 1982), pp. 21–41. As she points out, even assuming universal structures, their presence does not necessarily have motivating force, but actually may stifle practice.

13. Rorty, "Habermas and Lyotard on Postmodernity," in Richard J. Bernstein, ed. Habermas and Modernity (Cambridge, MA: MIT Press, 1985), pp. 165–166. As he adds (pp. 170, 173): if Bacon—the "prophet of self-assertion"—had been taken more seriously (instead of Descartes and Kant), "we might not have been stuck with the canon of 'great modern philosophers' who took 'subjectivity' as their theme" and might have seen that canon "as a distraction from the history of concrete social engineering which made the contemporary North American culture what it is now, with all its glories and all its dangers."

14. Jean-François Lyotard, The Postmodern Condition: A Report on Knowledge, trans. Geoff Bennington and Brian Massumi (first French ed. 1979; Minneapolis: University of Minnesota Press, 1984), pp. xxiii–xxv. I could have chosen as illustrative example also some facets of the work of Michel Foucault (especially aspects stressing rupture and discontinuity); but for present purposes Lyotard's approach seems particularly forthright and instructive.

15. The Postmodern Condition, pp. 4–5, 9–10. As Lyotard adds (p. 88, notes 34 and 35), speech acts for him are placed in the domain of the "agon" (or joust) rather than that of rational communication. The term "agonistics" is traced to "Heraclitus's ontology," the dialectic of the Sophists and also to Nietzsche's observations in "Homer's Contest."

16. The Postmodern Condition, pp. 11–13, 15–17. The term "nodal points" is adopted from the vocabulary of systems theory.

17. The Postmodern Condition, pp. 29, 31–32, 38–41, 46–47. As Lyotard observes (p. 43): "The principle of a universal metalanguage is replaced by the principle of a plurality of formal and axiomatic systems capable of arguing the truth of denotative statements; these systems are described by a metalanguage that is universal but not consistent" (that is, ultimately by ordinary language).

18. The Postmodern Condition, pp. 53–56, 59–61. As Rorty comments soberly: "Lyotard argues invalidly from the current concerns of various scientific disciplines to the claim that science is somehow discovering that it should aim at permanent revolution, rather than at the alternation between normality and revolution made

familiar by Kuhn. To say that 'science aims' at piling paralogy on paralogy is like saying that 'politics aims' at piling revolution on revolution. No inspection of the concerns of contemporary science or contemporary politics could show anything of the sort." See "Habermas and Lyotard on Postmodernity," in Bernstein, ed., *Habermas and Modernity*, p. 163.

19. Lyotard, *Le Différend* (Paris: Editions de Minuit, 1983), pp. 8–10.

20. *Le Différend*, pp. 10–11, 17, 27–29, 199–200. The study differentiates sharply between dialogue and agonal contest. There is a contest, we read (p. 46), "between the defenders of agonistics and the proponents of dialogue. How can this contest be settled? The latter say: through dialogue; the former: through the agon. If these positions are insisted upon, then the contest is perpetuated and becomes a kind of meta-contest: a contest over a manner of settling the contest regarding a certain definition of reality."

21. In *The Postmodern Condition*, Lyotard repeatedly places linguistic rules and the "social bond" on a contractual basis—which would seem to locate agonistics in the tradition of modern contractarianism (pp. 10, 43, 66). The same study also stresses the distinction between power and "terror" (pp. 46, 66)—but without clarifying their difference. As one may recall, Sartre's *Being and Nothingness* formulated a strictly conflictual model of the social bond—on entirely subject-centered and intentionalist premises. For critical assessments of Lyotard's political theory see Stuart Sim, "Lyotard and the Politics of Antifoundationalism," *Radical Philosophy*, No. 44 (1986), pp. 8–13; Seyla Benhabib, "Epistemologies of Postmodernism: A Rejoinder to Jean-François Lyotard," *New German Critique*, vol. 33 (1984), pp. 103–126; David Ingram, "Legitimacy and the Postmodern Condition: The Political Thought of Jean François Lyotard," *Praxis International*, vol. 7 (1987–88), pp. 286–305.

22. Gadamer, "The Universality of the Hermeneutical Problem," in *Philosophical Hermeneutics*, trans. and ed. David E. Linge (Berkeley: University of California Press, 1976), pp. 15–16 (translation slightly altered). For the German version see Gadamer, *Kleine Schriften I: Philosophie, Hermeneutik* (Tübingen: Mohr, 1967), p. 111.

23. Gadamer, "Replik," in Karl-Otto Apel et al., *Hermeneutik und Ideologiekritik* (Frankfurt-Main: Suhrkamp, 1971), pp. 289, 301–302, 317. I do not deny a certain vacillation in Gadamer's arguments—especially the fact that his emphasis on dialogue may privilege a consensual model (over agonal contest). For a fuller discussion of this issue see my "Hermeneutics and Deconstruction: Gadamer and Derrida in Dialogue," in *Critical Encounters* (Notre Dame: University of Notre Dame Press, 1987), pp. 130–158.

24. Martin Heidegger, "The Origin of the Work of Art," in *Poetry, Language, Thought*, trans. Albert Hofstadter (New York: Harper & Row, 1971), pp. 44, 48–50. A similar correlation is outlined in the Schelling lectures of 1936 between the dimensions of "ground" and "existence": "Ground is what sustains self-disclosing appearance and maintains it in its grasp. Existence, on the other hand, is self-transcendence and manifestation—a movement which is based on the ground and explicitly confirms the latter as its ground. Ground and existence belong together; only their linkage renders possible their separation and strife—which in turn yields a higher concord." See Heidegger, *Schellings Abhandlung Über das Wesen der menschlichen Freiheit (1809)*, ed. Hildegard Feick (Tübingen: Niemeyer, 1971), pp. 137–138.

25. Maurice Merleau-Ponty, *The Visible and the Invisible*, ed. Claude Lefort, trans. Alphonso Lingis (Evanston: Northwestern University Press, 1968), p. 263; *Signs*, trans. Richard C. McCleary (Evanston: Northwestern University Press, 1964), pp. 119–120. Merleau-Ponty in the latter context recommends a method which consists "in learning to see what is ours as alien and what was alien as our own" (p. 120). Compare also Heidegger, *Identity and Difference*, trans. Joan Stambaugh (New York: Harper & Row, 1969), and *Vorträge und Aufsätze* (3rd ed.; Pfullingen: Neske, 1967), vol. 2, pp. 23–24.

26. Bernhard Waldenfels, *Ordnung im Zwiellcht* (Frankfurt-Main: Suhrkamp, 1987), pp. 10–11, 29, 39, 43–46. For a more detailed discussion see Chapter 5 below.

27. Ernesto Laclau and Chantal Mouffe, *Hegemony and Socialist Strategy: Towards a Radical Democratic Politics*, trans. Winston Moore and Paul Cammack (London: Verso, 1985), pp. 93, 105–111, 122–129, 188. For a more detailed discussion see Chapter 6 below.

28. Merleau-Ponty, *Signs*, p. 139; Eric Voegelin, *Order and History*, vol. 4: *The Ecumenic Age* (Baton Rouge: Louisiana State University Press, 1974), p. 305. For some contemporary formulations of cross-cultural understanding, akin to "universal hermeneutics," see Alasdair MacIntyre, *Whose Justice? Which Rationality?* (Notre Dame: University of Notre Dame Press, 1988), esp. pp. 389–403, and David Tracy, *Plurality and Ambiguity: Hermeneutics, Religion, Hope* (New York: Harper & Row, 1987).

Further Readings

Alford, C. Fred. *Think No Evil*. Ithaca, N.Y.: Cornell University Press, 1999

Appadurai, Arjun. *Modernity at Large*. Minneapolis: University of Minnesota Press, 1997

———— (ed.). *Globalization*. Durham, N.C.: Duke University Press, 2001

Balslev, Anindita Niyogi. *Cultural Otherness*, 2nd ed. Atlanta: Scholars Press, 1999

———— (ed.). *Cross-Cultural Conversation (Initiation)*. Atlanta: Scholars Press, 1996

Barthes, Roland. *Empire of Signs*. Trans. Richard Howard. New York: Hill and Wang, 1982

Bauman, Zygmunt. *Legislators and Interpreters*. Cambridge, U.K.: Polity Press, 1987

Beck, Ulrich. *World Risk Society*. Cambridge, U.K.: Polity Press, 1999

Bell, Daniel A. *East Meets West*. Princeton, N.J.: Princeton University Press, 2000

Berger, Peter L. and Hsin-Huang Michael Hsiao (eds.). *In Search of an East Asian Development Model*. New Brunswick, N.J.: Transaction Books, 1988

Bhabha, Homi K. *The Location of Culture*. New York: Routledge, 1994

Bitterli, Urs. *Cultures in Conflict*. Trans. Ritchie Robertson. Stanford, Calif.: Stanford University Press, 1989

Breckenridge, Carol A. and Peter van der Veer (eds.). *Orientalism and Postcolonial Predicament*. Philadelphia: University of Pennsylvania Press, 1993

Buruma, Ian. *The Missionary and the Libertine*. New York: Random House, 2000

Butler, Judith, Ernesto Laclau and Slavoj Zizek. *Contingency, Hegemony, Universality*. London: Verso, 2000

Canclini, Nestor Garcia. *Hybrid Cultures*. Trans. Christopher L. Chiappari and Silvia L. Lopez. Minneapolis: University of Minnesota Press, 1995

Carrier, James G. (ed.). *Occidentalism*. Oxford, U.K.: Clarendon Press, 1995

Cheah, Pheng and Bruce Robbins (eds.). *Cosmopolitics*. Minneapolis: University of Minnesota Press, 1998

Chen, Xiaomei. *Occidentalism*. New York: Oxford University Press, 1995

Chow, Rey. *Ethics after Idealism*. Bloomington, Ind.: Indiana University Press, 1998

————. *Woman and Chinese Modernity*. Minneapolis: University of Minnesota Press, 1991

———. *Writing Diaspora*. Bloomington, Ind.: Indiana University Press, 1993

——— (ed.). *Modern Chinese Literary and Cultural Studies in the Age of Theory*. Durham, N.C.: Duke University Press, 2000

Clarke, John James. *Oriental Enlightenment*. New York: Routledge, 1997

Clifford, James and George E. Marcus (eds.). *Writing Culture*. Berkeley, Calif.: University of California Press, 1986

Cohen, Paul A. *Discovering History in China*. New York: Columbia University Press, 1984

Collins, Randall. *The Sociology of Philosophies*. Cambridge, Mass.: Harvard University Press, 1998

Creel, Herrlee Glessner. *Sinism*. Chicago: Open Court, 1929

Dallmayr, Fred. *Achieving Our World*. Lanham, Md.: Rowman & Littlefield, 2001

———. *Alternative Visions*. Lanham, Md.: Rowman & Littlefield, 1998

———. *Beyond Orientalism*. Albany, N.Y.: State University of New York Press, 1996

——— (ed.). *Border Crossings*. Lanham, Md.: Lexington Books, 1999

Dawson, Raymond. *The Chinese Chameleon*. London: Oxford University Press, 1967

De Bary, Wm. Theodore. *Asian Values and Human Rights*. Cambridge, Mass.: Harvard University Press, 1998

Derrida, Jacques. *Of Grammatology*, corrected ed. Trans. Gayatri Chakravorty Spivak. Baltimore: Johns Hopkins University Press, 1998

———. *On Cosmopolitanism and Forgiveness*. Trans. Mark Dooley and Michael Hughes. New York: Routledge, 2001

———. *The Other Heading*. Trans. Pascale-Anne Brault and Michael B. Naas. Bloomington, Ind.: Indiana University Press, 1991

Desan, Wilfrid. *The Planetary Man*. New York: Macmillan, 1972

Deutsch, Eliot (ed.). *Culture and Modernity*. Honolulu: University of Hawaii Press, 1991

Dharwadker, Vinay (ed.). *Cosmopolitan Geographies*. New York: Routledge, 2001

Dilworth, David A. and Valdo H. Viglielmo (eds.). *Sourcebook for Modern Japanese Philosophy*. Westport, Conn.: Greenwood Press, 1998

Dingwaney, Anuradha and Carol Maier (eds.). *Between Languages and Cultures*. Pittsburgh: University of Pittsburgh Press, 1994

Dirlik, Arif and Xudong Zhang (eds.). *Postmodernism and China*. Durham, N.C.: Duke University Press, 2000

Dussel, Enrique. *The Invention of the Americas*. Trans. Michael D. Barber. New York: Continuum, 1995

———. *The Underside of Modernity*. Trans. and ed. Eduardo Mendieta. Atlantic Highlands, N.J.: Humanities Press International, 1996

Eze, Emmanuel Chukwudi. *Achieving Our Humanity*. New York: Routledge, 2001

Fabian, Johannes. *Time and the Other*. New York: Columbia University Press, 1983

Falk, Richard. *Predatory Globalization*. Cambridge, U.K.: Polity Press, 1999

Fenollosa, Ernest. *The Chinese Written Character as a Medium for Poetry*. Ed. Ezra Pound. San Francisco: City Lights Books, 1936

Fleischackers, Samuel. *The Ethics of Culture*. Ithaca, N.Y.: Cornell University Press, 1994

Ferguson, Russell, Martha Gever, Trinh T. Minh-ha, and Cornel West (eds.). *Out There*. Cambridge, Mass.: MIT Press, 1990

Fukuzawa, Yukichi. *An Outline of a Theory of Civilization*. Trans. David A. Dilworth and G. Cameron Hurst. Tokyo: Sophia University, 1973

Gadamer, Hans-Georg. *Truth and Method*, 2nd rev. ed. Rev. trans. Joel Weinscheimer and Donald G. Marshall. New York: Crossroad, 1991

Geertz, Clifford. *Available Light*. Princeton, N.J.: Princeton University Press, 2000

———. *Interpretation of Cultures*. New York: Basic Books, 1973

———. *Negara*. Princeton, N.J.: Princeton University Press, 1980

Gernet, Jacques. *China and the Christian Impact*. Trans. Janet Lloyd. New York: Cambridge University Press, 1985

Giddens, Anthony. *Runaway World*. New York: Routledge, 2000

Glover, Jonathan. *Humanity*. New Haven, Conn.: Yale University Press, 2000

Gray, John. *Enlightenment's Wake*. New York: Routledge, 1995

Halbfass, Wilhelm. *India and Europe*. Albany, N.Y.: State University of New York Press, 1988

Hall, David, and Roger T. Ames. *Anticipating China*. Albany, N.Y.: State University of New York Press, 1998

———. *Thinking from the Han*. Albany, N.Y.: State University of New York Press, 1998

———. *Thinking through Confucius*. Albany, N.Y.: State University of New York Press, 1987

Hardt, Michael and Antonio Negri. *Empire*. Cambridge, Mass.: Harvard University Press, 2000

Harootunian, Harry. *History's Disquiet*. New York: Columbia University Press, 2000

Harrison, Lawrence E. and Samuel P. Huntington (eds.). *Culture Matters*. New York: Basic Books, 2000

Heidegger, Martin. *On the Way to Language*. Trans. Peter D. Hertz. New York: Harper and Row, 1971

Heisig, James W. and John C. Maraldo (eds.). *Rude Awakenings*. Honolulu: University of Hawaii Press, 1995

Huntington, Samuel P. *The Clash of Civilizations and the Remaking of World Order*. New York: Simon and Schuster, 1996

Husserl, Edmund. *The Crisis of European Sciences and Transcendental Phenomenology*. Trans. David Carr. Evanston, Ill.: Northwestern University Press, 1970

Jullien, François. *Detour and Access*. Trans. Sophie Hawkes. New York: Zone Books, 2000

———. *The Propensity of Things*. Trans. Janet Lloyd. New York: Zone Books, 1995

Jung, Hwa Yol. *The Question of Rationality and the Grammar of Intercultural Texts*. Niigata, Japan: International University of Japan, 1989

Kothari, Rajni. *Rethinking Development*. New York: New Horizons Press, 1989

Kristeva, Julia. *About Chinese Women*. Trans. Anita Barrows. New York: Urizen Books, 1977

Kristof, Nicholas D. and Sheryl WuDunn. *Thunder from the East*. New York: Alfred A. Knopf, 2000

Larson, Gerald James and Eliot Deutsch (eds.). *Interpreting across Boundaries*. Princeton, N.J.: Princeton University Press, 1988

Lewis, Martin W. and Kären E. Wigen. *The Myth of Continents*. Berkeley, Calif.: University of California Press, 1997

Liu, Lydia H. *Translingual Practice.* Stanford, Calif.: Stanford University Press, 1995
——— (ed.). *Tokens of Exchange.* Durham, N.C.: Duke University Press, 1999
Lyotard, Jean-François. *The Postmodern Condition.* Trans. Geoff Bennington and Brian Massumi. Minneapolis: University of Minnesota Press, 1984
Ma, Sheng-mei. *The Deathly Embrace.* Minneapolis: University of Minnesota Press, 2000
Macfie, A. L. (ed.). *Orientalism: A Reader.* Washington Square, New York: New York University Press, 2000
MacIntyre, Alasdair. *Three Rival Versions of Moral Enquiry.* Notre Dame, Ind.: University of Notre Dame Press, 1990
Mackerras, Colin. *Western Images of China.* Hong Kong: Oxford University Press, 1989
Maruyama, Masao. *Studies in the Intellectual History of Tokugawa Japan.* Trans. Mikiso Hane. Tokyo: University of Tokyo Press, 1974
———. *Thought and Behaviour in Modern Japanese Politics.* Ed. Ivan Morris. New York: Oxford University Press, 1969
Mehta, Jaswant Lal. *India and the West.* Chico, Calif.: Scholars Press, 1985
Merleau-Ponty, Maurice. *Texts and Dialogues.* Ed. Hugh J. Silverman and James Barry, Jr. and trans. Michael B. Smith *et al.* Atlantic Highlands, N.J.: Humanities Press International, 1992
Miyoshi, Masao and H. D. Harootunian (eds.). *Postmodernism and Japan.* Durham, N.C.: Duke University Press, 1989
Mohanty, Chandra Talpade, Ann Russo, and Lourdes Torres (eds.). *Third World Women and the Politics of Feminism.* Bloomington, Ind.: Indiana University Press, 1991
Mohanty, Jitendra Nath. *Reason and Tradition in Indian Thought.* Oxford, U.K.: Clarendon Press, 1992
Mohanty, Satya P. *Literary Theory and the Claims of History.* Ithaca, N.Y.: Cornell University Press, 1997
Moore, Charles A. (ed.). *The Chinese Mind.* Honolulu: East-West Center Press, 1967
——— (ed.). *The Indian Mind.* Honolulu: East-West Center Press, 1967
——— (ed.). *The Japanese Mind.* Honolulu: East-West Center Press, 1967
Nakamura, Hajime. *Ways of Thinking of Eastern Peoples.* Ed. Philip P. Wiener. Honolulu: East-West Center Press, 1964
Nandy, Ashis. *Traditions, Tyranny and Utopias.* Delhi: Oxford University Press, 1987
Narayan, Uma and Sandra Harding (eds.). *Decentering the Center.* Bloomington, Ind.: Indiana University Press, 2000
Nhat Hanh, Thich. *Interbeing,* rev. ed. Ed. Fred Eppsteiner. Berkeley, Calif.: Parallax Press, 1993
Nishida, Kitaro. *Fundamental Problems of Philosophy.* Trans. David A. Dilworth. Tokyo: Sophia University, 1970
———. *An Inquiry into the Good.* Trans. Masao Abe and Christopher Ives. New Haven, Conn.: Yale University Press, 1990
Nishitani, Keiji. *Religion and Nothingness.* Trans. Jan Van Bragt. Berkeley, Calif.: University of California Press, 1982
Northrop, F. S. C. *The Meeting of East and West.* New York: Macmillan, 1946

Nussbaum, Martha C. *Cultivating Humanity.* Cambridge, Mass.: Harvard University Press, 1997

Odin, Steve. *The Social Self in Zen and American Pragmatism.* Albany, N.Y.: State University of New York Press, 1996

Owens, Craig. *Beyond Recognition.* Ed. Scott Bryson *et al.* Berkeley, Calif.: University of California Press, 1992

Parekh, Bhikhu. *Rethinking Multiculturalism.* Cambridge, Mass.: Harvard University Press, 2000

Parkes, Graham (ed.). *Heidegger and Asian Thought.* Honolulu: University of Hawaii Press, 1987

Radhakrishnan, S. and P. T. Raju (eds.). *The Concept of Man.* 2nd ed. Lincoln, NE: Johnsen, 1966

Reid, T. R. *Confucius Lives Next Door.* New York: Random House, 1999

Robertson, Roland. *Globalization.* London: Sage Publications, 1992

Robinson, Fiova. *Globalizing Care.* Boulder, Colo.: Westview Press, 1999

Roland, Alan. *In Search of Self in India and Japan.* Princeton, N.J.: Princeton University Press, 1988

Sahlins, Marshall. *Culture in Practice.* New York: Zone Books, 2000

Said, Edward W. *Culture and Imperialism.* New York: Alfred A. Knopf, 1993

———. *Orientalism.* New York: Pantheon Books, 1978

———. *Reflections on Exile.* Cambridge, Mass.: Harvard University Press, 2000

———. *The World, the Text, and the Critic.* Cambridge, Mass.: Harvard University Press, 1983

Sakai, Naoki. *Translation and Subjectivity.* Minneapolis: University of Minnesota Press, 1997

Schrag, Calvin O. *Philosophical Papers.* Albany, N.Y.: State University of New York Press, 1992

———. *The Resources of Rationality.* Bloomington, Ind.: Indiana University Press, 1992

———. *The Self after Postmodernity.* New Haven, Conn.: Yale University Press, 1997

Schwartz, Benjamin I. *The World of Thought in Ancient China.* Cambridge, Mass.: Harvard University Press, 1985

Shweder, Richard A. *Thinking through Cultures.* Cambridge, Mass.: Harvard University Press, 1991

Silverman, Hugh J. (ed.). *Continental Philosophy, I: Philosophy and Non-Philosophy since Merleau-Ponty.* New York: Routledge, 1988

Spence, Jonathan D. *The Chan's Great Continent.* New York: W. W. Norton, 1998

———. *The Question of Hu.* New York: Alfred A. Knopf, 1985

Spivak, Gayatri Chakravorty. *A Critique of Postcolonial Reason.* Cambridge, Mass.: Harvard University Press, 1999

———. *In Other Worlds.* New York: Routledge, 1988

———. *Outside in the Teaching Machine.* New York: Routledge, 1993

Taylor, Charles. *Multiculturalism.* Ed. Amy Gutmann. Princeton, N.J.: Princeton University Press, 1994

Todorov, Tzvetan. *The Conquest of America.* Trans. Richard Howard. New York: Harper and Row, 1984

————. *On Human Diversity*. Trans. Catherine Porter. Cambridge, Mass.: Harvard University Press, 1993

Toulmin, Stephen. *Cosmopolis*. New York: Free Press, 1990

Tracy, David. *Plurality and Ambiguity*. New York: Harper and Row, 1987

Trinh, T. Minh-ha. *Woman, Native, Other*. Bloomington, Ind.: Indiana University Press, 1989

Tu, Wei-ming. *Centrality and Commonality*. Albany, N.Y.: State University of New York Press, 1989

————. *Confucian Thought*. Albany, N.Y.: State University of New York Press, 1985

———— (ed.). *Confucian Traditions in East Asian Modernity*. Cambridge, Mass.: Harvard University Press, 1996

————, Milan Hejtmanek, and Alan Wachman (eds.). *The Confucian World Observed*. Honolulu: The East-West Center, 1992

Turner, Bryan S. *Orientalism, Postmodernism and Globalism*. New York: Routledge, 1994

Venuti, Lawrence. *The Scandals of Translation*. New York: Routledge, 1998

Waldenfels, Bernhard. *Order in the Twilight*. Trans. David J. Parent. Athens, Ohio: Ohio University Press, 1996

Wallerstein, Immanuel. *Geopolitics and Geoculture*. New York: Cambridge University Press, 1991

Watsuji, Tetsuro. *Watsuji Tetsuro's Rinrigaku*. Trans. Yamamoto Seisaku and Robert E. Carter. Albany, N.Y.: State University of New York Press, 1996

Wu, Kuang-Ming. *On the "Logic" of Togetherness*. Leiden: Brill, 1998

Young, Robert. *White Mythologies*. New York: Routledge, 1990

Zhang, Longxi. *The Tao and the Logos*. Durham, N.C.: Duke University Press, 1992

Contributors

For the benefit of our readers, Asian surnames in some cases are italicized.

JUDITH BUTLER is Maxine Elliot Professor of Rhetoric and Comparative Literature at the University of California, Berkeley. She is the author of *Subjects of Desire* (1987), *Gender Trouble* (1990), *Bodies That Matter* (1993), *The Psychic Life of Power* (1997), and *Excitable Speech* (1997).

DAVID CAMPBELL is Professor of International Politics at the University of Newcastle in Great Britain. His most recent book is *National Deconstruction* (1998).

REY *CHOW* is Andrew Mellon Professor of the Humanities at Brown University where she teaches modern culture and media as well as comparative literature. Her works include *Woman and Chinese Modernity* (1991), *Writing Diaspora* (1993), *Primitive Passions* (1995), and *Ethics after Idealism* (1998).

FRED DALLMAYR is Packey Dee Professor of Government in the Department of Government and International Studies at the University of Notre Dame. He authored and edited many books including *The Other Heidegger* (1993), *Beyond Orientalism* (1996), *Alternative Visions* (1998), and *Border Crossings: Toward a Comparative Political Theory* (1999). Currently he is working on Jacques Derrida, and *Achieving Our World* (2001).

ENRIQUE DUSSELL has been in exile in Mexico from Argentina since 1975. He is currently Professor of Ethics in the Department of Philosophy at the Metropolitan Autonomous University in Mexico City. He is a prolific writer and philosopher of liberation. His works in English translation include *The Invention of the Americas* (1995) and *The Underside of Modernity* (1996).

HWA YOL JUNG is Professor of Political Science at Moravian College in Pennsylvania. His books include *The Crisis of Political Understanding* (1979), *The Question of Rationality and the Basic Grammar of Intercultural Texts* (1989), and *Rethinking Political Theory* (1993). Currently he is working on Mikhail Bakhtin, cultural hermeneutics, comparative philosophy (East Asia and West), environmental philosophy, and body politics.

KIM DAE JUNG is President of the Republic of Korea (South Korea) and received a Nobel Peace Prize in 2000. He has written many books in Korean, and *Prison Writings* (1987) is available in English.

LYDIA H. LIU is Professor of Comparative Literature and the Catherine and William L. Magistretti Distinguished Professor of East Asian Languages and Cultures at the University of California, Berkeley. She authored *Translingual Practice* (1995) and most recently edited *Tokens of Exchange* (1999).

KISHORE MAHBUBANI is a student of philosophy and history who has been with the Singapore Foreign Service since 1971. He is currently Singapore's Ambassador to the United Nations.

CHANDRA TALPADE MOHANTY is Professor of Women's Studies at Hamilton College. She is interested in cross-cultural, global women's issues. She is series editor of "Gender, Culture and Global Politics" for Garland Publishing and co-edited *Third World Women and the Politics of Feminism* (1991) and *Feminist Genealogies, Colonial Legacies, Democratic Futures* (1997). She has a book in progress, *Feminism Without Borders: Multiculturalism, Globalization and the Politics of Solidarity.*

MAURICE MERLEAU-PONTY (1908–1961) is a famed French phenomenologist. He was Professor of Philosophy at the Collège de France. His influence is worldwide. His published works in English translation include *Phenomenology of Perception* (1962), *The Visible and the Invisible* (1968), *Adventures of the Dialectic* (1973), and *Texts and Dialogues* (1992).

THICH NHAT HANH is a Vietnamese Zen Buddhist. He was the founder of the Buddhist "Order of Interbeing" in the mid-1960s. His writings include *Touching Peace* (1995) and *Living Buddhas, Living Christ* (1995).

NISHIDA KITARÔ (1870–1945) is the most renowned Japanese philosopher in the twentieth century. He founded the Kyoto school of philosophy. His nineteen-volume complete works—*Nishida Kitaro Zenshu* (1965)—are available in Japanese. His works in English translation include *Intelligibility and the Philosophy of Nothingness* (1958), *Art and Morality* (1973), and *An Inquiry into the Good* (1990).

BHIKHU PAREKH is Professor of Political Theory at the University of Hull, United Kingdom. Sir Bhikhu chairs the Commission on the Future Multi-Ethnic Britain. His publications include *Hannah Arendt and the Search for a New Political Philosophy* (1981), *Contemporary Political Thinkers* (1982), and *Gandhi's Political Philosophy* (1989) as well as *Rethinking Multiculturalism* (2000).

EDWARD W. SAID is University Professor of English and Comparative Literature at Columbia University. He is the author of *Beginnings* (1975), *Orientalism* (1978), *Culture and Imperialism* (1993), *Out of Place* (1999), and *Reflections on Exile* (2000).

CALVIN O. SCHRAG is now retired from teaching. He was George Ade Distinguished Professor of Philosophy at Purdue University. He authored *Communicative Praxis and the Space of Subjectivity* (1986), *The Resources of Rationality* (1992), *Philosophical Papers* (1994), and *The Self After Postmodernity* (1997).

TU WEIMING is Professor of Chinese history and philosophy at Harvard University and the Director of the Harvard-Yenching Institute. Numerous works he authored and edited on Confucianism include *Confucian Thought* (1985), *Centrality and Commonality* (1989), *The Confucian World Observed* (1992), and *Confucian Traditions in East Asian Modernity* (1996).

WATSUJI TETSURÔ (1889–1960) is a Japanese philosopher whose complete works—*Watsuji Tetsuro Zenshu* (1962)—are available in Japanese. His *A Climate: A Philosophical Study* (1961) is widely known and discussed in the West. His classic work *Rinrigaku*, originally published in three volumes (1937, 1942, and 1949) in Japanese, has now been partially translated into English as *Watsuji Tetsuro's Rinrigaku* (A Study of Ethics) (1996).

ZHANG LONGXI taught in the Department of Literatures and Languages at the University of California, Riverside and now teaches in the Department of Comparative Literature and Translation at the City University of Hong Kong, China. His major work is *The Tao and the Logos* (1992).